THE

PUBLICATIONS

OF THE

Lincoln Record Society

FOUNDED IN THE YEAR

1910

VOLUME 104

ISSN 0267–2634

THE CORRESPONDENCE OF WILLIAM STUKELEY AND MAURICE JOHNSON

1714–1754

EDITED BY

DIANA and MICHAEL HONEYBONE

The Lincoln Record Society

The Boydell Press

© Lincoln Record Society 2014

All Rights Reserved. Except as permitted under current legislation no part of this work may be photocopied, stored in a retrieval system, published, performed in public, adapted, broadcast, transmitted, recorded or reproduced in any form or by any means, without the prior permission of the copyright owner

First published 2014

A Lincoln Record Society Publication
published by The Boydell Press
an imprint of Boydell & Brewer Ltd
PO Box 9, Woodbridge, Suffolk IP12 3DF, UK
and of Boydell & Brewer Inc.
668 Mt Hope Avenue, Rochester, NY 14620–2731, USA
website: www.boydellandbrewer.com

ISBN 978 0 901503 98 5

A CIP catalogue record for this book is available
from the British Library

Details of other Lincoln Record Society volumes are available
from Boydell & Brewer Ltd

The publisher has no responsibility for the continued existence or accuracy of URLs for external or third-party internet websites referred to in this book, and does not guarantee that any content on such websites is, or will remain, accurate or appropriate

This publication is printed on acid-free paper

Printed and bound in Great Britain by
TJ International Ltd, Padstow, Cornwall

CONTENTS

List of illustrations	vi
Acknowledgements	ix
Abbreviations	x
INTRODUCTION	xi
Editorial conventions	lx
THE TEXT The correspondence of William Stukeley and Maurice Johnson, 1714–1754	1
Additional letters	199
APPENDICES	
1. Two dissertations on Lincolnshire topics by William Stukeley	217
(a) On the Alleged Burial of Danish Vikings at Threekingham, 14 March 1729	217
(b) On the Statues of the West Front of Croyland Abbey, 30 December 1746	223
2. Chronological order of letters in the Stukeley–Johnson correspondence	227
3. Spalding Gentlemen's Society members referred to in the letters	231
4. Contemporary tributes to Johnson and Stukeley	245
Index of people and places	253
Index of subjects	260

ILLUSTRATIONS

between pp.64 and 65

1. Maurice Johnson as a young man, artist unknown. (Spalding Gentlemen's Society)
2. William Stukeley; mezzotint by John Smith after a portrait by Kneller. (National Portrait Gallery, London)
3. Sketch of Johnson by Gerard Vandergucht, with obituary notes by Stukeley. (Spalding Gentlemen's Society)
4. Ayscoughfee Hall, Spalding, home of Maurice Johnson; watercolour by Hilkiah Burgess, 1818. (Spalding Gentlemen's Society)
5. Drawing by Stukeley of himself and his first wife, Frances (née Williamson). (Bodleian Library, Oxford)
6. The Grammar School, Spalding, where the SGS hoped to establish a museum; watercolour by Hilkiah Burgess, 1820. (Spalding Gentlemen's Society)
7. Sketch by Stukeley of his house in Boston, 1714. (Bodleian Library, Oxford)
8. Sketch by Stukeley of his garden in Grantham, in a letter to Johnson, 1728 (see **Letter 84**). (Northamptonshire Record Office)
9. The church of St George the Martyr, Queen Square, London, where Stukeley was Rector from 1747 to 1765. From Richard Tames, *Bloomsbury Past* (1993), 36.
10. Engraving showing arterial network of the spleen, from Stukeley's pamphlet, *Of the Spleen* (1723).
11. Detail from map of the northern edge of London, showing Stukeley's church in Queen Square, by John Rocque, 1746. (Spalding Gentlemen's Society)
12. Map of Spalding from Capt. Andrew Armstrong's map of Lincolnshire, 1778. (Spalding Gentlemen's Society)

between pp.128 and 129

13. Sketch of the 'Oxford dragon' by Stukeley, 1715 (see **Letter 5**). (Spalding Gentlemen's Society)
14. Sketch by Stukeley of a long-eared bat found in his house at Barn Hill, Stamford, 1743 (see **Letters 35** and **36**). (Bodleian Library, Oxford)
15. Letter by Johnson describing the view from the tower of Ayscoughfee House, 1712 (see **Letter 37**, 1744). (Bodleian Library, Oxford)

16. Drawing by Stukeley of the statue of St Guthlac on the west front of Croyland Abbey, 1746 (see **Letter 47**). (Spalding Gentlemen's Society)
17. Drawing by Stukeley of the carvings of St Guthlac's life, over the west door of Croyland Abbey, 1746 (see **Letters 47** and **49**). (Spalding Gentlemen's Society)
18. The carvings over the west door of Croyland Abbey today. (Photograph by Michael Honeybone)
19. Stukeley's family tree, drawn by himself sometime after 1737. (Bodleian Library, Oxford)
20. Stukeley's map of the Parts of Holland, Lincolnshire, 1723. (Bodleian Library, Oxford)
21. Engraving of a coin of the Emperor Carausius, showing the figure whom Stukeley assumed to be 'Oriuna', taken from *Paleographia Britannica or Discourses on Antiquities That relate to the History of Britain Number III* (1752), frontispiece. (Spalding Gentlemen's Society)

Illustrations 1, 3, 4, 6, 11, 12, 16, 17 and 21 are reproduced by kind permission of the President and Council of the Spalding Gentlemen's Society. Illustration 2 is reproduced by kind permission of the National Portrait Gallery, London. Illustrations 5, 7, 13, 14, 15, 19 and 20 are reproduced by kind permission of the Bodleian Library, Oxford. Illustration 8 is reproduced by kind permission of Northamptonshire Record Office.

The editors and publishers are grateful to all the institutions and persons listed for permission to reproduce the materials in which they hold copyright. Every effort has been made to trace the copyright holders; apologies are offered for any omission, and the publishers will be pleased to add any necessary acknowledgement in subsequent editions.

ACKNOWLEDGEMENTS

Thanks are due to the President and Council of the Spalding Gentlemen's Society and to their Curators past and present, especially the present Curator, Mr Tom Grimes, for providing access to the correspondence and other papers in their archives, and for permission to print some of their materials. We are particularly grateful to Mrs Marion Brassington for help with locating the eighteenth-century books in the Society's library.

We are equally grateful to the staff of the Special Collections section of the Bodleian Library, Oxford, for their untiring help in giving us access to their collection of Stukeley papers and permitting us to print some of them, including his letter-book which contains the letters from Johnson. The staff of the Parker Library at Corpus Christi College, Cambridge, have been most helpful in providing access to the Stukeley MSS in their collection.

Help has also been received from the libraries of Christ Church, Oxford, and Trinity College, Cambridge, the Lincolnshire Archives, Peterborough Archives, Northamptonshire Record Office, the library of the University of East Anglia and the Dean and Chapter Library at Norwich Cathedral, especially its Librarian, Gudrun Warren, and from John Smith of Stamford who introduced us to Stukeley's houses and gardens there.

The *Clergy of the Church of England Database* and the *COPAC* on-line catalogue of university libraries have provided valuable data. The Google index has allowed us to consult a wide range of eighteenth- and nineteenth-century books.

We are, as ever, grateful to our Editor, Nicholas Bennett, for his patience and encouragement.

ABBREVIATIONS

AS	Antiquarian Society; the early eighteenth-century name for the Society of Antiquaries (see also SA below)
Bodleian	Bodleian Library, Oxford
c.	circa
Correspondence	*The Correspondence of the Spalding Gentlemen's Society 1710–1761*, ed. D. Honeybone and M. Honeybone, LRS 99 (2010)
d.	died
fl.	floruit, i.e. was active
fol.	folio
FRS	Fellow of the Royal Society
FSA	Fellow of the Society of Antiquaries
LAO	Lincolnshire Archives
LCC	Lincolnshire County Council
LRS	Lincoln Record Society
MB1–6	Minute Book of the Spalding Gentlemen's Society, 1–6
MS(S)	manuscript(s)
n.d.	no date given on letter
ODNB	*Oxford Dictionary of National Biography*
PGS	Peterborough Gentlemen's Society
Phil.Trans.	*Philosophical Transactions of the Royal Society*
PRO	National Archives (Public Record Office)
r	recto
RS	Royal Society
SA	Society of Antiquaries
SGS	Spalding Gentlemen's Society
Surtees I–III	*The Family Memoirs of the Rev. William Stukeley* I–III, ed. W. C. Lukis, Surtees Society 73, 76, 80 (1882–7)
v	verso
vol.	volume

INTRODUCTION

This volume brings together the two sides of a correspondence, stretching over forty years, between two unusual and remarkable Lincolnshire friends, William Stukeley (1687–1765) and Maurice Johnson (1688–1755). Its publication originated in a series of fortunate discoveries, one of which occurred while we were preparing a calendar of the eighteenth-century correspondence of the Spalding Gentlemen's Society (known as the SGS from the time of its foundation) for publication by the Lincoln Record Society.[1] Among the correspondence we came across a group of letters to the Society's founder, Maurice Johnson, from his friend William Stukeley stretching across the years from 1714 to just before Johnson's death in early 1755. Sections of parts of them, and short quotations from some of them, had been included in various books on Stukeley, particularly three Surtees Society volumes,[2] but they had not been published in full. We decided to include short abstracts of the letters in the calendar but, given Stukeley's status as a pioneer archæologist and author, they seemed worthy of full transcription and separate publication to bring such valuable material into the public domain. The late Adrian Oswald FSA, a member of the SGS, had been working on a transcription prior to his death, but this was still only in its initial stages.

As part of our work on the SGS's eighteenth-century correspondence we also consulted William Stukeley's letter-books, now held in the Bodleian Library, Oxford. We became aware that by far the largest section in the volumes was composed of letters sent to Stukeley by Maurice Johnson of Spalding between 1714 and 1754. Many of these were written in response to Stukeley's letters in the Spalding collection, or asked questions to which Stukeley's replies were held at Spalding.

In this book we bring together the two sides of this correspondence as a continuous sequence of letters extending over the adult lifetimes of the two men. They begin when the writers were in their twenties, establishing themselves in their careers and setting out their hopes and plans for the future. They extend through their maturer years, covering Johnson's work as a lawyer in Lincolnshire and London and his development of his cherished project, the SGS. Stukeley's letters deal with his life and work as a physician, first in Boston from 1714 to 1717, then in London from 1717 to 1726, his move to Grantham in 1726, his change of career following ordination in the Church of England in 1729, his Stamford years and his eventual return to London in 1747 as incumbent of St George's church, Queen Square. The final letters follow their later years, in which both show disillusionment with the failure of some of their cherished schemes, but still remain positive and optimistic, Stukeley about his historical theories and

---

[1] D. Honeybone and M. Honeybone (eds), *The Correspondence of the Spalding Gentlemen's Society 1710–1761*, LRS 99 (2010).
[2] *Surtees* I–III.

publications and Johnson about the prospects for his society's continued success even after his own death.

Frequent references to the development and activities of the SGS are inevitably included in the letters, particularly those of Johnson, for whom the SGS was a major project throughout his life. However, it is not intended that this volume and its introduction give a complete history or description of the Society. This has already been provided in previous studies such as Moore's[3] and in two existing Lincoln Record Society volumes.[4] It is hoped that the SGS will shortly be making an electronic version of the eighteenth-century minute books available on-line via the Society's website and these will provide researchers and interested readers with a much more complete picture of the Society's activities.

The rest of this Introduction describes the content of this remarkable correspondence and relates it to the wide-ranging interests of the writers. A comparison of the two friends, in many ways similar but with differences, gives some biographical and contextual background, which continues to emerge in the following, more detailed consideration of the lives and concerns of Johnson and then Stukeley as separate individuals.

The text of the correspondence

Locations of the letters
The letters from Stukeley to Johnson are held among the eighteenth-century correspondence of the SGS which is preserved in the Society's archive in Spalding. The SGS's letter files were maintained by Johnson as the Society's Secretary and contained letters which would have been of interest to the Society's studies and were read out to them at meetings.

The letters from Johnson to Stukeley are in Stukeley's voluminous letter-books. They had originally belonged to Stukeley's daughter and descendants and were acquired during the nineteenth century by Captain Cragg of Threekingham (Lincolnshire). From him, they were passed to the Bodleian Library, Oxford, where they are now preserved in the library's Special Collections of English MSS, as MS Eng. misc. c.113 and 114. The two volumes[5] contain many of the letters written to Stukeley by a wide range of correspondents throughout his adult life, and the letters from Johnson comprise by far the largest section.

Three drafts of early letters by Johnson to Stukeley have survived among his papers in the Spalding archive; if undated, these can be dated by the completed letters sent to Stukeley, which are preserved in the Bodleian letter-books. Two are almost identical to the final text as sent to Stukeley and so have not been transcribed but are referred to in notes to **Letter 1** and **Letter 3**; the other is transcribed as **Letter 9**.

We have included seven further letters at the end, in Additional Letters. Two are addressed to Stukeley and are preserved in the Bodleian letter-books: one,

---

[3] W. Moore, *The Gentlemen's Society at Spalding: its Origin and Progress* (London, 1851).
[4] D. M. Owen (ed.), *The Minute-Books of the Spalding Gentlemen's Society 1712–1755*, LRS 73 (1981); D. Honeybone and M. Honeybone (eds), *The Correspondence of the Spalding Gentlemen's Society 1710–1761*, LRS 99 (2010).
[5] Bodleian, MS Eng. misc. c.113–114.

Letter 87 dated 15 February 1755, is from the Revd John Johnson, Maurice Johnson's third son, announcing his father's death to his old friend; John Johnson's second letter, **Letter 88** dated 30 March 1756, gives news of the SGS's activities. A third letter is in the Spalding archive, **Letter 89** dated 2 October 1756; it is from Stukeley to Dr John Green, Johnson's son-in-law and fellow-Secretary of the SGS, a man who shared Stukeley's interest in coin-collection. These letters show Stukeley's continuing interest in Johnson's society and family, with both of which he had had many years' contact. To ensure that the correspondence is as fully covered as possible, four further letters are also included. **Letter 84**, from Stukeley to Johnson in 1728, is in the Wingfield Papers at the Northamptonshire Record Office. The other three are from Johnson to Stukeley: **Letter 83**, dated 14 October 1719, and **Letter 86**, dated 21 June 1750, are printed in John Nichols, *Bibliotheca Topographica Britannica, Reliquiæ Galeanæ* (1781); **Letter 85**, dated 17 March 1744, is published in *Surtees* II (1876).

The correspondence and its contents
By bringing together the two components of a written conversation between lifelong friends it is possible to reconstruct the development of their shared interests, attitudes and opinions. They write on a remarkably wide range of topics, from their antiquarian and historical studies to current matters of interest. Some of these are national concerns: political scandals, financial disasters such as the South Sea Bubble, the threat of Jacobite invasions in 1715 and 1745. Others reflect the artistic and cultural life of the nation: the founding of the British Museum and Library, the latest operatic performances and singers, the work of artists and particularly the activities of the Royal Society and the Society of Antiquaries (the Antiquarian Society, as Johnson and Stukeley called it). Stukeley's periods of London residence from 1717 to 1726 and from 1747 onwards and his annual winter visits from 1740 to 1743 during his Stamford years kept him in touch with the life of the capital. Johnson, although a Spalding resident after his student years at the Inner Temple, made regular visits to London for the legal terms each year until his health deteriorated, and also kept in touch with London events and news through his many correspondents.

The letters also reflect the life of South Lincolnshire in the first half of the eighteenth century: local elections and politics, or social events such as recitals of music, race meetings and plays performed by travelling companies or a local school. The effect of the weather on crops and people is noted, with references to droughts, epidemics of sickness among cattle, the floods which were a constant threat to Fen-dwellers and the attempts of local landowners to drain the land. Local gossip brings before the reader a parade of characters, some easy to identify and others impossible to locate, marrying for love or money, building houses, succeeding or failing in their careers, encountering alarming accidents.

Naturally, these letters reflect the lives of the two friends. The reader becomes familiar with their hopes and plans for their careers, their concerns over finance and expenditure, their marriages and the activities of their children, their friendships, the difficulties and arguments which arise with neighbours and associates and all the minutiæ of small-town Lincolnshire life. Both were keen gardeners and proud of their gardens, whose development is described in detail, and we read of the improvements they make to their houses, a particular interest of

Stukeley's. Johnson describes with pride the splendid view from the tower of his house (**Letter 37**) and the activities of the wild-cat kitten which has become his pet (**Letter 15**).

Above all, the chief reason for the writing of these letters was to share their passion for the study of antiquity and their enthusiasm for spreading learned knowledge as widely as possible through sociable organisations. Both of these were significant features of the late seventeenth and particularly the early eighteenth centuries, a 'clubbable' period, to use the adjective created by that other great enthusiast for sociability and learning of the time, Dr Samuel Johnson (no relation to the Spalding Johnsons). Many provincial towns, as well as London, had clubs and societies at this period, some devoted to sharing discoveries in knowledge, some book-lending societies and some simply social gatherings such as dining or drinking clubs. Both Stukeley and Johnson preferred learned societies. They were members of these in the metropolis and in the East Midlands and Lincolnshire,[6] either as sole founders or as co-founders with a group of like-minded colleagues.

This correspondence is of special interest in illuminating a unique group of such learned societies which sprang up in South Lincolnshire and neighbouring towns in the first part of the eighteenth century, at a time when it was still assumed that all branches of learning, from numismatics and art to astronomy and calculus (or 'fluxions') were, and should be, accessible to study by groups of educated men in provincial towns. Indeed, as **Letter 32** indicates, Johnson considered including female members. This striking departure from the usual practice did not succeed, perhaps because of opposition from other members, though one of the societies to which both Johnson and Stukeley belonged in London in the early1720s, the Society of Roman Knights, did admit female members. The group of East Midland local societies was unique in being so numerous in such a small area, comparatively remote from the capital, and in the survival of a wealth of documentation connected with them, of which these letters are only a part. The extensive correspondence of the members of Johnson's SGS has already been calendared and the Society still possesses the six volumes of minute books dating from 1712 to the 1760s, which it is hoped will shortly be accessible to researchers via the internet. Two volumes of Stukeley's minutes of his short-lived Stamford Brazen Nose Society also survive and will form part of a projected future volume for the Lincoln Record Society, together with a transcription of the Peterborough Gentlemen's Society minute books.

The shared belief in access to all branches of knowledge led to a growing concern, felt by both Stukeley and Johnson in later life, about a current tendency towards specialisation. This was shown in the Antiquarian Society, which planned to set limits to its activities by specifying them in a Royal Charter. The Royal Society, already possessor of a charter, was beginning to concentrate its activities solely on those areas of natural philosophy which we today categorise as 'science', whereas earlier meetings had included topics such as geography, archæology and the study of languages. Stukeley summed this up in a memo-

---

[6] Stukeley's and Johnson's membership of London and Lincolnshire learned societies is discussed more fully below. Johnson was a member of the Wisbech Gentlemen's Society, the Peterborough Gentlemen's Society, the Brazen Nose Society of Stamford and the Deepings Club.

rable phrase in **Letter 75**, dated 24 April 1754, saying it would be 'prejudicial to learning in general, by dividing the Stream'. Johnson, in particular, felt that the pursuit of knowledge would be better served by the two major organisations, the Royal Society and the Antiquarian Society, joining together, particularly as a number of people were members of both societies.

Johnson's correspondence reflects his determination, detailed in the SGS minute books, to found and maintain in his home town of Spalding a society of the kind he had enjoyed while studying law at the Inner Temple in London. As described later in this introduction, he had been introduced to a remarkable group of wits and writers at Button's coffee-house. As his time in London drew to a close, Johnson appears to have expressed to the essayist Sir Richard Steele his regret at losing this experience of exciting discussion and discovery. Steele suggested that Johnson form such a club in Spalding on his return home to practise law there.[7] What was probably just a passing remark by Steele was taken by the young Johnson as a mission statement for his future life, and he returned home fired with enthusiasm for recreating in the provinces the life of thought and learned discussion he had met in London. His letters document the growth of the SGS from small beginnings as a conventional group meeting to read and discuss the latest London periodicals, to a wide-ranging organisation receiving reports from correspondents across Britain and abroad and documenting its active research into many areas including numismatics, biology and astronomy. His determination and support over forty years not only kept his society alive but secured for it an international corresponding network; his final letters show his satisfaction that it will outlive him as 'the Greatest Good I could propose to my Native place' (**Letter 81**, 19 January 1754).

Stukeley was an equally keen member of such societies. In particular, both were among the small group of antiquaries who met regularly in a London tavern during the initial years of the century to discuss antiquities and in 1717–18 re-activated the Antiquarian Society, which had lapsed since its original foundation in Elizabethan times and had informally begun to resume its activities in 1707. Its activities are frequently documented in this correspondence. As a physician with a background in science, Stukeley gained membership of the Royal Society in March 1718. He had hoped to become its Secretary in the early 1720s but his candidature was opposed by Sir Isaac Newton, who thought he lacked sufficient grounding in mathematics. Nonetheless, he remained an interested member; his later letters show him reading papers there following his re-election to membership during his London residence from 1748 to 1765.

This collection of letters demonstrates the repeated attempts to form learned societies wherever possible in Lincolnshire and neighbouring areas of the East Midlands. The letters throw light on the foundation in 1730 of the SGS's daughter society, the Peterborough Gentlemen's Society, which modelled itself on the rules and structure of the SGS. They provide evidence for the joint efforts of Johnson and Stukeley in creating a short-lived learned society at Ancaster in 1729 (**Letters 25–28**), Stukeley's own attempts to found and maintain a similar society in Stamford and revive it in the 1740s (**Letters 41**, **45** and **50**) and John-

---

[7] SGS, MB1, fol.30r.

son's unsuccessful attempt to found a similar society in Lincoln (**Letter 42**). One of the most fascinating aspects of this enthusiasm for learning and sociability appears particularly in **Letter 42**, where Johnson spells out his hopes for these societies to link up into a network of shared learning across the Fens and so provide what he calls 'An Academy of Arts and Sciences' for the Fens and South Lincolnshire, a remarkable visionary ideal.

These attempts illuminate the problems and difficulties of developing and maintaining such a group, and make Johnson's thriving Spalding society seem the more remarkable. Success appeared to depend on the regular presence of a leading figure in the local community who combined enthusiasm and organising skills with an equable personality, firm enough to prevent dissension and disruptive arguments but friendly enough to draw in and retain members. Perhaps this is why Johnson succeeded in this respect, in his home town at least, while the more fiery and enthusiastic Stukeley did not. Other societies, such as the early one at Wisbech at the beginning of the century, declined when a key figure left the area or died; in the case of Wisbech, Dr Richard Middleton Massey moved to London and Richard Lake died. This had a parallel at the Northampton Philosophical Society, which declined after a few active years (1743–51) when it lost two vital members, the Revd Dr Philip Doddridge who died and William Shipley who, like Massey, went to London.

This collection of letters, stretching over forty years, documents changes in knowledge, behaviour and outlook. Some of them arise from alterations in local or national circumstances and some reflect changing attitudes in two ageing friends. It is interesting to note changes in tone and style: in writing the early letters, both are aware that a letter containing discussion of learned topics could be passed on to other interested people to read, or could even be read out at a meeting such as the SGS or the Antiquarian Society. They therefore attempted a degree of dignified formality suited to the manners of the age. This gives way to an easier, more informal style as the friendship develops and as they pass to less formal topics. Sometimes the style becomes that of casual conversation, Johnson's sentences flowing together as in speech and Stukeley giving snippets of the latest London news and gossip. They still follow early eighteenth-century conventions in letter-writing: even in the most informal and friendly letters there is a degree of formality in the salutation and closing greetings, and in the signatures, surprising to a 21st-century reader. They are likely to begin with 'Dear Sir'; Johnson addresses Stukeley as 'Dear Doctor', and they conclude with a phrase such as 'I am, dear Sir, your affectionate friend and obedient humble servant'. Johnson is the more formal, probably because of his legal training in letter-writing. Throughout his father's long life, he always signs himself 'M. Johnson junior' or 'jun^r'; it is only after his father's death in 1747 that he signs himself 'M. Johnson'. Though Stukeley uses similar lengthy phrases at times, he also ends a letter 'Your affectionate W. Stukeley'.

The chronology of the letters is listed in Appendix 2 and shows periods of regular and frequent correspondence interspersed at times with months, or even years, when no letters occur in either collection. This may be because letters have been mislaid or lost, either at the time or later. For example, at the end of his life, the ageing and ailing Johnson does not seem to have filed and kept all the letters from Stukeley, while the fitter Stukeley, who survived his friend by over ten years, was still storing Johnson's letters. In 1719, one of Johnson's letters was apparently lent to someone else to look for an answer to a question it contained, and Stukeley does not appear to have received it back. Several of Stukeley's later letters dealing principally with coin-collecting, especially the 'Oriuna' question (**Letters 68**, **71**, **75**, **77**), were bound by Johnson into a volume, now in the Spalding collection, which he labelled 'Tracts' and which dealt with letters and other documents relating to numismatics, instead of being kept with the rest of his correspondence. Since the letter files that Johnson kept as Secretary of the SGS retained only correspondence of interest and application to the Society's activities, any of Stukeley's letters which were on purely personal matters may have been put among Johnson's personal papers, which were kept at his home and dispersed by later generations of his family. The minute books of the SGS record the reading of some letters from Stukeley which are not present in the SGS archive but may have been filed with Johnson's personal papers.

There were also times when letters, which were quite expensive for professional men without extensive incomes to send and receive, were not necessary. Stukeley and Johnson met frequently in London during the legal terms. When Stukeley was living in Lincolnshire, first in Boston at the start of the correspondence, then in Grantham and Stamford, it was possible for the two to visit each other or to meet. Stukeley retained family property in his birthplace of Holbeach, a few miles from Spalding, which he visited from time to time to check on its condition. The SGS minute books record Stukeley's presence at the Society's Thursday meetings on occasions; similarly, Johnson was a member of Stukeley's Brazen Nose Society in Stamford. The letters contain plans for meeting at Ancaster for their society there, and on expeditions to Crowland to study the Abbey ruins, and on other occasions. At times, it was the pressure of daily life that made them delay writing; the demands of careers, families and other commitments, familiar to many today, took time away from the creation of lengthy letters to old friends. As Appendix 2 indicates, after a regular correspondence from 1714 to 1720 the sequence shows gaps at times during the 1720s and 1730s, when the two were at their busiest and also had the most frequent occasions for meeting. The 1740s saw the resumption of regular correspondence, and in the final years, up to late 1754 when Johnson told his old friend that his health would no longer allow him to visit London, the letters were their main means of keeping in contact and sharing ideas.

William Stukeley and Maurice Johnson: similarities and differences

Lasting friendships can often derive from childhood. For them to survive into adult life, they are usually built on some degree of similarity of interests, tastes and attitudes, but do not necessarily require similarity of temperament. Johnson and Stukeley shared many similarities, but in some respects their lifelong friendship was an attraction of opposites.

Their family circumstances were alike. They were born within a year of each other, Stukeley in 1687 and Johnson in 1688, to fathers who were both lawyers in the Lincolnshire Fenland, John Stukeley in Holbeach and Maurice Johnson senior in nearby Spalding. Besides being professional associates, their fathers were fellow-officers in the local Militia regiment: Maurice Johnson senior was

Captain and John Stukeley his Lieutenant. Both Johnson and Stukeley remained conscious of their Lincolnshire origins and loyal to their county of origin: Johnson begins **Letter 15** by addressing Stukeley as 'Dear Countryman', that is to say, fellow-Lincolnshireman. This loyalty was perhaps stronger in Johnson's case, but Stukeley, who began his published work by devoting the first section of his *Itinerarium Curiosum* of 1725/6 to the antiquities of South Lincolnshire, and Holland in particular, kept his Lincolnshire connections and his Holbeach property and resided for much of his career in Boston, Grantham and Stamford. It was this sense of local loyalty that brought both of them into contact with Sir Isaac Newton, who on at least two occasions chaired dinners for the Lincolnshire gentlemen living in London and agreed to become an honorary member of the SGS because it was of benefit to Lincolnshire gentlemen.

Stukeley's godfather William Ambler lived next door to the Johnsons in Spalding; Stukeley's notebooks[8] speak of his riding alone to Spalding for the first time in 1700 at the age of twelve, which could have included a visit to Johnson. As **Letter 32** indicates, the two became friends at an early age. Perhaps one of the factors which drew them into a lasting friendship was their shared enthusiasm for collecting coins, particularly those of the Roman emperors. Both had a similar start to their education at local grammar schools, specialising in the Classics, and these coins gave them a tangible link to the world of ancient Rome with which their education made them familiar. Their training and skill in drawing, a necessary ability for recording antiquarian finds and sites, enabled them to make joint excursions, for example to Crowland to sketch the ruins of the Abbey. Another shared interest was in plants; Stukeley began by 'simpling' or collecting medically useful plants and Johnson's SGS developed a 'physic garden'. Both had the eighteenth-century passion for garden design and for growing the newly discovered species that were being introduced into England.

As professional gentlemen of the early eighteenth century, both Stukeley and Johnson were typically dependent on the support of aristocratic patrons. Stukeley gained the patronage of Lord Pembroke and later the Duke of Montagu who brought about his preferment to London in 1747. Johnson had the patronage of Francis Scott, first as Earl of Dalkeith and then as Duke of Buccleuch, a relationship which went back to their shared schooldays at Eton.

There were, however, some differences in temperament and circumstances which affected the course of their lives and careers. Although their backgrounds were similar, Johnson's family seems to have been more financially stable. Stukeley's father died at a comparatively early age, while Stukeley was at Cambridge, leaving him with family debts which dominated his early career. Maurice Johnson's father, on the other hand, seems to have married prudently, three times, and husbanded his resources so that he was able to provide his son with land on his marriage which ensured at least a portion of his income. Johnson's own marriage brought him more financial resources. Eventually his wife became co-heiress with her sister of the Ambler property, including the large Gayton House next door to Johnson's family home at Ayscoughfee Hall. Johnson was able to extend his education beyond the foundations given by a country grammar school when

---

[8] Bodleian, MS Eng. misc. e.121, fol.10.

the link with the Buccleuch family provided the opportunity of several years at Eton. After this, he followed his father and grandfather into the law, apparently willingly, and remained a Lincolnshire-based barrister throughout his life, encouraging one of his sons to take over his practice in later years. Stukeley's career was more varied. He was reluctant to follow his father into the law, insisting on studying natural philosophy and medicine at Cambridge. After years of practice in Boston, London and Grantham, he changed careers and was ordained into the Church of England in 1729, although he retained a medical interest in the production and use of his 'Gout Oils'.

Their circumstances affected their family life. Johnson was able to marry early, at the age of twenty-one. His bride was Elizabeth Ambler who was literally the girl next door, since she lived at Gayton House, adjacent to the Johnsons' family home of Ayscoughfee Hall in Spalding. It was a happy and successful marriage and Johnson remained a devoted husband and father to his very large family. Later, he faced the financial demands of ensuring their future in life, providing dowries for his daughters and establishing his sons in careers. Stukeley, who had to sort out his family's tangled financial situation, had to make his own way in the world. He did not marry until 1727 at the age of forty; although Frances Williamson brought him some money, he was left at her death in 1737 with a small family of daughters. His second marriage, in 1739 to Elizabeth Gale (sister of his friends Roger and Samuel Gale and co-heiress with them),[9] brought greater financial stability, financing the winter residences in London during 1740–3 and probably providing the resources for the self-publication of some of his later works, which was an expensive process.

The course of their professional and social lives was influenced not only by external circumstances but also by their personalities. While both were keen antiquarians, collectors and organisers of social groups, their approaches to their activities followed different patterns. Johnson's letters show him to be thorough and precise in investigating and recording details, as suited his legal training. One of his main characteristics was his conscientiousness, apparent in the care with which he recorded the minutes of the SGS's weekly meetings over many years and kept up the Society's correspondence. He was a man of steady loyalties to his friends and his intellectual interests, pursuing the same studies throughout his life and supporting the theories advanced by his associates in their publications. He appears to have lacked ambition to shine as a published author; his 'Decennium Carausii et Allecti', dealing with the coinage of the reigns of the Emperors Carausius and Allectus, while admired by colleagues, remained in MS form. His main ambitions, other than those for his children, were for his society in Spalding and he worked tirelessly to ensure its growth and success as a way of providing a benefaction to his native town. Unlike Stukeley, he had little enthusiasm for travel for its own sake. After an antiquarian journey to Bath as a young man in 1710, recorded in a Latin journal, he was contented with life in Spalding, his regular visits to London and the necessary journeys on the Midland Circuit on legal business.

---

[9] There are frequent references to the Gale brothers, particularly to Roger Gale, in the letters; further details may be found in the end-notes following the relevant letters and in Appendix 3.

Stukeley's enthusiasms were more intense and more changeable, leading to the rapid growth of convictions and theories. At times he would build great structures of conjecture from a basis of limited evidence, such as his later views on the Druids and on Lady Roisia's cave at Royston (**Letters 44** and **54**). It was this quick seizure of a new and exciting idea that could cause him at times to be misled, as by the alleged MS of 'Richard of Westminster' (**Letters 57–59**) and the coin whose inscription he read as 'Oriuna', of which Johnson took a more cautious view. However, he was capable of sound research, as in his work on the spleen[10] and his meticulous recording of archæological and architectural sites. His fiery responses to challenges had their value in leading him to attack those who were destroying some valuable sites, such as Avebury and the ruins of Croyland Abbey.

Stukeley's need for new stimulation was partly responsible for his changes of career and residence. He fluctuated between medicine and theology, between enthusiasm for solitude and preference for sociability, and between the charms of the peaceful countryside and the intellectual excitement available in the city, particularly in London. His final location, in Queen Square, which was on the extreme northern edge of London at that time, enabled him to combine the sociable mental stimulation of urban life with access to country pleasures. Unlike Johnson, the restless aspect of his nature made him a keen traveller, which provided material for his *Itinerarium Curiosum* and his archæological studies.

One of the advantages of a long-lasting friendship is that one is accepted by the friend without question and without hesitation. Despite the contrasts in their approaches to life and the changing circumstances that often kept them apart, these two men kept in touch with each other and maintained their remarkable friendship. The following two sections examine in more detail the background of the two correspondents.

Maurice Johnson (1688–1755)

Maurice Johnson was born into a family of Spalding lawyers. His grandfather Walter Johnson was a Justice of the Peace and attorney at law who married first Agnes Willesby and then, as his second wife, Katherine, née Downes, the widow of Thomas King of Moulton, also an attorney at law. Maurice's father, the son of Walter and Katherine, was born in 1661, the first of a line of six Maurice Johnsons. He became a barrister, having studied at the Inner Temple. This Maurice (from now onwards referred to as Maurice Johnson I or Maurice Johnson senior) had three wives, the first of whom was Jane Johnson, daughter and heir of Francis Johnson the owner of Ayscoughfee Hall, the great house on Spalding riverside, originally built by mediæval wool-merchants. Through her, Maurice Johnson I became the owner of Ayscoughfee Hall and it was the family home for generations of Spalding Johnsons. This first marriage was the only one to produce children; the elder of the two surviving sons of this marriage, born on 19 June 1688, was Maurice Johnson II (from now onwards referred to as Johnson, except where it is necessary to distinguish him from his father), the founder of the

---

[10] See Illustration 10.

Spalding Gentlemen's Society. His younger brother, John (1690–1744), became the Society's Treasurer.

Johnson attended the free grammar school of Spalding, an Elizabethan foundation held in a side-chapel of the nearby parish church of St Mary and St Nicholas, where the Revd John Waring was the schoolmaster from 1695 to 1716 (see Illustration 6). Here Johnson received a sound mathematical education in addition to the usual grammar-school curriculum concentrating on Latin and Greek. Johnson's MS index to the minute books is written on the blank pages of an old notebook from his schooldays, which still contains several pages of mathematical problems written in a young hand.

At some stage in his youth, Johnson went on to study at Eton College. This experience had a strong influence on him and he wrote a eulogy on the death of John Newborough, the headmaster of Eton from 1690 to 1711. This rather unusual step for the son of a provincial lawyer may have come about because Maurice Johnson I was the steward for the Spalding lands of the Duchess of Buccleuch. Her grandson, Francis Scott (1694–1751), later Lord Dalkeith and then Duke of Buccleuch, attended Eton in the early 1700s and it is likely that Johnson, a slightly older boy and already quite a promising scholar, was sent there at the same time to assist the young Scott in return for continuing his own education. Certainly Johnson refers to Scott as his schoolfellow, and Scott was prepared to become the patron of Johnson's learned society and to provide it with expensive books. In July 1738 Johnson drafted a letter to Scott, by then Duke of Buccleuch, 'you'll pardon me talking as a School Fellow … which makes Eaton ever Remembred by me with much more pleasure'.[11] Johnson evidently had an effective education, as is shown by his fluency in Latin, which he used at times for correspondence, and his familiarity with classical Greek.

In 1705 Johnson became a member of the Inns of Court, attending the Inner Temple in London, his father's Inn. His legal training as a barrister culminated in his being called to the Bar in 1710. This qualified him to become legal counsel at the assizes and to appear before Parliamentary committees to speak for or against Parliamentary bills. He became the official counsel at law for the Dean and Chapter of Peterborough. In addition to this he became a Justice of the Peace and was appointed chairman of the South Holland Quarter Sessions from 1713 onwards. The third area in which he applied his legal expertise was as manorial steward in Spalding, Crowland, Kirton and Hitchin. As chairman to the local Commission of Sewers he was deeply involved in clarifying the legal position in land drainage disputes, a significant matter in the Lincolnshire Fens.

Johnson consolidated his social position as a landed gentleman in Spalding by marrying in 1710, at the comparatively early age of twenty-one, Elizabeth, the daughter of his father's neighbour William Ambler of Gayton House, which stood until recently next to Ayscoughfee Hall, on the site of the present Council offices. Eventually Elizabeth became co-heiress of her father and as a result Johnson became, during the 1740s, the owner of Spalding's two greatest houses, Ayscoughfee Hall (see Illustration 4) and Gayton House. Johnson also took over

---

[11] *Correspondence*, 113 (letter 308), a draft in which Johnson explains to the Duke that the Society would like to receive a copy of Pine's new, expensive edition of the poems of Horace. This was later sent by the Duke for the Society's library and is still in its possession.

his father's role as steward of the main manor of Spalding, which belonged first to Anne Scott, Duchess of Buccleuch, and then on her death in 1732 to his former schoolfellow Francis Scott, second Duke of Buccleuch. His legal reputation and social position gave him prominence in the society of Spalding and district, which enabled him to give cachet and a very positive reputation to the learned society which he developed in Spalding. His use of the patronage system, which lay at the heart of English social, professional and cultural life at the time, derived from his association with the Duke, who was deeply involved in London learned society as a member of the Royal Society and the Antiquarian Society and also a major freemason.

Johnson and founding the Spalding Gentlemen's Society
His early experience of London life had a significant influence on Johnson, and he remained in touch with the life of the capital for much of the rest of his life through regular visits for the four legal terms each year. At these times he lodged in rooms in the city of London near the Temple, often using local coffee-houses such as the ones in Devereux Court as an address for receiving his mail when in London. The coffee-houses also played a vital part in the social life of the time, as they were the centres for meeting friends and discussing current topics of interest, serious as well as more light-hearted. A particular influence on the young Johnson during his time as a law student was the regular meeting at Button's, one of the best-known of the London coffee-houses in the early years of the eighteenth century, kept by the former butler of the well-known author Joseph Addison. As Johnson later documented in his account of the Spalding Gentlemen's Society's foundation, written in the Society's first minute book,[12] he was introduced to the remarkable club that met there, including such members as Addison, the essayist Steele and the poet Alexander Pope, by John Gay the dramatist, a friend of Johnson's since Gay had been secretary to the Duchess of Buccleuch. It was there that Johnson became inspired by the idea of a literary discussion meeting. He records that on one occasion, when about to leave London, and no doubt regretting the loss of the intellectual life of the capital, he was encouraged by Richard Steele to set up his own regular meeting in Spalding: 'as he assured Captn Steel, afterwards Sr Richard Steel Kn^t who and in the name of Izaac Bickerstaff published the Tatlers, when by his Encouragement he first had any thoughts of Instituting It [the SGS] determined steadily to attend and support It, wch that Gentleman advised him was the sine qua non, of such an Attempt, at Button's Coffee House'.[13]

As a result, Johnson began regular weekly gentlemen's meetings in Spalding from 1710 onwards, a remarkable feat for a young man in a provincial town. Meeting at first informally at a newly established local coffee-house, the doctors, clerics, lawyers, schoolmasters and merchants of the town and district began both to organise the repair and cataloguing of the Spalding parish library and to read and discuss another exciting new development, the essays in the London periodicals 'the *Tatler*, the *Spectator* and the *Lay Monks*'[14] which arrived regularly from

[12] SGS, MB1, fol.16r.
[13] SGS, MB1, fol 30r.
[14] SGS, MB1, fol.35r.

London on the coach that called at the White Hart inn in Spalding market-place. This became the nucleus of a society 'for supporting mutual Benevolence, raising and preserving & rendring of general Use a Publick Lending Library pursuant to the statute of the 7th of Queen Ann Chapt. 14th And the Improvement of the Members in All Arts & Sciences'.[15] As a London law student, Johnson would have noted the passing of this act in 1708 'For the better preservation of parochial libraries'. Section VII of this act, the first English act for public libraries, insisted that there should be a catalogue 'for the better preservation of the books'. As a result the Spalding parish church library, founded by the Revd Robert Ram in the 1630s, is today still in good condition and is looked after in the SGS's modern premises.

If Johnson's legal background gave the Society its first task, care of the books, his innate legalism also meant that from the start he gave a firm institutional framework to the meetings, insisting on a set of rules which were reviewed each year to provide a very precise constitution and recorded as such in the meticulous minute books which Johnson kept as Secretary. One topic of conversation was absolutely forbidden: the discussion of politics, as this could easily lead to destructive arguments.[16] Apart from this, the Society existed for any member 'to communicate any Thing in any part of Learning, Knowledge, Arts or Sciences which may to him seem Useful, New, Uncommon, Curious or Entertaining'.[17]

The significant word there is 'communicate': this was one of the key purposes of the Society. At the weekly meetings, which began on Mondays, then changed to Wednesdays but quickly moved to Thursdays, a minimum of five regular members (the quorum for a meeting) heard and discussed dissertations on a wide variety of learned topics or readings from the correspondence sent by members, examined specimens of plants and fossils or looked at the latest prints. Johnson quoted Persius's *Satire* I, line 26, 'a true old saying "scire tuum Nihil est, nisi Te scire hoc sciat Alter"' or in other words 'Your knowing is nothing, unless another knows that you know it'.[18] Johnson maintained correspondence with other learned societies, both locally and nationally, sending accounts of his Society's activities and discoveries to the Royal Society and Antiquarian Society, as well as the more local Peterborough Gentlemen's Society. He received reports from them in return, including the Royal Society's printed *Philosophical Transactions*.

He insisted that full minutes of all communications be kept; these have survived in full for the weekly meetings between June 1724 until the 1750s, when they became more intermittent, ending in 1758, three years after Johnson's death. It is hardly surprising that the minutes from 1709 to 1724 are incomplete, as these fifteen years were the period when Johnson was establishing his legal career and had regular absences from Spalding to go on the Midland legal circuit; but his letters to the Society show that he sent information to the Society even during

[15] SGS, MB1, fol.217r.
[16] SGS, MB1, fol.169r: 'No one whosoever may talk Politicks at the Society or read or report or offer or propose to be read or repeated any Political or Party paper.'
[17] SGS, MB1, fol.299r.
[18] SGS, MB2, fol.35r.

these absences.[19] Johnson's untiring efforts resulted in the Society's survival and growth: as the Revd Timothy Neve, Treasurer of the SGS and later founder of the Peterborough Gentlemen's Society, expressed it, 'Your Fame is gone abroad into the remotest corners of the Earth and your Names are mention'd, not only among the curious of our own Nation, but in both the Indies with great Honour. I believe there are not many Instances thro'out the kingdom of a voluntary Society of Gentlemen of different Parties & Perswasions, that have submitted themselves to strict Rules inviolably observ'd, for so many years and still subsisting in an amicable & ingenious Friendship.'[20]

Johnson's letters show that he developed a vision of the creation of a network of societies across the Fens and the nearby East Midlands, all corresponding with each other to share their knowledge and ideas. In **Letter 42**, written on 15 March 1746, he wrote to Stukeley, 'Now As Spalding is Naturaly Situat for It, I hope the Learning of Stamford, Peterborough, Boston & Wisbeach Will center in it, ... these like 4 Colleges of Arts will forme as it were an Academy of Arts & Sciences for this Gyrvian Tract [the Lincolnshire Fens].' Elsewhere he wrote of a scheme for 'assisting other Gentlemen my acquaintance and friends in Lincoln City, Peterborough, Stamford, Boston, Oundle, Wisbeach & elsewhere to Institute & promote the like Designe, and hold Correspondence with us'.[21]

Johnson had been a member of the early Wisbech Gentlemen's Society and considered that its revival, together with the creation of new societies at Peterborough, Stamford and other nearby towns, could establish such a web of contacts, with his Spalding society playing a significant role. He hoped that Stukeley's attempts to found and support his Stamford society in the 1730s and restore it in the 1740s, and the Revd Timothy Neve's Peterborough society, founded in 1730, could form elements of it. This ambitious scheme was not successful. Neve's society was the longest-lived, lasting as a 'learned society' for around twenty years until the early 1750s when it declined into a monthly book-lending club. Stukeley's Stamford society survived only a couple of years. A society at Ancaster failed after one meeting. Johnson's letters reveal attempts to encourage the founding of similar societies at Lincoln and Boston, though without success. These failures can be attributed to what appears to have been a common trend among such learned societies outside the metropolis: they tended to rely on the enthusiasm and stimulus provided by one man, generally the founder, and when this was withdrawn – because the main supporter left the area, or died, or was otherwise distracted from attention to the group – the societies either ceased to meet or became simply a social gathering. The constituent elements of the regional network that Johnson envisaged did not develop as he hoped they would. In addition, the pressures of his legal career absorbed the extra energy that would have been required to sustain this forward-looking scheme.

Johnson and the scope of the Spalding Gentlemen's Society
Johnson, like his friend Stukeley and many other people of the early eighteenth century, was a man of wide-ranging interests, at a time before the general accept-

---

[19] *Correspondence, passim.*
[20] Letter from the Revd Timothy Neve to Maurice Johnson, 5 March 1730, in the SGS archives.
[21] SGS, MB1, fol.73r.

ance of specialisation when it was still considered natural and acceptable for a gentleman to interest himself in the whole spectrum of knowledge, from electricity to classical literature. Accordingly, Johnson's society regarded the whole domain of human interests to be within its scope of study, as did other societies flourishing at the time, when even the Royal Society heard and published papers on such subjects as Grammar, Chronology, History, Antiquities, Music and Monsters.[22]

By 1725 Johnson was sufficiently highly regarded to be appointed legal counsel for the Lincolnshire Gentlemen in their Parliamentary fight against the 1725 Bedford Level Adventurers' Bill, intended to extend their draining activities. Fenland agriculture and navigation were perceived to be endangered by the silting up of waterways and the flooding of land due to the sinking of land as a result of current drainage techniques. In order to develop his role as a counsellor in drainage law, Johnson collected historical documents associated with the monastic drainage work in the mediæval period and with the continued work of the South Holland Commission of Sewers, which had been founded in the thirteenth century. He encouraged drainage engineers, particularly Captain John Perry (1669/70–1733), responsible for the closure of the dangerous Dagenham Breach in the banks of the River Thames in 1719, and John Grundy senior (1696–1748) to become members of the SGS, and the Society's minutes have frequent references to their work and plans. The SGS retains extensive MS collections relating to the Fens, and to Deeping Fen in particular, testifying to Johnson's determination to collect and preserve them for legal and historical purposes.

One group of MSS in particular has survived in the SGS's archive: maps. The early eighteenth century was a time of great interest in accurate mapping, and cartographical surveying techniques were widely taught. William Stukeley learnt triangulation and measuring methods as a young man, enabling him to create extensive local and national maps, notably maps of the drainage of the Wash area and of possible Roman roads in the area. Johnson encouraged him and also Thomas Badeslade[23] and John Grundy as map-makers and purchased their finished products. The original of Grundy's map of Spalding survives today in the SGS; it has been displayed on the wall of their meeting room since 1732 when Grundy created it. The SGS had contributed to the preparation of the map, deciding which buildings in the town were of sufficient importance to be illustrated in its margins. Maps were also of significance to Johnson in his work as Deputy Recorder for the boroughs of Stamford and Boston and as steward to gentlemen's estates across eastern England. In addition to managing the manor of Spalding for the Dukes of Buccleuch, he was steward of estates in Kirton and Croyland for the Earl of Exeter and for William Bogdani, lord of the manor of Hitchin, Hertfordshire, and gave legal advice to his kinsman Henry Johnson (1689–1760), lord of the manor of Berkhamsted. Johnson encouraged his fellow-stewards to join the SGS. The author of *The Duty of a Steward to his Lord* (1727), Edward Lawrence (1674–1739), was a friend of Johnson's who became a

---

[22] See J. Lowthorp (ed.), *The Philosophical Transactions and Collections ... Abridged and Disposed under General Heads in Five Volumes*, 4th edn (London, 1732).
[23] Thomas Badeslade (fl.1742), author of *Chorographia Britanniæ*: his extensive chorographical or map-making skills are only slowly being recognised today.

member. Perhaps the best-known of the surveyors who were friends or members was John Grundy junior (1719–83), who became the chief agent for the Deeping Fen Adventurers. John Landen (1719–90), the mathematician and surveyor, also became a member of the SGS.

This intense interest in surveying and practical calculation was related to drainage, but also had a connection with the abstract mathematics being developed across Europe in the first half of the eighteenth century. Johnson went to great lengths to gain Sir Isaac Newton's support for, and membership of, the SGS, though the aged Newton became an honorary rather than a corresponding member.[24] More significant in terms of the communication of mathematics was the work being done by Johnson's friends and associates in the 1730s on the application of Newton's calculus, or 'fluxions' as it was known. Among those who worked on this area of mathematics were John Grundy, William Bogdani, John Muller (1694–1784) – a colleague of Bogdani's in the Ordnance Department at the Tower of London, John Rowning (1701–71) who became an officer of the SGS, and George Lynn senior, Johnson's kinsman and a keen astronomer. The SGS's correspondence contains examples of working of problems in 'fluxions' and discussion of their application to the problems of water-flow in the Fenland rivers.[25]

Johnson shared his century's fascination with new machinery for research and for practical use. He was keen to develop engines and machinery which could move the water flooding the lands for which he was agent. He wrote careful minutes of Society meetings when engines were a topic of discussion, noting in particular the attempts by John Grundy senior to improve drainage engines. One of Johnson's many kinsmen was Dr Walter Lynn (1678–1763), George Lynn's brother, who was continuously endeavouring, without success, to get Parliament's support for his development of engines to drain mines. A machine actually designed and built for the SGS was an experimental air pump, like that shown in Joseph Wright of Derby's famous painting. It was created by Johnson's much younger step-brother Richard Falkner (1716/17–37). In 1735 Falkner, a medical student at Oxford, spent the summer working with Johnson and other SGS members on questions of natural philosophy derived from the experimental work of Newton and Boyle.

Johnson was an enthusiastic antiquary, fascinated by history and its tangible remains; this was one of the shared passions that kept alive his friendship with Stukeley. They were among a small group of antiquaries who had begun to meet informally in London from 1707 onwards. In 1717 this group was formally established as a re-foundation of the earlier Elizabethan Society of Antiquaries. Johnson usually referred to it as the Antiquarian Society, and we have followed his practice in this volume. Stukeley became its secretary and Johnson was appointed as its librarian, though a library was not brought together until permanent premises were established many years later. Johnson collected documents

---

[24] See Johnson's letter to Newton and account of his interview with Newton in *Correspondence*, letter 58.
[25] See Appendix 3 and *Correspondence*, appendix 2, for fuller details of these members, and the index to this volume for references to these engineering projects.

and charters, especially those relating to South Lincolnshire. He noted epitaphs in churches, as is shown in his report on Dunstable church (**Letter 12**).

One eighteenth-century passion which combined technical and antiquarian studies was the collection and study of coins. This enthusiasm is well explored in Rosemary Sweet's *Antiquaries*.[26] For professional men without the funds or leisure to undertake the Grand Tour abroad, a study of the Roman history of their own country was a possible substitute. They investigated Roman remains such as roads, the ruins of villas and the remains of mosaic pavements; indeed, in 1722 both Johnson and Stukeley were members of the Society of Roman Knights, whose aim was to preserve Roman remains in Britain. This study linked them and their locality with the great world of classical civilisation to which their education had introduced them, and coins provided the ideal portable artefact for doing so. Johnson, like Stukeley, was keen to use coins to sort out historical chronology and to do so he had to ensure that the coins were genuine and correctly dated. Together with other SGS members, in particular the expert numismatist Beaupré Bell (1704–41), another kinsman of Johnson's, he investigated methods of weighing coins and analysing their metal content, especially by hydrostatic methods. Ultimately Johnson was able to produce what was for him a satisfactory chronology of Britain from British and Roman times onwards from the coins he collected or those owned by his friends and contacts. In particular, he provided numismatic evidence for the situation in Britain between AD 285 and 315, the period including the reign of the Emperor Carausius and the proclamation in York of Constantine as Emperor in AD 306. This interest was partly encouraged by the belief held by Stukeley that Constantine was born in Britain; Johnson disagreed but tended to suggest, though incorrectly, a British origin for Carausius. This would have appealed to Johnson as a keen patriot, both nationally and locally. His interest in anything that reflected credit on Britain, on Lincolnshire and in particular on the Fens of South Lincolnshire, is clearly shown in his letters and minutes.

Another area of interest of Johnson's, which he shared with Stukeley and with many friends and SGS members, was the natural world, in particular its plants and animals. The SGS members brought in, or received from correspondents in other countries, specimens of flowers, seeds, shells and preserved insects among other botanical and biological specimens. Johnson was able to contribute to this from his extensive and well-maintained gardens at Ayscoughfee Hall. In his grounds Johnson created his 'canal', the centrepiece for a complex garden full of native and exotic plants, shrubs and trees. The yew trees still growing in the gardens at Ayscoughfee have been dated to his time. The letters in this collection demonstrate his interest in the development and extension of his gardens. In addition to his own gardens, he insisted that his society's premises should have gardens, with practical as well as attractive features. The premises in the Abbey Yard, occupied by the SGS from 1726 to 1743, had an extensive physic garden, much used by the Society's physicians and apothecaries. In order to establish it the Society considered the Oxford botanic garden and the physic gardens of the

---

[26] R. Sweet, *Antiquaries: The Discovery of the Past in Eighteenth-Century Britain* (London, 2004). For Johnson's work on coins, see Adam Daubney, 'Maurice Johnson: an eighteenth-century numismatist', *British Numismatic Journal* 82 (2012) 146–63.

Apothecaries in London. A series of garden utensils were purchased for the SGS Museum and Garden in 1727: 'a spade, trowels, rake, scythe, pruning knife, a pair of shears, a rolling stone, a hoe, a watering pott'[27] and several pots for plants. The Society also collected a range of dried plants in its extensive *hortus siccus*.

Perhaps the most widely used word in Johnson's references to his society's premises was 'museum' or his alternative spelling 'musæum'. The SGS deliberately used the Ashmolean Museum at Oxford as a model for their own creation. What early eighteenth-century intellectuals understood by a 'museum' was not just a collection but a place for active study and experiment; their classical education had informed them that a Muse was a presiding deity of a particular art or craft, so a museum was a place where the arts and sciences were practised. What the museum needed was materials and instruments for study. Consequently Johnson and his fellow-members purchased telescopes, compound and solar microscopes, magnifying glasses, prisms and thermometers. Apparently Johnson had his own museum at Ayscoughfee which presumably served as a model for that of the Society.[28]

It should not be surprising that a man engaged in such wide-ranging interests was a bibliophile. As already noted, one of the first concerns of the SGS was the repair and cataloguing of the Spalding parish library. Johnson went on to establish the Society's own library and this, as well as regular concerts of music, is dealt with in the following section.

Johnson and the survival of the Spalding Gentlemen's Society
Johnson was always looking for activities that would bind together the members of his society. A lending library was one of these. Johnson set about creating this by buying books through subscription from the Society's funds and also by requiring all members to contribute at least one book, to the value of at least £1, to the library as a condition of membership. Any members who were also authors were expected to contribute a copy of their works to the Society's library, and the SGS obtained a set of Newton's published works in this manner. Johnson always referred to this as a 'Public Lending Library', in contrast to Johnson's own private library held at Ayscoughfee Hall. The catalogue of the Society's library was immaculately kept, as one would expect since one of the origins of the Society was the cataloguing of the Spalding parish library following the 1708 Public Library Act ('public' in this case having its eighteenth-century meaning of one that was open for borrowing by authorised persons such as members, not one open to any member of the general public as today).

It was this insistence that the Society's library was a public library that proved the salvation of the Society itself as a result of a bequest in Johnson's will. He had always been reluctant to give the SGS a firm legal existence by purchasing, at great expense, a charter from the Crown, as the Royal Society had done in the 1660s. The Society of Antiquaries had followed this example in the 1750s, much to the displeasure of both Johnson and Stukeley because of the expense

---

[27] SGS, MB1, fol.162r.
[28] SGS, MB1, fol.75v. For an account of the Society's plans to build, see John Harris, 'Designs for the museum and library of the Spalding Gentlemen's Society', *Georgian Group Journal* 19 (2011), 39–49.

and the restriction which they felt a charter placed on a society's nature and activities. There was, however, a local corporation in legal existence, the Royal Free Grammar School of Spalding, which had its corporate existence from letters patent granted by Queen Elizabeth in 1588 and renewed by Charles II in 1674, and the governors of which were members of the SGS. Johnson granted to the school a chapelry that he owned at Wykeham Chapel, just outside Spalding, and the land associated with it, to augment the salary of the headmaster. He stipulated in his will that in exchange the headmaster would be responsible for the library of the SGS. This remains true today. The headmaster of Spalding Grammar School is ex officio librarian of the SGS (though the chaplaincy and income are no more), so that the library set up by Johnson, and added to by his successors, still legally survives.

Although Johnson did not state precisely when he first had the idea of an established librarianship for ensuring the survival of his society, he was always keen that the Society should continue to exist and prosper, and he was also particularly anxious that it should not decline into a dining or drinking club, which was the fate of many formal and informal social groups of the period. At the height of the Society's success, in the 1730s, a second binding factor was introduced, that of music. This was not unexpected, as a musical training was part of a gentleman's education in the early eighteenth century. Several members possessed musical skills and interests, resulting in the formation of a Friday music meeting, the 'concert', or 'consort' as Johnson called it. This was formalised in 1732 when it was officially agreed that the 'gentlemen of the concert' should be allowed to use the Society's rooms in the Abbey Yard on Fridays free of charge in exchange for providing an annual concert to celebrate the SGS's anniversary.

This music meeting worked closely with the SGS for approximately twenty years. Johnson's reasons for supporting the music meeting were explained by him in 1727, when a dinner had been organised to celebrate the anniversary of the drawing up of the Society's first formal rules in November 1712. Johnson found the idea of a celebratory dinner not to his liking: 'it proves a very Idle and Expensive method of celebrating the Anniversary of this Society as to feeding the Body instead of the Mind'. In a note added later he agreed that 'the Consort answered well and did the Institution Creditt and Service'.[29] Accordingly in January 1728 the anniversary was 'celebrated with mutual Benevolence & a consort of music'.[30] This became the annual pattern throughout the 1730s and 1740s.

The Society's musical director from 1735 to 1745 was Dr Musgrave Heighington (1680–1764), the organist of St Nicholas' church, Yarmouth, a few of whose music MSS survive in the library of Christ Church, Oxford. At the annual concert in August 1739 Heighington provided the music for 'An Ode for the Celebration of the Anniversary of the Gentlemen's Society', a setting of a poem by Maurice Johnson himself. Johnson was an active poet, writing in both Latin and English; one of his surviving Latin poems forms part of a preface to Stukeley's *Itinerarium Curiosum*, published in 1724/5. Johnson's verses are either

[29] SGS, MB1, fol.120r.
[30] SGS, MB1, fol.130r.

mannered imitations of classical poets he admired, such as Horace, or ironically witty, in the style of the early eighteenth-century wits whom he had known in London and enlisted in his Society. The best-known of these were Alexander Pope and John Gay. Johnson read Gay's poem 'Rural Sports' at an early meeting of the SGS on 19 January 1713.[31] Johnson also encouraged local poets such as William Jackson; as Jackson's patron, Johnson obtained a good post for him in the Boston customs. Johnson also made MS copies of many of the poems available at the time. He wrote out, in a variety of hands of which his legal studies had made him a master, three volumes of poetry, two of which have survived and are in the collection of Yale University, having been purchased at the second major sale of the Johnson family's private library and papers in 1970. They contain some of Johnson's own verses, including early poems to 'Miss E– A–', Elizabeth Ambler who became his wife.[32]

This careful collection of MSS points to the heart of Johnson's personal concerns: the preservation of learning through the effective organisation of books and manuscripts. As a result of his lifelong labours there survives in Spalding today an outstanding collection of documentation relating to the nature of knowledge and study in the first half of the eighteenth century. There remains also evidence of Johnson's own remarkable collections. In Bernard Quaritch's *Contributions towards a dictionary of English Book-collection* (1893), Maurice Johnson is listed as a major English bibliophile, and a study of the *Contributions* reveals that the family had been keen book collectors from the late sixteenth century to the nineteenth century. The titles of almost fifty books to which Johnson subscribed between 1710 and 1750 are known. Full details of his books can be found in the printed catalogues of their two sales by Sotheby's, the first in 1898 and the second in 1970.

Thanks to Maurice Johnson's knowledge and enthusiasm, four libraries were established and maintained in Spalding. The SGS catalogued, cleaned and maintained the parish library of theological works, kept in the vestry of the parish church. A new collection of classical texts was made to provide a library for the grammar school, also located at that time in the parish church. As already mentioned, a new library of books on a wide range of secular topics was created by the SGS for its own use, consisting of donations from members and books purchased from the Society's subscriptions. This collection still exists as a separate entity, known as the Original Collection, within the much larger library of the modern SGS. The fourth library, the personal collection built up by the Johnson family and held in Ayscoughfee Hall, has now been dispersed to libraries across the world following the two sales mentioned above.

Since the time of Maurice Johnson, the society he founded and maintained in Spalding between 1710 and his death in 1755 has survived and flourished, despite fluctuations in its fortunes over the intervening years. It is an unlikely survival in a small Fenland town. As is perhaps fitting, the reason for the Society's continuance to the present day has been the existence of its library. It was as a 'public lending library' that the Society kept going during the majority of the

---

[31] SGS, MB1, fol.30v, 19 January 1713.
[32] Yale University Library, Osborn Collection in the Beinecke Library, shelfmark c.229.

nineteenth century, although it was, of course, only available to its members. At the time when the family of the fifth and final lineal male descendant of Maurice Johnson decided to sell some of the family books at Sotheby's sale on 24 March 1898, the SGS was being most effectively revived and re-expanded into a learned society by the chief medical officer of the Johnson Hospital, Spalding, Dr Marten Perry. Accordingly, the Society purchased several remarkable volumes from the Johnson family library, and these are one of the most valued elements of an extensive library housed today in the buildings erected in 1910 in Broad Street, Spalding, to celebrate the Society's 200th anniversary.

Johnson and his family

No account of Johnson's life would be complete without reference to his family life. Johnson was a devoted husband and father. His letters pay tribute to his admiration for his wife, Elizabeth, particularly **Letter 33**. Of the twenty-five children born to them between 1711 and 1733 (several being twins), seventeen survived into childhood. Eleven of these, six girls and five boys, reached at least young adulthood and nine outlived their parents.[33] They are discussed in detail in the third tribute to Johnson quoted in Appendix 4. Johnson had hoped that his eldest son, also named Maurice, would join him both in his legal work and his enthusiasm for the Society. Although the young Maurice's name was entered in the books of the Inner Temple, the young man preferred a military career, becoming a captain and later a colonel in the First Regiment of Foot, though he became an SGS member and contributed frequent letters and drawings while on campaign in Europe. It was left to the second son, Walter, to share his father's legal work and become Treasurer of the SGS, and to the third son, the Revd John Johnson, who became minister of Spalding, to inherit the presidency after his father's death. Johnson's love for his family also extended to Ayscoughfee Hall, his home throughout his life; his letters provide frequent references to his development of its historical features and his work in supervising its extensive garden and grounds.

He also kept in touch with a wide range of relations, some close but many more distant, most of whom he referred to as 'Couzen'. Many of these were members of his Society, either attending regularly or contributing to its activities by correspondence from a distance. This distance could vary from nearby counties such as Northamptonshire (from where the Lynn family sent frequent letters) and Norfolk (the home of Beaupré Bell who regularly corresponded about numismatics), to Central America, where his cousin Henry Johnson was a merchant. Some of the most regular SGS members were related to Johnson by birth, such as his younger brother John, Treasurer for many years, or by marriage. Dr John Green, Johnson's co-secretary responsible for scientific correspondence, was also his son-in-law by his marriage to Johnson's eldest daughter Jane; another son-in-law was Robert Butter, a local merchant and proficient bassoonist who

---

[33] Following a visit to Johnson, Stukeley wrote to Gale on 14 October 1728, describing Johnson's collections and adding: 'I had like to have forgot his collection of children being no. X boys and girls of *equa portione*' (quoted in *Surtees* I, 208). John Nichols' *Literary Anecdotes* (1816) states, 'By her [Elizabeth] he had 26 children, 16 of whom sat down together at his table' (quoted in *Surtees* I, 89, n.7).

had married Johnson's daughter Elizabeth. Other family connections were with William Bogdani, Clerk to the Ordnance at the Tower of London and a regular correspondent, and Richard Falkner and George Johnson, both Oxford undergraduates. 'Couzens' would also encourage their friends to join and correspond with the SGS. The Revd Benjamin Ray of nearby Cowbit brought in his friend the scholarly Revd Samuel Pegge, and William Bogdani encouraged the mathematician John Muller to become a member.

This network of kinsfolk was a significant contributor to the continued existence of the SGS. Another factor which gave strength to the early Society and still maintains it today is the personal friendships at its heart. The third of the tributes to Johnson in Appendix 4 notes his friendly and sociable nature. Dozens of his personal friends in the Spalding area and from his legal work and social activities in London joined the SGS and often manifested their appreciation of his talents. One of the longest-lasting of the friendships Johnson formed and maintained throughout his life was that with William Stukeley.

William Stukeley (1687–1765)

'The Doctor is a very Learned Physitian Phylosopher Mathematician Poet and Antiquarian. He designs very well.'[34] This is how William Stukeley appeared to a Scottish friend, Sir John Clerk, who visited him in Grantham in 1727. Clerk had been one of the thirty-one Scottish commissioners in the negotiations which led to the 1707 Act of Union between England and Scotland. He was both the chief Scottish financial adviser in the treaty negotiations and a very rich antiquarian, composing during his long life a Latin paper '*De imperio Britannico*', a history of Anglo-Scottish relations.[35] When Clerk called in Grantham, Stukeley had been at work in his garden and 'never rural god appeared so rough and dirty'.[36] Clerk explained that during the visit Stukeley 'took a Scetch of my face which every body said was very like'.[37]

This meeting happened about halfway through Stukeley's life. He was born in Holbeach on 7 November 1687 and lived there until he went to Cambridge to study medicine in 1703. Clerk draws attention to Stukeley's central activities up to 1726, when he moved to Grantham where he lived from 1726 to 1729. Since there are several biographies of Stukeley in existence, this Introduction does not attempt to discuss them or provide another full account of his life, but concentrates on the aspects of it highlighted by Clerk and brought out in Stukeley's correspondence with Johnson from 1714 to 1754.

Stukeley was an extremely well qualified doctor, following his Bachelor of Physic degree at Cambridge in 1709, his Doctor of Physic degree in 1719 and his fellowship of the College of Physicians in 1720. His initial degree studies at Corpus Christi College had trained him as a natural philosopher and mathematician. Throughout his life he studied plants, becoming very knowledgeable in

---

[34] Quoted in S. Piggott, *William Stukeley, an Eighteenth-Century Antiquary*, revised edn (London, 1985), 76.
[35] Rosalind Mitchison, 'Sir John Clerk (1676–1755)', in *ODNB*.
[36] Piggott, *Stukeley*, 76.
[37] Piggott, *Stukeley*, 76.

their practical applications and in garden design and taking pleasure in creating gardens at his houses in Grantham, Stamford and later Kentish Town, then on the outskirts of London. Stukeley always held Sir Isaac Newton in great regard as a mathematician. When Stukeley lived in Grantham, he advised Newton on the possible purchase of Grantham House as his final retirement home, though Newton died before that could take place. As concerns poetry, Stukeley said of himself 'I had a fancy for Poetry';[38] his verses are not well known but he had an influence on later Romantic poetry. Both Blake and Wordsworth were careful readers of Stukeley's work on Stonehenge. Noah Heringman quotes[39] a line from Blake's *Jerusalem* about Stonehenge, 'The Building is Natural Religion and its Altars Natural Morality', a viewpoint possibly derived from Stukeley's views on early religion. Charles Rzepca has found exact associations between Stukeley's detailed statistics on Stonehenge and Wordsworth's poem *The Thorn*.[40] Certainly Stukeley was, and is, best known as an antiquarian, but his interests (as Sir John Clerk insisted) were remarkably wide-ranging.

Stukeley the physician
After Cambridge, Stukeley first served as a physician in Boston from 1710 to 1717, then in London from 1717 to 1726 and in Grantham from 1726 to 1729. He certainly had all the trappings of success as a doctor. After working in Boston for seven years, on Lady Day (25 March) 1717 he went 'to fix at London',[41] lodging in Ormond Street. He was admitted into the Royal Society by Sir Isaac Newton on 20 March 1718 on the nomination of Dr Richard Mead, his medical tutor under whom he had studied in London before qualifying. He then began immediately to present papers on a variety of medical topics such as that on fossil skeletons in February 1719. In July of that year he disputed for his Doctor of Medicine degree. A few months later he was admitted as a candidate into the Royal College of Physicians and was chosen as a member of the Council of the Royal Society on Newton's direction. In October 1719 he assisted in an operation on Mrs Banks' eyes and in February 1720 he read a paper at the Royal Society on the 'dichotomy of a woman'[42] which involved dividing the body into two parts. In that year he was also involved in the dissection of an elephant, as he explains in his letter to Johnson on 7 October 1720 (**Letter 17**), and a tortoise and he was extensively engaged in work on human anatomy as a demonstrator for Dr Stephen Chase, the anatomical reader and Gulstonian Lecturer at the Royal College of Physicians.

This work led to Stukeley's 1722 Gulstonian Lecture to the Royal College and his pamphlet *Of the Spleen*, published in London in 1723 together with his *Essay towards the Anatomy of the Elephant*. As Dr J. W. McNee explained, Stukeley 'recognised that this spongy organ [the spleen] when filled with blood, could by contraction empty itself again at pleasure. He thought it acted as a diverticulum

---

[38] Bodleian, MS Eng. misc. e.667/1, fol.1.
[39] N. Heringman, *Romantic Rocks, Aesthetic Geology* (Ithaca NY and London, 2004), 126.
[40] C. Rzepca, 'From relics to remains: Wordsworth's *The Thorn* and the emergence of secular history', *Romanticism on the Net* 31 (August 2003).
[41] Bodleian, MS Eng. misc. e.667/1, fol.9v.
[42] Bodleian, MS Eng. misc. e.667/1, fol.11v.

or safety valve to the general systemic circulation. "This necessary surcharge of blood is so regulated by the spleen, that no inconveniences arise from it" – truly an amazing prophecy of future discoveries.'[43] Stukeley said of the spleen ''tis a magazine of blood'; in remarkably similar language today the *Oxford Companion to Medicine*[44] says 'it acts as a reservoir of blood'. Stukeley's engraving of the arterial network of the spleen is reproduced as Illustration 10 in this volume: the spleen there is given its Latin name *lien*. Included in this publication on the spleen was a very popular poem on the subject by Anne Finch, Lady Winchelsea. Stukeley probably included the poem because she had died in 1720 and was the wife of Heneage Finch, fifth Earl of Winchilsea, one of Stukeley's patrons with whom he worked on numismatics in the Society of Antiquaries. *Of the Spleen* demonstrates Stukeley's skills in physic, poetry, antiquarian studies and drawing, and his deep involvement with his patrons.

Stukeley's best-known medical work, *Of the Gout*,[45] likewise reveals his diverse activities. Because gout appeared to attack rich people, it was a well-known and widely discussed medical condition in the eighteenth century, so much so that its nickname was 'the rich man's evil'.[46] The conventional explanation that gout arose from excess of heat as one of the four humours is neatly expressed in the sixteenth-century poem on gout by Barnabe Googe:

> The cause is plain and evident who listeth it to touch
> One reason is because that heat in man doth more exceed
> Which causeth that the humours pierce the sinews more with speed.[47]

Stukeley pointed out that 'It is contriv'd by our most wise author [God], that round about the commissure [junction] of all our joints, and upon the insertions of the tendons of the muscles, there should be plac'd many glands, to separate an oyly matter, wherewith to lubricate the joints and tendons in action.'[48] Whilst still accepting that 'The pain and heat, by degrees derive a vast flux of blood and humors',[49] Stukeley argued that 'this oyly matter of the joint and tendons thereabouts, becomes deflagrated [combustible], and the glands that secrete it, so spoil'd in texture, that they cannot further furnish a due quantity, either to lubricate the joint in walking, or to extinguish the matter of another fitt'.[50] Stukeley believed that the lack of this oily matter 'calcines the ends of the bones devoid of periosteum [outer bone tissue] into nodes and chalkstones [tophus or deposits of urates]'.[51] His medical solution was the application of 'our artificial oyls, analogous and succedaneous to the natural'[52] which would 'actually insinuate

---

[43] J. W. McNee, 'The Spleen: its structure, functions and disease', *British Medical Journal* (7 March 1931), 413–14.
[44] *Oxford Companion to Medicine* (1980), 1325.
[45] *Of the Gout, in two parts. First, a Letter to Sir Hans Sloan, Bart. about the Cure of the Gout, by Oyls externally apply'd: Secondly, A Treatise of the Cause and Cure of the Gout* (London, 1734).
[46] Simon McKeown (ed.), *The Overthrow of the Gowt*, by Christopher Ballista, translated by Barnabe Googe (1990), 9. The poem was first published in 1577.
[47] Googe, *Overthrow*, 16.
[48] Stukeley, *Of the Gout*, 14.
[49] Stukeley, *Of the Gout*, 15.
[50] Stukeley, *Of the Gout*, 15.
[51] Stukeley, *Of the Gout*, 16.
[52] Stukeley, *Of the Gout*, 16.

themselves to the part, and supply the use of the natural, by extinguishing this fiery drop, which gives the onset of the distemper.'[53] Stukeley was correct in his analysis of the problem of gout, as Nuki and Simkin pointed out in 2006. He had 'described the crystals [this fiery drop] from a topaceous joint'[54] which in 1776 were identified as uric acid, the build-up of which is acknowledged today to be the cause of gout.

Stukeley had begun to suffer from severe attacks of gout when he was a physician in London in the 1720s and he associated it with 'french wine, so that I was every winter laid up with gout: at some time for 3 or 4 months together'.[55] In 1729 Stukeley changed his vocation and was ordained. He was appointed to the living of All Saints, Stamford, where he met Dr Rogers, the creator of the 'artificial oyls'. Dr Rogers' brother had been Vicar of All Saints; he died in 1729 and as Stukeley said, 'providence directed me to the Cure of this parish in the year 1729, in which year in the month of May [Dr Rogers] first began to put in practice these oyls upon himself. I succeeded his brother and he himself became my parishioner.'[56]

As a student of physic Stukeley had studied the gout, 'this formidable *Goliath* of our Art: because I had a hereditary title to it. I read all the authors I could meet with, whilst I practis'd in the Metropolis.'[57] He wrote about gout only when he was sure he had a remedy which he himself had used extensively during his own sufferings. His pamphlet on the gout is 120 pages long and its chief virtue is its clarity of expression. Stukeley speaks directly to his reader about the nature of gout and the method of application of the 'artificial oyls'. Gout, he writes 'will lay hold on the most trifling occasion, any evacuation, a wrench, treading awry, a small blow, bruise, wound, a cold, excessive hot weather or cold, an easterly wind, an alteration of weather, a sitting up in the night, a little change of dyet, liquor, constitution, bad wine, *French* wine, stale drink, walking. From any of these the gout will frequently break forth.'[58] About the application of the oils, he wrote, 'Heat in a silver spoon, ladle or porringer … Shake the bottle first, embrocate the part affected with your hand, warmed, for a quarter of an hour before the fire … rub the oyls well in, and then wrap the part up in flannel.'[59] The pamphlet sold well in England and Ireland, going into a second edition; Stukeley assisted the family of Dr Rogers in getting an income from the oils for some time after Dr Rogers' death.

Although Stukeley ceased to practise as a physician in 1729 he remained involved in medical affairs for the rest of his life. However, having become a clergyman he could no longer hold office in the Royal College, where he had been Censor in 1725 during his early London years and for which he had carried out several design projects; notably in 1722 'he drew out the College of

---

[53] Stukeley, *Of the Gout*, 18.
[54] G. Nuki and P. A. Simkin, 'A concise history of gout and hyperuricemia and their treatment', *Arthritis Research and Therapy* (2006), 8 (Suppl. 1).
[55] Bodleian, MS Eng. misc. e.121, fol.28. This citation is from Kevin Fraser's excellent article 'William Stukeley and the Gout', *Medical History* 36 (1992), 165.
[56] Stukeley, *Of the Gout*, 33.
[57] Stukeley, *Of the Gout*, 38.
[58] Stukeley, *Of the Gout*, 90–1.
[59] Stukeley, *Of the Gout*, 118.

Physicians'.[60] Later in his life he wrote memoirs on smallpox inoculation and on the King's Evil,[61] and towards the end of his life he became concerned about the adulteration of flour by millers using alum, a topic which was to be of major concern to nineteenth-century public health officials.[62] Herbs and plants were of great medical interest and a lifelong interest of Stukeley's.

His involvement with plants derived from his early childhood when he went 'simpling' or searching for plants, particularly those of medical benefit, in the woods at Fleet, east of Holbeach, which 'knowing a pretty many plants, layd, I believe, the Foundation for my Inclinations to the study of Physic in that early age'.[63] David Haycock, in his outstanding study of Stukeley,[64] used the Royal College's archives to describe Stukeley's work to apply a 'cosmological theory to the practice of medicine'.[65] What Stukeley wanted to do was, as he said in his Botanic Lecture of 1723, 'restore the consideration of numbers in physic, especially in relation to plants, for in numbers as the Ancients thought, there lyes a great power and energy. Among the Pythagoreans numbers are the fountain, the principle and root of all things.'[66] What Stukeley was suggesting here is the numerical systematisation of plant collecting. He was applying his awareness of mathematical systems, derived from his Cambridge Newtonian contacts, to botanical studies a decade or so before Linnæus. He was also using early aids to plant collecting while at Cambridge. With friends he 'usd to range about once or twice a week the circumjacent country ... the frequent scenes of our simpling toyl, armed with Candleboxes & Ray's *Catalogus*'.[67] D. E. Allen points out[68] that these candleboxes would have been an early form of the vasculum or heated collecting box used by botanists.

Stukeley the gardener
Stukeley was at the heart of early eighteenth-century botanising and he maintained this interest throughout his life, particularly through his lifelong passion for gardening. While a doctor in Boston from 1710 to 1717 he 'built, planted a garden'[69] and established 'a botanic club. The Apothecaries and I went a simpling once a week.'[70] Following his move to Grantham in 1726 Stukeley became a dedicated gardener; he put up a bust of Newton in his newly created garden there. He drew sketches of his garden and the letters he wrote to friends during his years in Grantham, especially **Letter 84**, show that he loved creating the garden at his

---

[60] Bodleian, MS Eng. misc. e.667/1, fol.13v.
[61] Bodleian, MS Eng, misc. e.135 and e.139.
[62] Bodleian, MS Eng. misc. e.667/7, 1757. The use of alum as an additive by bakers was banned in 1875.
[63] *Surtees* I, 14.
[64] D. B. Haycock, *William Stukeley: Science, Religion and Archaeology in Eighteenth-Century England* (Woodbridge, 2002).
[65] Haycock, *William Stukeley*, 104.
[66] Cited in Haycock, *William Stukeley*, 104 from the Stukeley papers in Royal College of Physicians, MS 340/16.
[67] *Surtees* I, 22.
[68] D. E. Allen, 'Some further light on the history of the Vasculum', *Proceedings of the Botanical Society of the British Isles* 6 (1965), 105–9.
[69] *Surtees* I, 91.
[70] *Surtees* I, 122.

house, close to the site of the nineteenth-century Guildhall on St Peter's Hill. In the central part of the garden was to be 'a temple of the druids … When you enter the innermost circle or temple, you see in the center an ancient appletree overgrown with sacred mistletoe.'[71] John Smith, formerly Curator of Stamford Museum, has written an excellent article on Stukeley's gardening activies in Stamford.[72] Stukeley's London activities as a gardener towards the end of his life have been touched on by Todd Langstaffe-Gowan.[73]

Stukeley the Anglican antiquarian
Stukeley is best known today as a pioneer archæologist, though he would not have called himself an archæologist since the word did not exist then. He and his contemporaries would have regarded themselves as 'antiquaries' or 'curious in antiquity'. While Stukeley was living in Grantham between 1726 and 1729 he settled down to write up his archæological findings and to incorporate them into his Anglican Christian beliefs. He set about the process of understanding himself and what he had learnt from his activities in Cambridge, Boston and London and during his extensive journeys throughout England between 1717 and 1726. He wrote to his close friend Samuel Gale in February 1727: 'I now begin to fancy I could write somewhat to purpose, when freed from the hideous crys & nauseous noises of the Town.'[74] By leaving London, he created for himself the circumstances necessary to write up his antiquarian adventures and to give them the religious meaning which he felt Stonehenge and Avebury had. After living for three years in Grantham, and becoming a churchwarden at St Wulfram's church there in 1728, he wrote to the Archbishop of Canterbury, William Wake, as follows: 'I have long had thoughts of entering into Orders, but never ripened my resolutions until of late, nor have acquainted any mortal with it. I believe the retirement from the hurry of a City life, & the contemplative mood which a garden & the country disposes us to have forwarded my inclination that way.'[75]

Stukeley repeated the same sentiments in a draft letter to Samuel Gale when he was settled in Stamford as Vicar of All Saints: 'when the sweet tranquillity of country retirement; & self conversation in a garden, had given me leave to look into my own mind, I soon discovered again the latent seeds of religion'.[76] To his own satisfaction Stukeley interrelated archæology and early Christianity. For almost twenty years Stukeley lived in Stamford, saying afterwards, 'I employ'd all my facultyes, & all the skill I had obtained in ancient learning, in going to the sourse of religious antiquitys; & the harvest resulting therefrom, such as it is, is immense.'[77] The consideration of his work at Stonehenge and Avebury brings us to the heart of William Stukeley's life and experience. The period 1726–1747

---

[71] *Surtees* I, 208–9.
[72] John Smith, 'William Stukeley in Stamford: his houses, gardens and a project for a Palladian triumphal arch over Barn Hill', *Antiquaries Journal* 93 (2013), 353–400. See also Matthew M. Reeve, 'Of Druids, the Gothic, and the origins of architecture: the garden designs of William Stukeley (1687–1765)', *British Art Journal* 13 (3) (2012), 9–18.
[73] Todd Longstaffe-Gowan, *The London Town Garden, 1700–1840* (New Haven CT, 2001).
[74] *Surtees* I, 190.
[75] *Surtees* I, 216.
[76] *Surtees* I, 228.
[77] *Surtees* I, 77.

was a necessary time of reflection and writing, following the extraordinary years of archæological research and discovery between 1718 and 1726.

Stukeley's contribution to the development of archæology is now well known, thanks to the research and publications of Stuart Piggott, Michael Hunter, Peter Ucko and David Haycock. They approach his work from a modern perspective. However, this volume is concerned with his impact on his contemporaries as revealed in this selection of his letters. Stukeley explained his move, as a doctor, to Grantham in 1726 by saying he was

> a person of curiosity, who had spent a series of years in the metropolis, to cultivate his mind in the circle of sciences: and who avoyding the allurements which Fortune there threw in his way, to accumulate wealth: thro' an irresistible fondness of nature [and] the country life by a resolution which amaz'd all his acquaintance when his reputation was not a little, now in the prime of life, he quitted the Town in 1726.[78]

Three important words from this quotation reveal Stukeley to us: 'curiosity', 'science' and 'nature'. 'Curiosity' in the early eighteenth century meant an irresistible urge to investigate and learn; 'science' had the broader meaning of 'knowledge' or 'an intellectual discipline' and 'Nature' was the natural world about him.

Stukeley recorded that from 1712 he had always studied 'matters out of my [medical] profession, antiquitys, chronology, genealogy, astronomy, mathematics, philosophy'[79] and from the age of thirty, he recorded that he 'pursued the study of antiquity with great applause'.[80] Rosemary Sweet in her study *Antiquaries* points out how the methodology and language of natural history and scientific enquiry coloured that of antiquarian studies. She comments that 'at the heart of the antiquarian discipline was the need to compile, compare and contrast'.[81] Stukeley certainly compiled an extraordinary amount of data. Out of 149 separate collections of his papers in the Bodleian Library at Oxford, the first 19 alone contain 1,861 folios. His documents also survive in the collections of the Royal Society, the Society of Antiquaries, the Freemasons' Grand Lodge library, the library of his Cambridge college, Corpus Christi, the Royal College of Physicians, the National Archives at Kew, the Spalding Gentlemen's Society, Cardiff Central Library and Devizes Archaeological and Natural History Society, where his Commonplace Book is held.

It is not therefore surprising that Stukeley was described by Ronald Hutton as 'perhaps the most important forefather of the discipline of archaeology'.[82] This comment emphasises the twenty-first century appreciation of Stukeley's significance. What was, and what is the discipline of archæology, so strongly associated with Stukeley by Hutton? This understanding is crucial as there is an essential contrast between early eighteenth-century and early 21st-century views of the

---

[78] W. Stukeley, 'Stanfordia Illustrata', LAO, Cragg MSS, Microfilm MF/2/2/20/4. The original text is in the Parker Library of Corpus Christi College, Cambridge.
[79] *Surtees* I, 91–2.
[80] *Surtees* I, 92.
[81] R. Sweet, *Antiquaries*, 9.
[82] R. Hutton, 'The religion of William Stukeley', *Antiquaries Journal* 85 (2005), 382.

discipline. Archæology, according to Dr Johnson,[83] was a 'discourse on antiquity', that is to say a dissertation, either written or uttered, on some aspect of the past. Today, it is generally understood to be 'the study of man's past by scientific analysis of the material remains of his cultures'.[84] Both of these definitions are rather simplistic, as every individual archæologist was, and is, different in his or her relative emphasis on the discipline as an art, a craft or a natural science. No American positivist archæologist today would see Stukeley as a proponent of the scientific study of the past, yet Stukeley was one of the most scientifically minded people of his time.

To try to understand Stukeley as an archæologist we need to understand his agenda. Why did he travel the length and breadth of England between 1719 and 1724 and then self-publish the results of his journeys in 1725?[85] In his Preface, dated 26 December 1724, he writes 'The intent of this treatise is to oblige the curious in the Antiquity of Brittan [sic]: 'tis an account of places and things from inspection, not compil'd from others' labors, or travels in ones study.'[86] The 100 engravings it contains are central to *Itinerarium Curiosum*.[87] Stukeley's nationalist agenda becomes clear in engraving no. 8, 'The ground plot of the Ruins of Whitehall, June 14th 1718'. In his Preface, using his highly personal orthography, he explains the presence of this diagram as follows:

> I my self never saw the palace, but was pleas'd that I chanc'd to take this draught of its ruinous ichnography, but the very week before totally distroy'd. thus much I thought owing to the venerabl [sic] memory of that name, which is ever the word at Sea with *Brittish* ships, and which makes the whole world tremble.[88]

Stukeley was primarily concerned to trace the original inhabitants of Britain and its development into what he believed to be a central part of the great Roman Empire, viewed from his own time in the newly established kingdom of Great Britain – the result of the 1707 Act of Union between England and Scotland. His ideal of Britain in the eighteenth century was that it was a place where 'a gentleman may be lord of the soyl where formerly princes and emperors commanded'.[89] As Rosemary Sweet expressed it, 'This is a theme which we can trace through the antiquarian literature of the eighteenth century, as the rolling bandwagon of British chauvinism collided with the elegant artifice of classical culture.'[90] Like Johnson, Stukeley was proud of local links to the Roman Empire, hence their interest in those Emperors who had a connection with Britain, such as Constantine and Carausius, who they believed to be of British birth. Both

---

[83] S. Johnson, *A Dictionary of the English Language* (London, 1755).
[84] *Collins' English Dictionary* (1994).
[85] *Itinerarium Curiosum* was actually published in early 1725, in spite of the 1724 date on the initial pages. This confusion arises from the habit of starting the year from 25 March, which was common in England until the calendar change of 1752. See Stukeley's letter to Maurice Johnson, 12 November 1724 (**Letter 21**).
[86] *Itinerarium Curiosum* (1725), preface, first page.
[87] The best available modern publication of these engravings is Neil Mortimer, *Stukeley Illustrated: William Stukeley's Rediscovery of Britain's Ancient Sites* (Green Magic, 2004).
[88] *Itinerarium Curiosum*, preface, second page.
[89] *Itinerarium Curiosum*, 171.
[90] R. Sweet, *Antiquaries*, 121.

showed a rather ambivalent attitude, enthusing over the Roman connection but equally supporting the courage of the British inhabitants who opposed them. This ambivalence is shown in Stukeley's handwritten additions on page 49 of the 1725 edition of *Itinerarium Curiosum* in the Bodleian Library. With regard to the seventeenth-century monuments to the Manners family in Bottesford church, Leicestershire, Stukeley comments on how the earls of Rutland were portrayed to 'the life in marble statues and Roman habitts ... in armour'; he went on to write that 'the statuary has shown his taste of Antiquity by given 'em Whiskers after the mode of the antient Britains'.[91]

Stukeley was well equipped to pursue this archæological agenda, firstly through his classical background. He knew Latin and had the rudiments of Greek. He also attempted to learn Hebrew and tried, unsuccessfully, to read Egyptian hieroglyphs. He expressed the purpose of this in *Itinerarium Curiosum*: 'the moderns have exerted themselves in earnest, to rake up every dust of past times, mov'd by the evident advantages therefrom accruing, in the understanding their invaluabl writings, which have escap'd the common shipwreck of time.'[92] Stukeley's surveying and drawing skills, discussed in more detail below (pp.xlvii–l), also provided invaluable tools for his studies.

His education in topographical drawing led Stukeley to view the landscape both as a natural or created phenomenon and as a place populated either in the past or in his own time by real people. He almost always added living people to inhabit his drawings, on occasion even little portraits of himself in the act of sketching, as in his picture of Ludlow.[93] All this led him, as Rick Peterson points out, to 'create different representations of the monument which were more concerned with perceptions from within the landscape than the two-dimensional plan view'.[94] In other words, what Stukeley's antiquarian studies developed was the significance of an 'understanding of the landscape context of a site'.[95] His representation of places and features in hundreds of drawings arose partly from his intrinsic interest in what we now call phenomenalism, the term used by modern archæologists for an understanding of how a prehistoric monument fits into its landscape.

The best example is his discovery of the invisible Beckhampton Avenue leading west from the stones of the Avebury circle. According to archæologists working on the site in 1999 and 2000, Stukeley 'recorded much of the avenue during a concerted period of stone destruction between 1700–1725'.[96] Peterson has demonstrated how Stukeley combined a wide range of archæological skills to reconstruct a lost site. 'His primary recording tool appears to have been the "prospect", views of the current state of the monuments in their landscape. These were combined with field notes containing many compass bearings to allow the

---

[91] Bodleian, Gough Gen. Top. 58 (*Itinerarium Curiosum*), p.49.
[92] *Itinerarium Curiosum*, 2.
[93] *Itinerarium Curiosum*, plate 5.
[94] R. Peterson, 'William Stukeley, eighteenth-century phenomenalist', *Antiquity* 77 (296) (2003), 384–400.
[95] G. Lock, 'Human activity in a spatial context', in *The Oxford Handbook of Archaeology* (2009), 398.
[96] Southampton University Archaeological Research, 'The Negotiating Avebury Project'.

construction of generally three-dimensional views of the monument complex ... These drawings show the area around certain points in the monument complex in a way completely removed from the traditional landscape "prospect".'[97] In other words, Stukeley employed very highly developed artistic and mathematical skills to create a lost landscape; this was his unique contribution to eighteenth-century archæology.

He was, however, much more proud of his numismatic work and would have been happy that following his death his son-in-law and executor Richard Fleming published his final book, *Twenty Three Plates of the Coins of the Ancient British Kings* (1776). A picture of Stukeley's own numismatic collection by the end of his life can be drawn from the *Catalogue of the genuine collection of Coins and Medals etc.* published in May 1766: this is the catalogue of his coins put up for sale after his death in 1765, which can be seen in the British Library.[98] Among the wide range of ancient Greek, Roman and British coins that he possessed, he had 139 coins from the period of Carausius and Allectus, emperors in Britain in the late third century AD. In the eyes of later scholars, Stukeley's reputation was severely diminished by the controversy over the misreading of 'Fortuna' as 'Oriuna' on the reverse of a coin of Carausius, given by Stukeley's friend Richard Mead to the King of France. Stukeley was never able to see the actual coin and so, reliant on sketches and engravings and unaware of the damage to the coin at that point in the inscription, he interpreted the word as the name 'Oriuna', who he claimed was the wife of Carausius, usurper of the Roman imperial title in Britain at some time between AD 287 and 293.[99] An undamaged example of this type of coin, found in a hoard in Rouen in 1846, is illustrated in P. J. Casey's study of Carausius; had Stukeley seen this other example he would probably not have been misled.

Throughout his life Stukeley analysed his reasons for undertaking archæological, historical and literary study. His two volumes on Carausius[100] present his agenda, which is clearly stated in the preface to volume II, and is typical of him:

> Various is the purpose of this work, I. Moral; or if we please to call it so, religious ... to show, why Providence favour'd the Romans, so as to give them the empire of the world ... [II] political; to show that our emperor Carausius, a wise prince, was able to maintain himself in the government of Britain and the sovereignty of the sea against the whole power of the Roman empire ... [III] The third purpose is historical; the life of a great man, a Briton, a Roman; where Roman and Brittish history is united; and at that period of time, when Providence was bringing about the union of church, and state, the natural regimen of empires and kingdoms. [IV]

---

[97] R. Peterson, 'William Stukeley', 395–6.
[98] British Library, General Reference Collection 140.a.19. (1.).
[99] These dates and details are taken from the excellent study by P. J. Casey, *Carausius and Allectus: The British Usurpers* (London, 1994). This was written before several studies in the 1990s which have altered most historians' reactions to Stukeley's work and so it is still derogatory about him. Otherwise it is a highly recommended study.
[100] W. Stukeley, *The Medallic History of Marcus Aurelius Valerius Carausius Emperor in Brittain* I (1757), II (1759). Stukeley, like his friend Maurice Johnson, was convinced that Carausius was of British origins, which partly explains his interest in this emperor. This is further explored in **Letters 61, 68, 69** and **75**.

My fourth design is to propose a new scheme of medallic learning: to render it more useful to history.'[101]

Stukeley and sociability

Stukeley was able to collect details of the Carausian coins because of his extraordinarily extensive social networks; he knew the cabinets of coins of well over a hundred fellow-collectors.[102] He maintained contact with his fellow-intellectuals by two typical eighteenth-century activities: social clubs and letter-writing. His own account of his club membership is revealing. In 1709 or 1710, at the time when his friend Maurice Johnson was founding his own Gentlemen's Society in Spalding, Stukeley 'formd a weekly meeting of the young Physicians & Surgeons'[103] who were training alongside him in London. Moving to be a physician in Boston in May 1710 he 'erected a botanic club'.[104] In 1717 Stukeley, back in London, was immediately involved, as secretary, in the final re-foundation of the Antiquarian Society, together with Maurice Johnson. He later claimed, probably inaccurately, that he was 'the first person made a freemason in London for many years'.[105] In 1718 he became a member of the Royal Society and in 1720 a fellow of the Royal College of Physicians. On various occasions between 1720 and 1765 he held office in both these organisations. In addition he regularly set up small informal societies in London such as a 'vertuoso meeting in Avemary Lane ... another in Orange Street'.[106]

After his removal to become a doctor in Grantham in 1726 he set up a club at the Peacock Inn, Belvoir, at the foot of Belvoir Castle, whose owner the Duke of Rutland he claimed as one of his patients. He became churchwarden of St Wulfram's Church in Grantham and an active member of Johnson's Spalding Gentlemen's Society, maintaining this connection by correspondence even after his final removal to London. Together with Maurice Johnson, he did his best to establish a permanent social meeting at Ancaster to discuss intellectual concerns, associated with the judicial quarter sessions in his part of Lincolnshire.[107] Throughout his time in Stamford as Vicar of All Saints, from 1729 to 1747, he established weekly, fortnightly or monthly meetings, most of which lasted only a few months, though the Deepings Club seems to have maintained a longer existence.

Certainly he tried very hard, with Johnson's encouragement, to maintain his Stamford Brazen Nose Society which, like the SGS, held weekly meetings. He might have succeeded had he not been affected both by the death of his wife and that of Queen Caroline in 1737, and he attempted at least once to revive it (see their letters in March 1746, **Letters 41** and **42**). He said of this group, which met from June 1736 to June 1737, 'I endevor'd twice to erect a truly literary Society at Stamford, by the name of the Brazen nose society, but in vain. I filld some quarto books with the memoirs, but as at first I might say quorum pars magna

[101] Stukeley, *Carausius* II, pp.xxv–xxvii.
[102] Stukeley, *Carausius* I, pp.xxii–xxiii, lists these collectors who have helped him.
[103] *Surtees* I, 46.
[104] *Surtees* I, 122.
[105] *Surtees* I, 122: the truth of this statement is much disputed.
[106] *Surtees* I, 122.
[107] See below, **Letters 25–28**.

fui, in a little time I might say pars tota.'[108] In other words, he went from being one of a small group to being the sole remaining member.

Stukeley's comments on his Stamford society, unlike Johnson's thriving society in nearby Spalding, throw light on the normal state of the provincial sociable clubs of the eighteenth century.[109] 'Thus we enjoy', he wrote to his close friend Roger Gale 'this country truly; and that is true life, not the stink and noise and nonsense of London. We have two music clubs a week where I smoak a pipe, drink a dish of coffea and am well entertained.'[110] This was typical of the popular, but frequently ephemeral eighteenth-century clubs. The only ones that took root and survived were those with clear-cut aims and very determined administration. Isaac Newton, for example, dominated the Royal Society for the first quarter of the century by his overwhelming brilliance and firm personality. Maurice Johnson managed the SGS with remarkable persistence and determined weekly attendance, and by his social dominance in Spalding. Stukeley was a determined individual but lacked Newton's overwhelming personal stature and Johnson's genuine ability to relate to all manner of people. Wherever he lived, Stukeley organised societies for general interest. As Johnson stated to the SGS in 1752, both he and Stukeley insisted that 'dividing the Small Rivulets of Learning (as he ingeniously Phrases It) among us tends to ruin the stream'.[111] He did his best to bring about the union of the Royal and Antiquarian societies, but knew he had failed when the Antiquarian Society insisted on going to the huge expense of negotiating a royal charter in the 1750s, which cost over £300.

At the heart of Georgian society lay the concept of patronage and the Crown was the most impressive patron, but royal patronage was only available when the monarch was seriously short of cash. On the other hand, aristocratic patronage was more easily obtained. Stukeley was very conscious of this. He was at the heart of the establishment in 1721 of the short-lived Society of Roman Knights, which was patronised by Lord Pembroke, Lord Winchilsea and Lord Hertford; Maurice Johnson was a fellow-member. Its aim was to create enthusiasm for, and interest in, Roman antiquities. Equally short-lived and aristocratically patronised was the Egyptian Society, established at the end of 1741 by Lord Sandwich, whose members included the dukes of Montagu and Richmond and Lord Stanhope.[112] This group, as Rosemary Sweet points out, 'discussed the practice of patriarchal religion and the inheritance of the traditions of the Old Testament'.[113] Both these interests were at the heart of Stukeley's concerns, yet, in spite of his great enthusiasm for both Roman and Egyptian antiquities, neither the Roman Knights nor the Egyptian Society lasted as serious meetings for more than two years.

It is perhaps possible to understand the short life of so many of Stukeley's societies by reference to his mobile existence; until he came to Stamford he

---

[108] These quarto minute books are now in the Bodleian, MS Eng. misc. e.122/123.
[109] Peter Clark's wide-ranging study *British Clubs and Societies 1580–1800: The Origins of an Associational World* (2000) is valuable for the history of English clubs in this period.
[110] *Surtees* II, 292
[111] SGS, MB5, fol.96v.
[112] See below, **Letter 67** (Stukeley to Johnson, 16 June 1750).
[113] R. Sweet, *Antiquaries*, 130.

rarely stayed long in one place. Also of relevance is the nature of Georgian societies. Stukeley drew up a detailed list of the members of his Orange Street club mentioned above. It had around twenty members and of these at least six were closely involved in engraving: Herman Moll, the geographer, the Van der Gucht brothers, Elisha Kirkhall, John Harris and William Hulett.[114] Clearly, what kept this group together was serious professional activity by which they earned their living and all were friends or employees of Stukeley. A different yet significant society of the time was the Society of Dilettanti, which consisted of men who had been on the Grand Tour and who were both rich and well-connected. Stukeley's Orange Street club was a short-lived group of young professionals, meeting for friendship and mutual encouragement but disappearing as the members went their separate ways. In contrast, the Society of Dilettanti is still in existence, raising money for the study of Greek and Roman art. It was a society only for the richest gentry, which Stukeley could not afford to belong to: eighteenth-century societies were not open to everyone. The range of clubs between these two examples was enormous and Stukeley could only flourish in clubs where his priorities and interests were widely accepted. He was concerned with antiquarian interests, religion and philosophy; these concerns are best revealed in his correspondence and in his production and collection of books.

Stukeley as correspondent
As this book reveals, Stukeley was one of the most effective literary correspondents of his time. The survival of his correspondence is largely due to Stukeley's personal determination to save it for posterity. As a result, hundreds of letters to and from him survive, largely in the Bodleian Library and also in the archives of the SGS. Another reason for the existence of his extensive correspondence is the nature of the British postal service and its effective development in the early eighteenth century.

This explosion in correspondence is well illustrated in J. P. Jackson's occasional paper, written for and held by the library of the SGS: *Index of postal history items in the Society folios*. Letters could be handed in, pre-paid or unpaid, to the local postmaster, generally an innkeeper, or to a Receiving House, or even for incoming mail to a coffee-house, which charged for this service, usually a halfpenny per letter. From the London Post Office letters were delivered along six routes or Roads, each controlled by a Clerk of the Road. 'Each Clerk of the Road, in 1715, was given an assistant, called a Surveyor, to travel the road and be responsible for its practical administration.'[115] Marks, called Bishop Marks after the Postmaster-General Henry Bishop, were stamped on the letter recording the day and month on which the mail was handed into the post office.

In 1711 the official postage rate was 3d for up to 80 miles and 4d thereafter for a single sheet; it was double the rate for two sheets. This explains why the letters are often filled with writing on both sides of the paper and even in the margin, frequently making them difficult to read. Sometimes the writer adds 'A single sheet' below the address. MPs, government officials and other privileged persons

---

[114] *Surtees* I, 98.
[115] J. P. Jackson, *Index of Postal History Items in the Society Folios* (Spalding Gentlemen's Society, 2001), 3.

had the right to free postage. An example is a letter from Stukeley to Johnson on 20 December 1749 (**Letter 59**), franked 'Free R. Barbor' as a favour from the MP. At this time, the Secretary to the Postmaster General was George Shelvocke, who was made a member of the SGS in 1745.[116] He offered to free-frank the Society's foreign correspondence. As a result of these developments, postal correspondence became very widespread. William Stukeley was among the three main contributors of letters to the SGS; 75 letters from Maurice Johnson, 37 from Beaupré Bell and 33 letters and papers from Stukeley survive in the Society's archives and the minute books indicate that even more were received. Letters from over 150 correspondents of the SGS from the period 1710–1761 survive in the archives of the Society today.

It was through the publication of correspondence that studies of Stukeley and his work became widespread. A considerable number of Stukeley's letters and those of his correspondents were published by the Surtees Society between 1882 and 1887 as the three-volume *Family Memoirs of the Rev. William Stukeley M.D.* These letters survived partly because of Stukeley's extraordinary hoarding instincts and partly because he bequeathed them to his daughter Frances and her husband Richard Fleming. By a circuitous route these letters, covering the years 1704–1765, have now mostly reached the Bodleian Library, as is explained above. In addition to Stukeley's letters, the Surtees Society reprinted a remarkable range of eighteenth-century correspondence associated with him and with his major interests. The practices of nineteenth-century scholarship were such that, rather than publish complete letters, the Surtees Society's editor, the Revd W. C. Lukis,[117] often printed what he regarded as useful extracts: these illustrated the enormous range of interests of Stukeley and his intellectual milieu. In addition, Lukis modernised Stukeley's spelling and idiosyncratic punctuation. In this LRS volume we have attempted to transcribe the original eighteenth-century orthography as accurately as we can.

Stukeley as diarist, memoirist and author

Stukeley's letters are only a small part of the literary survivals of this most productive of writers. His personal diaries survive from 1730 to 1765 – sometimes as day-by-day entries – in notebooks, diaries or empty spaces in printed almanacs. These manuscripts are held by the Bodleian Library.[118] He frequently re-read his old diaries and personal memoirs, as did Johnson the minute books of the SGS, continuously adding details of earlier events and reflections on them in a much later hand. A simplified version of some of these records can be read in a publication by the Doppler Press, *The Commentarys, Diary & Commonplace Book of William Stukeley and Selected Letters* (1980). This is in effect a précis of volume I of the Surtees Society's publication and follows its convention of modernising spelling and punctuation, including the use of the strange

---

[116] See P. M. G. Bavin, 'George Shelvocke and the Free Franking System', in the *Bulletin of the Great Britain Group of the Postal History Society: The British Mailcoach* 15 (December 1977).
[117] Revd W. C. Lukis (1817–92) was an archæologist of significance in the nineteenth century, writing 27 articles and several books on prehistoric archæology, especially on dolmens.
[118] Bodleian, MS Eng. misc. d.119, e.125–141, e.196 and e.667.

nineteenth-century transcription of the eighteenth-century handwritten initial capital 'F' as 'ff'.

In addition to Stukeley's sixty-five personal notebooks that are now in the Bodleian Library, he also kept very detailed memoirs of meetings of the intellectual societies with which he was connected. The most intriguing of these are perhaps the eight volumes of memoirs of meetings of the Royal Society between 1740 and 1750 which he kept for his own use. He sent five of these volumes to the SGS for reading at weekly meetings; the other three are in the Bodleian Library.[119] The Bodleian holds a very interesting brief set of minutes of a short-lived conference that Stukeley masterminded in London for a year between April 1725 and January 1726, meeting once or twice a month in Ave Maria Lane. This conference studied artefacts located by the members such as medals, coins, pottery, seals, a spur, a 'small brass celt', intaglias, bells, and also a few 'natural curiosities'.[120] The Bodleian also has two volumes of very detailed minutes of Stukeley's Brazen Nose Society which met in Stamford from 1736 to 1737.[121] Perhaps his most significant minute-taking was his early minute books of the Society of Antiquaries.[122] His minutes of the Society of Roman Knights were listed as sold in Sotheby's sale catalogue of 19 February 1963, though their present location is difficult to determine. In addition, the Bodleian Library holds around eighty manuscript essays by Stukeley.[123] Further interesting sets of his dissertations are held by the Society of Antiquaries,[124] the SGS and the Library of Freemasons' Hall in London.[125] Finally, his old college in Cambridge, Corpus Christi, holds several essays by Stukeley, who was an undergraduate there from 1704 to 1709.

Using this very considerable amount of manuscript material, Stukeley published a wide range of books and papers. These can be conveniently divided into full-scale books, publications of pamphlet length and shorter pieces such as essays and sermons, published either independently or by the Royal Society. The process of publication is interesting as Stukeley was his own publisher, using a range of London printers and insisting on his own distinctive style of punctuation. His best-known and most successful books are his *Itinerarium Curiosum* of 1725,[126] his *Stonehenge* of 1740[127] and his study of Avebury, *Abury*,

---

[119] Stukeley's MS volumes of Royal Society memoirs held by the SGS have details for the years 1740, 1741, 1742, 1748 and 1750. His three Bodleian Library volumes (MS Eng. misc. e.124) give further record of meetings of the Royal Society between 1740 and 1742.
[120] Bodleian, MS Eng. misc. d.719/21: the meetings are recorded in Stukeley's hand at the end of the volume.
[121] Bodleian, MS Eng. misc. e.122 and e.123.
[122] Society of Antiquaries, SAL/MS/265 and 268.
[123] These essays are best listed in the Summary Catalogue of the Bodleian Library under Stukeley Papers 42243–42392. See also MS Eng. misc. e.667/7 for Stukeley's own list of his 'Tracts'.
[124] See especially SAL/MS/793.
[125] Freemasons' Hall, FM MSS 1130 Stu.
[126] *Itinerarium Curiosum, or, An account of the antiquity and remarkable curiositys in nature or art: observ'd in travels thro Great Brittain. Illustrated with copper prints. Centuria I*, by William Stukeley, MD, CML, & SRS. London. Printed for the author MDCCXXIV. (The book appeared in early 1725.)
[127] *Stonehenge, A Temple Restor'd to the British Druids*, by William Stukeley, M.D. Rector of All Saints Stamford. Printed for W. Innys and R. Manby at the West End of St Pauls MDCCXL.

of 1743.[128] His *Itinerarium* was successful partly because of its full range of illustrations; a second edition was published in 1776 after his death, with additional material relating to the invented text *De Situ Britanniæ* foisted upon Stukeley in his later years by Charles Bertram, discussed below. The two volumes on Stonehenge and Avebury were both very well received. Stukeley never published the remaining volumes of his history of religion, in which he intended to cover Moses, Egyptian learning, the ancient origins of the Christian faith, the learning of the ancients and Abraham.[129] Stukeley's other extensive publication was his history of Carausius, the Northern European usurper of the Roman imperial rank from AD 287 to 293.[130]

In addition to these four major studies, Stukeley published two important medical essays on the Spleen and the Gout, as discussed above, and three archæological pamphlets, one in 1720 on *Arthur's O'on and the Roman Vallum*, the second *Of the Roman Amphitheatre at Dorchester* in 1723, and the third *An Explanation of a Silver Plate found at Ripley in Derbyshire* in 1736. He had printed three detailed discussions of recent discoveries in British archæology: *Palæographia Britannica*, volume I in 1743, volume II in 1746 and volume III in 1752. The first two volumes discuss the underground chamber at Royston and the third concerns the well-known coin of Carausius with a picture of 'Fortuna' on the reverse, which Stukeley read as 'Oriuna' (see Illustration 21). In the later years of his life in London, Stukeley was central to two fascinating historical inventions. Charles Bertram invented a detailed description of Roman Britain, which he claimed to be the work of Richard of Cirencester, a fourteenth-century monk at Westminster. Stukeley wrote and later printed two papers for the Royal Society about it, publishing the map of Roman towns and roads that Bertram had invented and claimed to have found.[131] Stukeley, like many intelligent people of his time, was also impressed by the work of James Macpherson in 'discovering' early Scottish Gaelic heroic poetry supposedly written by the bard 'Ossian'. One of Stukeley's last published papers was a friendly and supportive letter he wrote to Macpherson expressing his pleasure in the poems of Ossian.[132] He also published several of his sermons: on *The Sabbath* (which had been preached to the House of Commons), in 1742, and *The Healing of Disease, a Character of the Messiah* (as preached to the College of Physicians), in 1750. Stukeley printed

---

[128] *Abury: A Temple of the British Druids with some others described. Wherein is a more particular account of the first and patriarchal religion; and the peopling of the British Island*, Volume the Second, by William Stukeley M.D. Rector of All Saints Stamford, London. Printed for the Author; and sold by W. Innys, R. Manby, B. Dod, J. Brindley, and the Booksellers in London MDCCXLIII. (In effect this was Volume II to *Stonehenge* which was intended to be Vol. I of a series of six books on Patriarchal Christianity.)
[129] The planned content of the series is described in the preface to *Stonehenge*, 2–3.
[130] *The Medallic History of Marcus Aurelius Valerius Carausius, Emperor in Brittain*, Book I, by William Stukeley, M.D. Rector of St George, Queen Square, Fellow of the College of Physicians, of the Royal and Antiquarian Societys London, Printed for Charles Corbet, Bookseller, over against St Dunstans Church, Fleet St. MDCCLVI and Book II MDCCLIX.
[131] *An Account of Richard of Cirencester, Monk of Westminster, and of his Works: with his Antient Map of Roman Brittain: And the Itinerary Thereof* (London, 1757).
[132] *A Letter from Dr Stukeley to Mr MacPherson, on his Publication of Fingal and Temora, with a Print of Cathmor's Shield* (London, 1763).

two theological pamphlets which he called *Palæographica Sacra*.[133] The first, number I, proved to Stukeley's satisfaction that Bacchus, the Greek god, was also the Jewish god Jehovah.[134] The second pamphlet was a collection of sermons on natural history, the Christian religion and sacred chronology, a topic of great interest at the time, which also fascinated Newton.

Stukeley gave many papers to the Royal Society and the Society of Antiquaries and several were published in their journals. His account of the cause of earthquakes was given to the Royal Society and then published twice in the 1750s, first in 1750 and then in 1756 as *The Philosophy of Earthquakes, Natural and Religious, Or an Inquiry into their Causes and their Purpose*. The Royal Society's *Philosophical Transactions* (volume 48) included his article 'An Account of the Eclipse predicted by Thales'. Two papers he read to the Society of Antiquaries, 'An Account of Lesnes Abbey' and 'An Account of the Sanctuary at Westminster', were later published in 1771 in *Archæologia*, the Society's first journal-style publication. Stukeley also had several, often anonymous, articles published by his friend and fellow-SGS member John Hill in Hill's popular journal *The Inspector*.

Finally, we are fortunate in possessing a very detailed *Catalogue of the Genuine Library of Books in Print and Manuscripts, and Collection of Prints and Drawings of the late Revd and Learned William Stukeley M.D.* (1776). The catalogue lists 1121 lots and it has been analysed briefly by Stuart Piggott[135] who draws attention to the books on medicine, architecture, gardening, classical literature, history and antiquities, numismatics and theology. A more detailed study reveals in addition extensive numbers of books on the etymology of languages, on astronomy and astrology, on chronology and travels, particularly map books. Not surprisingly, as a parish clergyman for thirty-five years, Stukeley amassed a collection of over twenty books of printed sermons. What is particularly striking is the widespread European authorship shown in the catalogue; Stukeley was clearly a member of the European republic of letters which thrived in the first half of the eighteenth century.

Stukeley the surveyor, draughtsman and artist
'I began childhood with a love of drawing and exercised it in practise continually.'[136] Throughout his life Stukeley developed the technical skills of surveying, drawing plans and map making and, more artistically, the drawing of buildings, landscapes and even portraits. For examples see Illustrations 5, 7, 8, 10, 13, 14, 16, 17, 19 and 20. To a large extent he used these skills to practical effect in connection with his wide-ranging interests, particularly in antiquities, geography and chorography.

---

[133] *Palæographica Sacra, or Discourses on Sacred Subjects by William Stukeley M.D. Rector of St George, Queen Square London* (London, 1763).
[134] *Palæographica Sacra: or, Discourses on Monuments of Antiquity that Relate to Sacred History. Number I: A Comment on an Ode of Horace, Shewing the Bacchus of the Heathen to be the Jehovah of the Jews* (London, 1736).
[135] Stuart Piggott (ed.), *Sale Catalogues of Libraries of Eminent Persons 10: Antiquaries* (London, 1974).
[136] From Stukeley's diary: F. Scoones, 'Dr William Stukeley's house at Grantham', *The Georgian Group Journal* 9 (1999), 158.

We have already discussed (pp.xxviii–xlii above) the way in which Stukeley drew landscapes as places that were populated by real people, and that therefore gave context for sites of antiquities. Also connected with his antiquarian interest was his keenness to record places and features that he perceived to be both of great historical significance and in danger of destruction. As a result we possess hundreds of images of eighteenth-century towns and sites drawn from an antiquarian as well as a human point of view. The fact that Stukeley recorded so many such sites that have now disappeared was the result of his often-expressed horror at the destructiveness of his contemporaries. An excellent example of this is his work on Arthur's O'on, the celebrated Roman building which formerly stood north of the Antonine Wall.[137] This now-destroyed temple near Falkirk in Scotland was the subject-matter of Stukeley's first published piece, *An Account of a Roman Temple and other Antiquities near Graham's Dike in Scotland*, printed in London in 1720. This Roman building was called a temple of Romulus by Stukeley, a chapel to Mithras by Alexander Gordon and a mausoleum by John Horsley. What is significant is that it was demolished in the 1740s, an act of 'gothicism' or, as we would say, vandalism. The culprit was Sir Michael Bruce, on whose estate it stood according to the 1806 edition of Camden's *Britannia*, who 'with aggravated Vandal barbarity, pulled it down to re-build a mill-dam'.[138] This quotation shows a critical eighteenth-century attitude towards the Goths and Vandals, who were seen as barbarians destroying the greatest culture the world had known, that of the Roman Empire.

The urge to stop the destruction of ancient buildings was paramount to William Stukeley. He was appalled by the dramatic destruction of the Avebury Stone Circle and sections of Hadrian's Wall; he, more than any other eighteenth-century antiquarian, detested and publicised this. Perhaps ironically, his own splendid house in Grantham disappeared in the nineteenth century, but thanks to his remarkable skills in drawing, a very good record of the rooms and gardens survives and has been published by Francesca Scoones.[139]

One element of Stukeley's library was 'geography' as it was then understood, defined as the study of the 'whole Globe of the Earth, or known habitable World; together with all Parts, Limits, Situations, and other remarkable things thereunto belonging'.[140] Stukeley brought to his studies of geography and chorography (the detailed study of a locality) his highly developed skills of topographical surveying and drawing.

The most popular and significant of all Stukeley's life's work is his extraordinary collection of chorographical drawings. A typical list can be drawn up from a manuscript notebook at the Bodleian Library covering his artistic output during a journey with his friend Roger Gale, which began on 13 August 1721 at 'Eaton College' and ended on 13 October at Colsterworth, between Stamford

---

137   T. G. Brown and P. G. Vasey, 'Arthur's O'on again: newly-discovered drawings by John Adair and their context', *Proceedings of the Society of Antiquarians of Scotland* 119 (1988), 352.
138   W. Camden, *Britannia*, ed. Richard Gough (4 vols, 1806), IV, 103.
139   Scoones, 'Stukeley's house at Grantham'. Her description of Stukeley's work, 'a set of charming naive watercolours', is a little patronising.
140   Nathan Bailey (ed.), *An Universal Etymological English Dictionary* (London, 1749).

and Grantham.[141] There are around 110 drawings, maps, plans, ground plots and prospects, all sketched as he travelled from London via Reading, Stonehenge, Ludlow, Derby and Nottingham to Grantham. It is interesting to go from these preliminary sketches to the finished etchings printed in early 1725 in his *Itinerarium Curiosum*. These copper prints have been reproduced endlessly during almost three hundred years since the originals were rapidly sketched as Stukeley travelled across England. A list of the journeys Stukeley took between 1721 and 1725 has been recreated by Stuart Piggott.[142]

As a young man Stukeley received careful tuition in topographical surveying. He 'used to converse very much with the [Holbeach] Parish Clerk, Wm. Pepper, a tenant of [his] Fathers who taught [him] something of the use of the Quadrant, & Dialling, & some Astrology [study of the stars' positions] withal, so that [he] could take the height of a steeple, & readily erect a scheme of twelve houses, & was very fond of the art, till the University corrected [his] Judgment in these matters'.[143] He also 'follow'd the trade of map making so [he] had delineated pretty good plans of [his] whole parish as far as [his] travels reachd, & by degrees made maps of the whole country [the Holland area of South Lincolnshire]'.[144]

Stukeley drew maps all his life. A good example is his map of the Antonine Itinerary, prepared in 1722, in which he records the fifteen journeys of the Iter Britanniarum along the roads of Roman Britain around AD 200.[145] He made many city maps, such as that of Lincoln (number 88 in the 1724/5 edition of the *Itinerarium*), which was used by the Archæological Institute of Great Britain and Ireland for its July meeting in 1848. His map of the 'Levels in Lincolnshire commonly called Holland' reveals a determination to create a unique plan of his home county (see illustration 20).

Stukeley was able to map any location he chose, to a high standard for the eighteenth century as a comparison with Thomas Badeslade's 1723 'Map of the River of Great Ouse'[146] demonstrates. His mapping skills were derived from his early training in surveying and mathematics, which he received as a trainee lawyer and surveyor in Lincolnshire and developed at Cambridge as a young man. He acknowledged this education in his account of Isaac Newton: 'We had then [1705] in our college, under the instruction of Dr Robert Dannye ... gone thro' an excellent course of lectures in mathematics and [natural] philosophy particularly the Newtonian.'[147]

Stukeley the Newtonian
Stukeley wrote of Newton, 'how many philosophers quietly sit down in their studies and invent an hypothesis; but Sir Isaac's way was by dint of experiment

---

[141] Bodleian, MS Top. gen. d.13.
[142] Piggott, *William Stukeley*, appendices I and II, 161–7.
[143] Surtees I, 15.
[144] Surtees I, 15.
[145] Bodleian, MS Gough Gen. Top. 56.
[146] In the SGS archive.
[147] W. Stukeley, *Memoirs of Sir Isaac Newton's Life*, ed. A. Hastings White (London, 1936). The MS on which this twentieth-century publication was based was finalised for printing by Stukeley in 1752, but he did not have it published.

to find out quid Natura faciat aut ferat [what Nature made or brought forth].'[148] We owe to Stukeley the story of Newton and the apple tree: 'this was the birth of those amazing discoverys whereby he built [natural] philosophy on a solid foundation to the astonishment of all Europe.'[149] However, what Newtonianism actually consisted of was extremely varied, so much so that, as Robert Schofield wrote, 'individual Newtonians, scattered throughout Britain, were left without constraint to present their separate and idiosyncratic versions of Newton's theory of matter and its action'.[150] Newton opened up the world of astronomy, mathematics, chemistry, sound, physics and the dynamics of gravity, natural history, mechanics and chronology. The overwhelming variety of these explanations of the natural and human world temporarily destroyed the notion of any straightforward system of thought acceptable to all as the basis of natural philosophy. This should be linked with the manner in which Newton's friend John Locke had written a 'plain unmetaphysical account of the workings of the human mind'.[151] Between them, Newton and Locke destroyed the Aristotelian system of classical philosophy on which European natural philosophy was based. As a result, the years 1700–1750 were a period when the whole notion of system was deemed inadequate. As the eighteenth century progressed, new systems became more acceptable. In particular, the Linnæan organisation of the natural world provided natural history with a framework which worked alongside that provided by Newtonian physics, a system which itself lasted until the time of Einstein. It is important to look on 1700–1750 as an era of open thinking; Stukeley took it upon himself to keep the stream of learning clearly directed. He joined Newton in searching for what George Cheyne called 'the whole Foundation of Natural Philosophy ... <u>Simplicity</u> and <u>Analogy</u>, or a simple, yet Beautiful <u>Harmony</u> running through all Works of Nature in an uninterrupted Chain of Causes and Effects'.[152]

Stukeley thought he found an understanding of this harmony in the music of the spheres. He worked intently on the planetary structure of the solar system and the universe, developing a cosmology of his own which has been studied in detail by Michael Hoskin.[153] Hoskin writes that 'Stukeley fills a "gap" in the history of theories of the Milky Way, for he antedated Kant and Lambert by three decades in seeing the Milky Way as the counterpart among the stars of the ecliptic in the solar system.'[154] In other words, Stukeley placed the sun and its planets firmly into the Via Galactica or Milky Way. In Stukeley's own words, he argued that 'the milky way is composed of infinite volumes of these starry orbs, such as we

---

[148] Stukeley, *Memoirs of Sir Isaac Newton*, 55.
[149] Stukeley, *Memoirs of Sir Isaac Newton*, 20.
[150] R. E. Schofield, *Mechanism and Materialism: British Natural Philosophy in an Age of Reason* (Princeton, 1970), 19 (cited in Haycock, *William Stukeley*, 53).
[151] J. R. Milton, 'John Locke', in *ODNB* (2004).
[152] George Cheyne, *Philosophical Principles of Religion: Natural and Revealed: in Two Parts* (London, 1715) I, 42, cited in Haycock, *William Stukeley*, 93. The ultimate destruction of system was Rousseau's work in *Emile* and *The Social Contract*, worked out in the 1750s, a real precursor of the French Revolution.
[153] M. Hoskin, 'Stukeley's Cosmology and the Newtonian origins of Olbers' Paradox', *Journal of the History of Astronomy* 16 (1985).
[154] Hoskin, 'Stukeley's Cosmology', 7.

see in a starry night; that these suns, whether collectively or separately, are placed in the quincuncial form, our starry orb making one of the infinite number.'[155] Stukeley called the diagram he created for his work on the Milky Way 'TO ΠΑΝ [the whole], his conception of the Universe', or his macrocosm, and it is part of his religious investigations into the nature of God's creation.

It is, in effect, an element of his Newtonianism. Throughout his life he was endeavouring to use a combination of his Newtonian natural philosophy and his own intellect to understand and describe God's creation. In his biography of Stukeley, David Haycock discusses this work in two chapters, 'The Microcosm, Doctor and Anatomist' and 'The Macrocosm, New Theories of the Universe'. One element of the microcosm that Stukeley investigated was the nature of corals. By briefly considering his comments we can understand both how he thought and why he sometimes arrived at what we know today are wrong conclusions. He read a paper on corals to the Royal Society in 1754, which they did not print. However, it did appear in the *Gentleman's Magazine* for September 1754,[156] and in it he demonstrates his method of working.

In this paper he discusses the new idea that corals were 'entirely made and fabricated by the little animals always found upon them; which generally are *polypuses*, like those we observe in our own fresh waters; and which so lately entertained the philosophical world when first discovered by M. Tremblay'. Clearly Stukeley was up to date with the 1740 discovery by Abraham Tremblay, via the microscope, of the polyp, 'a creature that lives by dividing and multiplying itself'.[157] However, he disagreed with the findings of Jean-André de Peysonnel that corals 'are entirely made and fabricated by the little animals always found near them',[158] the polyps. Stukeley argued that the coral was a plant, 'that these coral trees (as I must still call them) are no other than little huts, built as it were by these fishermen [the polyps] to live in while they exercise their trade'. In this Royal Society paper he argued that he had 'never been at the bottom of the ocean at coral fishing; have not had the opportunity of making researches into this particular branch of natural history; nor is there any need of it, to obtain satisfaction in the matter. I have seen both corals and polypuses, and must speak what reason loudly dictates against this novel notion.'[159] We now know that Stukeley was wrong; corals are indeed small, invertebrate sea animals but this appeared unreasonable to Stukeley.[160] He argued from reason and analogy as a technique of science: 'Analogy I approve of, as an excellent means, among others, to conduct us to the dark recesses of physical knowledge.'[161] He would have accepted Bishop Butler's assertion of 1736: 'And analogy can do no more, immediately or directly, than shew such and such things to be true

---

[155] W. Stukeley, 'The Phenomenon of the Milky Way accounted for', *Gentleman's Magazine* (October 1760), 466–7.
[156] W. Stukeley, 'The Coral Tree, a real Sea Vegetable: substance of a paper read to the Royal Society on producing the beautiful Coral Tree', *Gentleman's Magazine* (1754), 401–4.
[157] Quoted in D. Hollier (ed.), *A New History of French Literature* (Cambridge, Mass., 1994), 504.
[158] Stukeley, 'The Coral Tree', 401.
[159] Stukeley, 'The Coral Tree', 401.
[160] Jean-André de Peyssonel's research was based entirely on experiment and was eventually published by the Royal Society in the *Philosophical Transactions* (1753).
[161] Stukeley, 'The Coral Tree', 403.

or credible considered only as fact.'¹⁶² His analogy with fishermen's huts has been proved to be incorrect, but he maintained it throughout his paper, towards the end saying: 'Again I argue from analogy, and we cannot well have a surer basis ... Here is a true and precise analogy between the sea-water [coral] and the fresh water polypus [living on duck-weed]; the one is equally indebted to the plant in the brook, as the other to the coral in the sea. So providence wisely orders it.'¹⁶³ This account of his work on corals enables us to get to the heart of his activity as a natural philosopher. He listened to the latest research and then applied reason and analogy to make sense of the findings. Sometimes his evaluation was correct, particularly in medical research; sometimes he was later proved wrong. He was often in good company; the greatest French natural historian of the time, Réaumur, viciously attacked de Peysonnel's work.

Another example of Stukeley's ideas that would prove misguided is his investigation into earthquakes. He set out his views in a paper to the Royal Society on 22 March 1750 and he discussed it in a letter to Maurice Johnson dated 15 May 1750 (**Letter 65**). His approach to an earthquake was that 'we cannot help considering it in a philosophical as well as religious view'.¹⁶⁴ He continued, 'nor need we lose sight of the Theological Purpose of the amazing Alarms, whilst we endeavour to find out the Philosophy of them.' He drew attention to the 'Frequency of the Northern Lights and especially of that called Aurora Australis which are with us infrequent, and twice repeated, just before the Earthquake (being of such Colours as we have never seen before'.¹⁶⁵ On 16 November 1749 the Royal Society had heard Benjamin Franklin speak on electricity in clouds; from that talk Stukeley concluded: 'If a non electric Cloud discharges its contents, upon any part of the Earth, when in a high-electrify'd State, an Earthquake must necessarily ensue.'¹⁶⁶ He went on to say that before the 1750 earthquake in London 'coruscations in the Air were extremely frequent (which confirms us in the Notion of the Earth's being then in an electrify'd State).'¹⁶⁷ Stukeley was fascinated by the recent discoveries related to electricity and he had known about them from the earliest electrical experiments of Stephen Gray, with whom at Cambridge Stukeley had tried 'Various Experiments in Philosophy'.¹⁶⁸ Another friend from Cambridge, Stephen Hales, read a rather more detailed paper on electricity and earthquakes to the Royal Society on 5 April 1750. It contrasts with Stukeley's in that Stukeley adopts one idea totally and refuses to accept the possibility of earthquakes being caused by 'subterraneous Winds, or Fires, Vapour or Waters that heav'd up the Ground, like animal convulsions'.¹⁶⁹ Stephen Hales' work as a natural philosopher is more detailed than that of Stukeley and the contrast between the two helps us to clarify Stukeley's methods. He was excitable, determined and anxious to publish. This led to criticism at the time; as David Haycock points out, 'Horace

---

162 Joseph Butler, *The Analogy of Religion, Natural and Revealed* (London, 1736), vii.
163 Stukeley, 'The Coral Tree', 403.
164 W. Stukeley, 'On the causes of Earthquakes', *Phil.Trans.* 46 (1750), 641.
165 Stukeley, 'Earthquakes', 642.
166 Stukeley, 'Earthquakes', 643.
167 Stukeley, 'Earthquakes', 644.
168 Haycock, *William Stukeley*, 41.
169 Stukeley, 'Earthquakes', 642.

Walpole recorded "One Stukeley, a parson has accounted for [earthquakes] and I think prettily, by electricity. But that is the fashionable cause, and everything is resolved into electrical appearances."'[170]

A final earthquake-related aspect of Stukeley's natural philosophy is his 'Theory of the Earth'. Between 1757 and 1762 he wrote, but never published, a paper entitled 'The Philosophy of Springs and Fountains, or a Theory of the Earth'. He argued against the idea that 'the cause of Earthquakes was underground', stating that 'this never appears [as] the Chaneles that supply [springs] remain as before'.[171] Stukeley presented a perception of the earth as having at its heart 'the central abyss of freshwater made by percolation from the ocean'.[172] Above this central mass of fresh water, he argued, there was both a mass of stone 500 miles thick and a series of pipes 'thro' the body of the earth by which the moon attracts the freshwater from the abyss, into the cisterns or reservoirs at the surface of the earth'.[173] In this aspect of his natural philosophy Stukeley demonstrates his Newtonian understanding of gravity.

However, two other elements of his techniques for understanding the nature of the world are revealed in this paper. Firstly, he argued continuously from analogy: 'the Moon acting the part of an animal heart, the Moon thus keeps not only the ocean [by tides] but the whole liquid element, in perpetual motion ... this is the reason, why the ancients were so fond of making the earth to be a great animal & having life, & the like; expatiating on the analogy between the macro and the microcosm ... hence the sentiments of all ages have chim'd together in making the human body to be, as it were, a resemblance of the greater world ... the mass of blood is the ocean, and fountain of life, the rest a system of vessels, conduits, strainers directing the current of the fluids. Gravitation in the animal tribes, perpetuates the flux.'[174] In effect, Stukeley's natural philosophy derived partly from Newtonian discoveries but also from the ancient authors whom he and Newton had both read.

Their work was centred on the seventeenth-century approach to linguistic analysis. They were both working before the understanding of the development of Indo-European languages that followed the later eighteenth-century work of William Jones. The linguistic analogies Stukeley used were those of Newton and Bochart.[175] Newton's studies were not published in his lifetime, but Stukeley purchased the 1733 publication of the work on Daniel. Matt Goldish points out that 'by far the greatest influence on Newton [regarding the history of religion] was Samuel Bochart's *Sacred Geography*, in which outstanding features are the euhemerisation of ancient gods and biblical figures and Hebrew derivation of place names from all over Europe, Asia and Africa'.[176] Euhemerisation is the claim that gods were derived from heroes or kings who were worshipped and

---

[170] Haycock, *William Stukeley*, 225.
[171] This MS is held by Corpus Christi College, Cambridge (Parker Library, MS 623).
[172] Parker Library, MS 623, fol.62r.
[173] Parker Library, MS 623, fol.17v.
[174] Parker Library, MS 623, fol.36r.
[175] Isaac Newton, *Observations upon the Prophecies of Daniel* (London, 1733); S. Bochart, *Geographia Sacra* (Frankfurt am Main, 1681), copies of which were in Stukeley's library.
[176] M. Goldish, *Judaism in the Theology of Sir Isaac Newton* (London, 1998), 13.

deified. Goldish claims that 'Newton dabbled in his own Hebrew etymologies and he euhemerised even more, deriving all the pagan gods (following Bochart and Vossius) from Noah and his progeny.'[177]

One might conclude that the most important single influence on Stukeley was the scientific, linguistic, historical and geographical impact of the work of Sir Isaac Newton.

Stukeley and religion
Newton and Stukeley were closely associated in the 1720s, perhaps one of the most formative decades of Stukeley's life. During this time he created the foundations of his theological world-view. He met Newton frequently and very nearly became Secretary of the Royal Society; his bid failed only because Newton felt that Stukeley was not sufficiently skilled in mathematics for the post. Instead, in 1726 after nine years in London, Stukeley moved to set up as a physician in Grantham, became churchwarden of St Wulfram's church there from 1726 to 1729, and then in 1729 took orders, being ordained as a deacon and then as a priest by William Wake, Archbishop of Canterbury and previously Bishop of Lincoln. Why did Stukeley shift the focus of his life from medicine to religion?

The answer to this question is stated by Stukeley in his letter to the Archbishop requesting ordination, dated from Grantham on 3 June 1729: 'I have ever been studious in divinity, especially in the most abstruse and sublime parts of it; and my disquisition into the history of our Celtic ancestors, and their religion, have led me into them, and given me the opportunity of discovering some notions about the Doctrine of the Trinity which I think are not common. If I be not mistaken, I can prove it to be so far from contrary to, or above, human reason that 'tis deducible from reason itself.'[178] This is the result of Stukeley's belief in the efficacy of reason, which was at the heart of Newton's theology. Newton and Stukeley came to different conclusions about the Trinity. Newton as a mathematician could not accept the division of the one God into three. Stukeley could; he based his reasoning not on mathematics but on archæological and biblical etymological evidence.

The historian of culture Ronald Hutton has written at length about Stukeley and religion. Hutton claimed, following Stuart Piggott,[179] that 'a major change of attitude did occur at the time of his ordination'.[180] However, a careful reading of two earlier writings by Stukeley, his *Arthur's O'on* and an account of Stonehenge, suggests a different understanding. Both were written during the early 1720s: *Arthur's O'on* was published in 1720 and the manuscript on Stonehenge was written in 1723 though not published until 2005.[181]

In his study of the now-vanished Roman site known as Arthur's O'on, Stukeley presents a remarkable comparison between the small building in Scotland and the Pantheon in Rome, admitting however 'perhaps some may think we have

---

[177] Goldish, *Judaism*, 13.
[178] Letter from Stukeley to Archbishop Wake, quoted in *Surtees* I, 216.
[179] Piggott, *Stukeley*.
[180] Hutton, 'The religion of William Stukeley', 381–94.
[181] *Stukeley's 'Stonehenge': an unpublished manuscript, 1721–1724*, ed. Aubrey Burl and Neil Mortimer (New Haven, Conn., 2005).

done the Caledonian Temple too much Honour in drawing such a parallel.'[182] He agreed that the similarity between them was not a matter of chance: 'the Reader cannot but remark the repetition of one particular Proportion chosen thro' the whole, that of a Fifth, which is the most beautiful of all others and seems to have some relation to the Musical Concordance which is the sweetest as the most perfect.'[183] Here he describes in print for the first time his notion of the harmony of the world as expressed in music. In this, he related to Newton, who was particularly interested in 'the harmony and discord of sounds'.[184] After commenting on the Temple of Solomon, Stukeley goes on: 'the All-wise Author of Nature has constituted such and such Mixtures or Comparisons of Noises in Sound, to be harmonious and agreeable.' This is then put into its Newtonian context: 'a well founded Artist [the architect of Arthur's O'on] naturally and undesignedly falls into such symmetrical Measures, since others would offend according to the afore-mention'd establish'd Laws of Nature and the Reason of things, whereby Objects are proportion'd to their respective Organs of Sensation.'[185] He goes on to argue that the building on which he proposed that Arthur's O'on was based was the Pantheon, which he suggests was built 'according to the Etruscan taste, whence they [the Romans] derived their primitive religious rites. The Etruscans were the Progeny of the Celts, as is admirably well shown in Monsieur Pezron's Antiquities of that Nation,[186] the first, at least most considerable Inhabitants of the Body of Europe, who brought along with them the Manner of building Temples open at the Top, suitable to the conceptions of the Persians and more Eastern Nations from whence they came in the Infancy of Mankind.'[187]

In this pamphlet, Stukeley revealed his methods of thinking, his antiquarian approach and the origins of his theology. He was convinced that Western European thought and language were derived from the Middle East. He, more than any other English writer in the eighteenth century, created the concept of the Celts, speaking a language which he was sure had very close affiliations with Hebrew. He built his antiquarian and archæological ideas on a combination of two activities: study of built sites in their landscape context and linguistic analysis derived from the biblical accounts of the origin of mankind.

This combination of landscape observation and linguistic theology was typical of Stukeley throughout his life. A study of his original 1723 manuscript on Stonehenge[188] reveals a similar picture. Whilst he edited his own manuscript in his later years, it is possible to read his thoughts in the early 1720s. At that time Stukeley believed Stonehenge to be an ancient temple: 'Often when I have been in Stonehenge have I been rapt up in Jacobs soliloquy, how dreadful is this place

---

[182] W. Stukeley, *Arthur's O'on: An Account of a Roman Temple and other Antiquities near Graham's Dike in Scotland* (London, 1720), 19. We have used the copy owned by the Haverfield Library of Ancient History at Oxford, which was annotated by Stukeley in 1750.
[183] Stukeley, *Arthur's O'on*, 21.
[184] See *Isaac Newton's Papers and Letters on Natural Philosophy*, ed. I. B. Cohen (Cambridge, 1958), 177–235.
[185] Stukeley, *Arthur's O'on*, 21.
[186] Paul-Yves Pezron, *Antiquité de la nation et de la langue des Celtes* (Paris, 1703).
[187] Stukeley, *Arthur's O'on*, 23.
[188] Stukeley's *'Stonehenge'*.

this is none other but the house of God & this is the gate of heaven.'[189] He went on, 'The Druids in Stonehenge have a little more explicated their doctrine than elsewhere, which was much the same as that of the Ægyptians.'[190] Certainly by 1723 Stukeley was convinced of the connection between Stonehenge and the *prisca theologia* of the ancients: 'So our druids followed still the most simple manner learnt first from their master [the Egyptians].'[191]

Stukeley first makes explicit his notion of the Stonehenge Druids deriving their religion from the Jews and being precursors of Christianity in a comment he made on this manuscript, on page 111, referring to

> British women on the continent celebrating the origin of Bacchus crying *evole*. They had learnt it of later Phaenician traders who had it of the Canaanitish nations in imitation of somewhat they had observed in the Jews. A remarkable instance in our Druids of patriarchal institution, either they learnt it of Jacob, or they both learnt it from some common original, as of Abraham not unlikely, of crossing their hands in a religious way when they gathered the mistletoe as Pliny informs us. Their crucifying a man at one of their Great festivals & in the temple, is a wonderful tho' horrid notion of the sacrifice of the Messiah.[192]

This material has been discussed in detail by Ronald Hutton.[193] However, Hutton suggests that 'the same writings show an indifference to Christianity'[194] and proposes that Stukeley in the 1720s was a Deist, 'an umbrella term for somebody who believed in a single omnipotent deity whose works were manifested in the natural world and regarding whom Christianity did not necessarily offer the whole truth'.[195] Hutton draws back a little from his concept of Stukeley as a deist, saying 'to term him a deist would be defensible but misleading', but presents Stukeley's ordination in 1729 as a conversion, whereas Haycock sees it as a 'natural progression from the religious faith he had exhibited in all his work.'[196] Unfortunately Hutton's case is based on weak ground as he was taken in by Stukeley's entertaining banter in a frivolous letter to an ill friend, quoted in the Lukis collection of Stukeley material.[197] It is worthwhile to consider this draft of a letter, in which Stukeley says, 'hoping these few lines may not prove an unseasonable entertainment to you during the confinement of your indisposition.' The draft is not dated as it comes 'From Elysium'. The author claims to be in Heaven, having already died 'divers times before. I could tell you who I was once several ages agoe.' In other words, Stukeley is writing an entertaining pastiche to an ill friend, also a doctor. It is certainly no firm evidence for 'confusion of thought' as Hutton suggests, and he in no way 'proceeded to deny one of

---

[189] *Stukeley's 'Stonehenge'*, 26.
[190] *Stukeley's 'Stonehenge'*, 112 (p.101 of the original MS).
[191] *Stukeley's 'Stonehenge'*, 119 (p.109 of the original MS).
[192] *Stukeley's 'Stonehenge'*, 121–2 (p.111 of the original MS).
[193] Hutton, 'The religion of William Stukeley', 381–94.
[194] Hutton, 'The religion of William Stukeley', 386.
[195] Hutton, 'The religion of William Stukeley', 387.
[196] Hutton, 'The religion of William Stukeley', 389 (cited by Hutton from Haycock, *William Stukeley*, 152).
[197] *Surtees* I, 210–12 for the citations in this and the next paragraph.

its [Christianity's] key beliefs, by expressing a personal belief in reincarnation, buttressed by apparent personal memories of past lives'.[198]

The article by Hutton concentrates on what he calls Stukeley's 'conversion', deriving this from Stukeley's 1729 letter to the Archbishop of Canterbury in which he wrote that he had 'long had thoughts of entering into orders ... I have ever been studious in divinity.'[199] At the heart of his religious life was the widespread eighteenth-century belief in divine providence. According to Dr Johnson, the word *providence* meant 'the care of God over created things; divine superintendence'.[200] Stukeley's understanding of providence both supported his religious life and provided him with arguments to support Christianity. Stukeley would have agreed with Isaac Newton who wrote about prophecy and providence:

> The folly of Interpreters has been, to fortel times and things by this Prophecy, as if God designed to make them Prophets. By this rashness they have not only exposed themselves, but brought the Prophecy also into contempt. The design of God was much otherwise. He gave this and the Prophecies of the Old Testament, not to gratify men's curiosities by enabling them to foreknow things, but that after they were fulfilled they might be interpreted by the event, and his own Providence, not the Interpreters, be then manifested thereby to the world. For the event of things predicted many ages before, will then be a convincing argument that the world is governed by providence.[201]

In other words, aspects of the present world should be used to prove the truth of the Christian faith by comparing them with life in the past as revealed in both scripture and history.

This was Stukeley's purpose as a historian and an archæologist. He wrote in one of his many manuscript accounts of his life:

> I have all my life long perceiv'd that Providence favour'd my resolution.... Antiquity-studies soon got an ascendancy in my fancy, thinking wisdom was the product of former days, & thence to be recover'd.[202]

In the epitome of his writings, *Abury: A Temple of the British Druids*, Stukeley explained his understanding of the origins of the Christian faith before Christ. He asserted that 'creation is eternal fecundity,'[203] which was the exercise of the goodness, 'as it were, the essence of God. Then he can have no happiness but in the exercise of that goodness.'[204] He argued that 'the highest act of goodness which is possible, even for the supreme being, is the production of his like, the act of filiation, the begetting of his son'. This argument appeared to Stukeley as totally logical and reasonable. He then argued that the Druids arrived at this same view 'by ratiocination',[205] 'and when there was such a notion in the world,

---

[198] Hutton, 'The religion of William Stukeley', 389.
[199] *Surtees* I, 216.
[200] Johnson, *Dictionary of the English Language* (London, 1755).
[201] I. Newton, *Prophecies of Daniel*, 251. Stukeley possessed a copy.
[202] *Surtees* I, 79–80.
[203] Stukeley, *Abury: A Temple of the British Druids*, 87.
[204] Stukeley, *Abury*, 88.
[205] Stukeley, *Abury*, 89.

our Druids, who had the highest fame for theological studies, would cultivate it in some such manner as I have deliver'd, by the mere strength of natural reason'. Stukeley's view was that the Druids understood the patriarchal religion of Abraham:

> to our *British* Druids was reserv'd the honour of a more extensive idea and of executing it. They made plains and hills, valleys, springs and rivers contribute to form a temple of three miles in length. They have stamped the whole country with the impress of this sacred character, and that of the most permanent nature ... This I verily believe to have been a truly patriarchal temple ... and where the worship of God was perform'd.[206]

The archæological work Stukeley did on Avebury between 1718 and 1724 led to an intensification of his religious views and gave him the drive to preach Christianity. His belief in providence, coupled with an extraordinary imagination, an insistence on practical investigation and a wide-ranging awareness of ancient classical and theological writings, allowed him to extend the understanding of man's history and religion in his own unique manner.

In Stukeley, we have a portrait of a complex individual, enthusiastic, hardworking, combining practical observation and recording with a tendency to jump to conclusions, sometimes ahead of his data, and to relate them to grand, overarching schemes. The SGS were proud of their lively and hard-working member, supporting him loyally when he faced criticism or waded into controversial arguments and enjoying the dissertations which he provided for them. His lifelong friendship with Johnson, his letters and visits to Spalding and to the Society, ensured that they were able to follow with interest the career of a fellow-member whose views and publications kept him in the public gaze.

---

[206] Stukeley, *Abury*, 101–102.

EDITORIAL CONVENTIONS

The letters of this correspondence, despite some vocabulary and expressions which are now obsolete, present little difficulty to the modern reader. This section explains the conventions used in transcribing the letters for this volume. As an additional aid to understanding, each letter is followed by end-notes which elaborate details in the letters; they include information on individuals who are referred to. However, members of the SGS who are referred to have an entry in Appendix 3, with brief biographical details. Therefore they are not given an end-note when they appear in a letter, unless there is a point of particular significance for that letter connected with them.

The conventions adopted in editing and transcribing these letters for publication relate in particular to spelling, punctuation and the use of abbreviations. Changes in word-meanings did not present a significant problem, but if a word is used in a letter in its eighteenth-century meaning which could be misleading to a modern reader, or if an obsolete word is used, this is indicated in an end-note.

In transcribing these letters, we decided to adhere to the original spellings used by the two writers. Some earlier editors who have used extracts from Stukeley's and Johnson's correspondence have standardised the spelling, but we felt that something of the character of the original letters can be lost in this way. Their spelling systems are not such as to make for major difficulties in reading and understanding their letters. The early eighteenth century is a period of considerable interest to students of the English language, since the spelling of English was not yet fully standardised. The process of standardisation was hastened by the production of the dictionaries which were such a feature of the time, particularly Nathan Bailey's *Dictionarium Britannicum* in 1730 and the more famous Dr Samuel Johnson's *Dictionary* in 1755, the year of Maurice Johnson's death. The standardisation of spelling was also encouraged by the increasing use of English, rather than Latin, as a medium for serious publications as well as for popular texts. Sir Isaac Newton's practice was symptomatic of this; his *Principia* (1687) was written in Latin, but his *Opticks* (1704–6) was written in English.

Individual writers tended to develop their own, usually internally consistent system of spelling. Both Maurice Johnson and William Stukeley have individual and rather idiosyncratic spelling systems, which are generally consistent though each of them varies certain spellings from time to time. It is interesting to note that when they write in Latin, even when this is not quotation but original writing by them, the spelling is standardised, as it is in any brief quotations from classical Greek; no doubt this is the result of their early education in the Classics.

Stukeley, in particular, has his own distinctive spelling system. A notable feature of his orthography is the deliberate omission of the final 'e' in words such as 'judg' and 'nobl' and in the past participle of verbs, e.g. 'fastend', presumably on the grounds that this letter was no longer pronounced by the early eighteenth century. This contrasts with Johnson's regular use of the 'e' in participles such as 'danceing' and 'improveing' (which Stukeley also does from time to time), and his tendency to double a final consonant in words such as 'delightfull'. Johnson also adds an extra final 'e' to pronouns such as 'wee' and 'yee', perhaps to indicate the pronunciation of the vowel. Both men spelt surnames and place-names in different ways, sometimes even using two different spellings of a name within the same letter. For example, Stukeley's society at Stamford could appear as 'Brasen Nose Society' or 'Brazennose' or even 'Brazen Nose' and the antiquarian Thomas Hearne can also appear as 'Hearn'. We have retained the original spelling in all cases when transcribing, but in notes we have adopted a modern standard form and used the currently accepted spelling.

Abbreviations presented more of a problem. Both Stukeley and Johnson used abbreviations frequently in their letters, sometimes for speed or convenience, sometimes to fit into the space at the end of a line or to squeeze in a final message at the end of a letter, to avoid using a further sheet of paper which would increase the cost of postage. A single folded sheet, with messages written on all sides except the small area reserved for the address, was cheaper to send than a double sheet. Both men were accustomed to use abbreviations in their professional work. Johnson's arose from his legal training, as the legal documents of the period had a standard and extensive system of abbreviations for both English and Latin words. He and his fellow-members of the SGS produced an alphabetical catalogue of customary abbreviations in both languages, beautifully handwritten, which is still in the Society's archive. In some letters we have left abbreviations in the original form to give the full flavour of the letters: abbreviations such as 'S^r' for 'Sir', 'rec^d' for 'received', 'acc^t' for 'account' and 'fr^d' for 'friend' do not present a problem for the modern reader and can be understood easily from the context, as can frequently used abbreviations such as 'wch' for 'which' and 'yr' for 'your'. In some cases, however, we have extended the abbreviated forms into the full word. First, it was done if the abbreviation made it difficult to understand the meaning of a phrase or sentence. Secondly, if the abbreviation was written as one of the many graphic symbols used in the handwriting of the early eighteenth century, these present a problem both for reproduction by the printer and also for comprehensibility by the reader without the aid of Johnson's alphabet of abbreviations. Johnson, in particular, uses both the customary business abbreviations of the early eighteenth century and also abbreviations of Latin words, particularly of prefixes and case-endings, especially when discussing numismatics. In these cases, the word was inserted in its modern spelling.

The main occasion where a substitution was made was in the case where 'y' was written as a graphic device for representing 'th', as in words such as 'ye', 'yt' and 'ym', where the original writer and reader both understood that 'the', 'that' or 'them' was intended. In particular, to retain the spelling 'ye' can be misleading to a modern reader and give an impression of 'ye olde worlde' far removed from the dynamic and up-to-date ideas and lives of Stukeley and Johnson. We therefore reproduced 'ye' as 'the', ym as 'them' and 'yt' as 'that' throughout the transcription.

We also decided to keep the original punctuation of both writers. Johnson retained the early eighteenth-century practice of capitalisation of the initial letters of nouns. He sometimes applied this to other words such as adjectives, pronouns, adverbs and even verbs, especially as a means of signalling significance or emphasis, for example 'expecting to be Commanded to Flanders' and 'he is a Very Virtuous Industrious Young man'. He is not always consistent in this practice, as in phrases such as 'Acceptable and agreeable'. Stukeley, on the other hand, avoided capitalisation, not only at the beginning of nouns, as used by many of his fellow-writers in the early eighteenth century, but also at the beginning of a new sentence, following a full stop. We have retained this practice, as it reflects Stukeley's idiosyncratic presentation of his ideas in writing.

The sentence structure of the original writers has been retained, with the insertion of an occasional full stop in the interest of readability and comprehensibility. This is more necessary in the case of Johnson's style, which was formed by his study of classical Latin authors and by his training in the drawing up of legal documents. His sentences are usually long, periodic and complex, with several subordinate clauses, especially when he is writing on subjects of antiquarian interest or propounding plans for his society. His vocabulary then becomes formal and Latinate. When writing about more everyday matters, such as his family or his garden, both sentence structure and vocabulary become plainer and simpler.

Stukeley's style is equally shaped by his professional training, in his case as a natural philosopher and physician. His sentences tend to be much shorter and of less complex structure. His paragraphs are shorter, sometimes containing only a couple of sentences in contrast with Johnson's which can at times fill almost a page. His handwriting is simple and clear, contrasting with Johnson's bold hand which often uses flourishes and extended tails to letters. As a lawyer and antiquarian, Johnson was a master of many styles of writing; he was able to write court hand for documents and to copy the styles of the early manuscripts he collected and studied. The minute books that he kept up for the SGS for many years contain copies of earlier scripts which he made, on occasions using secretary hand or earlier mediæval writing styles or imitating black-letter printing. One interesting feature to note is that, as the two correspondents age, their handwriting increases in size to cope with problems of deteriorating eyesight. As his health deteriorated, Johnson's final letters were dictated to his clerk; the final one contains mistakes in spelling names which are uncharacteristic in his own writing.

Use of Latin

Both Johnson and Stukeley, in common with many writers of their time, had a good knowledge of Latin arising from their education at grammar schools which, according to the definition in Samuel Johnson's *Dictionary*, were schools 'in which the learned languages are grammatically taught'. The 'learned languages' were, of course, Latin and Greek. Maurice Johnson in particular, after his years at Eton, was a fluent reader and writer of Latin, and both he and Stukeley introduced Latin into their letters. This is most generally in the form of short phrases quoted from Latin writers, which educated eighteenth-century gentlemen would be expected to know and recognise from their education; indeed, some of them continued to read the Latin poets for pleasure. Johnson uses quotations most frequently, drawing on prose authors such as Cæsar as authorities when discussing early British history. He often brings in an apposite quotation from a Latin poet such as Virgil, Horace, Ovid or Juvenal to illustrate a comment or reflection on the events of his own times. He also quotes, sometimes at length, from mediæval chroniclers or from writers of the sixteenth and seventeenth centuries who wrote in Latin. On occasions, he can also quote in classical Greek, usually in connection with a point of historical or theological discussion. These letters show little of Johnson's ability to write original Latin, though the calendar of the SGS's correspondence records several letters in Latin to friends such as Roger Gale and Francis Curtis, and he wrote a Latin ode for the introduction to Stukeley's first volume of his *Itinerarium Curiosum*.

Stukeley also makes use of short Latin quotations and phrases, though less frequently than Johnson. His school education was less extensive and his Cambridge scientific and medical education, though drawing on some textbooks written in Latin, also used vernacular texts to a greater extent. However, he does offer, in **Letter 5**, a set of humorous Latin verses on Bobart's alleged 'dragon'.

Our policy has been to leave the short Latin quotations in place, without translation if they are well-known phrases. We offer, in the end-notes to the letter, a translation of less easily recognisable short quotations, either our own or an attributed version from a modern translation. On a few occasions, Johnson includes very long quotations in late Latin from history books and chronicles in his possession, usually in reply to a question from Stukeley about history or antiquities. Since these are not original writings by Johnson and are so long that they disrupt the flow of the letter, it was decided to omit them on occasion. In their place, we offer in the notes a summary of what the quotation contained, the name of the author and the work from which it was quoted, so that reference can be made to the quotation if required.

Dating of letters
Both Johnson and Stukeley were usually precise about dating their letters, so there were few problems in dating the correspondence and arranging the two separate sets of letters into their correct chronological sequence. The main difficulties encountered were:

(a) Letters written between 1 January and 25 March in any year until 1752. This can apply to any letter written in the first half of the eighteenth century, since the year officially began on 25 March, Lady Day. Thus a letter written on what we would call 18 February 1733 could be dated '1733' or '1732' or '1732/3'. In cases of ambiguity, the contents of the letter, referring to contemporary events or the publication of a book, enabled the date to be verified. The minute books of the SGS were also useful, since they record the arrival and reading at the Society of letters from Stukeley. In the text of the letters we transcribe the dating used by the writers, but in our own headings to the letters we have used the modern, post-1752 dating.

(b) Letters which are undated. **Letter 7**, a letter from Johnson in London, can be dated to 1715 by its contents and so can be placed into the sequence. Occasionally the surviving text is a fragment, missing the opening and closing where a date could be expected to occur. There are very few of these in this correspondence; the main one is **Letter 38**, from Johnson to Stukeley, which is filed at the end of the Johnson section in Stukeley's letter-book at the Bodleian Library as folio 360, following the rest of the correspondence. This is dateable from its contents to January 1744 as they relate to an Albano-ware dish; this is described in the minute book of the SGS where the date of the meeting at which it was shown is given.

(c) The other problem encountered was with one letter in the Bodleian collection. Maurice Johnson's letters to Stukeley, like all the other letters in Stukeley's letter-book, are mounted in a bound volume, in chronological sequence by date. In one case, however, the date of 1716 has presumably been misread by the person making up the volume as 1726 and the letter is placed out of sequence in the book, among the letters for the 1720s, as the folio numbers indicate. It was possible to insert it in this transcription in its correct place in 1716, as **Letter 10**, dating it from the fact that the letter is addressed by Johnson to Dr Stukeley 'at his house in Boston'. In 1716 Stukeley was practising as a physician in Boston, he left for London in 1717 and was living there in 1726, so the letter cannot be from 1726.

THE CORRESPONDENCE OF WILLIAM STUKELEY AND MAURICE JOHNSON

1714–1754

1. Maurice Johnson to William Stukeley, Spalding, 6 April 1714
Bodleian, MS Eng. misc. c.113, fols 295r–296v

To Dr William Stukeley

Dear Dr

Mr Aslak[1] gave Me Your kind Letter of Congratulation for which I heartyly thank You, And wish whenever You shall take a Wife to your bed the first Pledge of your Hymeneal Rites may be as Bouncing a Boy[2] as mine is: I hold my Self moreover obliged to You for wishing Us together: And as to the Noble Task you have wisely thought good to Assigne yourself,[3] I will assist You therein according to Your desire, all I can; whose Service You know You may freely command. I wish I could do It to your best advantage, but that requires an Abler Assistance. In Order thereunto however, I have sent you my Seldens Tracts,[4] a Book of Singular Use, as I have found, in that Affaire, I can spare it a fourteenight or thereabouts. The few MS animadversions are of my Own adding, & for my private Use; But if they any way divert or assist You, in reading the Author, they will give me more satisfaction than I proposed, As the little Unexpected Advantages my Friends any way reap thro my Meanes Do; You will percieve, Sir, they were added Occasionaly at Several perusals of the Book where you find 'em. But to the Purpose – I advise You carefully to peruse – Cæsaris Commen. De Bello Gall. Lib.6 as to the Druids and Religion (if Your Profession will permitt You to look into that),[5] and the Two former Books as to the State of this then Savage Country & the Bellum Britannicum – Taciti Historiarum Lib: 3, And his life of Agricola,[6] the Notes of our learned Countryman in English (Sir Henr. Saville's)[7] upon this Author are much esteemed. From the time of the Romans to the Norm: Conq: John Milton's Hist. of England[8] a thin quarto, a Scarce book, & worth 3 half Crowns, wherein that great man hath with immense Labour, & Judgement, greatly comended, extracted out of the Fabulous Monks the History of his Native Country down to the Conq: of Willm 1st over Harrold, Printed at London 1670 – Verstegan's Restitution of Decayd Intelligence,[9] Cambden's Discourses before his Britannia,[10] & Brady's Introduction[11] are worthy Your acquiring – And in the Useing these You may consult Dr Heylins Help to English History,[12] which last book I esteem extreemly necessary. I have here sent you One and begg the favour of You to accept It: You will find It a pretty exact Piece and of constant Use to You in the Series of Succession of our Kings, Bps, Nobles &c, As allso in the Chronological part, With which and Geography You must be duely acquainted, And conversant in thro' the whole Reading of History, Otherwise You will but little proffitt, and ill retaine what You read. Such was the Sentiment of Casaubon, Petavius, J. C. Scaliger and our great Locke,[13] all persons of Judgement and Sagacity; As for Geography Auntient & Modern Britain as described by Cluver, Cambden and Speed,[14] whose Mapps are comon, And much commended by some Gentlemen –

[p.2] Methinks I see You from Your Couché rise
Drive lazy Morning Slumbers from Your Eyes,
And seat Yourself to Study, And be wise,
All wide before You on Your Desk displayd
Some of our faithfull Old Historians layd,
Truth void of Dress adornes each honest Page,

The Reader various Passions engage,
The Turnes of Fortune, & the change of Fate,
So move his Soul, as erst the British State:

Methinks I see You at each Conquest pale,
The Britons lose the Day, Your Spirits faile:
As They to Mountains from the Romans flye,
Your Blood flows to your Heart by Sympathy;
But frequent Noble Acts revolvd will show
You're pleasd, And with returning Vigor glow:

Thus will the Sacæ Jutes & Angles grieve
Your Generous Breast, 'till Britons brave relieve
Such Cares assum'd, & you triumphing read
Our Ancestors with No small glory bleed:
With Joy, I see, you think the Lordly Dane
By Fair Uxorial Hands full timely Slain:
The Bastard's Conquest over Harald yields   [*William I*]
A Doubtfull pleasure, whilest their Native fields
Tilld by the English, from their Owners ta'en,
Their All, & left 'em even by the Dane,
Are without Right to Strange Norwegian Lords
Allotted, as the Purchase of their Swords:

[p.3] The Sacred Saxon Line almost ador'd
Is with Fitz Emprice happyly restord: [15]   [*Henry II, son of the Empress Matilda*]
With Henry Hereford I now suppose   [*Henry IV*]
You join, And Colour with his Reddning Rose,
And tho You mourne his pious Grandsons fate,   [*Henry VI*]
Yet can You not the Amorous Rival hate,
Or wish York's Snowy Rose should fade away,
Almost regretting Bosworth's bloody Day,
Tho Lancasters fourth Flower moist with that blood   [*Henry VII*]
Sprung up, and wide disclosed his Crimson budd,
Who joind to Yorks fair Sprigg Did wisely reigne,
Produceing that Bold Prince who dared restrayne   [*Henry VIII*]
Excessive Papal Power, Nor strove in vain
The Rights of his Emperiall Crown to gain:
His truly pious Son restor'd to Day   [*Edward VI*]
Religion, Pure from Errors chac'd away:

Thus whilest the wondrous Volumes you peruse
Unkend by any but the quick Eyed Muse,
Let auntient Chronos on your Right Side stand
With circling Eneantos[16] in his Hande,
By certain Æras dateing former Yeares
Whence unconfus'd fair History appeares:
Whilest on your Left Geography must Show

In Exact Plans what Watry Currents flow
Dividing Provinces, the Various Name
Each Province hath assum'd, the Land the Same,
Must fix the Boundaries each Century knew
Where Cities have been, And where Forest grew.

[p.4] 'Tis hence alone, Sir, that the Reading history can be retaind or profitt; And to Use Mr Lockes Words, It will otherwise be only a Jumble of matters of Fact confusedly heaped together without Order, or Instruction; 'Tis by these that Actions of Mankind are ranked into their proper places of times and Countries; Under which Circumstances They are not only much easier kept in the memory but in that natural Order are Only capable to afford those Observacions which make a Man the better, & the abler for reading Them: You See, Dear Sir, I am Somewhat particular in these matters and shall be more So when next I see you which I am pleasd in considering it will not be very long to, as you promise in yours.

I have something further to communicate, And that is what I was told by Mr Hutchinson of this Town,[17] who lately came from thence, that there hath lately been found at Blankney in this County the Skeleton of an Antient Briton I conjecture from certain smal rings of Iron found upon Strings near it, which I take to be the Lamina Ferrea of the Classicks, in which and other Baubles our Forefathers dealt – I don't know but It may be worth while to procure some of them which are in the hands of the honourable Mr Widdrington,[18] and of but very little value to any but Such Men, whom he may perhaps have preserved 'em for, the Curious in Antiquity: I think I have now held you a prodigious while in Discourse at this Distance, & that it is time to conclude, but first let me beg of you to present my humblest Services to Your ingenious Mr Kellsall,[19] whom I have more than Once invited to Spalding but never was so happy yet as to see him here, Mr Pimlow,[20] Mr Fawkner's Lady & her Daughter,[21] Mr Gonville,[22] Mister Wood & all the rest of the good neighbourhood whom You and I both know: Let me see You if You can on the morrow Seavenight at this Town, when You may enjoy the company of many of your Friends of these parts collected into a Society,[23] to which I invite you heartily, and am
      Dear Dr,
        Your assured Friend and most humble Servant
         Maur: Johnson junior

Spalding Tuesday
the 6th of April 1714

---

1 Mr William Azlacke of Boston is listed as a 'Benefactor to Spalding publick Libraries S.G.S.' in the SGS's library catalogue, for the donation of three volumes, all printed in the mid-1500s. He is also described in the catalogue as 'Guil. Azlacke Generosus de Sto. Botulpho' and described in a 1714 entry as 'Attorney at Law'. He does not appear to have become a member of the SGS, probably because at that early stage the Society accepted as members only those living in the vicinity of Spalding. The range of corresponding members developed later in the Society's history.

2 Maurice Johnson's eldest surviving son, also named Maurice, born 15 March 1714 (see Appendix 3). Johnson already had two surviving daughters, Jane and Elizabeth. He and his wife (née Elizabeth Ambler), who were married in 1710, had a large family of whom eleven survived into adulthood. See *Correspondence*, appendix 5 for a family tree of the Johnsons of Spalding.

3 Stukeley was setting about writing a chronology of Britain; see **Letter 2** below.

4   Maurice Johnson's personal library was very comprehensive; printed catalogues of its sale in 1898 and 1970 show its extent. It is interesting that Stukeley has evidently asked Johnson's advice for suitable reading on the history of Britain. The first reference is to John Selden (1584–1654), *Tracts* (1683): four of Selden's essays on the history of the common law of Britain and on testamentary law, translated from the original Latin. Selden's history sceptically dismissed early legends and contained much on the Druids, which would have interested Stukeley.

5   At this period, there was a tendency for doctors to take no interest in religion and even to be opposed to it; here Johnson teases Stukeley by suggesting he, as a physician, shares this view. Johnson recommends Cæsar's *Gallic Wars*, books 4, 5 and 6, which cover the two attacks on Britain and the nature of the Druids.

6   Tacitus, *Histories*, book 3 and *Agricola*, which cover the first century AD.

7   Sir Henry Savile (1549–1622), *Four Books of the Histories and Agricola* (1591).

8   John Milton (1608–1674), *The history of Britain, that part, especially now called England* (1670). In the first of six books Milton sceptically recounts the history of Britain up to Cæsar's invasion, 'leaning only on the credit of Geoffrey of Monmouth … whereto I neither oblige the belief of other persons, nor over-hastily subscribe my own' (p.24).

9   Richard Verstegan (*c.*1548–1640), *The Restitution of Decayed Intelligence in Antiquities* (1605), 'a seminal work of Anglo-Saxon scholarship' (*ODNB*). After a brief account of the origins of civilisation taken from the Bible, Verstegan begins his history with the origins of Germanic tribes, who were thought to have been descended from Japhet. 'English-men are descended of German race, and were heretofore generally called Saxons.'

10   William Camden (1551–1623). This could be a reference to Camden's *Remains of a Greater Worke concerning Britain* (1605) which was re-published frequently in the seventeenth century, particularly as *Remains concerning Britain* (1674).

11   Dr Robert Brady (1627–1700), *An Introduction to the old English history, comprehended in three several tracts* (1684), a discussion of 'Ecclesiastical and Secular Liberties in those ancient times' based upon an attack on the historical work of William Petit (1640–1707). The book culminates in 'A True and Exact History of the Succession of the Crown of England'.

12   Dr Peter Heylin (1599–1662), *Help to English History* (1641), a reference book which catalogues kings, bishops and lords. It was reprinted and extended in 1709, so this is perhaps the edition Johnson refers to. It is specified in the catalogue of Stukeley's library.

13   Isaac Casaubon (1559–1614), central in dating the Corpus Hermeticum to the post-Christian era; Dionysius Petavius (1583–1652), a great French Catholic scholar who worked on the historical reality of Christian doctrine; J. C. Scaliger (1484–1558), a late Renaissance classicist and natural philosopher; John Locke (1632–1704), the most significant European philosopher of his time, who taught that there were no innate ideas, only knowledge derived from experience.

14   Cluver (1580–1622), a German scholar best known for his *Universal Geography*; Camden: see note 10 above (Johnson and Stukeley frequently refer to Camden's *Britannia*); John Speed (1542–1629), best known for his county maps in *The Theatre of the Empire of Great Britaine* (1611), frequently re-printed.

15   A first draft of this letter, in the SGS's Spalding archive, contains these verses which are almost identical to this version, but include additional lines at two points, though these have been crossed out in the first draft and so are not included in this final version: (i) after 'happily restored' the original draft has 'Those Eight successive Reignes more pleasure bring/ than all the rest, so various was each King'; (ii) after 'Lancasters fourth flower' the original draft has a first version 'sprung from that plain/ who joind to Yorks fair Sprigg did wisely reigne;/ Producing him to whose stout Soul Wee owe,/ that Wee no grievous Roman bondage know/ And yield us that Bold prince …'; Johnson then deleted these lines and substituted the version given above.

16   In classical Greek mythology Eneantos was the personification of the year, represented with a horn.

17   This may be the Revd Samuel Hutchinson, curate at Sutterton in 1713 and member of the SGS in 1729.

18   The Hon. Ralph Widdrington (*c.*1640–1712) of Blankney (Lincs), briefly MP for Berwick in 1685, but probably never took his seat. He became a significant non-juror.

19   The Revd Edward Kelsall (1672–1719), MA (St John's College, Cambridge), was Master of Boston Grammar School from 1697 to 1702 and was then appointed Vicar of Boston. In 1710 he conducted a party of young gentlemen from Boston on a journey to Oxford, written up by Stukeley

as the 'Iter Oxoniense', which first introduced Stukeley to the ancient Rollright stone circle. This was similar to the 'Iter Bathonense' undertaken by Johnson in 1710: see **Letter 10**, n.2.

20 This could be either John or Ambrose Pimlow, friends of Stukeley's from his schooldays in Holbeach. Revd John Pimlow (c.1685–1729) was Lecturer at Boston; Revd Ambrose Pimlow (c.1687–1750), who had also been at Cambridge with Stukeley, became incumbent of Castle Acre (Norfolk).

21 Thomas Falkner was a merchant at Boston. After his death his widow Ann married Maurice Johnson's father as his third wife and came to live at Ayscoughfee Hall, thus becoming Maurice Johnson's stepmother.

22 See Appendix 3.

23 This reference to meetings of the SGS indicates that at this early stage (1714) it was meeting on Wednesdays, a day preferred by the Treasurer, Mr Atkinson. After Atkinson's death in 1719, the meeting day moved to Thursday and has remained so ever since.

[The Spalding archive contains a first draft of much of this letter (SGS/Maurice Johnson/2) which is almost identical to the final text as sent; it includes several further lines of verse, but these are crossed through by Johnson in the draft; see note 15 above. The Spalding version of the letter is incomplete, stopping at the beginning of page 4 of the above text, at '...those observations which make a Man the better & the abler for reading Them.' The remainder of the content is in note form, to remind Johnson of what to include in the final version: 'Skeleton at Blankney of a Brittain with Rings &c the familiar ferrea of the Classicks. Lamina'. This was enlarged in the finished letter, as above.]

2. William Stukeley to Maurice Johnson, Boston, 19 May 1714
Spalding, SGS/Stukeley/1

[Heading in Johnson's hand, added at a later date:[1]] Lr from Dr W. Stukeley FGS. About his Genealogico-Chronological Tables of our Kings & of the Druids – British antiq. found near Lincoln.

Dear Sir   Boston 19th of May 1714

I expected to see You to day, having appointed to meet Mr Ratcliffe[2] to end our affairs at Your house, but just now rec[eive]d a Note from him to postpone it till Tuesday next. I wish You could find time to come hither before then, I have returnd Selden[3] & an old Lawbook which is pretty antient but whether it be worth sending I can't tell. I have severall more by me which You should have If You likd 'em. I now begin to think much with spending any further time or pains with my Geneological Scheme[4] & design shortly to paste the peices together & spend this Summer in the more immediate Studys of my profession for Business comes in upon me apace. I think what I have done will not be useless, because as I have drawn the Pedegrees of every Prince that ever wore a Scepter in any parts of this Isle & that up to the highest traces of Time which as far as any books I could meet withal could direct me to any certainty, together with the year of their Reign & all in a cotemporary method, as likewise their Arms, & a little Sketch of History along with 'em: I conceive it will give one a lasting & unconfusd Train & memory of the British history, & be serviceable in finding out the founders of Churches &c by the coats of Arms. & their Antiquity. I must own I have a mighty love for Antiquity & there is no greater Satisfaction to me than being lost as it were in the dark recesses of Old Times. in following thro' mazy obscurity the bright shadow of Truth, till with a joy superior to any the other Sciences are ready to afford You, You embrace if it be but the appearance of the Lovely Goddess.

Our old Father Brute or Brito[5] makes a considerable Show in my Paper & whatever Mr Selden & several more grave [p.2] Authors think ~~that~~ who, its likely, took a distast at first sight against that old History & never thoroughly examin'd into it, I must needs with the Great Milton say that he & his Progeny, defended by many, & persons of great capacity in Antiquitys, denyd utterly by few, that the account of those old & inborn names of successive Kings so long handed down, cannot be dischargd from Existence without too strict an incredulity. The only way I thought in this Case to arrive at Truth was very fairly & carefully to compare the evidences on both sides, which to the best of my Judgment prodigiously preponderate in favour of our Illustrious Ancestor. Tis true there is some reason to imagine him a Descendant of the Gaulish & German Monarchs from the Continent, & evidence I think from thence alone sufficient to vindicate him from annihilation, but whoever reads the collections I have made about him must (I think) beleive him to be descended from the blood royal of the Trojans. & where I pray You is the insuperable difficulty of believing so old a Tradition when almost every Roman Writer mention the reliques of the Trojans being scatterd in Italy Spain Gaul, nay that Ulysses himself landed in his rambles upon this Island. Tis not to be denyd by an Ipse dixit gratis,[6] or some inconnexions of Geography chronography or some mixtures of the improbable or even impossible, for even fables have something at the bottom, of Truth. nor must suspend my belief to so narrow a Scantling with those that acknowledge nothing true of our Island before or but what Cæsar has told us, who himself tells a great many lyes in his own favour, & for the same reason may tell lyes to depreciate the honour of his Enimys the Britons. must I think so meanly of our old Druids that were Tutors even to the Gaulish Priests that for a great many ages used the Greek characters which shews they were able & why not willing amongst their other Magnificent Studys, to transmitt the memory of their Kings Great Men & actions to posterity, when Cæsar tells us Multa [p.3] Dryades de sideribus & eorum motu, de Mundi & terrarum magnitudine, de rerum natura, de deorum immortalium Vi ac potestate disputabant & Iuventuti tradebant.[7] Can they be so ingagd in these great, remote & difficult Speculations as wholly neglect those nearer easier & more obvious Matters of Fact of Government Wars & Councels all which they had so great a hand in themselves. but I'le say no more on this head. however in confidence of the Truth of this Descent from Æneas I have endeavourd to unravell his pedigree thro' all the Labyrinths of Grecian Fable up to Noah wherein one way or other is comprehended some part at least of all the famous Men & Kingdoms of Greece Italy & Ægypt. where there is any mutual relation by Marriage or descent. & this will be particularly usefull to me in reading Classics.

I have been rambling of late about Lincoln side, we were two or three days at Sir Edwd. Husseys[8] who has a very good library. We went to Mr Widringtons[9] to see the old beads & reliques of the Britons buryed there, some were of Amber some of Glasse & some of clay enammeld with curious colours, there were brass rings, bits of bridles & other trinkets of brasse.

I am Dear Sir

Your very humble servant
Wm Stukeley.

To Maurice Johnson Esqr
at Spalding

---

1   Stukeley was living in Boston at this time, practising as a physician. Johnson's annotation was added some years later, while he was organising the papers of the SGS, as Stukeley is referred to as 'FGS' (Fellow of the Gentlemen's Society) but he did not become a member or 'Fellow' until 1722 by which stage he had left Boston.
2   Mr Ratcliffe is presumably a local solicitor.
3   See **Letter 1**, n.4.
4   Stukeley's genealogical scheme at the time consisted of an attempt to create accurate lists relating to what Dr Samuel Johnson later (1755) defined in his *Dictionary* as 'pertaining to the history of the succession of houses', particularly the royal houses of Britain and England.
5   The myth that Brutus, the descendant of Æneas the Trojan, founded Britain is first written about in the *Historia Britonum* of Nennius (*c.*830) and more fully developed in the work of Geoffrey of Monmouth (*c.*1100–*c.*1150), *Historia Regum Britanniæ*, which was being regarded by the more sceptical historians of Stukeley's time as a mythical account.
6   This phrase implies that the historical account of Brutus is merely an assertion, without proof. Stukeley is concerned to suggest that even fables or myths have some foundation in truth, as he goes on to say.
7   Stukeley has transposed the 'Dryades' from earlier in the passage; Cæsar wrote 'præterea' ('besides this'). 'The Druids debated many things: about the stars and their movements, about the size of the world and its lands, about the nature of things and the strength and power of the immortal gods, and passed this on to their young people', Cæsar, *De Bello Gallico* IV. Cæsar adds 'Græcis litteris utantur', which is where Stukeley learned that the Druids used Greek letters.
8   Sir Edward Hussey, probably the third baronet (1661–1725), MP for Lincoln. His seat was the Old Hall at Caythorpe (Lincs).
9   See **Letter 1**, n.18.

3. Maurice Johnson to William Stukeley, Spalding, 8 November 1714[1]
Bodleian, MS Eng. misc. c.113, fol.297r–v

Sir

I was at Lincoln when the Letter you intended me came hither; And as no Man of Spirit can take pleasure in being slighted, So I assure you it was a Satisfaction to me to find you therein protesting that which I could not but imagin might be so, the Misreport of the Silly Fellow who should have brought Mr Paceys answer to Mr Atkinson;[2] by which I had avoided an ineffectual Journey Speaking relatively, the true intent of it being to wait upon Mr Kellsall[3] that Revd. & Learned Pastor, with You & so have enjoyd both your companys.

The Value I have for you I need not speak it, you yourself can, And the great opinion I have concieved of that Worthy Clergyman, with whom was I honoured in an acquaintance, would more frequently draw me to Boston; Alltho I seldom stirr abroad, But upon Business or for the sake of conversing with men of Learning and worth in which alone I take all the Pleasure I have out of our own Door.

As my Friendship is very sincere, whenever I profess to have any, So I was very glad to read in your Letter that you have Interest & Employment in a neighbouring parish; I heartyly wish your business may encrease upon your hands. And question not but You have it in your power both to engage & serve.

I returne you thanks for the Draught & description of the Golden Ring you communicated to Me. You may not I think suppose it as you do with ambiguity to have been either a Roman or British antiquity: but must suppose It to have been of the former, unless you'll say that by the Stature of our Gigantick ancestors, It might belong to some British Gentleman after they were Romanized and came into the fashion of their Conquerors, as the Romans called Themselves – For I meet not with the use of the Annulus[4] amongst the auncient Britons.

The Lamina[5] which They are by Cæs. (L.v de Bell. Gallic.) said to have used for money were ferrea and I suppose flatt thin plates of that mettal, of like Shape but Golden were those menconed in the Notes to Gibson's Ed. of Cambd. Britann.[6] in Wales and they are the only portable things at all like the Ring which have occurred to me. And that but very little the Diameter of the hole being much les & the Circle broader in plate wise, strung upon Cords & hung round the Hero upon his Breast, as our modern heros at eating Custards the Aldermen of London wear their Golden Chaines.

But to come to the Romans: Pliny tells us the Annulus distinguished the Equites a plebe[7] and Aul: Gell:[8] hath a curious passage Li.x Cap.x in Solution of the Question why the Greeks & old Romans wore their Rings upon the next finger to the little one of their Left hands as our Wives do, & marryd men have used according to that Monkish Verse counting from the Thumb

Miles	Mercator	Stultus	Maritus	Amator[9]
1	2	3	4	5

as Perhaps you may not have that author by you, and it is to your purpose, who are a physician ergo Abstrusionis Rei Naturalis investigator,[10] I will transcribe, being allso [p.2] desireous to know whether It be true or Erroneous.

Veteres Græcos annulum habuisse in Digito accepimus sinistræ manus, qui minimo est proximus, Romanos quoque homines aiunt sic plerumque Annulis usitatos. Caussam esse huius rei Appian in libris Ægyptianis hanc dicit: quod insectis apertisque humanis Corporibus, ut mos in Ægypto fuit, quas Græci ἀνατομας appellant, repertum est nervum quemdam tenuissimum ab eo uno digito, de quo diximus ad Cor hominis pergere ac pervenire. Propterea non inscitum visum esse eum potissimum digitum tali honore decorandum; qui continens & quasi connexus esse cum principatu cordis videretur.[11]

As to the size of the ring, It is very large but I would not have you rashly add that to your other Arguments of Mankinds being dwindled since the time Wee may suppose It to have been used. But you must remember That tho made of that shape yet not therefore of Consequence to be worn upon either finger or Thumb: The Key rings are all you know of like Shape but very inconvenient for wearing.

Besides remember vast great Rings were once much in fashion amongst the auncient Romans as by that of Juvenal.

   Tyrias humero revocante Lacernas
Ventilat æstivum digitis Sudantibus aurum
Nec sufferre queat majoris Pondera gemmæ[12]

So Effeminate were that people as to weare a lighter Ring in Summer & heavier in Winter, of which Sort you may Conjecture what you see to have been. I could wish Sir you had allso communicated the Weight, Colour of the gold with the description of the head sett in It, of what stone, & allso whether It was Sunk in as our Seales or cutt out in Relievo, these you may in your next.

I thank God our Society prospers, wee should be glad to see you, favour me in presenting my respects to Mr Kellsall & my other Friends, let me know how you relish these conjectures & your thoughts more particularly upon that passage in A. Gellius, And before Wee part let me tell you how the late facetious Thom: Brown[13] translated the 2 last lines of the 58 Epigram of the 2nd book of Martial

Te tamen ut Videam, duo Millia non piget ire

Ut te non videam, quatuor ire piget.

To go two Miles to see you I thought civill

But to go Four to miss you is the Devill;

This is only by the way and you may be assured you have in me a true Friend & humble Servant

Spalding Monday 8th Novr. 1714   Maurice Johnson junr

---

[1] There is in the Spalding archive a first draft of this letter, dated 7 November. The text is virtually identical.

[2] See Appendix 3. The incident referred to here cannot be traced.

[3] See **Letter 1**, n.19.

[4] A technical archæological term for 'a ring'. Stukeley's letter describing the gold ring is not present in the Spalding archive.

[5] Thin plates of metal.

[6] Edmund Gibson, later Bishop of Lincoln, translated into English and edited a new version of Camden's *Britannia* which was very widely read throughout the eighteenth century.

[7] The wearing of a ring distinguished the Roman knights from the ordinary people or 'plebes'.

[8] Aulus Gellius (second century AD), *Noctes Atticæ*, a very important and popular handbook of knowledge.

[9] Soldier; merchant; fool; husband; lover.

[10] 'Therefore an investigator into the hidden areas of natural knowledge.'

[11] 'We understand that the ancient Greeks had a ring on the finger of their left hand, which is nearest to the smallest [finger], and they say that many of the Roman men had the custom of using such a ring. Appian says this about the reason for this practice, in his book about the Egyptians: that when human bodies are cut open, as was the custom in Egypt, which the Greeks call 'anatomas' [anatomy], a certain very thin nerve is found, going from that one finger, which is said to go to the heart of man. Because of this, it is not unlikely that this powerful finger was adorned with such honour, as it contains and is connected to the supremacy of the heart.'

[12] 'Wearing a Tyrian cloak around his shoulders, waves about a summer gold ring on his sweaty fingers, as he cannot bear the weight of a large jewel', Juvenal, *Satires* 1.

[13] Sir Thomas Browne (1605–82: see *ODNB*), physician and author. 'Facetious' in the eighteenth century meant 'witty'.

4. Maurice Johnson senior[1] to William Stukeley, Spalding, 6 February 1715
Bodleian, MS Eng. misc. c.113, fol.298r

Sir,

I suppose you have your fathers will & probate upon your mothers administring – and Ad[ministra]con to you de Bonis non of your father – and Adcon to your Mother – It is convenient they should be at the heareing[2] – I intended to have put you in mind of sending them – and any other papers as Bonds &c which you have in your hands and make any claime under. But was interrupted & concluded my short note to you & fear I omitted it. However you may send them by some of your neighbours who goe to London sealed up in a cover addressed to

                 Sir Your humble servant

Spalding 6 Febr. 1715   Maur. Johnson
To Dr Stukeley
att Boston
   These

---

¹ This letter was written by Maurice Johnson senior (1661–1747), the father of Maurice Johnson junior. He was a lawyer who was handling the legal matters arising after the death of Stukeley's father, John Stukeley, in 1706. It was presumably kept with the letters of Maurice Johnson junior, on the assumption that Maurice junior had written it. The letter is mistakenly filed in the Bodleian archives as written by Maurice Johnson junior, but it is written in a mid-seventeenth-century hand such as his father used.
² Stukeley's mother died in 1707, the year after her husband, and it took Stukeley many years to establish his inheritance fully. He had to appear in Chancery on several occasions in connection with his ownership of land; this letter presumably relates to one of them.

5. William Stukeley to Maurice Johnson, Boston, 23 July 1715
Spalding, SGS/Stukeley/2

[Later heading in Johnson's hand:] A Letter from the Learned & Ingenious Dr Wm Stukeley. In Praise of the Study of Antiquities with a Drawing with the Oxford Epigram thereon.

Dear Sir,

   I rec[eive]d Your obliging letter. I perceive it is Sir Rich: Steele that writes the Censor¹ & he has given us a pretty short delineation of a Classical Study. I am so byassd in Favour of Antiquity that I cannot but think There were greater Men in all Sciences & capacitys in Former Ages than any we have seen since,² & if we add to the account the vast advantage of their Labours whereby We might reasonably expect larger proportionable advances in our Moderns, My Judgment is that the longer Mankind continues thro the Intemperance & corruption of our Nature all the Facultys of our Mind are debasd & depravd along with those of our bodyly Organs Whence we cannot come up to that Vastness of Soul those Sublime Stretches of Fancy & Invention, thos [*sic*] deep & sagacious reserches into the Nature of Things that inimitable way of Thinking &c which are presented to our admiration in the Writings & other Monuments of the Antients Those delitious Morsells which are Snatchd from the Mouth of Time as Sir Rich[ar]d has it.³ How commendable then must their Endeavours be who labour in preserving the Scatterd remains of that Universal Shipwrack & please us with the view of any worthy peice of our Venerable Ancestors.

   I often reflect within my self that the Study of Antiquity is a very great Argument (but I reckon Youll think an odd one) of the Immortality of the Soul, For that Ætherial Spark thro the excellency of its Essence is always breathing & thirsting after something that is beyond its bodily Prisons, seeks more extensive views & Endeavours a more capacious Scope of thought than the present scene of things about us presents it with, hence a solution of that universal superstitious desire of Mankind to pry into futuritys, an inclination that loudly proclaims the descent & lineage of the Soul, its relation to the Great Fountain of all Being & Knowledge: I need not explain my meaning by reflections of our propensity to Astrology divinations Almanacks & a thousand old wives conceits to foretell things to come nor the use the Devill made of it in formerly [*sic*] Times in bringing People to his Oracles & then fastning them down to his service & devotion: Now the Judicious Antiquary seeing all this & knowing tis beyond our Power resolves to assimilate himself as much as possible to the Divinity & therefore endeavours to become Immortall a parte post, what is to come is absolutely out of our reach, what is past there is a possibility of knowing & therefore he ransacks the confusd abysse of Fled Ages & picks up the disjointed Memorialls of past Persons & things in order to frame some intelligible Scheme of what he proposes to himself by his Study, here with inexpressible Pleasure he converses with Antique grave Sages, Oracles of Witt & knowledge, The most disinterested Counsellors the most agreeable Companions most desireable Friends. & because this World is nought but a Revolution, thro mature consideration & comparison of [p.2] Former Causes & effects he boldly pronounces a great many future events & Contingencies which Time future confirms in his behalf in reward to his former reserches. And who can pretend to be a divine without the knowledge of the Divinity of the old World which is the same as if I should say without his Bible that most Excellent & most antient History, who can pretend to be a famous Statesman that is not throughly drenchd in the noble Volumes of old Greek & Roman Historians, who can pretend to acquitt himself in any station whatever with satisfaction to himself & reputation amongst others without this Study of antiquity. Our Minds are a dark & empty Table[4] & receive Ideas & notices of Things only from the View of the Ambient world & reflections & compositions of those Ideas, & how short his knowledge must be that converses only with the present times how imperfect & wretched, is too obvious to insist upon.

I agree with you that Sir Rich[ar]d banters Dr Woodward[5] about his Roman shield & ranks it with that merry conceit of Hortensius, i.e. Mr Bobart [6] keeper of the Physick Garden Oxon. who when I was there amongst his other Curiositys showd us his Draco Monoceros catchd in the Garden which is what is meant in the Censor by the stuffd Ratt whos picture as near as I could remember I have exhibited in the Margin

[*Sketch of a 'dragon', reproduced in Illustration 13.*]

with this the Comical old Gent. amused for some time the whole University pretending it to be a winged Dragon catchd by his catt, & of the same species of those depicted in the books of the writers of natural historys of creatures at the same time pulling down a large folio Author of that sort with the picture of a Draco alatus exactly answering to this, when it was nothing but a ratt which he had dryd & prepared, by cutting off the two hinder legs & turning the ribs up in form of Wings, the verses following were made upon it at that Time.

Pray give my humble respects to Your Society.
       I am your humble Servant
        W. Stukeley
              July 23 1715

In Dracunculum Monoceraton Bobartianum
An Omnis Generatio sit Univoca   Affr.

Exhibet ex Mira Monstrum Bobartius Arte
   Dum stupet Ambiguam Turba Togata Feram.
En Caput armatum, En Cornuta Bellua Fronte
   Mentitasque Draco sibilat Ore Minas!
Torquet ut inflexæ sinuosa volumina Caudæ
   Et volat Alata Pelle Biformis Avis.
Parturit en Monstrum & Mutatur Ridiculus Mus
   Iam Feli terror, terror & ipse sibi.
Ludicra non Mixtam Speciem Natura creavit,
   Sed probat Artificem Machina ficta Manum.[7]

To Maurice Johnson Esq
at Spalding

[Cover sheet later annotated by Johnson 'Dr Stukeley July 1715 Draco Monoceros epigramma. Study of Antiquitys'.]

[1] The publication *The Censor*, which appeared from 1715 to 1717, was actually edited by Lewis Theobald (1688–1744). It was a literary journal, similar to the *Tatler* which had been edited by Addison and Sir Richard Steele, hence the mistake; Steele also wrote for the *Spectator* and *Guardian* and was also involved in setting up 'The Censorium', a theatrical organisation in Villiers Street, London. Johnson had known them both in London when he was studying law at the Inner Temple. The number of *The Censor* discussed here was No.5, dated Wednesday 20 April 1715; it was in praise of 'contemporaries [who] busy themselves in retrieving the sacred Monuments of their Fore-fathers from Obscurity and Oblivion' (p.29).

[2] Here Stukeley is in agreement with *The Censor* in the ongoing controversy between the Ancients and the Moderns, which is at the heart of early eighteenth-century historical and literary studies. Stukeley preferred the older knowledge because he believed it had not been defiled by later corruption. 'Sciences' here has its eighteenth-century meaning of 'branches of knowledge'.

[3] This is a direct quotation from *The Censor* 5, 30.

[4] Here Stukeley refers to John Locke's philosophical work in which he describes the mind as a *'tabula rasa'* or 'blank slate' at birth. Stukeley sees himself as 'the Judicious Antiquary' who 'resolves to assimilate himself as much as possible to the Divinity'.

[5] This issue of *The Censor* was aimed at 'those Gentlemen, who make it their business to impose false witness upon the ignorant, under a Pretext of Learning and Antiquity' (p.32). Theobald attacks 'Celsus the Naturalist' by whom he means Dr John Woodward (1665–1728: see *ODNB*), who was being ridiculed for falsely claiming a sixteenth-century shield he had purchased in 1693 was Roman. See J. M. Levine, *Dr Woodward's Shield* (Ithaca, 1991).

[6] Theobald also attacks 'Hortensius' or Jacob Bobart junior (1641–1719: see *ODNB*), the botanist and gardener in charge of the Oxford University Botanic Garden. Stukeley had met him on a visit to Oxford in 1710. It is useful to have Stukeley's sketch of the 'dragon' (see Illustration 13) to complement this account of what appears to have been a well-known practical joke.

[7] 'On the small, single-horned dragon; is everyone universally agreed about it? Bobart displays a monster made by wonderful art, while the gowned crowd is amazed by this ambiguous creature. See the armed head, the beast's horned brow; the dragon appears to be hissing threats through its mouth! It twists the sinuous coils of its curving tail and this double-formed bird flies with wings of fur. A monster is born and a ridiculous mouse is mutated [this is a deliberate pun on a well-known line from Horace, Epistles II, 'Parturient montes, nascetur ridiculus mus', 'the mountains will be in labour but only a ridiculous mouse will be born'] now the terror of a cat and a terror to itself. Nature never created a mixed species, even in jest; but the artificial creature proves to be the work of a craftsman's hand.'

6. Maurice Johnson to William Stukeley, Spalding, 28 July 1715
Bodleian, MS Eng. misc. c.113, fols 300r–301r

Dear Dr,

Since I did my Self the honour of writeing to you I had that of seeing Mrs Heron[1] at Spalding, who with pleasure told me You had done her the favour of your Company pretty often of late; & who that had any time to Spare would not chuse to Spend It with so fine a Lady, so agreeable a Companion? For certainly the more delightfull the Ideas are raised in our Minds by the Object conversd with, the more entertaining & engageing must the Conversation be: This the Gentlemen of your Faculty are so very Sensible of That I never know a Physician yet, who had not rendered himself well with some more eligible Fair One; & so long as Vapours are not Unfashionable They will secure your Interest with that Tender Sex, & preserve Its attachment to You. When You can prevaile upon Yourself to Step a few miles on this Side Cressy[2] I shall be glad to see You, & the Sooner perhaps the better haveing something of moment to Communicate to You, which I deem not So safely done this Way, & when I can wait upon You at Boston is uncertain, as my Excursions ever are, thô I intend my Self that Satisfaction as oft as I may enjoy, haveing no where greater Encouragement than from your Friendship & Company & that of Your learned & candid Friend the Revd. Mr Kelsall,[3] whose hands I should be proud to kiss here & now the Weather & Ways are tollerable I live in hopes of seing [sic] with You, & what I have said to induce You is a point of my sincere Friendship & not a Draw or Fetch to bring You hither meerly for my own Indulgence but what I am so uneasie to apprise You of, that if I find by your Answear, You can't be here of a pretty while, I will endeavour to wait Upon expressly about It, & I fantcy You will think the Consideration pertinent, when You shall weigh It well. He, I think, deserves not the name of Friend who is not watchfull for the Good of those persons, who give him that Title & for whom he professes Friendship upon common occasions.

[p.2] In my Answer to Yours which I mentioned before & hope You rec[eive]d I took no other notice of your Translation of Higden & Trevisa[4] than to say I was glad the Book was fallen into good hands, as the Labours of all learned Men do when You, Sir, possess Them with your usual diligence; as You wrote me Sometime since That You had Bp Nicholsons[5] Engl. Library which I commended to your perusal, I shall only desire you, for your better Satisfaction about Caxton and Trevisa, to peruse the S inked in the margin R Higden part 1 fo: 65 & fo: 69 at the Top, where You will meet with a more Satisfactory Account of those books and be convinced that even the great John Selden[6] (who is allowd by the very Authors of the Hereditary Right[7] to be a very proper Judge of the Historical Books of England fol: 40 ibm.) can be now & then grossly mistaken. But Humanum est errare,[8] & therefore if at any time You are mislead by the Conjectures, or what your Brother Thomlinson[9] calles the Feble Conatus's, of Your humble Servant: I hope, & trust, You will accept my Intentions as good, & pardon that in a little Fellow which Wee must excuse in So great a Man (or if you please Men) as I have lately mentioned. My Brother, Couzen Johnson &c recommend Themselves to You as Your Servants, & indeed our whole Society have, & express a great Value for you, & was extreemly pleased with the account of the Urne you Communicated to Us – I have herewith Sent you a little book conteining 2 Scarce Treatises for your peruseal, but must desire you'll returne It me forthwith, the first is I believe done faithfully, the last chiefly from Rishanger[10] a very scarce piece, & an Historian of good Credit with many being, Historiographer Royal to the Kings Son whose Troubles & uneasie Reigne are there related, and Liveing in those perilous ~~Times~~ Dayes, which are now to be paralelld a 2nd time.[11]

[p.3] The Clouds which hang over this Distracted Divided Island are Dark & Gloomy, & each moment threaten Its Destruction. – Repellit Vim Vis,[12] but too frequently in Conclusion the Repulse done, the protectd are Enslaved by the military hand; & they who with best Reasons boast their being Freeborn, have most cause to apprehend a Stratocracy.[13] The Times are now Arduous & will be still more & more so; Tho by all the Accounts I have yet heard, this County (I thank Heaven) is not in any Commotion: only I am troubled to hear of Some Differences arisen in Your Town thro' the Indiscretion of some persons, who anyone would have Imagined had had more prudence, Let affaires of State go as providence directeth.

Ambiguam tellure nova Salamina futuram[14] is the worst any man of Spirit will say with Teucer's Apollo, In such matters the les said the better being (as the proverb hath It) soonest amended, but with Friends Wee may be freer than with Informers, which my Lord Coke hinted, when he tells Us the Common Law calls such pessimum hominum Genus Anglice,[15] the Vilest Scoundrels, out of whose power to harm you I wish You may have the Guard upon your Conduct ever to preserve yourself: You'll resieve this by a Safe hand who will favour me with the carrying of your answear allso, & the Book back again with my Lhyd & Caxton[16] if you can Spare Them. tho I did not know of the opportunity They have given Me 'till I had gotten thus far allmost, than which my Paper will allow me to go no farther, only to add what you shall ever find me

Dear Dr: Your assured Friend and most humble Servant

Maur: Johnson junr.

Spalding Thursday – 1715 July the 28

P.S. I had almost forgotten to tell you that our Marquess, (with the Other New Titles he takes or hath conferred upon him rather,) is, as I hear, to be created Viscount Spalding or of Spalding.[17]

Wee returne You many thanks for your kind & ingenious Elucidation of the Censor & the Epigram upon Monsr. Bobarts Draco renatus,[18] & Such only of a somewhat larger Size were those mentioned by Livy & conquered by More of More hall.

To Dr William Stukeley
at his house in Boston
These.

---

1   She is presumably the wife of Henry Heron (1673–1730) of Cressy Hall (Lincs), who was the Tory MP for Boston 1713–22 and then for Lincolnshire 1722–27. While Stukeley was living in Boston, a Tory town, he accepted Tory principles, probably under the Herons' influence, but was later a Whig like Maurice Johnson.
2   Cressy Hall, north of Spalding.
3   See **Letter 1**, n.19.
4   Ranulf Higden (fl.1364: see *ODNB*); he wrote the *Polychronicon*, one of the last and most popular chronicles of ecclesiastical and general history. It was translated from Latin by John Trevisa (*c*.1342–*c*.1402) and printed by Caxton in the fifteenth century; it was significant in opening up ecclesiastical history to lay readers.

5   William Nicholson (1655–1727), Bishop of Carlisle (1702–18) and later Archbishop of Derry (1718–27), author of *The English Historical Library* (London, 1714), which calls Higden 'a downright plagiary' (i. 65). His book is very critical of all mediæval historiography but contains an excellent survey of county histories.
6   See **Letter 1**, n.4.
7   George Harbin (1665–1744: see *ODNB*), a non-juror and author of *The Hereditary Right of the Crown of England* (1713); this reference is to fol.40.
8   'It is human to make mistakes.'
9   Dr Thomlinson, a well-qualified medical doctor in Spalding in 1715; referred to as 'brother' in the profession since he and Stukeley are fellow-physicians. For further details see *Surtees* I, 31.
10 William Rishanger (*c.*1250–*c.*1312: see *ODNB*). His best-known book was *The Chronicles of the Barons' War* describing the events of Henry III's reign and the role of Simon de Montfort.
11 The reaction to the threat of the Jacobite invasion against the new Hanoverian regime was the Riot Act of 9 July 1715. Fighting took place in Scotland and the north of England, culminating in the Battle of Preston.
12 'Force wards off force', a Latin proverb, said by Nectarius to Stilico in Act 1 Scene ii of *Magister Bonus sive Arsenius*, an anonymous Latin play published in 1614 which was well-known at the time.
13 A military dictatorship.
14 'A new Salamis will be like the old one' (Horace, *Odes* VII, book 1).
15 'The worst kind of English person' as stated by Sir Edward Coke (1552–1604: see *ODNB*); Lord Chief Justice of England famous in Johnson's time for his *Reports* and *Institutes of the Laws of England*.
16 Edward Lhuyd (1660–1709), botanist, linguist and antiquarian, best known for his *Archæologia Britannica* (1707), much used by Stukeley. We cannot be certain which Caxton volume is referred to here; the 1898 sale catalogue of a portion of Johnson's library lists 'Folio ccclxxxi of Caxton's edition of Higden's Polichronicon by Trevisa, printed *c.*1482'. Bernard Quaritch noted that 'The nine Caxtons … were, when in the Johnsons' hands, bound together in two volumes, five in each' (*Contributions towards a Dictionary of English Book Collectors* (1969), 176).
17 No creation of such a marquisate can be located for this period; Johnson may be speculating before the expected event which did not take place.
18 See **Letter 5** for details of the 'dragon'. More of More Hall was a legendary figure who killed the Dragon of Wantley; the story was turned into a satirical opera by Henry Carey in the 1730s.

7. Maurice Johnson to William Stukeley, London, undated but dateable to 1715[1]
Bodleian, MS Eng. misc. c.113, fols 387r–388r

Inner Temple

Dear Sir,

The last token of your Friendship came Safe to me here, a Place Sometimes the Seat of the muses when as in Rome, the Empire stands Settled, But alass my old Friend matters go not So with Us, and the Literæ humaniores Armis cedunt,[2] Scarce any Symphony is good without a Drum, and the Tour of Hide Park Camp leaves the Theatres very Thin, that Learning is somewhere cultivated with more earnestness Your Indefatigable Reserches evince, and 'tis a Pain to me that I cannot of some time more Effectualy answear some parts of Your Ingenious Letter, as what you did me the honour to comunicate was a pleasure. The first opportunity I shall have from my own Study, shall serve You, & in the mean time give me leave to tell You Your Acquaintance Mons. Schwitzer's designe of making his Treatise of Gardening [3] publick answers as Yet, my Bookseller tells me not So well as might be expected; from the cleverness of his proposeal to reduce Whole Lordships into gardens, or Villas of Elegance. Mr Trapp[4] has also

proposed a Designe to the Classical Gentry of publishing the Æneid in blank Verse, but Virgil hath worne too many Suits of English & Scotch Cloaths, to make a plain one render him readily acceptable. If I can learne any thing from Mr Kemp[5] or Coll. Guige[6] two learned Antiquarys of my Acquaintance to Suit Your Taste, You shall be sure to have It handed You, by
Dear Sir – Your very much obliged humble Servant
                                  Maur Johnson junr
P.S. favour me with your answer by my wife who will transmitt It me readyly.

To
Dr William Stukely at
his house in
Boston
Lincolnshire

[1] It is possible to date this letter to 1715 by the reference to Switzer's book (see below) and the comment on the military camp which was in Hyde Park, London, from July to November 1715 ready to defend London against the Jacobite invasion.
[2] 'The Arts give place to arms.'
[3] Stephen Switzer (1682–1745: see *ODNB*), author of *The nobleman, gentleman, and gardener's recreation, or, An introduction to gardening, planting, agriculture and the other business and pleasures of a country life* (1715). The SGS library owned a copy of the second edition. Switzer was a very well-known gardener and landscape designer; Maurice Johnson ordered plants from him for his garden at Ayscoughfee Hall.
[4] Joseph Trapp (1679–1747: see *ODNB*), first professor of poetry at Oxford. His blank-verse English translation of Virgil's *Æneid* was published in 1718 and 1720.
[5] John Kemp FRS (1665–1717: see *ODNB*); an account of his antiquarian activities was published in 1719–20 by Robert Ainsworth.
[6] This is probably the significant military figure General John Guise (1682/3–1765: see *ODNB*), who was captain, then lieutenant-colonel in the 1st Foot Guards in 1706 and commanded a battalion in the Vigo campaign of 1719. He was elected FRS in 1716 and was famous for his collection of paintings which he left to Christ Church, Oxford.

8. William Stukeley to Maurice Johnson, Boston, 6 June 1716
Spalding, SGS/Stukeley/3

[Later heading in Johnson's hand]: Dr Wm Stukeley with an Acc[oun]t of Telescopes & Sir Chr. Wrenns Sphære. a Model of Stoneheng – Roman red earthen Pot found at Boston & a plated Key – with Drawings

I did not answer your letter sooner because I was always in expectation of seeing You here. when I was at Peterburgh my Brother Hill[1] told me (last Year) of his new improvements of the Telescope, I should be glad to have a particular Account of the matter upon Tryall, & would have One of them if it answerd, but if he can make one of four foot give as plain & clear a view of the Planets as one of fourteen, than [*sic*] by the same reason he can make one of forty foot that shall answer one of four hundred & thereby deserve the reward offerd for the Longitude.[2] The Convenience of a short Telescope is very great because easily manageable & one of a moderate length might be usd at Sea, the satellites of Jupiter will be a constant guide for the Longitude. I lately at Lyn had the Opportunity of peeping thro' thos long spectacles into the World of Jupiter & Venus upon their conjunction on Good friday[3] & likewise into the Sun where we observd some remarkeable Spots. We saw two of Jupiters Satellites but the most curious sight was that of Saturn for I had a very fair View of that Wonderfull Planet, could see his Ring distinctly & one of his Satellites & the Shadow of the ring quite across his body as in the Margin. [*Sketch of Saturn with ring in the margin of the letter*] Now we are upon thes [*sic*] Celestial Speculations, it puts me in Mind of a curious Selenography[4] which Sir Christopher Wren[5] made when he was a young Man or a globe so cut that by turning it to the light it represented the true Phases of the Moon together with the Mountains, Valleys, Seas &c all shadow'd naturally as that Satellite of ours shows herself in a Telescope & I have lately been playing such a trick my self for happening to fall into a Set of thoughts about Stonehenge in Wiltshire, by a prospect of Loggans[6] which I met withal, I undertook to make an exact Modell of that most noble & stupendous piece of Antiquity, which I have accomplisht, & from thence drawn the groundplott of its present ruins & the view of it in its pristine State, & propose from thence to find out the original Architectonic Scheme by which it was erected, together with its design Use founders &c & thereby doe justice to so wonderful a Curiosity which Mr Camden[7] passes over so slightily (as usual in things antienter than the Romans) with such a wretched anile account, as its hard to say whether that or his draught of it be most false & trifleing.

Mr Tho. Falkner's[8] Workmen that found the Roman urn whose losse I so much regretted found since a little Earthen Pot about 6 inches high of red clay with a narrow mouth which for ought I know might be one of their Sacrificeing vessels, [*sketch of pot in margin of letter*] & some more bitts of Pots, very deep & an old key of Iron seeming to have been overlayd with Silver. when I was with You last I took a very rude draught of your Boadicia[9] I wish you would send me an exact One & of what other Bryttish coyns or curiositys You have by You or should chance to see. I am

Dear Sir

    Your obliged & most humble servt
        Wm Stukely
          June 6 1716

[*Sketch of ornate key.*]

To
Maurice Johnson Esq.

[1] His brother-physician Dr Theophilus Hill (1680–1746), a Peterborough physician; for a romantic view of Dr Hill, see George Rousseau's biography of Theophilus's second son, Sir John Hill: *The Notorious Sir John Hill* (2012).
[2] The Longitude Prize proposed by a 1714 Act of Parliament for an effective way of measuring the longitude of a ship's position at sea.
[3] Conjunctions of Venus and Jupiter are fairly common events; this probably refers to March–April 1716. Good Friday was on 30 March in 1716.
[4] The study of the lunar landscape.
[5] Christopher Wren (1632–1723: see *ODNB*), when a student at Oxford, created a map of the moon's topography on the surface of a globe. He became Professor of Astronomy at Gresham's College at the age of twenty-five.
[6] David Loggan (1634–1692: see *ODNB*), official engraver to the University of Oxford. Stukeley

wrote, 'indeed before ever I had seen Stonehenge, only from Loggan's two prints I made a model of it which satisfied me it couldn't be a hexagon'. Quoted in A. Burl and N. Mortimer (eds), *Stukeley's Stonehenge: An Unpublished Manuscript 1721–24* (2005), 51.

[7]   See **Letter 1**, n.10. 'Anile' means 'feeble'.

[8]   See **Letter**, 1 n.21. A letter from Stukeley to an unidentified correspondent, dated 'Boston, June 22, 1715', giving details of the loss of the urn, is printed in *Surtees* I, 257.

[9]   A coin dating from the reign of Queen Boudicca in Maurice Johnson's collection.

9. Maurice Johnson to William Stukeley, Spalding, undated but dateable to just before 6 October 1716; unfinished draft[1]
Spalding, SGS/Maurice Johnson/6

British Coine of Boadicea penes M Johnson

Dear Dr

I haven't been long returnd from London, where I proposed to have served you farther in Your Enquirys about the Antiquities of our Ancestors the Britains but met not one Soul of my old Acquaintance versed in those matters in the very Short Stay in that Place, after I Did my Self the honour of answearing yours which I made but 4 or 5 Days upon Terme Ending, That I might enjoy Home the longer before the Circuit, The Gentleman whom I principaly relyd upon was Mr Kemp[2] a Curious Collector of all Sorts of Antiquities, & he was out of Town, You know the Affection I bear to all Literati & the particular esteem I have for Your self, so I proceed, without apologys for not doing what I proposd, since not in my Power, to give an Account of the Boadicea in my Collection which You was pleased to require, but as I told You, I had not by me when I received yours but in my Boxes here: where, Upon Your Judgement of It, joynd with that of the Keeper of Bp. Laud's Collection at Oxford,[3] who compared It with 2 others there, & very obligeingly gave mine the preference, and of several other Learned men, I placed It as that Heroines chronologically in my box of the 1st Imperial Medals, & am, whenever I view that Series of monstrous Men, highly pleased to reflect upon the true bravery of that Fair Princess,[4] brought into my mind by this Amulet (for so Sir I begg You'll give me leave to call It) as the learned Lord Almoner[5] hath taught me from Cæsar & Bartholini.[6]

–Thus farr I had written before I went the Circuit,[7] but Business of one sort or other prevented me Finishing It, which give me leave to Do, with thanks for yours the other day & assuring You I am Your much obliged humble Servant now Safely returned from my Legal Ramblings, & should be heartily glad to See You, But in the meane time, not to forget Boadicea, give me leave on behalf of the Bishop of Caerlisle,[8] & myself to observe upon tis amulet That It Is of the Size of such as have commonly passd for British money Viz. Between that of the middle, & little Copper, not broader than our milled Testons, but rather thicker than an Halfpenny as you may see by these Figures:

[*Two sketches, to give an impression of the size of the coin, one of the front view and one of the side view, though the first is shown blank.*]

No.1 The Surface of the Amulett
No.2 The greatest Thicknes of It,

Now haveing Seen the Dimensions & Bulk, let us consider the Shape of this odd piece, which was I suppose intended to have been circular, & is pretty near so, And struck convex on the one side & concave on the other as I have seen several Eastern pieces, & as all ours which claim the name of British which I have seen have been, & I remember in Some of the Acts of the Royal Soc. to've seen an account of Some very large Rude & unintelligible pieces (I think of Silver) found in Ireland ascribed by the Gent. who communicated It to the antient Brittains ~~upon~~ for That very ~~account~~ Reason. I say struck, & not cast, or if cast struck afterwards by which meanes It is very much crack at the Edges, the metal being hard, & so resisting the stroke.

[*This draft letter ends at this point, as the foot of the page is missing and appears to have been torn off. The letter was not sent in this form; a second draft, which is also in the SGS archive at Spalding (SGS/Maurice Johnson/7) was written almost immediately afterwards, containing this information but expanding it considerably. This second draft is virtually identical to the next transcribed letter (Bodleian, MS Eng. misc. c.113, fols 311r–312v), which was the one actually sent to Stukeley.*]

1   This draft can be dated by its contents which are virtually identical with those of **Letter 10**, dated 6 October 1716.
2   See **Letter 7**, n.5.
3   Archbishop Laud founded a collection of coins at Oxford University in 1636. Thomas Hearne (1678–1735: see *ODNB*) catalogued this collection in 1702.
4   At the time of Boudicca's revolt in AD 61 there were many Iceni silver coins, often showing a warrior wearing a feathered headdress. It is interesting to note Johnson's comparison of the Roman emperors as 'monstrous Men' with the 'Fair Princess' Boudicca.
5   The Revd William Wake was Lord Almoner in 1715; his function as such was to distribute the King's alms. Wake was Bishop of Lincoln from 1705 to 1716 and then became Archbishop of Canterbury.
6   'Bartholinus informs us that Danish women, before they put the new-born Infant into the Cradle, place there, or over the Door...Amulets.' See John Brand, *Observations on popular antiquities* (1813), 7. Erasmus Bartholin (1625–98) was a Danish scientist.
7   Johnson, as a lawyer, attended the Midland Circuit, one of the legal circuits of royal judges.
8   The Bishop of Carlisle in 1716 was William Nicholson; see **Letter 6**, n.5.

10. Maurice Johnson to William Stukeley, Spalding, 6 October 1716
Bodleian, MS Eng. misc. c.113, fols 311r–312v

[*This letter is misfiled in the Bodleian collection by the original compiler of the letter-book of Stukeley's correspondence, as though the date were 1726, hence the folio numbers. This is contradicted by two factors: (i) the virtually identical first draft of the letter, in the Spalding archives, is clearly dated '6 8ʳ [October] 1716'; (ii) it is addressed to Stukeley 'at his house in Boston' whereas by 1726 Stukeley was not living in Boston but in London, where he moved in 1717.*]

Dear Dr

That I have not been more Expeditious in answering Yours than to have two in arreare, could be owing to nothing but Engagements of my Profession, goeing the Circuit & attending the Assizes at Wisbech.[1] This you'll allow a Sufficient Excuse

& Give me leave after condoling with You for the Loss of our late Learned Friend & honest good Man Mr Warren[2] to Let you know Wee have in his place a very good tempered Ingenious & I believe truely an honest Church Man & who hath a true taste of polite Literature, his name's Timothy Neve[3] he was of Cambridge but I believe your Junior he's a Native of Shropshire. I have long purposed to give my Self the pleasure of seeing You in Your Musæum, where I ever find such Entertainment as Suits me, So that as soon as I may You shall have me whether You have dissections or no, my Father told me of a MS he had read of written by Bishop Skyrlaw[4] which he intended to send you word of as worthy Your perusal in the curious research You're now Upon, lest his Letter should not have come to Your hands take the account of it from the Book, which is Dr Ayliff[5] a Civilian's history of the Univ. of Oxon. where page 252 speaking of University College in the University sub. AD 1403. He says designeing to speak of especial Benefactors who have increased the Number of Fellows & Scholars in It by bestowing on 'em Liberalities in a les degree such was (he goes on) Walter Skirlaw Bishop of Durham who, on a purchase of the Mannor of Rothyng in Essex gave It to this Coll. for the Maintanance of 3 Fellows born within the Diocesses of York or Durham, & to be chosen (contrary to the Durham Statutes) without respect to any Degree; Yea tho under Graduates provided They be of approved Moralls & Learning: & besides other bounteous Acts he gave some MSS & amongst them his own Treatise about Generation & Corruption; & dying March 24th 1406 the Soc: were formerly wont every Yeare to say a solemn Mass for his Soul with a Deacon & Sub Deacon on the 23^{d} of February: thus farr the Dr. & hence It is reasonable to Suppose the MS worth consulting. however both my Father & I thought It very well worthy the communicating this account to You. Permit me Sir, to add in this place that Mr John Richards[6] who intends to study the Science You have with good Success prosequuted is an Ingenious Young Gentleman & of a very Sweet Temper, & if Your affairs would permitt You to do a Countryman that Service proposed, I believe You'd meet his gratefull Returne. [p.2] You tell me that in Your Expedition on the Bordering Counties of Rutland & Nottingham amongst other Coynes there you Sawe one of Agrippa, I have a peice in honour of him as Admiral, with a Neptunus cum Tridente on the Reverse, It is of mezzo bronzo Size. You saw allso a Julia, but what my Friend had you seen her as Naso did when he burst out into that pathetick Rapture Ecce Corinna venit &c.[7]

If You've never been at Thorpe Hall near Peterburgh the seat of Sir Francis St John[8] It's worth Your while to Visitt the Statues in that Garden. They're all of white marble but have suffer'd exceedingly by the moistnes of the air, & injudicious Scituation They're plac'd in the Statue Garden lyeing to the North, In the Midst of 4 quarters Stands a Gigantick Livia uxor Imp. Octavii[9] the Posture is Noble & truly Imperial the flesh round & soft & the Drapery neatly perform'd in the 4 quarters are a Gladiator, an Orator & 2 Roman Statues of Diana & Amphion & upon the Terras a Hercules Hydram Superans the lest affected by the weather of any & I think an Admirable peice, Bateing that It hath that Fault which I have observed in some original paintings of Albert Durer of that Demy God. the Clubb is much too small for the notions the poets have impress'd of Its Service & its Masters Strength[.][10] They told me there that the Livia cost Three score pounds carryage from London & Setting up, there are some good pictures in the House particularly that of old Sir Oliver who built It & a Noble Bust in Copper over the best Parlour Chimney – a very Fine Library well stocked – & in the Court 2 Equestrian Statues in Copper upon Stone Pedestalls of H IV Galliæ Rex & Don Juan d'Austria.[11] – Here you must likewise at a Small distance from the House see the Fishponds which are very Fine with handsome Walks of Firr, & a very lofty Holly Hedge – I forgot to add two things more remarkable within Doors that there are over most of the Door Cases the Busts of Several Romans particularly an admirable Bassianus Caracalla[12] in Alablaster & in the Gallery whence you goe out Upon the Top of the House by a pair of winding staires, a large Mapp of Venice with the Solemnity of Doges Espousing Hadria & a picture of the Bucentaure in Colours not very ill done.[13]

[p.3] As to my Boadicea of which you was pleased to require an Account in a Letter which came to me to London, which I wrote You I had not by me there, but It was in my Boxes placed, upon your Judgement joyn'd with that of the Keeper of the Laudean Collection of Medalls at Oxon[14] (who compared It with 2 others there & very obligeingly gave mine the preference,) As that Heroines chronologicaly in my Box of the 1st Imperial, & whenever I view that Series of Monstrous Men, It gives me great pleasure to reflect upon the true & Undaunted Bravery of that Royal British Widdow, brought into my mind by this her Amulett (for So Sir I begg You'll give me leave to call It) as the Learned Lord Almoner[15] hath taught me from Cæsar & Bartholine It is of the Size of such as have commonly pass'd for British Money viz. between that of the Mezzo Bronzo & silver Sextaries of the Romans, not broader than our Milled Testons, but rather Thicker than a Half penny as you may see by These Figures:

[*Two sketches, one of the front face of the coin, though depicted blank, simply to show its size; one of the side edge to show its thickness.*]

No.1 the surface of the Amulett
No 2 the greatest Thickness of It.
Now haveing seen the Dimension & Bulk let us consider the **Shape** of this odd peice which was I presume intended for exactly Circular and is somewhat so. It is Struck Hollow i.e. the one side which I shall call the ~~surface~~ Impress convex & the other (the Reverse, as I take it) concave, Thus have Wee seen most of the Asiatick peices & as all ours which claim the name of Brittish (that I have ever yet met with) have been, & I remember in Some of the Acts of the R.S.[16] to've seen an account of Some very large & rude & unintelligible pieces (I think these were of Silver & larger & thicker than our Crown pieces) found in Ireland Ascribed by the Gent. who communicated that account to the antient Britains for that very reason. I use the word Struck & not cast, or if cast struck afterwards by which means It is very much cracked as described at the Edges, the Mettal being hard, & so not yeilding easily to the Stroke & this too You may have frequently observed in Antient Coines. for I take the **Matter** of which this is made to be Gold, as those were in the Laudæan Collection Although the **Colour** be very pale yet it is of a different Yellow from Brass of any Sort I've observed, & It's **Weight** much greater (not to mention that other way of trying It by the Touchstone) which It also had by old Mr Couzins a Goldsmith formerly in Stamford who declared to the Person I had it of that It was pure Gold & would have bought It as such, The intrinsick weight of the Amulet is a Dramme & and half & four Grains – the difference of Its Specifick Gravity in Proportion to the best Hammerd Lead 2 grains, this sufficiently proves It weightier than Brass,

I have not had the opportunity of ponderating It hydrostaticaly against redder Gold, I must own It brings into my mind the Electrum of the Antients which my Lord St Albans [17] sayth had in It $^{1}/_{5}{}^{\text{th}}$ of Silver to the Gold & made a Compound metal as fitt for most uses as Gold & more resplendent, & more qualified in some other properties Vid: Dr Rawleys Ed: of the Sylva Experiment 798 fol 168.[18] Of this Pausanias. [*illegible*] το δε άλλο ήλεκτρον (in opposition to the natural) άναμεμγμένος έσώ Αργυρώ χρώσος [19] & of this the Civil Law takes Notice in Several [p.4] places as of the Nummi Electrini & the Vasa Electrina[20] which the Goldsmiths like those of Syracuse would now & then be for putting off as all Fine Gold – but this is meerly Philological. to conclude, That you may have the fullest account I can give you of this thing take here 2 perfect Draughts of It.

[*Two sketches, showing the front and reverse of the coin.*]

No.1 the surface of the Impress which is Convex & I chose to place in this position because It seems as It were at bottom to have an Exergue.
No. II the Reverse which is Concave & looks as Camden[21] has observd of some of the British Amulets most like an Horse & behind it something like a Wheel which brings into my mind that of the Poet
Esseda festinant pilenta, petorrita, Naves
Captivum Portatur Ebur, &c.[22]
where he enumerates the Different sorts of Gallick Carriages, But Omitts the Temo which was the Currus Falcatus as I have read in a Schol. Upon Juvenal aut de Temone Britanno Excidet Arveragus i.e. Arbila.[23]

Before I part with you let me Communicate a Comment in the Margin of my Camden Brit.[24] written by my Great Grandsire[25] over the picture of Stoneheng which you found such fault with, he hath put this Lemma: In Memoria Baudiceæ als Bunducæ. The Marginal is This: Stoneheng probably supposed to have been erected by the Britans as a Magnificent Moniment in Memory of Boadicia here slayne vd. Phl Thoalcan. in Vita Boadiceæ. Which author here cited I must own I never ~~before~~ heard of before nor ever met with the like account, Camden being in Memoriam Ambrosii & I have heard my Mother – I mean my Fathers present wife[26] say That when she was in Wilts: with her former husband Andrew Philipps Esq. a Councellor at Law and Philizar[27] of many Counties & a Gentleman of good learning that He told her there was upon One of the Great Upright Stones an Inscription in Saxon Characters as she thinks he said Importing that there lay several thousands of Young men who intended to repent when they were old. I must not conclude without using this Small remainder of my paper to let you know that I purchased the cause of this long harangue at Wansford (or Walmesford secundum Camden) in Northamtonshire near to whose famous Bridge [28] It was found of which the [*illegible*] Poet
Ausonias juxta Ripas qua cogitur Unda
Ferre jugum & famam debet Wansfordia Ponti &c.
  I am in hopes of seeing You as Soon as I can come to Boston or You to Spalding till when believe me to be
                Dear Doctor
                your assured Faithful Friend
                    Maur. Johnson junr

Saturday the 6th
October 1716

P.S. Since I wrote this I understand my Fathers came to You & he hath received your answer.

To Dr William Stukely at his House
in Boston
These

1   Wisbech was one location of the autumn Assizes of the Midland legal Circuit. Johnson's professional commitments had prevented him from travelling to Boston to see Stukeley's 'musæum', his study or library, as defined by Nathan Bailey, *English Dictionary* (1730).
2   This must be the Revd John Waring, Master of Spalding Grammar School, who died in 1716; the SGS bought his books for their library. Johnson's 'Iter Bathonense', an account in Latin of a journey to Bath made in 1710 by himself and a group of other young Spalding gentlemen, was dedicated to Waring.
3   See Appendix 3.
4   Bishop Walter Skirlaw (*c.*1330–1406: see *ODNB*), educated at Oxford, Bishop of Coventry, then Bishop of Durham in 1388, a significant cleric and royal administrator. He had given the college an estate at Roding (Essex).
5   Dr John Ayliffe (1676–1732: see *ODNB*), legal historian and author of *The Ancient and Present State of the University of Oxford* (1714).
6   See Appendix 3.
7   Ovid's *Amores* 1.5: 'Look, Corinna comes'.
8   Lord Chief Justice Oliver St John built Thorpe Hall near Peterborough in the Cromwellian period. A descendant, Sir Francis St John (*c.*1680–1756) had his seat there and maintained the classical statues which had come into the park in the seventeenth century. This account by Johnson is a crucial early account of the hall, gardens and statuary; the hall, now in possession of the Sue Ryder charity, remains, but the statues are no longer there.
9   Livia (58 BC–AD 29), wife of the Emperor Augustus, deified by her grandson the Emperor Claudius as Augusta.
10 All classical deities: the Roman goddess Diana, known to the Greeks as Artemis, the goddess who killed the Greek deity Amphion; Hercules, whose second labour was to kill the nine-headed monster Hydra. In Dürer's picture (1496) of Hercules killing the Molionides, his club is shown as rather short. Dürer painted several images of Hercules.
11 Henri IV (1553–1610), King of France 1589–1610, and Don Juan of Austria (1547–1578), half-brother of King Philip of Spain, famous for defeating the Ottoman fleet at the Battle of Lepanto in 1571.
12 Lucius Septimius Bassianus (AD 186–217) who became Roman emperor as Caracalla.
13 The Doge of Venice, each Ascension Day, went on board his galley, the Bucentaur, to celebrate the 'marriage' of Venice to the Adriatic Sea, here referred to by its Latin name 'Hadria'.
14 See **Letter 7**, n.5.
15 See **Letter 9**, n.3.
16 At this stage the SGS was not receiving the *Phil.Trans.* so Johnson, usually meticulous in giving references, has to refer to his memory of seeing someone else's copy.
17 Francis Bacon (1561–1626: see *ODNB*), created Viscount St Albans in 1621.
18 Dr William Rawley (1588–1667), Bacon's chaplain. He edited Francis Bacon's *Sylva Sylvarum, or a Natural History* in 1627.
19 'The other metallic substance is a mingling of gold and silver.' This quotation comes from Pausanias's description of a statue of Augustus: 'native amber [electrum], of which the statue of Augustus is made, is … very rare … but the other electrum is an alloy of gold with silver'. See Pausanias, *Description of Greece*, 5.12.7, quoted in K. W. Arafat, *Ancient Artists and Roman Rulers* (1996).
20 'Vasa electrina' was the name given to amber vases set with silver; 'nummi electrini' is amber

set in gold, or coins made from an alloy of gold and silver; see J. W. Mollett, *Illustrated Dictionary of Words used in Art and Archæology* (1883). Johnson is attempting to differentiate between the confusing Latin words for 'amber' and 'gold-silver alloy'.

21   See **Letter 1**, n.10.

22   'Chariots, carriages, wagons and ships hurry along/ Burdens of captured ivory …' (Horace, *Epistles*, book II, epistle 1, lines 192–3, trans. A. S. Kline).

23   From Juvenal, *Satires* 4, lines 130–1: 'Or Arveragus falls from a British chariot-pole'. Arviragus was a mythical British king of whom this reference by Juvenal is the only evidence. 'Currus falcatus' means 'a chariot with scythes'.

24   This is a specific reference to William Camden's popular *Britannia, or a chorographical description of Great Britain and Ireland*, published in Latin in 1586 and in English in 1610. Here Camden briefly discusses the revolt of 'Boodica' and the attempts by Aurelius Ambrosianus to defeat the Saxons.

25   This is probably Martyn Johnson (1589–1651), attorney-at-law in Spalding.

26   Elizabeth Johnson, née Oldfield (d.1724), second wife of Maurice Johnson I, whom he married after the death of the mother of Maurice Johnson II.

27   Or 'filizer', a legal officer responsible for organising legal writs for a group of counties.

28   Wansford Bridge, the famous and still-surviving packhorse bridge across the River Nene at Wansford, built in 1577. The poet William Dillingham (1617–89) published in his *Poemata varii argumenti* the poem, addressed to the Earl of Westmorland, of which this is an extract.

11. William Stukeley to Maurice Johnson, London, 13 June 1717
Spalding, SGS/Stukeley/4

[Heading in Johnson's hand]: SGS No 39
Dr William Stukeley on his fixing in London, And of the Anatomical Wax Works

Dear Sir

I had a mind to let You know that I am now fixd in Ormond Street in Lodgings at one Mrs Machens, & have not yet seen cause to be sorry at my removal hither, being in hopes I shall have an opportunity still to see my Friends I valued in the Country among whom You have the chief Place, as often as I did when nearer. I found sufficiently by 7 years experience it was not worth my while to stay longer in Lincolnshire,[1] as my abode, if I have but the 10th part of business I left behind me it will be worth 20 times as much to me, & instead of dirty roads & dull Company I need not tell you what we meet with in London, especially in my Scituation, On one side of my lodgings We have a beau Street & those sort of entertainments it affords, & in my Study backwards I have a fine view to Hampstead, & the rural Scene of haymakers, Mugitusque boum[2] &c. next door I have the beautiful sight of Lord Powis's house the most regular peice of Architecture of any house in London[3] & a Sharp fresh Air, so that I enjoy a perfect Rus in Urbe. I have been engagd this day or two at a most incomparable Curiosity lately brought from France, Several bodys anatomically dissected composd of Waxwork where the internal as well as External fabrick of the human Frame is most inimitably performd, every part in its proper Colour, form, & the branching ramifications of the Nerves, Arteries, Veins &c most accurately shown, I have drawn out a peice or two of it as much as the Man would permitt Me.[4] As for News I think we are in a more unsettled condition than we have been this 20 years, & the Court & Parliament can by no means throughly agree. here has been long debates & hard Words about the Dutch troops,[5] particularly that there should be so disproportionable an Account between their importation & exporta-

tion as £4000 & £14000, & all we can conclude is that we had a Dutch markett. My Lord Oxford[6] is now to be tryed & My Lord Chancellor[7] is appointed Lord High Steward. I beleive Mr Heron[8] & His Lady will be down before You come up: they are well. I hope we shall see You here this next term, when I shall be glad to be introduced into some Antique Acquaintance. Our old friend Mr Gay[9] author as tis said of the Censor has laid down his Wand. Pray give my service to all your Family & Friends at Spalding I imagine you know Sir John Elwill[10] is dead. I am with Sincerity & respect
    Your most obedient servant
      Wm Stukeley
      13 June 1717

To Maurice Johnson Esqr
at Spalding
Lincolnshire

Ancaster Free

[1] Stukeley worked as a physician in Boston from 1710 to 1717 then returned to London until 1726.
[2] 'The lowing of cattle'; Stukeley's lodgings with Mrs Machin, in the recently built Ormond Street, Bloomsbury, were at this time near the northern edge of London.
[3] William Herbert, 2nd Marquis of Powis, built his famously attractive house (now destroyed) on what is today the north side of Great Ormond Street, close to Queen Square. This locates Stukeley's London lodgings exactly.
[4] Anatomical waxworks first came to London from France and Italy around this year.
[5] There was much discussion on 21 May 1717 about the cost of transporting Dutch troops used to help in defeating the 1715 Jacobite uprising.
[6] Robert Harley (1661–1724) first Earl of Oxford, was tried before the House of Lords on 23 June 1717 and acquitted; he had led the Tory government at the end of Queen Anne's reign so he was attacked by the new Whig government.
[7] William Cowper (1665–1723), first Earl Cowper.
[8] See **Letter 6**, n.1.
[9] See his entry in Appendix 3.
[10] Sir John Elwill, created a baronet in 1701, died 3 May 1717.

12. Maurice Johnson to William Stukeley, from Woburn, Bedfordshire, 10 March 1718
Spalding, SGS/Maurice Johnson/8[1]

[Later note by Johnson:] To Dr Stukeley [written]about Dunstable

Dear Dr:
 I have twice since I had the pleasure of being in your Company been at your Lodgings[2] to wait upon You, but hadn't the Satisfaction of Spending an Afternoon & Evening with you as I proposed, I told the Gentlewoman where you lodge that That was all the Buisnes I had, & so it was indeed, for I ever thought It very well worth my while to make It my Busyness to cultivate a Friendship with you & Enjoy the Improvements such Conversation affords. I was in great hopes of meeting with you at the Society last Wednesday, where Wee had a Great Deal of Good Company, but were at a loss for our Secretary,[3] I question not your

haveing from better Hands an Account of What was then & there transacted; If in my Circuit Travailes any thing Occurrs to me I can fantcy worth communicating You shall have It, Were It not for the Decency of Attendance due from a Young Lawyer, I believe for buisnes I might have Leisure Enough, but Wee must shew our Faces a long time to the Practizers, before they'll be known to Us, let Us know them never so well;[4] In my Journey hither I rode thro St Albans but thought It not so absolutely necessary to stay there after the Copious remarkes You obliged me with upon your returne from thence, So joggd on to Dunstable in the Way plain to a proverb:[5] whilest the Mutton was dressing I learnt there accidentaly from Such a Sort of a Dr as that place affords (who was refreshing himself at the Door of my Inn) for there are Men of all Sorts stiled Drs & Lawyers, that the Priory of the place was dedicated to St Peter. The Scite of It is pretty large, & on part thereof where Sober Recluse used to walke, the Brother permits Sundery Madd Folks under his care & Cure to take a limitted Parade: the Church is of but a Soft Sort of Stone, consisting now of 3 Isles, the Steeple a Low Tower, embattelled as is all the West Front, & on the North side that End stands a low Tower Steeple, on the South a small Embattelled Turrett to lead to the Leads of the Roof, 2 Doors, a Large one Circularly arched to the Nave, & a les to the North Isle – several vulgar hic jacets[6] Such a one of Dunstaple, with such an One his wife, on brass in 1400 & odd; My Female Sacristan told me that Under a Stone from off which the Basen [sic] Inscription is stolen there lyes a Woman who had 13 children at 3 births but knew not her Name, Tradition haveing not delivered that to her. On a screen of Oak between the Antichoire or Rood Place & the South Isle consisting of 7 pillars are the Implements & Emblems of the Passion not Inelegantly carved, but from the manner of the work, & which is Some of it hollow too I fantcy pretty old, the Great & Little Portals of the Priory or Religious house are remaining on the South side of the Church. There are at the upper End of the North Isle Several Modern Monuments & Inscriptions of the Marshes a Gentleman's Family of that Town, & one of a relation of theirs Mr Chew, who the £300 worth of Marble tells you was an Esq., a Tradesman, Cittizen, Fined for Sheriff of London & served that Office for that County. Take the only One I had leisure to be punctual in, as haveing something in It worth remembering, tis cut in Brass, over It in the Stone which is a large Cours black Marble the figures of the Man & his Wife in Brass,

Hic iacent Nichus. Lane quondam p.sidens frat'nitat sci Johis Bapte de Dunstaple qui obiit ii° die mens Decembri Anno Dni m° cccc° lix° Et Agnes ux. ei quorum aiabus p.piiciet. de. amen.[7]

You'll take this hasty Scribble on the road as meant for an amusement. Let me know Dear Dr how You go on now & then, if you favour Me with an Answer this Weeke direct for me Upon the Midand [sic] Circuit at Lincoln, the next at Derby, & I shall recieve yours in time. I am with my humble Service to Mr President & all the members

                My Good Old Friend
                    Your most humble servant
                    Maur. Johnson junr.

Woebourn
Bedfordshire
Monday 10° Martii 1717/8

P.S. Mr Brother John Johnson who hath been a Barraster of the Inner Temple these 4 yeares is very desireous of being admitted a Member[8] but tho in Town with Me, he is So very modest, I could never bring him along with me, I believe yourself knew him so well as to recommend him to the President & Members, which I desire You'll do, & Enter him (if they please to admitt him) & pay down his Subscription for this Month, & likewise his & mine till One of us see You next (each first Wednesday in the month) When They shall be with many thanks to Your honour repayd; & pray advertize me of his admission, if the Society think fitt to recieve him amongst 'Em.

For Dr William Stukeley at
Mrs Machines in Ormond street
near Red Lyon Square
London
These

[1] This letter was probably returned to Johnson by Stukeley for inclusion in the papers of the SGS because of the information about Dunstable church that it contains.
[2] See **Letter 11**, n.3; Johnson was in London for the legal Term.
[3] This tactful comment by Johnson refers to Stukeley's role as Secretary of the Society of Antiquaries.
[4] A useful explanation of how young lawyers got legal work by regular attendance at the Circuit Courts.
[5] The *Universal British Directory* (1791) quotes the proverb 'As plain as Dunstable road'. The entry also mentions the woman referred to later by Johnson, who had the remarkable number of children, though it implies three sets of triplets and three single births.
[6] This full description of Dunstable Priory in 1718 is useful, as is his account of the memorials, or 'hic jacets'. The priory, founded as an Augustinian priory in 1132, is now St Peter's, one of four churches in Dunstable.
[7] Johnson has written this inscription in Gothic script, copying that in which it was written. The abbreviations may be original or Johnson's own; many of them are typical abbreviations used in such funerary inscriptions. The full version would read: Hic iacent Nicholaus Lane quondam præsidens fraternitatis sancti Johannis Baptistæ de Dunstaple qui obit iio die mensis Decembri Anno Domini m° cccc° lix° Et Agnes uxor eius quorum animabus propicietur Deus: Here lie Nicholas Lane, formerly president of the guild of St John the Baptist at Dunstable who died on the 2nd December AD 1459 and Agnes his wife, on whose souls may God have mercy.
[8] Maurice Johnson's younger brother John became a member of the Antiquarian Society in 1718.

13. William Stukeley to Maurice Johnson, London, 10 April 1718
Spalding, SGS/Stukeley/5

[Later heading in Johnson's hand:] SGS No. 54 A Letter from Dr W Stukeley FRS & one of the Restorers and Secr. of the Antiquarian Soc. in London to Maurice Johnson Junr Esqr another Restorer & Member thereof concerning its progress. Silver eight square Saxon key with a Saxon inscription thereon explained by Tho. Warkhouse of the Temple Esq a Member

10 April 1718
Dear Sir
    I recd. Yours which is reposited Amongst the Letters of the Society[1] who give their thanks and remember their Services to You. Mr Warkhouse[2] has favour us

with an Interpretation of the Silver key which I have at large transcribd into the Book It is in short This

Thurla Mawtharl eregen taste alefeist b egi u Argent
Fora Foramen Æreæ Capsæ modo licet tuum est Argentum
Open the Lock of the Silver Cabinet & the Money is Yours.

he thinks Æreæ is generally meant of all Metals & because of the Smallness of the key the Chest may be probably of the Same Metal with It. They have admitted Mr Brown Willis[3] who is putting out the Catalogue of all the Abbots Pryers &c of every Religious house he has Got the Pryors of Spalding compleat. Your Bror Mr John was admitted according to request. We are now to the Number of 40, good Members. We want nothing but Materials which at present come in but slowly. They have desired Me to publish my Map of Holland[4] at the Common Expence, & I have been thinking that if You proceed to take what is still remaining in Our Churches We may between Us make a little Tract to preserve the Monuments of our Own Country. I have some Sheets by Me which I had thoughts of Communicating to the Bp. of Lincoln[5] but in Case You like it I will reserve 'em for our own purpose. Mr Heron[6] I believe will give Us a Print of his house & Mr Trafford[7] perhaps one of his for its furder [sic] Ornament if We could out of every Parish raise Contribution for one of their Churches, it would make a pretty thing & the first of its kind. This is purely my present Imagination which I submit entirely to Your Judgement. But Something must be got together for publication by the Years end, & We intend Every One shall take a Subject what they Please to give Us their Thoughts upon. Mr Gale[8] & I & two more are going for Easter holydays to Colchester I gott 3 guineas this Week which I tell him will bear the expence of the next. Honest Mr Bertie[9] was with Us last Night, & We drank Your health &c. As for News it seems to Me as if We should have Peace thro'out Europe this Year, which I hope will take off our Apprehensions of 4s. Tax next Year which People conjecturd to be necessary seeing so large a Naval Armament upon our Stocks. Poor Mr Director[10] is so taken up with his Mrs that We seldom have [*letter continues sideways in left margin*] his Company, & Nothing is yet done towards Rich. II. We have got a pretty many Prints by the Contributions of Members which Serve the Company to Stare at. Tho. Hearn[11] is miserably afflicted by the Vicechancellors Court & he Swears he will retract nothing which he verily beleives to be true as he dos all that he has publishd, a good reason for printing. Mr Rawlinson has sold Dr Mead[12] a compleat & perfect Holinshed[13] I beleive the only one in the World for 25l. Modest Mr Curl[14] calls himself Printer to the Antiquarian Society but he has been terribly mawld by Mist in his weekly Journal he calls printing bawdy Curlicism a Word which has obtaind much in Town. Commend if you please my respects to all Friends at Spalding particularly your Society & beleive Me Sir
        Your humble servant
        Wm Stukeley
        Ormond street Apr. 10 1718

To Maurice Johnson Esqr
at Spalding
Lincolnshire   Ancaster   Free[15]

[*An attached sheet in Johnson's hand has a drawing of the key, annotated 'a Silver key found in Derbyshire now in the possession of Mr Thornton of Bloxholm in Lincolnshire 1717' and a copy of the inscription as given by Stukeley in this letter, with an epigram:*
'On the Antiquarian Society
Wee've eight square Keys for Saxon locks
And Alfred's apoplectick Box
– Countess of Winchelsea's Letter to the Lady Viscountess Weymouth at Longleat']

[*This letter also has notes made by Johnson about a coin of Henry VIII and a sketch of the coin, noted as being 'apud Johem Chichley' and drawings of two signet rings, one with the initials 'WA' and a note about them in Johnson's hand: 'a Silver Ring & Seal the Rim of a great Breadth & thick as a Shilling Produced by Mr Vertue*[16] *4 Febry 1717/8. It seems to have been the Secretum Sigillum of some Prelate perhapps WA stands for Willus Abbas and it may be some Abbat of Winchester.'*]

1   The Society of Antiquaries of London, or as Johnson usually called them, the Antiquarian Society.
2   Thomas Warkhouse, a gentleman of Norfolk, a member of the Antiquarian Society in 1718.
3   Appendix 3.
4   See the map of South Holland (Illustration 20).
5   Dr Edmund Gibson (1669–1748: see *ODNB*), Bishop of Lincoln (1716–23), then of London (1723–48). He published the popular edition of Camden's *Britannia* in 1695.
6   See **Letter 6**, n.1.
7   Sigismund Trafford (c.1644–1723), builder of Dunton Hall (Lincs) and uncle of Sigismund Trafford, the Fen drainer (1694–1741), SGS member 1724.
8   This is probably Roger Gale (1672–1744: see *ODNB* and Appendix 3) as he was the elder brother and Vice-President of the Antiquarian Society; Stukeley was in correspondence with him at the time. He was a customs official and keen antiquarian, Treasurer of the AS from 1717 and SGS member 1733, also FRS 1717.
9   See Appendix 3.
10 John Talman (1677–1726: see *ODNB*) was Director of the Antiquarian Society in 1718.
11 Thomas Hearne (1678–1735: see *ODNB*), the Oxford antiquarian, printer of manuscripts and diarist.
12 Thomas Rawlinson (1681–1725), book collector, agent and friend of Hearne and Richard Mead, member of the AS 1718; Dr Richard Mead (1673–1754: see *ODNB*), well-known physician and book-collector, under whom Stukeley had studied, see Appendix 3.
13 Raphael Holinshed (c.1525–1580: see *ODNB*), author of *Chronicles of England, Scotland and Ireland* (1577).
14 Edmund Curl (1675–1747), bookseller and publisher; Nathaniel Mist (d.1737: see *ODNB*), published *Mist's Journal*, a Jacobite periodical opposed to Walpole, from 1716 to 1737.
15 In the eighteenth century MPs were entitled to free postage and were able to extend this privilege to professional associates.
16 George Vertue (1684–1756: see *ODNB*), painter and engraver. His engraving of the portrait of Richard II, dated 1718 and made for the AS, is now in the National Portrait Gallery. See Appendix 3.

14. William Stukeley to Maurice Johnson, London, 19 June 1718
Spalding, SGS/Stukeley/6

Dear Sir
    I received Yours & The Society return their Thanks As well for your Information about Ely Minster &c As that You are so mindful as to drink our Healths On

Your Club Nights which Mr Gale says is a Cell to the Miter.[1] We have finishd the Plate of St James' Font[2] to the General Approbation, & another of an old Horn given by Ulphus Prince of Deira to the Church at York.[3] Mr Vertue has now gott a fine Drawing of King Rich[d] II.[4] We subscribe 7s 6d a peice towards It. We have thoughts of taking a Room in the Temple & laying up Liquor in it as You doe, We have bought towards Furniture a good Picture of Ed.III[5] & shall have several other Pictures &c presented to us. I hope to see You in Town soon till when with my service to All Friends I remain your Friend

& most humble Servant
Wm Stukeley

Ormondstreet 19 June 1718

[p.2] All the World here are in great Expectations of the Event of Affairs in Italy & Hungary[6] tho' the Prints say the Spaniards are landed in Milan yet Wagers are laid that a Peace between the Emperor & Sultan will be made first, Mr Dutchman must be forcd into our fourcorded Alliance. Jemmy Garnon a Surgeon of Boston & I drank Your healths at Dinner t'other day with your Uncle Green.[7]

Pray with my Service to Your Father tell him I desire he would not fail to bring up all my Bonds & Papers relating to my Aunt Stukeley this Term for I shall want them very much.

Yours W:S:

Now the Southwark Pudding wonder is over[8] The City is all in an uproar about the Election of a Chamberlain[9] like a Country Corporation for Burgesses where roast Pigg & Beef & wine is dealt about freely at Taverns & Advertisements about it more voluminous than the late celebrated Bangorian Notifications[10] tho' not in a calm & undisturbed Way.

To
Maurice Johnson Esq[r]
    at Spalding
        Lincolnshire

[1] Roger Gale refers to the SGS as a 'Cell to the Miter' meaning the AS, which met originally at the Mitre Tavern in Fleet Street, London. Stukeley was Secretary of the AS at the time.
[2] The font of St James' church, Westminster, was sculpted by Grinling Gibbons.
[3] The tenth-century horn of Ulf is preserved in York Minster.
[4] See **Letter 13**, n.16, above.
[5] The Society of Antiquaries does not possess a portrait of Edward III as far as we can ascertain. There is a late seventeenth-century engraving of Edward III in the National Gallery's collection, by Michael Vandergucht, father of Stukeley's friends and associates, Gerard (1697–1776) and Jan Vandergucht (1699–1730).
[6] In 1718 the Ottoman Empire relinquished control over Hungary. Following this the Quadruple Alliance was formed between the Holy Roman Empire, France, England and Holland to defeat the Spanish armies and navies which had invaded Sicily and Sardinia and threatened to take the French throne.
[7] James Garnon was listed as a surgeon in Boston in P. J. and R. V. Wallis, *Eighteenth-Century Medics* (1988). Dr Edward Green (1665–1728), a London surgeon, was Maurice Johnson's relation by his grandfather's first marriage; when setting up the Spalding society, Johnson wrote to him for advice about publications they should subscribe to.
[8] In May 1718 James Austin, a London ink-dealer, created an immense plum pudding which was paraded through the streets of London and eventually stolen and eaten by the inhabitants of Southwark Mint, a debtors' sanctuary in London.

9   The Chamberlain of the City of London elected in 1718 was Sir George Ludlam who served until 1727.
10 The Bangorian Controversy was an intense theological debate over whether power in the Church was held by the sovereign, appointed by divine right, or by the people, who received revelation directly from God. Stukeley uses 'advertisement' in its early meaning of 'information'.

[83. Maurice Johnson to William Stukeley, 14 October 1719
This letter is not part of Stukeley's MS collection in his letter-book in the Bodleian Library but is transcribed and published in John Nichols, *Bibliotheca Topographica Britannica*. We have reproduced it as **Letter 83** in the Additional Letters section.]

15. Maurice Johnson to William Stukeley, Spalding, 23 November 1719
Bodleian, MS Eng. misc. c.113, fols 302r–303v

Spalding 23rd Novr 1719

Dear Countryman[1]
I once thought I should have seen You in Town this Terme of St Michael[2] But It will now be St Hillarys e'er I leave the Country where by so long an Absence from the Mitre,[3] I shall scarce be known by or know the faces of the worthy Members of the most agreeable Society I ever had the honour to be a member of. tho' I wrote to You but lately and since I had the honour of a Line from You my Friend Yet as I presumed you might Expect me in Town this Terme and so think an Answer in Writing needles being about the time I should have been with You had not I been deteined here by something of certain Profitt to me, I thought fitt to give You a Second Epistle to begg a double Answear in Your own good time to them both together: Since I wrote to you last I have lost an Old Friend & special good Client Mr Atkinson,[4] who is dead and buryed, he has left no Children, unles his Widdow be with Child, whom he has provided for very handsomely in the Short time of his Practice, & after her decease the house wherein he dwelt (which he had fitted up very neately) with stables Brewhouse & other Offices & a pretty Garden & Orchard under It he has by his Will given to the Masters of the Free Grammar Schole of this Town in which he was brought up & to which and his good Parts & Industry he ow'd in great Measure the Estate he dyd possessd of. But this Bequeast is but conditional if she have no Issue by him who live to Enjoy It, for she is with child as most people think. Our Town is very bigg with Expectation from a Play which is to be Acted on O Sapientia[5] by the Young Gentlemen at our Free Schole for which the Gentlemen & Ladys have raised 'em a Stage in the Town house & Very Fine & tall Scænes are painting here by a good hand for 'em & Several Suits of gay Cloaths making up – Mrs Heron[6] & some other people of good Fashion have taken Lodgings in the Town for That Week our Roads being bad to travaile at this time as you know full well thô but a few miles Backwards & forwards. They are to have a Prologue which is promised 'em by the Best Poet in Cambridge, & Every Night a Consort of Corelli & Albinonis Compositions performed by Gentlemen of this Town & from Norfolk & North'tonshire seaven Violins 3 Bases a Bassoon & a Trumpett all very good performers[7] with a Ball on the fourth Night & Assembly

for the Ladys & Gentlemen given by the Master of the School in Compliment to the Company & publick Exercises in Verse & prose in English, Greek & Latin by way of Declamations & Gratulations. I wish I could then Enjoy your good Company here to share these Diversions with Me & your Brother Parker of Peterburgh[8] whom I expect at that time as my Guest with our friend Jos. Sparke[9] who is one of the Consort; & my Brother Ambler[10] who is much at your Service as is my Father Johnson & Bro[11] & your Godfather[12] who had had this Illness preceded by a Soar Throat & that by a Pain in his Eare & deafness: Thus far of [p.2] our Health. Now I must tell of an odd Creature I keep in my Study which I think as necessary there as in a Daiery, since the ratts presumed one terme in my Absence to knaw me many Books parchments &c which is a Ketten as Yet & sent me a mighty & rare present out of the Forest of Rockingham,[13] being of the Savage Race, & striped like a Tyger with large Black lists round the leggs & thighs & Neck the Furr very deep & of a light Sandy colour, with very large Eyes the Balls of each foot jett Black & a large Taile, But being a Female I feare It will not be so Large & Some of the wild Breed are, which the Woodmen, Keepers & Gentlemen themselves when a Shooting frequently destroy as Vermin in the Forest, They being most detested by Sportsmen as Killing more Leveretts & Young Pheasants than any other sort of Creature in the Woods, haveing had this Beast before It could eat Flesh, or could well See & shift for Its Safety & kept It continually & till very lately tyd up in a Bass[14] in my Study, I have made It as tame as any Creature can be when only I am with It but if any other Person comes into the room It bounces away & lyes lurking in an hole untill the Strange Face disappeare, & then will come to Me again, & is fond of Me even to being very troublesome till I turne It down off my Desk or Table when I'm intent on any Thing – in short my Puss is like Bezas Mitissa in his Epigramm,[15] Neither could the Sieur Michel de Montaines[16] be more fond or a Grimalkin of better Sence nor could Bickerstaff be fonder or more Indulgent to his.[17] – Lest my Former to You should ha' miscarry'd I begg leave to repeat in this the Request I made in That of your presenting my most humble Services to Mr Le Neve[18] & enquireing of him for Me the Sence & meaning in a Liberal Explicacion of these Termes or Words used in Domesday in Lincolnshire – Tailla – & Berew.[19] which later Ingulphus him Selfe renders Manerium, but what Sort of Manor I want to know for Im Confident It couldn't be Manerium Capitale from that Abbats Instance in his History.[20] My other Queries to that Learned Gent. were about Coats of Armes, But I trust my Letter came to your hands. I long mightyly to know What forwardnes all your Learned Labours towards the Expediteing whereof my Subscription is cast in are: I recounted them to you in my former & referr to that, in which was allso Enclosed my Collections for that of the Fleet family your great & Noble Antecessor ex materna in these parts for the sake of which Labour principaly I hope you received It Safe. It would be very obligeing in you if you happen to have mett with any thing relating to mine who came originaly from the North Northumberland & Yorkshire into Norfolk & Suffolk & there remained till unsettled by Popery & a branch of It came into these Fenny Tracts to Shirke about & hide from Persecution and the threatening rage of Superstition.[21]

[p.3] You heard perhapps that Sir Wm Massingbeard at the Peacock & Mr Richd. Ellis[22] at the White heart feast the Burghers of Boston their Wives sons & Daughters dayly & Nightly, & give large presents, the later is at Mr Nettletons house Et omnia Botulphiis sicut olim Romæ venalia[23] – I've something farther to Communicate which is that next Sunday Young Dr Luddington[24] as the Folk call him the Learned Curate of Fleet is to preach our Charity Sermon which wee Expect will be such an One as has not yet been heard on that Occasion – Mr Serle[25] the Chappelain of Cowbitt has buryd his Wife who dyed in Childbed. My Service to David Atkinson when You See him, that Man servd him very ill[26] & I was an Ignorant means of his So doeing unwitting & unwillingly I became so. For I'm Sure as I've great reason, so I am a great Lover of my Countryman & Brother whom I take to be a very worthy honest Gentleman, but they say Serle is in quest of a Woman with some money already & then he'll leave the Fenns, & go into his neighbourhood, which Yet I believe he scarce dare do had he a good Fortune to back his Villany. There has been a report here of Young Hargate of Duckhall's[27] marrying Serle's Wife's Eldest Daughter, but my Bro. Ambler says the young man himself denys It. You whom I have ever found ready to do more than I coud ever desire of You will excuse the prolixity of my Epistles who can write but seldom, And am then willing to give you what Account comes to Me of Matters transacted in the Country, of which I had almost forgot to tell you the last I heard, that Upon Your Brother Tomlinson's[28] recommendation Mr Heron has taken Jack Rishton who formerly kept the White heart in this Town[29] into his house as a Domestick Servant.

Ps Dear Dr I begg of you to read the enclosed [*document no longer present*] relateing to what follows & then if you please to send It by the Penny Post as directed sealed up with your Seale. Now my Friend I begg your Patience, to hear me tell my own Story in relation to a matter between Me and a Neighbour of Mine and Acquaintance of yours Mr Richard Pacey[30] who has Entertaind in his Service a Person as a Clerke to whom I think my Selfe as I wrote him to have a much better Tytle: You must know I am resolvd not to be imposd upon neither woud I do any thing willingly to disgust my Countryman & Brother Pacey. The case it this, last Isle of Ely assizes holden at Wisbech Wee were almost allways together, and therefore I presume he must hear and be privy to My Discourse concerning this Fellow whose name is John Woodbine, he had been Clerk with one Mr Lewhurn Lestrange[31] a Fellow residing in & Bursar of Caius College in Cambridge & a Councillor, this last Gentleman useing to Attend the Isle Assizes the very last time he came was last winter assizes at Ely & there upon my being with him in his Chambers I saw some Court Rolls & other Writeings of his Clerks and liked 'em so well as to Engage his Master if ever he parted with him for anything Not a Notorious fault to let me have him if he was willing to serve Me; Well, since that time I neither saw nor heard from Mr Lestrange with whom I had no other acquaintance nor Correspondence but as a Brother practicer at the Isle Assizes, Upon Enquireing last Wisbeach Assizes of Dr Balam[32] & Mr Comissary Bramston[33] why he wasn't there They told me he was they thought so Sick he could not come & apprehended his Illness would prove fatal to him, this I think passd in the Company of Mr Pacey but am not sure It was so, but Wee were generaly together & I beggd of those Gentlemen to do me the favour if Mr Lestrange Dy'd to Engage his Clerke Woodbyne to Serve me & to Send him forthwith to Me & told 'em what had passed between his Master and Me at Ely the Assizes before, I had their Promise but not performance Dr Balam indeed tarryd in the Isle till sometime after Mr Lestranges Death, but I heard nothing from Commissary Bramston, nor that Lestrange was Dead till Some Short time

since accidentaly, so I immediatlywrote to a trustier Friend of Kings Colledge to make Enquiry after the Young Man for me who sent Me word to my very great Surprize that he was hired by Mr Pacey: to whome I wrote about him but have had not so much as the favour of a Line in answer. I hope & think that I treated the affair with good Manners & as became a Gentleman in my Letter to him, but the Servant I have being not qualifyd to do my Court Rolls &c I pressd him as farr as I could with decency to Spare me a Person, to whom I think I have so just & fair pretensions, I begg the Friendshipp of You Doctor to take the trouble of calling upon Mr Pacey and as his busyness is not so Urgent in probability as mine to Engage to let the Young Fellow come to Me Sometime in the next Tearme with his good will & Candour. It will be time enough for Me and I am willing to Stay so long for him. I begg of you to know what Wages he was to have had of him by the by and send Me word in your answear f[*gap caused by removal of seal*] very willing I find to Serve Me who am
        Dear Dr your very much obliged and most humble
            Servant Maur. Johnson jun^r

To Dr Stukely at Mrs Machins
in Ormond Street
London

Frank H. Heron.[34]

---

[1] In the eighteenth century this meant the county or region in which one was born or resided, in this case a fellow-Lincolnshire man or fellow-Fenman.

[2] Michaelmas Term was one of the four short terms of the sittings of legal courts: Michaelmas in autumn, Hilary in winter, Easter in spring and Trinity in summer. Each lasted a few weeks. Maurice Johnson usually went to London during Term on legal business.

[3] See **Letter 14**, n.1.

[4] Willliam Atkinson; see his entry in Appendix 3.

[5] 'O Sapientia' (O Wisdom) are the first words of the antiphon used on 17 December at Evensong or Vespers. The Master of Spalding Grammar School was the Revd Timothy Neve; he produced a play on that day with a special prologue which he composed, which remains in the SGS archive.

[6] For the Heron family, see **Letter 6**, n.1.

[7] The Spalding musicians met regularly every week in a similar manner to the SGS.

[8] This is perhaps Revd Dr William Parker (c.1684–1730), a contemporary of Stukeley's at Cambridge, whose memorial is in Peterborough Cathedral.

[9] The Revd Joseph Sparke: see Appendix 3.

[10] Joshua Ambler: see Appendix 3.

[11] Johnson's younger brother John, later Treasurer of the SGS from 1729 to 1744, also a barrister and Clerk to the Court of Sewers in the Spalding area. See Appendix 3.

[12] Stukeley's godfather was William Ambler.

[13] This young wild cat from Rockingham Forest was perhaps given to Johnson by his relations, the Lynn family of Southwick near Rockingham.

[14] A straw-stuffed mat or cushion.

[15] Theodore Beza (1519–1605), the Calvinist theologian whose *Poemata* included many epigrams.

[16] Michel de Montaigne (1533–92) wrote in his *Apology for Raymond Seboul*, 'When I play with my cat, how do I know she is not playing with me rather than I with her?'

[17] Grimalkin or Greymalkin is a name for an old female cat; one of the witches in Macbeth says, 'I come, Greymalkin'. Isaac Bickerstaff was the pen-name of Richard Steele in the *Tatler*, which was also known as *The Lucubrations of Isaac Bickerstaff*. Steele was sometimes pictured with a cat.

[18] This is probably Peter Le Neve (1679–1740: see *ODNB*), Norroy King of Arms or Herald from

1704 to 1729. He was also Richmond Herald. He was a keen antiquarian, one of the group that re-founded the SA in 1717 and its first President.

[19] Both terms are used in Domesday Book. 'Tailla' today is regarded as a land tax or tallage imposed on towns; 'Berew.' or in full 'berewica' is an outlying place attached to a manor. In the Lincolnshire Domesday, Tydd St Mary is listed as a berewick of Spalding.

[20] Johnson was using the Latin chronicle of Croyland Abbey, known as 'Ingulf's Chronicle'; the version which Johnson referred to is still at the SGS.

[21] A letter from Johnson to Stukeley has apparently not been preserved by Stukeley; without it the complex genealogical history of the Johnsons discussed here cannot be unravelled.

[22] Sir William Massingberd, unsuccessful Tory candidate at the Boston by-election in 1719; Mr, later Sir, Richard Ellys (1682–1742: see *ODNB*), MP for Boston 1719–1734 and a patron of Stukeley; see Appendix 3. They were using Boston inns as centres for hospitality in support of their election campaigns.

[23] 'And everything is for sale in Boston as formerly in Rome'. Johnson is punning on a quotation from Sallust's *De bello Iugurthino*.

[24] The Revd Thomas Lodington (1686–1729), Rector of Fleet (Lincs), son of Dr Thomas Lodington, Vicar of Horncastle from 1679 to 1724. There is a portrait in the collections of North Lincolnshire Museums Service showing the younger Thomas Lodington with Fleet church in the background.

[25] Revd Radcliffe Searle (1692–1757), Cambridge (1711), curate at Crowland (1716), curate at Cowbit (1717), Rector of Thoresway (1719), Vicar of Tetney (1732).

[26] David Atkinson: see Appendix 3.

[27] Duck Hall was a property in the south-west Spalding area in the eighteenth century, where presumably the Hargate family lived. It was recorded in **Letter 73** (11 May 1751) as having been demolished; Johnson obtained some stone steps from it which he used in his 'canal' in his garden.

[28] Stukeley's medical associate; see **Letter 6**, n.9.

[29] The principal hotel and coaching station of Spalding. The French philosopher J. J. Rousseau stayed there for ten days, 5–14 May 1767.

[30] One of Stukeley's London associates was a lawyer, Mr Pacey, who introduced him to Lord Macclesfield in April 1725 (*Surtees* I, 76).

[31] Mr Lestrange, fellow of Caius College, is recorded as having been buried in St Michael's church, Cambridge, on 19 August 1719.

[32] William Balam LLD (1642–1725), Lincoln's Inn (1672), Cambridge University (1682).

[33] Dr William Bramston (d.1734) of Queens' College, Cambridge, was the legal Commissary of the University of Cambridge in 1718.

[34] This is presumably the MP Henry Heron.

16. William Stukeley to Maurice Johnson, London, 29 November 1719
Spalding, SGS/Stukeley/7

[Later heading in Johnson's hand:] Letter from Dr Stukeley about Stoneheng: the Deaths of many learned Men – Great Character of Sir Godfrey Kneller Bart[1] primier Portrait Painter to our Kings & Queens for many Reignes.

Dear Sir,

I am asham'd you should have so much reason to provoke Me to answer Your letters, both which I received. The first Mr Hare has had ever since to find out the Coats of Arms which he has not yet done. All Your directions & Quæries were proposd & deliverd, according to Your request. the word Tailla I don't find any of them know what it is, but Berew is agreed to signify a Farmhouse.[2] I am vastly indebted to You for the elaborate account You have sent me of the Fletes. & am sorry It will ever scarce be in my Power to answer it with a return of Memorandums of Yours, because I shall have no opportunitys of conversing with the

Genealogical Books for want of time but beleive You may when in Town have what Satisfaction is possible in that Way in my Lord Oxfords Library[3] where I saw vast numbers of Such as well as in the College of Arms. I scarce ever allow my thoughts to range into Antiquitys more than what is the consequence of Conversation & the Mitre Society,[4] only one thing I beleive I must be forcd to bring to some kind of a head which is Stonehenge, My Lord Pembroke,[5] in whose Neighbourhood that Noble Antiquity Stands, & I, have had a deal of talk about it & he generally either comes to Me or sends for me two or three times a week to discourse concerning it. he has been three times this Summer & taken accurate measures of it which my short stay would not permitt me & given me thereby an opportunity of finishing my Drawings, & his Lordships great reading & Judgment has put so many notions into my head & so improvd what I had thought about it that its probable I may as soon As leisure permitts throw my Conceptions together. I much commend the Spirit of your Town in improving the common Mirth of the approaching Season by Plays & Balls &c. I think Madam Heron[6] much in the right to lodge in the Town in order to partake of the Diversions. I envy Your happyness in the Conversation of so agreeable a Lady & am sorry we shall not see her in Town this season. We are all running Mad with singing by Mrs Robinson[7] & Plays & Balls & Masquerades & Musick Anthems & the Lord knows what whereof I shall have but very little share having no great taste for publick ways of Diversion, If I meet with [p.2] a pretty Lady that sings well & can perform upon the harpsichord tis ten times more satisfaction to me to spend an hour with her than all the Nicolinis, Margaretas &c[8] united Consorts. for such is the natural slowness of my Genius that I cannot bear such a tumult of Pleasure. tis like the Sun striking upon the eyes when we come out of a Dark Room, his too dazling beams proving painfully glorious. I was born in the Night this month of November, so fancy I was thence determind rather to be sensible of & most affected with silent, soft & solemn agreeables, like the Majesty of Moon shine or the moving Scene of a Starlight night. which acts upon the exterior organs more tenderly & chiefly puts one into a pleasing indolence & fitt of meditation. The Sieur de Talman[9] whom we call the Abbott of Henxworth is so wrapt up in the pleasures of a Country retirement & of a pretty Ladys Arms that he is not yet arrivd at Fumopolis[10] as our Treasurer calls it. Poor Mr Mickleton[11] was buryed this week at St Clements, his dire fate is much lamented, being unhappily drownd in the Thames, he had been courting an agreeable Lady at Chelsea this summer & was near marrying as its thought. A miserable accident happend too, to a Clergyman this week Minister of Silchester[12] where Mr Gales's & I were this Summer & calld upon him, he was drowned in Fleet Ditch. a Person of Learning & who only knew & collected the Antiquitys of the Place. Mr Keck[13] one admitted into our Society, dyed at Paris this summer a very pretty young Gentleman of great Fortune I took my leave of him just upon his Departure, he gave £500 to the Royal Society. My Lord Pembroke told me that Mr Chichley[14] had a very bad fall from his horse but without any certainty. There has likewise been a Legacy of £40 per annum left our College of Physicians & £10 per annum to the Royal Society by another hand. I had the honor this week to dine with our Illustrious Countryman the Great Sr Isaac Newton, & was surprizd to observe him read the Smallest Print for an hour together without Spectacles. I likewise this week [p.3] sat by whilst the Great Sr Godfrey Kneller painted the great Dr Mead[15] & afterwards dined with them & was infinitely delighted with the agreeable Company of that famous Limner. Tis surprising to see his peices, what Charms dos he inspire into the fair sex what Spirit & Fire dos he lay upon the Canvas what inimitable Attitudes dos he put his Figures into, You see the very Souls of Persons in his Tables. I observd he had very artfully placd a most incomparable Picture at full length all done by his own hand, of the famous Beauty Mrs Chetwynd[16] now Lady Blondel at the end of the Room which I imagind was to put the Dr into good humor who has too much sense to be untouched by Superior Graces in the Fair Sex. This Lady when single putt both our Universitys into a general Combustion like a Comet. Mr Baxters Etymologicon[17] has been published several Months & is a curious fund & new resourse of Bryttish Antiquitys. I beleive Yours is at Mr Thomas's at the Royal Society, I think too I heard Mr Gale say he had a book of Tho. Hearns[18] for You. our Richmondshire business[19] is near finished, it is printed by Mr Gosling. We goe on at the Miter much in our old way & never forget the Cell at Spalding. Mr Hill[20] is not yet returnd from Herefordshire. We have got a very fine new Steeple sett up at St Clements[21] but all the New Churches are at a Stand the Exigences of the Government diverting that Money into another Channel. Now the Town is taken up with discourse about the new Peerage Bill[22] which (I am sorry to relate it) will certainly pass. Lately the Missisipi Fairy Phantom[23] diverted us, & our own Lottery, where blind Fortune deals her favors about, as usually injudiciously. I have most of my ticketts yet to draw & can only say I am no loser at present, But my motto is si sit Prudentia – Mr Singleton who married our Countrywoman has by my advice publishd an admirable Print of Dr Radcliffe[24] by which I beleive he will gett £50 clear. Pray give my humble Service in general to all my good Friends at Spalding & beleive me to be sincerely

    Dear Sr
     Your most obliged humble Servant
      Wm Stukeley
29 Nov. 1719 Ormond street

A Tender of my humble Respects to Madam Heron will from your hands be acceptable
I have deliverd Your Messages &c to Mr Pacey but shall not concern my self any other ways.

To
Maurice Johnson Esqr
 at Spalding
  Lincolnshire

[*This side has sketches of decorative motifs, probably by Maurice Johnson.*]

1 Sir Godfrey Kneller (1646–1723: see *ODNB*), famous as a portrait painter; his ink and wash picture of Stukeley is in the National Portrait Gallery.
2 This is evidence that Stukeley had received the first letter from Johnson referred to in **Letter 15**, see n.15. His response here refers mainly to the Domesday Book references in that letter. He has apparently handed over the first letter to Mr Hare who has not yet returned it. This is probably John Hare (1668–1720), Richmond Herald of Arms and a founder-member of the refounded Society of Antiquaries in 1717.
3 This is the very extensive library of Robert Harley, first Earl of Oxford, which became known as

the Harley Collection; with the additions made by his son the second Earl it was sold to the Crown in 1753 and became the nucleus of the British Museum's library, now the British Library.

4   See **Letter 14**, n.1.

5   Thomas Herbert, eighth Earl of Pembroke (1656/7–1733: see *ODNB*), of Wilton House. He was an early patron of Stukeley; this paragraph is a useful account of the development of the patronage relationship between Stukeley and Pembroke. Later his son the ninth Earl became Stukeley's patron; Stukeley's book on Avebury was dedicated to him.

6   See **Letter 6**, n.1 and **Letter 15**.

7   Mrs Robinson, née Turner (d.1741), sang at Drury Lane Theatre from October 1719 to March 1720, then left the stage to rear a family; both her children later sang in performances of Handel's works.

8   Nicolino Grimaldi Nicolini (born *c.*1673), a Neapolitan singer, came to London around 1708 and led the enthusiasm for Italian opera until around 1718. Margherita Durastanti arrived in London in 1719 to begin a successful career singing in Handel's operas.

9   John Talman (1677–1726: see *ODNB*). He was the first Director of the AS and had married Frances Cockayne of Hinxworth (Herts), in 1718.

10   This was a popular contemporary nickname for London, referring to the smoke from coal fires.

11   James Mickleton (1688–1719), drowned 23 November 1719; a lawyer and founder-member of the re-founded AS.

12   Thomas Betham (d.1719), Rector of Silchester (Hants), a place of interest to Stukeley because of his studies of Roman sites. He had visited it as part of his tour with his fellow-antiquaries Roger and Samuel Gale.

13   Probably Robert Keck (1686–1719); the AS records state that 'his election is the second that stands recorded in the minutes'. FRS 1714, admitted to the Inner Temple 1701, died 16 September 1719.

14   John Chichley, an original member of the re-founded AS in 1717, studied at the Middle Temple.

15   Dr Richard Mead (1673–1754: see *ODNB*). There is a wash drawing of Mead by Stukeley in the Royal College of Physicians. We cannot trace a named portrait of Mead by Kneller, though it has been suggested that his fine portrait of William Cheselden (1688–1752) in the possession of the Royal College of Surgeons in fact represents Mead (*ODNB*, 'Kneller, Godfrey').

16   Mary Chetwynd (d.1756) was the daughter of John Chetwynd of Grendon (Warwicks). In 1709 she married Sir Montague Blundell, Bart. (1689–1756), MP for Haslemere; he became Viscount Blundell in the Peerage of Ireland in 1720.

17   William Baxter (1650–1723) published his *Glossarium Antiquitatum Britannicarum*, a dictionary of British antiquities, in 1719. In 1733 Stukeley and Edward Lhuyd worked together on a second edition.

18   Thomas Hearne, librarian and later independent scholar at Oxford, well known as an acerbic critic of his fellow-scholars. See **Letter 9**, n.3.

19   Roger Gale published *Registrum Honoris de Richmond* in 1722 by subscription, under the auspices of the AS. Johnson, Stukeley and the SGS are all listed among the subscribers. The book transcribed Domesday entries and later documents relating to the Honour of Richmond in Yorkshire. 'Our' here refers to the AS. Robert Gosling (d.1741) was a London printer.

20   James Hill (1697–1727: see *ODNB*), FRS, FSA. He worked until his death on a history of Hereford, which was never published.

21   St Clement Danes church, London, was built by Sir Christopher Wren in 1682; the steeple was added by Sir James Gibbs in 1719/20. The 'New Churches' is a reference to the churches built following the 'Commission for Building Fifty New Churches' of 1711 to provide enough churches for the expanding population of London; some were new buildings, others re-building of earlier mediæval churches. The 'New Churches' scheme extended and altered St George's church, Queen Square, of which Stukeley was to become Rector in 1747.

22   The Peerage Bill of 1719 aimed to maintain the social exclusion of the House of Lords. It was defeated in March 1719 and again in December 1719 by the determination of Robert Walpole.

23   This was the financial scheme set up by the Scotsman John Law and the French monarchy to develop French Louisiana. It encouraged over-speculation, turned out to be a financial disaster like the English South Sea Bubble of the following year, and collapsed in 1720, ruining many investors.

24   Dr John Radcliffe (1650–1764: see *ODNB*), physician and benefactor. He is best remembered today by the Radcliffe Camera Library and Radcliffe Observatory in Oxford; the John Radcliffe

Hospital in Oxford was named after him. Many prints of him were published, including in 1720 prints by Vertue and Michael Vandergucht.

17. William Stukeley to Maurice Johnson, London, 7 October 1720
Spalding, SGS/Stukeley/8

[Heading in Johnson's hand:] Lr from Dr Stukeley dissection of an Elephant

Dear S^r

The affairs of Learning suffer under the common Calamity of South Sea drooping[1] all Discours & thought is turnd to the retriving Public Credit & private Losses, not the Improvement of the Mind or cultivating Arts. Our Antiquitys among other things have for some time been at a Stand partly by reason of People being out of Town partly because We have been deprivd for some time of Mr Gales Company his Lady[2] dying in Cambridgshire of the Small Pox & was carryd into Yorkshire for enterrment. We have lately been busy in dissecting an Elephant that dyd in Town, at Sr Hans Sloans,[3] & I made drawings of all the remarkeables. Dr Bentleys[4] New Testament is coming out which is supposed to be a very fine Work to show how great a value we put on that Work It Dr Mead[5] has promised to get him 40 Subscribers. The Lord knows whats become of Jos. Sparke[6] I have not seen him a long time. Your Coz. Manningham[7] is well, Mr Johnson[8] is chose into the Society. I am, in hopes of seeing You soon, very much
    Your humble Servt
    Wm Stukeley

  7 Oct: 1720 Ormond street

To Mr Maurice Johnson Junr
 at Spalding
   Lincolnshire
Free Percy[9]

[*Notes by Maurice Johnson.*][10]
For Dr Stukeley
Dr of Spalding Town Hall
& Half penny
Inscription of Mr Henry Eagle
sacram^t of Marry[age] on a bottle dugg up in the gardens of Ayscoughfee hall.

---

1 The South Sea Company was established in 1711 to develop trade with Central and South America and to take over part of the National Debt. Its shares suddenly shot up in 1720 following peace with Spain, the expectation of improved trade and the complete takeover of the National Debt by the South Sea Company in April 1720. This led to extraordinary speculation with the price of a share rising from around £150 to nearly £1,000 in late August. The inevitable collapse back to £150, which ruined many of those speculating, came during September 1720.
2 Roger Gale's wife, Henrietta, daughter of Henry Roper of Kent.
3 See Appendix 3.
4 See Appendix 3.
5 See **Letter 13**, n.12.

6   See **Letter 15**, n.9.
7   Probably Sir Richard Manningham; see Appendix 3.
8   Johnson's brother John Johnson became a member of the AS in 1718.
9   There was no MP of that name at this time; the free post name may be one of the officials of the UK Parliament.
10 Johnson's notes are to remind him of some drawings [Dr] and information to send to Stukeley.

18. Maurice Johnson to William Stukeley, Spalding, 14 October 1720
Bodleian, MS Eng. misc. c.113, fols 304r–305v

Dear Doctor,

For Your Sake & some other very Good Friends and Relations of mine I am heartily Sorry the Calamity[1] You mention has been so general, but Striking in the Naile beyond the Head must needs one time or another make the work intended to be fastend, give way: I condole with Mr Gale[2] on his Loss, for hes a Gentleman of the greatest Candour & worth, and for whom I have a just Esteem; & his not comeing amongst You must be felt by a Society, were It even fuller of men of Learning & Tast. Your talking of the Elephant You dissected[3] brings Dr Blair (now my Neighbour) into my head, who They tell Me meets good Encouragement for a Man who is not understood by all who Converse with him. I have seen his Account of that he dissected in Scotland in the Acts R. Soc.[4] & I have had the pleasure of an Account of that stupendous Creature from the Dr himself. I promise my Self a great Encrease of this pleasure from Your Draughts which So judiciously, artfully, & faithfully describe whatever You think worthy your Pencill. Our Soc. by their Secretary here[5] returne You thanks for communicating So much of the little Store of Learned Novelties now Stirring, but if wee have not now & then (as You Sir can catch the leisure for It) Something of this Sort from You, who have the pleasure of knowing & the reward of being known by the Conizeurs[6] & Literati of the Age, from whom can Wee hope It: – Since the Gentlemen of the Faculty have thought good to Encourage the work which you mention & to which the quondam Master of our Poor Grammar School is Equal,[7] even after what Dr Milles & Stephanus[8] performed, I hope a Lawyer or 2 may be Excused if They be desireous of forwarding So great an Undertaking for the Universal Benefitt & Creditt of our other Orb – As Medaglions are placed at the Head of Collections. The Gospell may well be Sett first on a Shelf of Law books & you may expect to find Canons & Decretals, Succeed with decency, as they ought to be grounded only upon It: I have lately had 2 Such accessions to my Collection of Medalls as to render the surveying It much more pleasant to the Judicious in the Metallick Affair.

[p.2] You'll oblige Me, Good Sir, In presenting my humble Service to my Couzen Johnson[9] & his Brother Manningham[10] & letting Mr Johnson know that my Bro: & I went to Thetford to meet him, where I received his Letter which I answered, but not hearing from him Since doubt whether he received It or No. At Thetford Wee were exceedingly entertained by Mr Martins[11] Library & Collections, that Young Gentleman is an Ornament to our Society of Lovers of Antiquity: 'Tis incredible what paines he has taken in the Affaires of his Native Town & 'tis pity but the World should be told by him what Sitomagus[12] has been; I presume nothing has fallen in your way of that Sort of Enquiry I made of you regarding my own Family,[13] and alltho I hope to See You in a very Short time, Yet I shall take It as a favour if in answer to this You'll be pleased Sir to Send Me the observations which Mr Norroy & the late Richmond Herald Mr Hare[14] made upon the Queries relateing to Some Coates of Armes I sent you formerly an Account of to Enquire of Those Gentlemen to whom They belonged, & which They answered but I never had the account from You yet. I read the P.S. of Yours to my Father, who presents his Service to You & will bring up what writeings he has of those you there mention along with him to London this Michaelmas Terme, of which I will remind him at the time He putts up his papers for that Journey, being even more willing and ready to do You all the Service in my Power; even in Amusements too, of which I may reckon Advertisements of all sorts of Literature & the Politer Studies, & for the Thoughts of yourself and any Gentleman You shall think It worth your while to communicate them to, I'll here give you an account of a few of my Collection the Remarkes you make on them as I veryly believe 'em genuine Peices, will much oblige me & my Thursday Companions,[15] whom (I must needs say It of them to my great pleasure) I find come very kindly into enquiries of this Sort. But we have no Occo's Augustino's Ursinus's[16] to consult here.

[*Johnson includes here sketches of six Roman coins from his collection and a sketch of a pointed implement, with a note: 'Question whether this Instrument of Brass & thrice as big be a Stilus.'*]

[p.3] Time permittes Me not to be more accurate now in my writing and drawing but as a word to the wise is sufficient, So such Hints may perhapps serve to unfold, what I understand not, farther that they are Family medals or Coins, & where Shadowd, much obscured by being worn away. I must allso Send you Sir the exact Size & shape of a Large flying Animal which hath 6 Leggs & is of a light Yellow Collour & shadowd with a dark brown

[*Detailed sketch of a winged insect from the underside.*]

this Creature was catched here by a boy playing in the feilds, but whether It be of the moths, [*illegible*] or what other Sort of Fly you can better determine than I am able.

Our Gentlemen & Ladies are about fixing certaine Seasons of Diversion here as one Week in the yeare for Plays, an other for Races, & a monthly day for Assembly for Daunceing & Cards, & They Say I must make One at these their Pastimes: But nothing they've Sett Up gives me the pleasure which the Consort dos at their Musick meetings, which are weekly, & their Conversation Upon Thursdays where wee are now numerous enough, and never faile of Good Company from which a man may realy Improve, if he will; & such is what a rational Creature ought to covett, & is what makes one So desireous of enjoying as much of yours as can be allotted to
    Dear Doctor
        Your most humble Servant
            Maur. Johnson

Spalding Saturday the 14th of Octob 1720

PS.[17] I begg You'll make my Service acceptable to all the Members at the Mitre: Especially my Couzen Johnson, & tell him I thank him for his last which is an answer to what I wrote to him upon my return from Thetford, & which I received just now; & that I'll do as he desires Me in it: Lett the Gentlemen at the Mitre know (I pray) that I have gotten the Inspeximus I promised very fairly transcribed & examined with the E[arl] of Exeters Original, for the press as an Appendix to Registr: Hon Richmond but I believe I needn't feare being too late for the publishing It.[18]

Note to William Stukeley from Adlard Stukeley[19]
Added as postscript to Johnson's letter.

P.S. Dear Doctor

Mr Johnson being so kind to let me have this Opportunity I readily Embrace it to Acquaint you that I should be always glad to see a Letter from you and do hope when you are at Leasure you will be able to give me an ~~acquaint~~ Account of your Success with the Colonell & I should be glad to heare of a Reason from Mr Sowthy why another persons affaire don't go on with more dispatch[20] – All our Freinds in the Country are well & I remain
                                Your Obedient Kinsman
                                Adlard Sq. Stukeley

To Dr William Stukeley
at Mrs Machins in Ormond street
London

1 The South Sea Bubble: see **Letter 17**, n.1.
2 See **Letter 17**, n.2.
3 See **Letter 17**, n.3.
4 Dr Patrick Blair (1680–1728), a Scottish Jacobite surgeon, finally settled in Boston around 1720. He had 'anatomized' or dissected an elephant in Dundee in 1706 and wrote an illustrated account for the Royal Society's *Philosophical Transactions* 27 (1710), 117–68.
5 Maurice Johnson was the SGS's Secretary from 1712 until he became President in 1748.
6 Johnson's spelling of 'connoisseur'; the word was spelt as 'connoiseur' in Bayley's *Dictionary* (1730).
7 See **Letter 17**, n.4. The Gentlemen of the Faculty are the London physicians encouraged by Dr Mead to purchase Bentley's proposed new critical edition of the Greek New Testament. Bentley had been Master of Spalding Grammar School; see Appendix 3.
8 Dr John Mill (1644/5–1707), Principal of St Edmund Hall, Oxford, and author of an edition of the Greek New Testament, published in 1707 and used by Bentley; Robert Estienne (1503–59), French scholar and printer, produced four editions of the Greek New Testament between 1546 and 1557. For full details of Bentley's efforts to produce a new edition of the New Testament, see B. F. Harris, 'Richard Bentley and the text of the Greek Testament', *The Evangelical Quarterly* 34(4) (Oct.–Dec. 1962), 214–20.
9 See Appendix 3.
10 See **Letter 17**, n.7.
11 Thomas Martin (1697–1771: see *ODNB*), Norfolk antiquarian, AS member (1719), SGS (1733).
12 Thomas Martin, *History of Thetford*, ed. Richard Gough (1779), 7: 'But that Thetford continued to be one of the most considerable towns in these parts of England, is manifest from the very name the Romans gave it SITOMAGUS'. Martin derived that name from the Antonine Itinerary (second century AD), where Sitomagus is listed as the first settlement on the road from Venta Icenorum (Caister St Edmund near Norwich) to London. It is now tentatively identified as Ixworth (Suffolk).

13 See **Letter 15**, n.21; the family matter appears to have been discussed in the missing letter, so cannot be identified.
14 Peter Le Neve (see **Letter 15**, n.18); John Hare (c.1668–1720), joint Richmond Herald of Arms 1704, member of the AS in 1717 and associated with Roger Gale in his work on the Honour of Richmond.
15 By this time the SGS was meeting on Thursday evenings, as it still does.
16 Adolpho Occo (1483–1537?), the Spanish bishop Antonio Agustin (1516–86) and Fulvius Ursinus (1534–83) were all numismatists. This gives an idea of the breadth of Johnson's reading.
17 Johnson's postscript is written sideways in the margins of the three sheets of the letter. It has been transcribed in one complete piece at the end of the letter, since Johnson squeezed it into any spare space after the paper had been filled.
18 Roger Gale's work on the documents connected with the Honour of Richmond, *Registrum Honoris de Richmond*, was published in 1723.
19 Adlard Squire Stukeley (1698–1768), William Stukeley's cousin, lived in Holbeach, Stukeley's home town. The details of his letter relate to rentals in Holbeach where Stukeley owned land.
20 Both these matters are unknown.

19. Maurice Johnson to William Stukeley, Spalding, 3 April 1721
Bodleian, MS Eng. misc. c.113, fols 306r–307v

Dear Dr

When Your very obligeing & most Ingenious Letter came hither I was upon the Midland Circuit, from whence I returned not time enough to acknowledge the Favour Sooner than by this Post; & I now heartyly thank You for It, Sir, not only in my own name, but allso in the Name of our Society, to which I am Deputed by the Office I bear amongst Them: They're Senceible in an high Degree of the great honour the Society of Lovers of Antiquity Do Them in So constantly beareing in their Remembrance at their Learned Assemblys So minute a Detachment from the Literati as They are, but assure Yee That They hold well together, Do as much good as is in their Small power, towards the promotion of Learning, & as They encrease considerably for the place in Members, So allso in Reputation, Spalding being the Seat of the Muses in the Fenns; & I assure You the Society of Lovers of Antiquity at the Mitre[1] is as Constant a Toast There every Thursday, as the brightest Belle at Court is with the Gay men of the Town. I am particularly obliged Dear Sir by the Remaines You Sent Me of our poor departed friend Mr Hare,[2] & am Very gladd to have Them, thus makeing much to my Purpose; But can't forbeare Saying I think the Noble Harleyan Library[3] would have been but at a reasonable rate adorned with the Monumenta Vetustatis Kempiana,[4] at the Price I am told the late Possessor left 'em to that most Learned & most Illustrious Family: when Your Leasure permits me The Favour of another Epistle, I begg to be enformed whether the designe of publishing the Draughts of those Curiosities be layd aside [p.2] Or be proceeded in. I have the Latin Account of Them, & think if our Soc. of Lovers of Antiq. could obtain of the proprietors Leave to have them drawn out & engraven by the best hands, It would [*sic*] an Undertaking worthy of that Learned Body. It would render that Clever Account of Them much more Entertaining, be of great use to Designers, & Spread the English name more amongst Foreigne Academies than any thing, as I imagine, They can Undertake; I doubt not but Dr Tanners Seales[5] will be very Curious, & well worth haveing, I long for his New Edition of the Notitia, how gos that on? Doubtles the Remaines of Greece are wondrous, & realy to Me what You relate Surprizeing, But I creditt

You, & from what I read in Sandys, Hill, Prideaux[6] & other Authors of Creditt am convinced the East in every point outshone the rest of the World. So that Horace might justly Say Upon the Conquest of his Countrymen
Græcia capta ferum Victorem cepit, & Artes
Intulit Agresti Latio etc[7]
I lament the loss of the Inscription You mention, & perhapps this Instance of noyseing a thing of that Sort amongst the Barbarians may render It impracticable to gett over any thing more thô even of les value than the Boustrophedon;[8] the instances of monuments so inscribed are rare, as I apprehend; some I have read of; & presume Wee shall at lest have this drawn out & transcribed, I believe You told Me but I have forgotten the Subject of It.

[p.3] My Lord the E[arl] of Pembroke[9] is a most Illustrious Hero, & in all Respects a truly great Man. I recieve aboundance of pleasure from the thoughts of Your Enjoying the Friendship & Conversation of So Learned & Communicative a Scholar & So Incorrupt a Patriot: I much admired the Greatness of the Undertaking of Sforza Duke of Milan related in the Life of Leonardo da Vinci lately published before his Treatise of Painting[10] to lead Water so farr to his Capital, but the Stupendous Aquaducts of Antioch communicated to You by that noble Lord, & the Sicilian Temple of Castor make me cease to wonder at the Labours of that Italian, The Dome of Milan & Church of St Peter are no longer Miracles: Turne but the Eyes of your Imagination Towards Memphis & Babilon, & Europe can afford nothing that can make You Stare. Thô every thing You apply to my Friend comes with satisfaction out of Your hands & I shall (I promise my Self) recieve much from Your reserches in Greece, Yet I must own I could have wishd You had not for the more beautyfull & stupendous, have deserted the Enquirys You was Upon relateing to our brave, or great Ancestors the ~~brave~~ rough, the bold, the Honest Britons. as to your Querie concerning the Scotch Temple[11] You was pleased to favour me with an Etching of, whether It might have been designed a place sacred to Terminus?[12] I find no mention of any to that Deitie amongst the many recounted by Du Choul[13] in his Discours de la Religion des Anciens Romains. Nor in Natalis Comes[14] where he more particularly notes the Several Orders appropriate as It were to the Temples erected to particular Deities. But I find this remarkable passage in Vincentius Chartarius his Imagines Deorum Qui ab Antiquis colebantur, In quibus Simulacra Ritus Cærimoniæ, magnaque ex parte Veterum religio Explicatur. Quarto Edit. Lugduni 1581 pag.23. Fabula de Saturno/ de Lapide a Saturno devorato – Quare scribit Pausanias, in Apollinis Delphii Templo Lapidum non admodum grandem extare, maxima religione custoditum, quem loco Jovis a Saturno devoratum dictitarent, hunc ubi quotidie, sed festis præcipui diebus, aliquid Olei instillassent lana illota circumlegebant. Romani autem eum esse crediderunt,[15] qui pertinaciter cæteris omnibus Diis abeuntibus, Solus in Jovis Capitolini Templo persistere voluit, ideoque pro Termino Deo postea est habitus. In allusion to this (I presume) are the words: Cedo nulli upon the Signet of Erasmus[16] on each side the Figure of Terminus, which was his Cognizance or Device, I have not all his works but in the Catalogue of Them the last as Dr Patin in his Edition of the Morias Encomion[17] tells You is a Treatise De Deo Termino, in which perhapps You may find full Satisfaction as to this point, whether the Auntients ever Erected Temples to that Deitie or no, Ovid as I remember thô he speaks purposely of him in Lib.2 Fastorum affirmes not that he had any peculiar Temple, but only his old place in the Capitol, for there mentioning the Sacred Rites performed to Terminus every where by the Proprietors of the Ground on each Side of him in the Open Air, as Crowning him with Garlands &c the Poet Speaking of the Capitol Says of Terminus

[p.4]   In Æde
 Restitis Et magno cum Jove Templa tenet
Nunc quoque Se Supra ne quid nisi Sidera cernat
 Exiguum in Templi tecta [18]foramen habent
Termine post illud Levitas, tibi Libera non est.
 Quâ positus fueris in Statione mane
Nec Tu Vicino quicquam concede roganti
 Ne videare hominem preposuisse Jovi
Et seu Vomeribus, Seu tu pulsabere rastris
 Clamato, Tuus est hic ager, ille Tuus &c.[19]

[18]foramen habent. Serv. L.ii
Unde in Capitolio Supra pars Tecti patet quæ lapidem ipsum Termini spectat: nam Termino non nisi sub Divo sacrificabatur. Non tamen huic Soli: Cuivis enim Numini, Cui in loco aliqu fulgurito ara erecta, Sine Tegmine Veteres faciebant Sed his plerumque Vid. Vitru. L I Cap. II Neapol

Hence I conjecture there were no Temples erected to that Deitie, & that the Foramen in the Capitol here mentioned , being allso like that in Arthurs Oon, has given Occasion to Some Gentlemen to fancy this a Temple consecrated to Terminus; but you Sir, who are so Conversant with architecture know there were other Rotundas with such Foramens, & my Commentator referrs to Vitruvius Lib. I cap.II[20] – But enough of these wo[o]den Gods.

I am with great respect a most humble Servant to the Gentlemen of the Mitre and most particularly
Dear Doctor Your obliged and obedient
humble Servant and faithfull Friend
        Maur. Johnson jun[r]
Spalding Monday the 3[d] of April 1721

Our old acquaintance Mr Hardy[21] is Very well, I had the pleasure of [his] company for Some Hours at Nottingham, he's about publishing part of Plato – I begg of You to present my service particularly to my couzen Johnson and Dr Manningham.

To Dr William Stukeley at
Mrs Machins near Powys House
Ormond Street
London.

[1] See **Letter 14**, n.1.
[2] John Hare (see **Letter 18**, n.14) had committed suicide on 14 May 1720 by throwing himself into the Thames. In 'the Remaines' Johnson refers to the extensive bibliography of books and manuscripts owned by Hare.
[3] The Harleian Library belonged to the first and second earls of Oxford, the Harley family. In 1753 it was purchased by the Government to form the basis for the British Library.
[4] *Monumenta Vetustatis Kempiana*, ed. Robert Ainsworth (1720) was the account of the antiquarian

collection of John Kemp (1665–1717). This collection was offered to the Harley family for £2,000 but was refused and it was eventually sold at auction for £1,000 in March 1721.

5   Dr Thomas Tanner (1674–1735: see *ODNB*). He was Chancellor of Norwich Diocese and later Bishop of St Asaph, and worked for years to produce a new edition of his *Notitia Monastica* which updated Dugdale's *Monasticon*. It finally appeared in 1744. His other published work was an account of British and Irish authors, *Bibliotheca Britannico-Hibernica*, published in 1748.

6   George Sandys (1578–1644: see *ODNB*), wrote the very popular *A relation of a journey begun an. Dom. 1610*, published 1615, about his travels in the Middle East, which was widely read throughout the seventeenth century; Aaron Hill (1685–1750: see *ODNB*) wrote *A full and just account of the present state of the Ottoman Empire* (1709), a lavishly illustrated volume in which he described his visit to the site of Troy; Humphrey Prideaux (1648–1724: see *ODNB*) wrote *Marmora Oxoniensia* (1676) which included an appendix on Greek chronology.

7   'Captive Greece took her savage victor captive, and introduced the Arts into rural Latium' (Horace, *Epistles* 2, lines 156–7).

8   'Boustrophedon' is a writing style which writes alternate lines in opposite directions, i.e. the first line starts on the left and the second line starts on the right, and so on, 'as the ox turns [when ploughing]'; it was often used in very early Greek writing.

9   See **Letter 16**, n.5.

10   Johnson is referring to *A Treatise of Painting, by Leonardo da Vinci, Translated from the original Italian and adorn'd with a great number of cuts To which is prefix'd the author's life done from the last edition of the French* (London, 1721), 8–9.

11   In 1720/1 Stukeley published his study *Arthur's O'on*, discussing the Roman temple just north of the Antonine Wall, near Falkirk, Scotland, pulled down in 1743. This is best read in Stukeley's proof copy held by the Ashmolean Museum, Oxford. A recent study of Arthur's O'on by I. G. Brown and P. G. Vesey was published in the *Proceedings of the Society of Antiquaries of Scotland* (1989), 353–60.

12   Terminus was the Roman god of boundaries, an appropriate dedication as the Antonine Wall represented the most northerly boundary of Roman territory in Britain.

13   The frontispiece of Guillaume du Choul (1496–1555), *Discours de la Religion des anciens Romains* (1556), shows a circular Roman temple. The evidence he presents is largely derived from illustrated coins and medals.

14   Natale Conti (1520–82) was the author of *Mythologiæ sive explicationis Fabularum*, 10 vols, first published in Venice in 1567; this was the prime European book on mythology in the sixteenth and seventeenth centuries. His approach was via allegory, seeing characterisation in myths as being representative of human ideals. Stukeley in particular used this approach to the past, believing one could locate some of the historical origins of humankind in myths.

15   From this point onwards, the text is written in the margins of the pages, working backwards towards the beginning of the letter. It has all been brought together in this transcription.

16   The motto of Erasmus (*c*.1466–1536) was 'Concedo Nulli' or 'Cedo Nulli': 'I yield to none'. According to A. H. Wesseling, this was 'inspired by an antique gem depicting Terminus, a gift from Alexander Stewart (d.1513), illegitimate son of King James IV of Scotland whom Erasmus tutored for some time while in Italy. The gem reminded Erasmus of the ancient legend recounted by Livy that the sanctuary of Terminus in Rome could not be removed to make way for a temple to Jupiter.' See A. H. Wesseling, 'Devices, Proverbs, Emblems: Hadrianus Junius' *Emblemata* in the light of Erasmus' *Adagia*', in *The Kaleidoscopic Scholarship of Hadrianus Junius 1511–1575: Northern Humanism at the Dawn of the Dutch Golden Age* (Leiden, 2011).

17   *Morias Encomion, or The Praise of Folly* (1st edn 1511), later edited by Dr C. Patin (1633–93) as *Stultitiæ Laus* (1676). Patin was a French physician who worked in Italy and was an expert numismatist. In this edition he produced the first catalogue of Erasmus's work.

18   Johnson has inserted an asterisk at this point in the verse, to refer Stukeley to the quotation which immediately follows the verse. The word 'foramen' means an opening, in this case a circular opening in the roof of a building.

19   A quotation from Ovid's *Fasti* II, lines 669–78, describing the temple of the Roman god Terminus as open to the sky.

20   Vitruvius, *Ten Books on Architecture*, book I, chapter II, refers to the elements of architecture as: order, arrangement, eurythmy, symmetry, propriety and economy.

21   See Appendix 3. Hardy was known as a scholar but did not publish on Plato as far as can be discovered.

20. Maurice Johnson to William Stukeley, Spalding, 3 August 1722
Bodleian, MS Eng. misc. c.113, fol. 308r

Spalding the 3rd of August 1722

Dear Sir

I have been but a very little while come off from the Circuit, where at Nottingham I had the pleasure to See our Friend Mr Hardy[1] well, he presents his Service to You, & I begg leave to joine my Brothers and my own with his to all the Gentlemen at the Mitre:[2] I received the honour of a Letter from Mr Gale[3] with an Enquiry after a Town, or Mannor called Drayton, & describd to be in Marisco de Holand, to which I returnd him as Speedy an answer as I could, & wish It had been in my Power to have done It to his Satisfaction & my own, but I can neither hear of nor find in any Papers &c upon the best Enquiry & Search I have been able to make, any Place whatsoever of that Name in all our County, I begg the Favour of you Sir to present my best Services to that worthy Gentleman &, to assure him from Me that I have done my best Endeavours, hope he'll accept the Intention, & excuse the Hast in which I was forced to write to him.

I am very much delighted with the hopes of being So Soon Master of a Sett of your Maps of this our Native Country[4] which will be a Treasure, both usefull and ornamental; My Brother has been very Industrious to promote your good Designe, & has written to every Gentleman in the Commission residing in Elloe to whom he could transmitt your Proposals, & spake with all those who live in this Town, and given to each of 'em one of your Papers. & you may be sure Sir both my Brother & I will do what lyes in Us to make Them, & other Gentlemen Satisfied That this laudable undertaking of yours is of great use and general Advantage, but there are few who know how to Set a just Value upon the Labours of the Learned, even in Matters of so great Importance. This I am convinced of from the Answears my Brother allmost universaly received to your Proposals, for allthô the greatest part of the Commissioners were willing to have one mapp, yet scarce any body but he & I woud come in to take Setts of them, for They Say, What should They do with more than One & propose to buy them Single at Mr Molls shop[5] when they are published: The World is so unworthy of such publick Benefits That I should now be as farr from persuading my Brother to undertake the exceeding usefull and realy very much wanted Work of a Compleat Collection of the Inquisitions, Statutes & Laws of Sewers, with the Historical Account of the Dreyning preservation and Improvement of our Country, which I acquainted you with, & for which he hath not only the greatest number of Materials, but allso I may (I believe) Say the best abilities of any one private Gentleman, as ever I was desireous of haveing It undertaken by him. – He presents his best Services to you Sir and desires me to let you know That allthô he received your Letter the last of June, yet he could not get your printed proposeals from Baker[6] till Yesterday morning, and ever since he had them he has employd his time in writing to the Commissioners who live out of Town, and in goeing to those in Town, from whom he mett with no better reception than What I have before told you. Wee're told you propose to See Lincolnshire sometime this month, which I am very gladd of, & you shall be most heartyly wellcom to Me; Indeed to make your Mapp correct It would be necessary to take the distances true, which You know may be done in this Levell Country with greater Exactnes than in others, and Yet in all the Mapps I have, or have ever Seen, I think the Towns &c are more misplaced in the parts of Holland, than they're any where else. I have little New to tell you except that about a Fourteenight agone a Woman (sent to Lincoln Gaol from Cowbitt sometime before the last assizes upon the Coroners Committment) was executed by Fire for the murder of her husband, pursuant to the Sentence for that Petit Treason[7] & that one Green of Moulton an old Fellow of Threescore is Committed for a Rape committed since the assizes on the body of is own Daughter, a Girle of about 17 – Our Schole-Masters house is got up the 2^d Story & will be a very neat & Commodious habitation, which he very well deserves[8] – Mr Bott[9] lately a dissenting teacher at Holbeach is or was lately in London to be ordeind by the Lord Bishop of our Diocess & has given out (as I'm told) that my Lord Chancellor will preferr him in the Church – the 17th of last month I received a Letter from my Couzen Johnson dated at Carthagena[10] 10th of January, he tells Me he's very well & grown fatt and that the Country agrees with him of which he gives a pretty long and handsom account and desires me to present his Service to you Sir and all the Gentlemen at the Mitre, He was then to set saile for Porto Bello in about 2 months. When you see Sir Richard Manningham[11] I pray present my Service to him & let him know this & that That Gentleman desires me to remember him to him & his Lady.

    I am Dear Dr
    Your much obliged humble servant & faithfull friend
    Maurice Johnson jun^r

P.S. I have communicated your Queries to Mr Britain[12] & some other Gentlemen of learning and observation of which you know Wee haven't vast numbers, & if you yourself don't come down I begg you'll send me one plate [*of the map*] in the enclosed Frank that Wee may insert what observations I can pick up from them or be able to make my Self and transmitt It to you. I've sent a few of your proposeals to distant parts of the County & both by Letters and in Conversation done all that lyes in my power to Serve you, and the publick indeed for whos benefit this difficult undertaking can only be.

To Doctor William Stukeley
at Mrs Machins in
Ormond Street
London
Fr: Sam. Bracebridge[13]

[1] See **Letter 19**, n.21.
[2] The members of the Antiquarian Society.
[3] For details of this letter from Roger Gale, the elder of the Gale brothers, see *Correspondence*, letter 43 (pp.22–3), which discusses the Domesday Book entry for Drayton in Marisco de Holand, i.e. the village of Drayton by Swineshead (Lincs). After further enquiries, Johnson was able to answer Gale's question satisfactorily.
[4] Stukeley's fine 'Map of the Levels in Lincolnshire commonly called Holland' was finally printed in 1723 (see Illustration 20). Johnson's phrase 'our Native Country' meant the area in which he and Stukeley were born, South Holland in Lincolnshire.
[5] Herman Moll (1654–1732: see *ODNB*). He was called by Stukeley 'a German Engraver on copper' (*Surtees* I, 134). His shop was in Devereux Court, by the Inner Temple and close to Johnson's London lodgings.
[6] There were in London at the time several printers called Baker. However, this might be a reference to Benjamin Barker who worked with Moll on his *Atlas Geographicus* (1709).

7   The murder of a husband was regarded as a 'petty treason' for which the penalty could be burning. The last such execution was in 1726.
8   The Schoolmaster's House still exists in Spalding, in Church Street opposite the church of St Mary and St Nicholas. At that time, the grammar school was housed in one of the chapels of this church.
9   Stukeley, as a Holbeach landowner, would have known of Mr Bott; unfortunately it has not proved possible to identify him further.
10 See Appendix 3. He was waiting at Cartagena in Spain for a ship to Panama, where he was a merchant.
11 See **Letter 17**, n.7.
12 See Appendix 3.
13 Samuel Bracebridge (1673–1735), Tory MP for Tamworth 1710–1723, barrister of the Inner Temple and consequently an associate of Johnson's, for whom he provided this letter-franking.

21. William Stukeley to Maurice Johnson, London, 12 November 1724
Spalding, SGS/Stukeley/9

[Heading in Johnson's hand:] Dr Stukeley writing about publishing his Itinerarium

Dear S^r

I am much disapointed not seeing you in town this term that you might have lookd over what I have wrote to you being the first letter of my itinerarium.[1] tis what occurd to me of our holland,[2] as a comment on the map. likewise a discourse of its former state under the romans & all that I could throw together of that natur. I begin printing after christmas.[3] if you have any thing to add in this part or any other that I have traveld, pray send it before then. I likewise expect according to the good old custom that you send me a modest copy of verses commendatory of such works to be prefixt.[4] Dr Genevier[5] is printing his life of Carausius at Paris to be dedicated to my l[or]d viceroy of Ireland. 16 decr. next I set out with our l[or]d president & vice-president[6] to Wilts. to dig up an old roman city or villa which they have discoverd. Our Society[7] now begins again to meet & fill, where all things goe well. they send their benediction to the cell of Spalding & I my humble service to them & you, being your most affectionat servant

Ormondstr. 12 Nov. 1724   Wm Stukeley

[p.2] pray remember to send me the inscription round Mr Herons[8] br[gap] eagle, & any thing of that sort you have. or of roman antiquitys in holland, what cisterns are those found at Spalding? which I make to be a roman ~~road~~ town, & that a roman road came [to] it directly from clowscross, so passing by herring brig to brig-end causey.[9] I dont desire to infring upon your own work of the state of literature there, but rather to provoke you to publish it. but you will easily guess whats for my purpos as a traveller, & distinguish it from a professd local history. You have many coyns & things found in our parts which prove the romans abode there such like I judg pertinent. as also an account of nobl [sic] familys that formerly dwelt among us, genealogys &c. I have inserted that of the Wakes & Craons.[10] or any particularitys of religious houses dispersd about the country. I am only fearful of incurring a censure I pass upon others, knowing least nearest home, which makes me desirous to pick up somewhat about our native parts.

Dr Jurin is married.¹¹

To Maurice Johnson Junr
  at Spalding
    Lincolnshire
Free Percy

1   The first *Iter* of Stukeley's *Itinerarium Curiosum* (1725), 1–34, is addressed to Johnson.
2   'Our Holland' may be the whole of the Parts of Holland, one of the three old 'Parts' or divisions of Lincolnshire, or perhaps South Holland, the area in which Stukeley and Johnson grew up.
3   The actual publication date of the book was the following year, 1725.
4   Johnson complied with this request, writing what became the third of five Latin commendatory verses published at the beginning of the *Itinerarium Curiosum*.
5   Dr Claude Génébrier (fl.1720–40) was a French physician and numismatist who eventually published his work on the Roman Emperor Carausius, *Histoire de Carausius Empereur de la Grande Bretagne*, in 1740. For Carausius, see **Letter 22**, n.5. Génébrier was to dedicate the book to John Carteret (1690–1763), first Earl of Granville and Viceroy of Ireland.
6   The 'Lord President' of the AS was Algernon Seymour (1684–1750), Earl of Hertford and later seventh Duke of Somerset, President of the AS 1724–49. The Vice-President was Roger Gale: see **Letter 13**, n.8.
7   The AS, of which Stukeley was still Secretary.
8   Henry Heron, MP: see **Letter 6**, n.1. This is some form of Roman antiquity that he owns, probably a coin.
9   Clows Cross is two miles south of Crowland; Herring Bridge is in the parish of Pinchbeck, north of Spalding. Bridge End Causeway is further north, across a noted marshy area on the road between Grantham and Donington. It dates from early mediæval times, when it was maintained by a cell of Gilbertine monks and lay brothers attached to Sempringham Priory.
10   The family of Wake of Lincolnshire, of French origins, became associated in the popular mind with Hereward the Wake after Charles Kingsley's nineteenth-century novel. The Craons were another mediæval Lincolnshire family of French origins.
11   See Appendix 3.

22. Maurice Johnson to William Stukeley, Lincoln,¹ 8 March 1725
Bodleian, MS Eng. misc. c.113, fol.309r–v

                        Lincoln Monday the 8th of March 1724/5
Dear Doctor

Since I had the pleasure of seeing you I received the following Account of the Roman Coines found at Wells [*sic*]² an Antient Barony near Allford in the Wolds of this County with about 100. of Them all very fair from my Friend Mr Gonville of Allford³ – They are chiefly of Gallienus, Victorinus, Claudius Goth. & the Tetrici⁴ with one of Carausius⁵ & another of a young Prince, happly his Son – Thus much of his Letter is to your purpose – 'As some Labourers were at work ditching upon Well walk about half a quarter of a mile from the house they found in an earthen pott about a foot deep between Six and Seaven hundred such peices of Coin as these I herewith Send you which are all I could pick up & near that another pot with coins in it which they took to be Silver but they all Mildred to powder when they touched them – they carry their work on in a direct line and have found Severall places in the earth blacker than the other & in those black places dig up Cinders & ashes & in One a large square Stone like an hearth Stone which makes me beleive there has been some Roman Camp there – the pot is broke to peices Soe that I could not get any of it to send You. If these peices be of any Vallue to you be pleased to let me know & I'le get all I can of 'em, pray let me know what I may venture to give a peice for them' – Sir I entreat you to make my Service acceptable to the Soc.[6] & have little to add but that the present Abbot of Croyland[7] complaines that the Tenant of the Grantee of the Scite of the Convent makes a Trade of digging out the Stone Coffins of his Venerable Prædecessors & selling them for Hogg Troughs – I once hoped I should have been proprietor of the Medal of Carausius which fell into Captn Pownall's hands,[8] he haveing expressly promised Me, that if ever he parted with It, It should be to Me: but notwithstanding that, & what you was so kind to say to him on my behalf, he hath dispos'd of It to another: so that being carryd out of the Country & [p.2] in the hands of a Man of Great Fortune to whom I am entirely a stranger I Question much whether I may ever see it again, therefore as I think You told Me you toke a drawing of It (which I had not Leisure to do here,) I begg of you Sir to Send Me down a Copy of your Drawing in Answer directed to Me at Spalding where I shall be in less than 3 Weeks: Which I desire you to tell Dr Degg[9] with my humble Service & Lady Oldfeilds – and that he is admitted a Member of our Little Soc; which hopes much for the Honour of Your & his presence this Summer: as also my Couzen H Johnsons & Sir Richard[10] another (Two other of our worthy Members) to whom & to Sir Richard You'll much oblige Me in presenting my Services – But for the future my Friend I shall excuse you & my Self so much of this recommendatory part & taking It for granted you'll do me this good Office to Such gentlemen as you know Me attach'd to – Endeavour to use Time & paper more to your Satisfaction.

The Bishop of Derry's Son, Mr Nicholson, is made Chancellor of this Church of Lincoln in the room of Dr Mandeville.[11] They say our Bishops son Mr Reynolds[12] is to be made Archdeacon of Lincoln. I think I have told You all the news I know and am

      Dear Doctor
       Your very much obliged &
       Faithfull humble servant
        Maur Johnson junr

To Dr Stukeley at Mrs Machins
near Powys House in
 Ormond street
  London.

[1] Johnson is on the legal Circuit, attending the Midland Assizes at Lincoln.
[2] Well, south of Alford. In 1725 two urns containing 600 Roman coins were found, according to Thomas Allen, *The History of the County of Lincoln* (1834), 169.
[3] See **Letter 1**, n.22.
[4] Later Roman emperors of the third century AD: Gallienus (lived approx. 213–68) held imperial power in the West from 253, killed as Emperor in 268; Victorinus controlled the breakaway Gallic empire (Gaul, Germania and Britannia) from 269 to his death in 271; Claudius Gothicus (213–79) became Emperor on the death of Gallienus in 268 and died of smallpox; Tetricus I followed Victorinus as ruler of the Gallic empire from 271 to 274 and was deposed by the Emperor Aurelian; Tetricus II, his son, ruled the short-lived Gallic empire but was deposed together with his father in 274. Both of the latter survived and held minor offices in the re-united Roman Empire. These dates help to date this hoard of coins as a whole.

5   Carausius (see his entry in *ODNB*). Between AD 286 and 293 he successfully controlled imperial Roman power in Gallia and Britain. He was a central figure from Roman times for Johnson and Stukeley, who used numismatic evidence to clarify the role of Carausius and his successor Allectus, who murdered Carausius in 293. Modern scholars have concluded that Carausius was not a native of Britain, as Stukeley suggested, but probably from what is today Flanders. See P. J. Casey, *Carausius and Allectus* (1994).
6   The SGS.
7   The Rector of Crowland in 1725 was the Revd Barnaby Goche, SGS 1723; Robert Hunter was Lord of the Manor of Croyland in the 1720s. See Appendix 3 for their entries.
8   William Pownall (1692–1735), army officer, lived in Lincoln and collected coins and books, particularly the Anglo-Saxon Blickling Homilies which he sold to Sir Richard Ellys (see **Letter 15**, n.22) in the 1720s.
9   See Appendix 3.
10 Sir Richard Manningham.
11 The Revd Joseph Nicholson MA LLD, Prebendary of Lincoln (1714), Rector of Mareham le Fen (1714–28), Chancellor of Lincoln Cathedral (1725–28); John Mandeville (1677–1725), Chancellor of Lincoln Cathedral (1695–1725).
12 The Revd George Reynolds LLD (1677–1769), Archdeacon of Lincoln (1725–69), Subdean of Lincoln (1732–69).

[*The document SGS/Stukeley/9A, kept with the Stukeley papers at Spalding is: 'Extract from my Journal Friday July the 15th 1726'. It is not a letter, but an account of a visit to Repton and a meeting with an 88-year-old man who, forty years previously, had helped to excavate stone coffins containing human skeletons. It is not in the handwriting of either William Stukeley or Maurice Johnson. The identification with Stukeley is made in a pencil note 'P Stukeley' written probably by a previous SGS officer.*]

[84. William Stukeley to Maurice Johnson, Grantham, soon after 13 April 1728
This letter does not form part of the SGS archive of Stukeley's letters. It is in the Wingfield Collection of the Northamptonshire Record Office. We have included a transcription of it as **Letter 84** in the Additional Letters section.]

23. Maurice Johnson to William Stukeley, Spalding, 16 April 1728
Bodleian, MS Eng. misc. c.113, fols 313r–314v

My Dear Friend   Spalding 16 April 1728
  Thô this my Congratulation[1] come late thrô my being disappointed by Unforeseen Busyness of the Pleasure I proposed to my Self of giving It You by Word of Mouth, as absent Friends may Still in some measure by this meanes Supply that defect which our being So Severd (thô in the Same Province) causes. And I've long Enjoy'd the Sweets of Such a Correspondence with You: Believe me my Friend as You've ever from our Infancy had my hearty good Wishes, So in Nothing more than in what You have now the Enjoyment of a Bosom Friend, a Constant Partner of your privat houres, One who can render Even darkness less disagreeable, In whom You may on the Grandest & on the most trivial affaires of Human Life talke freely & Confide in for her own Sake: I now must go on and add my farther Wishes for your fullfilling the Sequel of Entring in this happy

state: May you be blessd with a Numerous Issue, that Cement of Love, & pledge of Affection. The rare Endowments & Qualifications of your Spouse must render her a most agreeable Consort: To her I must presume, You now leave the politer Studies, and haveing put 'Em into good hands say Musas colimus Severiores[2] – Your profession tho pleasant in the Study must be painfull in the Practice. The Miseries of human Nature & your Compassion must make It So to You, & you'd need have Some Relief: You've long since discarded the Muses And Mr Gale tells Me you've left off the pursuit of Antiquities – But I understand It only of taking those pleasant Tours round the different parts of our Island. – Not that you're capable of despising a Knowledge which you have gaind with So much labour, & can't but be of some Use in Every State of Life & thrô a dry Study is Even a Relief to Me after the Toiles & Fatigue of one which has the less of Amusement in It of any. I long to See You & could my Spouse Travaile, (but She's generaly disqualified for that,)[3] Wee would wait on You & Your Lady this Summer: when You bring her to see Your Relations in these parts, Wee shall hope for the Honour of your Good Company here: I thought It hard that you shoud be over and not let me See you, but suppose you made no stay here abouts. The Weather has So mended our ways that It will soon be good Travailing and I must to London again next Month:[4] I doubt not of Homes being as delectable to You as It can be to Me & In that You have the advantage, Your Avocations from It are not So farr, nor Your absences from your family for So long a time together. After Terme I come hither charmd with the Delights of Nature, thô It be Nature in the Fenns. I a good deale cultivate Vegetables[5] of all Sorts from the Oak to the Sedums, and have so Encouraged a Love for Gardening in my Children that Wee are a Family of Botanists, and perhapps It's better for Us that our bounds are Contracted by a River, a Churchyard &c that tho Wee may praise the more Spatious Wee have but Small Ground to Cultivate. Between that & my Study which [*illegible*] I spend my Time, & rarely Very rarely Seek any Field sports or take the Diversions [p.2] of this Town Which are Bowling, Billiards &c for I seldom (but to Visitt a Neighbour) Stirr from home (when I can be there) Except on Thursday Evenings to our Society the Members whereof Especialy my Father & Brother[6] are much at your Service: Wee have fitted up an handsom Square Roome Sufficient to hold Two dozen Commodiously. It is pressed Round,[7] & under lock & key. Each class[8] has Something for the Rudiments of a Musæum which Encreaseth Weekly and Wee have a pretty little Garden Spott & a Good Cellar belonging to It: there Wee take a Sober Glass are Chearfull together & Communicate Our thoughts to Each Other in a quiet & Sociable way Once a Week. I usualy take the Opportunity of makeing my Visitts before the Company meets there, & have the rest of the Week pretty much to my Self. Wee have lately lost Three great Men who honoured us with their Names Amongst the list of Honourary Members Sir Izaac Newton,[9] Mr Green the Surgeon[10] & the Dean of Durham.[11] But have the Honour of a Supply of our present worthy Diocesan my Lord Bishop of Lincoln,[12] & his Excellency the Governor of Jamaica,[13] & the Dean of Peterborough,[14] Who have all been amongst us, & much approve our Society, to my great Consolation; Every man having an Affection for his own Product. In this I hope I may hereafter be thought to have been a Friend to the whole Neighbourhood & a Sort of Father to this place, if by this Meanes the Arts & Sciences are advanced in It, & the People betterd by It. I am certain Our publick Library[15] is very much encreased, and frequented; Our Free Schole well accommodated with good Editions of the Classicks &c & Wee converse weekly with young Gentlemen at the Society who are the Ornaments of It now, and were Children in their Accidences[16] when I had the good happ to Lay the foundations of our first meeting together on the foot It now Stands in 1709/10, our first Proposals were subscribed in 1712: I hear Sir you have formd a Soc. in your Neighbourhood & am gladd of It[17] – some Gentlemen at Stamford whereof Dr Coleby is one have done the like,[18] that which was at Wisbeach (I hear) is droppd.[19]

[p.3] You'll oblige Me Sir in Spareing me So much of your Leisure now & then as to let Me know how You Do and Permitting Me to renew that Correspondence, which by Your Removal from London, And the Important affaires of Marrying and Fixing your Family & with the fitting up Your House & Gardens, Has been a while Interupted and the longer by my haveing been now a Second time prevented the pleasure of Renewing It in person. As to the State of Physick & Physicians in our Parts Your old Friend Dr Nutton[20] is Still alive & gives his Advice to Such patients as Attend him at home & there only, for He very rarely is Seen abroa'd. Our Country tho' much Overflowd of late is Now very healthfull. Dr Dinham has bought your Couzen Hinsons house which he before was Tenant to;[21] Dr Mitchell[22] is Sometimes here & at Other times at Boston, I have heard his Relations in London are desireous he should go & fix there. At Peterborough they told Me Dr Parker in a great Measure declines busyness as dos Dr Muzard at Oundle, which brings Dr King of Stamford into a pretty many Familys thereabouts.[23] Wee had not long Since an Irish Gentleman who was bred at Montpellier cast away & lay long sick here, he on his recovery was Introduced to the Soc. & read Some Lectures there on an Arm prepard & sent from London by young Mr Mitchell, and on the Nose, Eye & Eare. the Soc. complimented him with a peice of Money. He professed Chyrurgery & Chemistry and was (as he sayd) going to read Lectures at Cambridge. I heare he has since fled, having been in danger by taking a body out of Croyland Church yard to dissect at Thorney. The Church warden of Croyland whose Son is Apprentice to a Chyrurgeon at Thorney is under prosecution about it.[24] When You See him pray present my Service to your Neighbour Mr Doughtie[25] of whom I have had now & then the Satisfaction of hearing of your Health.

   I am My Friend
     Your very much Obliged and Faithfull Servant
      Maur Johnson junr

P.S. All our Family particularly my Spouse present their humble Services to You & Your Lady and wish You much Joy. Let the seale of this Letter [*seal missing*] remind you of our antient band of Farther Friendship with those Noble Lords of the Elder of which Mr Vertue is Engraving a good Likeness.[26]

To
Dr Stukeley at his House
 in Grantham
  Lincolnshire
Turn at Stilton   Present.

---

1 William Stukeley married Frances Williamson of Allington near Grantham on 19 December 1727.

2   'We follow the more serious Muses' or 'Muses of a graver spirit', a quotation from Martial, *Epigrams* IX, xi, 16–17.

3   Mrs Elizabeth Johnson was frequently pregnant, giving birth to well over twenty children (records suggest twenty-five), sometimes twins, and was consequently very restricted in ability to travel.

4   In May he would be in London for the legal Term.

5   He uses 'vegetables' in the eighteenth-century sense of 'plants' which included trees. He cultivated trees and plants in his extensive gardens at Ayscoughfee Hall, particularly flowers newly introduced into England.

6   See Appendix 3.

7   'Fitted with cupboards and bookcases all round'.

8   Johnson refers to the SGS's locked bookshelves, where the books were classified by subject-matter.

9   Sir Isaac Newton became a member of the SGS in 1724. For an account of Johnson's interview with Newton, see *Correspondence*, 26–7 (letter 58).

10 Edward Green: see **Letter 14**, n.7.

11 The Revd John Montague (1655–1728). See Appendix 3.

12 The Revd Richard Reynolds (1674–1743). See Appendix 3.

13 See **Letter 22**, n.7.

14 The Revd Francis Lockier (1669–1740). See Appendix 3.

15 He refers here to the books of the SGS library and those of the parish church library which the Society looked after. 'Public' here means available to members of the Society or close associates, not its current meaning.

16 He means those just starting their education by learning Latin grammar.

17 In 1727 Stukeley organised a club which met monthly, first at Croxton Kerrial (Leics) and then more regularly at the village of Belvoir, by Belvoir Castle on the Leics/Lincs border.

18 Dr Dixon Coleby MD (1680–1756), physician at St Martin's in Stamford, became a member of the SGS in 1733. Johnson refers here to the first attempt to found a learned society in Stamford in the 1720s. Stukeley eventually re-established a society in Stamford, the Brazen Nose Society, which flourished in 1736–1737.

19 The Wisbech club was established around the same time as the SGS; its library was catalogued by Dr Richard Middleton Massey and Richard Lake in 1718. Johnson was a member. Its closure came about when Dr Massey left Wisbech for London and Lake died.

20 Dr John Nutton MD (?1657–*c*.1732), a doctor in Spalding.

21 See Appendix 3. He bought the house on London Road from Captain Joseph Hinson, who became a member of the SGS in 1742.

22 It is impossible to ascertain which Dr Mitchell is referred to here; four Dr Mitchells were members of the SGS. This is most probably Dr Robert Mitchell, called 'Scoto-Britannus' in the SGS members' list, whose medical training was at Reims and Leiden; he later moved to Epsom in Surrey, but corresponded with the SGS from there.

23 Dr William Parker, who trained at Leiden, was a physician at Peterborough during this period; Dr Philip Musard MD, who trained at Utrecht, lived in Oundle where his wife Ann died in 1737; Dr John King MD (1696–1728: see *ODNB*), SGS member in 1725, was a Stamford physician and classical scholar. He died of fever in October 1728.

24 This story is recounted in SGS Minute Book 1, fol.121r. On 28 December 1727 a Mr Burck attended the meeting, 'a professor of Anatomy & Chemistry [he] was Introduced from Mr Michael Mitchell ... of whom he had procured a left Arm of an human Body to the Muscles very curiously prepared so as thereby he demonstrated their use. Also that of the Nerves leading to the Eye etc., the Eare & Nose & Braine And the structure of the Braine & Eye from those of a Calfe. The Soc. ordered the Treasurer to give him half a Guinea.'

25 In June 1729 Stukeley as trustee signed letters of administration for the will of William Doughty Gentleman of Grantham.

26 See **Letter 13**, n.16. Vertue made hundreds of engraved portraits, so without the seal it is not possible to identify this one.

24. Maurice Johnson to William Stukeley, Spalding, 31 January 1728/9
Bodleian, MS Eng. misc. c.113, fols 315r–316r

Spalding the last of Jany 1728/9

Dear Dr

I return you many Thanks for, but not till this very morning did recieve, yours dated 18 of last Month, So Long have I been delayd the pleasure Mr Beatniffs[1] Arch Letter and your adequate Account have given Me. Go on my Friend to Cultivate your Villa, Sacred (as mine) to Sence and the Taste of the Few. I long to Enjoy the Improvements you've made, to take a turn in that Sylva Academi[2] & in your Druid Temple Querere Verum, prepared by that profound Silence & those Sentiments the very Sight of the Cenotaph of the reverd OTÜS[3] must Inspire & Command; I have not so Sacred a soulcase to record, but having lately retrievd for 6d of Croyland Guzzle (where I spent the last week on a Commission of Chancery)[4] the Convex Capital of a Column of the Benedictine Order or none, but of as grand & simple a Taste as the Asiatick one given Us by Tournefort[5] from a Temple of Juno at Samos somewhat of this Form: (*sketch of a carved capital*) I purpose to place the same in the Centre of our Coach Yard and thereon A Vase of Ely Earth conteining an Aloe that Type of Longevity so helpefull to our Most useful Animal the Horse, And thereunder (on her decease) to repose my Belle-Savage[6] who from Kitten small was taken out of our Neighbouring Forest has For these half Score Yeares last past been the Vigilant Guard of Our Study & Garden, Defending this from Hares, Shrews & all Vermine which would have preyd on the Vegetables, & those from Rats & Mice; who thô they could not have devourd my Fossils, Petrifactions or Metallick Treasures might the many Curious Communications & drawings I possess of Your hand & by Your Favour & Value more being Attended with those Illustrations: – Our Society so much my Pride & Care being more peculiarly my production is a Thriving Girle: & has of late had many Topping Woers; Women especialy at her Age of 18 yrs[7] must be bashfull – but It being Notified that his Grace the Duke of Bedford & my Good Lord the Earl of Oxford[8] have Gallant Inclinations towards her, Wee the Regular Members, her Counsell & Guardians, have made an Order that those & the following Patrons Shall be Invited, & on Acceptance notified by a Regular Member be, & become Members thereof Either Regular, or Honorary as they please.

[p.2] The Other Gentlemen Wee would willingly associate are –[9]
Our Countryman His Grace the Lord Archbishop of Cant. sometime our diocesan – our Countryman His Grace the Duke of Ancaster, G.C. our Lord Lieutenant – our Neighbour the Earle of Westmorland First Lord Com. of Trade – our Countryman Mr Dymock Champion of England, Lord of Scrivelsby – the Lord Bishop of London, sometime our Diocesan – our Countryman Mr Gardiner, Subdean of Lincoln, a Good divine, Poet and Florist, our Countryman Mr Chancellor Newell, Chancellor and VG of the Dioces, Revd Dr Stanley Dean of St Asaph, a Generous good Man, Dr Michael Stanhope DD both Landed in our Parts & the Rt honble the Earle of Lincoln: For who's Family & Father's Memory Wee have aboundant Esteem: you See Sir Ambition like Other Strong Weeds grows & thrives rankly in a Fenn Village. But without these Great Names we have had Those of [10] Newton, Britain, King, Lake, Green, Waren, Curtis, Bellinger, the Honble Dr Mountague Dean of Durham & Moreton all Good & worthy Members deceased. As Wee're

honoured with those of the Living: Bertie of Sutton, Lord Coleraine, Degg, Ellis of Grantham, Roger Gale, the Gays, Gilby Recorder of Lincoln, Green student in your Profession, skillful in Botany & a Good General Scholar, Draughtsman & Penman & my Brother Secretary of our Soc:, Major General Hunter, Governor of Jamaica, Hardy, Hepburn of Stamford, Heron, Holmes, Jurin, the Lynns, good Lawyers, Astronomers & draughtsmen, Dr Francis Lockyer dean of Peterborough, Dr Reynolds our Lord Bishop, & his son our Proctor in Convocation, Massey, Mitchell, Your own & another dear old Friend of Mine (who must also be an Ornament to any Society, being beloved by all who know him) [p.3] Mat Snow of the Middle Temple Esq, Protonothary of the high Court of Chancery, the Honble Talbot Touchett, Trafford, Toller, Sir Fr. Whichcott, Wesley the divine Bard & Coll. Williamson Governor of the Tower, cum Mult. of Lords and private Gentlemen of all Professions; But these I've named evince a Subject of any rank, rather recieves the Honour by associating, & That the Ballance of the Dowry is of the Girles Side who's so Amply provided for.

Wee highly Good Sir approve the proposal of a meeting[11] at ~~Brigg End Causeway & if that House or those nearest can Furnish but half a dozen Bedds~~ Sleeford a Town of good Accommodation and where I should chose [*sic*] being the place Wee always Baite at & on all Accounts most Convenient. Wee may there spend 2 days Each Spring, another each Summer Season without any Inconveniences which I desire may be the Thursdays in Lincoln Assize Weeks which allways beginning on the Monday usually holds till Thursday morning. You Sir will be pleasd to Engage the learned & Worthy Gentlemen you Mencion,
1. The Revd Mr Masson of Aswarby[12]
2. "   " Mr Vernon[13]
3. Capt. Pownall[14]
4. Mr Hardy[15]
5. & Mr Warburton to come[16]
6. with your selfe thither at those times & I'll endeavour to Engage Sir Francis Whichcote   7.[17]
the Revd Mr Neve our Treasurer   8.
Revd Mr Milles   9.
Mr Bolton of Grey's Inne   10.
my Brother a Templar   11.
All Members of our Society as a detachment thereof and For promoting learning in Lincolnshire to Give you and your Friends these 2 Annual Meeting [*sic*] there with Dear Dr
Your most Affectionate Friend & humble Servant
         Maur Johnson junr 12.

P.S. as You was pleased to name but half a Dozen I sett just as many down against you. But lest they should Some of them faile; to make our Meetings fuller, I will name to You 6 more on our Side, which if you approve of making up 24 Send Me the Rest of the Names directed in your Answer for me at the Widdows Coffee house in Devereaux Court London, whither I go on Monday: Joseph Banks of Revesby Esq,[17] George Lynn junr of the Inner Temple Esq, Mr Stevens, Revd Mr Ray, Mr Richards & my Brother Secretary young Dr Green – adieu & Let Me have Your Answer.

All our Family services attend your Lady and your Self, Wee're putting Mr Bullen[18] in a Way of Living –

[p.4] I lose the Lest Bit of the Paper, but Entertain you with an Epigram of good Lady Hertford's[19] on the Stream you've so well delineated at Marlborough Mount being frozen up:

Poor Stream held Captive by the Frost
Thy Current numb'd, Its' brightness lost,
Compell'd thy Journey to delay,
& in these narrower Borders stay.
Thy Fortune is to mine ally'd
Both by Superiour Force are ty'd:
Different Captivities Wee prove,
You're bound by Cold, & I by Love.

To Dr Stukeley
At his house in Grantham
Lincolnshire
Turn at Stilton

[1] This is probably the Revd Samuel Beatniff (c.1703–81), curate and later Rector of Gaywood (Norfolk), who lived at King's Lynn; the letter, which would have given more information, has not survived.

[2] As **Letter 84** indicates, Stukeley made extensive improvements to the gardens of his house in Grantham, describing them in a letter to Samuel Gale (*Surtees* I, 208–9). See also Francesca Scoones, 'Dr William Stukeley's house at Grantham', *Georgian Group Journal* 9 (1999), and Matthew Reeve, 'Of Druids, the Gothick and the origins of architecture: the garden design of William Stukeley (1687–1765)', *British Art Journal* 13(3) (2012).

[3] 'Otus' is the Latin name for the horned owl; the Duchess of Ancaster had sent one to Stukeley but it died and he buried it in his garden. See *Surtees* I, 118.

[4] Johnson had apparently purchased the capital of a stone column surviving from the ruins of the Benedictine Abbey of Croyland; for a sketch of it, see SGS, Minute Book 2, fol.3r. In the minutes, Johnson recorded that he 'purchased and procured this Capital to be imported by boat & placed in Ayscoughfee hall Court Yard'. Johnson and Stukeley were anxious to preserve the remains of the Abbey, which were being destroyed by some local people.

[5] Johnson gives the source of this comment in SGS, Minute Book 2, fol.3r: 'vide Tournefort's Voyages to the Levant vol.1 p.318'. The title of the first edition of 1718, presumably the one used by Johnson, is *A Voyage into the Levant Volume I*, by Joseph Pilton de Tournefort.

[6] Johnson's wild cat, now tamed by him, which protects his documents from mice and rats: see **Letter 15**.

[7] Here Johnson is happy with the date of 1710 for the formation of the SGS, though it was not formally organised until 1712.

[8] On 30 January (see SGS, Minute Book 2, fol.3r), the Society ordered 'That His Grace the Most Noble Prince Wriothesley Duke of Bedford ... & the Right Honble Edward Earle of Oxford & Earle Mortimer ... be Invited' to become members. Edward Harley, third Earl of Oxford (see *ODNB*) accepted membership but there is no record of the Duke of Bedford becoming a member.

[9] None of this group accepted membership: William Wake (1657–1737: see *ODNB*), Archbishop of Canterbury, who later ordained Stukeley; Peregrine Bertie (1686–1742), second Duke of Ancaster – however, his namesake and distant relative, a lawyer living in Leyton (Essex), did join the SGS, which can lead to confusion; Thomas Fane (1683–1736), sixth Earl of Westmorland, though his brother John Fane the seventh Earl did become a member in 1744; Lewis Dymoke of Scrivelsby (Lincs), hereditary Champion of England; Edmund Gibson (1669–1748: see *ODNB*), Bishop of Lincoln (1715–23) and then Bishop of London (1723–48); James Gardiner (1689–1732: see *ODNB*), Subdean of Lincoln (1704–32), author and translator, interested in studying and growing flowering plants, which is the eighteenth-century meaning of 'florist'; George Newell, Vicar-General and Archdeacon from 1708;

William Stanley (1642–1731: see *ODNB*), Vice-Chancellor of Oxford (1693–94), Dean of St Asaph (1707–31) – Thomas Hearne made unpleasant comments about him, which indicates he was a capable person; probably Dr Michael Stanhope (1681–1737), Canon of St Paul's Cathedral and later Canon of Windsor; George Clinton (1718–1730), eighth Earl of Lincoln, son of Henry Clinton the seventh Earl (1684–1728), Paymaster to the Forces (1715–20) – still only a boy but son of a well-known and popular father. All of them were intended to be honorary members to bring lustre to the SGS. This is an ambitious recruitment programme, though Johnson was successful in acquiring some high-ranking noble and ecclesiastical members.

[10] This second list is of forty men who had accepted membership of the SGS. For details of the most significant of them, see their individual entries in Appendix 3.

[11] There follows Johnson's suggestion for a new learned 'literary' society to meet at the time of the Lincoln Assizes. A meeting was arranged for establishing it at Ancaster; see the following letters. Stukeley and Johnson were to provide an equal number of suitable members.

[12] The Revd John Masson, Rector of Aswarby near Sleaford (1714–47), not an SGS member.

[13] Probably the Revd Edward Vernon, Rector of Muston (Leics), not an SGS member; he was a member of a society at Belvoir (Leics), organised by Stukeley in the late 1720s.

[14] See **Letter 22**, n.8.

[15] The Revd John Hardy: see Appendix 3.

[16] William Warburton (1698–1779; see *ODNB*), author and clergyman; educated at Newark (Notts), ordained in 1723, receiving the living of Brant Broughton (Lincs) where he became a friend of Stukeley who was living in Grantham. Later he became Bishop of Gloucester.

[17] The next five proposed members of the new society were all SGS members, as were the six people on the following reserve list in the postscript; see their individual entries in Appendix 3.

[18] Mr Bullen has not been identified.

[19] Frances, Countess of Hertford (1699–1754), wife of the Earl of Hertford, who lived at Marlborough; she was a poet and patron of poets, particularly James Thomson and Stephen Duck 'the Thresher Poet'.

25. William Stukeley to Maurice Johnson, Grantham, 15 February 1729
Spalding, SGS/Stukeley/10

[Heading in Maurice Johnson's hand:] Dr Stukeley for forming a general Society of Literati to meet at Ancaster

Dear S^r

I rec^d yours & since then have seen Dr Musard,[1] Mr Hibbins[2] & Mr Arnet[3] who met at Grantham by appointment. I told them of the scheme projected between you & me.[4] they approve of it much but desire the place may be Ancaster[5] where we shall not be so much exposd to vulgar observation; & have as good accommodation. tis not above 5 mile out of your way & all heath road, which is but an hours ride. beside tis a roman castle seated in the very bosom of the most delightful heath imaginable. I admire the place every time I see it. I shall meet you there on the thursday of the assize week by noon. but I expect the first time that you come home with us at night, to make me a visit. bring capt. Pownal[6] along with you. I shall bring Mr Smith[7] our lecturer, a very good scholar & order as many as I can to meet us. the verses you sent me of Lady Hertfords produc'd the following answer.

Hail to thee, Kennet, gentle Stream,
of Hertfords Muse the happy theme!
'twas not chill frost that caus'd thy stay,
in wonder thou forgot'st thy way.

Soft as thy wave her tuneful voice,
thy Splendor yeilds to her bright eyes.
Nor grieve ye, at your kindly fate,
by being fixt more fortunate.
for thou cans't from thy watery glass
reflect the image of her face.
Nor could she liberty approve,
stedfast in noble Seymours love.[8]

Pray remember me to my Antiquarian friends, such as I beleive have some kind remembrance of me, which are but a few.
    I am Your most obliged
      & obedient Servant
      Wm Stukeley
    Grantham 15 Feb. 1728–9

To Maurice Johnson Esqr
  at the Widows coffeehouse[9]
   Devereux court
  Strand near Temple barr
   London.

[1] See **Letter 23**, n.23.
[2] Probably James Hibbins, an associate of Stukeley's in Holbeach where his son James, who later became a successful London doctor, was born in 1712.
[3] This may be the Revd George Arnet MA (Edinburgh), Vicar of Holbeach (1711–21).
[4] See **Letter 24** for the projected society of South Lincolnshire gentlemen which was to meet at Ancaster at the time of the Lincoln Assizes.
[5] The Society held only one meeting, despite the convenience of Ancaster as a meeting-place on Ermine Street (or the High Dyke), the old Roman road south from Lincoln to Grantham and beyond.
[6] See **Letter 22**, n.8.
[7] The Revd William Smith MA, Lecturer or Reader at St Wulfram's church, Grantham, appointed in 1717.
[8] See **Letter 24**. Stukeley would appreciate the references to the River Kennet which passed near Avebury and to Frances Seymour, wife of his patron Edward Seymour, Earl of Hertford.
[9] Johnson was meeting fellow-barristers in London to transact business during the legal Term, using a popular coffee-house near the Temple as his *poste restante* for his mail, as was the custom.

26. Maurice Johnson to William Stukeley, London, 15 February 1729
Bodleian, MS Eng. misc. c.113, fols 317r–318v

          Tuesday the 15 of Febry 1728/9
Dear Dr
 On receipt of Your Last favour & farther Recollection I find Frydays in Lincoln Assize Weeks must be the days of Biennial Converse the Judges sometimes in this Assize not leaving Lincoln till that morning So let the Days be Frydays & for Your reasons who allways give good ones to Me. The place of our Meeting together be Ancastre as You propose, thô Sleford be more in Confinio Paludum & Bruere, Inter nos.[1] I'll remember to Let Pownall[2] know your Commands. But as

Wee shall be most of Us Members of our Society at Spalding which as Mr R Gale says like a lively Young Girle has Outgrown her Mother[3] with submission to you as a Brother Fennman & Member thereof I desire the Sanction of that Worthy Sett of Gentlemen which will in my Opinion give Us & our Soc. Assembling as a Committé of that Body of Literati great Creditt & therefore On my return home I shall propose the same to them to Induce some Very Valuable Members thereof to Attend It at so great a distance & that I may Let my Darling Project see I have Interest enough through my Friendship with you & other Friends on your side the County to do it Creditt. I Can't hear any thing has been done since I was in Town last Terme at Either Society here[4] worth sending You. I'm obliged to You for Your fine Answer to the fine Ladys Epigram & say with Ovid – Quam celere e toto redit mens Orbe Stiveclus – instead of Sabinus.[5] Mr Banks[6] has a good picture of the Old Countess of desmond. I hope the Earl of Oxford[7] will become a Member & Patron of our Society at Spalding his Lordship having declard in our favour. The Honble and Revd Mr Cecill[8] shewd Me this day some fine Intaglias & Medaglions he has brought from Greece. My Brother & Cousin G. Lynn[9] with Me are
        Yours affectionatly
        Maur Johnson[10]

[fol.318v]
To Dr Stukeley at
his House in
Grantham
Lincolnshire

[In Stukeley's hand:][11]
Mr Hardy
Mr Peck
Warburton
    Vernon
    Gibber
    Smith
    Bacon

[1] 'On the boundaries of the Fens and the Heath, between us': Johnson had originally preferred Sleaford as the meeting-place for the new society.
[2] See **Letter 22**, n.8.
[3] This is a reference to a comment by Roger Gale that the SGS was now more flourishing than its 'parent' society the AS; for a transcription of Gale's letter to Johnson, see *Correspondence*, 39–40.
[4] The RS and the AS in London.
[5] This is Johnson's version of a quotation from Ovid's *Amores* 2.18: 'Quam celer e toto rediit mens orbe Sabinus …' ('How quickly Sabinus has returned with replies from across the whole world'). Johnson substitutes 'Stiveclus', a Latinised form of 'Stukeley', for 'Sabinus'.
[6] This is either Joseph Banks MP (1665–1727) or his son Joseph Banks MP (1695–1741), both owners of Revesby Abbey (Lincs). One of these became a member of the SGS in 1722 and the latter, who became High Sheriff of Lincolnshire in 1735, was the uncle of the famous naturalist Sir Joseph Banks (1745–1820) who became a member of the SGS in 1768. The portrait is of Katherine Fitzgerald, Countess of Desmond (c.1530–1604 but claimed to be a centenarian). Her portrait is in the National Portrait Gallery, London.
[7] Edward Harley, second Earl of Oxford, did become a member of the SGS in 1729.

8   The Hon. and Revd Charles Cecil (1695–1737), Rector of Bishop's Hatfield (Herts); Bishop of Bristol (1733–4), Bishop of Bangor (1734–7).
9   George Lynn Senior. See Appendix 3.
10   This is an unusual form of Johnson's signature; he usually signed himself 'M (or Maur.) Johnson junior' until his father's death in 1747.
11   This is Stukeley's list of proposed members for the Ancaster society. For John Hardy, see his entry in Appendix 3; for Francis Peck, William Warburton and Edward Vernon, see **Letter 24**; for William Smith, see **Letter 25**. It is not certain which member of the extensive Lincolnshire and Norfolk Bacon family is mentioned here, and Mr Gibber cannot be identified.

27. William Stukeley to Maurice Johnson, Grantham, 13 March 1729
Spalding, SGS/Stukeley/11

Dear S^r

This morning M^{dm} Welby[1] of Denton sent for me in hast to one in her family ill. which unluckily deprives me of the pleasure of meeting you at Ancaster. but hope & beg that you would come to Grantham to night. I have enclosd a discourse[2] I designd to have read to you if you have nothing better you may read it for me & send it again. My Service waits on all the gentlemen there & I am (in hast)
       Yours W Stukeley
       13 Mar. 1728–9

To
Maurice Johnson Esqr
 at Ancaster

1   The Welby family lived at Denton Manor (Lincs) and were among Stukeley's aristocratic patients.
2   Stukeley was thus unable to attend the Ancaster meeting. His paper on the history of Threekingham (Lincs) was read for him by Johnson and is kept in the SGS archive.

[*SGS/Stukeley/10A, dated 14 March 1728/9, is a paper written by Stukeley on the history and name of the Lincolnshire village of Threekingham, which Stukeley had intended to read at the meeting of the Ancaster society. As his letter of 13 March 1729 makes clear, he was unable to attend and so sent the paper to Johnson to be read in his absence. It is transcribed in Appendix 1.*]

28. Maurice Johnson to William Stukeley, Spalding, 24 March 1729
Bodleian, MS Eng. misc. c.113, fols 319r–320r

          Spalding Monday the 24 March 1728/9
Dear Dr
 Tis with much pleasure I think of & returne You many Thanks for the most agreeable Reception & Entertainment I received so very lately at Your house & the favouring Me with your learned Discourse prepared for our Ancaster Congress which I had the pleasure last Thursday of reading to our Soc. Who present You Sir with their Services & thanks for the honour done them in remembering them

in so advantageous a manner for which I in particular am the more obliged to You, & thô the distance of 20 Miles[1] prevents our So frequent meeting as Wee wish, Yet I trust these projected biennial meetings at Ancaster if they take effect and hold as I hope they may, & the Meanes of entercourse thus afforded us by the Post will keep up a mutual notice of what occurs worthy of It in Holland, or Kesteven in which you're so pleasantly seated and as You desir'd be pleased to take what has occurrd to Me concerning Grantham.

GRANTHAM, Lincolnshire, Grantham wap[entake] Kesteven Spelm[an]. Villare Angl[icum].

Post Paunton, visitur Grantham, oppidum non infrequens,1. Schola a Richardo Foxo Wintoniensi Episcopo & 2. Templo Specioso exornatum cujus Sacra Pyramis admirandam in Altitudinem surgit, & Fabulis est famigerata.

Cl. Camden Brit. Corit. 478 which Holland translates literally without any addition fo. 537.[2]

[*Two inserted notes by Maurice Johnson, referring to 1. and 2. above*] 1. Fuller says fo.157 of his Worthies that this Bishop was born at Grantham & dyd 1528. You have a good Picture of him at the College at Grantham & another in C.C.Oxon.[3]

2. 'Tis height makes Grantham steeple stand awry. Cleveland p.66[4]

Remigius Episcopalem sedem a Dorkester Lindum transtulit, & nobilem illam Basilicam Lindensem, quæ nunc exstat condidit. Inveniuntur frequenter ab Aratoribus ultra superiorem partem Urbis, 3. numismata vetustissima unde Inditium est ampliorem olim in ea parte fuisse Civitatem, & conjectura est recentiores ad Urbis partes inferiores, aquæ gratia, descendisse. Qui enim inferiora loca habitant Eyia circumdantur. Est autem Eya flu[men] Withamo fluvio nomen præripiens.

[*Inserted note by Johnson, referring to 3. above*] 3. penes Domino Ricardo Ellys Bart & MJ[5]

Withamus, sic dictus ab Witham op: oritur 4. octavo supra Grantham miliario tami fonte & cum Granthamum alluit nec latus, nec profundi Alvei est. Sed multis auctus rivulis antequam Lindum perveniat celebris est, navicularum piscatoriarum patiens, sed prope Lindum nomine mutate Eya vocatur. Eoque in loco, ubi nomen mutat, brachium expandit, quod Urbis inferiora loca circumvagatur, excursoque uno aut duobus miliaribus corpori parenti se sociat. Hinc forte, Eya flu: dictus quod Urbis inferiorem partem insulam faciat. Nec me interim fallit, quosdam esse qui Eiam pro simplici aquæ vocabulo accipiant.

Sunt qui adfirmant Lindim oriri apud Witham, aut non longe ab eo pago. Witham autem 4 passuum millibus distat a Granthamo in ipsa pene via quæ ducit a Londinio Grantamum. Sunt qui Lindim flu: Ree Ang: appellant. Sed illud generale magnorum apud Anglos fluminem nomen.[6]

Lelands Collectanea Tom.III pag. 33 Ed [*illegible*][7]

Ey signifies an Island as in Shipisey & Ea or Eau a Water or River as Wee find frequently in our Records Brun Ea, Suth Eau, Aqua de Welland, Aqua de Glenn, & so described in the boundaries of our old Deeds & Inquisicons & Verdicts for ascertaining the boundaries of this County & Its divisions.

[p.2] CANTENNIS: Ita enim ausus sum reponere in Antonino pro vitioso Causennis, vel Gausennis, ut edidit Simlerus, quod nihili esse necesse est. Solutè quis scripserit Cant en (vel an) isc, sive Ambitus vel Flexura Aquæ. Hæc urbs hodie

Grantham est in Majoribus Icenis sive Lindensi Conventu. Siquidem idem sonat Britannis Grant quod & Cant, sicuti nos supra docuimus in voce Ad Tavum: Et Grantham etiam ibridâ compositione profertur pro Grant avon, Amnis scilicet curvatura. Camdeno videtur esse Brig Castreton, sive Arx ad Pontem in Iceno[rum] dynastiâ Rotelandiâ, sive Regione Putri[norum]. Verum repugnant Antonini Milliaria.
Baxteri Glossar Antiq. Britan. P.65, 66, & supra 55[8]

This is a New Light, but by which I own I am not much informed. I find nothing which seems to me like It on Ptolemey's Tables & Anonym. Ravenno.[9] Mr Gales Itinerary of Antoninus from Suritas Ed. At Colen 1600 1 Vol fol 742[10]

Iter a Londinio Luguvallum ad Vallum M.P. ccccxliii. Inter Durobrivas M.P. xxxv. Causennim M.P. xxx. Lindum M.P. xxvi.

In the next Tour Iter à Londinio Lindum M.P. CLVI. No mention of It where I should most have expected to have met with this Cantennis if Grantham there. from Leicester Ratis (Ratæ or Ragæ) the rout runs thus: Ratis M.P.XII Verometum M.P. XIII Margidunum M.P. XIII Ad Pontem M.P. VII Crococolanum M.P. VII Lindum M.P. XII.
And in Var. Lect. Suritæ ad Calcem addit. no notice of any name of any other place in any MSS or of any Various Reading to Countenance this Conciept. I may here add thô something remarkable is noted of most great Towns, & even of some less (as Spalding for instance) in that Venerable Monument of middle aged Authority the Sax. Chron.[11] Yet on diligent Search I cannot therein find any mention of Grantham, As I do of most other Towns of any note in the County. Nor in Venerable Bede, Gildas, Asser Menev., Matt. Paris, Walsingham, the X scrip. & 3 Volls of our old Historians published by Bishop Fell & Dean Gale [12] in the well compiled Indexes of all which I searched for It. Not but that I believe Grantham has long been a Burrough & Mercat of good consideration as such I find It sent

    1 Ed. 3. to a Councell at Westminster Ralph Browne Will Game & John de Barnaby

MSS Collect. Brown Willys me penes[13]

    Ed.4 7. Parliament at Westminster Will. Husee was returnd for Grantham the only Burgess. Perhaps the same Sir William Husee who 2 4 Ed. was Lord C[hief] J[ustice] of the King's Bench; [14]

    12. Parliament at Westminster John Harrington & Gilbert Husee.[15]

    From hence to Edward 6 time the publick Records furnish no Accounts of the Burgesses (if any were) returnd for Grantham to any Great Councell or Parliament for which therefore as Mr Willis writes me You must Consult the Archives of the Burough.

[p.3] In the 4th yeare of King Henry IV [1403] the Townsmen, Homines Villatæ, of Grantham in Lincolnshire were charged to the king in a Roll of Escheate with certain goods taken upon a Felon. They are charged by the name of John del Botery & Sociis suis Constabulariis Villæ de Grantham & John de Harryngton & others Men of the same Town. They are impleaded in the Exchequer at the

1. Maurice Johnson as a young man, artist unknown
   (Spalding Gentlemen's Society)

2. A mezzotint by John Smith c. 1720 from the portrait of Stukeley by Sir Godfrey Kneller. This engraving was given to the SGS to show that Stukeley had been a Mason and the portrait frame has the following screwed-in title: REV. WILLIAM STUKELEY, M.D. INITIATED 1721 Presented by BRO A. F. CALVERT P. G. Std
(National Portrait Gallery, London)

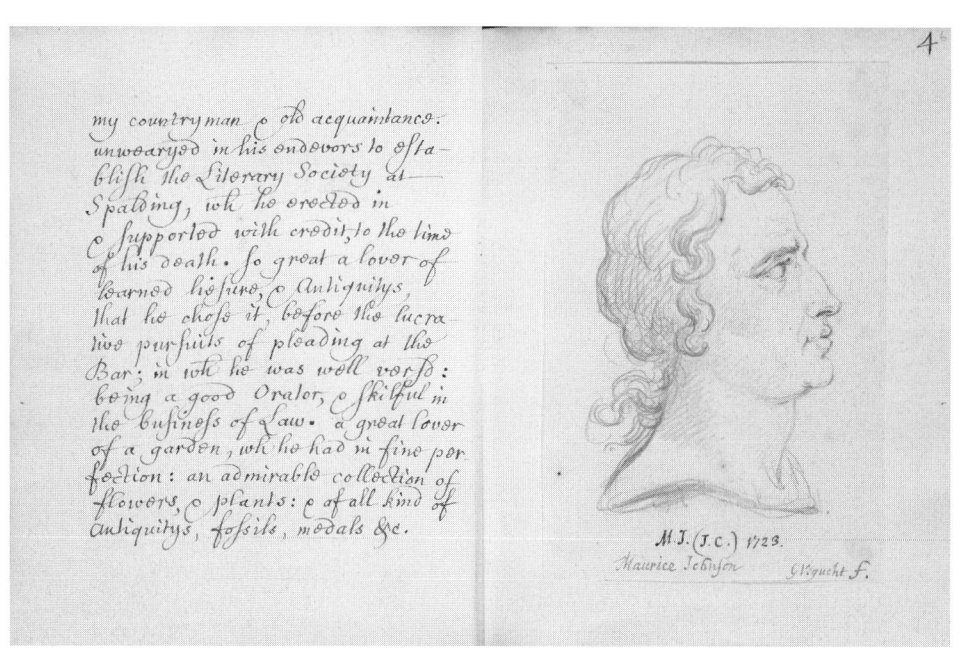

3. Sketch of Johnson by Gerard Vandergucht, with obituary notes by Stukeley
(Bodleian Library, Oxford)

4. Ayscoughfee Hall, Spalding, home of Maurice Johnson; watercolour
by Hilkiah Burgess, 1818
(Spalding Gentlemen's Society)

5. Drawing by Stukeley of himself and his first wife, Frances (née Williamson) (Bodleian Library, Oxford)

6. The Grammar School, Spalding, where the SGS hoped to establish a museum;
watercolour by Hilkiah Burgess, 1820
(Spalding Gentlemen's Society)

7. Sketch by Stukeley of his house in Boston, 1714
(Bodleian Library, Oxford)

is a bason or amphitheater 100 foot diameter 5 foot deep: planted with tall fruittrees of various sorts, as apples, pears, plumbs, walnuts, mulberrys, services, medlars, cherrys. this makes an agreable shade & is the sylva academy for philosophers to walk in. tis underfoot grass only. quite round all this is a broad grass walk, & the wall is high enough only to exclude thieves but not to hinder the prospect of the country. for I have raised the whole accordingly. the little diagram I have sketched out will make you understand the nature of it. I have a great deal of gardenroom more to the east & north planted much with fruittrees &c but I have done nothing at them yet. & the river runs at the bottom. the corners by the amphitheater have alcoves & seats to the south of the house is my hermitage vineyard, so call'd because the walls are all planted with vines, & in the wall I have built a grotto or cell sufficiently romantic. the plain of the garden is full of the most odoriferous herbs. herein is a stone terrestrial globe set conform to the true globe. & my roman altar from northumberland in a ragged niche overgrown with ivy &c. in a wall I have placed this inscription cut in large letters. in a battering wall (as technically call'd) which I built to support my terrace to the east I have plac't the following. it faces the river.

by these things you may guess I have throughly fixt my lares my fortune, my ambition. & truly no one was ever more satisfyd with their change of their station than my self. not having the least inclination ever to see London again. but treat it with the utmost contempt, or as the angel says in Milton and with retorted scorn his back he turnd on those proud towers to swift destruction doom'd.

in the time I spent there I took a full draught of what London could

on this side lyeth a long Orchard 110 [...] on the S side lyes a long slope & a Parterre

N

feet

100

yard

Hall [...] hermitage

I had ye pleasure of being this retirement every [...] at [...] in 1729 1728

W

BEATAE
TRANQVILLITATI
P.
W: STVKELEY 1726

FLVMINA
AMEM
SILVASQVE
INGLORIVS.
CHYNDONAX.
1726

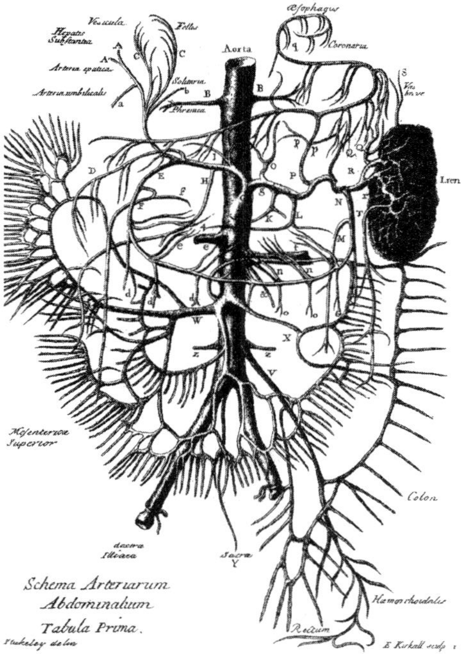

10. Engraving showing arterial network of the spleen, from Stukeley's pamphlet, *Of the Spleen* (1723)

9. The church of St George the Martyr, Queen Square, London, where Stukeley was Rector from 1747 to 1765. From Richard Tames, *Bloomsbury Past* (1993), 36.

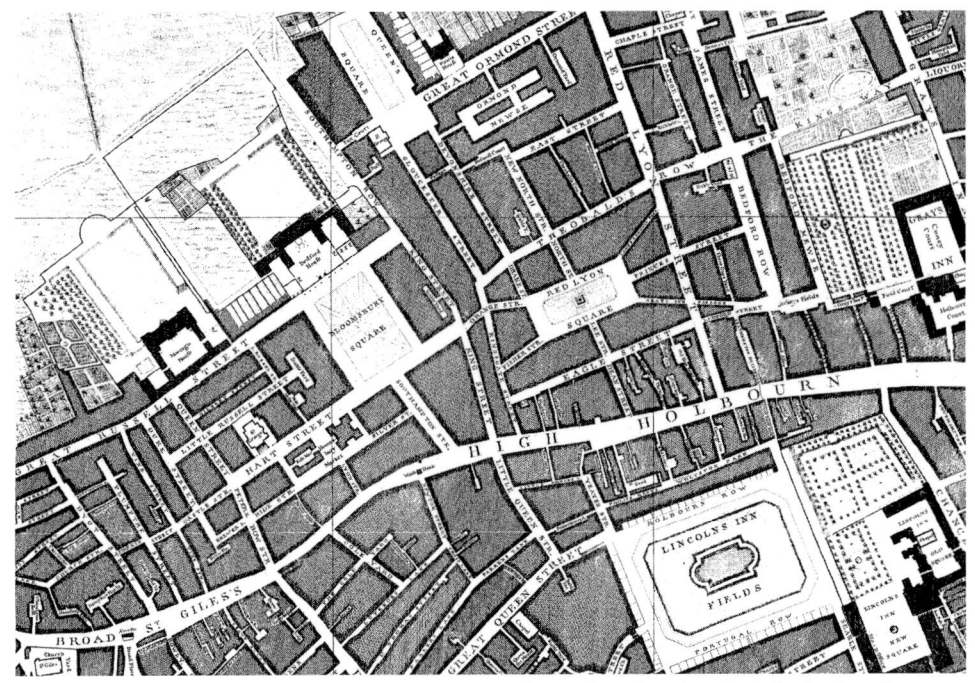

11. Detail from map of the northern edge of London, showing Stukeley's church in Queen Square, by John Rocque, 1746
(Spalding Gentlemen's Society)

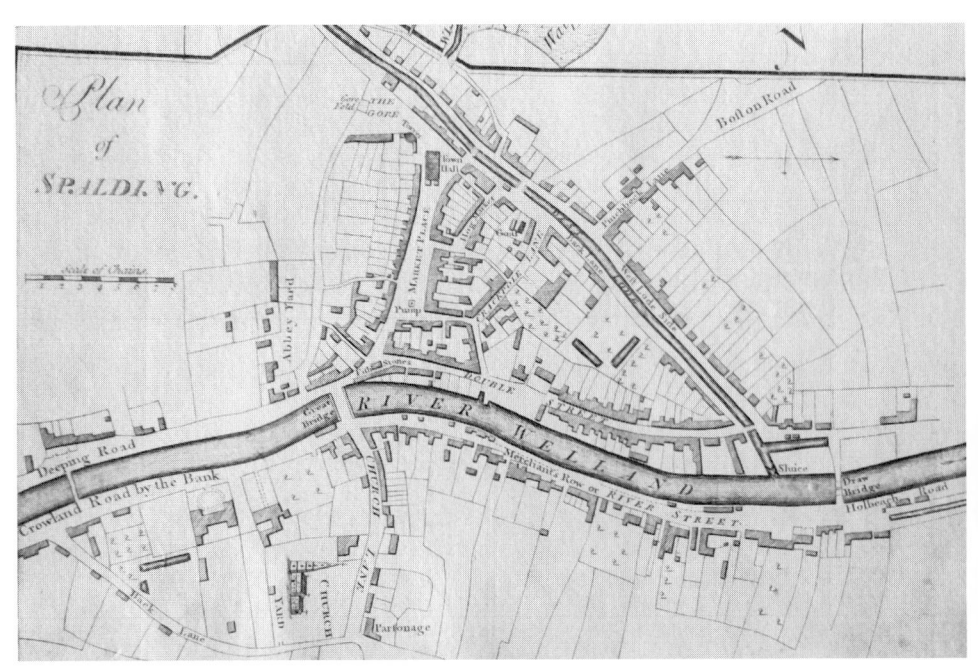

12. Map of Spalding from Capt. Andrew Armstrong's map of Lincolnshire, 1778
(Spalding Gentlemen's Society)

Kings suit by that Name or Style. And in the Exchequer Judgement is entred, That the said John del Botery & the Constables & Other Townsmen of Grantham be discharged of part of the said Goods And That They be charged with the price of Other part thereof.

Maddox of the Cities Towns & Buroughs of England Cap. X S.xix fol. 188.[16] the Record is Very long & there set forth at length from Mich. Commun[ar]ia 4 H. 4 Rot.37.[17]

To prove that In fact Particular persons Members of Corporat Bodies have been chargd by the King with a Debt due to him from their Corporal Community. the like Instances are given in the same Chapter of London, Lincoln, Stamford &c. Hill 40 Eliz.R[egina] I have this Memorandum in a MS Extract. Notar. & Receptor Scaccar. ex Rememorator. Rs remaner. de div[er]sis Chartis olim Moyle Farmer Protonotar.

De Diversis Finibus & Amerciamentis impositis sup[er] Johannem Blewett in Cur. Baron. de Grantham una. cum causis impositionis Eorundem his miss. & tre de Certiorar. Ro. 174 Eodem MS fo. 44 No.xxii[18]

AD 1523 26 H[enry] 8 Cap. 14. By the Statute for Nomination of Suffragans (Bishops) & Consecration. Grantham is one of the Towns enacted to be taken and Accepted for the See of a Bishop Suffragan of this Realme, or Coadjutorial (Gibs. Codex Tit. V. cviii. 155) the Rt Revd Father in God John Longland S.T.P. Confessor to the King and Chancellour of the University of Oxford then Lord Bishop of the Diocees of Lincoln. (Godwyn 310. Heylin 118.)[19]

But I have not read of any person ever appointed Suffragan of Grantham.[20]

Upon revising my Transcripts of Domesday book, I find, the parts of Kesteven are wanting, I haveing only Some part of Lindsey, and what relates to Spalding cum Membris.[21] but as I have never met with any other place called Grantham be pleased to observe. That in the charter of Osmund Bishop of Sarum & Chancellor of England he (the said Bishop) bestows on that Cathedral Church Ecclesias de Granham (perhaps for Grantham) cum decimis cæterisque ibidem adjacentibus Anno Domini 1091.[22] for the provision of Canons sæcular called in King H. II's Confirm. Ecclesiam de Graham. I know not if Grantham be thereby meant. Vide Dugdale 2 part of Monasticon Anglican. fol.375/431 378/21.1[23]

  This is all I can at present send you with the Services of all our Family to your Lady and Self Who am
Dear Dr
     Your very much obliged and affect. Friend
      Maur. Johnson junr.

To Dr Stukeley at his House
in Grantham
Lincolnshire
Turn at Stilton.

---

[1] Twenty miles from Spalding to Grantham; part of the route, near Bridge End, was very marshy at the time, which would have made it a lengthy journey.

[2] Philemon Holland (1602) translated this passage from Camden's *Britannia* as: 'After Paunton we come to Grantham, a town of good resort, adorned and set out with a schoole built by Richard Fox,

Bishop of Winchester, and with a faire Church, have a spire-steeple of a mighty height, whereof there goe many fabulous tales' (Holland's translation, ed. Dana F. Sutton, 2004). In this letter Johnson is supplying Stukeley with quotations relating to the history of Grantham, from books which Johnson owns but to which Stukeley does not have access.

3   Richard Fox (1447/8–1528: see *ODNB*), Bishop of Winchester; born at Ropsley near Grantham and a pupil of Grantham Grammar School. He founded Corpus Christi College, Oxford, in 1517. Johnson's numbering for his additional notes has been left full-size, to distinguish it from the present editors' end-notes.

4   John Cleveland (1613–58: see *ODNB*), poet and author of *The Works of John Cleveland* (1687). This quotation comes from Cleveland's poem *An Elegy upon the Archbishop of Canterbury* about the death of William Laud, Archbishop of Canterbury, executed in 1645. The poem ends: 'No churchman can be Innocent and High,/ 'Tis height makes Grantham Steeple stand awry'. The very lofty steeple of St Wulfram's church, Grantham, is not 'awry' or crooked, but the church has one pinnacle of the tower slightly thicker than the others, to contain a spiral staircase, which gives it a somewhat uneven appearance.

5   'In the possession of Sir Richard Ellys, Baronet, and M[aurice] J[ohnson]'; both were keen numismatists, specialising in Roman coins. For Sir Richard Ellys, see Appendix 3. The quotation from Leland continues after this inserted note.

6   A quotation from John Leland (1503–52: see *ODNB*), *Antiquarii de Rebus Britannicis Collectanea*, ed. Thomas Hearne (1711), iii. 33: 'Remigius transferred the Episcopal seat from Dorchester to Lincoln and founded that noble Cathedral which now stands. Beyond the upper part of the city ploughmen often find very old coins, which indicate that once there was a larger city in those parts and it is conjectured that the more recent inhabitants have descended to the lower parts of the city for the sake of the water. Those who live in the lower areas are surrounded by the river Eye. The Eye takes over the name from the River Witham. The Witham, so called from the village of Witham, rises eight miles above Grantham, in a spring, and when it flows through Grantham it is neither broad nor deep in its bed. But, increased by many streams before it comes to Lincoln, it is famous for carrying fishing boats, but near Lincoln its name is changed and it is called the Eye. In that place where its name is changed, it puts out an arm, which flows around the lower parts of the city, and having branched off for one or two miles it rejoins the body of its parent. Thence perhaps it is called the Eye because it makes an island of the lower part of the city. I also know that some people call it the Eye because this is simply a word for 'water'. [Johnson's Note 3 occurs here: see n.5]. There are those who claim that the Lindis rises in Witham, or not far from that area. But Witham is four miles from Grantham, on the same road which leads from London to Grantham. There are those who call the river Lindis 'Ree' in English. But the other is the most generally used name among the English.'

7   The quotation from Leland ends here; the following paragraph is Johnson's own comment.

8   This quotation is taken directly from Johnson's own copy of William Baxter, *Glossarium antiquitatum Britannicarum* (London, 1719): 'Cantennis: I have dared to put this into the Antonine Itinerary [see note 10] instead of the incorrect Causennis, or Gausennis, as Simlerus edited it, because they are not necessary. The answer is that someone wrote "Cant en (or an) isc", or "the circuit or bend in the water". This town is today Grantham in the region of the Greater Iceni or Lindissi. Probably Grant and Cant sounded the same to the Britons, just as we learned in the pronunciation of Ad Tavum: And Grantham shows a hybrid composition of "Grant avon" that is to say "a curve in the river". Camden thought it was Brig Casterton or the Citadel at the Bridge in the Icenian domain of Rutland, or the Rotten Region [Baxter's misreading of the first syllable 'Rot' referring to 'red soil']. The Antonine list of miles refutes this.' Johnson's note on p.55 of Camden says 'Certe Saxones Britannicarum Originum ignari, sæpius mutabant Avon in finibus Nominum, in suum Ham, veluti in Grantham pro Grant avon, & similibus aliis.'

9   Johnson is attempting to make sense of the quotation from Baxter which offers the rather spurious claim that 'Cantennis' is a hybrid Celtic/Latin name for Grantham, based on an explanation that it means 'a bend in the river'; this would offer evidence for a Roman origin for Grantham. Unfortunately for Baxter, the Witham's course through Grantham and area is relatively straight; the major bend towards the coast comes much further north, at Lincoln. Johnson cites authorities who do not use this name: Claudius Ptolemy's account of the British Isles, written in the second century AD, was first printed around 1480; the Ravenna Cosmography was a list of hundreds of place-names collected in the seventh century by a cleric in Ravenna, then the capital of the western Roman Empire. 'Causennæ' is now accepted as the Roman name for Ancaster, but see **Letter 83**, n.12 for further discussion of its situation.

10   Thomas Gale (1636–1702: see *ODNB*), Dean of York and father of Roger and Samuel Gale,

friends of Johnson and Stukeley. Thomas Gale prepared an edition of *Antonini iter Britanniarum* [The Antonine Itinerary], published in 1709 by Roger Gale. Johnson refers here to several of the fifteen journeys listed in this work, particularly Iter V and Iter VI. These journeys were Roman military routes between Londinium and Lindum Colonia [London and Lincoln]. Johnson and Stukeley were attempting to locate the names listed in them in relation to the towns and villages of their own times. They mistook 'Ad Pontem', now accepted as East Stoke (Notts), for Ponton, south of Grantham, and this led to complex misunderstandings as they tried to make the final stages of the route use Ermine Street instead of the Fosse Way to which the Antonine route evidently refers. All the place-names mentioned in the Antonine routes can be found correctly placed on the Ordnance Survey map of Roman Britain. Jerome Surita (1512–1580), a Spanish historian, edited the Antonine Itinerary, published in Cologne in 1600; this text was referred to by the Gales in their publication.

11   The Anglo-Saxon Chronicle.

12   Johnson has also searched other authoritative documents in vain for the name 'Cantennis': Bede (d.630), *Ecclesiastical History of the English Nation*; Gildas (*c.*504–70), *The Ruin of Britain*; Asser (d.908/9), *Life of King Alfred*; Matthew Paris (*c.*1200–59), a Benedictine monk, cartographer and author, known for his *Historia Anglorum*; Thomas Walsingham (*c.*1340–1422), Prior of Wymondham (Norfolk), who wrote his *Chronica Majora* around 1400–20 as a continuation of Matthew Paris's work; Bishop John Fell (1625–1708), Bishop of Oxford and Dean of Christ Church, patron of Thomas Gale's and William Fulman's publication of *Historia Anglicæ Scriptores*, three well-known volumes of transcriptions of British historical writings in Latin (1684, 1687 and 1691). The third volume of the latter contained the first printed version of Nennius's *Historia Brittonum*. This gives some indication of Johnson's breadth of reading.

13   This happened in 1327, i.e. the first year of the reign of King Edward III. Johnson's note means '[In the] manuscript collection of Browne Willis, in my possession'. For Browne Willis, see Appendix 3.

14   Sir William Hussey senior (1443–95: see *ODNB*), Chief Justice of the King's Bench. His grandson William Hussey (*c.*1490–1556) was MP for Grantham in 1529.

15   This refers to a Parliament held at Westminster in the twelfth year of the reign of Edward IV, i.e. 1473. The *History of Parliament* volumes for 1422–1504 have not yet been published.

16   Thomas Madox (1666–1727) became Historiographer Royal in 1714. He published an account of the Exchequer of the Kings of England in 1711. The volume referred to here is *Firma Burgi, an historical essay concerning the Cities, Towns and Boroughs of England, taken from Records* (1723), an account of the process of taxation of English towns and boroughs, yielding income either to the Crown or to individuals.

17   This is a reference to documents from the year 1403, quoted in *Firma Burgi*.

18   The year specified is 1598; unfortunately the documents cannot be located.

19   This refers to efforts in 1523 to develop bishoprics in England by the appointment of suffragan bishops, in effect assistants to the diocesan bishops. Bishop John Longland (d.1547) was Bishop of Lincoln 1521–47. The reference to 'Gibs. Codex' is to *Codex Juris Ecclesiastici Anglicani* by Edmund Gibson, later Bishop of Lincoln.

20   Johnson was correct here; the first suffragan bishop of Grantham was Welbore MacCarthy, appointed in 1905.

21   Johnson did not have transcripts from Domesday Book (1086) of the entries for the Parts of Kesteven, which include Grantham. Stukeley certainly referred to these in his research.

22   'The churches of Gran[t]ham with the tithes and those adjacent to them'. The Prebends of North and South Grantham were both in the gift of the Bishop of Salisbury: see M. Honeybone, *The Book of Grantham* (1980), 76, for an explanation of this.

23   Johnson refers here to William Dugdale's monumental study, *Monasticon Anglicanum* (3 vols, London, 1655–73).

29. Maurice Johnson to William Stukeley, Spalding, 2 October 1730
Bodleian, MS Eng. misc. c.113, fols 321r–322r

Spalding 2d October 1730

Dear Dr

I take the Opportunity by our Gardiner who brings You this, & will e'er he returns from his Fathers on Tuesday Morning early wait upon You for an Answer, of Enquiring after Your & Your Ladys health, And acquainting You That I propose to my Self the pleasure of meeting You at Deeping[1] with my Kinsman Mr Ray[2] (who expresses himself highly Obliged to You) the Next time, when he has given our Society hopes of bringing from You to communicate to Them a Dissertation of Yours on a passage in the Evangelist,[3] Unus eorum Surgens nomine Agabus signicavit per Spiritum λιμον μεγαν μελλειν εσεσθαι εφ' όλ[*illegible*] quæ fuit sub Claudio Cæsare as St Luke records in the Acts of the holy Apostles Cap.xi v.28.[4] Illustrated by some Medal or Coine of that Emperor, In the Account of whose Life by Suetonius Wee read Urbis Annonæque curam solicitissime Semper egit, And again sub AUC 797 L:V Arctiore autem Annona ob assiduas Sterilitates, detentus quondam medio Foro a turbâ, convitiisque ac simul fragminibus panis ita instratus+, (+Instead of Instratus, Bapt. Egnatius says in his Edition It is sometimes read Infestatus.) ut ægre nec nisi postico evadere in Palatium valuerit,[5] on this last passage Jos. Scaliger says Duce Fames notabiles sub Claudio, Altera Claudio Aug II C. Licinio Cæcina COSS. Altera Consulibus Suffectis Rufo & Pompeio Silvano, Imperatore Claudio Cons. IV designato, quo tempore Regina Adiabenorum Helena, coemptâ ex Ægypto annona, famem Judææ levavit. Auct. Josepho Lib. xx. cap. 3. Atque hæc (says that Great Man) est Fames illa quam prædixit Agabus. Triennium interest inter utriusque Famis tempus.[6]

Aurelius Victor in Cæsaribus de Claudio says just as he has spoken of the Conquests of his Generals & his British Expedition: Adhuc Annonæ egestas composita quam Caligula induxerat, dum adactis toto Orbe Navigiis pervium mare theatris curribusque damno publico efficere contendit. Corn. Tacitus Annales. LXII having related many Prodigies at Rome about the time (sub AUC 804) that Nero was brought into favour with Claudius by Agrippina, says Frugum quoque egestas, & orta ex eo Fames, in prodigium excipiebatur. Nec oculis occulti tantum questus. Sed jura reddentem Claudium circum vasere clamoribus turbidis, pulsamque in extremam Fori partem urgebant, [p.2] donec Militum globo infestos prorupit. Quindecim dierum alimenta Urbi non amplius superfuisse constitit, magnaque Deum benignitate & modestia Hiemis rebus extremis subventum. At hercule olim ex Italiæ regionibus longinquas in provincias commeatus portabant. Nec nunc infecunditate laboratur, sed Africam potius & Ægyptum exercemus navibusque & casibus vita P.R. permissa est. on which the learned Lipsius observes Quindecim dierum alimenta, Id est, Canon dierum XV. It might not be so general, but in Caligulas time there was once a less provision for subsistence in the City, when they had not for above 7 or 8 days. Seneca ad Paullinum c.18.[7]

Adolph. Occo MD in his Numism.Impp. Rom. 73 says in Claudius' reigne: Anno Orbis 4007 U.C. 797 Anno Domini 44. Ingens fames hoc Anno per universam Europam & Asiam cœpit, quæ aliquot Annos perseveravit, ut constat ex historiis & Actis Apost. c.xi & under the next yeare Claudii Tr. p.vi Cos.

iii Design.iiii Imp. xi, xii, xiii gives this Account of a brass coine or medal TI. CLAUDIUS CÆSAR AUG. (reverse) Vas quoddam frumentarium PON. M. TR. P. IMP. P. P. COS. III & 5 yeares after this Inscription on a Silver one of the same Emperor (reverse) S.P.Q.R. P.P. OB C.S./Corona quercea/ Fruges Italiæ pleno diffudit copia cornu – seu Frugibus ac Alimentis Urbi ac Italiæ diffusis, sometimes signified by a Modius or such like Vessell with Eares of Corne out of It. as Spanh[eim] de Usis Numism. Diss iii fo.154. Largitio – Locupletat Tribus – Locupletator orbis Terrarum – Munificentia Princ. Congiarum datum P.R. ibm 156. Annona miseræ data plebi – Liberalitas Aug. CERES AUG. Walk. c. vi. p.83, 84. Claudius being the first Emperor who Seconded Julius Cæsars impious Attempt on Us & coming hither in Person, Wee have more of his Coines found here than of any of his Predecessors, but one on the Subject of his Relieving the City distressed by that noted dearth must be more rare inasmuch as I concieve that began after his returne from his British Expedition, but It lasted Several years It administered frequent Occasions to him of exerting his bounty & liberality. Justness in designing & beauty of Sculpture came in under his Successor. The Sax. Chron. says he reduced great part of Britain & the Orcades in the 4 yeare of his reigne. 7 on þis ylcan geare geweard se mycela hungur on Syria þe Lucas recđ on þare boc Actus Apostolorum, sub AD 46. And in that same yeare there happend a great Famine in Syria which Luke recordeth in his Book of the Acts of the Apostles.[8]

[p.2] If when You're revising your Dissertation, any Hint from these few Notices on a subject well worthy your elaborate Discussion, may prove of Service, I shall think, as you mayn't have all these Authors, or not in the same Editions at hand, my time in turning to Them well spent, and shall long to see so remarkable a Prophecy so well Illustrated as by your hand, who can exhaust the Subject. In the meanwhile give me leave my Good Friend to request Your Sentiments on these few Queries? Why were the Hebrews Leviticus xi of Four Sorts of Beasts whereof some Chew the Cudd only[9] – 2dly Others have only the Foot cleft – 3dly Others Chew not the Cudd Nor have the Foot cleft – the fourth sort both Chew the Cudd & have the Hoof divided, forbidden to each of the 3 former as unclean? or even to touch their Carkeises. Why of Fish all that had not Finnes or Scales? since the Tench is [*gap in text*] & why amongst Birds (as of Prey) is the Swan expressly forbidden. [10] The Haire, Henn & Goose, as wee commonly translate – Leporem, Gallinam & Anserem,[11] our Auncestors the Britains eat not, as wee're told, but kept them for pleasure – the Hair & Rabbit are expressly forbidden to the Jews, & perhaps under the Swan all the Anatiles.[12] What of these were abstained from by the Egyptians, & Assyrians? I concieve the Haire & Rabbit having not Claws for Offence or Defence nor preying on any Other Animal – and the Anatiles feeding chiefly on Weeds & Insects could not be forbidden as Beasts creatures eating of & so partaking of the flesh of forbidden Animals, except It may be sayd of the duck kind That they'll devour Froggs which are indeed forbidden, but I believe Neither Swans nor any of the short round billed Anatiles eat fish. I don't wonder at any Nation abstaining from Such Animals as they had make [*sic*] the Symbol of the Deitie, or payd adoration to. But I wonder the Hebrews should follow the Egyptians in symbolizing their Creator by the Image of an Animal which was used in All Sacrifices and eaten by them[13] – These things have been more in Your way of Thinking and Enquiry than mine, And Your Thoughts on them will much Oblige

                    Revd Sir
                    Your affectionate Friend and humble
                    Servant   Maur. Johnson junr.
To the Rever^d
Dr Stukeley at his House
in Stamford
    Present.

1   Stukeley was ordained priest by the Bishop of Lincoln on 9 November 1729 (LAO, Reg. 38, pp.214–15) and was instituted on the following day to the living of All Saints' church, Stamford (see the address of this letter). In 1730, soon after he came to Stamford, Stukeley joined a gentlemen's club at Market Deeping; it lasted until he moved to London in 1747. Johnson attended its meetings on occasions. No records from the club still exist. It is possible that it was the remnant of a club formed in Stamford in the 1720s, of which Johnson had been a member.
2   Revd Benjamin Ray: see Appendix 3.
3   The majority of this letter is Johnson's response to suggestions by Stukeley about his theological work. Apparently Stukeley was working on the coins and medals of the Roman Emperor Claudius which commemorated a famine during his reign (AD 41–54), and looking for other sources from that period which referred to it. This was probably part of a concordance of the four Gospels, supported by external historical evidence, which Stukeley was compiling at this time; it is today in the library of Trinity College, Cambridge. In the first three paragraphs of this letter, Johnson offers extensive quotations from a wide range of sources in classical literature, the New Testament and the Anglo-Saxon Chronicle on the subject of famine during Claudius's reign, to assist Stukeley in his studies. This gives some indication of the breadth of Johnson's scholarship and the extent of his library.
4   The final part of this quotation is illegible. The version of this phrase given in the modern edition of the Greek New Testament is λιμον μεγαν μελλειν εσεσθαι εφ' ὁλην την οικουμενην ('And there stood up one of them, named Agabus, and signified by the Spirit that there should be great dearth throughout all the world: which came to pass in the days of Claudius Cæsar'): Acts of the Apostles 11:28.
5   This quotation comes from Suetonius's *History of the Twelve Cæsars* written around AD 120; the fifth book deals with Claudius and para. 18 refers to Claudius's efforts to relieve famine in Rome; see, for example, Robert Graves' translation, *I, Claudius* (1979), 171.
6   Joseph Scaliger (see **Letter 1**, n.13) refers to Josephus (AD 37–100), *The Antiquities of the Jews* (written around AD 94), book 20, chapter 2 (not chapter 3 as Johnson states), which described 'how Helena queen of Adiabene [in modern Iran] and her son Izates embraced the Jewish religion and how Helena supplied the poor with corn when there was a great famine at Jerusalem' (William Whiston's translation). Scaliger proposed that this famine is the one referred to in the Acts of the Apostles.
7   In this paragraph Johnson draws attention to the question of grain supplies and famine in the texts of Aurelius Victor (AD *c*.320–*c*.390), *Liber de Cæsaribus* (ch.4), Tacitus (AD 56–117), *Annales* (book 12, ch.43) and Seneca (4 BC – AD 65), *Ad Paulinum de Brevitate Vitæ* (ch.18) and to the fact that the city of Rome was left with only enough food for fifteen days.
8   In this paragraph Johnson offers further references to classical texts and also to Roman coins, citing Adolpho Occo (see **Letter 18**, n.16), *Imperatorum Romanorum Numismata a Pompeio Magno ad Heraclium* (1579). The final reference is to a passage from the Anglo-Saxon Chronicle (9th–10th century AD), Cotton Tiberius MS, under the entry for AD 47. The entry continues 'þe wæs fore-witegad on Actibus Apostolorum þurh Agabum þone witegan' (which was foretold in the Acts of the Apostles by Agabus the prophet).
9   The four sorts of beast were the camel, rabbit (or rock badger), hare and pig.
10 The tench has extremely small scales and a very thick skin; presumably this apparent absence of scales explains why Johnson raises the question of its acceptability to the Israelites. Later translations of the Bible such as the New English Bible (1970) do not include the swan; the problem here is the translation from the original Hebrew into English equivalents in the Authorised Version.
11 Latin for 'hare, hen and goose'.
12 Anatiles are the Anatidæ, the biological family of birds that includes ducks, geese and swans.
13 This refers to the worship of the golden calf by the Israelites in the desert (Exodus 32:4–7); a calf was a creature they were permitted to eat by their dietary laws. Johnson found this problematic

and so passed the question on to Stukeley as it was 'more in Your way of thinking and Enquiry than mine'.

30. William Stukeley to Maurice Johnson, Stamford, 9 October 1730
Spalding, SGS/Stukeley/12

[Annotated by Maurice Johnson:] Letter from the Learned & Revd Dr Wm Stukeley of the distinction in the Levit. Law &c of <u>Clean</u> & <u>Unclean</u>.

Dear S^r

I thank you for your extracts about Claudius's famin.[1] The affair of the creatures forbidden to be eaten under the Mosaic dispensation, I have never consider'd. I know that the distinction of clean & unclean is much older than that time. because Noah took of clean & unclean creatures into the ark in different proportions. & that was done without regard to eating, but to sacrifice. for some creatures were not acceptabl to god almighty in that service: when eating of creatures was not practised. & undoubtedly god at first order'd what creatures he thought proper, what not, which went afterward, under the notion of clean & unclean. Sacrificing is as old as the creation. the coats Adam & Eve first wore, were stript, without question, from the backs of sacrific'd animals. Sacrificing animals was a positive ceremony order'd by God, chiefly with a future view to the great & divine sacrifice to be made 4000 year after.[2] god was so good as to provide a timely remedy immediately after the taint receivd so probably the inhibitions of Moses were positive orders that had no intrinsic meaning, but respected something in a future & more perfect dispensation. for certainly every thing that comes out of the creators hands are compleat works, perfect & clean. but god thought fit to lay an injunction then which was to vanish along with all types & prefigurations at the glorious dayspring & liberty of the Gospel. I happen at this time to have a great hurry upon my hands, which I desire you would allow of, for an excuse, that I am so short at present but always most affectionately your humble Servt

        Wm Stukeley
My most humble service Stamford 9 Oct 1730
waits on the society at
Spalding.

I brought this with me to Deeping[3] on tuesday last expecting you there. I read your letter over on Munday at our meeting. The gentlemen were pleased with the hopes of seeing you there. & still hope for that Satisfaction. they give their thanks for the letter.

To
Maurice Johnson Esqr
 at Spalding
Turn at Stilton.

---

[1] See **Letter 29**. Stukeley's spelling of 'famine' is typical of his idiosyncratic orthography; he rarely wrote a final 'e' if it was not pronounced.

2   According to chronologies calculated from the Old Testament and accepted at this time, the crucifixion of Christ took place 4000 years after the creation of the world by God.
3   See **Letter 29**, n.1. Stukeley read **Letter 29** to the meeting of the Deepings Club on Monday 5 October 1730, having received the letter from the hands of one of Johnson's servants who was visiting his father in Stamford, thus saving Stukeley having to pay for the letter, as the postal system of that time required the recipient, not the sender, to pay. Stukeley had hoped that Johnson would attend the meeting so he could hand over this reply and thus save Johnson the cost of postage.

31. Maurice Johnson to William Stukeley, Spalding, 20 April 1731
Bodleian, MS Eng. misc. c.113, fols 323r–324r

Spalding 20 April 1731

Dear Dr

It was a great satisfaction to Me to hear by Mr Augustin Manby your Neighbour Hepburnes apprentice who brings You this,[1] Upon my Enquiry after You, That You're got well home again before Your Lady lyes in, I thank God mines Very well & abroad again:[2] I hope Sir from his Account That Your Arm is as well as ever & to have the pleasure of seeing You can write & that You'll now finish & favour Us with the promised & so long expected Curious dissertation Upon the Annonal Medal of Claudius,[3] Or in the Interim any thing that Occurrs. I assure You wee're[4] So Strong as to have 3 or 4 Letters at a time Comunicated from One Member or Others. Correspondence is the Thing that best keeps up the Spiritt of such Societies the same or more Elaborate Dissertations when printed please not so much. the Novelty of a Letter excites the Curiosity of all who know the Writer, besides theres usually some Modern Occurrence interwoven. I wish much to See You here, had none of your Company when You called last in Xmas time, I think then You sayd You should See these parts again some time this Summer And if So You'll be a Judicious Witness of my Piety who with the good Assistance of the younger Collins[5] Painter to our Society, have restored 7 antient Family Pictures to a good Degree of their primitive Beauty religiously preserving their Beards, Hair, Habitt, Amongst Them one by Holbein, and another by Paolo Veronese, a most beautyfull Profile of some Lady I presume of the family of Bassan to whom I am related & who came out of Italy in Queen Elizabeth's time, this being on Pannel, but diminished by careless keeping Wee have eked out & embellished with suitable Decorations taken from Ænea Vico Parmensi. That [p.2] which on the Concurrent Judgement of my good Friends Mr Bogdani, Bell & Collin I call an Holbein has some token of an Order in a red Ribband & may Probably be an Ancestor of mine of both my Names[6] who as my Good Friend Mr Brown Willis assures me under his hand from the Records he searchd for his Compiling the Notitia Parliamentaria served as Burgess for your Town of Stamford with David Cecill [*gap in text caused by removal of seal*] Parliament at London H. VIII which was in 1523. You Sir Who know how to set a just Value on Such Treasures will be pleased to see them so well preserved probably for some Centurys, for the Spirit of drawing being got into our Family, all my Younkers practice It, & truly my Eldest Son & daughter with good Success for their time. As our Family was formerly in Stamford & my Grandfather[7] dwelt there sometime whilest he was building that house in which his Grandson my Kinsman Parson Johnson[8] now lives near the Chain Bridge & as my Mothers Family was renderd eminent by the great & beneficent Arch-Deacon Robert Johnson[9] in Your Neighbourhood

& I believe truly both but branches Originaly from the same Stock You'll oblige Me in collecting any Memorials which may fall in Your way relating to them as I have done for You Sir in my reading relating to your own Family & Kinred: The Pedigree in Wrights history of Rutland Shire[10] is so perplexed & Confused that It is unintelligible both to Mr Peck Mr Johnson of Olney & my Self & I am confident there are some errors therein but cannot with all my Diligence Set them right which I wish to be able to do before Peck can publish his intended 2d Vol of Acad. Tertia Anglicana: for which purpose I long Since wrote & received a Very Civil Letter from that Ingenious Author.[11]

[p.3] I'm almost Persuaded to fix our Museum[12] in the lower part of the Building now all used for our Free Grammar School which being thirty foot high will Admitt of Dividing by a Floor layd partly in the Middle into 2 Noble Rooms & useing the upper for the School saves double Cieling & the Lower for the Museum makes It readyer of access & saves a Stair Case. What think You of this proposicion, for our purpose 20 feet clear wide 25 long & 15 feet high. Wee can have no greater height but can reduce the width by sett forward the Cases if 20ft be wide in proporcion to the length – or can lengthen It 3 feet, as advised. Wee erected a New Class[13] in the Free School, & therein placed the proper Philological Tracts & Classicks which were in the Vestiary & at the Museum, & I have surveyd & find them all forthcoming after 20 yeares use of many & a curious Sett of Classickes in very usefull Editions. Seign^r Collins has presented us with a drawing of Your Kindswoman the Beautyfull Queen Anna Bolleyn[14] in our Minute Book from a Cast in Lead in my Collection found in dorsetshire as broad as my Palm. & I gave them a short dissertation under It on that Lovely, Virtuous, Ingenious, unfortunate Lady; the drawing will take you much. But I must leave you to look over a Charge I'm to give at our first Great Annual Court of Sewers[15] this day where our Engineer Captn Perry is to move for Leave to Stopp the Navigation of the Welland for Some Time this Summer whiles he with 200 Spade men deepens Its bed & Channell thro this Town for 2 Miles towards the sea Grande Sane Opus est valde necessarium nautis, by which means wee Expect to see Vessells rideing at our High Bridge (One day for Grandeur of a single Arch to rival the Rialto) of Double the Burden that can now come up by reason of the Sand Beds & Carrs he will remove.[16]

I am ever Revd Sir with my Father & Brother yours
        Maur. Johnson junr.

To the Revnd
Dr William Stukeley
At his House in
 Stamford
 These Present

[1] Again, Johnson is saving Stukeley the cost of postage by organising hand delivery by an apprentice of Stukeley's neighbour Hepburne.

[2] This is the pregnancy of Frances Stukeley, née Williamson. Their second child, Mary, was born on 2 May 1731; she died in 1732. Johnson's wife Elizabeth had had many pregnancies, a number of which resulted in still-births or short-lived infants; she had recently given birth to their ninth surviving child, Anne Alethea, born in 1731, who married Richard Wallin, an SGS member and a merchant trading to the West Indies.

3   This coin or medal of the Emperor Claudius is the focus of **Letter 29** above, which offers evidence from Johnson to help Stukeley with his dissertation on the coin.
4   The SGS. Johnson explains his reason for his determination to expand the correspondence of the Society.
5   Richard Collins (d.1732), appointed official painter to the SGS in 1727; see his entry in Appendix 3.
6   Johnson was keen to preserve his family portraits, and to teach his children, 'my Younkers', the important art of drawing. It is impossible to authenticate any of these remoter ancestors of Maurice Johnson apart from 'an ancestor of mine of both my names', Maurice Johnson (c.1480–1551), a dyer and the Alderman of Stamford 1518, 1528 and 1539, and also MP for Stamford in 1523, 1529 and 1536. He owned land in Stamford and Shropshire and at the time of his death leased shops on Thorney Abbey property. Johnson points out, at the end of this paragraph, his difficulty in understanding the family tree.
7   Walter Johnson (1620–92), JP of Spalding and father by his second marriage of Maurice Johnson I, the father of Maurice Johnson II, who is writing this letter.
8   Revd Walter Johnson: see Appendix 3.
9   Revd Robert Johnson (1541–1625: see *ODNB*), the son of the Maurice Johnson referred to in n.6 above. Of Puritan inclinations, he was Archdeacon of Leicester and held four canonries, including being a Canon of Windsor for fifty-three years. His income allowed him to found two grammar schools in Rutland which evolved into public schools: Oakham and Uppingham.
10 James Wright, *The History and Antiquities of the County of Rutland* (1684), has a genealogy (p.38) of the Stamford Johnsons, including Maurice Johnson the MP and Archdeacon Robert Johnson. Aspects of it are, as Maurice Johnson says, impossible to understand because of omissions.
11 Francis Peck (1692–1743: see *ODNB*), *Academia tertia Anglicana; or the Antiquarian Annals of Stamford in Lincoln, Rutland and Northampton Shires* (1727), to which Johnson subscribed. Peck did not produce a second volume on Stamford, but did publish in 1732 and 1735 his two-volume *Desiderata Curiosa*, full of complex historical details.
12 The SGS's museum was housed from 1727 to 1743 in the Society's rooms in the Abbey Yard, which they rented from Joseph Sparke. In 1725 it had been unsuccessfully proposed to use the upper section of the Grammar School on the south side of the chancel of the parish church as a museum. Johnson is now taking up this idea again, but the scheme, like later schemes to build a museum nearby, met with local opposition and proved unsuccessful until 1911–12 when the present Society building was constructed. See a detailed article on this, John Harris, 'Designs for the Museum and Library of the Spalding Gentlemen's Society', *The Georgian Group Journal* 19 (2011), 39–49.
13 A further bookcase for those of the Society's classical texts that could also be of use to the school.
14 For Richard Collins' drawing and Johnson's short dissertation, see SGS, MB2, fol.46v. Stukeley's mother was Frances (née Bullen), daughter of Robert Bullen, gent., and thus he claimed kinship with the Boleyns (originally Bullens).
15 Johnson was Chairman of the South Holland Commission of Sewers, the group of local gentlemen who had met since the thirteenth century to attempt to solve local drainage problems. The drainage of the Fens by the Adventurers, agreed to by Acts of Parliament, frequently caused major local problems of flooding. Johnson was involved as Chairman and as a barrister in pleading in Parliament against proposed bills relating to draining sections of the Fens that would have had unfavourable results for South Holland.
16 Johnson optimistically hopes that Capt. Perry's dredging schemes will improve facilities for Spalding shipping; he describes it as a 'great work and very necessary for the sailors'. Perry had been successful in several previous schemes, including closing the Dagenham Breach in the north bank of the Thames in 1719.

[SGS/Stukeley/13, dated 5 July 1731, is a letter, not in Stukeley's hand and therefore probably a copy, from Stukeley to 'the Rev. Gregory Hinson (Dean of Stamford) respecting the Choice of a Warden of Brown's Hospital in Stamford.']

[SGS/Stukeley/13A is a sketch of a section through a Roman road, labelled in Stukeley's writing 'a section of the Hermenstreet road at Wothorp Park corner by Stanford. Sept. 26. 1732' and in Maurice Johnson's writing 'as View^d by the

learned Dr Stukeley wᵒ drew this 27 & he communicated to SGS 28.7': see SGS, MB2, fol.72v.]

32. Maurice Johnson to William Stukeley, Spalding, 8 January 1733
Bodleian, MS Eng. misc. c.113, fols 325r–326r

Spalding 8th January 1732/3

Dear Dr

Thinking It very long since I either See or heard from You & being informed You're leaving the Country to live in London,[1] I hope Your good & great Friend My Lord Archbishop ha's found the usual Argument for induceing You to draw nearer to Lambeth, & shall be very glad & desire to know if It be So, I purposed indeed to have seen Stamford last Summer but had not Opportunity, if You Should Stay there 'till next I hope I may haveing no Friend whos Conversation I take more delight in than yours & frequently regrett our not having had the Opportunity of being more together as Wee were Neighbours born & contracted an Early Acquaintance. I have done & still do all I can to inspire a Love of learning in the Gent. of this Place, Especialy the Youth, and our Soc. is constant, flourishing, & a Very agreeable Amusement to Me and some Other of them every week. Wee began It very Early in the afternoon last Thursday, being the first in the New Yeare, by Opening It with a Concert of Musick[2] performed by Gent. (chiefly Members) who pay that Annual Tribute for the use of our Museum on Frydays, and wee had a Room next adjoyning which by keeping the doors open Wee layd to the Musæum, and there had the honour to Entertain the Ladies who love Musick with It & Tea & Coffee & a Glass of Wine as celebrating the Anniversary of our Institution. Wee have addressed his Grace the Duke of Buccleuch[3] who is a Member of the Royal Soc. a Grand Master of Free Masons & now Lord of our Mannor, & invited him from being a Member to become our Patron; He is a Prince of great Candour & Humanity, whom I have the honour & pleasure to serve as Steward of his Mannors in Lincolnshire & hath a very Considerable Estate in our Parts of the County and [p.2] can if he pleases fix Us upon as Sure a Basis as human Institutions are capable of, without being at an Immoderate Expence, and I own to You haveing been the Founder & Parent, I have so much fondness for the designe, that I wish to see It So Settled as to be likely to be continued to after Ages and late Posterity may have reason to thank Me who would thereby reap the fruits of my much labour & paines, and I am still ready to Contribute more & be at Some Expence to obteine the Possession of a proper place of our Own, that Wee may Enjoy Free from all future Charges & preserve our Books and all our Implements together and ready at Hand on all Occasions. But I find It a true Observation that without a Cheerfull Glass & sober Pipe Wee Englishman [*sic*] can't well keep up Conversation therefore I not only admit them but as a farther Inducement Musick too and would have every Soc. begun with an houre or Twos Concert, And am so much of my Countryman St Gilbert of Sempringhams Mind,[4] that I would have a Mixture of Female Members, Women sweetening and softening our Rugged Sex and being capable of Musick and Poetry and all parts of the Arts of designeing and It's very rarely that at Such Meetings which are to relax the Mind from Buisness & Severe Studys that any thing Occurrs which They cannot enter into, You see Sir how I'm extending my Social Scheme, but

It is our Singular felicity here that, Wee're not divided nor Suffer party to enter, politicks being the only Subject prohibited & that Very positively by our Laws. As I assure you I rely much on Your Judgement and Wee toke the paines jointly to refound the Soc. of Antiquarys[5] together and Draw up their Rules, I mention these my Notions to you for Your Opinion therein, And had one such assistant as You resident here to act with joynt vigour, should not doubt of accomplishing this my Grand designe for a Villager to meditate. Who has had no Extra-Ordinary Assistance either of Power or Pelf[6] to do what has been done – But by pursuant the Scheme of taking fines of the Resident (who are the only paying Members) as the Royal Soc. has done, I hope I may raise Money Sufficient. [p.3] In the Mean time Wee have Enough from hand to Mouth 28l. 14s. 9¼d in our Treasury And in Contributions from promoters of our Museum 56. 15. 0 towards It. But Wee wait 'till Wee have had our Great Man down here to see his [*gap in text*] & the Circumstances of this place, and according as he and the Members agree the Matter shall Endeavour to fit up or build a Museum for our Meeting.[7] But as Correspondence is the Spirit of all Societys theres nothing Wee more covet, and You who used to promote such good designes very much that way & from whom I used to have now & then the favour of a Letter seem to have quite forgott Me, Who am forced as well as I can, in the midst of Various buisness, to carry on a Correspondence with the Members at distance. And which I do the more readily as advised by Sir Iz. Newton. Every thing New, Uncommon, or Curious and perhaps unobserved before give a Life and Vigour to Company, Sets them on thinking of It and furnishes Matter for Conversation. I have carefully lately read the Fortuita Sacra cum Commentario de Cymbalis[8] and am much pleased with them. The Author I think shews a great deal of Learning and Judgement. I pray are the Celtick characters different from the first Greek characters; & where is there an Alphabet of them & on what Authority, if you have one be so good as to transcribe It for Me. What dos Dr Chishull[9] in his Inscriptia Sigea fo.15 mean by Etruscæ inversæ, which he makes very like the old Greek & latin Letters. I thought nobody had understood the Hetruscan, Punick & Celtick Languages now. thô doubtles many things were wrote in Them worth understanding and many monuments may I presume be remaining which want explaining that have their Characters, and some the old Egyptian on them, both the Sacred & Civil as Capt. Lethelliers[10] Apex of a Pyramid which I see. My Bro. Amblers[10] marryd at York to one Mrs Hather a Lady of that Country & related to Archbishop Sterns Family, he's still there – My Wife & all our Family Present You & Your Lady with all the Good Wishes of the Season and I am

    Dear Dr
      Your affectionate Friend and
      Obedient humble servant Maur. Johnson junr.

To
the Revd Dr Stukeley
At his House in Stamford
 Turn at Stilton

---

[1] In fact, Stukeley stayed in Stamford until 1747 when he obtained a living in London. During the later 1730s and early 1740s he spent part of the year in London, and then settled in Stamford, in a house he had bought on Barn Hill. During his Stamford years, however, he did attempt, through his patrons, to gain promotion in the Church, such as canonries at several cathedrals, but without success.

2   The SGS had annual music concerts from 1732 to 1746. Johnson preferred this method of celebrating the Society's anniversary to the original scheme of a dinner for members.
3   Francis Scott (1695–1751), second Duke of Buccleuch; see Appendix 3. He agreed to become the SGS's Patron in 1733.
4   St Gilbert of Sempringham (*c.*1083–*c.*1189: see *ODNB*), created Sempringham Priory around his living in Sempringham (Lincs), and established the double order of Gilbertines, which was unique in Britain and very unusual in Europe in housing both canons and nuns in the same establishment, though in separate quarters. The Gilbertine order spread through eastern England, particularly Lincolnshire and Yorkshire.
5   In late 1717 and early 1718, Johnson, Stukeley and a group of like-minded antiquaries put the Society of Antiquaries on a permanent footing, with Stukeley as Secretary and Johnson as Librarian (though at the time the Society did not as yet possess a library). It had been founded during the reign of Elizabeth I but had ceased to meet; this re-foundation grew out of an informal meeting in London of several people interested in antiquities, including Peter Le Neve and the Gale brothers, Roger and Samuel.
6   'Money'. This section gives the clearest expression of Johnson's hopes and plans for his Society. He hoped to build a permanent museum and meeting place and the reference to St Gilbert of Sempringham indicates his wish for the company of men and women in intelligent discussion. Both he and Stukeley had been members, in the 1720s, of the London-based Society of Roman Knights, which had a particular interest in Roman antiquities in Britain and included women among its members. Johnson's hope for female members in the SGS was finally realised in 2007, following a resolution of December 2006, with the admission of women to full membership.
7   This could be either the Duke of Buccleuch or Lord Coleraine, a keen antiquarian. The minute book entry for 25 February 1731 (SGS, MB2, fol.43v) records a letter from Johnson to the Society from London, expressing the hope that Lord Coleraine, an SGS member, will support their plans for building a museum.
8   Sir Richard Ellys (see Appendix 3 and *ODNB*) published *Fortuita Sacra* (1727), a detailed philological and theological analysis in Latin of a range of disputed New Testament texts.
9   The Revd Edmund Chishull (1671–1733), Anglican clergyman and antiquary, published *Antiquitates Asiaticæ* in 1728, following his visits to Ephesus and Asia Minor. In the section on an Etruscan inscription, the 'Inscriptio Sigea', he discusses whether the Etruscans wrote from right to left, since many of the letters of their alphabet appear to be Greek letters reversed; on fol.6 he writes: 'Græcis inversis literis sinistrorum scripta' and on fol.14: 'multi inverse scripti', concluding on fol.24: 'Etruscæ vero Phœniciis vero similiores … sinistrorsum sunt ducendæ'. There was considerable interest in attempting to translate the few remaining Etruscan inscriptions at this time as part of the fascination with ancient scripts such as Egyptian and Phoenician.
10 Captain (later Lieut.-Gen.) William Lethieullier FSA (1702–1756) was very interested in ancient Egypt and donated an Egyptian mummy to the newly established British Museum on his death.
11 Joshua Ambler (1694–1734), a founder member of the SGS, was the brother of Johnson's wife Elizabeth; he married on 16 December 1732 at York, Mrs Alice Hather (or Heater). Joshua's sisters inherited Gayton (or Holyrood) House, next door to Johnson's home at Ayscoughfee Hall (see **Letter 37**, n.3). Richard Sterne (1595/6–1683), Archbishop of York (1664–83), to whom Ambler's wife was related, had a family of thirteen children.

33. Maurice Johnson to William Stukeley, Spalding, 13 July 1739
Bodleian, MS Eng. misc. c.113, fols 327r–328v

      To Dr Stukeley
                    Spalding 13 July 1739
Dear Dr
  Your Mercury gave me long hopes of my having a Letter from You before I had that pleasure, which I assure You I received with much, as renewing a Correspondence with One of the oldest Friends I have, the more valuable as you so litle like Our Parts, thô Your Native Place, as rarely to favour them with Your

Company; & You know my affaires permitt me to see Your pleasant place but Seldome, having that I know of never been there since You was but I did my Self the pleasure of Spending what time I could with You; Wee have no other Method of more frequently than this by Letter a Method which in our Younger Yeares wee long pursued with mutual satisfaction, & I hope and trust haveing renewd may So Still, I'm the speedyer Sir in acknowledging Your favour, that as You say, Your going with Your Lady (to whom all our humble Services) to wait on our good Friend her Brother,[1] You may take mine and all our Societys Services along with You to Scruton, which thô I should be glad, shall hardly ever have the Opportunity, to See. I content my Self imis immersus Paludibus[2] with a few good Companions & many good Books, a man so fixd down must remember Est Ulubris, Animus modo te non deficit, Felicitas,[3] and make himself easie, that is, happy. I forward my Family as fast as I can, having My Eldest Son an Ensigne in the first Regiment of Foot Guards, & now here raising Recruits for his Company. my Second bred under Me, of the Temple, to Succeed me in my Court keeping. my 2 Eldest Daughters marryed to mine and their Satisfactions[4] and I thank God the rest of my Children all healthfull and promiseing to be usefull to the World and blessings to me and their Dear Mother by whom I had 25[5] and I thank Heaven both that Good Woman (who joins with me as doth my Cousin Benj: Ray[6] in our Services to You and Your Lady), and I are very well. I wish to shew you some litle Improvements I have projected and Executed in part in our Gardens particularly my Perambulation Walk ~~of~~ planted with all kinds of Forest & Trees round the Extreem Compass of our little Territorye wherein Some Oaks of my own raising [p.2] Do Dominum juvant Umbrâ,[7] My Father, (Your's Ancient Acquaintance & now for many Yeares Survivor)[8] is to my advantage and, (I hope) may many more Yeares continue hearty and in all respects both of Body and Mind firme & well; He uses Moderate Exercise Still whenever the Weather permitts on Horseback with Some or Other of his Grand Children to whom his kind Instructions are of great advantage and truly I see Small difference that has made in him but in his Houres, he retires to his rest earlyer and rises not so soon by a few howers. I myself am turned 50 and have Two Grandsons, the Sons of my Eldest Daughter by her good Husband Dr Green which to talk, more Avito[9] are fine Boys. Now, when You can after You come off of Your Northern Expedition let Us See You and come & See whether our Garden may not afford Something farther curious to furnish Your delightful Hermitage,[10] and It shall be at Your Service, I allmost fancy You'll be prevailed on by Your Good Brother and tempted by Sir John Clark[11] to make the Tour of Edenburgh, where I wish my good Lord his Grace the Duke of Buccleuch who not Long Since passd through Town for Dalkeith had had commands for Mee, who have perhaps all my life made It too much a Rule to Me not to stir from home Unless unavoidable Busyness and Such as would defray the time and Expences actualy drew or draggd Me hence, not even in my Neighbourhood, and in this I have been indulged and Encouraged by a Wife whose Conversation I with just reason delight in above all, and who has spent all her Mornings in her Nursery, but if Wee live to see our Youngest, which is a Boy, very Sprightly, & 5¾ old[12] [sic] grown Manlike I've insist on It with his Mother that then She and I will go abroad and visitt our Relations and Friends. In the Interim London and Lincoln twice a Yeare are Journeys I'm in some measure obliged to take, where and from a few learned Corresponding Members I gather that Honey which in a great Measure susteines the Hive here, whos Swarme & their Improvement is (Exclusive of my Family) the great Concern and amuzement of my Life. [p.3] By this You'll Understand I mean our Gentlemens Society, or Cell, now arrived to some degree of Esteem in the learned World having had the honour to be taken notice of by the Royal & Antiquarian Societies, not on my Motion, who am no Member of the former and was not present at the later when those worthy Centum viri[13] presented our Museum with all their works, as the former gave orders Wee should have their Transactions gratis as they're publish [sic] to place in our Publick Library which Wee have augmented to 700 Volumes. Our Meetings are for the Size & Situation of the Town well frequented and our Annual Celebration of our Institution (which has Some Yeares been fixed and is held on the last Thursday in the Month of August) is realy Splendid tho with our much Expence, being renderd agreeable by the Appearance of the Ladies and the Performance of a good Consert by the Gentlemen, those of this Place and Neighbourhood having the Use of our Room every Friday and one Class[14] in it for their Collection of Musick to Encourage that heavenly Science, Musgrave Heighing[15] [sic] Dr of Musick an Oxford Man & Orgainist of Yarmouth is Maister of our Band and a Beneficent Member of our Soc. He is an Ingenious Composer, an Elegant Scholar and has Attended us Annualy these 3 yeares past. Besides some of the Newest & best Italian Musick, Wee have allways performed some Odes of Anacreon & Horace in their own words, & One suitable to the Occasion, which (as the Laureats Birthday Ode) is renewd yearly by Some Cibber of our Own;[16] but not being fond of exposing him wee never print Them. To shew You Sir how much Wee Love Musick to encourage our Consert Wee've lately contributed to an Excellent Harpsichord[17] and at a Soc. held 28 ult. had read a short dissertation upon the Invention of That Instrument and the Improvement of It into an Orgain; with Some account of the most remarkable Orgains, Either for Expence in the materials and making as those of pure Gold, Or for the Vast Size of the Pipes. of this Wee have pretty full minutes entred as of Every thing Wee've had communicated from 1712. and if I'm prevented being there to do that Office my Bro. Secretary Dr Green does.[18] I believe you may remember the Antient and Very polite Minister of our Parish is our President. my Bro^r Treasurer and Mr Michael Cox a Chyrurgeon & Apothecary Operator. and my quondam Clerk Wm Stagg who is a good Florist is our Housekeeper, Brewer, Gardiner and Coadjutor in Omnibus, he has a Key to our Presses or Classes & hard Names to all our Nicknacks & Curiosities, which by shewing sometimes causes an Increase of them

[p.4] But above all our Greatest Glory is having had our Countreyman Sr Iz. Newton[19] a Declared Approver and a Member, and the having his Grace my Lord the Duke of Buccleuch Lord of our Mannor our Patron and Benefactor who has bestowed Langley's or the Free Masons Architecture from Vitruvius to the present time, and Pines Horace on Us.[20] Works of too great Expence to have been Otherwise expected to be Seen in this Village. At a Soc. 7 June last Mr Everard a Member Communicated to Us a Letter to him from Mr Robert Flower Master of Bishop Stortford Writing School in Hertfordshire with the draught of an Abacus or Board,[21] where by small dice of Black, White & Red Colours, running in paralell lines by their being grooved in & so made moveable backwards & forwards by a Stylus or Bodkin Arithmetick is perform'd without Nombers or Figures by Colours instead thereof & by their Motion & View of them instead of Mental Reckoning by the mocion of 252 whereof backwards &

forwards, on the 21st of the Same Month at another Soc. Wee See him performe exactly and in less time than a Very expert and daily Practising Arithmetician & Algebraist, many difficult Questions Wee then Set him in Addition, Subtraction, Multiplication, Division, Involution, Evolution &c On which Occasion Wee had a Dissertation on the Abaci of the Antients, viz. of Pythagoras or the Abacus Factorum, which nothing but a Multiplication Table, that of Euclid, for Geometry shewd with Smal [*illegible*] of use before Slates. of the Chinese Coloured Bedes strung on Paralell Wires & most resembling this of Mr Flowers in the Intention & Operation, but not go so farr, the American Cords of Various Colours with Knotts on them at certain distances whereby Those of Lima & Truxillo calculated – and of the Invention of Draught Boards Backgammon & Chest [*sic*] the Noblest of all Sedentary games. And I could not forbeare reminding Our Younger Members, of their Friend Persius's remonstrance –

  Nec qui Abaco Numeros, & Secto in Pulvere Metas
  Scit risisse vafer, multum gaudere paratus
  Si Cynico barbam petulans Nonaria vellat –[22]

Be pleased to make my Services acceptable to Mr Gale & give him the enclosed Answer to his last Letter &

Believe me Dear Dr to be your faithfull friend as ever

          Maur. Johnson junior

---

[1] Stukeley married his second wife, Elizabeth Gale (1687–1757), in 1738. She was the daughter of the Revd Thomas Gale, Dean of York, and sister of Roger and Samuel Gale, both close friends of Stukeley and Johnson. Roger, the elder, inherited his father's manor of Scruton in the North Riding of Yorkshire.

[2] 'Immersed in the deepest Fens'.

[3] 'Happiness can be found in Ulubræ [a small marshland town] as long as the spirit is not lacking', based on a quotation from Horace, *Epistles* I.

[4] Johnson is giving the latest news of his eldest children: the 'Ensigne' is Maurice Johnson (1714–93), eventually a colonel in the 1st Regiment of Foot; originally Johnson had intended Maurice to follow him into the law, but he had preferred an army career. The second son, Walter Johnson FSA (1720–79), followed his father by becoming a barrister. Jane Johnson, the eldest surviving child (1711–54), married Dr John Green, Second Secretary of the SGS; Elizabeth Johnson (1713–84) married Robert Butter, merchant of Spalding, SGS member and keen bassoonist.

[5] Everard Green's pedigree of the Johnson family mentions twenty-seven children of Maurice and Elizabeth Johnson, but two are not named. Thirteen boys and twelve girls are named, and by 1739 all the children had been born: so Johnson's figure of twenty-five children seems to be correct. Eleven of them survived to adulthood.

[6] Revd Benjamin Ray, see Appendix 3.

[7] 'Help [or please] their master by their shade', from Horace, *Epistles* I, xv.

[8] Maurice Johnson I (1661–1747) had been a close friend of Stukeley's father John (1657–1706); both were local lawyers and fellow-officers in the local Militia.

[9] 'In a grandfatherly manner'. As Johnson was born in June 1688, he was fifty-one at the time of this letter.

[10] Stukeley created a hermitage garden in Stamford between his home in St Peter's Street and the Town Meadows.

[11] Roger Gale, Stukeley's brother-in-law, had a house at Scruton in North Yorkshire. Gale visited Scotland in the company of Sir John Clerk (1676–1755): see Appendix 3. The Duke of Buccleuch (see **Letter 32**, n.2) had a house at Dalkeith, just south of Edinburgh. There is a hint in this letter, unusual for Johnson, that he perhaps regrets not having travelled more widely in his younger days.

[12] Henry Eustace Johnson (1733–*c*.1764), Johnson's youngest child, became an assistant secretary to the East India Company in Madras. Specimens of his penmanship survive in the SGS's archive.

[13] The members of the Society of Antiquaries. The original 'centumviri' were the officials of the

chancery court of ancient Rome. The Royal Society ('the former') regularly sent their published *Transactions* to the SGS, and they are still preserved in the Society's library. Johnson was proud of the Society's growing library, augmented by the donation of a book by each new member; his catalogue survives in the SGS's archives and the 'Original Collection' is still kept together.

[14] One bookcase.

[15] Musgrave Heighington (1680–1764): see Appendix 3. Some of his settings of Latin odes are held in the library of Christ Church, Oxford.

[16] Colley Cibber (1671–1757: see *ODNB*), actor and theatrical entrepreneur, was appointed Poet Laureate in 1730. Johnson may feel some loyalty towards Cibber as he was educated in Lincolnshire, at the King's School, Grantham; local loyalties are often evident in comments on people, both by Johnson and Stukeley.

[17] SGS, MB3 (28 June 1739), records that 'The Society paid Five Guineas towards the Purchase of the said Harpsychord' which is described in detail.

[18] Dr John Green. The President was the Revd Stephen Lyon (c.1668–1747), perpetual curate of Spalding (c.1710–1747), of French Huguenot descent. His portrait is in the SGS. The Treasurer at this time was Johnson's brother John Johnson (see Appendix 3); the Operator or curator was Michael Cox, a local surgeon and apothecary, and his coadjutor, or assistant, was Johnson's legal clerk William Stagg, who was the SGS's official gardener and lived in the Society's premises in the 1740s. The meaning of 'florist' at that time was a person who grew, and had a good knowledge of, flowers.

[19] See Appendix 3.

[20] The Duke of Buccleuch gave the SGS a copy of Batty Langley's *Ancient Masonry both in Theory and Practice* (1736), tracing architecture from Vitruvius to Sir Christopher Wren, and of John Pine's expensive and beautiful illustrated edition of Horace, bound in gilded leather (pub. 1737). Both are recorded in the eighteenth-century catalogue and are still in the SGS's archive.

[21] There is a very full account of Robert Flower's abacus in SGS, MB3, fols 34–35 (entry for 7–21 June 1739). Flower brought his abacus to the Society's meeting on 14 July and there was extensive discussion which Johnson outlines in this letter. A Revd Robert Fowler (1712–59) from Wainfleet was ordained deacon at Lincoln in 1734; a Revd Robert Fowler was briefly Master of the Grammar School at Bishop's Stortford, but it is not certain whether either of these is the person referred to here.

[22] Not some crafty fellow who's used to jeering at maths
On the abacus, or diagrams drawn in the furrowed dust,
One ready to howl with delight when some insolent whore
Tugs at a Cynic's beard

    Persius, *Satires* I, lines 131–3, translated by A. S. Kline and quoted by kind permission

34. Maurice Johnson to William Stukeley, Spalding, 21 August 1741
Bodleian, MS Eng. misc. c.113, fols 329r–330r

21 August 1741 Spalding

Dear Dr

Your Mercury Man lately on my Enquiry after your Health gave Me hopes wee might have the pleasure shortly of seeing You here in your way to or from Holbeach,[1] & if you propose Us that pleasure (which Wee shall be glad of at all times) I thought it worth while to Acquaint You that On thursday Next being the last in the Month and the 26 Instant, Wee shall (as has been some Yeares past & is appoynted to be continued) celebrate the Anniversary of our Institution with a good Concert of Musick in our Town Hall[2] – in my Mind the noblest Entertainment that can be: as a member if you notify it to Mr Hepburn the Chirurgeon, who is also a Brother[3] & has been at some of our anniversarys 'tis not Unlikely he'll bear You Company hither. You used as I remember to love Musick, a Charming & Divine Science, our Method is to have 3 Acts of It. the first begins at 5. The 2^d at 6. The 3rd at 7. after each a pause & the Gentlemen & Ladies are Entertaind with a Glass of Wine.[4] Every Gentleman Except Musick Masters pays a Shilling as at ordinary meetings of our Soc. the Communications whereof conclude the Day with with [sic] a Sober Glass and a Pipe. Wee generally have another Concert the day following and the Young People after that stay & spend the Evening in danceing which reconciles our Institution greatly to the Gayer part of the World who do not so farr Enter into & therefore not so well relish the Philosophical & Historical Part of It as You & I my Friend do. I had last post but one a Long Letter from Your Brother Gale[5] with the Author of Eboracum Francis Drake's account of the Antiquities lately discovered without Micklegate; & his Own Judicious remarkes thereon – and Dr Drakes account of the remains of the once Sumptuous Abbey of Mailross built by St David King of Scots.[6] Amongst the peices of Antiquitie found near York Mr Drake mentions [p.2] a Lamp of Red Earth impressed with the Image of an human body with a Swines Head, a Scymetar in the Right & a Globe in the left hand. This I take was a representation of Hecate not always Tergemina, but Hoggheaded, the Daughter or Energy of Nox ruling half the Globe.[7] this was one of those strange deities borrowd from Egypt as I believe which abounded in Images of human bodys with Heads of all kinds of Animals, Picart[8] in his Religious Customs &c exhibits the like both from the Easter & Western Indies, in very elegant Sculptures. the Abbé Pluche, and P. Montfalcon as well as Natalis Cimes[9] give us many like of Egyptian contrivance or derivd from thence. I have from that delightful Book the said learned Abbé's History of the Heavens and such other Lights as Caussinus, Bochart, de Brie, Walton, Castell, Montfaulcon, Krantzius and Munster[10] have furnishd Me, drawn up a Sheet to Sheet at One View the original & rise of all the Arts of Designeing and of Writing & Accounting by Numerals or Figures of any kind, which I wish You whom I know to be deeply read and for whos Judgement I have a deference would as a Friend when we see you here peruse; but 'tis too tedious to transcribe and I drew It up as it is. and intend to enter it before Our Alphabetical Plagiæ, Markes, Artists names &c of our MSS A.B. of Arts & Science[11] as a proper Introduction thereunto. this has given me the Study and pleasure of much Oriental learning, which is highly delightfull and improveing to my Mind. [p.3] I want and much wish I could obtain sketches of the Signes of the Zodiack, the Seven Planetts, and Capitals Constellations as represented by the Antient Syrians, Egyptians, Nubians, Arabians and Chaldæans or any of them from all whom the Greeks borrowd, as the Romans from the Greeks. if you have any Author who gives them lend It me or favour me with Sleight Sketches from It, with Citations and those references thereto. for the Greeks horribly belied those great & learned People and their ingenious devices & works, & misled the Romans: the Dioscuri[12] are a remarkable Instance of this, for the remoter East knew them Not; but Gemini were Twyn Kids, first Sheep, then Cows and after them the Goats produced their Young – hence 1.Aries 2.Taurus 3.Gemini.

Wee have received from Mr Norcliffe[13] a Merchant at Frederickshall and an Ingenious Corresponding Member of our Soc. a Natural History of Greenland published last Year at Copnhagen by the Rever^d Mr Egede that Kings Superintendent there interleaved & translated by that worthy Gent. into English for our Entertainment, being a curious account of the Inhabitants, Beasts, Birds, Fishes, Amphibious Animals, Vegetables there produced, in Quarto finely printed in the Danish Language and dedicated to the present Prince of Denmark with a New map of the Country and Coasts in a pretty large Scale, a Valuable Present and Attended with a Collection of all the Metals & Minerals of Norway. and fossil Shells found deep & unpetrified there, and On the coast of Sweeden. of Escalops, large Muscles &c. And Very full Narratives of the Success of the pious Missionaries sent from Denmark to Instruct the ignorant natives in Xianity. & of their Manners, Laws, Customes, Habits and Commerce. which you may See at our Museum, which has lately been also enriched with the skin of a Rattle Snake from Maryland.[14]

I am with our humble services to Your Lady
                                    Dear Dr
        Your affectionat Friend and obliged Servant
                                Maur. Johnson junior

To the Reverend
Dr Stukeley at his house
    at Stamford
        present

---

[1] An extract from this letter is transcribed in *Surtees* III, 342. The letter had been delivered by a servant who was visiting Stamford, to avoid the high cost of postage paid by the recipient. Stukeley still needed to visit his home town of Holbeach as he had property there, inherited from his father and cousins.

[2] The SGS held annual concerts of music to celebrate the anniversary of their foundation. They drew on the services of the local music club, who were permitted to rehearse in the SGS's meeting room in return for providing the concerts; some of them were SGS members. See also **Letter 32**, n.1. The date of the planned concert was, in fact, 27 August (as SGS, MB3, fol.88r shows). The Town Hall, now demolished, was built *c.*1620 by John Hobson of Spalding.

[3] Dr John Hepburn (*c.*1685–1766): see Appendix 3.

[4] The Society's minute book (entry for 27 August 1741) gives a full account of the concert programme (SGS, MB3, fol.88r). The Society's concerts were composed of instrumental items, usually by Italian composers such as Corelli and Locatelli and by contemporary English composers, and songs, some of which were settings of Latin and Greek odes and others of specially composed verses, including some by Maurice Johnson. The composer of the music for these was Musgrave Heighington, the SGS's musical director; see Appendix 3.

5 Roger Gale's letter to Johnson, dated 9 August 1742, is summarised as letter 399 in *Correspondence*. The SGS's archive holds the original, together with the account from the *York Courant* of 2 June 1742 about the discovery of Roman antiquities at York.

6 The letter describing the ruins of Melrose Abbey in the Scottish Borders is actually from Francis Drake of York to his cousin the Revd Thomas Drake of Norham near Berwick upon Tweed. It is summarised as letter 396 in *Correspondence* and is in the SGS's archives.

7 The goddess Hecate, usually connected with the underworld and night (Nox), was represented in several forms, particularly as a three-personed figure ('Tergemina') or as a woman with an animal's head, often that of a boar.

8 Bernard Picart (1673–1733) published *Cérémonies et coutumes religieuses de tous les peoples du monde* between 1723 and 1743.

9 The breadth of Johnson's reading and the extent of his library is shown in his references to a range of authors in this letter: the Abbé Nicolas Pluche (1688–1761) wrote *Spectacle de la Nature* (1732–42) and *Histoire du Ciel* (1739). The former popularised everyday understanding of nature and the latter connected the latest work on astronomy with the writings of poets and philosophers. Both books were very popular across Europe in the 1730s and 1740s. Bernard de Montfaucon (1655–1741) wrote *Antiquity Explained and Represented in Diagrams* (1719); Natalis Comes, or Natale Conti (1520–82), an Italian historian and poet, wrote *Mythologiæ* (10 vols, 1562), a standard source for the study of mythology in Johnson's time.

10 A further list of authors referred to for this study; the most significant are Nicolas Caussin (1583–1651), author and editor of several popular books on the symbols associated with Egyptian inscriptions; Samuel Bochart (1599–1667), who wrote on the sacred geography of the Middle East from his very wide knowledge of the past and current languages of the region; Albert Krantz, or Krantzius (c.1448–1517), German monk and historian of Northern Europe; Sebastian Münster (1488–1562), author of *Cosmographia*, a well-illustrated description of the world by a Hebrew scholar.

11 The SGS began a project, 'the Alphabet of the Arts and Sciences', which included English and Latin abbreviations; this ambitious scheme was not completed.

12 Castor and Pollux, twin sons of Zeus and Leda, associated with the constellation Gemini.

13 Richard Norcliffe (fl.1740s): see Appendix 3. As a merchant in Norway he came across the *Natural History of Greenland* by the Norwegian, Revd Hans Egede, first published in Danish in Copenhagen in 1741. Egede (1686–1758) was the first Lutheran missionary to Greenland and became Bishop of Greenland in 1741. The SGS proposed to publish Norcliffe's translation of the book but did not have sufficient funds. Dr John Green, Second Secretary of the SGS, communicated a summary of the book to the RS; see *Phil.Trans.* 42 (1742). An English translation of Egede's book was published in 1760.

14 This may be the snake-skin shown in the drawing of the SGS's rooms (*Correspondence*, Illustration 7, between pp. 203 and 217).

35. William Stukeley to Maurice Johnson, Stamford, 27 November 1743
Spalding, SGS/Stukeley/14

Stamford 27 nov. 1743

My dear friend,

the bearer Mr Gale, a relation of my wifes,[1] coming to Spalding, I desir'd him to call on you & inquire after your health & familys. I have been busy, all this year & am still, in preparing my ground for a garden,[2] which pleads an excuse for me, in not being able to wait on you, at the same time, that it makes a request for any plants you can spare, & send me by our market folks, which I thankfully shall receive & interr immediately.

I lately met with an odd kind of batt with ears an inch & a half long, a live.[3] the ears are double, too, a thing, I suppose common to all. I am most affectionately, with my service to all friends

Yours intirely
Wm Stukeley

To
Maurice Johnson Esqr
  Spalding

[On reverse, notes in Maurice Johnson's writing:]
Dr Wm Stukeley   SGS 15 Decr 1743   and per the Secr. MJ
The within relations of Batts vespertiliones

Messrs Grundys their History of R Wytham & Schæme with Calculations for Restoreing the Navigation from Boston to Lincoln and for dreyning the Lords^{ps} on the Town Row on the W. Side of Lincoln heath. with a Mapp 6 f long by 2 f by a Scale of 2½ – Miles with proper & Curious decorations, the Levels taken in ab^t 400 Stations the Stations in the Water marked in Red & those on the Land in Black figures & compared wth the Surface of the River at Low water marke.[4]
   There is in Spirits an extraordinary Batt of the Sort called Regina Vespertilionum, In the Philos. Trans. of RS some Account of very large Bats and in the Voyage Writers. But the most monstrous are those Bats which Mr Emelie a Gentleman lately returned from Naples (where he long resided) assured Dr Mortimer Secr. RS Mr Mark Catesby a Member of the same & my Self that he & Others Particularly Dr Atwell F.R.S. with him see down in the Subterraneous City of Herculaneum now Portici – near Naples, which he affirmed to be as large as Doves; by which wee'll suppose he meant the Turtle Dove the lest of the Pidgeon kind: (these Bats he also at the royal Soc. on the 8th of decr. 1743 gave the like Acc^t of & that the [*sic*] flew ab^t on their goeing down into & ab^t with lighted flambeaus, but went not up into the passage out, but hid themselves after awhile when he shewd the Soc. the Statue Vases & Capital I sent this Soc. a Sketch & account of[5]   MJ

[1] Presumably a cousin or nephew of Stukeley's second wife Elizabeth, née Gale.
[2] This is Stukeley's garden at his newly purchased house in Barn Hill, Stamford.
[3] Probably the brown long-eared bat, *plecotus auritus*. Johnson's notes at the end of the letter refer to vespertiliones, a sub-order of bats. See Illustration 14 for Stukeley's drawing of the bat.
[4] Johnson refers here to the proposals by the Grundys, father and son, both drainage engineers, for restoring the navigation of the River Witham, 1742. The plan is illustrated in M. J. Honeybone, 'The Spalding Gentlemen's Society: the communication of science in the East Midlands 1710–1760' (unpublished Open University Ph.D. thesis, 2001), I, pp.98–99.
[5] The *Phil.Trans.* (1742–3) shows no published details of these. They are all mentioned in SGS, MB3 (entry for 15 December 1743).

36. William Stukeley to Maurice Johnson, Stamford, 5 January 1744
Spalding, SGS/Stukeley/15

[Annotated by Johnson:] Letter from the Rev^d & Learn'd Dr W Stukeley <u>Druidion</u> apud Shap in Westmorland – <u>Vespertiliones</u> – of <u>Dormant Animals</u>, & <u>Birds of Passage</u> – of the <u>Comett</u> now appearing & its site & Course here 5° Jan 1743/4

My dear friend,
   I received your letter directed to the Gentlemans Society at Stamford, for which I return you thanks. I can't say in relation to the Society, <u>quorum magna</u>

pars fui,[1] being indeed the whole. in relation to Mr Ames's subscription, we poor authors give our own manufacture reciprocally. my last work of Abury[2] is the subscription price.

our friend & brother Roger Gale[3] is in pretty good health, & has promised to come & see me in the spring. I am to return with him, & we are to go together to Shap in Westmorland: in our way to Scruton. when I was at Shap, with him in 1725 I discern'd one of our Druid temples of the serpentine order[4] there. for we rode a mile along one of the avenues, being part of the snake, made with great stones, as usual, set upright. you may imagin it gave me great pleasure, as being at that time, ripening my notions about them, at Abury: & discerning the internal meaning of them. but Mr Gales business would not then permit him to stay at the place. therefore I was forced to leave it: & hope now for a [p.2] new pleasure in the review of that most venerable work.

There are very many Druid temples & other works of theirs in the north, many whereof I have seen. those gentlemen were driven northwards in the Roman persecutions, along with the Christians. I shall describe some of them, if ever I live to publish my third & last volume concerning them.[5]

the long-eared bat, which you call regina vespertilionum I have dry'd & hung up in my hall, where perhaps it may have reigned many years in its dormant state.[6] I admire the creature as one of the beautys of the forming hand of Providence. in divers respects tis a passage between birds and reptiles. no doubt its long ears enable it to hear very acutely, & at great distances. it is likewise double ear'd, as all bats are. this makes them an emblem of a minister of state, a king. I apprehend, these large ears assist the animal in its flight, for in substance they are like its wings.

the fabric of the bat is admirable. it suspends its self either with its head upwards or downwards.

but we cannot omit looking on the creature, among others, as presenting us with an example of [p.3] that sleeping & seperate state, we our selves are once to undergoe, in the grave, till we awake at the general resurrection. snails do the like, dormice, & many more. toads entombd for centurys, in stone, marble, wood. Providence hereby puts a jest upon infidels, as unphilosophical gentry.

Somewhat akin to this are the birds of passage, that point out the 4 great seasons or conversions of the year, the two solstices & equinoxes, by their wonderful & unaccountable migrations: just as old jacob[7] when question'd of Pharaoh concerning his age, most elegantly calls his life, a pilgrimage regarding a better & heavenly country to which he aspired: as interpreted by the excellent author of the epistle to the hebrews. So well were the antients acquainted with the doctrin of a future state: contrary to my friend Warburtons assertion,[8] in his divine legation. for tho' this knowledg was no part of the institutes of Moses, no more than of our acts of parliam^t yet assuredly the Jews knew a future state, as well as the Egyptians & all other heathens.

last night I saw the comet[9] between Andromeda & pegasus, between the stars Sceat & Mirach. it is going to the sun. I am thoroughly satisfy'd, that the principal purpose of comets, is to furnish a faggot to the sun, when wanted, to keep up its heat & quantity. & tis a contrivance as amazing as those enormous bodys. therefore they are matter extremely dense & solid; which now & then drop into his fiery vortex: at proper seasons [p.4] as originally projected by their almighty author. at other times they pass by, & go into the boundless regions of space, very slowly to return.

I am now busy in laying out my garden which will be very forastiere & wild. Mr Gale & I (my curate I mean)[10] propose waiting on you in the spring. my service to your Gentlemens society concludes me

                    Your faithful
                    humble servant
Stamford 5 jan. 1743–4   W Stukeley

To Maurice Johnson junʳ Esqʳ
        Spalding
Turn at Stilton

[1] 'Of which I was the greater part'. By 1744 Stukeley was the only remaining member of the Brazen Nose Society, or the Gentlemen's Society of Stamford, which he organised from 1736 to 1737. Johnson had also been a member.
[2] Stukeley published his book on the Avebury circle, *Abury, a Temple of the British Druids*, in 1743.
[3] See Roger Gale's entry in Appendix 3.
[4] In a letter (dated 24 September 1743) to Gale, who encouraged his work on stone circles, Stukeley described the stones at Shap as 'another huge serpentine temple, like that at Aubrey. The measure of what are left extends a mile and a half …'. There is a full contemporary decription of the Shap stones, dated 7 May 1743, by Thomas Routh (see *Surtees* III, 237–8). The stones are today regarded as Neolithic; many have been destroyed or removed since Stukeley's time.
[5] This volume, dealing specifically with Druid temples, was not published.
[6] Stukeley discovered the bat in his newly purchased house at Barn Hill, Stamford, in 1743; see **Letter 35** above. Later in this letter he refers to his work on his new garden at Barn Hill.
[7] Genesis 47:9; the later reference to the Epistle to the Hebrews is probably to ch.11.
[8] Stukeley's friend William Warburton (1698–1779: see *ODNB*), then incumbent of Brant Broughton and later Bishop of Gloucester. He argued in *The Divine Legation of Moses Demonstrated* that the Hebrews in the time of Moses were not aware of the doctrine of a future state.
[9] The great comet of 1744, the sixth brightest in recorded history, had a fan of six tails. Stukeley recorded it early in its appearance in Europe, which lasted from December 1743 to April 1744.
[10] William Gale (*c.*1716–89), a cousin of Roger and Samuel Gale and of Stukeley's wife, confrater at Browne's Hospital, Stamford; later Rector of Careby and Braceborough, Lincolnshire, and chaplain to the Earl of Wigton.

37. Maurice Johnson to William Stukeley, Spalding, 9 January 1744
Bodleian, MS Eng. misc. c.113, fols 331r–332v

                                        Spalding 9 January 1743/4
Dear Dr[1]

That I may contribute to the pleasures of your projected Gardens,[2] you tell me you're now making: I've herewith Sent you what Variety I had in my Nursery of Flowering Trees and Shrubs to Yield Sweet Odours, & give a Beauty to your Boscage, being planted before Your taller Trees. I shall Sir be glad to See You & Your Lady & Kinsman (to both whom my humble Services) when Yee come into these Parts. I'm greatly Amused with planting all my grounds as well those formerly as now in My power, by my Wifes Brothers Widow's death;[3] with forrest and the larger fruit Trees, mindful of Silvester's saying[4]

                He who delights to Plant and Sett,
                Makes after-Ages in his Debt.

which was the Case in this Country of our Auncestry: The Ogles, Sharpes, Gamlyns, Oldfeilds, Wilsbyes, all which Families I'm so nearly related to, as well as the Johnsons,[5] having planted most of the Timber in this and the Neighbouring Parishes, as yours did at Holbeach. I'm so much devoted to Timber, that I think it horrid (as the Druids of old) to fell Oakes: & foreseeing that's likely now to be the fate of Some here planted by Sir Anthony Oldfeild, to preserve those on my Side the River Welland purpose to purchace the land they grow on: they flanking my Feilds, which I greatly delight in; having laid them now together on the East side my house from It to the Church Drove, or Antient Kings highway from Spalding to Cowbitt: for that other by the River Side (which is now the [p.2] most frequented) is part of the Landowners Estates and only by them (Upon long sufferance, and for the Sake of the Trade & Commerce of this Town) permitted to be Used by all Men. My Method is to supply all the defects where my Fields (which are Seven in Nomber,) are not planted about: then to plant Willows, Osiers, & Sallows next the Ditches. this is the 3rd yeare I've been on this Work; and I propose in places most proper to plant some Clumps of Ash flanked with Scotch Firrs here and there for taking some noble Objects from certain Stations. As Croyland Abbey, Moulton Spire &c – about 5 Yeares hence (if wee live) You may applaud my Designe: Nothing of this Sort having been attempted hitherto in these Parts since Symon Lord Pryor of Spalding planted his Villa at Wykeham;[6] Nor then (I believe) after my manner, especially as I apprehend most Suitable to our Soil, of setting all my Trees (Save the Aquatick) above Soile, & raising a Small Tumulus round the Stemm of Each. I can have finer terminations of View than Any the greatest modern Gardiner can pretend to build: And tho they're too farr distant to be taken into It on the ground, have my Sight from the Turrett a top of my house[7] terminated S by Peterborough Cathedral, & N. by Boston steeple, which Appeares as at the Extremitie of a Visto, like a most Stately Egyptian Obelisk, & along a side of It the meandres of the Welland to It's Outfall beyond Fossdyke, & ships at sea. thence Mr Lynn[8] and I with a Mapp & Compass, viewed, and on the [p.3] 5th Septr. 1712 Sett down these Sumptuous Objects & their Bearings, and formes of appearance. first just under our Eyes.[9]

N.E. Spalding Parish Church & Free schole — a lofty Spire
antiently St Thomas's Chapell & built before the Church
Wykeham Hall and stately Chapell   a double Cube or
the Villa of the Lord Pryours of Spalding   Paralellagram
Fossedyke Chapell   a low Towr
Spalding Northern Corne-Windmill
A large Farme House coverd with red Tyles
Cowhorne Ferryhouse on the River Welland
with the Turnes of that River, and Vessels lying in It or On It in various Parts – or under Saile
BOSTON Church & Towr,   a most Stately Obelisk
Kirton Church   gives name to the Hundred   a large Towr
Sutterton Church   a Spire
Surfleet Church   a Spire
Quadring Church   (an Elegant building)   a Windmill, a Spire
Donyngton Church   Markett Town   a Spire
Gosbertown Church   a stately Spire

	Pinchbeck (called so from the bright Glen stream) Windmills	
	& parts of the Great Northern Road	
	Pinchbeck Church	a stately Towr
N.	Spalding High Bridg, Town & Town hall	
N.W.	Helpringham Church a neat Building	a Spire
W.	Rippingale Church	a Spire
	Remaines of Spalding-Prioury	
	The River of Welland; and other parts of Spalding Town called Windsover and Monkshall	
[p.4]	Grimesthorpe Parke, his Grace the Duke of Ancasters	
	Dieping Churches 1. a Market Town 2.Spires & a Town	
	Clipsham Parke & Woods	Matth. Snows Esq
	Stretton Woods	Mr Horsemans
	These Woods intercepted our View of Stamford Churches	
	Burleigh Parke and Wottrop Groves	E. of Exeters
S.W.	Spalding Southern Corne-Windmills	
	Parston Church[10]	a Spire
	PETERBOROUGH St Jno. Baptists Ch.	a fine Spire
	The Cathedral	Spires & Towr
	Yaxly Church	a Spire
	Stanground Church	a Spire
	THORNEY Abby Church	a Towr with 2 high Embatteld Turretts
	CROYLAND Abby Church	a Pyramid
	& in those Lordships several Dutch Water Engines	
S.	Cowbitt Chapell	a Towr
		Windmill
	Bellsmore	2 Water Engines
	Whittlesea Church	a lofty Spire
S.E.	Moulton Chapell	an Octagonal Cupola
	many Coppice Woods & a Windmill	
E.	The Churches of Weston, Moulton, Whapload, Holbeach, Gedney, Fleet, & Sutton were not then discernable but may be seen thence when the Trees are bare of leaves.	

So much for Gardening and Views: thank you for Your most ingenious & learned Letter. favour me with more at your best Leisure who am
Dear Friend Your most faithfull Servant
M. Johnson junior

---

[1]   Johnson's writing has increased in size compared with his earlier letters, probably as his eyesight alters with age. Stukeley's writing in his later letters is also growing larger.

[2]   This is Stukeley's newly developed garden at Barn Hill, Stamford, of which he drew many plans. See John Smith, 'William Stukeley in Stamford: his houses, gardens and a project for a Palladian triumphal arch over Barn Hill', *Antiquaries Journal* 93 (2013), 353–400.

[3]   The death of Mrs Johnson's brother's widow led to Johnson's possession, via his wife's inheritance from her brother Joshua Ambler, of the house next door to Ayscoughfee Hall, Gayton or Holyrood House, which for the next ten years became the meeting-place of the SGS.

[4]   Johnson refers to the poet Joshua Sylvester (1563–1618); 'Silvester' relates to the Latin *silvestris* meaning 'wooded'.

5   Johnson's fascination with his family history appears in many of his letters to Stukeley, who knew these family genealogies. Sir Anthony Oldfield (1626–68) was the major landholder of his period; see P. R. Seddon (ed.), *The Letter Book of Sir Anthony Oldfield 1662–1667*, LRS 91 (2004).
6   Trees still survive around the site of Wykeham chapel, north-east of Spalding.
7   See Illustration 4 for the turret, still surviving on Ayscoughfee Hall.
8   Probably Dr Walter Lynn; see Appendix 3.
9   For most of the following locations, see Stukeley's 'Map of the Levels in Lincolnshire commonly called Holland' (1723), Bodleian, Gough Gen. Top. 56, reproduced as Illustration 20 in this volume.
10 Paston, then a separate village and now a district of northern Peterborough.

38. Maurice Johnson to William Stukeley, undated fragment[1] dated to 9 January 1744
Bodleian, MS Eng. misc. c.114, fol.360

My Son writes me from Brussells[2] That at Liege he had the good fortune to procure a round Dish 12in in diametre of old Albano Ware, whereof he sent Me a drawing. within a Rim of Foliage Work representing a Frame in high relief – is represented the Decollation of St Jno the Baptist in a prison, the daughter of Herodias recieves his head in a Charger from the Executioner – Another prisoner Manicled by seems shuddering at the Apprehension of like fate. It seems after Mich. Angelos Manner. I hope he'll pick up some good Academy drawings at least those of the Flemish School, which now for Statuary & Tapistry exceeds the Roman. I have an Oval Dish of Albano ware which was a Legacy to my Wife by her Mistress who's Great Great Grandfather Coll. Ram brought It with him thence the subject – Venus between Bacchus & Ceres Sine quibus frigesceret. Sir Rd Ellis[3] had one of Curtius taking the fatal Leap after Julio Romano. Sir And. Fountaine[4] is rich in very many Vessels of many kinds of that ware which he keeps in a Clossett by themselves as a great Treasure. Martial says – Dives erat Porsena fictitibus [5]– he has also many Etruscan Vases, but their beauty is not Comparable to that of these more modern Crokery. Dresden China, and that made in the East on European designs Draughts & Modells do indeed farr excel all others. For elegance the Siameze excel the Japeneze, as much as the later do the Chinese, in general. But when they any of them do their best to follow European orders & directions They will be well paid for their Performances – of which I've seen some to Imitate Insects & Natural Flowers in Alto Relievo so Natural & Just both in [*gap in text*] as to Vie with Myron's Works[6]

To the Reverend Dr Stukeley at his
house in Stamford
– with 6 Parcells of Trees
present

1   In Stukeley's letter-books in the Bodleian Library, this is filed separately from the other Johnson letters, as an unidentified fragment, since it is not signed or dated. It is in Maurice Johnson's handwriting. Since the reverse of the sheet bears Stukeley's address and the message about the 'Parcells of Trees', it must be the cover sheet to **Letter 37** above, which refers to 'Flowering Trees and Shrubs'; Johnson has added an unsigned postscript on this cover sheet.
2   The letter from Johnson's eldest son Maurice, which describes the dish discussed in the letter and sends a drawing of it, is dated 22 December 1743 (see *Correspondence*, letter 424). The younger

Johnson was in Flanders with his regiment, the 1st of Foot (the Guards). The drawing he sent his father is a good reproduction of this dish of Albano ware, a form of majolica.

3   See Appendix 3. Marcus Curtius was a legendary hero of early Rome; according to Livy, he leapt on horseback into a widening chasm in the Forum, so saving the city by his sacrifice.

4   Sir Andrew Fountaine (1676–1753: see *ODNB*), a great antiquarian and collector, whose 'collection of majolica was the finest outside Italy'.

5   'Porsena was rich in painted ware', one of Martial's epigrams.

6   Myron of Eleutheræ (*c*.480–440 BC), the Athenian sculptor.

39. William Stukeley to Maurice Johnson, Stamford, 18 February 1744
Spalding, SGS/Stukeley/16

Dear S^r

I received your trees,[1] & hope they will be able to return you the tribute of their agreable odors: when you give me the pleasure of seeing you here. in the mean time be pleasd to accept of my hearty thanks, for your so liberal a donation.

while Dr Bradley[2] gives us his accurate account of the wonderful comet which now appears, both even & morn; I have sent you the inclosed scheme, as settled by the astronomers with us. its tail is above a million of miles long, even before it comes to its perihelion. the line of nodes is the place where the plane of the comets parabolic orbit, cuts the plane of the earths circular orbit, in an angle of about 40 degrees. at its perihelion it will be 20 millions of miles distant from the sun.[3]

I have been infinitely delighted with the view & contemplation of this stupendous appearance, one of the magnalia Divinæ potestatis.[4] I hope in the Spring to wait on you & am

	Your most faithful
the comet appears in a	humble servant
morning, by reason of its	W Stukeley
great northern latitude	Stamford 18 feb. 1743–4

To Maurice Johnson jun^r Esqr
        Spalding
Turn at Stilton

[*Enclosed: diagram of the comet's orbit in relationship to the Sun and to the earth's orbit, with dates of its position at intervals from 23 December 1743 to 19 April 1744. Annotated by Johnson: 'A Description & Plan of the Comet which appeared in 1743 By the Reverend & learned Dr Wm Stukeley a Member of the Royal Society Lond^n & the Gentlemens Society in Spalding.'*]

1   See **Letter 37** above; Stukeley acknowledges Johnson's gift of trees.

2   James Bradley (1692–1762: see *ODNB*), Savilian Professor of Astronomy at Oxford and Astronomer Royal in 1742 following Edmond Halley. Bradley made detailed notes of his observations of the comet of 1744, which was extremely bright, equalling 'the brightness of Jupiter at times'.

3   The comet's perihelion was on 1 March 1744; it was indeed 20.5 million miles from the Sun.

4   'The wonders of the Divine power'.

[**85. Maurice Johnson to William Stukeley, Spalding, 17 March 1744**
This letter is not in the Bodleian collection of Johnson's letters. It has been published in *Surtees* II, 285–7. It is included in this volume as **Letter 85** in the Additional Letters section below.]

40. Maurice Johnson to William Stukeley, Spalding, 14 July 1744[1]
Bodleian, MS Eng. misc. c.113, fols 333r–334v

Spalding 14th July 1744

Dear Dr

The Indisposition I left you under, I hope's long since gone, and that you and your Lady & family (to whom our Services & thanks for all favours when lately so frequently with you) are Well. & to your kinsman Mr Gale.[2] On our Return Wee found my Son Green[3] likewise from his Uncles, Red Mershal in Durham, who last Thursday entertaind Us with a Journal thither[4] and sketches of a Cross near Doncaster built (I believe) by Otewel son of Hugh E[arl] of Chester about 1110. Castellain of Tickhill & Lord of that Honor hard by: +I:CESTES: LA: CRVICE: OTE:D: TILLIA: KI: ALME: DEV: ENFIACE:MERCI:AM+[5] & description of the Great Church of St George in Doncaster, with Its panelled Roofe, painted with Scripture histories, as Boston once was[6] – York Cath[edral]; Castle, & assembly Room, a Vine at North Allerton extending it Self 47 Yards. The Parish Ch.[7], Parsonage, Rectors house, & an Antient Monument in Marble, of Sir Jeremy Claxton, & his Lady in a vast headdress, her haire Set up on Each Side & confined in a Caul of Network, his Defaced; of her & the Ch. & a Chancel wherein they lye, calld Claxton's Porch, about 1270 and the Parsonage House, he made sketches [p.2] also of the S. View of the Church of Tuxford in the Clays in Notts. antiently written Tokesford, wherein as appears by Pat.31 Ed.3 p.1 m.25 John a descendant of Thomas Lord Longvillers (about A.Dni 1356) founded a Cell in his the [*sic*] Parsonage house for 3 Chantry Priests to celebrate Mass in this Church & 2 in New Sted Priory in Shirewood – Dugd: 2 Bar: fo.144/ 3 Mon: Angl: fo.90. Tanners Notit: fo:412.[8]

The new Edition of Pataroli[9] (which Dr Green has got,) does not come up to what B. Bells Tabulæ Augustæ would give Us, if Trinity Coll: (which ought) would publish them. They have the MS ready prepared (to my Knowledg) for the press & promised his Executors to do justice in honour to his Memory as a Benefactor to their Library in printing them: and I believe Kirkhall had engraved by far the greatest Part of the Heads, & (to my knowledge) he had plates of others done by other good Hands, Mr Commissary Greaves talkd of urging them to It.[10]

[p.3] Wee shall be greatly beholden to you for transcripts at Your Leisure of our Brazennose Coll. Society minutes[11] or Such of them, or Such Parts of them as You Can now & then Conveniently transmitt me. which as Ben. Ray[12] & I, & some Others of our Soc. here are also Brother Members of that You'll esteem us the worthier of, & in some degree entitled to the favour, as You, Sir, are to Ours and wellcome to Command what you please of them, and the free Use of any Of our Papers and Things, which I wish You to See how decently I have procured to be reposited for daily & ready Use, & even Ornament. bring your Couz. Gale with you, whom wee should be glad to have a Member,[13] being a Worthy, ingen-

ious Gentleman. And with the humble Services of all our Family to You & yours believe me to be Dear Friend
   Your much obliged & obed^t Servt
    M Johnson jun^r

PS. be so good as let your Servant carry the Enclosed to Dr Colbys & when you See them give my Services to Cous. Wingfields[14]

 I know there was a Family of the Name of Tilliol of Scaleby Castle in Cumberland, but know of no Town, or Seat of that name, presume they might be descended from this Otewel or Otho who being a natural son of Loup could not properly take his Syrname, but might that of this Honour & Honourable Office, which he held. He was Shipwrecked says the Saxon Chron: with 2 of the Kings Sons, & other persons of great Quality AD 1120.[15]

 I understand the Inscription of the Cross by Doncaster, thus Hanc Crucem Otho de Ticilliâ: f.f. Cuj. Animam Deus desponset mi[sericordi]æ. Amen

 The Normans could not pronounce, therefore detested, and Alterd the Harsh Spelling of many Saxon Words where Several Consonants came together as in our Lincoln, by them as Mr Baxter[16] notes perridicule mutatum in Nicol – So here I presume for like reason Tickhill into Tillia, if my Conjecture be right. There is the River Till, in Northumberland, whence our antient family of the Tillneys, Tilleneaus, took their Name as I apprehend.[17]
    Adieu.

---

[1] Part of this letter is transcribed in *Surtees* III, 352–4.
[2] Presumably the Revd William Gale; see **Letter 36**, n.10.
[3] Dr John Green, Maurice Johnson's son-in-law; see Appendix 3.
[4] He and his wife Jane had been to visit their uncle, the Revd Walter Johnson, formerly of Spalding but now Rector of Redmarshall (Co. Durham); see Appendix 3. He gave detailed accounts of his journey at SGS meetings.
[5] The British Museum holds a print of Doncaster Cross by George Vertue, with the inscription 'Ices: Est La Cruice: Ote: D: Tillia: Ki: Alme: Dev: En: Face; Merci: AM.' The Cross was replaced at the end of the eighteenth century by Hall Cross, a copy of the original cross.
[6] The mediæval church of St George in Doncaster was destroyed by fire in 1852 and rebuilt to designs by George Gilbert Scott.
[7] Dr Green is now describing St Cuthbert's, the parish church of Redmarshall. The effigies he refers to are now thought to be those of Thomas de Loughton and his wife from the mid-fifteenth century.
[8] In 1386 John de Longvilliers gave the living of Tuxford (Notts) to the priory of Newstead to establish three chantry chaplains at Tuxford and two at Newstead to celebrate mass daily. Following the Reformation, the income went to Tuxford Grammar School. See Dugdale, *Monasticon Anglicanum* III, 90, and Tanner, *Notitia Monastica*, 412.
[9] Lorenzo Pataroli (1674–1727), *Opera Omnia* (1740) contains Pataroli's account of early Roman imperial coinage.
[10] Beaupré Bell (see Appendix 3) bequeathed his manuscripts to Trinity College, Cambridge, where they still remain. They included his 'Tabulæ Augustæ', a precise account of the coinage of the Emperor Augustus, which the college agreed to print. The publication was eagerly awaited by numismatists, and is still awaited; the MS as it stands has only the first section of text in its final form for printing; the remainder has its final corrections but is not in a fair copy and it would require a considerable amount of editing. Elisha Kirkall (c.1682–1742), who had prepared the illustrative plates for the publication, was a prolific and innovative engraver working in London. William Greaves (c.1703–87), Commissary of Cambridge University, who attempted to encourage the publication, had married Bell's sister and heiress, and succeeded to Bell's estate at Outwell (Norfolk).
[11] The minutes of the meetings of Stukeley's Brazen Nose Society of Stamford in 1736 and 1737 were read at the SGS. The minutes survive today in two MS volumes in the Bodleian Library

(MS Eng. misc. e.22 and 123) and it is planned to transcribe them for a forthcoming volume to be published by the LRS.

12   The Revd Benjamin Ray: see Appendix 3.
13   A member of the SGS. There is no record of William Gale becoming a member.
14   Dr Dixon Colby (1680–1756), a Stamford physician; see Appendix 3. Johnson was related to the Wingfield family of Stamford and Tickencote.
15   Richard Tilliol was granted the manor of Scaleby in Cumberland by Henry I. For a full account of the Tilliol family, see Carole Rawcliffe, 'Tilliol, Sir Peter', in J. S. Roskell, L. Clark and C. Rawcliffe (eds), *The History of Parliament: The House of Commons 1386–1421* (4 vols, Stroud, 1993), IV, 614–17. Johnson refers to the sinking of the *White Ship* in 1120.
16   William Baxter (1650–1723), author of *Glossarium Antiquitatum Britannicarum* (1719 and 1733): see p.153, 'Normannis denique perridicule Nichol appelatur hæc urbs'. See also **Letter 16**, n.17.
17   Modern etymology derives 'Tickhill' from 'Tica's hill'.

41. William Stukeley to Maurice Johnson, Stamford, 8 March 1746[1]
Spalding, SGS/Stukeley/17

[Annotated by Johnson:] 1745 the Reverend Dr Stukeley with the 1st Vol of Acts & Observations of his Soc. Æneanasensis[2] & about restoring the Said Society –

Dear Sir,
   I received yours on a Saturday even at 5 a clock, whence you will easily judg, I cannot well write a long answer, seeing I do all the duty at my church my self at all times. otherwise it would be a pleasure to me to be copious, thô tedious. I will endeavour to show your daughter all the respect that can be.[3] I have long meditated & at last resolvd to set about restoring our Æneanasense Society here at Stamford. I am determind not to be deceiv'd about it, therefore hope nothing from it: knowing the difficulty of doing these things in the country. & I have learnt to be easy about such matters, <u>nil admirari</u>. a little amusement contents me. I have sent you the first volume of our Memoirs,[4] & propose to see you in Spalding [p.2] as soon as the fine weather comes.

   My wifes service & mine wait on your good family & I am
                                            Your affectionate friend
                                                      W Stukeley
Stamford 8 mar.
       1745–6

To Maurice Johnson esq^r

1   This letter was discussed at a meeting of the the SGS (MB4, fol.33v, entry for 13 March 1746).
2   This, and the later reference in Stukeley's letter, relate to Stukeley's attempt to revive the Brazen Nose Society, a learned society at Stamford similar to those at Spalding and Peterborough. He had instituted the Society in 1736 and it operated until 1737. His attempt to revive it in 1746 was unsuccessful. It is referred to here by its Latin title; the title-page of the minute books recording its meetings in 1736–7 states: 'Æneanasensis Societas Stanfordiæ Fundata 18 junii 1736' (The Society of the Brazen Nose of Stamford, founded 18 June 1736).
3   Johnson's daughter Elizabeth, known in the family as 'Madcap Bet', stayed with Stukeley and his

family in Stamford in May 1746 (see *Correspondence*, letter 460). She later married Robert Butter, a Spalding merchant, amateur bassoonist and SGS member.

4   See **Letters 36**, n.1 and **40** n.11 above. For a full discussion of Stukeley's minute books and his attempt to establish a learned society in Stamford in the 1730s, see SGS, MB4, fol.33 (entry for 13 March 1746).

42. Maurice Johnson to William Stukeley, Spalding, 15 March 1746
Bodleian, MS Eng. misc. c.113, fols 335r–336v

Spalding 15 March 1745[1]

Dear Dr,

I'm much obliged to You and return you thanks for your kind professions of regard towards my Daughter, and never doubt of Your Shewing them to Me or Mine: but take it to be prudent to have the Recommendation of a Friend to a Friend whenever one goes for a while to any place, it makeing some houres pass more pleasantly, & as I've few Acquaintance of nearer Intimacy & longer Continuance than You Good Sir,[2] so I value that of none more than of Yours Your Lady and Daughters to whom You'll farther favour Me in makeing mine & my Wifes & Families Services Acceptable & agreeable: I hope Wee shall keep up a Constant correspondence, recieved your first Vol of the Acts & Observations of our Brasennose Society safe, am glad you're determined to restore it with Vigour, to which I will contribute all in my Power, & hope I may do good, as I willingly would to a Town where I & my Auncestors long since have excercised a Jurisdiction[3] and my Familie flourished in my Namesake thrice Chief Magistrate in 1518, 1528 & 1539. & in 14 Parliament of King H[enry] VIII AD 1523 was with David Cecill Esq Burgess for the same. Robert the Arch Deacon founder of Okeham & Uppingham Schools sometime resided there in Q.Eliz. & King J[ames] I time. & my Grandfather Walter whilest he rebuilt the far greatest Part of his House by the Chain Bridge here[4] in King C[harles] 2d time dwelt with his Numerous Family at Stamford. Where when I had the Honour to be Deputy of John Earle of Exeter Lord Recorder, I proposd the Instituting a Literary Society[5] Whereof Mr Richards a Steward of his Lordships who resided then in St Martins, was So great a Promoter as, with the leave of our Soc. here, He had our Rules; the Last whereof is the onely one necessary as I find by Experience to all such Undertakings, and I therefore accordingly recommend it to you to insert

No one is to talk sing read or repeat any Politicks or what relate to the State-Affaires & Government; Nor to enter into Disputes in Religion here: Other-wise to Communicate whatever may be thought useful or Entertaining.

How they Came not to keep It up, had they observed this Rule inviolably, notwithstanding Elections I enquire not, But was Informed My [*sic*] Principal that Earle and the then Burgesses Mr Cecil & Mr Bertie became Members thereof & contributed both Money & Books towards It as also Mr Atwood Mr Blackwells Dr Coleby Mr Denshire Sen[r] Mr Hepburne and Others[6] and that those Books were reposited in one of the Churches. I wish if there be such that you had them revised & rendered safe & useful there, if you cannot get them removed in that fine Room you shewd me in Browns Bead House,[7] which I should think the best and hope you'll prevaile to have It for Your Place of Meeting, being Spatious and Pleasant: But if as You Seemed to doubt these Cannot be obtained you can for one day in the Week accomodate the Company with the Room adjoyning yet detached from your house[8] [p.2] which were I to chuse I would much rather do than hold It in a Publick House, at least 'till Your Company and Books with the Supellex encrease so as to require larger Accomodation, as they may in time. The main thing is to engage Some if they be but few to be staunch and constant Attendants, Do all by Ballott, as to Admitting Members & making or altering Rules, Save matters of necessary Expence let them be left to the President & officers of the Soc. as a Councell and standing Committee, as ours are. Wee brew our Own Ale & have a Cellar & Pipes & Tabacco, for there must be some Ale with some History, as they say at Oxford, & old Peter le Neve[9] used you know to Say He could not be Conversable without a Pipe, which is the Case of others,

For there Each Science Sir should reare Its Type

History her Pot, Divinity its Pipe.[10]

if any one chuse he may drink wine with us, paying 1s., otherwise Wee pay but 6d a Meeting & onely the Residents who are Regular Members pay 12s. a Yeare that is 1s per Month, if not elsewhere on Some Duty, for defraying Expences of the Rooms, Coales, Candles, And Attendance, which Small Contribution with what Testons[11] are collected at Every Meeting pays for our Malt, Hops, Brewings, Glasses, Pipes, Tabacco & keeping our Garden too. But by 35 Yeares Various trials & Experience[12] and the Prudent Care of 3 good Treasurers Wee had in that time[13] Mr Wm. Atkinson, the Reverend Mr Timothy Neve, & my Brother, (whom my Son Walter succeeds in that Office, as in Others & all his Buisyness) Wee're got into the best & cheapest Method of manageing. Wee have 2 Secr.[14] One for Natural History, Physick, Philosophy, Mathematicks, Anatomy, Botany Chemistry, & the Other for Divinity, Law, History, Antiquity, Architecture & the Arts of designeing: the Senior Secr. Annually audits our Treasurers Accounts who against that day collects all the Monthly payments. Wee have an Operator (ever a Chyrurgeon & Apothecary) having an Hortus Siccus,[15] a Collection of Specimens of the Materia Medica, Embryos & Many Animals in Spiritts. these have been here Dr Francis Bellinger, Mr René Mitchell, Mr Peter Bold, Mr Harry Bayley & now Mr Michael Cox. As I have the Honour to be Senior Secretary which I have ever been Ive corresponded in the Artificial Sciences if Wee may So call them, as Dr Green our other Secretary in the Natural. Wee had at our beginning change of Presidents as my Father & Revd Mr Waring but have long fixed in our Antient Minister, whose V.P. is the 1st in standing of 5 at the Meeting which No. with Us makes a Society to do Busyness by majority of Balls[16] if an Equal Number be present then the President or V.P. has 2 Balls. Tantum de hoc onely I should Add That as Wee have but one Church here & therein Over the Porch were at our Institution in 1709/10 a parcel of old Books which wee mended & with all our Divinity Church History, Canon Law, & Ethicks keep in 6 Classes under Lock & Key in the Vestiary being for more immediate use of our Clergy the Minister as Librarian & his Curate & the School Master, (who has another of Fine Classicks & Gramarians at hand in our Grammar School) as Deputys. All our Other Books are with a Fine Collection of Musick & Some good musical Instruments in 5 more such Classes in our Museum & our Collection of Supellex Literaria[17] in 4 more Classes there ready for Use and for our Operators Care and Under the Custody and Direction of the Secretaries with many MSS. Some of the Members compiling Others written by the Secretaries or their Register, & amongst them Several Curious Drawings & Plans.

God give you good Success my old Friend in all your undertakings, in this Laudable one in particular which has Occasiond my Prolixity which as You declare you dislike not I took the more Paines or rather I may truly say, pleasure in, hopeing some Hints may be of use: I am endeavouring to Excite the Vicar & Schoolmaster with some Gentlemen at Boston, & in that Neighbourhood (who are Members of our Soc. here) to Institute Such a Society There, of which Corporation having likewise had the like honour to be Deputy Recorder, and having Relations and Friends dwelling there I hope to have the Honour to be a Member. They have a good Publick Library Over their Church Porch ready & neatly fitted up, and a Fine pleasant publick Room in their Markett Place which they may have the Use of & Space at one End for 2 Closeetts [sic] for Repositories, highly commodious without any Expences. if wee bring these things to bear and our Meetings there, with you & at Peterborough be kept up but with the assiduity Wee in this Smallest & less advantaged Town of the 4 keep up ours; the Easy & Constant meanes of circulating our Notices will vastly Enspirit them all & circulate Knowledge So, as that these like 4 Colleges of Arts will forme as it were an Academy of Arts & Sciences for this Gyrvian Tract. Yet thô the lest Wee must not give up the point of Antiquity to Any of the Four, & for Standing insist on being acknowledgd the first, so long held up to the tenor of the Institution in England for I have made diligent Enquiry and can find not One out of London & the Universities[18] which has subsisted So long, but abroad especialy in Italy & France these Sort of Literary Societies (commonly called Institutes) are frequent & almost in Every considerable Town, and Sir Izaack Newton, when he deigned to do us the honour on Our application to him by me to become a Member, Not onely Approved our Rules, which I read Over to him, but declared he wishd the like in Every Markett Town.

[Note by Johnson at foot of page:] I recom^d my Son the Revd Jno Johnson BA. of St Jno Coll. Cambr. & Curate of Ramsey to be a Memb^r with us of your Brazen Nose Society.[19]

[p.4] Lincoln being our Metropolis the See of our Diocesan the Consistory Court of his Chancellor & that of the Highshireff of the County kept there, the Dean & Chapter a Corporate body of long Standing their Archives well stored with Antient Records and their Library a Spatious & well furnished Room I would fain Have had a Society therein fixed[20] and 1720 proposd the Instituting Such by Dr Mandeville then the Chancellor of that Church, Mr Gardener Sub Dean Mr Trimnell Chanter & what they called Masters most comonly resident together with Such of the Canons as could and would come into It – and Sr Edward Hales Mr Scroop, Mr Newell Chancellor of the Diocese, Mr Howson, Mr Register Porter, Captain Pownell, Mr Disneys [sic], Dr Pakey, Mr Sibthorpe, Dr Greathead, Mr Gilby their Recorder Dr Nelthorpe, Mr Harvey the Town Clerk, Mr Pert Clerk of the Court of Sewers Mr Beck Clerk of the Court of Justices of Peace. and Others of my Acquaintance then living there And the Lord Bishop should be the Patron of It, as he properly is of the Chapter. and the High Sheriff for the time being President. & the Chapter Clerk their Secretary. but this Schæme alltho' they had & have Ten times as many Noblemen Clergy and Gentlemen within a ride to their News house took not effect, which yet at Race times, Assizes & Elections might have been frequently very numerous, besides what the attendance on the Bishops & Sheriffs Courts & those Other Courts must bring to that Town. Now As Spalding is Naturaly Situat for It, I hope the Learning of Stamford, Peterborough, Boston & Wisbeach Will center in it, <u>being partly equidistant from Every of them.</u>[21] they have a Library & some sort of remains of an Institute, but almost discontinued Since our friend & fellow Members Dr Massey left them and Mr Richard Lake died who published the Catalogue of their Parochial Library & augmented It greatly, before which are the Names of their Members Benefactors thereunto. Dr Bull their Minister is Super Annuated & I have few tho Some Relations and Acquaintance now left there, but if I live to spend a day or Two I will endeavour to revive It, at lest as their Coburgesses have now & then Meetings, which gave Us meanes of some Care being taken of their Books to have them reviewed & put in good Order (which I hear they want) & engageing a Member or Two at lest to Correspond with Us as you Dr & Couzen Lake used to do. Your See Dear Sr How Zealous I Continue to be in the Cause of Enlargeing Knowledge, which I'm certain will not render this long Conversation disagreeable to You. & you'll be convinced I have been true to my undertaking when I assure you if nothing from Correspondents has been communicated, Or by Members at home produced, I've Never failed from my Own Study to furnish the Company with something to create Conversation and note in our Minutes for as long as Wee kept any[22] which was soon after Sr Richard Steele layd down his Spectator which with the Tatlers, Lovers & Lay Monks[23] Wee took in as they Came Out & read at our Meetings and have them all in Single Papers.

    I am Dear Dr Your most obliged & affectionate friend

                                  M Johnson jun^r

[1] This letter would be dated '1746' today; its contents show that it is a direct reply to Stukeley's letter of 8 March 1746 (**Letter 41** above). At the time, the year officially began on Lady Day (25 March) and correspondents could date a letter written between January and 25 March 1746 as either '1745', '1745/6' or '1746'. This practice ceased on the reform of the calendar in 1752. This letter is invaluable in providing an extensive account of the functioning of the SGS and Johnson's hopes and plans for a network of corresponding learned societies in the East Midlands, particularly in the Fens of Lincolnshire and neighbouring counties. All the aspects of the SGS and its activities are documented in the Society's minute books, museum and library.

[2] The friendship between Johnson and Stukeley went back to their childhood, when their fathers were local lawyers and fellow-officers in the Militia. See the discussion of this in the Introduction (at pp.xvii–xviii).

[3] For details of Johnson's ancestors in the Stamford area, see **Letter 31** above. Robert Johnson (1540–1625: see *ODNB*) was Archdeacon of Leicester and son of Maurice Johnson, MP for Stamford.

[4] Walter Johnson JP (1620–92); his heir was the Revd Walter Johnson, his grandson, who owned the house by the Chain Bridge in Spalding.

[5] This was in 1721, the first of three short-lived attempts to found a learned society in Stamford; the other two were Stukeley's in 1736 and 1746. The SGS minute book (entry for 9 October 1721) records, 'In ans[wer] to a Lr from Mr W Richards of Stamford to the Secr. he has leave to transmit for the use of the Gent[lemen] of Stamford (who as Wee're informd desire them for the establishment of a Soc. there) a Copy of the Rule & Orders of the Soc.[SGS]' (SGS, MB1, fol.57v). On 22 May 1746 Johnson added a further note (SGS, MB4, fol.47; see **Letter 43** below). Johnson was Deputy Recorder to John Cecil, sixth Earl of Exeter (1674–1721), who was appointed Recorder in 1720 and died in December 1721.

[6] The two MPs for Stamford, the Hon. Charles Cecil (c.1683–1726), MP 1705–22, and Charles Bertie (c.1674–1730), MP 1717–27. The other members of this first Stamford society were: the Revd Dr John Attwood (c.1681–1733, Rector of St Andrew and St Michael, Stamford, and the Earl's chap-

7   Browne's Hospital or Bedehouse, Stamford contains a common room, chapel, confraters' room and audit room. Johnson is probably referring to the Audit Room, the business room of the Hospital.
8   This is the room which Stukeley planned to be attached by a covered bridge to his house in Barn Hill, Stamford.
9   See **Letter 15**, n.18 above.
10 Johnson adapts a quotation from Pope's *Dunciad* (book III, lines 195–6): 'But where each science lifts its modern type,/ History her Pot, Divinity her Pipe'.
11 An old English coin, worth one shilling in the sixteenth century but only 6d by the eighteenth century. This was the subscription paid by regular members at each meeting they attended.
12 This puts the foundation date of the SGS to an informal origin in 1710, generally accepted today. The formal articles of association were signed in 1712.
13 For all the members of the SGS mentioned in this paragraph, see their individual entries in Appendix 3. 'My brother' is John Johnson; 'my Father' is Maurice Johnson (senior); 'our Antient Minister' is the Revd Stephen Lyon.
14 Maurice Johnson was the only Secretary for some years; later Dr John Green became Second Secretary, dealing with the sciences and medicine as listed here, while Johnson remained as First Secretary, dealing with the humanities, law and antiquities. In 1748 Johnson became President on the death of the Revd. Stephen Lyon and Green remained as Secretary.
15 A 'dry garden' or herbarium, a collection of dried specimens of herbs and plants in their museum.
16 For voting on business matters and the election of members, the SGS used, and still uses, a ballot box in which members place a ball signifying their decision. A white ball signifies assent and a black ball signifies a negative vote.
17 Additional literary material such as library catalogues.
18 The SGS is today the longest continuously surviving provincial society of its kind. In London the Royal Society predates it; the Society of Antiquaries had an earlier foundation but ceased to meet until re-founded in 1717 by a group including Johnson and Stukeley. There were other provincial societies of a similar age, such as the Dublin Philosophical Society, but these were short-lived in Johnson's time, although some of them were re-founded at a later date. Here and in the following paragraph Johnson spells out his plans for an extension of learned activity in Lincolnshire and the surrounding area through a connected network of learned societies all communicating their knowledge to each other; unfortunately this was not achieved.
19 This is a note to Stukeley to include Johnson's son, Revd John Johnson, as a member of the Stamford Brazen Nose Society. See John Johnson's entry in Appendix 3.
20 As a magistrate and lawyer attending the Lincoln Assizes, Johnson was in close touch with the intelligentsia of the City and Cathedral of Lincoln. He proposed several sources for membership, giving a list of suitable members of the Cathedral clergy and officials and another of fellow-lawyers and physicians from the Lincoln area. As an assize town, Lincoln could also potentially have drawn in members living in the country but attending the Assizes, on the pattern of the society he and Stukeley attempted to form at Ancaster in the late 1720s. He was much saddened by this failure to establish a learned society there, with which his own SGS could have corresponded. Those he lists as potential members are: Dr John Mandeville (d.1725), Chancellor of Lincoln Cathedral (1695–1725); Revd James Gardiner (d.1732: see *ODNB*), Subdean of Lincoln (1704–32); Revd Dr David Trimnell (1675–1756), Precentor of Lincoln (1718–56); Sir Edward Hales, third Baronet (1672–1720); Gervase Scrope of North Cockerington (d.1741), High Sheriff of Lincolnshire (1721), High Steward of Louth (1737–41); George Newell LLB, Vicar General of Lincoln Diocese (1708); Thomas Howson (1668–1737), Registrar to the Bishop of Lincoln; probably Thomas Porter, Proctor of Lincoln Diocese and Rector of Bassingham; Capt. William Pownall (d.1736) of the Lincolnshire Militia, a keen antiquarian; either Daniel Disney JP or the Revd John Disney JP (1677–1730) or, since Johnson uses the plural, perhaps both of them; Dr Robert Pakey (will dated 1738), Lincolnshire physician who owned land in Holbeach; Gervase Sibthorpe (d.1749); Dr Edward Greathead (1673–1743), Lincoln physician; William Gilby (1669–1744) of Gray's Inn, Recorder of Lincoln (1721); probably Dr Edward Nelthorpe MD (Reims), will proved 1738; Francis [?] Harvey, Town Clerk of Lincoln; probably Robert Peart (1684–1732), Clerk to the Court of Sewers; Thomas Becke, attorney (1690–1757), Sheriff's clerk (1720).
21 Johnson's underlining. As a Spaldonian and the originator of a successful society, he sees Spalding as the centre of Fenland learned activities. 'It' in the next sentence refers to Wisbech, where the first

of the town's literary societies was founded in 1712; Dr Richard Middleton Massey and Mr Richard Lake (see Appendix 3) were recorded as members of the Wisbech society in 1718, and Maurice Johnson was also a member. A catalogue of their library was published in 1718 and a copy is now in the Bodleian Library, Oxford. The Revd Dr Henry Bull (1683–1750) was Vicar of Wisbech 1721–50. The Wisbech society ceased to meet when Massey moved to London and Lake died; it was revived at the end of the eighteenth century.

[22] The eighteenth-century minutes of the SGS begin in 1712 but are continuous only from 1726 to 1758. They record the extent of Johnson's supportive contributions to the Society's meetings, either in person or by letter if he was absent from Spalding. The Society owed much of its early success to his continuous support and to his efforts in securing a wide range of corresponding members; this probably helps to explain why the SGS flourished while other local societies declined.

[23] Johnson refers to the early editions of the London-based magazines *The Tatler* (1709–11) edited by Captain (later Sir) Richard Steele (one of Johnson's inspirations in founding the SGS), Addison and Steele's *The Spectator* (1711–14), *The Lover* (1714) and *The Lay Monk* (1713–14) edited by Sir Richard Blackmore. They were an important ingredient of the early SGS meetings; the Society began as an informal group which read and discussed these papers, sent down from London by coach. A full account of these Whig journals is given in Brian Cowan, 'Mr Spectator and the Coffee House Public Sphere', *Eighteenth-Century Studies* 37(3) (2004). The current periodical *The Spectator* began in 1828.

43. William Stukeley to Maurice Johnson, Stamford, 14 May 1746
Spalding, SGS/Stukeley/18

Dear S^r

We in our way have at present a deal of business upon our hands. particular discourses to make, for Whitsunday, Trinity Sunday, a thanks giving sermon, two lecture-sermons in my church upon the Sacrament. beside we are now engag'd in attending Mr Griffis's[1] experimental philosophy lectures, which he performs exceedingly well, & with a very fine apparatus of instruments.

all this I mention, to apologize for my not writing a long letter to you, as otherwise I should. yesterday at our deeping club[2] I read your letter. Mr Archdeacon Payn[3] gave us the reason, why the literary society broke up here, which you mention. the books were reposited in S. Marys church & Birdmore[4] the incumbent then, whilst a fine library was making for him in his own church, was so poor a dog, that he would not contribute a penny toward it. [p.2] he mention'd some more oddityes, of some acquaintance of yours here, which broke off the Society. we still have a monthly book-club, but divide the books amongst ourselves. I have long known the oddityes of mankind, which makes me very slow in beginning any thing of this sort, & very tame about it. I believe, I shall do it, & am sure not to be dissappointed, for I hope for nothing.

I shall be heartily glad to see you. your daughter is a fine girl.[5] the volatility of her spirits, is a prejudice to her health. & I endeavord to persuade her to be sensible of it, & spare them. I hope she will find benefit here.

      I am,
      Your very affectionate
      servant
      W Stukeley

I shall send Mr Hill an abstract of my description of Aaron's breast-plate according to your desire.[6]

      Stamford 14 may 1746

To Maurice Johnson Esqr
  Spalding
Carr. Paid.

1 William Griffis (or Griffith) published his syllabus for *A Course of Experimental Philosophy consisting of five parts* in 1740. He lectured on the sciences across the Midlands of England.
2 Stukeley's Deepings Club met regularly during his years in Stamford, though it ceased at his departure. It was more of a social and dining club than an active learned society, though papers were read there at times. Johnson also visited it.
3 Archdeacon Squire Payne (*c*.1676–1751), Archdeacon of Stow (1730–75), son-in-law and biographer of Richard Cumberland, Bishop of Peterborough. For an account of his life, drawing on his memorandum and account book, see A. Tindal Hart, *Country Counting House* (London, 1962).
4 Revd Ralph Birdmore (d.1743), Rector of St Mary's church, Stamford (1726–38) and Rector of St George with St Paul, Stamford (1734–43).
5 Johnson's daughter Elizabeth, 'Madcap Bet'; see **Letter 41**, n.3.
6 For Stukeley's essay on the Pectoral of Aaron, see Bodleian, MS Eng. misc. e.553. The Mr Hill he refers to here is almost certainly [Sir] John Hill, MD, FRS; see his entry in Appendix 3.

44. William Stukeley to Maurice Johnson, Stamford, 17 December 1746
Spalding, SGS/Stukeley/19

[Annotated by Johnson:] the Revd Dr Stukeley to M Johnson jun^r with his Antiquitates Royston for SGS // of the Earths Rotation.

Dear S^r

  I sent you last tuesday my new book *Origines Roistonianæ pars altera*.¹ both parts are bound together, as it is designed for a publick library. I beg you would present it, in my name to your learned Society.

  I was obliged to print it at Stamford, for the sake of correcting the press. & the rather, because I would honor our old University² as much as I am able; whose origin, I give an account of, in the book. I wish we could have printed it better. Howgrave³ your neighbour of the most delightful Flora hills, did his best. & if the matter be but agreable to you gentlemen, who are judges, I must be content. I own, I have been a little severe, ~~merely~~ because a pert fellow⁴ had nothing to say upon the subject, but [p.2] merely to trouble the world with new & arbitrary conjectures, without any reasonable foundation. & this treatment of an antiquity subject, must needs reflect upon the study in general, & render it contemptible.

  I my self, in my own mind, am fully satisfy'd, that my hypothesis is more than verisimilitude. it was the fashion of that time, for the ladys to amuse themselves in working tapistry in historical figures. & these of Roiston, probably, lady ROISIA⁵ cut, as the first sketches of a design of that nature. & I doubt not but she lived to execute it, & gave it for a present to some of the religious houses, whereof many, she had a hand in founding.

  I have a great deal more to say on the subject, [p.3] expecting my fancy antagonist will reply. & then I shall be able to anoint him properly. at present I look upon his whole book as a rhapsody of stuff. & I am told by his neighbors, that the whole has a jacobite aspect.⁶

  when I parted with you, I took horse & passed thro' Littleworth;⁷ & was extremely delighted with the sight. I really thought my self, in some new American plantation.

Tis expected our neighbour N – I[8] will be made a judg; I wish you would make interest to get among us again, as recorder. by that means you & I might have a quarterly ramble together, very agreable, in this fine country.

I have got a taste for viewing churches. I was lately at Edmondthorp,[9] where are some admirably old & fine painted glass, coats of arms & figures of knights [p.4] in their surcoats armorial, not far from the conquest.

in the same place, I saw some huge & perfect escallop shells, antediluvian, in the stone. you know Leicestershire consists of a red stone, brim-full of the petrify'd shells of the old world; especially all around the bottom of the great cliff, which generally bounds Lincolnshire & that county.[10]

Tis easy to conceive, that when the whole face of the country was as an ocean, that this cliff of ours, which begins at Hambledon in Rutland, & ends at Lincoln, stopt these shells from rolling down with the declining waters of the cataclysm into the sea, & so left 'em incrusted in the stone. I know this is the case, all along the bottom of the cliff. my service waits on your Society & I am

> Your affectionate
> W. Stukely [sic]

Stamf[d] 17 dec. 1746

---

[1] *Origines Roystonianæ Part II*, also called *Palæographia Britannica*, was printed by Francis Howgrave in 1746. Stukeley wrote this as a defence of his original account of the caves discovered in Royston (Herts), which he had first published in *Palæographia Britannica* I (1743).

[2] Stukeley worked extensively to develop the historical fact that during the early 1330s there had been a serious attempt by Oxford students from the north of England to establish a new university in Stamford, Lincs. The Crown, under Edward III, completely defeated this and closed it in 1335. Graduating Oxford students had to take a Latin oath promising not to teach in the University of Stamford until this was repealed in 1827. For a full and thorough discussion of this, see N. J. Sheehan, *Stamford University: The Stuttering Dream* (Stamford, 2012).

[3] Francis Howgrave (d.1771) was a Stamford apothecary who became the printer of the *Stamford Mercury*. He printed in 1726 *An Essay on the Ancient and Present State of Stamford*. See n.1 above.

[4] Revd Charles Parkin, Rector of Oxborough, Norfolk, published in 1744 *An Answer to, or Remarks upon Dr Stukeley's Origines Roystonianæ, wherein the Antiquity and Imagery of the Oratory, lately discovered at Royston in Hertfordshire, are truly Stated, and Accounted for*. Parkin argued that the oratory was 'an Hermit's cell at Royston in the Saxon-Age ... of some one, or of a Body of Hermits, and continued ... 'till its Dissolution in the Reign of King Henry VIII' (p.75). Recent research suggests that it dates from the fifteenth century and was perhaps a hermitage.

[5] Lady Roisia's existence has yet to be proved historically. Parkin replied to Stukeley's criticism in 'A Reply to the Peevish, Weak and Malevolent Objections brought by Dr Stukeley in his *Origines Roystonianæ No.2*' (Norwich, 1748) in which he argued 'Royston proved to be an old Saxon Town, its Derivation and Original; and the History of Lady Roisa shown to be a meer Fable and Fragment' (A1). For more details of Lady Roisa see **Letter 45**.

[6] The Jacobite rising of 1745 was still fresh in people's minds, so Stukeley uses this derogatory term to diminish the impact of Parkin's criticism. Parkin's parish contained many Roman Catholic families associated with the recusant Bedingfelds of Oxburgh Hall.

[7] Littleworth, an area to the south-west of Spalding, was being opened up as a settlement and agricultural district between the North and South Droves, following the improvement in Fen drainage by Capt. Perry and John Grundy (see Appendix 3) in the 1720s and 1730s. Stukeley refers to Littleworth in his diary for 1745–48 (Bodleian, MS Eng. misc. e.126, fol.42).

[8] This is presumably William Noel (1695–1762), a neighbour of Stukeley's on Barn Hill in Stamford, MP for Stamford, Judge of Common Pleas and Deputy Recorder of Stamford. Maurice Johnson had been Deputy Recorder of Stamford and would therefore have had to attend the Stamford Sessions four times a year.

9   The church of St Michael and All Angels, Edmondthorpe (Leics), has a fifteenth-century chancel screen and fine sculpted memorials to the Smith family, lords of the manor.
10 Stukeley shared the belief of natural philosophers of his time in the Great Flood. His careful study of the topography of eastern England led him to find fossil scallop shells on the Lincolnshire Cliff, which supported the theory, feasible at the time, that they had been deposited by an overwhelming flood.

45. Maurice Johnson to William Stukeley, Spalding, 20 December 1746
Bodleian, MS Eng. misc. c.113, fols 337r–338v

Spalding 20 Decr 1746

Dear S^r

When Your Neighbour brought Me for our Society's Library Your Learned and very pleasing present your Palæographia Britannica conteining your Account of Royston,[1] Origines Roistonianæ Of the Lady Roisia de Veres Cross, Oratory & Sepulchre there Hers, her Husbands Families, their Descendants, King Henry II whom they served and the highly probable Meaning and Intent of the Sculptures in her Oratory together with the Second Part being Your Defence of all those persons & of Your Account of them and the Imagery I happend to be So Urgently engaged in busynes that required dispatch as not to be able any other way than Verbaly to the Person who brought them to return You my Thanks. I am now Good Sir to add Those of our Society by Order of the Company there last Thursday to whom I had the honour to Communicate an Abstract of the Whole and of the Norfolk production which administred Occasion to Your farther Improveing our Understanding Te defendendo.[2] with us You carryd All points, I had with delight and attention perused Your No.1 when, the Answer as Its called by the Author Or his Remarkes came out I had that and perused it fairly as I cou'd Compareing It with Your Account. The few Remarkes that Occurred to me then Or have since I send You that You See Sir I enabled my Self to say Something as I ought of It, when from You I presented Your agreeable Performance, abounding in Ingenuity and illustrating a dark Intricate and Singular Designe of such Remote Antiquity, with much of Other Science.

[p.2] I think Your reasons good for rejoyning and for printing the II N^{o3} where you could with most ease to Yourself correct the Press, the Execution whereof in so out the way difficult matters & of So great Variety is commendable, and dos honour to our Soc. Æneanas.[4] My Bro. Secretary Dr Green and I were charmed with your draw[in]g of Lord Abbot Turketyl.[5] & wonder not from that fine Head and Your deducing the Origin of Cambr[idge]. as well as Stamf[or]d Universitys from Our Abby of Croyland[6] and Your Accounts of that and of them that You have as I allways thought You had a Taste for Viewing Churches Who have for the Many Yeares of our long and happy Acquaintance Viewd them & Every Work of Art, as well of Nature so as to be on every Occasion able to apply what was to be observed from them to the best uses the advancement of Knowledge and Virtue, & the Honour of the Maker of them or of the Almighty Maker of us all who endued us with a Capacity to imitate or aim at understanding his works and made the great Originals for our Use and Imitation – Remember Your kind Engagement to me as soon as the Ways & Weather are inviting Let me Meet You on my Confines at old Croyland[7] bring all your sketches of It or Its parts, I'll bring mine Wee'll Compare 'em on the spot and then Ill conduct You to Your Apartment in this Old fabric where Wee'll adjust them & I promise my self much Joy in our Conferences.

[p.3] Your Curious discourse of Ordinary Bearings & original of our Coats of Armes thence Assumed is New to me and most of Us and what Wee're much obliged to You for evincing how the Individual or leader himself was distinguishable, as his Banner did his Troop or Company.[8]

Yesterday I had the Satisfaction to assist in the Actual inducting my Kinsman, our fellow Member, Mr Benj. Ray[9] into and giving him personal Possession of Cowbitt Chapell, a Donative Centum Annis worth 80l. per annum: & he's this day gone for Bugden to have his Lordships Licence for Preaching – whither my Son John Went to'ther day in order to obteine Priest's Orders[10] and a Like Licence under our Ministers Title being his Curate at 35l. per annum. I thank God he is a Very, Virtuous Industrious Young man his Tutor thought him too Studious & his Companions esteem him as a Good Scholar good Temperd and Ingenious, & a constant good Member of our Meetings here, as indeed all my Sons are when at Home. The Captains[11] lately gone up to Town expecting to be Commanded to Flanders. My son of the Temple may hereafter perhaps make a Tender of his Services for the Office you kindly wish Me restored to,[12] without the Occasions It might administer I hope Wee may meet more frequently than affairs have of late Yeares permitted which will ever be a great Comfort to Dear Friend

Your faithfull & affectionate

M Johnson jun[r]

To
the Reverend
Dr Stukeley
  at Stamford
Carryage pd.
     Present.

---

[1] See **Letter 44** above. The 'Norfolk production' referred to later in the paragraph is Parkin's published attack on Stukeley.

[2] 'In order to defend you'.

[3] See **Letter 44** above.

[4] The 'Societas Æneanasensis', Stukeley's Brazen Nose Society in Stamford. See **Letter 41**, n.2 above.

[5] Abbot Thurcytel, ODNB, advisor to King Eadred, grandson of King Alfred, restored Croyland Abbey around 950 after it had been destroyed by the Danes. A statue on the west front of the ruins of the Abbey was identified by Stukeley as Turketyl and he sent a drawing of the figure's head to Johnson.

[6] Stukeley linked the supposed origins of Cambridge University to Croyland Abbey, basing this on the fifteenth-century *Continuation of the Chronicle of Croyland* which said that monks from Croyland went in 1109 'every day to Cambridge and hired a public barn there, openly taught their respective sciences and in a short space of time, collected a great concourse of scholars' (see *Ingulph's Chronicle of the Abbey of Croyland*, trans. H. T. Riley (London, 1854), 237). There was also a claim that an earlier university than the attempt in the 1330s had been created in Stamford partly on the initiative of Croyland monks.

[7] Johnson was Steward of the Manor of Croyland for Maj.-Gen. Robert Hunter. Both he and Stukeley made notes and sketches of the ruins of Croyland Abbey. Stukeley claimed that Johnson was responsible for restoring the distinctive three-arched bridge in Crowland.

[8] There is an extensive analysis of heraldry and coats of arms in Stukeley's volume *Palæographia*

Britannica, Part II; this was discussed at the SGS meeting on 18 December 1746 (see SGS, MB4, fol.85v).

9   Johnson's kinsman the Revd Benjamin Ray: see his entry in Appendix 3.

10   Revd John Johnson: see Appendix 3. The Bishop of Lincoln was frequently resident in his palace at Buckden (Hunts), since the Diocese of Lincoln stretched from the Humber to the Thames.

11   Captain, later Col. Maurice Johnson, eldest son of Maurice Johnson: see Appendix 3.

12   The 'son of the Temple' is Walter Johnson, who studied law there as his father had done: see Appendix 3. The 'Office' is presumably that of deputy recorder of Stamford: see **Letter 44**, n.8 above.

[*SGS/Stukeley/9α is reproduced in Appendix 1 (b) in this volume. It is a dissertation by Stukeley, dated 30 December 1746, on the identification of the statues on the West Front of Croyland Abbey as historical figures connected with the history of the Abbey and is accompanied by detailed drawings. It relates to the correspondence about the Abbey, particularly* **Letters 45** *and* **46**.]

46. Maurice Johnson to William Stukeley, Spalding, 10 January 1747
Bodleian, MS Eng. misc. c.113, fols 337r–340v

Spalding 10 January 1746/7

Dear Dr

Your curious and I believe just Explication of the Statues on Croyland Abby Front I received safe yesterday was a senight[1] had the weather permitted I had had them & read them On New Yeares day to our Company, which I did the meeting after on Thursday last,[2] and the Gentlemen were highly pleasd therewith and with the drawings illustrating the same[3] you did them the Honour to inscribe to them, as that Explication to me for which they Sir & I returne you many Thankes. In discourse thereof I could as You was pleasd to Say, and accordingly did Confirm & somewhat enlarge upon Your Sentiments, but see nothing to Correct but that in your description in words of 1st Statue viz. of King Æthelbald you say he has a <u>Scepter</u> in his right hand, which in your Drawing seems a <u>Sword</u>, and I forget which It realy is in the Original. – what were the 2 large Statues on each Side the Door under these – the 2 Heads or Bustos by them and what the Particular Acts of St Guthlake in the 5 ap Compartements? for I have no life of him to explaine them. but at your best Leisure should be glad to know. I think the Abby was dedicated to the B.V.M. St Bartholomew and St Guthlake. Which are the 10 Apostles overhead?

[p.2] Mr Emanuel Mendes da Costa[4] a Merchant & Member has Sent Us Watsons Letters on Electricity[5] & various Specimens of Petrifactions, Metals & other Fossils with some Shells and a White Orobus from the E. Indies but one growing single in Each Pod. & that the size of our common Pea. also those New Microscopical Observations by Turbervill Needham[6] a Gent. residing in Portugal which I read with Pleasure & an Extract thereof to our Company as I believe they'll give you pleasure have sent them for your perusal you'll be so good to return them by the Bearer (but charge you let me pay him) for some of our Members will be enquiring for them & I keep them a While so as in my Use.

There is an Odd anonymous Author whose work is entitled Gesta Romanorum[7] Several Copies are in the Bodleyan & Royal & other Libr. MSS. I have one printed 1507 from 58 Cap. of this book, written by whom Wee know not, nor can find out. Archdeacon Parnell[8] took his Plan of that divine Poem of his Hermit. neither Vossius nor Casley[9] give any Account of this Author, farther than that in Bibl. Reg. is a french translation of It written in XV Century, my Edition has neither Author Name nor Place nor printer.

[p.3] Be pleasd with Needham's Microscopical Discoverys to return me the MS Letter I've layd in the Title page for your perusal. D° Johanni Urry[10] (of Chr. Ch. Ed. of Chaucer) De Ode in POCOCKIUM. Why Halberdarie? where any such ode written by Edmund Smith (vulgo vocatus Captn Ragg author of Phædra).[11] Tis a very humorous thing and neat Imitation of Types, as such shew it with my Service to your Printer Mr Howgrave[12] if you please, but You'll not let it be soild.

Wee heartily wish You and Your Ladie and Daughters all the good Wishes of this, many of these Seasons. Mr Jn° Hill[13] the Apothecary son of our old ingenious Friend the Dr Theophilus Hill[14] who published Theophrastus περι λιθων, is about publishing Dioscorides and Galen on the same Subject, his Theophrastus has met with great Approbation. He has discoverd & before the R.S. I see him prove from those Authors, Pliny, and Chemical Experiments a certain green Sandlike Substance lately sent to Sr Hans Sloan, to be the true Crusocolla,[15] and affirmd It had answerd in Medicin & Sodering Gold when tryed.

[p.4] The Fossil Kingdom is much sought after as a fashionable Study by many Members of Fashion of the RS at this time, who are making Collections of Specimens thereof from all Parts. there is & always has been fashionable Study, as well as Dress, Exercise &c, But if the Amusement be but Innocent 'tis well, & the more Improveing the better. I think theres none in Politicks & therefore could not but wonder whence that Strange Scurrilous Libell came to Me,[16] who never deal in them But detest & abhor them and by barring 'em as much as in my power from the Conversation at our Meetings have hitherto kept us together in Amity as I hope & trust I may able [*sic*] to do with the good assistance of Your & other Friends Correspondence so long as I live And so long at lest I hope to be Dear Dr

Your much obliged Servt & sincere friend.

M Johnson jun^r

To the Rev^d Dr Stukeley.

---

1   'A week ago yesterday'. A 'senight' or 'sennight' is a period of 'seven nights', as 'a fortnight' is a period of 'fourteen nights'.
2   The SGS's weekly Thursday meeting (see SGS, MB4, fol.88r, entry for 8 January 1747).
3   The SGS's archives still hold Stukeley's drawings of Croyland Abbey, two of which are reproduced as Illustrations 16 and 17 in this volume.
4   Emanuel Mendes da Costa (1717–91): see Appendix 3.
5   William Watson (1715–87: see *ODNB*). He published *Experiments and Observations Tending to Illustrate the Nature and Properties of Electricity* (1746); it had four reprints.
6   John Turberville Needham (1713–81: see *ODNB*). His *An Account of some New Microscopical Discoveries* was published by his brother Francis in 1745. He was at the heart of European natural philosophy in the mid-eighteenth century. The book is still in the SGS library's Original Collection.
7   *Gesta Romanorum*, printed in England by Wynkyn de Worde in the early sixteenth century, was a collection of stories from the classical world, probably prepared for clerics as a source for sermon illustrations. Johnson had a 1507 edition in his own library. The British Library has a version published in Venice in 1507, *Ex gestis Romanorum hystorie notabiles collecte de viciis virtutibus tractantes cum applicationibus moralisatis et mysticis*.

8   The Revd Thomas Parnell (1679–1718: see *ODNB*). His *Poems on several Occasions* was edited by Pope (1721). He was Archdeacon of Clogher in Ireland and an associate of Swift and his circle.
9   Gerardus Vossius (1577–1659: see *ODNB*), a Dutch scholar who had many connections with England in the 1620s and 1630s. His *De religione gentilium*, a major work on pagan religions, was popular in England. Johnson owned another of his books. David Casley (1681/2–1754: see *ODNB*) was the librarian of the Cotton Library and published *Catalogue of the Manuscripts of the King's Library* (1734); Johnson's own copy of this was sold at the 1898 Sotheby's sale of Johnson's books.
10 John Urry (1666–1715: see *ODNB*), of Christ Church, Oxford; he edited *Chaucer's Works* although the edition did not appear until after his death. Johnson owned a copy printed in 1721. 'In Pocockium' is a poem on Dr Edward Pococke (1604–91), also of Christ Church and the outstanding Oxford Arabic scholar of his day.
11 Edmund Smith (1672–1710) was a poet, dramatist and member of Addison and Steele's coffee-house set in the first decade of the eighteenth century. He had been at Christ Church in 1691 as an undergraduate at the time of Pococke's death and was a friend of Urry. Earlier, Urry had been a sergeant in the University regiment, raised to combat Monmouth's rebellion, and had received a halberd. On Pococke's death, Urry got Smith to write a Latin ode, *Pocockius*, which Dr Samuel Johnson later described as outstandingly good. Smith's nickname was 'Captain Ragg' because he wore his ancient, ragged scholar's gown. Presumably Urry's halberd is mentioned in an epistle about the poem. Smith was best known for his play *Phædra and Hippolitus*, an adaptation of Racine's *Phèdre*; for this and the poem, see *The Works of Mr Edmund Smith* (1729).
12 Francis Howgrave: see **Letter 44**, nn.1 and 3.
13 John Hill (1714–75): see Appendix 3 and *ODNB*. His first publication was on geology, a translation of the classical Greek author Theophrastus's *History of Stones* (περι λιθων) in 1746. Hill had two papers published in the RS's *Phil.Trans.* in 1746, one on the seeding of mosses (pp.60–6) and one on Windsor Loam (pp.458–63). For a discussion of Hill's work and the RS, see Kevin Fraser, 'John Hill and the R.S. in the eighteenth century', *Notes and Records of the Royal Society* 48(1) (January 1994).
14 Dr Theophilus Hill MD (1680–1746), father of John Hill, a physician in Peterborough and a member of both the SGS and PGS.
15 A blue-green hydrated copper silicate mineral. The name was first given by Theophrastus.
16 The nature of this 'scandal' is unknown.

47. William Stukeley to Maurice Johnson, Stamford, 20 January 1747
SGS/Stukeley/9β

Stamford 20 jan. 1746–7

                                    To Maurice Johnson esq^r &c
S^r

I return your book, & the epistle to John Urry, upon Pocock;[1] which is a great curiosity; being wrote with a pen, in imitation of printing.

I have in complyance with your command, sent you my conjectures upon that elegant carving, over the west door of Crowland abby: accompanied with a drawing of it.[2] tis curiously done, in basso relievo, but was injured by the parliament-soldiers, when they took the kings garrison here, 1644.

it consists of 5 compartiments; of the history of S. Guthlake.[3] the 1. or lower-most exhibits his arrival at Crowland. for he was the first english anchorite. & resolving to get, [p.2] if possible, out of the world, penetrated into the then dismal & uninhabited recesses of the very center of the fens; & there pitchd his station for life; where now the abby stands. the very spot of his cell was on the southwest corner, on the outside: where there is some brickwork, & a door to the north, by the great door of the church.

the sculpture exhibits S. Guthlake in the boat, which carryed him along the river, with his companion, & the boatman. he sits in the stern, as in conference with Cissa in the middle. Cissa was a gentleman & very rich, but forsook the world & his estate, for love of religion; was ordained a priest & accompanied S. Guthlake, & became a hermit with him, in Crowland. the boatman is Tatwin, who carried him to the place. & he likewise became religious, along with him.

[p.3] These, after S. Guthlake was dead, & the abby founded, remain'd still in their cells, near S. Guthlak's cell, to their deaths. & were buryed ~~by~~ near him, in the east end of the choir: Cissa on the south side of S. Guthlakes shrine: Tatwin on the north side.

the boat is represented as coming to land, where lyes a sow & pigs, under a tree. for S. Guthlake was directed (by the Spirit) to fix his cell by a place, where he should find a sow & pigs.

this story, I doubt not, was taken from Virgils Æneid III where Helenus the priest & prophet directs Æneas in like manner.[4]

> Signa tibi dicam, tu condita mente teneto.
> cum tibi sollicito, secreti ad fluminis undam,
> littoreis ingens inventa sub illicibus sus,
> triginta capitum fœtus enixa jacebit:
> alba, solo recubans, albi circum ubera nati;
> is locus urbis erit, requies ea certa laborum.

[p.4] the monks of this time read the classics; & took passages of this nature from them, which they apply'd^x to historys in their legends

[Stukeley's note on blank facing page:] ^{x}for sake of the marvailous^x

a like influence of this nature, we have in our great ancestor Hengist, building Stamford castle: as I have shown in a manuscript discourse wrote some years ago, at the request of our friend Roger Gale, intituled <u>Origines Stamfordienses</u>.[5]

Hengist, after he had beaten the Scots & Picts at the Roman ford, just by our nunnery, beg'd of the Brittish king Vortigern, some ground to build a fort on, wherein to keep his prey, which he had got in great abundance by this victory, from the plundering enemy.

he, with the modesty of a soldier of fortune, ask'd but as much ground, as he could compass with an oxes hide; which being granted, he cut the hide into long thongs, which took in a considerable quantity of ground: whereon [p.5] he built his castle: which in reality is our Stamford castle.

the truth of the matter is this. Hengist askd of the king a hyde of land; a Saxon word implying a midling farm: or as much as would maintain a family in tillage.

hence the monks reading the story in Virgil, of the ground which Dido bought of Hiarbas king of Lybia, apply it to Hengists castle.

> mercatiq[ue] solum, facti de nomine Byrsam
> Taurino quantum possent circumdare tergo. Æn. I [6]

The second compartment is the middle one, being a picture of S. Guthlake driving the devil away, with his discipline. this discipline of his was kept in the abby, after his death, as a relique of great value.

hence the arms of the abby 3 knives & three whips quarterly. the knives[7] relate to S. Bartholomew: & the halfpence coined by the tradesmen at the time of the Restoration, had these arms.

[p.6] The third compartment shows to us S. Guthlake dead, extended on his shrine. the person over him is embalming his body.

The fourth compartment is of two females by the shrine of S. Guthlake: possibly she sitting, may be S. Edelfreda[8] daughter of king Offa of the Mercians. She was espoused to Ethelbert king of Essex, who was perfidiously murdered. afterwards she had a cell in Crowland abby on the south-side the high altar: & was buryed near S. Guthlakes shrine.

If this be not the truth, it was some famous miracle wrought at his shrine, which we cannot now recount, for want of the historys of his life.

[p.7] The 5th or upper compartment contains the apotheosis of S. Guthlake. he being dead is carried up into heaven. or at least the devil contends for his body. an angel holds him by the head, a devil by the feet. above, is another angel on the wing.

The two great images on the side of the west door are very finely carv'd: but their heads & arms & symbols being destroy'd by the reforming rabble,[9] we cannot pretend to say[x] who they were. I observe the pedestals whereon they stand are carv'd with a good taste.

[Stukeley's note on blank facing page:] [x]with certainty[x]

Upon the pedestal on the right hand or north side of the door is carv'd Adam & Eve in paradise. the pedestal of the other, is composd of angels well carv'd. [p.8] from these circumstances, I conjecture the former figure represents the second Adam, our blessed Savior: the other is the virgin Mary.

the abbots heads hard by, probably mean the abbots then living, when this noble front was built. but from the indistinct account of the several builders of the several parts of this once magnificent structure, one cannot exactly point out the times & persons.

W. Stukeley
Stamford 20 jan. 1746–7

To fill up a vacant page, I have sent you a drawing of S. Guthlac, in a larger scale.[10]

[p.9] [*Drawing of St. Guthlac, with caption:*]
Sanctus Guthlacus Gyrviorum Antonius, ex pulcherrima ejus statua in fronte Ecclesiæ Croylandensis, Anno 1746. W. Stukeley d.[11]

[*Caption over drawing of West Door carvings:*]
Societati Literatorum Spaldingensium monumentum hoc vere venerandum, Actorum beati Guthlaci, ex archetype delineatum, in fronte Ecclesiæ CROY-LANDENSIS, offert W. Stukeley. 1746.[12]

1 See **Letter 46**, n.10.
2 See Illustrations 16–18 in this volume, which show Stukeley's drawings of the carvings and a picture of their present state. Stukeley sent his drawings of the Croyland Abbey carvings, which are still in the SGS's archives. Stukeley's interpretations of these carvings are always interesting if perhaps regarded as at times a little over-imaginative today.

3   St Guthlac (674–715: see *ODNB*). He was a member of the Mercian royal family but gave up military and court life to establish a hermitage in the Fens at Crowland around 700, arriving on St Bartholomew's Day. His *Life* was written *c.*740 by Felix; this successful eulogy made Guthlac one of the most significant of the late Anglo-Saxon saints, producing church dedications and bringing renown to Croyland Abbey, which grew up on the site of his hermitage.

4   'I shall give you a sign and you must keep it deep within your heart: when in an hour of perplexity by the flowing waters of a lonely river you find under some holm-oaks on the shore a great sow lying there on her side all white, with her young all white around her udders, that will be the place for your city' (Virgil, *Æneid*, book 3); see David West's translation (Penguin Classics, 1991), 59.

5   For the stories of the Saxon hero Hengist in Stamford, see Sheehan, *Stamford University: The Stuttering Dream* (Stamford, 2012), xiii and 9–10. For 'Stanfordia Illustrata', Stukeley's work on Stamford's history dated by Stukeley 1735 and prepared for Roger Gale, see Corpus Christi College, Cambridge, Parker Library MS 619. Stukeley imaginatively expands Bede's very brief references to Vortigern and Hengist in *Ecclesiastical History of the English Nation*, xiv–xv. Stukeley drew also on the Anglo-Saxon Chronicle, Nennius's *Historia Britonum*, Geoffrey of Monmouth's *Historia Regum Britanniæ* and Henry of Huntingdon's *Historia Anglorum*.

6   'They bought a piece of land, called the Byrsa, the animal's hide, as large an area as they could include within the hide of a bull', Virgil, *Æneid*, book 1, lines 365–367; this was an area of land that could be encompassed within strips cut from a bull's hide. Stukeley's interpretation of 'a hide' as 'adequate land for a family for a year' is still generally accepted.

7   St Guthlac is said to have received a whip from St Bartholomew to defend himself against the devils of the marshland; the knives represent the martyrdom of St Bartholomew, traditionally by being flayed alive. The monks of Croyland Abbey gave gifts of small knives to visitors as a symbol; Stukeley's MSS record gaining possession of several of these, which were often found by local Crowland people.

8   Etheldrida was the daughter of Offa, King of Mercia. According to the Croyland *Chronicle* she lived at Croyland around 830 'as a recluse in one part of the cell situate on the south side of the church of Croyland, over against the great altar there'. See *Chronicle of the Abbey of Croyland*, trans. H. T. Riley (1908), 15.

9   Croyland Abbey was peacefully dissolved in December 1539 and began to become dilapidated, except for the section of the north aisle that was converted into a parish church. During the Civil War the Abbey was fortified as part of the defence of Crowland against Parliamentarian troops. Elements of the building were damaged by the besiegers, the 'reforming rabble' during the siege.

10 See Illustration 16.

11 'St Guthlac, the [St] Antony of the Gyrvii, taken from the very beautiful statue of him on the front of the church of Croyland in the year 1746. W. Stukeley drew [it].' St Antony the hermit was one of the early Desert Fathers of the Church.

12 'W. Stukeley offers to the Society of the Learned in Spalding this truly venerable monument of the Acts of the blessed Guthlac, drawn from the original on the front of the church of Croyland. 1746.'

48. William Stukeley to Maurice Johnson, Stamford, 28 January 1747
SGS/Stukeley/9β

Dear Sir,

I omitted sending you the drawings of the acts of S. Guthlac, & thrô hurry, did not advertize you. but to make you some amends I have now sent it with a parcel of loose prints,[1] which I beg your society to accept of.

by this means, the drawing comes safe, without wrinkles, which could not well be done with the former conveyance. my complements wait on all friends at Spalding & I am

Your most obedient
W Stukeley

Stamf[d] 28 jan. 1746–7

To Maur. Johnson esq[r]

[1] This outstanding set of Stukeley's drawings is still among the SGS's prized possessions.

49. Maurice Johnson to William Stukeley, Spalding, 6 February 1747
Bodleian, MS Eng. misc. c.113, fols 341r–342v.

Spalding 6 February 1746/7

Dear Dr

I return you our Thanks for Your Discourse on the Compartments carved over the West doors of Croyland and exhibiting as You well explain them the Miracles & death of St Guthlake which I received time enough to communicate to our Company their last Meeting in last Month as You happend to Omitt sending the Drawing with them,[1] having a Sketch drawn at my Instance there in Sept. 1731 by Wm Bogdani Esq[2] a worthy Member I carryd It with me & shewd them that: As yours in a much larger Scale Yesterday, for which they also Thank You and attending the Dissertation much illustrate it, and indeed Nothing is more edifying and pleasant, than ingenious Accounts of Antient monuments So illustrated by Sketches or Draughts of them. They save many words & make Stronger and more Adequate impressions than Words alone can. The late Earl of Oxford[3] had St Guthlakes Life in a Velom Roll illumined formerly I think our old friend Peter le Neve Norroy, but I never See It only I have this memorandum of It. the Passion or Legend of St Guthlake in the Harley Library Olim P. le N. norroy 21 Novr. 1722. The fullest account I have Seen of him is but short in Jno Bromtons[4] Chron int. X Scriptores 797 (18) to 798 (7) but thence I could no way have explain these, indeed I have met in Dugdales Imbanking[5] something about his driving away the Devils with his discipline from Felix a monk of Croyland who wrote his Life in tolerable Latin Verse. But that Wee have not and wish Wee had a better Store of Books to consult on all Occasions.

[p.2] I have for our English history as best coinciding with my Profession a pretty good Collection, For the rest I've done My endeavours to store our Publick Librarys in our Church, Free School, & Museum, with Good Editions of the most Usefull standard Authors, and some curious.[6] From about 100 I've by means of our Society allmost by donation of single authors raised them to 1000. Opus proh Jupiter! Grande & Laboriosum.[7] Besides Some MSS 4 Portofolios of Prints & Drawings & 2 Cabinetts one of Natural the Other of Artificial Curiosities as a Necessary Appendix to a Library. Supellex Literaria[8] in which are many good Specimens of our Materia Medica, And of the Fossil Kingdom, a Study become very fashionable & at this time much cultivated by many Men of ample fortunes. Mr Hill (son of our Old Friend Dr Theophilous Hill[9] of Peterb[orough]) who last Yeare publishd Theophrastus of stone &c is this yeare publishd Dioscorides, with what Aristotle, Galen and Pliny have on the same Subject, his former Book being very well recieved, and with the assistance of the Collections of the Royal Society, Sr Hans Sloane, the Duke of Richmond (his principal Patron) Dr Parsons, Mr Da Costa & others[10] he hath Opportunities of not only seing, [sic] but trying and proving by all manner of Experiments every kind of Fossil body, and thereby hath discovered and retrieved to Us the Chrysocolla of the Antients, as I see demonstrated at his own house and afterwards at the Royal Society by Experiments confirming the description given of It by those antient Authors greek & Latin.

[p.3] My daughter Mary's[11] goeing again to Your Town for change of Air, by which only she finds benefitt, to be with Mrs Fullers who are my Wifes acquaintance and so obligeing to let her board with them. She presents her Services to You Your Lady & daughters and proposes pleasure to her Self in sometimes waiting on You and takeing a Walk in your Garden. Wee had yesterday brought in at our Meeting a present from Mr Neve[12] Fellow of CCC Oxford and a Member, Archdeacon Battelys Opera Posthuma[13] there printed conteining a new Edition of Antiq. Rutupinæ with many Additional Copperplates and St Edmund St Edmunds Bury [sic] published by his Son Oliver Battely & dedicated to the Lord AB of Canterbury in 2º a very Entertaining Usefull & elegant Work. a Grasier from Wisebeach told me this morning that at the Wells in Marshland Norfolk[14] in that neighbourhood they have lately lost by the distemper 1700 head of Cattle: & Wee apprehend it's Spreading from that Quarter hitherwards. My Eldest son the Captain is Embarked with the Duke[15] for Flanders. God send them a prosperous Campaigne: He took a Man and Three strong Horses 2 of this country breed, with him, the 3rd an Hardy good Sized White Croppeard Scot, which He has used to Stand fire and knows to be hardy & Serviceable, having Servd him a Campaigne before. My Sister Ambler[16] this Lady day breaking up house keeping, I should be glad of a good Tenant & Neighbour at next door in her Stead, where there's room enough [p.4] and a Large Garden, Good Offices, Stable, Brewhouse, Coachhouse &c Near the Church, Freeschool, & Mercat, and to a Bookish-Man 'twould be Very agreeable to be so near our Collections, as to have the Society under the Roof, but if he wants the Whol House, those Wee must remove elsewhere: there's as 'tis the Use of a paved Hall, handsom Parlour, and an Other Room, Great Stair Case, Kitchen, Pantry below stairs and 4 Good Chambers & a large Closett, with Garretts Over the whole House. Recommend them if you can, who knows the House, formerly your Ancestors the Hobsons,[17] and the neighbourhood for the Sake of   Dear Dr   Your much obliged Friend

                M Johnson junr.

To the Reverend
Dr Stukeley at
  Stamford
    Present

---

1 See **Letter 48** above.
2 See Appendix 3.
3 The Guthlac Roll, today in the British Library. Drawn *c.*1200, it is a set of eighteen roundel drawings in a parchment roll, depicting the life of St Guthlac. Johnson refers here to Edward Harley, second Earl of Oxford, SGS 1729 and antiquarian collector, who died in 1741. In 1752 his family sold his library, including the roll, to be part of the founding collection of the British Museum. For Peter le Neve, see **Letter 15**, n.18 above.
4 Johnson's source is R. Twysden (ed.), *Historiæ Anglicanæ Scriptores* X (1652). Twysden edited ten mediæval chronicles, the sixth of which was *Chronicon Johannis Brompton Abatis Jorvalensis*. John Brompton (fl.1436–64) was Abbot of Jervaulx and did include an account of St Guthlac which is printed in Twysden (797–8) as Johnson specifies. This chronicle was probably written after 1340. According to *ODNB*, 'scholars in early modern England drew on it heavily'. Brompton probably organised the transcription from a range of earlier sources.
5 William Dugdale, *The History of Imbanking and Drayning of Divers Fenns and Marshes* (1662). The SGS did not own a copy in the eighteenth century, nor is one recorded in the sale catalogues of Johnson's books.

6 This is one of the specific eighteenth-century meanings of 'curious': here it means something particularly detailed and valuable as well as hard to find.
7 'Oh Jupiter! A great and laborious work.'
8 The four portfolios of prints and drawings exist today in the SGS archives and have been added to in later years. The contents of the cabinets have mostly disappeared but several eighteenth-century cabinets are still present at the SGS. 'Supellex Literaria' means the equipment necessary to maintain a learned collection.
9 Dr Theophilus Hill: see **Letter 46**, n.14, above. For his son John Hill, see **Letter 46**, n.13. Chrysocolla, hydrated copper silicate, a mineral of a striking blue-green colour, was anciently used in soldering gold; deposits were found in Cornwall at this period. For more details of chrysocolla, see **Letter 46** and also G. S. Rousseau, *The Notorious Sir John Hill: The Man Destroyed by Ambition in the Era of Celebrity* (2012), 42.
10 Charles Lennox, second Duke of Richmond and Duc d'Aubigny in the French nobility (1701–50). For Sir Hans Sloane, James Parsons and Emanuel Mendes da Costa, see their entries in *ODNB* and in Appendix 3.
11 Mary Johnson was probably born in 1723; she married Thomas Archer and had a daughter Anna Maria Elizabeth Charlotte Archer, born in 1752. She had died by 1755 when her daughter, Johnson's granddaughter, is mentioned in his will.
12 See Appendix 3; this is Timothy Neve junior, son of the Revd Timothy Neve, former Treasurer of the SGS and later Secretary of the PGS in Peterborough. Both were SGS members.
13 John Batteley (1646–1708: see *ODNB*), Archdeacon of Canterbury; his nephew posthumously published his *Antiquitates Rutupinæ* (1745), containing a history of Bury St Edmunds. This volume was presented by Timothy Neve junior as his present to the SGS on becoming a member in 1746.
14 There was a very severe outbreak of cattle distemper or murrain in 1747 which led to an Order in Council in March 1748 controlling the movement of cattle across the country.
15 Following the Battle of Culloden in 1746, the Duke of Cumberland returned to the European mainland in 1747, accompanied by Captain Maurice Johnson as an ADC. The British army was defeated at Maastricht at the Battle of Lauffeld in July 1747 and this led to the Peace of Aix-la-Chapelle in 1748.
16 Johnson's wife Elizabeth, née Ambler, had a sister Mary Ambler (1696–1754) who was joint heiress with her of Gayton House (later Holyrood House) next door to Ayscoughfee Hall, following the death of their brother Joshua Ambler in 1734. This is a helpful description of the house, which no longer exists and has been replaced by the Council Offices. The SGS had its meeting rooms there from 1745 to the death of Maurice Johnson in 1755.
17 Stukeley claimed descent from the Hobson family, who lived in Gayton House from 1600 to 1654: see Nancy Snowdon, *Ayscoughfee: A Great Place in Spalding* (2007), 79. Stukeley owned a drawing and a print of 'Old Hobson', the famous Cambridge carrier Thomas Hobson (1544–1631): see *Surtees* II, 34–5.

50. Maurice Johnson to William Stukeley, Spalding, 20 June 1747
Bodleian, MS Eng. misc. c.113, fols 343r–344v

Spalding June 20th 1747

Dear D[r]

Since I sent you My Neighbour Ravenscrofts reasons for declineing What he had enclined to,[1] He has been served with a Spâ at the Motion of his plaguing Antagonist Mrs Fish to revive her Suit against Him, She imagineing He has intermedled, as Wee presume, in his Aunt Digby's Affaires, for she had Surceasd before, as I told you, and Seemed to Acquiesce to have dropd all further Demands against Him: Had You therefore proceeded to revive in his Name, You see she had more handle than He trusts She can have had given her, for attacking him again, and giveing him fresh trouble & renewing Expences: which had They been by You occasiond, would have been to You imputed, & required & expected by

Him to be born by You. Dr Hutchinson here on Thursday Morning gave Us some, but not so full Account of Your Burgessing,[2] but not what I hoped to have heard from Him that Yee had made any Progress in restoreing a Gentlemans Society at Stamford like ours[3] (the Accommodations whereof I shewd him) as Yee proposd.

[p.2] As to the Subject of your Last[4] relating to his Lordships intended Conduct haveing been pretty much Used to negotiating matters passing thrô Great Mens hands Nothing's Surprizing, thô it may seem Mysterious: You and my Old Friend your Brother Dr[5] are so Well enclined to See Me something oftener, youd have Me have an Unavoidable Occasion of It which when his Lordship by the Town Clerk gives me his Commands, (if he does think fitt to give 'em) In obedience to Him, and duly to my Family, Especially my Son the Templar[6] I shall readily Submit to. In the Interim I hope Dr Coleby's well & with many Thanks to him for his Friendship give him my Compliments, who am greatly Obliged to Him for permitting me Such share of his Thoughts, as to have me perpetually in Mind – Be these things as They may, my Trust is to See You and your Daughter here when Yee take the Journey You proposed which I hope will be e'er long, being told Your Couzen Stukeley[7] is upon returning home from London where I suppose He has sometime been.

[p.3] By a Letter commun[icated] to Us at our Meeting on Thursday last[8] by order of the Soc. of Antiq. our Friend Vertue has engraved a Compleat Hypocaust & Bath discoverd lately at Hovingham in the Wap[ontake] of Ridall in the North Rideing of Yorkshire with a Pavement tesselated & some few Roman Coines found near It. Also another Discovery of Roman Roades & the Station of Delgovitiæ, with an Elaborate discourse thereon, which were shewn and read at the Mitre[9] attended with an Accurate Draught of the Town, as when Roman their Buildings & other Works there & that Robert Fenwick Esqr has been at the expence of publishing an Historical Account of Overbury, Brementonensis, compild in 2º by the late Revd and Learned Mr Rauthmell,[10] with some plates. Mr Professor Ward[11] of the Court of Wards and Liverys whereof Mr Vertue has engraved a plate [sic]. this Overbury should be called Over Burrow in Lancashire I presume, said by Camden to've been a City, & not Overbury, which the Index Villaris places in Worcestershire.[12] Two posts agone Mr Professor Ward (inter alia) advised us of Mr Folks[13] have [sic] thrô his diligence in Searching the Cottonian Library been so fortunate as to discover the Coines published by Speed supposd in the report of the Comittee of the house of Commons to've been lost in the Fire at Ashburnham house in 1731.[14] whereof the Judicious Gent. will make good Use in the Types he is publishing to his accurate Tables.

[p.4] By a Letter from a Reverend Member of our Soc.,[15] of whom We desired some Account of the Literary Soc. said to be at Doncaster in his Neighbourhood he was pleasd to give Us It & that they buy books But have a Rule restraining them from purchaceing any in Divinity, Law or Physick. I should think this the most Lucky season for Yee unanimously to restore Your Soc. & Set Yours Now of Stamford at the Head under whose Patronage & his Heireapparents May It flourish is the sincere Wish of
Dear Dr Your most obliged & affectionate Friend & Servt
      M Johnson jun[r]

To
 the Reverend
Dr Stukeley at

Stamford
Carr. pd.

1   George Ravenscroft of Wykeham Grange, Spalding. There was a complex legal case, Digby v. Ravenscroft, which began in 1687. Presumably 'spâ' is an abbreviation for 'subpoena', a writ instructing a person to attend a legal hearing as a witness.
2   Dr Samuel Hutchinson, a Lincolnshire man, a Stamford physician and a Fellow of St John's College, Cambridge, who was a candidate for the Cambridge Professorship in Anatomy in 1746. His father, Revd Samuel Hutchinson, became an SGS member in 1729; Dr Hutchinson became a member in 1746. The 'Burgessing' was the election of MPs for Stamford which took place on 29 June 1747.
3   See **Letter 36**, n.1, above; in 1747 Stukeley attempted to re-start his short-lived Brazen Nose Society of 1736–7 but without success.
4   This letter is not present in the SGS archive; it possibly refers to Lord Burghley, the new MP for Stamford.
5   Presumably Dr Dixon Coleby who is mentioned a few lines later; see Appendix 3.
6   Maurice Johnson's second son Walter, a member of the Inner Temple of the Inns of Court like his father.
7   If this is Stukeley's first cousin it will be Squire Adlard Stukeley, born 1698, a JP living in Holbeach. Stukeley refers to him elsewhere as 'couzen Stukeley'. Stukeley and his daughter, either Frances or Anna, are to visit Holbeach.
8   A good example of communication between learned societies in mid-eighteenth-century Britain (see SGS, MB4, fol.106r). For George Vertue the engraver, see Appendix 3. The Roman bath at Hovingham which he had engraved was discovered in 1745. Delgovitiæ or Delgovicia was near Market Weighton (East Yorkshire). Vertue's letters to the SGS have not survived.
9   The meeting place in London of the Antiquarian Society at the time.
10 Revd Richard Rauthmell, *Antiquitates Bremetonacenses or The Roman Antiquities of Overborough* (1746); it has a dedication to Robert Fenwick.
11 John Ward; see Appendix 3. His letter to Johnson, referred to several lines later, is reported in the SGS minute book (MB4, fol.104r, entry for 28 May 1747); it is summarised in *Correspondence*, 173.
12 There is the site of a Roman fort at Calacum or Casterton in Over Burrow or Burrow-in-Lonsdale (Lancs). Overbury is a village in Worcestershire by Bredon Hill. The spelling of place-names was still in the process of standardisation, which could cause confusion at times.
13 Martin Folkes: see Appendix 3. His *A Table of English Silver Coins from the Norman Conquest to the Present Times* was published in 1745; he was presumably producing illustrative examples as a supplement to it.
14 In the fire at Ashburnham House, Westminster, which housed the Cottonian collection of ancient books and manuscripts, a number of significant books were destroyed. The remainder of the collection formed the nucleus of the British Library.
15 This letter from Revd John Romley (see Appendix 3) was read at the SGS on 11 June 1747 (SGS, MB4, fol.105r). It gave a full account of the Literary Society at Doncaster which was sometimes held at Bawtry and sometimes at Blyth, both near Doncaster. The letter does not appear to have survived in the SGS archive.

[*SGS/ Stukeley/19A is not a letter but a copy of a paper by Stukeley on the African city of 'Ras Sem', addressed to the Revd Dr Shaw, President of St Edmund Hall, Oxford. The SGS paper is a copy in Stukeley's handwriting, presumably made for Johnson and the Spalding Gentlemen's Society.*]

51. William Stukeley to Maurice Johnson, Stamford, 21 September 1747
SGS/Stukeley/20

[Annotated by Johnson:] SGS 24 Sept 1747 from the Revd Dr Stukeley of a Rom[an] Villa Tesselated Paviam[en]t at Winterton, Tanned Corps in a Yorkshire Moor of a Woman with Sandals; British Weapons of Brass

To Maur. Johnson esq^r

Dear S^r

I received a Letter lately from Geo. Stovin esq^{r1} of Crowl yorkshire, inviting me to come to the opening a Roman tesselated pavement lately found on his ground, at Winterton by Humber in our county. since then, he sent me a very rude drawing of it; it was 35 foot long, 12 broad. beside, there were fragments found near it, tore up by the plow. so that is was in shape, much like that at Coterstock.[2]

these places were villa's or summerhouses, built by the Roman governors here; near a spring, & a wood, with a good prospect, southward. I find this observable of them all.

they were built of timber, one story high, coverd by tile. & were burnt by the Scots & Picts, when the Romans left us; or by the Saxons afterwards, when they made themselves masters of the island.

since then Mr Stovin calld on me,[3] & show'd me [p.2] many fragments of glass &c found thereon. he further acquainted me; this summer he found a female body,[4] above 6 foot deep in the moors of yorkshire. the skin tann'd like a piece of doe leather, & stretchd like it. the hair on the head, & nails on the fingers. she had sandals on, lac'd on the top of the foot: made of a raw hide, which too was tann'd like as the woman's skin. they had a seam at the heel, sowed with a thong of the same hide. 5 loops cut in the whole leather, on each side, & twelve small ones, at the toe; so that it drew up at the toe, like a purse mouth.

Mr Whichcot our member[5] put one of the sandals on, & says, they are very light, & easy to dance in. Mr Stovin says, the water of the moor is like tanners ooze, in color & quality, by reason of the great quantitys of oak under ground, in it. & he supposes, this has tann'd her skin, & buskins. & that she may be some hundred years old: I add some thousands. he says, he dug up in that moor, some brass british celts (as called) a dart, & two daggers: so that, no doubt, this was a british lady.

I am Yours &c
W Stukeley
Stamford 21 sept. Mauritii die^6 1747

1   George Stovin (1696–1780), born in the Isle of Axholme, lived at Tetley Hall, Winterton. For details of the Roman villa, see an article by I. M. Stead, *Antiquaries' Journal* 46 (1966), 72–84. Stovin discovered the villa in 1747 and reported it to the Royal Society.
2   Cotterstock Romano-British villa (Northants), discovered in 1736 on the land of Mr Campion. For a modern interpretation, see Stephen Upex, 'The Roman villa at Cotterstock', *Britannia* 23 (2001).
3   Stukeley described his contacts with Stovin in diary entries (quoted in *Surtees* II, 344–5), giving a full account of the discovery.
4   This is the Amcotts Moor Woman, uncovered by George Stovin. It is discussed by R. C. Turner and M. Rhodes, 'A bog body and its shoes from Amcotts, Lincolnshire', *Antiquaries' Journal* 72 (1992). A shoe still survives. The body was dated to AD 200–400.

⁵ Thomas Whichcote (1710–76), MP for Lincolnshire (1740–74).
⁶ St Maurice's feast day is today celebrated on 22 September. On 24 September 1747 Stukeley attended the SGS Thursday meeting and reported on Stovin's finds (see SGS, MB4, fol.121v).

52. Maurice Johnson to William Stukeley, Spalding, 24 October 1747
Bodleian, MS Eng. misc. c.113, fols 345r–346v

Spalding 24 Octr 1747

Dear D^r

As I know no greater pleasure than Serving a Worthy Friend by any fair meanes in a man's power; I take the Liberty I trust your friendship and our long acquaintance allow Me of Begging your good Interest & assistance for that purpose with his Grace the Duke of Mountague as Master of the Ordnance: requesting your Recommendation of our good Friend Mr Wm Bogdani,¹ Who has many yeares been an Industrious, Juditious, & Faithfull Clerk in that Office. That He may succeed Edward Short Esq who (the Mercury² says) died as on last Wednesday morning, Principal Clerk in that Office: I presume of an Apoplexy, of which He had had some strokes & being renderd incapable of doeing the duty of his Office Mr Bogdani (who was next Clerk under him) has for some time done both his Own, & that Gentlemans with great paines & diligence. No Man can be more firmly attached to the Government than our friend Mr Bogdani, and no Man is so well qualified for this Office, as his Grace well knows, whom I cant but wish You Sir might happen to See, or would at lest take occasion of writing to & recommend as he has by Many Yeares Services in the Office he being Next in It to the deceased, Merite of more than ordinary.

[p.2] The Autumn Feaveur³ has afflicted me and every one of our family my Father not excepted, they're got something better but many of them farr from being well yet. And the Small Pox Spreads in this Town so, that wee apprehend It will become general, but proves of a favourable kind. The Infection amongst our horned Cattle is not Yet ceased.⁴ And in these Parts few are left alive. So that the poor grasiers & their Landlords will be reduced greatly: Wooll, Hemp, Flax & Horse Corne bearing no Price. Since Wee had the pleasure of your Company at our Societys last meeting in the last Month I gave the Company 1st Octr instant an Account of what related to this place more particularly in King Edward IV reigne⁵ & of the Elloe Stone an Antient Cross, long since gone, but which stood in a Quadrivium⁶ between Moulton and Whapload frequently occurring in our Records the Sheriffes holding their Turnes there and the Kings Escheators sometimes takeing Inquisitions post mortem near it. where was a Seat sometime belonging to the Lord Wells and a family formerly of good Note in this County took their Name Elloestone from It. from my Son Butter⁷ at Rippon

[p.3] Wee had the Epitaph of Hugh Ripley 1637 who was the last Wakeman & thrice Mayor, by whose good Endeavors the Town of Rippon first became a Mayoraltie. And of Colonell Jordan Crosland of Nubie Kn^t Governour of Scarborough Castle for Kings Charles 1 & 2 ob. 20 Aug. 1670.

8 Inst I related what memorable had occurred to me here in my reading temp. RR. E[dward] V & R[ichard] III and Mr Hursthouse a beneficent Member presented Us with Doyly & Coulsons Edition of Pere Calmetts Bible Dictionary.⁸

15 Inst Dr Green⁹ gave us 2 MSS of the late Capt. Thomas's deceas'd here.

One containing the Rules of Navigation, & Astronomy as thereto relating & his Voyages 1698 to Venice, Zant & Cephalonia, with Draughts of the Appearances made at Sea of sundry Iselands Capes & forelands. The other a tract of Sailing by John Cox and Journal of a Voyage to Minorca by Captn Willm Ashton And home again in 1678 with a fleet under the Command of Sr John Narborough Admiral. Last Thursday I continued my historical Notice under King H[enry] VII and took notice of a Remark made by Mr Folkes his Tables of this being the first of our Kings whose Coin beares a true Similitude to his Pictures, & that done en Profile and a Remarke both of Mr Talmans[10] & Seign^r Grisonis (from whom I had a Letter from Florence last post & he's removing to Pisa for the sake of his Son who is there studying the Law) That the Roman Coniseurs do not rely on any resemblance in Any Coine or Medal of the Popes before Martin V de Colonna,[11] who began his Pontificate in 1415 and dyed about 1431 under whom the Arts revived there.

[p.4] In a Letter from Dr Rutherforth[12] of St Jno Coll. Camb. he says he apprehends Tanning human Bodies or Parts of them may formerly have been One Method used to preserve them. And that at Sudbury he had been shewn what they told him was the head of Simon Sudbury[13] so preserved. this was that AB of Canterbury slain in Wat Tyler & Jack Straws Insurrection in 1381. who Weaver & from him Fuller says was interred at Sudbury in Suffolk.

I am My Good Friend Your most obliged & affectionate
Servt M Johnson jun^r

To
the Reverend
    Dr Stukeley
    at Stamford
Turn at Stilton

---

[1]   William Bogdani: see Appendix 3. This demonstrates the system of patronage at the heart of social life in the eighteenth century. In 1737 Edward Short was Chief Clerk and Deputy to the Clerk of the Ordnance; Bogdani was a clerk in ordinary but hoped for preferment, which **Letter 53** below indicates that he gained. By 1755 Bogdani was signing documents as Clerk of the Ordnance. Stukeley's main patron at this stage was John Montagu, second Duke of Montagu, who was at this time presenting him to the living of St George's church, Queen Square, London. The Duke was Master of the Ordnance and therefore had final control over appointments to offices in the Ordnance, the supply organisation for guns to the army and navy.

[2]   This is presumably the *Stamford Mercury* for October 1747.

[3]   Autumn fever or fall fever was a name for leptospirosis; symptoms, lasting for three to seven days, are fever, pain, vomiting and exhaustion. The bacteria involved are particularly spread through contact with animal urine. Smallpox was commonplace and varied in intensity. Stukeley deliberately exposed himself to the disease in youth before training to be a physician, to acquire some immunity. Direct inoculation or variolation with smallpox was well known in 1747 but it did not become widespread until after Jenner's development of cowpox-based vaccine in 1796.

[4]   There was a nationwide outbreak of cattle plague or rinderpest in the 1740s; see C. A. Spinage, *Cattle Plague: A History* (London, 2003).

[5]   Stukeley had attended the SGS as one of the Vice-Presidents; see **Letter 51**, n.6 above. At the following meeting on 1 October 1747 there was a long account of the life and reign of Edward IV given by Maurice Johnson (see SGS, MB4, fol.123r).

[6]   This account of the Elloe Stone is taken from SGS, MB4, fol.123r. It is today on Spalding Gate, Whaplode, having been moved from its earlier position. It is thought today that it marked the site of the local Hundred Court of Elloe Wapentake.

7   Johnson's son-in-law Robert Butter; see Appendix 3. Hugh Ripley (d.1637) was the last Wakeman of Ripon (Yorks) in 1604 and first Mayor in 1605. Sir Jordan Crosland of Newby (c.1617–70) held Helmsley Castle for the King during its siege in the Civil War and was made Governor of Scarborough Castle by Charles II in 1665.

8   This is an account of one evening's meeting of the SGS. The minute book has a full account by Johnson of the reigns of Edward IV and Richard III; he offers the conventional view of the murder of the princes in the Tower by Richard Duke of Gloucester (SGS, MB4, fol.124v). John Hursthouse, a Spalding mercer, became an SGS member in 1742. He presented to the Society Augustin Calmet, *An Historical, Critical, Geographical, Chronological and Etymological Dictionary of the Holy Bible*, trans. Samuel D'Oyly and John Colson (1732).

9   This meeting is recorded in SGS, MB4, fol.125r. The donation by Johnson's son-in-law and fellow-Secretary, John Green (see Appendix 3), is listed on fol.176v in Part III of Maurice Johnson's MS catalogue of the SGS's libraries, 'Catalogue Libro. & Bibliothec. Societatis Generosæ Spalding.' commenced in 1715. It is a folio MS volume, 'Ashton and Cox MS of Astry. Navig: & Voyg. To Minorca Captn Ashton & Jno. Cox 1679'. Admiral Sir John Narborough (1640–88) commanded an English fleet in the Mediterranean against North African pirates in 1678. The meeting also continued Johnson's survey of English history. For Martin Folkes' Tables, see **Letter 50**, n.13, above.

10 John Talman (1677–1726) was the Superintendent of Drawings, Prints, Plates and Books of the Society of Antiquaries. For Giuseppe Grisoni, see Appendix 3. In 1725, when Johnson hoped to build a new museum and library for the SGS, both Talman and Grisoni submitted design sketches. See John Harris, 'Designs for the museum and library of the Spalding Gentlemen's Society', *The Georgian Group Journal* 19 (2011), 39–49.

11 Pope Martin V (1368–1431) became Pope in 1417. He stabilised the papacy after the Rome–Avignon split and reorganised the papal coinage.

12 The Revd Dr Thomas Rutherforth; see Appendix 3. The letter is summarised in *Correspondence*, 175.

13 Simon Sudbury (1316–81) was the Archbishop of Canterbury from 1375 to his assassination during the 1381 Peasants' Revolt. His skull has been at St Gregory's church, Sudbury, since the year of his death. Johnson has referred to John Weever, *Ancient Funerall Monuments* (1631), presented to the SGS by James West, and to Thomas Fuller, *History of the Worthies of England* III (1662), of which he possessed a copy.

53. Maurice Johnson to William Stukeley, Spalding, 6 November 1747
Bodleian, MS Eng. misc. c.113, fols 347r–348v

Spalding 6º Novr 1747

Dear D^r

Since I addressd you for your good Interest on behalf of my Friend Mr Bogdani I've received an Agreeable Letter from that Gentleman Who has had the happyness to be benefitted on the Occasion I mentioned to his Content: I acquaint you therewith that if You've not applyd to his Grace, You may Spare giveing your Self that trouble:[1] If you have apply'd his Grace must have the better opinion of Him for being So recommended, which can't but be a Creditt to Him, having Servd long & faithfully And brought the Busyness of that Board and kept It to in the greatest Adroitness and regularity, by Sorting, binding up, Indexing and rendring all their Papers usefull & lodging them as Records in so rational a manner in the Offices as that They may readily had [*sic*] recourse to anything there that They can have Occasion for, which in the Confusion those things was a Laborious and Tedious Task. which with our having been Intimate from our Childhood, allmost as long as You & I, induced me to recommend him.

[p.2] I had been up in Town this Term e'er this time but that my poor Father declines so the Dr Green thinks him near his End, so shall not go up, my Son being gone,[2] with whom I was last Saturday at Grimesthorpe:[3] which His Grace has vastly improved especialy the Environs & the south grand Apartment, and the Chapell. I was there told a Sumptuous Monument for his Father is prepareing At London to be Erected at Edenham, the Chancell whereof his Grace purposes to Enlarge for the better reception of that & others. which indeed are frequently not Seen to best advantage when crampd in too Low and narrow a Compass. the whole South Aisle of our parish Church, Save what was taken into the adjoyning Free school for a Chapell of St Thos of Beckett that Blissful Martyr,[4] belongs to 3 Mansions[5] in this Town for Buryal places Viz^t the Upper End where my Mothers monument Stands to our house, Ayscoughfeehall, which came to Us by Her, the Middle part to my Couz Johnsons called antiently the Swanshouse and that next the door to my Couz Wilsbys Berquery House and no other people bury there. I have in right of my Wife another Buryal place belonging to the next door house sometime Gaytons,[6] afterwards [p.3] Sr William Rigdons, who enlarged It with materials of the Wardens of the Guild of the BVM. & St Thos of Beckett the Merchants Saint, & I believe S^r W^m was a Merchant of the Staple at Callis, this House afterwards belonged to the Hobsons, who built our Town Hall, & are of Your worthy kinred One of whom lyes interred in this buryal place at the SW Corner of the Church under a Black Marble whereon are his Armes & Inscription. I have likewise right of Sepulture my Self Wife and descended from her as She descended from Sir Andrew Oldfeild Grandfather – Anth. who purchasd the Rectory of the Crown & Sold It to the Inhabitants of this Place with that Special Reservation in his Deeds. these are all in bad Condition but if my kinsmen will joyn with me I'll endeavour to have them all made neat and fitt to be Seen, which is but a decent Piety in any private Person. Shall when See You next desire Your good Advice therein, an [sic] in the Interim with all our Compliments to Yourself Lady and the Young Ladys Your Daughters   Dear D^r

    Your most obliged and Obed^t Friend and Servant
        M Johnson junior

What think you of the Images dug up in Mr Beridges Garden at Algarkirke?[7]

To the Reverend Dr Stukeley
  at Stamford
      These
Carryage p^d

---

[1] See **Letter 52**, n.1, above. Bogdani appears to have gained the promotion in the Ordnance Office that he was seeking. Bogdani's relationship to Johnson is not clear, though Johnson claimed him as a kinsman.

[2] Johnson's son Walter has gone to London instead of his father to conduct the necessary legal business during the term. Dr Green was the family doctor as well as the husband of Maurice Johnson's daughter Jane. Johnson's father Maurice Johnson senior died on 8 November 1747, aged eighty-six. For a family tree of the Johnsons, see *Correspondence*, Appendix 5.

[3] Johnson and his son Walter attended the Duke of Ancaster at Grimsthorpe as his legal representatives. This is the third Duke, Peregrine Bertie (1714–78), who had succeeded his father the second Duke, also called Peregrine, in 1742. The monument to the second Duke in St Michael and All Angels' church, Edenham (the parish church for Grimsthorpe), is by Roubiliac.

[4] Spalding Grammar School met in the eastern end of the south aisle of the parish church of St Mary and St Nicholas, in a separate chancel chapel.

[5] This is a useful account of the ancestral family burial places in the south aisle of the church. The three families referred to are the Oldfields, Johnsons and Wilsbys.

6   Gayton House, later known as Holyrood House and Fairfax House, next door to Johnson's home at Ayscoughfee Hall, was built around 1500. It eventually came into the possession of the Ambler family until the death in 1733 of Joshua Ambler, when it passed to his two sisters as his heirs; one of them was Elizabeth, the wife of Maurice Johnson. Eventually Johnson used part of it as a meeting-place for the SGS and it became the home of his son Walter on Walter's marriage. It was demolished by the Town Council in the 1960s and replaced by the Council Offices.

7   Algarkirk, a parish south-west of Boston. The Beridge family were lords of the manor and rectors from the seventeenth to the nineteenth century. The nature of the 'images' is unfortunately not recorded.

54. William Stukeley to Maurice Johnson, Stamford, 25 May 1748
SGS/Stukeley/21

[Annotated by Johnson:] 25 May 1748 From the Reverend Dr Wm Stukeley to the Presid^t with a Present of Fossils – of Petrifactions, Instruments & Peices of Urns, Pateræ &c to the Museum & promise of his Communications from London.

My dear friend,
   I have sent you here, by Mercurius Spaldingensis, a bag of fossils, & Roman fragments, & some, probably Saxon.[1] I am extremely busy, packing up bag & baggage for London; where, I hope, we shall have many opportunitys of seeing one another, durante vita.[2]
   To my daughter, I propose next week, to show the new city of little worth:[3] in our way to Holbech. she will have great pleasure in viewing the innumerable beautys & curiositys of your garden.
   I have long agoe sold my house to Mr Noel:[4] & he will not suffer us to finger a flower. one of my chief amusements in London, is going to the Royal Society. Brown Willys esq^r[5] tiezes me to goe thence to the Antiquarys. I always tell him, I cannot possibly do so absurd a thing, as to goe to two feasts together.[6] insted [p.2] of that, I goe directly home; & over a contemplative pipe, I recollect all that is past, at Crane court; & make memorandums of it. this I write down more particularly, next morning.
   this method I have practisd, all the times I have been there, since I left the Town. & now shall continue it for life.
   I intend, when I am got thro'ly fix't in my new scituation, <u>to transcribe all my papers of this sort, & send 'em to you</u>; for the amusement of the gentlemen of your Society.[7]
   for tho' I goe again to live in London, for my final remove: yet I carry the same mind along with me. I can't goe from one public entertainment to another : & never be easy, but when in public company. on the contrary, I love solitude in London. & the beauty of living there, is, that we can mix company & solitude, in a just proportion. whilst in the country, we can have nothing else but Solitude. in Stamford, I so find it: almost equal to that of our friend Guthlakes at Croyland.
   [p.3] I leave here, a most elegant place. & now tis not my own, I may praise it. for I think, considering, this is but its 4th year. it is as pretty a seat, as I ever saw. beside my temple of Flora, I made a Temple of Bacchus. the upper part of it, was a great window into my study. <u>I have contriv'd it so, as</u> <u>that</u> in a year or two, <u>I should have had</u> a strike or two of <u>grapes within doors: ripe a month or</u>

two, or more, sooner than the English season. a place it would have been, beyond measure pleasant, & elegant.[8]

now Mr Noel designs to pull it down. His views & mine are quite different.

Just before I left Town, my evil genius Parkin put out what he calls a reply to my objections, about Lady Roisia's sepulchral chapel at Roiston. by his title page, one would suppose, <u>he</u> had wrote first, & I had answer'd <u>him</u>. from so nonsensical a title page,[9] the world, I beleive, expects nothing material. for I saw it keep its station, from day to day, unmolested, in Tryes show-glass. & they tell me, my answer to his objections is so full & just; that I ought not to give him any thing further. they that have read it, say it consists altogether of scandal & abuse, but no argument.

I have not read it nor ever shall: but from some friends of mine in his neighborhood, I know his character to be such, that like a puppy, you may beat him, & he will still yelp on, till he dyes.

I saw your friend Mr Hill.[10] he is now engag'd in a laborious work. & by what I hear he holds Osborn with a strait rein. which is a rare thing in an author. for I think the London booksellers & Drs. are generally people <u>sine animis</u>:[11] at least their souls are sinecures.

I am with service to all your Society, your sincere friend & Servant

W Stukeley

Stamford 25 may 1748

---

[1] Stukeley's present to the SGS was acknowledged at the meeting on 2 June 1748 and recorded in SGS, MB5, fol.15r. Stukeley and Johnson maintain the joke of the messenger who carried letters and parcels between them as 'Mercury' the messenger of the gods. It may have been an individual messenger; if it was the regular carrier, the joke may refer ironically to the slowness of his travel.

[2] Stukeley was moving in 1748 to live permanently in London where he had been presented to the living of St George's church, Queen Square. He hopes to maintain his friendship with Johnson by seeing him on Johnson's London visits 'as long as they live'.

[3] See **Letter 44**, n.7, above.

[4] See **Letter 44**, n.8, above. Stukeley had been living in his house in Barn Hill, Stamford, for around four years. As Stukeley's neighbour, Noel was glad to purchase his house and garden. He had been in dispute with Stukeley about a bay window which looked over Noel's garden. This is referred to more fully later in this letter. For a full account of Stukeley's Stamford garden and his quarrel with Noel, see John Smith, 'William Stukeley in Stamford: his houses, gardens and a plan for a Palladian triumphal arch over Barn Hill', *Antiquaries' Journal* 93 (2013), 353–400.

[5] See Appendix 3.

[6] At this time the regular weekly London meetings of the Royal Society and the Society of Antiquaries had come to be held on the same day, though at different times. The Royal Society met from 1710 to 1780 at Crane Court, just north of Fleet Street, in a property similar in size to the SGS's Spalding meeting room. When resident in London, Stukeley felt unable to attend both and came to prefer the Royal Society; he made full notes on his return home and sent copies of these to Spalding where they were read at SGS meetings; they ran to five bound volumes which are still in the SGS archives.

[7] There is a note in Johnson's hand: 'I more particularly request a Copy of the Drs MS Dissertation & drawings of the Shecinah & Urim & Thummim.' These relate to early Jewish theological concepts of the presence of God and to the symbols on the robes of the High Priest. Stukeley wrote a dissertation on the pectoral (or breastplate) of Aaron, the first High Priest, which is in the Bodleian Library (MS Eng. misc. e.553). The Freemasons' Hall Library, London, holds MS 'Shechinah' by Stukeley, 'Enquiry into the nature of the appearance of the divine Shechinah' and 'Bazaleel or Pectoral of Aaron', all in MSS under call number 1130 STU.

[8] There is a note by Johnson: 'Q. that I may put the same in practice in what was my Study & is to be a Greenhouse?'

⁹ See **Letters 44** and **45** above, particularly **Letter 44**, nn. 4 and 5. The Revd Charles Parkin's forty-page reply to Stukeley's book on the Royston cave was entitled *A reply, to the peevish, weak and malevolent objections brought by Dr Stukeley, in his Origines Roystonianæ, no.2*. Stukeley claims that Parkin's book, shown in the Stamford bookseller's window, was not selling.

¹⁰ John Hill: see Appendix 3. Hill's printer, referred to here, was Thomas Osborne (1704–67) of Gray's Inn. See G. Rousseau, *The Notorious Sir John Hill* (2012), 92–7.

¹¹ 'Without souls'.

55. Maurice Johnson to William Stukeley, Spalding, 27 May 1748
Bodleian, MS Eng. misc. c.113, fols 349r–350v

Spalding 27 May 1748

Dear D^r

By your Mercury I received the Bagg of Philosophical & Antiquarian Wares & Merchandize various in Sorts & very agreeable: expect There shall share them with our Corpus Literatum,¹ on which his Grace our Lord Patron² t'other Day bestowd Dr Mckenzys 3 Voll in fol. printed at Edenb. of Scots Authors from the first to the beginning of last Century a Judicious & become rare Work: & Rocque Plan of London, Westminster & Southwark engraven by Pine & Tinney a most Laborious, Noble, & useful Performance on 24 sheets of Imperial Paper with a 2° Index to Shew the ready finding Every Place & thing therein. his Grace was So good to Subscribe for 2 Copies, that Wee might be enrichd with this no doubt very Expensive as well as absolutely Necessary Instruction to an English Library & Museum, and judiciously sent it us as of most service in Sheets. He was pleasd to add to these great Guifts, Professor Spences Polymetis (whereof Lord Viscount Falkland³ made our Museum his donation as a Member) to be lodgd in our School Class for the ready use of the Master &c. I acquaint You with these Accessions as I know what contributes to the wellfare of our Institution gives You pleasure Whom I've frequently wished fate had fixed here with Me, where I Am Once every week endeavouring to Cultivate mine and provide for future Generations. & am as often refreshed with the Charmes of the most Heavenly Art of the best composd human Musick Both which I begg You earnestly to Partake with Your good Lady ⁴& all your Daughters, whom I shall Every day expect till I see Yee here, where as My Dear Spouse desires Me with her Compliments, & with those of my Son Walter & all our family to add Yee shall be most heartyly wellcome to Us.

[p.2] I take Your Intention of Communicating to Us at your Leisure Houres the transcripts of Your Literary observations most kindly,⁵ & must by our antient Friendship above all request I may have a transcript with Sketches of your own MS Dissertations on the Shecinah & Urim & Thummim the Ephod & Breastplate of Aaron,⁶ wherewith in only a Cursary view & Perusal I was extreemly Delighted & I think edified, being you must know, now & then Something of a Rhapsodist my Self; at lest admiring Such as were So, & taking great delight in the Sublime. I must engage You to leave me (to whom all the rest of that, & those Croyland Statues belong by Free guift of my Friend Beverley Butler Esqr the Owner) the Head of that Abb[o]t which I will have replaced again without a Dionysian Miracle.⁷ And shall be much obliged to You if You'd give me leave to be the Purchasor of the Two Peices of relievo of St Jn° Bapt., & St Ethelreda, or Either of them:⁸ which things I wish for & may be left safe for me with the old

Roman altar with my old Gardiner Mr R^d Ashlynn , I'll give You the full Value for them & place the one in my Garden the Other in my House as Ornaments, & if You've taken down Your painted Glass & don't intend to put it up in London (where nothing lasts long) I'ld buy & put that up with what I've Collected in my hall windows.[9]

[p.3] You must take these requests, not as coveting your Goods or as Unmannerly proposals, or as begging the things. the Head belongs of right to Me, and if You'll take Equivalent in Money or Goods for the Other things, Wee may be both better Suited. such sort of things being lost in London, where theres plenty of New & more Excellent carvings, & Glass painting which except in a few Churches, is rarely Used now a days.[10] And if you chuse to keep them, or make Other Use of Them, I am but where I was, & [will] not take it ill, but would have you understand I don't want to have 'Em for Asking for, & would Set a Value on them. So as to preserve them perhaps Some Centurys longer which that Aiscough-Feehall may last, I'm doeing many Necessary repairs to It, & not only so, but towards restoring It to Its original Designe. My Gardens are realy now Very pleasant, When the Captn[11] comes from Flanders, will be highly Improved in a Manner to his Tast, which I think a good one & what will much lighten the Expence in their keeping & not destroy the plan they were made on neither, which would by no meanes be to the satisfaction of my Dearest Friend,
    Your most affectionate & faithful Servant
     M Johnson[12]

PS. I would also buy Your Statues & the Pedestals, if not disposed of

To the Reverend
Dr Stukeley at
   Stamford
Carryage payd.

1 'The body of literate people', i.e. the SGS.
2 Francis Scott, Duke of Buccleuch: see Appendix 3. A generous benefactor, his gifts recorded here were: George Mackenzie MD, *Lives and Characters of the most eminent Writers of the Scots Nation* (1708); John Roque, *Survey of London, Westminster and Southwark* (1746–7); Joseph Spence, *Polymetis: An Enquiry concerning the Agreement between the Works of the Roman Poets and the Remains of Ancient Artists* (1747). These are still in the SGS library.
3 Lucius Carey, seventh Viscount Falkland (1707–85) became a member in 1738.
4 Stukeley's second wife Elizabeth, née Gale, sister of Roger and Samuel Gale, whom he had married in 1738.
5 A reference to Stukeley's transcripts of his notes on the Royal Society's meetings; see **Letter 54**, n.6, above.
6 See **Letter 54**, n.7, above.
7 This refers to St Denis, the third-century Bishop of Paris who was martyred for his faith shortly after AD 250. The abbey of St Denis was built over his burial place. His legend claimed that after he was beheaded he picked up his head and walked ten kilometres, preaching his last sermon.
8 Johnson offers to purchase some of the surviving carvings from Croyland Abbey, including a head which Stukeley identified as that of Abbot Turketyl, which Stukeley had taken to Stamford.
9 Much of Johnson's collection of stained and painted glass survives today in Ayscoughfee Hall. It is discussed in fuller detail in **Letter 58** below.
10 Johnson's comments indicate the relatively rare placement of stained or painted glass in English churches in the first half of the eighteenth century.
11 Johnson's eldest son Captain Maurice Johnson.

[12] During his father's lifetime, Johnson signed himself 'Maurice Johnson junior' to distinguish himself from his father, also confusingly called Maurice. Since his father's death he no longer uses the 'junior' as he is now the senior member of his family.

56. Maurice Johnson to William Stukeley, Spalding, 10 April 1749
Bodleian, MS Eng. misc. c.113, fols 359r–360v

Spalding 10th April 1749

My Good Friend

Tis So long since I had any Conversation with you That I cannot longer deny my Self the urgeing you to indulge me in that pleasure. When I proposd to be had [sic] It personaly last on my being in London Your Lady told Me you was Enjoying the Pleasures of the Country with your Great Patron his Grace of Montague in North[amp]tonshire.[1] I have heretofore had the pleasure of seing Boughton whose Gardens I much admired for the Vast Command of Water. an Element absolutely necessary to render Gardens or Fields Agreeable to me, who have enough of it for 3 parts of the Yeare sometimes too little in the Hottest season, thô had Wee as Wee ought but half the Water should Come down the Welland to Us, and that Command of the Glen Wee might have by Westload[2] I should Never Want or Wish for a Spring. – Wee have have [sic] here been so Enterprizing as to devise a Triumphal Arch[3] to be placed on the Stone Steps where Whilom a Sumptuous Cross stood in our Mercatplace to be illuminated with Fixed fireworks Against the Thanksgiving for the Peace. when Wee intend to have a Concert of Musick and Assemblie for the fair Sex at our Towns hall which will this Yeare be new fronted with a Grand pair of Valvæ of Oake, & a Venetian Window over them, all to be set in ashler Stone work of Ketton stone, & the Embasement Rusticke Worke. Mr Wm Sands Architect & Free Mason qui invenit perficiet.[4] I hear Sir Edward Bellamy late Father of the City,[5] has Left his Eldest Daughter Couz. G. Lynn of Southwyks Lady a large addition to the Handsom Fortune he formerly gave him with Her, of which They Both are very deserving. My Son the Captn. has been with us a While, & brought home with him many excellent Sketches & some Drawings from Brabant. amongst them one of the Tower of St Michaels Church near Glastonbury commonly called the Torr, a Turre, taken near it in Indian inke by some forreigner on his Travels here as seems by a memorandum on It in bad English and a forreigne hand, as appears to Me, but worth preserving. [p.2] It seems to have been build on a Stone Vault of 3 Arches, and to have been Open to the Nave or Body of that Church, which adjoined to It Eastward, & was I believe a pretty Spatious edifice. Our Country is pretty dry, old Mr Grundy Master of Mathem[atics], Engineer & Agent for our Lords and Others Adventurers for Dreyning our Fenns is dead, & his Son succeeds him,[6] a much more Ingenious Man better Scholar & neater Draughtsman than his Father. He has lately drawn on Velom, surveyd & taken the Levels of, Shire Drain & South Ea &c for Mr Hunter Lord of Croyland,[7] Tycho Wing[8] is doeing the same for the Duke of Bedford, or for the Corporation of Bedford Levells. They would preclude my Friend & Patron from his & the Crowns antient rights of running their Waters off Postland Croyland Lordship and destroy or exceedingly Lessen the Values of his & Our Friend Beverley Butlers & 1000 Other Estates there & thereabout. Whereupon Wee've had a

Commission in Chancery for a Week past depending here for Examination of some Antient Witnesses in perpetuam Rei memoriam.[9]

Mr Sands has purchased of Mr Hurne Spalding-Towns End-Mannor-Hall here commonly called Duck Hall.[10] & taken great part of It down: that Mannor sometime belonged to Dr Joseph Moor a Physician here of whose Heir Mr Hargate the famous Decoy Man bought It & built this House, having gotten an Estate of 500l. per annum by Decoys: Cressey hall's in a Way to be ruined for want of being Kept in tenantable Repaires.[11] I wish you know any good Gentlemans family wanted to hire an House here of 3 or 4 Rooms on a floor with 5 Chambers & as many Garretts for I believe my Sister Ambler leaves my house at next door,[12] Which is What I mean, next Lady day. & this Part of It with the Garden she had. if a Tenant wou'd have more Id let him the Whole & 4 acres of Pasture for 24l. per annum. But [p.3] I would rather let it, as I do, reserving the Great Parlour & use of the Hall for Our Society, & the Stone Building in the yard to Our Servant which makes the rent 10l. per annum easier and more Commodious to me: but Rather than Not have a good Tenant, if I can get one, I will make way for the Society in my Own house, and fit them up what was my Father's Study to meet in.[13] Wee've there been of late highly entertaind with some elegant Latin Translations in Verse from the Prophets and Psalms sent in by my Couz Walter Johnson Rector of Redmarshall in Durham composd by his Son George Johnson of Durham School, an excellent Poet & who next Yeare goes to the University. and I believe to St John's Coll. in Cambridge whether most of our Family have been sent who had an university Education.[14]

I pray who is publishing the Antiquities of France in English with Father Montfaulcon's plates, & are [sic] to be any additional Plates to this Work?[15] Mrs Johnson & all my Family joine with me in our Regards to you & yours, who Wee hope Enjoy good health: And that at your best Leisure You will be so good to me as to remember your kind promise at our parting of Sending Me transcripts of what I so much desired. for there's no man whom I more esteem than Your Self Sir, nor whos thoughts and manner of treating Subjects I enter into with so great delight. from certainly a sameness of Turn of Mind and Disposition natural to Us in Common. Nunc pauci sumus[16] – of which Number let me ever remaine Dear Friend

        Your most affectionat Servant   M Johnson

P.S. The Owner of our Navigation Toll to Stamford and the Lords Adventurers are like to have a strong Contest about the neglect of these laters Duty therein, as the Farmer of these Tolls, one Mr Ward Tenant to Lady Feast, suggests.

To the Rev^d Dr Stukeley
At his house by St George's Church
in Queen Square near
   Ormond Street
      London

---

[1]   Stukeley's current patron was John, second Duke of Montagu (1690–1749); his country house was Boughton House in Northamptonshire.

[2]   At the time the Westlode was still a stream on the surface in the town of Spalding. Today it flows under New Road and Westlode Street.

3   The SGS archive contains drawings and notes relating to the Spalding celebrations of the Peace of Aix-la-Chapelle. The celebrations were delayed until six months after the peace treaty in 1748. The national celebrations are best remembered today in Handel's *Music for the Royal Fireworks* (1749). For details of the Spalding plans, see *Correspondence*, 178–80.
4   Spalding Town Hall was built by John Hobson in 1620. Its earlier form can be seen in the margin of John Grundy's map of Spalding. The new Venetian window and the new oak doors (Johnson's 'Valvæ') can be seen in Hilkiah Burgess's 1822 engraving of Spalding Market Place. Both are reproduced in *Correspondence*, Illustrations 2 and 3. William Sands (d.1751), the architect, became an SGS member in 1745; for details of his life see Howard Colvin, *A Biographical Dictionary of British Architects 1600–1840* (1995). The Latin phrase means '[he] who designed it will complete it'.
5   Sir Edward Bellamy (d. 28 March 1749), Lord Mayor of London in 1734, Master of the Fishmongers' Company and a director of the Bank of England, was elected to SGS membership in 1735. Johnson's son Maurice married Elizabeth Bellamy, Sir Edward's second daughter, in 1749. Her sister was already married to George Lynn junior (1707–1758), a relative of the Johnsons; see Appendix 3.
6   John Grundy senior (1696–1748) and his son John Grundy junior (1719–83), both drainage engineers; see Appendix 3.
7   Thomas Orby Hunter (c.1710–69) was granted the inheritance of the Manor of Crowland by Act of Parliament in 1752. He became an SGS member in 1734 and was a Government minister.
8   Tycho Wing (1696–1750), a surveyor, astronomer and astrologist, worked with his son John Wing in surveying the estates of the Duke of Bedford and the lands of the Corporation of the Bedford Levels. His family eventually lived in Thorney Abbey.
9   'In perpetual memory of the matter'. As a drainage lawyer, Johnson worked on behalf of Hunter and Butler in Crowland against the Corporation of the Bedford Levels. This indicates the extent to which the drainage work by the Bedford Levels Corporation interfered with the rights of estates contingent to the land held by the Bedford Levels Corporation; it is the age-old dispute among those involved in drainage as to where the water should be sent when it is drained from a particular area of land.
10 See **Letter 15**, n.27, above. Town's End Manor was south of the town of Spalding via the London road. A drawing of a duck decoy such as those used by Mr Hargate is reproduced in William Stukeley, *Itinerarium Curiosum* I, 18. The house was finally demolished in 1751.
11 Cressy Hall, Gosberton, no longer exists in its eighteenth-century form. Sir Henry Heron, who died in 1695, built the house to which Johnson refers; it was burnt down in 1792 (for a report of the fire, see M. Beardsley and N. Bennett (eds), *Gratefull to Providence: The Diary and Accounts of Matthew Flinders, Surgeon, Apothecary and Man-Midwife II, 1785–1802*, LRS 97 (2009), 114).
12 See **Letter 53**, n.6, above.
13 The Society remained at Gayton House until Maurice Johnson's death in 1755, and then had to move from the premises described here to Mr Cox's Rooms by the High Bridge on the opposite side of the river.
14 Although St John's College, Cambridge, was the most popular college for South Lincolnshire families, George Johnson went to Brasenose College, Oxford, and then became a Fellow of Magdalen College; see Appendix 3.
15 See **Letter 34**, n.9, above. There was a 1750 publication of a version of Montfaucon's work in two volumes, printed by W. Innys, J. and P. Knapton, R. Manby and H. S. Cox, entitled *Regal and Ecclesiastical Antiquities of France, with upwards of Three Hundred Large Folio Copper Plates*.
16 'We are now few.'

57. Maurice Johnson to William Stukeley, Spalding, 19 April 1749
Bodleian, MS Eng. misc. c.113, fols 361r–362v

My Good Friend
   Your accurate account of the great Treasure you have prudently & happyly for the British Nation our Native Country procured from Denmark of the Work of Richard of Westminster[1] I congratulate you and all our Learned Countrymen in, being assured It could in no hands turn to so good Account. Leland, Camden,

Speed, the Gales father & son, Selden, Spelman, Gybson, Horseley, Nicholson, Lluyd, Draiton, Hollingshead, Somner,[2] are all gone, as well as this our Richard: but you (thank God) remain to do him, & his, and your Country the right to retrieve him from ruin and restore him by our friend Wm Bowyer's[3] press to the Public: being (as I concieve with you) an inestimable Jewel, & bringing into my mind our old Acquaintance Bishop Kennett's Motto to his Catalogue of antient Authors, from Æsop Upon the Dunghill was found a Pearle, & alluding to that sayd upon Terence [gap in text] Ennius, Aurum extraxit e Stercore Ennii.[4] This Author[5] by his Name [gap in text] seems not to have been much known to any of our Criticks, even the most diligent and Inquisitive. Let me give You the fruits of my enquiries about him sime I was last post favoured with your kind Letter[6] and assure you with grateful acknowledgement of your kind Intentions towards Me & our Society here of sending us your Literary memoirs, I am well Content they have been & should longer be postpon'd on So grand an Occasion as Your making your Self Master of this most rare, curious, and useful Author hopeing You'll Impart the same entire to the public, enriched & illustrated with Comments by your Self than whom None ever more Consulted or I believe so well has understood & to me explained the Chorography, as well as the general Geography of Britain and the Roman stations, and Saxon, Danish, & Norman Towns, Castles, Forts & other Tectonical Operations of those Several People:

Gerard John Vossius de Historicis Latinis[7] Lib. III Ed: Wendelius Mærsalti Francofurti ad Mœnum in Quarto Anno 1677 pag. 532. Sub aut circa AD 1340:

His temporibus Richardus Cicestrius[8] Anglus, monachus Westmonasterii Benedictinus, multum Industriæ posuit in rebus Anglosaxonum colligendis: quas quinque Chronicorum Libris comprehendit. Aliis vocatur Richardus de Cirencestria, [p.2] Opusque eius dicitur Speculum historiale. Opus illud inchoat ab Hengisti Saxonis in Britanniam Appulsum: qui in ann. incidit 448. Exinde per 9 seculor: Seriem progressus ad Annum pertingit 1348. Hoc est 22 ann. Regis sui Edwardi 3. Et hoc Opus est bipartitum. Pars prior incipit Post primum Insulæ Britanniæ Regem &c. Atque hæc ab Auctore Vocata est SPECULUM HISTORIÆ & complectitur Libros 4.

Altera pars dicitur ANGLOSAXONUM CHRONICON: Estque Continuatio partis prioris.

Codex is manui exaratus apud Cantabrigienses reperitur in Bibliotheca publica – Int.Libr: MSS in Catal: MSS fo: 168 N2304. (14) Summa Richardi Historia Bruti Pr. Britannia Insularum Optima. In fine Libri (ait Dr Thos. James[9] ins Librarius anno 1600) habentur hæc verba: Reges vero Saxonum Geo. Malmesburiensi Henrico Huntingdoniense p.mitto, Quos de Regibus Britonum tacere jubeo, cum non habeant Librum illius Britannico Sermonis, quam Walterus Oxenfordensis Archidiaconus ex Britanniâ advexit; quem de Historiâ eorum veraciter editum, in honorem predictorum Principum hoc modo in Latinam transferre curavi.

Procedit Vossius: Sed est in Collegia Sti Benedicti apud Cantabrig. Scilicet MS conspicitur Chronicorum Epitome: quæ et ipso Richardum hunc Auctorem in titulo præfert.

NB Int Libr. MSS in Catal. MSS fo:134. No. 1343 (66) Epitome Chronicorum Angliæ

2. Epitome Chronicorum Ric. Cic. Monachi Westmonasterii.

of this Author my old Friend Archbishop Nicholson[10] in his Historical English Libr. Folio Ed. p.1 65:

I agree with You that Sr. Richd. bantors Dr. Woodward about his Roman shield & ranks it with that merry conceit of Hortensius i.e. Mr. Bobart keeper of the Physick Garden Oxon who when I was there amongst his other Curiositys shew'd us his Draco Monoceros catch'd in the Garden which is what is mount in the Consor by that stuff'd Ratt whos picture as near as I could remember I have exhibited in the Margin.

with this The Comical Old Gent. amused for some time the whole University pretending it to be a winged Dragon catch'd by his catt, & of the same species of those depicted in the books of the writers of natural historys of creatures of the same time pulling down a large folio author of that sort with the picture of a Draco alatus exactly answering to this, when it was nothing but a ratt which he had dry'd & prepar'd, by cutting off his two hind or leggs & turning the ribs up in form of Wings, the verses following were made upon it at that Time. Pray give my humble respects to Your Society

I am your humble Servant

W. Stukely

July 23 1715.

13. Sketch of the 'Oxford dragon' by Stukeley, 1715 (see **Letter 5**)
(Spalding Gentlemen's Society)

The eared bat, taken at Barnhill house 6. nov. 1743.

14. Sketch by Stukeley of a long-eared bat found in his house at Barn Hill, Stamford, 1743 (see **Letters 35** and **36**)
(Bodleian Library, Oxford)

5 Sept.r 1712. Sett down these Sumptuous Objects & their
Bearings, and formes of appearance? first just under o Eyes
NE. Spalding Parish Church & Freeschole — a lofty Spire.
  anciently S.t Thomas's Chapell & built before the Church   double   grand
  Wykeham Hall and Stately Chapell — a Cube or Parallella,
  the Villa of the Lord Priory of Spalding
  Fossedyke Chapell . . . . a low Towr.
  Spalding Northern Corne = – Wind Mill.
  a Large Farme house cover'd w.th red Tyles
  Cowhorne Ferry house on the River Welland
  w.th the Turnes of that River, and Vessels lying in It . or
  On It in various Parts — or Under Saile
  BOSTON Church & Towr, almost Stately Obelisk.
  Kirton – Church Gives name to the hundred. a large Towr
  Sutterton Church . . . . a Spire.
  Surfleet Church . . . . a Spire.
  Quadring Church a (an Elegant building) Windmill a Spire.
  Donnington Church Markett Town a Spire.
  Gosberton Church . . . . . . a Stately Spire
  Pinchbeck (called so from of bright Glen stream) Windmills
  & parts of the Great Northern Road
  Pinchbeck Church . . . . . . a Stately Towr.
N. Spalding High Bridg, Town & Town hall —
NW. Helpringham Church a New Build a Spire.
W. Rippingale Church . . . . . a Spire
  Remaines of Spalding = Priory
  The River of Welland, and other parts of Spalding Town
  called Windsover and Monks hall —

15. Letter by Johnson describing the view from the tower
of Ayscoughfee House, 1712 (see **Letter 37**, 1744)
(Bodleian Library, Oxford)

16. Drawing by Stukeley of the statue of
St Guthlac on the west front of
Croyland Abbey, 1746 (see **Letter 47**)
(Spalding Gentlemen's Society)

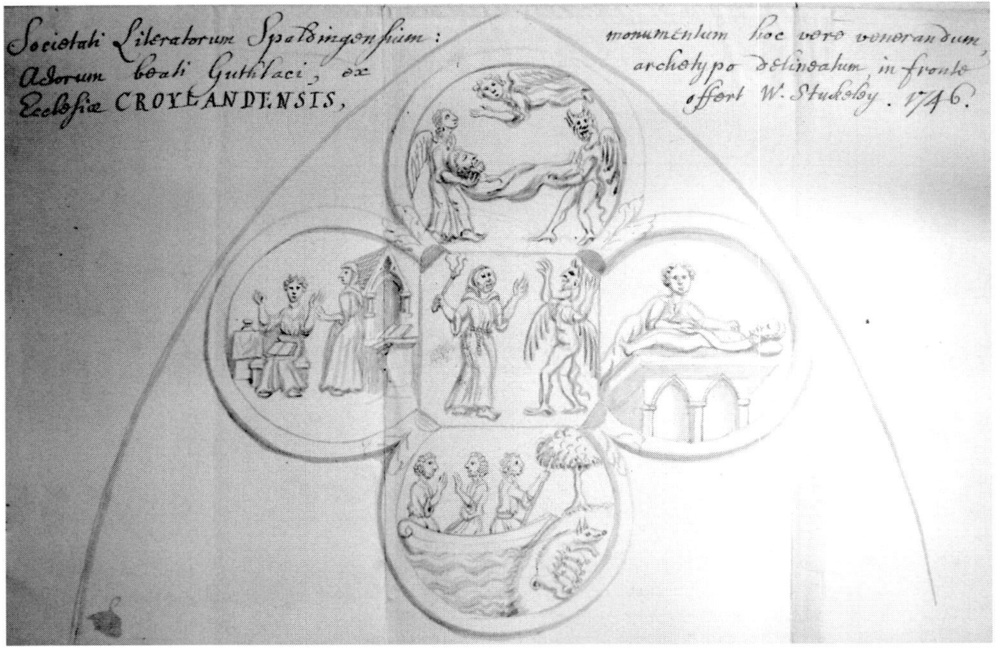

Societati Literatorum Spaldingensium:
Asylorum bonæ Gulthlaci, ex
Ecclesia CROYLANDENSIS,
monumentum hoc ære insigniendum;
archotypa Delineatum, in fronte
offert W. Stukeley. 1746.

17. Drawing by Stukeley of the carvings of St Guthlac's life, over the west door of Croyland Abbey, 1746 (see **Letters 47** and **49**)
(Spalding Gentlemen's Society)

18. The carvings over the west door of Croyland Abbey today
(Photograph by Michael Honeybone)

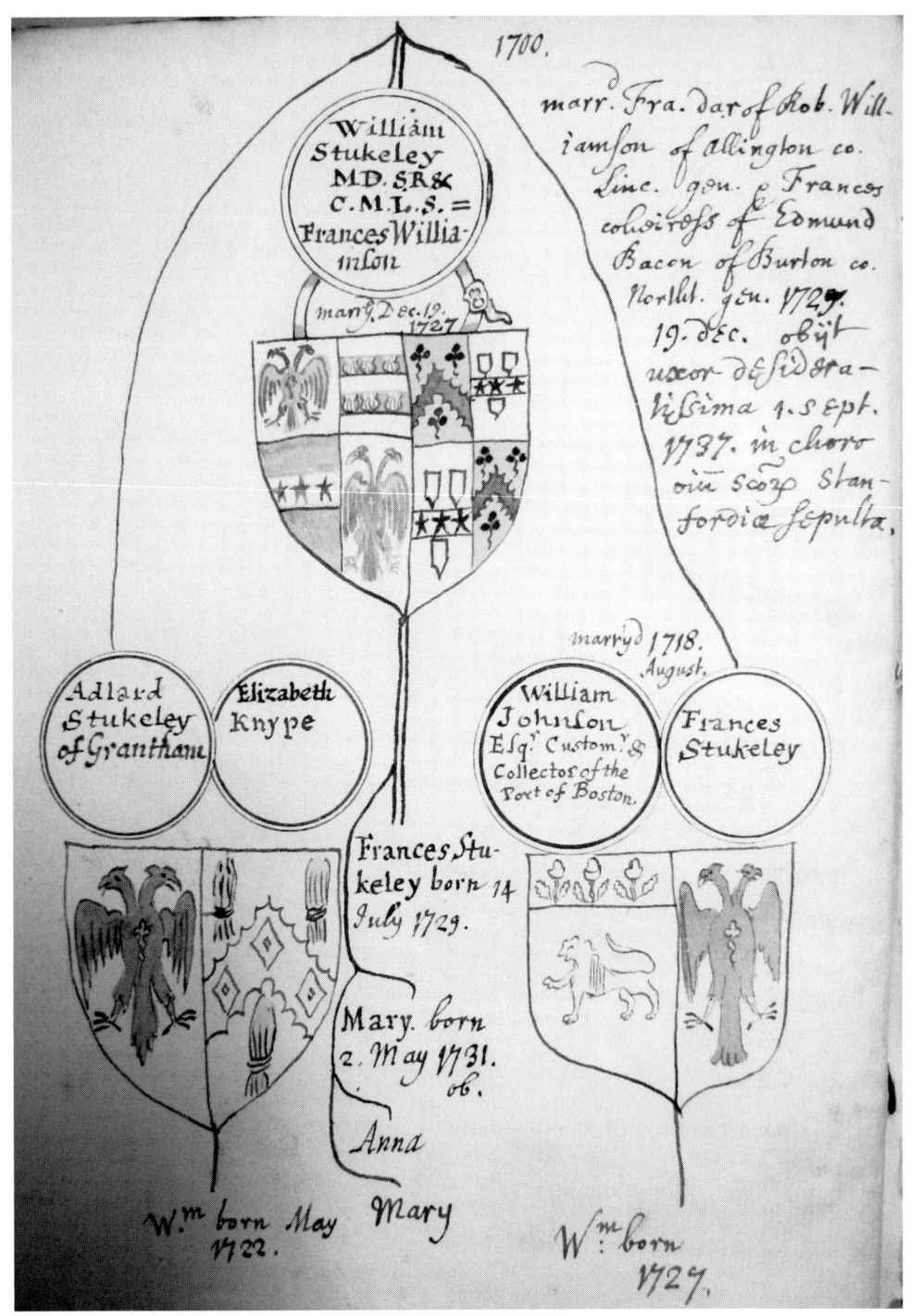

19. Stukeley's family tree, drawn by himself sometime after 1737
(Bodleian Library, Oxford)

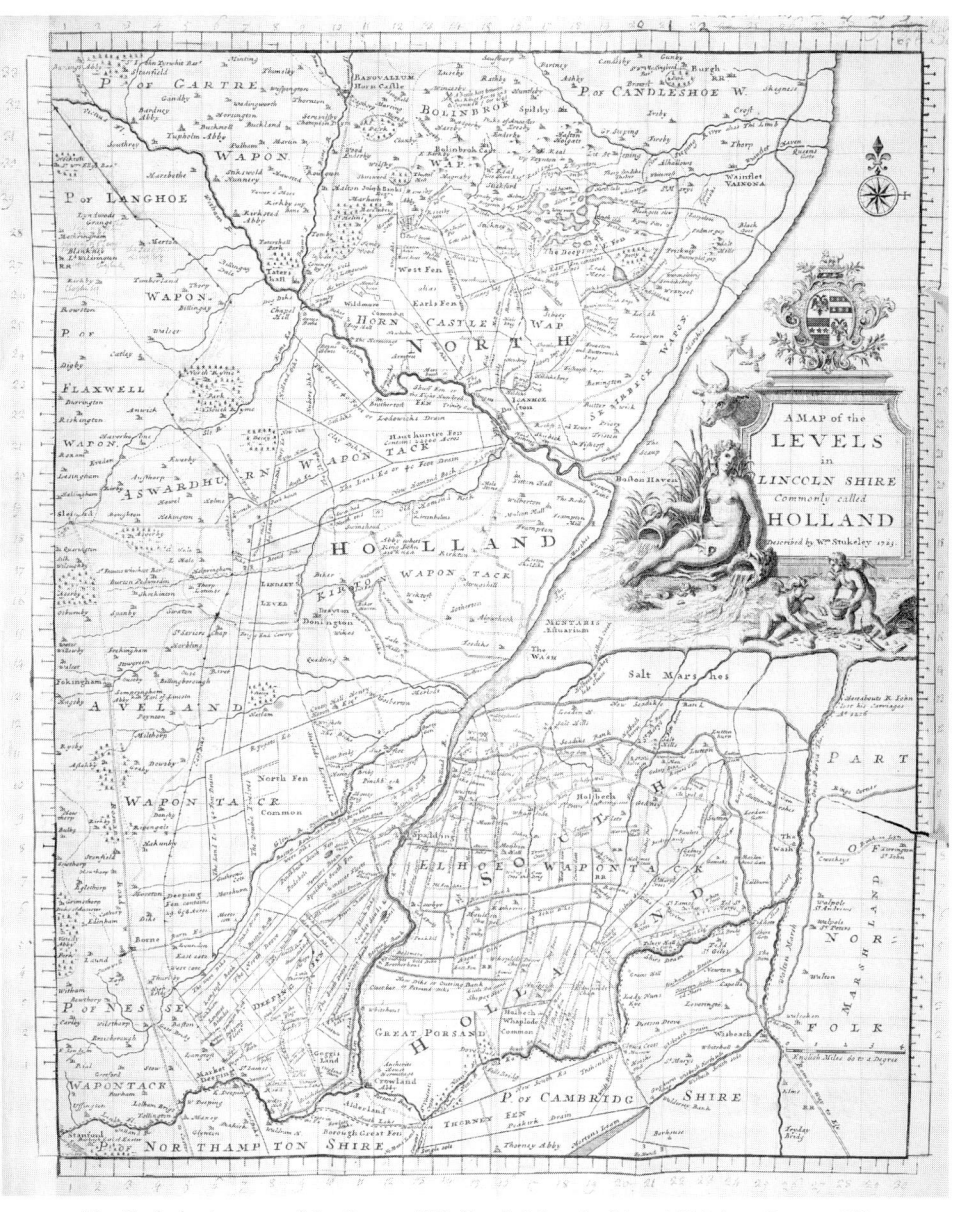

20. Stukeley's map of the Parts of Holland, Lincolnshire, 1723 (see **Letter 13**)
(Bodleian Library, Oxford)

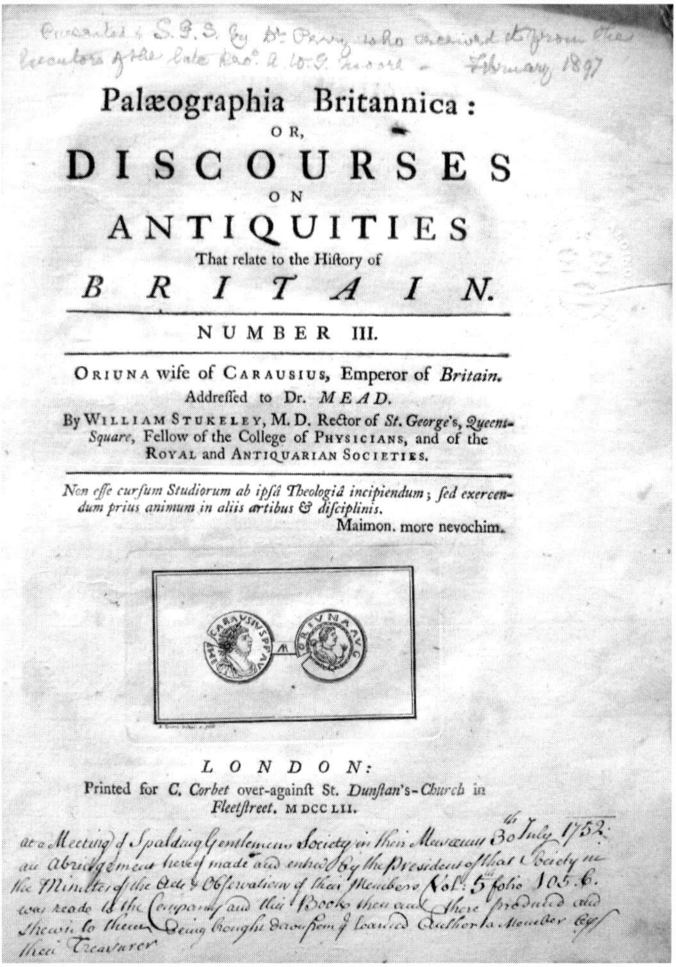

21. Engraving of a coin of the Emperor Carausius, showing the figure whom Stukeley assumed to be 'Oriuna', taken from *Paleographia Britannica or Discourses on Antiquities That relate to the History of Britain Number III* (1752), frontispiece (Spalding Gentlemen's Society)

– Nor have I any more to say of Richard of Chichester [*sic*] than what John Pitts[11] has told Me [Fo.438] that He was a Monk of Westminster AD 1348: That he travelld to most of the Libraries of England & out of his Collections thence compiled a Notable History of this Kingdom, from the comeing in of the Saxons down to his own time. but it seems he treated too of much Higher Times.

This Sir seems to be Your Man, thô you have Other & better works of him, than they knew. [p.3] I'm so quick in my Answer not knowing but hopeing the result of these my Enquiries may be of Some service, or at lest of Satisfaction to You in relation to So great on Author & So little known, to whom all the weight and authority of good Testimonies which can be had, should in this Sceptical Age, be given. The Value of this book must be great. I never see an Higdens Polychronicon[12] with a Mapp in It, thô I think old Mr Bagford of the Charterhouse told me, that Monke (who flourished about the same time with this Author) was the first he had Seen with a Mapp. this of Richards Britannia faciei Romanæ with the Cities Towns Stations Rivers & Coasts as he describes them in Words must be very entertaining and instructing too. I begg a Sketch of so much of It from You as this County and its Environs or adjacent Parts.

This ex opposito[13] probably intends his excellent Chronological History of Britain the Emperors, Generals, Legats, Proprætors who made expeditions hither. Which being concise & full of matter may more likely have been translated into Elegant latin from some old British Author or Authors now lost, or whom Wee knew not: Not but that there are as my learned Friend Mr Morgan Powell MA,[14] Curate of Kirton and a worthy Member of our Society here, assures me, several MSS historys in the Libraries of the Welch Gentry, Written in the British tongue: Concise, full of matter, believd by them to be genuine, & highly Valued by them, thô not yet published: of One of which that Curious Gentleman, has courteously engaged to give Us an Account, & an Epitome, which he is preparing to bring with him against the next Meeting of that Company whereat Wee are to have him present. and I shall Consult him concerning this retrieved Author Richard of Westminster & you shall recieve his Sentiments from
Dear Dr
Your affectionat humble Servt
M Johnson
Spalding 19 April 1749

[p.4] PS. A part of the Waters which now come down the Welland went antiently by the Well-stream into the Ouse But (with submission) the Welland was ever a Natural & Navigable River calld by some such name by the Britains, by the Romans Lenda fl., by the Saxons Veland. It came from Springs rising near Silvertoft under Rockingham Castle joyned by many others in Northamptonshire receiving all the Waters of Rutland by the Guash flowed by Stane-ford & made thereby that Borough and Pills Gate haven vulgarly calld Pillgitt near Burleigh whereunto in Antient Times the Saltwater als Tides flowed up befor any of our Marshes were Imbanked and this Town stood by the Sea Side, now thereby many miles from It. in the Roman Imbankations the Præfectus Prætorio Catius joyned the Neen with It by his Cutt still called Catwater. & Lollius Urbicus made Lollham Bridges. on authority of John Brittain MA SGS.S.[15]

Adieu.

To
the Reverend Dr Stukeley
Rector of St Georges Queen Square
    Ormond Street
        London

1   This is the first reference in this correspondence to Stukeley's association with Charles Bertram (see *ODNB*), an Englishman living in Denmark, who created a MS about Roman Britain, *De Situ Britanniæ*, from a complex range of sources, claiming that it was based on the work of Richard of Westminster, a monk of Westminster who lived in the fourteenth century and had written historical texts. During the nineteenth century, first German and then British historians proved this MS to be an eighteenth-century invention, though Stukeley was certainly not alone in accepting it as authentic.
2   Johnson lists the most significant long-dead British historians writing on Roman Britain who were read in the mid-eighteenth century. Bertram would have used these sources and his own creative imagination to produce his MS and map of Roman Britain.
3   William Bowyer (1699–1777: see *ODNB*): he was a well-educated London printer and publisher who particularly encouraged works of scholarship and who became the Printer of Votes for the House of Commons.
4   'He extracted gold from Ennius' dunghill', a comment attributed to Virgil. White Kennett (1660–1728), Bishop of Peterborough, was known as a historian for his three-volume *Compleat History of England* (1706) and *Register and Chronicle Ecclesiastical and Civil* (1726), a collection of historical documents.
5   The quotations which follow are Johnson's offerings from his own reading to Stukeley, to help in identifying Richard, the monk of Westminster and purported author of the MS which Bertram created. Johnson identifies him as Richard of Cirencester (*c.*1340–1400: see *ODNB*) who wrote *Speculum historiale de gestis regum Angliæ*; this survives in a fifteenth-century copy and consists of four books.
6   The letter from Stukeley announcing Bertram's contact with him about the MS has not survived in the Spalding archive.
7   Gerardus Vossius (1577–1649) wrote *De Historicis Latinis* in three volumes. Johnson's quotation would have been taken from his own copy which was sold at Sotheby's sale of his library in 1970.
8   'At that time Richard of Chichester, an Englishman, a Benedictine monk of Westminster, put much effort into collecting matters relating to the Anglo-Saxons, which made up five books of chronicles. By others he is called Richard of Cirencester. His work is called "Speculum Historiale". That work begins with Hengist the Saxon being brought into Britain, which happened in the year 448. From there it proceeds through a series of nine centuries and arrives at the year 1348. That is the 22nd year of his king Edward III. And this is a two-part work. The first part begins after the first king of the island of Britain etc. And that is called by the author "Speculum Historiæ" [The Mirror of History] and is composed of four books. The other part is called "Chronicle of the Anglo-Saxons": and it is a continuation of the first part. This document, produced by hand, may be found at Cambridge in the Public Library – [here follows the library reference to the MS]. At the end of the book (says Dr Thomas James the Librarian in the year 1600) are these words: [There is a sketch in margin of a hand pointing to this quotation to indicate its importance.] "I take the Kings of the Saxons from Geoffrey of Malmesbury and Henry of Huntingdon, who are silent about the Kings of the Britons because they did not have a book in the British language, which Walter the Archdeacon of Oxford had brought from Britain; which I have translated into Latin in this way from their History, truly set down, in honour of the aforesaid Princes." Vossius goes on: "But at St Benet's College [Corpus Christi College] at Cambridge there is an abridged version of the Chronicles: which carries the name of that same Richard in the title.' [Here follows the library reference to the MS.]' The modern library references to these two volumes are: in Cambridge University Library, MS FF 128; in the Parker Library of Corpus Christi College, Cambridge, MS 427.
9   Dr Thomas James (1572–1629: *ODNB*). He became the first Bodley's Librarian at the University of Oxford in 1599 and published in 1600 a catalogue of the MSS in the college libraries of Oxford and Cambridge, *Eclogia Oxonio-Cantabrigiensis*.
10 Archbishop William Nicholson (1655–1727: see *ODNB*), Bishop of Carlisle, then of Derry, appointed Archbishop of Cashel in the year he died. He published *The English Historical Library* (1696), a contemporary account of MSS and printed books on the topography and history of England.

¹¹ John Pits (1560–1616), a Roman Catholic priest working on the Continent, wrote *De Illustribus Angliæ Scriptoribus* (1619). 'Higher' here means 'earlier'.
¹² Ranulf Higden: see **Letter 6**, n.4, above. John Bagford (1675–1716) was a bookseller and book-collector specialising in the history of typography. Maps accompanied copies of Higden's *Polychronicon* from *c.*1400. Bertram sent Stukeley a copy of his map of Britain in 1749. In 1755 Bertram drew and engraved his map, which Stukeley re-engraved and published in 1755 in *An Account of Richard of Cirencester, Monk of Westminster and of his Works: with his Antient Map of Roman Britain, and the Itinerary Thereof*. For nearly a hundred years Bertram's invented map was generally accepted as the work of Richard of Cirencester.
¹³ There is a sketch of a pointing hand in the margin, referring back to the reference on p.2 of this letter to Henry of Huntingdon (*c.*1088–1157: see *ODNB*), who wrote a ten-volume *Historia Anglorum* between 1110 and his death.
¹⁴ Revd Morgan Powell: see Appendix 3.
¹⁵ Revd John Brittain: see Appendix 3. In the eighteenth century it was assumed that Lollius Urbicus, pro-prætor of Britain in AD 144, was responsible for building bridges and roads across Britain. It was argued that he had built the Lolham Bridge to take King Street across the Welland area, west of Maxey and south of West Deeping, and north of Helpston.

58. Maurice Johnson to William Stukeley, Spalding, 16 December 1749
Bodleian, MS Eng. misc. c.113, fols 351r–352v

Spalding 16 Decr 1749

Dear Doctor

Having had the pleasure as He compiled them to recieve from Couzen Beaupree Bell his Tabulæ Augustæ¹ and with his Leave to read them to the Company at our Meetings many of whom subscribed to him towards the Publication of them after Seign^r Paterolis² manner 16 yeares since: having now stayd so long expecting some of Trinity College³ should publish Them as they purposd on recieing [*sic*] his MSS & Collection of Coines, but not finding the Work any forwarder: Wee sent lately an humble & modest proposal to the worthy Vice Master Dr Walker our Acquaintance to Lay before the Master & Coll. That if [*sic*] would permitt us the Use of the MS & Plates prepared for that Purpose Wee would publish the work for the Credit of the Author Many Yeares a Member, Constant Correspondent & kind Benefactor to our Society, Whereto Wee have as yet recievd no Answer, but supposing them not to comply with our request thô little but Care is wanting to the fitting It for & bringing it forth from the press, Would It not become & be well worth the while of Our Society of Antiquaries to offer to publish the same, which would be an acceptable Acquisition to all our Gentry studious in the res nummaria, his accounts of the women being fuller, & his Socii Reges a most noble & useful Augmentation to All the schemes of the Imperial Series I have seen. What renderd the thing tedious, & prevented his publishing It himself was – His not sticking to the Icons he first chose, but changeing them frequently for Others, sometimes for such as were not so good, but he fancyd spake the Spirit of the Person better, as he had from their Cotemporary authors given their Characters. – His being in a mind to give the longlivd Princes in the 1st Middle & last stage of their Reignes – & Mr Kirkhall his Engravers Delays, which he frequently complained of to me, but I know he had most of them done by him & some few by other good hands, & have the Proof plates of them my self which at sundry times he was So kind to send Me, & had he thought Us worthy of the Beneficence he bestowed on that College the work should have come out long eer this to his Honor if Mr Bowyers Accurate Press & Our and our Friends Care and good assistance could have set it forth: A proper Introduction and Indexes were all that were wanting when I last see the sheets as to the printing Part.

[p.2] Have you yet, my Friend taken any and what steps towards publishing Richardus Londiniensis[4] or the valuable MSS Topography & history of Britain, You were happy in retrieving from Denmark, & so obliging to give me large Extracts from. wherein I was greatly disappointed in not finding some notices of any place in these parts of England, nothing in all Holland which was certainly Embanked & taken in at 3 different Periods by the Romans: those Banks remain a Proof of this Assertion particularly their Raven – or Roman Bank[5] which leads quite thrô the very lowest inland tract towards Cambridgeshire. & it continued thence into Norfolk. I have restored and painted my Great Old Dineing Room[6] & furnished it with my Family Pictures. So that I daily converse with some of my Ancestors for whom Wee ought to have a grateful respect. therein I have put up what Historical Painted Glass I had preserved out of other windows in this House and which came out of the Chapel (formerly on the Garden Side of It long since demolished) in the South window, representing a top the Host of Heaven, the Trinity, BVM, Angels, Prophets, Apostles, Sts, Confessors, and Martyrs, with Blew Under & separating them from – The Sacrament of Confirmation as It was antiently called as Performing by a Bishop. & that of Marryage of King Henry V with his Queen Katherin of France – to fill the Window I have thereunder in larger Proportion on one side the Virgin within an Iris & several heads of Sts. On the Other our B.S.J.C.[7] as he appeared to St Thomas or as they call It Noli Me Tangere – 'tis his Appearance showing his wounds after his resurrection – Either to that doubting Apostle, or to a faithful Woman. As I've shut this Window up with Doors & have but One & that a Very large window to the Room I've taken the Advantage in placing my Pourtraits to give them all a good & most of them a right Light (which is difficult to do) and my room thô spatious is light enough. In it Wee live for constancy, & keep 2 rooms next the Garden for recieving Company, Other 2 next them I use for Studys in One I have Law Books, Records and Writeings in the Other All other sorts of Books. I should be greatly glad to recieve you here my good Friend to shew you these, and what Improvements I've made in my Gardens, which I've pretty much Opend, and made a Walk thrô my Orchard and Kitchen Garden answering that which Crosses my Parterres whence I look upon my Fields & over the Country as farr as Weston Hills –

[p.3] There have been a pretty many Saxon Coines found lately at Okeham[8] whereof some of the Edwards Harald & the Conquerors have been shewn us at our Society. I procured one of Edward the younger or Martyr as I take it to be coined by Colgrum on Efor i.e. of York exceed [*sic*] perfect and well preserved, Dr Green has One or 2 I think of Edw[ar]d the Elder and W. the Conqueror. I am defective mostly in Saxon Coines, beginning too late to think 'em worth having whereas they continue the Series & Chronologie, but I have Some, and endeavour to get more, especialy would procure all I could of our Mercian Kings & Princes, & all the Monarchs from Egbert: I begg of you to assist me with what duplicates you can if you have any such, and Casts in silver or the best Pewter of any others or any You can borrow with a permission to take Casts of, which I would gladly pay a Silver Smith for making, and they'd make several in their large flasks at a time Whenever You could find leisure to get me It done.

& such would be especially if made of Silver partly as good for my purpose as the Originals: and could do them no Injury: I'll get as much done for You here, if Wee have any Coines or Medals You would have casts of.

There is in the last Gentlemans Magazine a Picture of a Sea Dragon with wings & in shape like Bobart's flying dragon,[9] but with Cloven feet said to be taken on the Coast of Suffolk & shewn about that County & Norfolk & when dryed to be 4 feet long, I pray have Yee had any Notices of It at the Royal Society Or is it some such deception as that was whereof You many Yeares agoe gave me a Sketch and a Very witty Latin Epigram under It – if this had been in a News paper I should have concluded It intended as an Enigma but Sylvanus Urban or the Editor, gives some farther reasons to assure his readers that Some Strange Marine monster hitherto undescribed was actualy taken in a Net and long exposd to the View of many. Another rare phænomenon has appeard and is to be seen at Okeham, and his works in many noble Men and Gentlemens handes thereabouts, one Mr Samuel Goodwin[10] a Country farmer of a great Genius for works of Designing who draws Correctly & Colours naturaly, and who being only self taught has taken up painting as a Profession for his lively [*sic*] & paints all things, but succeeds greatly and gets good Prices for his Peices in Still life – & has made many Pictures of a White wood Cock shot in Eaton Park. Dr Green and young Mr Jno Wingfield who have frequently seen him & several of his peices give us this account of him & them at our last Meeting.

[p.4] The Distemper is returned amongst our Cattle and at our last Great Court of Sewers for the Yeare Called the Certiorari Court held in our Town Hall for this Wapentack of Elloe on Tuesday last wee had dismall Accounts of the havoc It makes as well for some of our Principal Graziers who are Commissioners as from the Surveyors and Dikereeves in all the Towns & Hamletts.[11]

I have good Hopes of my Eldest Son the Captains[12] continueing and Supporting my Family by a marryage. The Treaty whereof is concluded with the younger daughter of the late Father of the City, they're at her Elder Sisters house, my Couzen Lynns of Southwyke, where I have reason to believe it will be consummated these Holydays, not dareing (for his Brother dyd there but lately of a malignant Small Pox) to go thither, I gave them a Meeting at our Cell in Deeping,[13] and there adjusted all requisite preliminaries of the marryage Settlements: and it is much to the Satisfaction of all parties on both Sides; the Captain has a pretty house in Mortimer Street, Cavendish Square; He was So long before I could induce him to think of entering into the State that I was sometime apprehensive, and feard He would have declind It. But he has made Choice of an Excellent Woman with all requisite qualifications to make him happy.

I am Dear Dr your affectionate Friend & Servant

M Johnson

To the Reverend
Dr Stukeley at his house in
  Queens Square
      Ormond street
         London
a Single sheet.

---

[1] See Bell's entry in Appendix 3; for his proposed publication see **Letter 40**, n.10, above.

[2] Lorenzo Pataroli (1674–1727), author and philologist. See **Letter 40**, n.9, above.

3   This account of Johnson's efforts, determined but unsuccessful, to get Trinity College, Cambridge, to organise the printing of Bell's book on Roman imperial coinage throws light on the problems of organising and financing publication in the eighteenth century. Bell's papers are still in the library of Trinity College but the final extensive revision, which he appeared to be undertaking around the time of his death, was not completed, which may explain why they were not printed.
4   Richard of Cirencester: see **Letter 57**, n.1, above for Charles Bertram's inventive account of Roman Britain.
5   'Fleet had Hurdletree Bank, Saturday Dyke (also called Raven's Bank) ... Tydd St Mary had Raven's Dyke', H. E. Hallam, *Settlement and Society: A Study of the Early Agrarian History of South Lincolnshire* (1965), 4. It appears that Raven's Bank was often also called Roman Bank.
6   The rooms that Johnson refers to are still visible and open to the public in Ayscoughfee Hall, Spalding. The painted glass in the window is a significant feature. For fuller details see Nancy Snowdon, *Ayscoughfee: A Great Place in Spalding* (2007).
7   Our Blessed Saviour Jesus Christ. 'Noli me Tangere' or 'Do not touch me', words spoken by Jesus in John 20:17 to Mary Magdalene immediately after his resurrection.
8   In 1749, 300 Anglo-Saxon coins were discovered at Oakham (Rutland). For a list of these, see Kenneth Johnson, *Viking-Age Hoards and Late Anglo-Saxon Coins* (1987) and Blunt and Lyon, 'The Oakham Hoard of 1747 deposited *c.*980', *Numismatic Chronicle* 7/19 (1979), 111–21.
9   *The Gentleman's Magazine* (November 1749), 506 and figure C. For Stukeley's account of Bobart's alleged 'dragon', see **Letter 5** above and Illustration 13.
10 It has not proved possible to find further information on the painter and farmer Samuel Goodwin. The account of him was not minuted at the Thursday meeting on 14 December 1749 when the minutes were written up by Dr John Green, whose notes are more concise than Johnson's. Gilbert White mentions a white woodcock in his *Journal*, 399–400.
11 The issue of *The Gentleman's Magazine* for November 1749 also contains a 'Treatise on the distemper of the horned cattle': see below and **Letter 49**, n.13, above.
12 See **Letter 56**, n.5, above. Captain Maurice Johnson married Elizabeth daughter of Sir Edward Bellamy, former Lord Mayor of London, in December 1749. The marriage took place at Southwick (Northants), the home of her elder sister who was married to George Lynn junior of Southwick, a relative of the Johnsons, whose brother John had been Chaplain to Bellamy. It is probable that Elizabeth, as well as her sister, had obtained a good inheritance on her father's recent death; George Lynn and Elizabeth Bellamy were joint executors of his will, 2 July 1748, probate granted 14 April 1749.
13 Both Johnson and Stukeley record regular meetings of a society at Deeping, of which they were members.

59. William Stukeley to Maurice Johnson, London, 20 December 1749
SGS/Stukeley/22

[Annotated by Johnson:] A Letter from the Revd Dr Wm Stukeley to the President SGS concerning a curious enameld antient Shrine supposd of the Abbat & Monks of Croyland murderd by the Pagan Danes AD 870 / 2º The Drs MS Memoires of his Observations made at R.S. London, Antediluvian Skeleton, & blew Stone Hatchet ./ 3 a Basso Relievo Sculpture in Stone of Mithras sacrificing a Bull at the Veral [*sic*] Equinox found at Micklegate in York. the 25 December celebrated with horse Races on Knavesmire as Natale Invicti Mithræ.

My dear friend

it was a great pleasure to me, to hear from you. I heartily wish, our friend beauprè had left his coyns, plates, & manuscripts to your Society. then we might have hoped for the publication of it, to his honor, & the public utility.[1] I know not whether it would have fared better in the antiquarian society. for as long as they keep at a tavern, & on thursday night, I never can be with 'em.[2] nor doe they doe much; as far as I hear. Lord Colrane gave his prints, & books of prints, to 'em, by Will.³ but they have no benefit therefrom, as being nothing more than a name.

I exhibited at the royal Society, a curious enameld, antient shrine, which I beleive, belong'd to your neighbor Croyland:⁴ representing the murder of the abbot at the high altar, & his monks, by the Danes, in a[nn]o 870. as Ingulfus relates the barbarous tragedy. when it is ingraven, I will send you a print. the shrine was found in Mr Pullens possession, of St Neots, who dyed lately. he never show'd it, in his life time; & we know nothing of it, but by conjecture.

Richard of Westminster⁵ is not out of my thoughts; tho' at present, I can't say any thing about printing it, because I know the charge, & trouble, & small hope of a return. had my master Montagu lived, I know he would have made the charge very easy. but he has not left behind him, his fellow. he has brought me into good company, & then left me: at a time when, like you, I enjoy'd the sweets, the tranquillity of rural retirement. sed quo fata vocant, sequamur.⁶

[p.2] I must now content my self, with supplying gardens, & hills, & purling streams, with the show, & gawdys of the Town: but much rather with the meetings of the Royal Society. that is, an entertainment indeed. & what was a great inducement to me, to come hither. & that I may help a little to impart some of that pleasure, to the Spaldingensian society, I have filled a quarto volume of 64 pages, in transcribing my Memoirs there, as I promised you. this I hope to deliver into your own hands, next term. you are to read it at your Meetings: & but one on a night. & I shall endeavour to continue it.⁷

last thursday we had there exhibited by Dr Shaw of Oxford,⁸ a bit of the arm of a man, part of a whole skeleton, blown up in a rock at Gibraltar, lately. it was observed, that human exuviæ of the deluge, are not so common as fishes, & other things. My friend Mr Reveley⁹ lately come from yorkshire, has a blew stone hatchet, with a hole in it, found in the midst of a quarry of stone. I take it to be antidiluvian. the stone is become such, since the hatchet was introduc'd there. these matters were cover'd over, at the ceasing of the Noachian deluge; by the retiring waters covering them over with earth, which is, since then, become stone.

we have lately admitted the Duke of Newcastle, of Grafton, Lord Cardigan, Walgrave¹⁰ & more of the quality who pay us 20 guineas down. they in some mesure strengthen, & adorn. we had a very splendid appeareance at our annual feast on S. Andrew. D. Newcastle, Grafton, many Lords, & great folks present. I, as usual, was chaplain. I always retire, as soon as grace is said. the president told me next day, they wanted me to give extreme unction to Hawksbee,¹¹ who was got dead drunk. I told Hawksbee last thursday, that I would have marked him [p.3] with a S. Andrews cross, that S. Peter might know him, otherwise he would have small hopes of entry.

a year before I left Stamford, I received from my friend Fra: Drake¹² of york, a drawing of a basso releivo on stone, lately found at micklegate, 10 foot under ground. he knew not what to make of it, & desired my opinion. I sent him word, it was the image of Mithras sacrificing the bull, at the vernal equinox, according to patriarchal usage. I gave him a large account of the matter, as it arose to my mind, off hand, upon the curious subject. lately he wrote to me, & return'd the account I gave him, desiring, it might be read at the Royal Society: which was done.¹³

I have since reconsider'd the thing, & wrote a copious dissertation thereon.

I have order'd a graving to be made of it, & think to print it soon, as a 2ᵈ No. of *Palæographia Sacra*.¹⁴ for the whole subject is extremely curious: but the york sculpture has more curious particulars in it, than any other yet discoverd. it shows, the Mithriac sacred [*sic*] were much cultivated in Brittain. & that at York, on the neighboring knavesmire, they celebrated annually, a most magnificent horserace, to the honor of Mithras, on 25 december, called Natale invicti Mithræ:¹⁵ thinking thereby to efface the solemnity of our Saviors birth day, in the growing times of christianity.

I am delighted in your account of fitting up your great old dining room, hope in june next, to sit there, & contemplate the shadows of your ancestry there: & the splendors of the painted glass. I congratulate you on the fair prospect of the captain, at last buckling to, & preserving your family. your most elegant garden, you still continue to render, more elegant.

I am acquainted with your new lord Prior mitratus¹⁶ [p.4] Mr Gideon, & have been to do homage.

they are now, at Cocks auction room, selling the spoils of our deceased friend Geo. Holmes.¹⁷ a vast sight of coyns, books, prints, raritys of all sorts. I look at these things, but never buy, having no room, for what I have already.

inclosed is a paper¹⁸ I wrote, the morning Mr Folkes & I walked to kentish town to take our last leave of my great Patron. I wish you many & happy new years & am

                    Your most obedient
                    humble servant W: Stukeley

London 20 dec. 1749

To Maurice Johnson Esqʳ
    Spalding
        Lincolnshire

Free
R Barbor¹⁹

---

¹ Stukeley picks up Johnson's reference to Beaupré Bell's unpublished MS on Roman imperial coinage, a subject of great interest to numismatists of the period: see **Letter 40**, n.10, and **Letter 58** above.

² Stukeley would not attend meetings of the Society of Antiquaries at this time as they met at the Mitre Tavern on the same day as the Royal Society. At sixty-two he is apparently less energetic than in his earlier years.

³ Henry Hare, third Baron Coleraine (1693–1749: see *ODNB*). By a codicil to his will he granted his British drawings and engravings to the Society of Antiquaries, but since they lacked a legal, chartered existence the donation was problematic. Eventually his companion, Rose Duplessis, donated them to the Society and this encouraged the Antiquaries to obtain a charter in 1751. This decision is discussed below by Johnson and Stukeley, not always with approval.

⁴ Maybe Stukeley did organise an engraving of this shrine. Drawings of it exist, listed as two coloured drawings of a Becket shrine found in Mr Pulleyn's house at St Neots, by Frances Stukeley 1748 (*Surtees* III, 504). Frances was Stukeley's eldest daughter, born on 17 June 1729. This explanation is more likely than Stukeley's claim relating it to Croyland Abbey.

⁵ Richard of Westminster or Cirencester is discussed in detail in **Letter 57** above. Stukeley's plans for publication are facing financial difficulties and he regrets the death of his patron the Duke of Montagu who had recently died and who, he is sure, would have financed the printing. It is thanks to the Duke's influence that Stukeley now has the living of St George's, Queen Square.

⁶ 'But where the Fates call, we follow.' Stukeley was always attracted to somewhere where he was

7   Stukeley kept his promise; the SGS today possesses five MS volumes of Stukeley's records of the meetings of the Royal Society which he attended and these were read out at SGS meetings during the early 1750s, as the minute books record.
8   This is most probably Thomas Shaw FRS (1694–1751), a famous traveller and author. He was principal of St Edmund's Hall, Oxford, and left his collection of natural curiosities to the University of Oxford. Stukeley addressed his dissertation on an African city, 'Ras Sem', to Dr Shaw; see the note on document SGS/Stukeley/19A following **Letter 50**. 'Exuviæ' are skeletal remains.
9   Councillor Reveley of Bedford Row, London, who owned an estate in Yorkshire. For more details of this, see *Surtees* III, 362–3.
10 Thomas Pelham-Holles, first Duke of Newcastle (1693–1768), FRS (26 October 1749); Charles Fitzroy, second Duke of Grafton (1683–1757), FRS (23 November 1749); George Montagu, Earl of Cardigan (1712–90), FRS (7 December 1749); James Waldegrave, second Earl Waldegrave (1715–63), FRS (14 December 1749). All were significant Whig politicians.
11 Francis Hauksbee (1688–1763), nephew of the famous instrument-maker of the same name who died in 1713; housekeeper and Clerk to the Royal Society, which precluded him from becoming FRS. He was an instrument-maker, demonstrator and lecturer.
12 Francis Drake (c.1696–1771); see Appendix 3. He became FRS in 1736.
13 'Account of a Bas-relief of Mithras found at York, explain'd by the Rev. Dr Stukeley, FRS, communicated to the RS by Mr Francis Drake of York Antiquary and FRS', read 23 November 1749 (*Phil.Trans.* (1749), 46, nos 491–6, 214–17).
14 Stukeley did not publish his second number of *Palæographia Sacra* until 1763 and it did not contain an article on Mithras. However, he did write an 'Account of the sculpture of Mithras found at York 1746', which is in Bodleian, MS Eng. misc. d.453.
15 'The birthday of the unconquered Mithras'. York Races moved to the Knavesmire site in 1731, though they did not appear to have taken place on 25 December.
16 'Your mitred Prior', a humorous title for Samson Gideon (1699–1762), a well-known London banker who purchased in 1749 the manorial rights of Spalding, which had belonged to the Prior of Spalding before the Dissolution. A mitred prior was the head of a priory which was significant enough for him to have a seat in Parliament. Gideon made his name by his level-headed behaviour during the South Sea Bubble and became the chief Government adviser on the financing of loans, particularly during the Seven Years' War, see Appendix 3.
17 George Holmes (1662–1749: see *ODNB*) FSA, FRS; Archivist and Keeper of the royal and Government records at the Tower of London, SGS member 1728. See Appendix 3.
18 Stukeley's paper is not with the letter today in the SGS's archive. There is a note by Johnson at this point: 'a Meditation in the Fields on seeing the Duke of Mountague's Herse setting forward from London for his Interrment at Warkton in Northamptonshire 18 July 1749'. John Montagu (1690–1749: see *ODNB*), second Duke of Montagu, had been Stukeley's patron; see n.5 above.
19 Robert Barbor (d.1761), MP for Stamford 1747–61. Stukeley was able to use Barbor's franking, giving him free postage. Barbor was the chief agent for Brownlow Cecil, Earl of Exeter.

60. Maurice Johnson to William Stukeley, Spalding, 8 January 1750
Bodleian, MS Eng. misc. c.113, fols 353r–354v

Spalding 8 January 1749/50

With many Thanks to You, My Good Friend, for your kind regards towards me & my Family, & your Promise of favouring us with your good Company in June, when I shall with much pleasure expect you, and in the interim of favouring us with your MS Memoires:[1] I'm to acquaint you that tho my Son be married,[2] and fixed in as pleasant a part as any about Town, where I want no Inducement I can wish to go up & see them, and all my old friends & Acquaintances; Yet my Age and Infirmities[3] will not permitt me to take that pleasure, therefore must beg the favour of you to consigne that valuable Quarto (you're so generously enclined to trust Me with) to me; Seald up & directed for me, & sent to my Bookbinder Mr Christopher Norris[4] at the Bible & Crown in the Chapter House alley in St Pauls Churchyard at your own best Leisure, from whom I shall recieve It safe in a Box, the first Occasion he has after of sending down to me. As you occasionaly pass that way if you've leasure to call in on that honest good old Workman (whom I've many Yeares employd and found faithfull,) you'll think he may be trusted with It & if you be pleasd so, or by a peny post Letter, to Let him know when he may wait on you for it, or leave it out ready for him, when he calls, He'll wait on you for It, or take it, if left out, & you should happen not to be at home.

You tell Me my Friend you intend a Dissertation on the Mithriac Sacred Rites & a Bass Relief found at Micklegait York[5] illustrating them as there Exhibited for 2 N° of Paleographia Sacra, permitt me to hint that I Concieve one on Shrines, might be Very Useful, Copious, & entertaining, & might be aboundantly embelished with designes, from the rich remains of such as have adorned Our English Churches, Towards which I find Several Notices in our Minute Books of the Acts and Observations of the Members of our Soc. here, looking into our Index[6] thereof which I, with no small paines, compiled: They were at first I believe in imitation of the Ark of the Covenant, & what was therein Conteined: as the Mystica Sacra of Ceres, Cybele & Bacchus, were, (from thence assumed) Portable – Cistæ – the Cistoforus or minister who carryed it; & some parts thereof, when built & fixed with Marbles, Sculpture & Mosaics of bulk & magnificence, continued still movable: Even of the Shrines of the Sacred Sepulchre, in Linc[oln] Cath[edral] since stiled Bishop Remigius's Tomb – and in the Churches of Heckington[7] &c. And of our Tutelar Patron Sts, these Smaller Portable Parts were carryd in processions occasionally, & again with great Care & reverence reposited in Loco, the rest permanent, as a Pavilion, Catafalco, or Cabinett for recieving and conteining the Same: all these were gilded, usualy too adorned with much Pinacle work, & carving of Wood in foliage gilded or coverd with Plates of Silver or other Metal & gilt. and in many parts set off with Ouches,[8] or Gemms Pearles & pretious Stones in Various figures. [p.2] Such a Subject would well suit the Interest of your Paleography being sacred and copious enough to make one No. of Them. what our Minutes of Acts & observations of SGS or my Adversaria may furnish on the Occasion you may readyly command. And I would hint this farther that perhaps in some of the Philos. Trans. of RSL[9] or amongst their Papers You may find a drawing and Estimation of the Gemms set in Gold in a part of a Pinacled Shrine I remember when a Youth to've seen at Sir Hans Sloanes[10] in his almost inestimable Collection of Curiositys, but have no Memoire of in writing now by me: Dr Mortimer (best I believe now) acquainted with those Treasures, & with any Account may have been communicated to RSL of such part of a Shrine, or others at any time to that Learned and illustrious Body can most ready assist you Sir with farther information, but as I remember It was rich in Rubys or red Gemms, & in Emeralds, and cost the liberal Owner a large Summe. I have my Self what I shew you & sent Sir Richard Ellys a full Account of whereto I received his concurrent opinion [*gap in text caused by removal of a seal*] a Plate of Very thick deep blew or Azure glass encaustionisd with a Saxon inscription in Capital Characters Coeval in Gold with the time of King Ethelreds retireing to his Convent of Bardeney in our County[11] on the cruel murder of Queen Estritha his Wife by the Pagan Danes which I take to have been Part of a Shrine sacred to him on so devout an Occasion, and seems to speak the same in it's Phraze and Brevity, Ethelredus Rex apud Templum. to which, on that mournful Event from an Active Soldier & perhaps too severe a Conqueror, he entirely turned, and devoted Himself, great part of his Substance & all the remainder of his Life.

As I'm hopefull, and think not without probability, that a Paragraph in a Letter I was this morning favoured with from Couz. H. Johnson of Great Berkhamstead may happly prove of Great Creditt, honour and Advantage to My namesake your sisters son,[12] by the late William Johnson of Boston Esq., whom I had sometime the pleasure to be known to, and to know to be an ingenious Gentleman, therefore Dear Friend for Your Sake, Your Nephews and Sisters I send it You to make what farther Enquiries and use thereof, You, who're in the best place in the universe for gaining full satisfaction in such a Point, shall think proper – My Kinsmans Words are – as follow on the Other Side the paper – that you may take it off, or communicate it if Occasion be without more from my Good Old Friend

   Your most Affectionat & faithful Servant

            M Johnson

PS all our Compliments attend your Lady Self and the young Ladies your Daughters.

[p.3] [*Copy by Johnson of paragraph from Henry Johnson's letter*] 'I was last Summer for a few Weeks with my Wife and Daughters at Tunbridge Wells, where I met with a very worthy Gentleman of Our name (vizt) Leiutenant Gen[eral] Johnson,[13] who has servd his Country in almost every Action from the Battle of Almanza to the last that was fought in Flanders. I did not know him 'till this last summer, He has a country house in Surry, is a marryd man, & no children. his Arms however are quite different from Ours, but seems to have the same Inclinations with us in making researches into his Name & family. Amongst other things He told me, He had had a letter last Spring from the Governor of Boston in New England[14] acquainting him That there was at that very time One of the greatest Estates in that Country plac'd out in Trustees hands for the Benefit & account of its right Heires when the same should be found: This Estate was originaly the Property of Isaac Johnson Esqr. who married Arrabella the Daughter of the Earle of Lincoln from Boston in Lincolnshire.[15] who in the reigne of Charles Ist left England together with his Lady and Family, & was the Founder of the fine City of Boston the Metropolis of New England, which he called Boston from the Place of his or his Ladies old Abode, & at that time he became Master of the Estate above mentiond which since his time has been so much improved, as to become the most considerable of any in that Country, and as his Heires have failed, the same is now in Trust, according to the Custom of that Country, to be taken up, when a Right Heire shall offerr for that Purpose.'

[*Note by Maurice Johnson*] Dugdale in I Baron. fo. 533 says that Thos. Clinton Ld Clinton Earle of Lincoln who died at his Castle of Tatshall 15 Jan 16 Jac. 1 1618 had Issue 7 sons & 9 Daughters whereof One was named Arabella.[16]

To the Reverend
　　Dr Stukeley in Queens Square
　　　　by Ormondstreet
　　　　　　London
A single sheet.

1   See **Letter 59**, n.7, above.
2   See **Letter 58**, n.12, above.
3   Johnson was now aged sixty-one; later letters discuss the health problems which were curtailing his activities. He had given up the work of Secretary of the SGS to Dr John Green and had become President on the death of Revd Stephen Lyon in 1748.
4   Christopher Norris, stationer and bookbinder of St Gregory by St Paul's, London, Master of the Stationers' Company 1762; see his will dated 12 August 1763 (PRO, PROB 11/891/90). Two volumes owned by Johnson and bound by Norris are recorded at the British Library, shelfmarks Davis 157 and Add. MS 35157. Norris was binding Stukeley's memoirs of the RS for Johnson.
5   See **Letter 59**, n.4, above. Johnson suggests that Stukeley should write a dissertation on shrines for the next edition of *Palæographia Sacra* and so supplies information which could be helpful for this.
6   A search of the MS index compiled by Johnson and still held by the SGS reveals four entries under 'Shrines' relating to MB2, fol.142r; MB3, fols 27 and 29 and MB5, fol.51v. Johnson's comments show a post-Reformation attitude when shrines could be studied for their antiquarian interest; during the period 1547–1660 they were frequently destroyed by iconoclasts.
7   St Andrew's church, Heckington (Lincs) is most famous for its fourteenth-century Easter Sepulchre and sedilia.
8   An old English word meaning 'settings for gems'.
9   The RS did publish Stukeley's paper on 'an Ancient Shrine belonging to the Abbey of Croyland' which he wrote in November 1748 (*Phil.Trans.* (January 1748/9), 45, 485–90).
10 Hans Sloane (1660–1753: see *ODNB* and Appendix 3) 'was always ready on proper Notice to admit the Curious to the sight of his Museum'. This collection, combined with that of Edward Harley, second Earl of Oxford, became the founding collection of the British Museum.
11 Æthelred, King of Mercia (fl. *c.*700), married Osthryth, niece of St Oswald, King of Northumbria. He founded Bardney Abbey and St Oswald's remains were buried there. The Latin phrase means 'King Ethelred at the temple/church'.
12 Stukeley's sister Frances married William Johnson of Boston, a customs collector; their son William Johnson was born in 1727. Johnson copies the paragraph referred to here, at the end of his letter.
13 This is Johnson's copy of Henry Johnson's letter. The person he met is probably Lieutenant-General John Johnson (d.1753), Colonel of the 33rd Foot (later the Duke of Wellington's Regiment). He lived at Burhill (Surrey).
14 William Shirley (1694–1771), Governor of Massachusetts Bay, which was administered from Boston (Mass.).
15 Thomas Clinton, third Earl of Lincoln (1568– 1619), married Elizabeth Knyvett and had, among other children, a daughter Arabella or Arbella. She married Isaac Johnson (born *c.*1600 in Stamford), grandson of Archdeacon Robert Johnson, founder of Oakham School; it is presumably this connection with the Rutland Johnsons that interests Henry and Maurice Johnson. The couple emigrated to New England along with John Winthrop; the flagship of Winthrop's fleet was called the *Arbella* in her honour. She died in Salem (Massachusetts) in 1630. Her husband moved with Winthrop to the new site of Boston (Massachusetts), where he was the richest man in the colony.
16 William Dugdale, *Baronage of England* (3 vols, 1675–6); Johnson owned these and they were sold at the first Sotheby's sale of his books in 1898.

61. William Stukeley to Maurice Johnson, London, 16 January 1750
Spalding, SGS/Stukeley/23

[Annotated by Johnson: Letter from Dr Stukeley with his Memoires of transactions at RS, taken memoriter, And sent for the benefit of SGS to the President.]

My dear friend,

I received your last, wherein are the memoirs of that remarkable piece of history of the Johnsons of Boston, who chiefly had a hand in founding that flourishing metropolis of the same name, in our w.indies.[1] The troubles in k. C[harles] I time, was the inducement for them to undertake such a task; to leave their native country, torn in pieces by domestic troubles & convulsions. they nam'd all the circumjacent new villages Kirton, Freeston, Frampton, & the like, as these near our Boston. the minister of the town then, the famous Cotton,[2] who wrote a concordance, went with them. some of his descendants lived lately at Frampton, having a fair estate, in my time.

I am very much chagrined, that you should talk of not coming to London again. we that are isochronous,[3] need not either of us yet, plead age & [p.2] infirmitys. when I remov'd to London, I consider'd, that I remov'd into the world; where I could not fail of opportunitys of seeing all my friends: & still hope of seeing you here.

the few old acquaintance I had left here, are dropping off, every day. Lord Pembroke[4] was well on Sunday. our president Folks[5] din'd with him. on tuesday 6 a clock, he was dead.

We have had an exceeding mild winter here. no snow. scarce any frost. I find, a removal of a degree more south, is an advantage to us, in ætate vergente.[6] that made me blame our friend Roger Gale,[7] who was born by Cambridg; going to Scruton in old age, 200 mile north.

I shall take an opportunity of calling on your son, & new daughter.[8]

I have sent to you & the gentlemen of your Society, my memoirs of the royal society.[9] not doubting of your favourable acceptance: & [p.3] of taking it merely, as it is, a matter of memory: which cannot possibly, have any correctness: but must have innumerable errors. it serves only as a sort of index, to help us to find out any particular, we want to be better apprized of.

I come home directly from Crane Court[10] & taking my contemplative pipe, I minute down, what I remember, of all that passes. this is one reason, why I never go to the antiquarians, who have foolishly alterd their meeting, to the same night. so that by mixing two entertainments, they remember nothing distinctly of either.

hence therefore I desire you would never read above one night of my memoirs, at a time. be they long, or short.

Dr Mead[11] had 2 gold Allectus's; more than any body else had. he gave one to the french king. not content with this [p.4] indiscretion, he sent him an unique silver coyn of Carausius; on the reverse, his wife ORIVNA AUGUSTA.[12] & this without so much as a drawing taken of it.

this I look upon as an irreparable loss to our nation, which is only concern'd, in those coyns.[13]

Mr Richardson of queen square an ingenious gent. pictoris celeberrimi filius,[14] & I have agreed to visit you in june next.

I wish you many happy new years, & am with my respects to the gentlemen of the Society,

Your faithful friend
Wm Stukeley
queen square 16 jan.
1749–50

To Maurice Johnson Esqr

1   See **Letter 60** above, especially nn.12–16.
2   Revd John Cotton (1585–1652: see *ODNB*). In 1633 Cotton left St Botolph's church, Boston (Lincs), to become pastor in Boston (Massachusetts). The biblical concordance ascribed to him by Stukeley, *A Concordance to the Whole Bible: According to the Translation Allowed by his Late Majestie of Great Britaine*, was published by Clement Cotton, *c*.1630; John Cotton does not appear to have published a concordance.
3   Of the same age: Stukeley was born in late 1687 and Johnson in 1688.
4   Henry Herbert, ninth Earl of Pembroke (1689–1750), died on 9 January 1750; he was the son of Stukeley's earlier patron, Thomas Herbert, the eighth Earl, for whom see Philip Ayres, *Classical Culture and the Idea of Rome* (1997).
5   Martin Folkes: see Appendix 3.
6   'Inclining towards old age'.
7   Gale died in 1744. Scruton is approximately 200 miles north of Cambridge.
8   The newly married Captain Maurice Johnson and Elizabeth Johnson, née Bellamy: see **Letter 58**, n.12, above.
9   See **Letter 59** above. The SGS read Stukeley's notes on RS meetings, one meeting at a time as instructed, during the early 1750s.
10   The RS had rooms in Crane Court, off Fleet Street, London, from 1710 to 1780. The Society of Antiquaries met at the Mitre Tavern nearby until 1753. The two societies now met on the same day, though at different times, so that attendance at both would have been possible; Stukeley's earlier prodigious energy is evidently beginning to flag as he ages.
11   Dr Richard Mead: see **Letter 13**, n.12, above, and Appendix 3.
12   Stukeley and Johnson were particularly interested in Carausius (d.293) and Allectus (d.296), Roman army officers who ruled over Britain and northern Gaul as usurpers, because they shared the widely held but incorrect belief that both men were of British origin. Stukeley misread the inscription on this coin of the Emperor Carausius, found at Silchester, though he had only seen a hastily drawn sketch of it before the coin was given to King Louis XV of France. The controversy over this coin concerned the possibility that the woman depicted on the reverse of the coin was the wife of Carausius. The coin was chipped at the beginning of the inscription; Stukeley assumed that it read 'ORIVNA' which he took to be her name, Oriuna. He then created a complex story around Carausius and his putative wife, which he published in 1752, *Oriuna wife of Carausius Emperor of Britain*. Other readings were suggested: the more familiar 'FORTUNA' and Johnson's own idea, which he added as a note on the text of this letter, 'formed from ORIENS AUG. as I verily believe & wrote him word with a Note of Several of Carausius Coins with that Devise'. In a note written after 1749, on a letter from Dr Patrick Kennedy on the subject (originally received in 1734), Johnson wrote: 'Dr Richard Mead his Maj. Kg. G II physician in 1749 as Dr Stukeley then wrote me word presented His most Christian Majesty [Louis XV of France] with a Silver Denarius of Carausius & ORIVNA AUGUSTA his wife & Empress. Which I take to have been made out of one of his with ORIENS AUG on the reverse & so I sent the Dr word 12 Mar. 1749. Some conjecture It to be made out of a pretty frequent legend on coins FORTUNA AUG.' The whole story is well told in P. J. Casey, *The British Usurpers Carausius and Allectus* (1995), 180–4. For a contemporary engraving of the coin, see Illustration 21.
13   Johnson added a note here: 'if So it is no loss, Not that I doubt of Carausius having had both a Wife (as on Sir Richard Ellys' Bijugate Coin of them) & a Son whom I have'.
14   Jonathan Richardson (1694–1771), son of the painter Jonathan Richardson (1667–1745: see *ODNB*). George Vertue linked Richardson with Kneller, Michael Dahl and Charles Jervas as the top four portrait painters of the period. The son lived in his father's old house in Queen Square and was

buried in Stukeley's church of St George's with a Latin epitaph calling him 'son of the most famous artist'.

62. Maurice Johnson to William Stukeley, Spalding, 3 March 1750
Bodleian, MS Eng. misc. c.113, fols 355r–356v

Spalding 3º March 1749/50

Dear Friend

It would give me great concern if what I communicated to you the 8th of last January from my Kinsman Mr Johnson of Berkhamsteads Letter to me to me [*sic*] concerning your Nephew Johnson had given you offence, who have not been used to discontinue to me the favour of an Answer So long[1]: As I sent you Sir that Notice with a good designe, if it proved of no Service, it at lest shewd my good wishes that It might, & I concievd some probability of Its turning out so, knowing not any Gentleman more likely than your late Brother in Law[2] to have been related to the Estate in question kept in Trust for the right Heire Considerable enough to make it worth any mans while to make out a proper claim to, that could do It justly and with such proofs as the Law requires. I've been since informed that there was a Gentleman of our Name,[3] but whether of the same family enquird after I could not be informd, Coll.[1] Richard Johnson of Spilsby (or Bilsby near Alford rather, as I believe) who's only Child a Daughter was a Very great Fortune, & married to Sir Hardolf Wastneys[4] of Headon hall in Nottinghamsh[ire] Baronett; that Ladys name I'm told was Judith & she and her Husband are both dead lately & without leaving any Issue. I had the honour to be known to Sir Hardolf, being my Client in some Causes many yeares since relating to part of his Ladies Lincolnsh[ire] Estate in our Woulds; but I never knew her Ladyship, nor any of her Family. I have frequently found that the Antient Methods of Inquisitions post mortem of Men of Estates taken by the Escheators in Every County before the Kings Court of Wards and Liveries was abolished; as also the Heralds Visitations, or Entries made of Genealogies, Pedigrees & Memoires taken by the Provincial Kings of Armes were of great Use for comeing at, ascertaining and determining Rights to Estates as well as to Titles of Honour, and think If such had continued this great Estate had not wanted an Heire so long: but a just Title and true claim might probably have been easyly made out to It. Tis true that the Books in the College of Armes (which is a corporate Body by Patent of Ph[ilip] and Mary[5] & Act of Parliam[en]t confirming the same) are open and People may if they please to pay for it as some few Families have done, have their Pedigrees inserted therein. But formerly, nay even since the Restoration, several Visitations were made by the Proper Offices in the County Towns & at Noblemens & Gentlemens Seats where they recieved and Entred full Accounts of their Families.

[p.2]The Revd Mr Ray[6] lately communicated to our Society a Letter to him from the Revd Mr Pegg of Godmersham a Member, wherein he charges a great Man[7] with a Very considerable Error in the Chronology of the Death of Herod Agrippa confounding it with that of Herod the Great in his Medica Sacra. a mistake as it seems of about 43 yeares by the acc[oun]ts of the Succession of the Kings of the Asmonæan race. Wee have been much obliged to another Member Mr Zachary Brookes BD of St J[oh]n's Coll. in Cambr[idge][8] for his learned

Thesis for that Degree in defence of the Miracles of the Primitive Christian Church for some Centurys after the Apostolick Age, & for his Vindication of himself and that, against Dr Middleton, & his Abettors, the Scepticks of this unbelieving Generation, in his Examination of that Drs free Enquiry into the Miraculous Powers of the primitive Church. The Medica Sacra is not yet come to hand here, but remembering what your Sentiments are of it, makes me les desireous of seing it. Wee had a very pretty Agate shewn us by Dr Green at our last meeting, an Intaglia, cut with J. Cæsars head & having a thick white Vein in It, so managed as to look like an Hood or Vestment of the Pontifex Max:[9] coming down from the side of the face. It seems to me to have been designed as a Bulla or Jewel to wear on the Neck or perhaps in a Bracelet, the Inscription not being cut backward, but so as to be read on It as these Letters C.I. CÆSAR. D.PP. for Caius Julius Cæsar Dictator perpetuo, the resemblance Very like to those on his Denarii. perhapps by the dipthong done long after his time in honour of him and his family by some of the Julian race. it is Oval and above the Size of a Common Seale, but very thin. The Saxon Coines lately found at Oakham in Rutland-shire,[10] being Pennys of some of our later Mercian Kings, being well preserved, thô wretched work, have some of them come into Dr Green's, and one into my Possession, but there is not any great Erudition to be Expected from them. But I wish I had had the picking them, to take but one of a Sort, to supply my Series in a Chronological Order; and truly that's the best use to be made of Them. I have carryd Mr Smith of Woodston's[11] List of Shireffs up to Alfreds time, the Saxons all are called Vicedomini, by the Normans Vice Comites: & have added the Domini; & an Introductory discourse of the Dignity, Use & Power of those Officers.

I shall long to recieve you here in June as you've been So kind to promise me, & hope my old Dineing [sic] and Gardens thô not in the present fashion, will please You, who can't think every think the better for being in the mode: but are, like me for Moribus Antiquis. I am intending to seperate my Books and placeing such as are of Arts & Sciences, History and Poetry in Presses in the Study I have fitted up for my self for the remainder of my Days to leave them so to my Eldest Son, Give my Law Books to my Second, & have given what valuable I had in Divinity to my third Son our Minister.[12] but I grow So indolent that I long talk of things now before I find spirits to accomplish them, the Cata-loguing such a small parcel as I'm possessed of & pasting my Armes in them appearing somewhat laborious to me now, who should a few yeares agone done out of hand with delight, but as the warm weather advances I may resume some activity. My Bookbinder old Mr Christopher Norris[13] at the Bible & Crown in Chapter-house-Ally by St Pauls Church has a parcell to send me down in a Box, and if you please good Sir to trust the MS Q[uart]o of your memoires taken at the Royal Soc. intended as kindly told me for the Use of ours with him directed to be sent to me, with the Books he is to send down, I dare say he will take great Care of It and send it me safe. which I shall joyfully recieve, to be read one Dissertation or Division at a Meeting of our Company and so on throughout the whole. Wee are not So much beholden to any Benefactor to our Institution as to You Sir. Correspondents are, (as Sir Iz. Newton told me, when he deigned to do us the honor of Accepting our Invitation and became a Member)[14] what can best give Spirit to such an Undertaking, but how few are those who will find leasure to write such Letters as are improving as well as Entertaining, how fewer Still who

care to Carry on a Correspondence of this sort, whence they can only propose to benefit Others, for alas our Situation, occurrences & abilities permitt us not to make adequate Returns, Such as Wee have, I ever was ready to transmitt, and to no friends with more pleasure than to your Self, being Dear Doctor with all our Compliments to you your good Lady and Daughters
 Your very much obliged and most obedient Servant
 M Johnson

To the Reverend Dr Stukeley
  at his house in Ormondstreet
    Queens Square
      London
a single sheet.

---

1 See **Letter 60** above. Presumably Stukeley had packed his letter of 16 January with his bound MS of his Royal Society memoirs, ready for the bookbinder to send to Johnson, but this was delayed until early March: see Johnson's letter of 12 March 1750, **Letter 64** below.

2 William Johnson, late husband of Stukeley's sister Frances. Both Stukeley and Johnson took family history seriously.

3 Richard Johnson (c.1630–99), of Bilsby (Lincs): Militia Colonel and significant landowner in Virginia.

4 Hardolf Wasteneys, 4th Bt (1675–1742), MP; married Judith Johnson, daughter of Richard Johnson of Bilsby and niece of Thomas Johnson of Bilsby: see University of Nottingham MSS and Special Collections (Eyre of Grove MSS).

5 Philip of Spain and his wife Queen Mary granted the College of Arms a new charter in 1555.

6 Revd Benjamin Ray attended the SGS meeting on 8 February 1750, which is recorded as follows: 'A Lr was communicated from the Revd Mr Ray to the President dated from Cowbit 20 ulto with some Account of Sir Hardolf Wastneys of Headen Hall in Nottinghamshire Baronett and of Spilsby in this County and Judith his Lady, Daughter and heiress of the honble Coll. Rd Johnson of Bilsby by Alford & an Extract of a Lr to Mr Ray from the Revd Mr Pegg a member & the late Bp Smallbrookes Character & of a Gross Error in Chronology as to the death of Herod Agrippa in Dr Meads Medica Sacra.' (SGS, MB5, fol.54r)

7 Dr Richard Mead's *Medica Sacra* (1740) comments on diseases mentioned in the Bible. Chapter XV discusses the disease suffered by King Herod; the 1745 edition removes the confusion between Herod Agrippa and Herod the Great.

8 Zachary or Zachariah Brooke (1716–88: see *ODNB*); SGS 1746. His BD thesis was published as *Defensio Miraculorum* in response to the sceptical approach of the theologian Conyers Middleton (1683–1750: see *ODNB*), who was best known for his liberal Anglicanism and his *Life of Cicero* (1741). For Zachariah Brooke see Appendix 3.

9 More detail of this gemstone is given by Dr Green as Secretary in his minute of 1 March 1749/50 (SGS, MB5, fol.55r) which is almost a full folio page of information about the intaglio. Cæsar is represented as the Pontifex Maximus or High Priest, a title later taken over by the popes.

10 See **Letter 58**, n.8, above.

11 Revd Robert Smyth did not live to complete this work, which is described in John Nichols, *Illustrations of the Literary History of the Eighteenth Century* IV (1822), 355–7. See Appendix 3.

12 Johnson's sons Maurice, the eldest, Walter, the second, who had followed his father into the law, and John, now minister of Spalding. The division of the books reflects their interests.

13 See **Letter 60**, n.4, above. Norris was binding Stukeley's MS notes on RS meetings, for the use of the SGS at their weekly meetings.

14 See Johnson's comment in **Letter 32** above. Johnson's account of his meeting with Sir Isaac Newton is in *Correspondence*, 26–7.

63. William Stukeley to Maurice Johnson, London, 9 March 1750
Spalding, SGS/Stukeley/24

[Annotated by Maurice Johnson:] Letter from Dr Stukeley to the Pr[esident] SGS[1] concerning the 2d Earthquake felt at London in 1749/50

My dear friend

I remember, I took notice of the revd Mr Cotton vicar of Boston, being one of the first founders of Boston, in new England. which is evidence enough, I did not neglect the notice you sent me, about the Johnson estate there.[2] but tho' your intention in it was kind, yet I could not take any further thought about it; as knowing my bro[ther] Johnson was a yorkshire man, & had no pretence therein: & his son, I fear, is a worthless lad.

I long agoe deliver'd my MS of the royal Soc. memoirs, to your old book-binder,[3] who knew me very well. you cannot be long without it. & by that time you have gone thro' it, I shall have another, somewhat larger, ready for you.

I am angry, that you grow so unactive, & fancy your self such an old man. Dr Willis[4] calld on me. he is still trader-mad. he has [p.2] printed his book of the parliament men, & dedicated it to the Duke of Richmond now made president of the Antiquarians.[5]

Mr Giffard[6] near me, is saxon coyn-mad & bought many of the Rutland ones. has a good collection of such.

we have a piece in the press, by the revd Mr Borlase[7] of Cornwall, an acquaintance of your friend Mr de la costa.[8] tis an account of the works of the druids there. they found some british gold coyns lately, in that country.

last thursday morning soon after 6 a clock we had another shock of the earthquake,[9] more sensible than the former. & at night a ridotto,[10] as much crouded as the masquerade, before. for now our people, especially the women are so stark mad of their diversion, that they would not scruple to step over a yawning gulf to goe to 'em. nay so audacious are they grown, as to call their game-meetings; whirlwinds, & earthquakes. I am
      Your affectionate humble servant
         W: Stukeley

Lond. 9 mar 1749–50

To
 Maurice Johnson Esqr
  Spalding
   Lincolnshire

Free
 John Lincoln

---

[1] Maurice Johnson became President of the SGS in 1748 following the death of Revd Stephen Lyon, Rector of Merewith (Kent) and also Perpetual Curate of Spalding 1710–48, who had been President for much of that time.

[2] See **Letter 60** and **Letter 61**, n.2, above. Stukeley's 'brother Johnson' was the husband of his sister Frances.

[3] See **Letter 60**, n.4, above.

4   Browne Willis (see Appendix 3) was particularly interested in collecting traders' tokens. He had just printed the third and final volume of his *Notitia Parliamentaria*.
5   Charles Lennox, second Duke of Richmond (1701–50); he succeeded the Duke of Somerset (who died early in 1750) as President of the Society of Antiquaries, but died himself in November 1750.
6   Revd Andrew Gifford DD, FSA (1700–84) lived in Queen Square, London, and thus was a neighbour of Stukeley's. A Baptist minister at Eagle Street chapel, London, he was a significant numismatist and became sub-librarian at the British Museum. For the Saxon coins, see **Letter 58**, n.8, above.
7   Revd William Borlase FRS (1696–1772: see *ODNB*), author of *Antiquities ... of the County of Cornwall consisting of several Essays on the First Inhabitants, Druid-Superstition, Customs* (1754).
8   Emanuel Mendes da Costa: see Appendix 3.
9   Stukeley wrote this letter on Friday 9 March 1750, after the earthquake recorded on 8 March which followed an earlier earthquake on 8 February.
10 A social assembly for music, dancing and cards. Stukeley had expected that the shock of these earthquakes would have made people adopt a serious mode of life.

64. Maurice Johnson to William Stukeley, Spalding, 12 March 1750
Bodleian, MS Eng. misc. c.113, fols 357r–358v

Spalding 12 March 1749/50

Dearest Dr

Last Fryday I received by our Carrier your kind Communications from my old Bookbinder with a Parcell & intended to've carryd in & read the 1st of the memoires[1] next thursday & then have returnd you as I now do Our Societys & my Own Thanks but your repeated favour of a 2nd letter by this day's post[2] calls for my Earlyer Acknowledgement. So Sir for the first, first; your enclosed kind Letter dated 16 January ulto. Wee have in our Museum Soc. Gen. Spalding a Q[uart]o, but Imperfect, history of New England Canaan perhaps compild by the Revd Mr Cotton, you mention, [*gap in text*] Authors name being to it, Its elegantly printed, & has aboundance of Poetry therein by Benjamin Johnson, not the Laureat to J[ames] I, but another good Poet of the same names for the Verses therein in honour of the first planters, Called the Worthies of that Settlement I esteem excellent. In our Catal[ogue] it is indeed attributed to Thomas Norton of New England, thus his NEW ENGLAND CANAAN, published by Elliott, under whos name too as I find there remarked that book has gone, printed at Amsterdam 1637. & is here bound up with Rams Herbal,[3] or an Epitome of Dr Reimb. Dodcon's by Ram being of the same Size and of the gift of Mr Benj[amin] Cook Register of SGS in 1746. as in my Catalogue of their Libraries fo:136 & 240 and I find there fo: 12 in Q[uart]o Cotton Jno. of Boston in New England of Infant Baptisme printed by Cotes at London 1647[4] bound up with Stephen Marshall BD his Defence of Infant Baptisme in answer to Tombes, printed by the same R. Cotes the yeare before and given by my Uncle Martin Johnson Esq a worthy Justice of Peace, Father of my good Kinsman the Rector of Red Marshall in Durhamshire And Elder Brother of my Father.[5] all great Benefactors to the same ibm. fo:12 & 48 & passim per Catalogum. Thô you & I my Good Old Friend are as to Time indeed Cotemporarie Creatures, You have the advantage of me greatly in Strength both of mind and Body, mine having been So shatterd with several Severe & longlast fitts of the Stone & Gravell as to render Traveling impracticable for Me, and even being Conveyd the gentlest way very Irksom & hazardous.[6]

[p.2] You may pity but cant blame, my not Seeing an Eldest Son in prosperity at his own house & in our Metropolis, & so many Kind Friends as I might there Enjoy: He may & will this Summer I hope bring our Daughter[7] to wait on her Dear Mother in whom my Life love & felicity here on Earth centres. Wee shall recieve them, and all Friends with gladness, amongst whom I Esteem You Good Sir One of my Principal & with You Your Ingenious & worthy Neighbour Mr Richardson[8] whom I trust I have what will entertain, and from whom (as I wish & want) I doubt not but to recieve Satisfactory Information as to some Pourtraicts & other paintings which have long been Ornaments of this old house, thô never perhapps rightly understood by Any Posser [sic] of them hitherto with some reasons I can give him Conjectures which his Knowledge & Experience may Confirme or direct me better. this great matter I've made it my Busyness to be certainly well acquainted with, How they every One of them came into any of my Ancestors hands & have (when but a Youth, Out of a natural affection to the Art of designing) had them Cleaned, repaired, framed, & preserved a Ma puissance.[9]

I purpose to perpetuate on them the 1. Persons, 2.dates, with their 3.Armes & 4. Painters Names, a good rational & highly satisfactory Method. Am meditating fitting up a Gentlemans Family Library for my Son & Sons Son as Such came to Me from my Great Grandfathers Grandfather to remain ad Seros Usque Nepotes[10] – & hope to have it ready against I may recieve yee here, with some illumined MSS therein And a most Noble Collection of Royal Charters and other highly Useful Records, Mapps, Charts & plannes of these Parts. Our friend your Brother Gale

[*Section of text missing here; perhaps it was on a separate page, now lost. The text continues with a page of quotations from books, in Latin, relating to the Emperor Carausius, his family and which of them were portrayed on his coinage.*]

[p.4] 'Tis great Pity liberal Patrons should be imposd upon, but their Bounty frequently makes ingenious Knaves set themselves to work to feign or Counterfeit or some way falsify & render rare & so desirable Inscriptions, Sculptures, Statues, Medals, Coines & Pictures, whereof I am assured our Cabinetts & Collections afford numerous Instances; whereof in my small Cognizance it has been my hap to detect not a few – I am glad the Gentleman you informe me of Mr Borlase[11] on whose ancestor I have a MS Poem of B.[*gap in text*] as I think in giving some Account of our British ancestors in the West of England, & when publishd shall be obligd to you for a farther Account of his work. You know I pretend[12] to possess a Cassivelaun, is that if so an Unique Incomptum Caput ex parte Ærei projecta, [on reverse] Equus cum Esseda sive Essedæ Rota ex parte Cavâ eiusdem Ærei minuti – cum [*symbols similar to the letters CAS*] an hæc sint Celticæ?[13]

For News. One John Sawden on to'therday here fell into a Brewers vat & dyd last night as the Coroners Inquest have found of that Scald. The Brewers man perished in like manner not long agone. By neglect of repairing the Haven Bank by Wormgate,[14] the same was broken by last high tyde & I'm told near a thousand acres are overflown, & what might have been prevented (& was Cautiond against) for fifty shillings will cost five times as much in damages & to repair – This I had from our School M[aste]r who is a Boston man.[15] Wee let the tide up our Wash & It went as high as Croyland & Dieping, or it had topd our Banks in some parts, as it did those of Wrag Marsh.

My Garden shews & smells delightfully with the Bloom of fruit Trees in

Blossom & Vernal flowers. I wish you was walking in It to be regald with their odors with your most affectionat friend   M Johnson

To the Reverend
Dr Stukeley Rector of George's [*sic*]
at his House in Queen Square
  Ormond Street
    London

1   Stukeley's memoirs of the RS meetings have at last reached Johnson.
2   It appears that Johnson received **Letter 63**, written on 9 March, on Monday 12 March. **Letter 61**, written on 16 January 1750, had been enclosed with the parcel of memoirs and had arrived in Spalding on Friday 9 March, so Johnson received two letters very close together. The delay in receiving **Letter 61**, in reply to Johnson's **Letter 60** about the possible land claim in New England, explains Johnson's concern, expressed at the beginning of **Letter 62**, that he might inadvertently have offended Stukeley by referring to his family concerns.
3   Thomas Morton (d.1646/7: see *ODNB*) wrote *New English Canaan or New Canaan, containing an Abstract of New England* (Amsterdam, 1637). The book is listed in the eighteenth-century catalogue of the SGS library, fol.136. Morton, a settler in New England, was in favour of the American Indians and was in conflict with the Puritan Massachusetts Bay Company. The Spalding copy was bound together with *Ram's Little Dodoen: a brief epitome of the new herbal or history of plants* (1606), an English version by William Ram of a herbal by the Flemish physician Rembert Dodoens (1517–85). Originally entitled *Cruydeboeck* (1554), this fully illustrated herbal was one of the most popular books in the late sixteenth and early seventeenth centuries, known across Europe.
4   The exact reference in the SGS's eighteenth-century book catalogue (fol.12) reads 'Cotton Jno of Boston in New Engld of Infant Baptisme Cotes London 1647 [presented by] Martin Johnson Esq NB this is bound up with Marshall of the same subject'. Marshall's book is Stephen Marshall (1594/5–1655), *A Defence of Infant Baptism*. Martin Johnson was Johnson's uncle.
5   The Revd Walter Johnson: see Appendix 3.
6   This account by Johnson of his physical health at the age of sixty-two explains his declining activity.
7   Johnson's daughter-in-law Elizabeth, née Bellamy, who had married his eldest son Maurice. This letter emphasises the closeness of Johnson's family relationships, particularly his devotion to his wife.
8   See **Letter 61**, n.14, above.
9   'To the best of my strength', a widely used motto.
10 'To my remote grandchildren/descendants'.
11 See **Letter 63**, n.7, above.
12 'Pretend' is used here in its eighteenth-century sense of 'claim'.
13 Johnson thinks his coin is from the reign of the British leader Cassivelaunus; it shows a horse-drawn chariot and has letters which may be a form of 'CAS'; he is enquiring whether they are Celtic letters.
14 A defensive bank north-west of Boston, going towards Coningsby. Boston suffered from repeated tidal floods.
15 The Revd Samuel Whiting: see Appendix 3.

65. William Stukeley to Maurice Johnson, London, 15 May 1750
Spalding, SGS/Stukeley/25

[Annotated by Maurice Johnson:] Letter from the Rev^d Dr William Stukeley Rector of St Georges Queen Square Ormond street F. Coll of Phys. & of the R & SA Socs London to the President of SGS. 15 May 1750. That Earthquakes are electrical Vibrations.

Dear S^r,

Perhaps you will be glad to hear of an old friend after we have here seen & felt two most sensible shocks of an earthquake; where every house in London trembled, in an astonishing manner. I was sensible of it, at the first: & began then to perceive the cause of it, & mention'd it, at one of our weekly meetings, in this neighborhood: that it was certainly an electrical vibration; & nothing under the earth that caus'd it.[1]

We have here 3 friendly conversations in the week where a collection of us meet at 5 in the afternoon; over a dish of thea, & nothing else. they were on foot, before I came here. one at Dr Hills, son to Dr Hill of Peterborough;[2] Another at Dr Parsons's in redlyon square. another at Mr Sherwoods, devonshire street, surgeon: beside Dr Mortimers[3] on a fryday, in queensquare, which is a sort of eccho to the Royal Society. so that we have literal conversation enough. the 3 last are in my own parish. Dr Hill lives in Blomesbury: & sends his service to you. he is ill of the gout.

I gave in a paper to the Royal Society, being my opinion about the cause of earthquakes, decrying the vulgar solution of subterraneous vapors. for I was angry to see 100 papers read, being only circumstantial descriptions, without any attempt to the solution. I suppose they all acquiesc'd in the old mumpsimus notion.[4] some only puzzling themselves in finding out, which way the vapor mov'd: but with infinite contradictions to one another. others busyed themselves & horses, to find out [p.2] to an inch, the extent of the trembling. others in relating circumstances merely trifling & ridiculous.

I thought it became us to inquire into the cause of so wonderful a phænomenon. upon reading my paper,[5] no less than 5 rose up to speak against it. the president Lord Macclesfield, Mr Burroughs, Dr Squire, & de la costa with a stale joke. I laught at 'em: my friends were excessively angry. the next week I gave in a much larger paper, with a gentle reproof, & full confirmation of my opinion. all was hush.

at the same time, I preachd a sermon upon the occasion in my own church. my friends, both philosophical & christian, who were hearers in both places, tiezed me very much to print all the discourses. & I have left a copy, a present for you, at your bookbinders.[6]

I see your Lord Gideon[7] now & then, & he speaks civilly to me, & invites me to come, & see him. here the *malesana cupido*[8] of getting more, prevails, on all hands, together with ambition. what else could induce my lord of London[9] at his age, & with his infirmitys, & great fortune, to take so laborious a task upon himself. last thursday at the Visitation at St Pauls, he gave us a most excellent charge, which will be printed.[10] Dr Chapman has given an excellent charge against infidel Middleton, in Suffolk, which will be printed.

Your antiquarian Society have got the Duke of Richmond their President, & are busy getting a charter. I was at the feast the 23 april, the only time I can be with 'em. Your friend Browne Willis Esqr LL.D.[11] is in a most deplorable languishing way. he has finished his book of members of parliament.

The College of Physicians under their new president [p.3] Dr Wasey[12] having appointed me to preach the Crounian sermon on 20 sept. next, I am diverting my self occasionally, on that account. Our old friend Dr Jurin disobliged me. nor did I regret the loss of him, tho' the oldest acquaintance I had in London. the critics have mauld my friend Warburton[13] most cruelly, with a battery of 24 pieces of cannon, against his edition of Shakespear. he provokd 'em sufficiently. I hear lord Orfords[14] admirable collection of pictures are condemn'd to be sold by auction, next winter.

let me tell you, that you may take the clovelike seed you sometime find among thea, & raise it on a hot bed. Dr Hardisway[15] has one of his own raising, now a yard high, & in full bloom. tis to be seen at Master Edwards's (master in canc.) at his seat at Wimbledon.

Our bridg[16] is almost now cover'd, I mean the two arches. & tis a most noble work. I cannot be reconcild to your notion of seeing London no more. Your son living here ought to be inducement sufficient.

I am in hopes I shall take you in my way from Stamford to holbech, in june or july: & that Mr Richardson my neighbor will accompany me.[17] he is a great rider, a sensible, pleasant man: but a little slippery in performance of distant promises.

We have all the world in our neighbourhood to day, at the foundling hospital, to hear Handel's Messiah;[18] at half a guinea tickets, which raises £700. thus the modern taste is to mix religion with their diversions. & half the company have not been at a church these 20 years; perhaps not in their lives. all the pleasure I have from it, is to take a walk in the field, solitary; & see the company; the gay, the foolish world; & enjoy the pleasure of my own thoughts, along with the sweet air of the fields. I am Dear Sir,

      Your faithful servant
       & affectionate friend
        W Stukeley

S. Geo. 15 may 1750

To
Maurice Johnson Esq\
 Spalding
  Lincolnshire
   single sheet

---

[1] Stukeley refers to the two earlier earthquakes in 1750, those on 8 February and 8 March. Following these, Stukeley's letter to the President of the RS 'concerning the Causes of Earthquakes' was read at the RS on 5 April 1750.

[2] John Hill: see Appendix 3.

[3] Dr James Parsons (see *ODNB*), SGS 1746, Appendix 3, lived in Red Lion Square, London, just south of Stukeley's rectory in Queen Square; Dr Noah Sherwood FRS (1700–64) lived in Devonshire Street which crosses Harley Street south of Regent's Park; Dr Cromwell Mortimer: see Appendix 3 and *ODNB*, SGS 1737.

[4] 'Old mumpsimus' means a traditional and incorrect explanation which should be replaced by modern, up-to-date evidence. It goes back to a story of a mid-sixteenth-century priest who misread the Latin 'sumpsimus' in the liturgy as 'mumpsimus' and continued to use his misreading despite attempts to point out the correct version.

[5] Stukeley first spoke at the RS on earthquakes on 22 March 1750 (see *Phil.Trans.* 46, 641–6; this was a letter to the President dated 13 March 1750). His second piece was read on 5 April 1750 (*Phil. Trans.* 46, 657–69). Immediately following this, Stephen Hales' paper agreed with Stukeley. Stukeley's views were criticised by the President of the SGS, Martin Folkes, George Parker, second Earl of Macclesfield (1698–1764: see *ODNB*), who became President in 1752; James Burrouw (1701–82), a legal reporter, later President in 1768 and 1772; Dr Samuel Squire (1713–66), in 1750 Clerk of the Closet in the Prince of Wales' household and later Bishop of St Davids; and Emanuel Mendes da Costa (SGS member), see Appendix 3.

6   Stukeley's book, *The Philosophy of Earthquakes, Natural and Religious* (1750). There was a later edition in 1756.
7   See **Letter 59**, n.16, above.
8   'Unhealthy greed'.
9   Thomas Sherlock (1678–1761: see *ODNB*), Bishop of London from 1748 to his death in 1761 aged over eighty.
10 Thomas Sherlock, *An Examination of the Consequences of Dr Middletons Free enquiry etc To which are added, some observations, in order to confute what he has objected to the Lord Bishop of London's Discourses on the use and intent of prophesy* (1750), a 36-page response to Dr Conyers Middleton, *A Free Enquiry into the Miraculous Powers, which are supposed to have subsisted in the Christian Church* (1749).
11 Browne Willis; despite Stukeley's concern, he lived until 1760; see Appendix 3.
12 Dr William Wasey (1691–1757: see *ODNB*). He was elected President of the Royal College of Physicians in April 1750 on the death of Dr Jurin. Dr James Jurin (see Appendix 3) had been President from January to March 1750. Stukeley had known Jurin since Stukeley's early days as a trainee physician in London. Stukeley preached his Crounian Sermon on 20 September 1750; it was published as 'The treating of diseases, a character of the Messiah, being the anniversary sermon preached before the Royal College of Physicians London' (1750).
13 Revd William Warburton: see **Letter 36**, n.8, above and *ODNB*. He published his much-criticised edition of Shakespeare in 1747.
14 The sale of Sir Robert Walpole's outstanding collection of paintings did not happen until 1779, when it was sold to the Empress of Russia, Catherine the Great, by Walpole's grandson the third Earl of Orford. A catalogue was published in 2014.
15 Dr Peter Hardisway contributed several pieces to the RS's *Phil.Trans.* Mr Edwards is recorded as Master in Chancery in 1750.
16 Westminster Bridge was being built and was finished in 1750. Prior to that, river crossings from Westminster had to be made by boat.
17 See **Letter 61**, n.14, above.
18 Handel's *Messiah* was first performed in Dublin in 1742 and in London in 1743 at Covent Garden, but was not at first successful as it was not thought proper to perform a religious work in a theatre. It then achieved enormous success following this 1750 performance at the Foundling Hospital, a short distance from Stukeley's house in Queen Square. The libretto of *Messiah* was written by Charles Jennens (1701–1773 ODNB) SGS member in 1748.

66. Maurice Johnson to William Stukeley, Spalding, 13 June 1750
Bodleian, MS Eng. misc. c.113, fols 363r–364v

13 June 1750

Dear Dr,

I've gotten my House and Gardens in good Order and shall be proud of recieving You and your good Lady and all your Daughters here as Soon and for as Long time as You'll please to favour Us with your Company, which you've proposed very kindly should be about this time which is also of most leisure to Me. According to his promise I hoped to have seen Dr Browne Willis Esq. here before now, but you Account but too justly I fear for my disappointment in that Expectation, I hope You'll keep Mr Richardson Steady to his Accompanying yee, & will endevour shewing him something or Other worthy the Speculation of a Cognizeur.[1] Our Convers at this Season turns much on Horses & Horseraces, with Cockings and Assemblies the concomitant Entertainment of the Season. To'ther day I had a Severus Alex[ander][2] M [*illegible*] F, large Brass, on reverse Mars gradiens brought me, plowd up hereabouts. & My Son Walter (the Antiquary of my House),[3] purchased an Antient Gold ring dug up in our Abbey yard, wherein is a pointing Hæmatite or greenish bloodstone: which I suppose might

have been part of some relique or shrine of a St set for whatever virtues might thence, or in case of a flux of blood, be imagined in It, I'm sure It could never be worn as Ornamental. I have the true Citisus Virgilii[4] in full blow, and 'tis a very beautyful low shrub with french yellow flowers of which he sings
Florentem Citisum sequitur lasciva capella.

[p.2] Wee're much concerned for Dr Hills[5] ill state of health fearing It may prevent his publishing his other 2 Volumes of Plants, & of Animals, which if Wee had as well done as that of Fossils Wee should esteem ourselves possessd of a Compleat history indeed of all Sublunary natural bodies. but, with our best Compliments to that Learned & ingenious Gentleman, Wee hope he is not so Severely handled by the Gout, as to disable him from carrying on those good intended Works. – Not long since died at Baston near Langtoft the widdow of the Revd Mr Standish[6] sometime School M[aste]r of Peterborough, after that a Minister in South Carolina, where he made a prety large Collection of Indian Armes & Instruments & of the Exuviæ of Beasts & Birds & Shells of fish, and of Nuts of the Country, the Remaines whereof have furnished Mrs Townsend & some other Ladies with materials for Rock & Grotto works, & some of our Members have augmented their Collections thereout. Dr Green particularly who shewd us an Elegant Light blew, spotted with black, large Nasuform beetle, not in Moufett, Ray,[7] or 2 Authors of the Indies in Folios he has, but whose names I've forgotten, or any other He consulted, and some fine specimens of rare Shells. this Gentleman was a Correspondent of Sir Hans Sloanes many yeares, & dyd abroad.

Mr Muscut School M[aster] of Boston[8] sent us lately as his Donation to our Library Dr Perry's View of the Levant, in which is a Print of a Granate Trough wherein he conjectures they prepared the mummies adorned with Hieroglyphical Figures both within and without, a curious Vase & the most Singular thing in that whole great Folio this Print is under a Sistrum[9] inscribed to the Ægyptian Society – [p.3] I pray my Good Friend what is that Ægyptian Society?[10] and who are the Members? and where do they meet? and what is become of that great dealer in Hieroglyphicks, Mummies and Canopus's, our quondam Brother Member & your Successor Alexander Gordon MA?[11] talking of these things, however ashamed Horace might be of that useful Invention the Knatt net, or Conopy,[12] being seen by daylight amongst M. Anthony's military Equipage: they are things of good use to Us a'nights here, & might be so to any Roman General, who was susceptible of feeling in any Country abounding with stinging flyes thô Lewis Desprez Interprets his
>   Interque Signa (turpe!) militaria
>   Sol aspicit Conopeum

as encreasing the indignity ex eo quod muliebre tabernaculum erat pro Prætorio Seu Imperatorio tentorio.[13]

Mr Smith of Woodston[14] by Peterb[orough] has sent me (from monuments & painted Glass in 30 Churches he has lately Viewd about Lincoln) many Corrections of the Armorials of our County Shireffes, in a Letter, and I trust his historio-heraldico-chronological List of those great Officers for this Shire will come forth as compleat, as that for any other, perhaps more so. I've not yet had the pleasure of recieving what you kindly left for me with my Bookbinder he deteining it to send with some other things, in the interim Sir I return you many thanks – There is a literary Meeting, wee are assured, forming at Boston begun by a dissenting Teacher there but I can yet learn no more of it than that a Gentleman or 2 belonging to their Custome House[15] & an Apothecary & surgeon (perhaps one man both) are Members, a Gentleman who has lately been there tells Me the Haven is choaked up so much with Sands that the Navigation up to the Town is lost, So is that down from Lincoln, nothing they say but Violent Flood can relieve them & should such next winter come unless they strongly embanked the Borough 'twill be overflowed.

[p.4] Some Improvements my Son Walter has made in 3 ~~yds~~ fields (conteining 12 acres & adjoyning to mine) which he has some Beasts and Sheep in, will I perswade my Self please you my Friend, as they do me, makeing by variety & difference from the form of a Garden, a grateful amusem[en]t by casting up some ditches, planting Quick, with Elmes & Willow sets intermixed, & sowing the banks with infinite variety of Poppies, Marygolds and many other flowers, many of which are in full blow. He has renderd them very agreeable, and more So, as they are different from those that lye about Them. Wee intend to improve them yet farther by planting here and there Some Scotch firrs in them.[16] I long to have you here to take a Walk in them with your old affect[ionate] Friend and faithful Servant

M. Johnson

To
the Reverend Dr Stukeley
Rector of St George's
   Queensquare by
     Ormond Street
       London

---

[1] The early eighteenth-century spelling of 'connoisseur'. For Richardson, see **Letter 61**, n.14, above and for Browne Willis see Appendix 3.

[2] Severus Alexander reigned over the Roman Empire from AD 222 to 235 in succession to his cousin Elagabalus. Johnson prefers the study of coins to local entertainments such as 'cockings' or cock-fights.

[3] Walter Johnson became Treasurer of the SGS and an active member.

[4] The broom, Cytisus scoparius. The reference is to Virgil's *Eclogues* 2, 64, 'the lascivious she-goat follows the flowering cytisus'.

[5] In 1750 Hill was writing his attacks on the RS and its President, Martin Folkes, which ensured that he was never elected FRS. No illness in 1750 is mentioned in George Rousseau's *The Notorious Sir John Hill* (2013).

[6] Revd David Standish, Usher of Peterborough Free School 1708, Master 1721–24. He went to South Carolina in 1724, becoming minister of St Paul's parish, Colleton County, from 1724 to 1728 when he died. Mrs Townsend may have been a relative of the SGS member Revd Thomas Townsend, Vicar of Pinchbeck, or his son Revd Charles Townsend; both became SGS members, the father in 1727 and the son in 1734.

[7] Dr John Green, by now SGS Secretary, had a natural history collection so he as able to add the Black Spotted Blue Beetle, common in North America. The books consulted were Thomas Moffet, *Insectorum sive Minimorum Animalium Theatrum* (1634) and John Ray, *Historia Insectorum*, edited by the Royal Society (1710); a copy of Ray's book was owned by the SGS. Sir Hans Sloane (see Appendix 3) was in the Caribbean from 1687 to 1688 starting his collections.

[8] The Revd James Muscut was Master of Boston Grammar School from 1745 to 1759. He was probably the same person as the Revd James Muscut, Fellow of Corpus Christi College, Oxford, and Rector of Little Staughton (Beds), where he was buried in 1759. His gift of the book by Charles Perry MD, *View of the Levant* (1743), is still in the SGS library.

[9] Discussion about a sistrum, or Egyptian ceremonial rattle, brought about the friendship between Stukeley and the Duke of Montagu at a meeting of the Egyptian Society; Stukeley explained its

function as being used at sacrifices 'in warm countries to drive away birds of prey, by a rattle, from devouring the sacrifice' and to warn off those who should not attend the ritual (*Surtees* I, 55).

[10] The short-lived Egyptian Society (1741–43), founded by John Montagu, fourth Earl of Sandwich, with Dr Perry, Dr Richard Pococke, Martin Folkes and Stukeley among its associate members. According to Stukeley, 'the purpose of it was to inquire into Egyptian antiquities' (*The Medallic History of Carausius* II, vi). **Letter 67** below contains Stukeley's fuller explanation of the Society and its activities.

[11] Alexander Gordon: see Appendix 3. He had been Secretary of an earlier Egyptian Club in the 1730s as well as Secretary of the Society of Antiquaries in 1736 before going to Carolina in 1741.

[12] Johnson refers to the use of mosquito netting in the Fens as a protection against 'knatts' or 'gnats', mosquitoes carrying malaria, known as marsh fever or tertian ague. The Fens were renowned for their gnats and mosquitoes before major drainage reduced the amount of marshland.

[13] Horace, *Opera: Interpretatione et notis illustravit*, ed. Ludovicus Desprez (1691), 274. This quotation is from *Epode* IX, 'To Mæcenas'. A. S. Kline translates it as 'While the sun looks down on his shameful pavilion/ Among the warlike standards'. Desprez's footnote suggests that Antony's tent with mosquito netting was undignified for a warrior because it was a woman's tent used for the imperial headquarters; the protective hangings were probably made of silk. See also **Letter 67** below.

[14] Revd Robert Smyth (d.1761), Rector of Woodston, assisted Edmund Carter in his *History of Cambridge* (1753). See *Correspondence*, Letters 465, 466 and 468 for details of Smyth's work.

[15] This is important evidence for the rather brief life of the eighteenth-century Boston Literary Society. The Customs House member was probably William Jackson, poet and member of the SGS.

[16] Walter Johnson, the second son of Maurice Johnson, appears to have shared his father's enthusiasm for gardening as well as for the law and the activities of the SGS.

67. William Stukeley to Maurice Johnson, London 16 June 1750
SGS/Stukeley/26

[Annotated by Johnson:] Letter from the Rev^d Dr Stukeley to the Pres. SGS of the Egyptian Society in London, Founded 1740. the Camisa or Arabian Vestm[en]t, Use of Rings of Metal. Tyn early known. The Tyrian Hercules planted Britain.[1]

Dear S^r

I was glad to receive yours: & to find you was well. for my Landlord & your Sovereign Gideon,[2] walking together, he told me, you was ill of a cold. I thank you for your kind invitation. if I come, it will most probably be solus. as for wives & daughters, their business is at home; for I have no caravan for female pilgrims. & I my self can propose only to stay one evening with you; & lodg at an inn (as usual) I don't travel now for pleasure but business. home is most agreable, at our time of life.

I grieve very much for the loss of Boston;[3] owing to great stupidity; in letting the water of Lincoln river run by a cutt below the bridg; insted of coming thro' the town.

Dr Perry[4] I was well acquainted withal; those 4 winters I lived in Glocesterstreet 1740. 41. 42. 43. then it was, we founded the Egyptian Society, Lord Sandwich president.[5] it subsisted whilst I was in London. then it drop'd. I have the memoirs of it, as taken by my self. & there it was, that the Duke of Montagu took me so much into his favor; as pav'd the way for my being now in Town, for the rest of my life. nor have I ever repented it' tho' I greiv'd exceedingly for the loss of the Duke: even as much as Horace did, for that of his Mecænas. & I equally lost my Mecænas.[6] for I frequent no levees: nor trouble my self with any ambitious views, but enjoy a vast deal of solitude: not running, as the rest of the world dos here, from one public company to another, from morning to evening. just as our folks do, running from the Royal Society to the Antiquarians; the same evening.

Insted of that, I retreat, every night at 6 a clock, to my contemplative pipe; & that is more enjoyment to me, than [p.2] the company of the preceding day.

When I came first to my house in Glocester Street,[7] Mr Wm Torkington who was one of the gentlemen pensioners, came to visit me. his ancestor marryed the heiress of our family, of great Stukeley. he offerd to introduce me to Lord Sandwich, then lately come home from his Egyptian travels. my Lord put on the habit of the Arabs, inhabiting those oriental countrys, the same as their founder Ismaels.[8] tis calld *camisa*, a black short gown with open sleeves; loose; a slit on the breast for convenient putting on: reaching down only to the knees. the body & legs otherwise naked. many rings of pewter put upon the neck, small of the legs, wrists, earings, noserings. the antient arabians had these ornaments from Brittain.[9] for the first hero's that undertook voyages, went in quest of metals. & our Cornish tyn mines were found out very early, for this reason; by the first adventurers, under the conduct of the Tyrian Hercules, the planter of our island. Tyn is mentioned by Moses, & by Job. this was their habit.

[*Sketch by Stukeley of a person wearing the clothes and jewellery described above.*]

[p.3] The 11th of December 1741 I met Lord Sandwich at Lebecks head chandois street; when his Lordship, Dr Pocock, Dr Perry, & Captain Norden the Dane[10] declar'd the purport of that assembly was to form themselves into an Egyptian Society, for the promoting, & preserving Egyptian, & other antient learning: they all having been in egypt. at the same time they nominated, Mr Folks, Dr Stukeley, Dr Milles, Mr Cha. Stanhope, Mr Dampier, & Mr Mitchell[11] associates of the same; who together with them were styled founders of the Society.

22 january 1741–2. the Duke of Montagu, Richmond, were admitted of the Society. the Duke of Montagu, asked me the meaning of that egyptian rattle (as his Grace calld it) lying before us. I answerd, it was not without reason that he calld it so: for the sistrum[12] so famous in antiquity, was really so: tho' not properly understood in authors. in the antient world (continued I) when the sacrifices were laid on the altar, they waited with impatience for the descent of celestial fire; in token of the divine acceptance. in the mean time, in hot countrys, they were oblig'd to hold a sistrum in their hands to drive off the birds, & beasts of prey. thus did Abraham in his famous federal sacrifice with God almighty: Genesis XV. II. the Egyptians therefore could not fail, taking this instrument into the principal of their sacred utensils. the rattling it, was equivalent to crying out procul este profani.[13]

the ~~solution~~ Society approved of this solution. & soon after I drew an account of it, up at large, & presented it to the Duke of Montagu. from which time, his Grace was pleasd to take me into his particular favor, & friendship. & tho' the Society drop'd, after I left the town, in the summer of 1743: yet the Duke orderd me to come to Boughton that summer: & constantly ever after, invited me by letter under his own hand, to meet him there. & his kindness toward me, increasd every year, extremely.

[p.4] thus Dear S^r I have answer'd your demand, & given a short account of the famous egyptian Society: which flourished extremely for the 3 first years. as to its dissolution, I suppose, when ambition seizes the minds of mortal men, literature flys, of course. I have very large memoirs about it.[14]

sawny gordon[15] before that time, went secretary to the governor of Carolina.

London is the only place, where we can enjoy one another: therefore I still live in hope of seeing you here. I am Dear S^r

Your faithful servant
W: Stukeley

S. Geo. 16 jun. 1750

To
    Maurice Johnson Esqr
        Spalding
            Lincolnshire

[Annotation by Johnson:] Gouldman[16] says Camis, Camisia, is an Arabic word, & (from Isidor) seems to think it was a sort of shirt to lye in, quod in his dormimus in Camis (cama signifying a low or truckle bed a χαμαι huius) thence says he in Camis i.e. in stratis – hinc Chorion, externa Fœtûs membrana, veluti domicilium, Camisia Fœtus dicebatur a Mart Some say It was of Linen & the inward vestment worn next to the skin, therefore frequently make use of for a Shirt, shift or Smock. The Intusium or Indusium Virorum & Subucula Fæminarum.

1 See **Letter 66** above for Johnson's queries about the Egyptian Society. Johnson added these summaries of the contents of Stukeley's letters for ease of reference when preparing material for SGS meetings.
2 See **Letter 59**, n.16, above. He had purchased the Lordship of the Manor of Spalding and was also a landlord of Stukeley's in London and the most successful Government financier of the early eighteenth century.
3 See **Letter 66** above for Boston's problems with the River Witham, which were affecting its success as a port.
4 See **Letter 66**, nn. 9 and 11 above.
5 This is a valuable account of the short-lived Egyptian Society; see *Surtees* I, 326 for a letter by Stukeley about this society.
6 Gaius Mæcenas was a wealthy Roman patron of the Emperor Augustus and the poet Horace. The *Epode* IX by Horace, quoted in **Letter 66**, was devoted to Mæcenas, who became a well-known symbol of cultivated and extremely generous literary and personal patronage; he is therefore linked by Stukeley to his patron the second Duke of Montagu, who had died in 1749.
7 Stukeley rented a house in Gloucester Street, London, in the early 1740s while he lived at Stamford; he stayed there while visiting London during the winter months of 1740–43. Mr Torkington of Stamford's ancestor was Dr William Fullwood of Huntingdon, who owned land in Great Stukeley, the ancestral home of Stukeley's family.
8 The traditions of Islamic history, particularly relating to the Prophet Muhammad, name Ishmael as the first ancestor of the Arab people. The Book of Genesis speaks of Ishmael as the son of Abraham and Hagar.
9 Tin mining began in Cornwall in the Bronze Age; the considered view of modern historians is that tin was exported across the Channel and then perhaps carried south to Mediterranean ports for further trans-shipment. Heracles or Hercules, the son of Zeus, was a Greek-Roman form of the god worshipped by the Phœnicians of Tyre as their protecting god. The association between the Tyrian merchants and the transport of tin ingots led to the widespread notion in the sixteenth and seventeenth centuries that Britain had been colonised from Phœnicia.
10 The founders of the Egyptian Society, who had all visited Egypt, were John Montagu, fourth Earl

of Sandwich (1718–92: see *ODNB*), an active traveller, politician and government minister, credited with the invention of the sandwich; the Revd Dr Richard Pococke (1704), Bishop of Ossory and a famed traveller, particularly in Egypt; Dr Charles Perry (d.1780; see **Letter 66** above) who dedicated his book of Egyptian travels to the Earl of Sandwich; Capt. Frederick Norden (1708–42: see *ODNB*), a Danish naval officer who travelled in Egypt in 1738–39, making outstanding plans and drawings, published by the RS in 1757. He served in the English navy and was elected FRS and FSA. A footnote to the account of Stukeley's life in John Nichols' edition of *Anecdotes of William Bowyer* states: 'Of this Society ... the following short history by Dr Stukeley is preserved in the Dedication to his Carausius, p.vi, "dec.11 1741, an Egyptian Society was begun, under the presidentship of Lord Sandwich. The purpose of it was to enquire into Egyptian Antiquities; Lord Sandwich was met by Dr Pococke, Dr Perry, Capt. Norden the Swedish gentleman, all having been in Egypt: they nominated Mr Martin Folkes, Mr Charles Stanhope, Dr Stukeley, Dr Milles, Mr Dampier, Mr Mitchell associated, and with them founders of the society, The Dukes of Montagu and Richmond, Lord Stanhope, Mr Dayrolles, and some others, were nominated candidates. A sistrum was laid before the president as the insigne of office. At one of these meetings, Jan. 22, 1742, the Duke of Montagu was pleased to ask me the purport of that celebrated instrument. I spoke of it to the satisfaction of those present, but particularly of the Duke, and he requested me afterwards to give it him in writing."' See also *Reliquiæ Galeanæ*, 102–316 where it appears that the meetings were held at the Lebeck's Head in Chandos Street.

11 The associate members, who were interested in Egyptian antiquities but had not visited Egypt, were, in addition to Stukeley: Martin Folkes; Revd Jeremiah Milles FRS and FSA (1714–84: see *ODNB*), a cousin of Richard Pococke and a great traveller, and eventually President of the AS; Charles Stanhope (1673– 1760), politician and FRS; Thomas Dampier (d.1777), Dean of Durham; probably Sir Andrew Mitchell (1708–71: see *ODNB*), traveller and politician; the second Duke of Montagu (see *ODNB*) who, as Stukeley explains, became his patron as a result of meeting him at this society; and Charles Lennox, second Duke of Richmond (1701–50), FRS and a founding supporter of the Foundling Hospital in Great Ormond Street, close to Stukeley's London house.

12 See **Letter 66**, n.10, above.

13 'Keep far away, you uninitiated ones'; Stukeley refers to Virgil's *Æneid* VI, line 258, 'procul o procul este profani', spoken by the Cumæan Sibyl before uttering a sacred prophecy.

14 Stukeley uses 'literature' in the early eighteenth-century sense of 'learning'. He was not the Secretary of the Egyptian Society; 'The Minute Book of the Egyptian Society', 1741–43, was kept by the Revd Jeremiah Milles and then by the Revd Richard Pococke and is in the British Library, Add. MS 52362.

15 Alexander Gordon; see **Letter 66**, n.12, above.

16 Johnson adds a note for his own reference, about the origins and meaning of the word 'camisa' used by Stukeley for the Egyptian men's costume and related to 'chemise'. Francis Gouldman (1607–88/9: see *ODNB*) published works on bilingual lexicography, particularly *A Copious Dictionary in Three Parts*, and helped to edit *Critici Sacri* (1660), a nine-volume collection of essays on biblical interpretation. Stukeley refers to a shirt-like garment. Johnson traces the etymology back to a word for a low bed, so implying a garment like a nightshirt. His final phrase defines it as a 'men's tunic and women's undergarment'.

[86. Maurice Johnson to William Stukeley, Spalding, 21 June 1750
This letter is not part of Stukeley's collection in his letter-book in the Bodleian Library but is transcribed and published in John Nichols, *Bibliotheca Topographica Britannica*. We have reproduced it as **Letter 85** in the Additional Letters section below.]

68. William Stukeley to Maurice Johnson, London, 13 September 1750[1]
SGS/T1

[In Johnson's hand:] Letter from the Rev[d] Dr Stukeley to the Pr.[2] concerning Carausius with a Drawing of the reverse of a curious Denarius of that Brave Emperor. Quamvis non dubito quin Carausius Uxorem Augustam & Imperatricem atque Etiam ex eâ Liberum habuerat. Hanc fuisse nisi sub Imagine & Specie Deæ Orientis, seu Auroræ, inde forsan ORIVNA dicta valde dubitandum est[3]

[*At the head of the letter is a drawing by Stukeley of both sides of a Roman coin, discussed in detail in this letter.*]

[In Stukeley's hand] A silver coyn IMP CARAVSIVS PF AUG <u>imperatoris caput laureatum.</u>[4] The reverse as above. This coyn, was offered to Dr Carausius (als. Kennedy)[5] for 3 guineas. he shuffling about it, as usual with him, Dr Mead bought it for 10 guineas: & without showing it to us, or having a drawing taken of it; gave it to the french King. for which excess of vanity, I have often accused him of the crime of <u>læsæ-majestatis Brittanniæ</u>.[6]

with a good deal of trouble, I came at a sorry drawing of the coyn: from whence I took the above: & could not help giving you the pleasure of it. Du Bose the french king's librarian has sent Kennedy all Genebriers[7] prints of the life of Carausius, which he bought. I wish Kennedy was equal to the work.[8] He has the greatest collection of his coyns anywhere. [p.2] I gave him 14 of his very best. but he has not even the gratitude to own it. our antiquarians seem mightily disconcerted in the loss of the Duke of Richmond. I have now lost 3 great friends out of white hall in 13 months space. on thursday next I preach before coll. Med.[9] at Bow church. Dr Ayscough one of Dr Radcliffes itinerants[10] has long been in Greece. he was 2 months in Athens. where are more noble antiquitys than at Rome: & nigh as many. he has brought home a considerable number of bass relievo's, busts, coyns, inscriptions & MSS.

3 Sept. last dy'd my schoolfellow & our worthy countryman Ambrose Pimlow,[11] in norf[ol]k. the last of my schoolfellows. I divert my self now & then with making notes on Ric[ard]us de Cirencester monachus Westmonasteriensis,[12] I find the MS is an extraordinary curiosity. I design when I print it, to take subscriptions without payment, till delivered. for I am determin'd to have nothing to do with booksellers. but this may be some years first. the world is run mad after pleasure, more than learning. a friend of mine was lately translating Venuti's account of Heraclium.[13] but the bookseller, according to custom, used him ill. then they were forced to get a sorry hack to do it. Your Lord Gideon the ruler[14] has a great taste for pictures, & buys many. our bridg[15] is nigh finished, according to my design. [p.3] I hope you have got my book on earthquakes, which I left for you. we hear they have had a shock at Grantham & at Stamford.[16] the booksellers now being deserted by all writers, plague the world with magazines upon magazines: every one possessing himself of one, stolen out of every book, & from one another. I am heartily Your most affectionate servant,
W. Stukeley
s. Geo. qu. Squ. 13 sep. 1750

To
> Maurice Johnson Esqr
> Spalding
> Lincolnshire

1   This letter and the two following from Stukeley are bound in Johnson's MS volume of 'Tracts', kept in the SGS's archive. This volume contains, among other papers, Johnson's dissertation on the coinage of Carausius and Allectus, together with letters on this and other aspects of Roman coinage from Stukeley, Beaupré Bell, Dr Patrick Kennedy and Roger Gale. Stukeley's letters are significant in illustrating Stukeley's determination to write on the history of the Emperor Carausius (d.293), Emperor in Britain and Gaul from 283 to 293; Johnson and Stukeley thought, incorrectly, that Carausius was a native Briton. For a modern discussion of this, see P. J. Casey, *Carausius and Allectus* (1994).

2   The President of the SGS, i.e. Maurice Johnson. Johnson made a number of interlinear and marginal notes on this letter, probably to draw attention to sections intended to be read and discussed at SGS meetings.

3   'Although I do not doubt that Carausius had a wife as his consort and Empress and that he even had children by her; this [i.e. the image on the coin] was only the image and sign of the Goddess of the East, or the Dawn; thence perhaps it is very doubtful that she was called ORIVNA'. Johnson is here expressing his doubts about Stukeley's identification of the female figure on this damaged coin of Carausius as the Emperor's wife 'Oriuna'.

4   P. J. Casey located 240 coins with this inscription struck at Rouen around AD 286 (Casey, 107). As Stukeley notes, they show the head of the Emperor crowned with a laurel wreath.

5   Dr Patrick Kennedy (d.1760: see *ODNB*), a numismatist who worked on the coinage of Carausius (hence Stukeley's nickname for him) and sold this coin to Dr Mead. The coin had a slight nick in it, thus damaging part of the inscription. Today the inscription is taken as the customary 'Fortuna' but both Kennedy and Stukeley read it as 'Oriuna', taking this to be the name of the female figure shown on the coin. Stukeley decided that she must be the wife of Carausius. Kennedy wrote two studies, *A Dissertation upon Oriuna* (1751) and *Further Observations upon Carausius* (1756), which the author of his *ODNB* entry suggests 'are still of interest'. Johnson did not accept this, preferring to read the damaged inscription as 'Oriens'; an engraving of the coin is reproduced here as Illustration 21.

6   'Treason against the British king'. There is a note in Johnson's hand: 'Dr Kennedy about giving an History of Carausius, chiefly from Coines'.

7   Claude Genebrier, *Histoire de Carausius Empereur de la Grande Bretagne...prouvé par les Medailles* (Paris, 1740). Stukeley probably copied some of Genebrier's plates for his own *Medallic History of Marcus Aurelius Valerius Carausius Emperor in Britain* (2 vols, 1757–59).

8   This sentence was underlined in red by Johnson, who added a note, 'see his letter to me. MJ'. Johnson presumably shared Stukeley's doubts about Kennedy's abilities. Kennedy's letter and a draft of Johnson's reply are summarised in *Correspondence*, 92–3.

9   The Royal College of Physicians.

10   Dr John Radcliffe (1650–1714: see *ODNB*), physician and philanthropist. He used his considerable wealth to help establish the Radcliffe Infirmary and Radcliffe Observatory in Oxford, and also two travelling medical fellowships for students of University College, Oxford. Dr Ayscough was one of these fellows. There is a note in Johnson's hand: 'Dr Aysough's [*sic*] arguments in Greece'.

11   Revd Ambrose Pimlow (*c*.1687–1750), son of Ambrose Pimlow, Vicar of Holbeach, and one of Stukeley's oldest friends. He attended Holbeach Grammar School and Cambridge (Queens' College) at the same time as his friend Stukeley. He was ordained priest in 1708, becoming Vicar of Castle Acre (1710–50), and Rector of Great Dunham (1722–50), both in Norfolk. Stukeley had regular meetings with Pimlow and another old Cambridge friend, George Burton.

12   See **Letter 57**, n.1, above. There is a note in Johnson's hand: 'the valuable MS of Richd of Westmr'.

13   Cavaliere Marchese Don Marcello de Venuti's *Descrizione delle prime scoperte dell'antica citta d'Ercolano* (1750) was translated in 1750 and printed by George Woodall. There is a note in Johnson's hand: 'Venuti's account of Heraclium'.

14   See **Letter 59**, n.16, above.

15   Stukeley was involved in some aspects of the design and building of the new Westminster Bridge in London.

16 Extensive earthquakes were recorded across the east of England in August and September 1750, including one in Spalding on 23 August (see SGS, MB5, fol.63r). Stukeley's pamphlet *The Philosophy of Earthquakes, Natural and Religious* was printed in 1750.

69. Maurice Johnson to William Stukeley, Spalding, 22 September 1750
Bodleian, MS Eng. misc. c.113, fols 365r–366v

Spalding 22^d Septr 1750

Your description Dear Dr. with your drawing[1] of Carausii denarius, on reverse oriuna Aug? (which seems something like his Oriens Aug.) of 13th Inst. I was favoured with timely, and to'ther day at our first Meeting after I received It pleasurd Our Company by communicating so great a Curiosity to them, thô I doubt not of that Brave Emperors having a Wife & Child, having myself no fewer than Two small brass or quarter asses[2] I take to be of his Son Carausius Cæsar, on reverse Princeps Iuventutis – and as I allways thought the female head on Sir R[ichard] Ellis's sometimes my Bijugate of Carausius[3] was that of his wife I know not but that Ladies name might be Oriuna, & think this with the Pearle Diadem and necklace (an Ornament never seen by me on a Male Image) not unlike that in features. However I am greatly obliged to You for the Sketch of It, which has enriched my Adversaria Decennii Impp. Carausii & Allecti.[4]

Young Mr Wm Dodd[5] Fellow of Emanuel, Son of the Minister of Bourne who is giving us an Elegant english translation of Callimachus, has obteind the favour of Dr Ayscough for Mr Young (als Parson Adams as Fielding calls him)[6] to collate a very fine MS by him brought from the Levant as he told Us last tuesday when here to see a drawing of a Busto of that Poet by B.Bell dedicated & presented to my late Dear Brother, & Lascharis first Greek Ed[ition] at Florence by Aldus, my friend John Hardy gave me for a keep sake with a Limning therein done therefrom by my son the Captain.[7] Couz. B.Bell was giving us an Edition with Latin Translation and Comment of his own on that Poet whom he greatly admired; and by my information thereof from our Minutes of SGS enterd many Yeares agoe from Mr Bells own information. Mr Dodd has employd a friend to Apply to Dr Mason Woodward Professor & to the Librarian of that Coll[ege] for the use of those papers, Which should be (as bequeathed) there whence we find it impracticable to Obtein the loan of his Tabulæ Augustæ (thô corrected here by Us) & the plates to publish for his honour & the subscribers' benefit.

[p.2] Wee had read at our said last Thursdays Meeting transcribed & communicated by Mr John Newstead from the Maker Mr Tho. Hawkes of Norwich a Tinman painter Astronomer Mathem[atician] Mechanic & Land surveyor there a description of an Orrery placed within a Celestial Sphære, 25 Inches in Diametre, a most curious Machine & elegantly decorated placed on a Carved Mahogeny frame 30 inches high. Whereto from Ingulphus Bishop Fells Edition fo:98[8] I added his of the Pinax presented to Lewis IV Outremarin of France to Abbot Turketul when on an Embassy to him at Paris about 947. Melted & Consumed in the fire of their Library of Croyland wherein they lost 300 Original, & about 400 other Books. this present is mentioned in Sir Harry Savills Ed. folio 499.32.[9] That Sphære there called Pinax Pulcherrima, and said to be a Nader not parallelled throughout all England was very sumptuous being adorned properly with all the

Metals Suitable to the concieved Natures of the planetts – the Colures & Signes of the Zodiac expressed by enamelled figures allso according to their Names and decorated with multiplicity of Gemms or Pretious Stones, that sad Accident of the Fire wherein these Treasures were destroyed and lost happend about the yeare 1091.

From shelf to shelf when flames did greedy Roll
And lick up all the Physic of the Soul.[10]

Wee've got to your 21 No. of MS Memoires of the Royal Society, for which my Good Friend Wee've been vastly obliged to You. & can't but express our Wishes of the Sequell, and in Your own good time those of the Egyptian Society – Cujus Pars Magna fuisti – for You see Sir Est Animus Ulubris – modo Mens non deficit.[11] Wee hold up, and with Your good help chiefly, & some Other Correspondents flourish with Equal or rather higher Spirits than wee set out full fourty Yeares agone.[12]

[p.3] About the time I expected you here (as You gave me the pleasure to hope) I had the satisfaction of Your Nephew from Grantham,[13] who gave Us an agreeable Account of many things He had observed in the Expedition to the East Indies whither I'm in hopes of getting my Youngest & only Son now on my hands[14] to put out in the world. if You've Acquaintance with any Director of that Company begg You'll Speak a good word on his behalf his Name is Henry Eustace Johnson age 17. Writes finely & readily, Casts Accounts accurately and wishes to be taken into their Service & sent abroad by their Next ships which go out about Xmas for India, as a Writer, which Mr Anthony Birks[15] of Gosberton a famed M[aste]r has for near two yeares been qualifying him for, or any Busyness requiring abilitys in Penmanship and Arithmetick beside some knowledge of History Chronology Geography Geometry Astronomy & Surveying, Mensuration, & Calculations of all Weights Measures & Foreigne Coine compard with our Sterling.

The late Earthquake[16] was sencibly felt here at Spalding throughout all the Vintings of the Parish & for many Miles chiefly North & South in direction upon Thursday the Twenty third day of August 1750 at about seven o'Clock in the Morning: Wee had for a fourteenight before It very mild & calm weather. And a Deep reed Aurora Vertical covering the Cope of heaven one Evening which looked very terrible & was Succeeded on the 12th about 10 o Clock in the Morning by a Violent Hurrican & storm of wind which blew me down 2 vast tall old Ash Trees which grew between my house & the Church, & several Large Branches, which It tore off from my Wallnutt Trees but lasted but a little while. Several other Timber Trees that grew in the Wad [sic] of It suffered & some were blown down. Mr Da Costa (to whom when you see him our services) had the Account of It as then given us. from Dear Dr. with all our Compliments to your Lady and family

Your much obliged & most affectionate friend & servant

M Johnson

PS. On Thursday next against the Orgainists grand Concert at Boston[17] He with Mr Muskutt school M[aste]r there who assists him on the Tenor, came hither to our Yesterdays Concert the Members whereof furnished them Out of their Collection with many Volumes of written Concertos of all the best hands in parts to the number of about 60 Volumes and some of Our performing Members have been engaged to go over them to lend them their hands, and they've occasionaly done at the Celebrations of the Anniversary of the Institution of our Society which for their having the Use of our Rooms Every fryday thro the yeare The Gentlemen of the Concert are by antient Pact & Convention if required obliged so to Celebrate for Entertainment of the Ladies & our foreigne[18] Members.

To
    the Reverend
    Dr Stukeley at St George's
    Queen Square
        Ormondstreet
        London.

[1] This drawing (see **Letter 68** above) was numbered No.47 in Stukeley's Catalogue and listed in Stukeley's *Carausius* II, 187 (shown on plate 23 no. 4).

[2] An 'as' was a bronze and later copper coin of the Roman Republic and Empire. The latest numismatic scholarship records no son of Carausius's called Carausius Cæsar. The British Museum's Portable Antiquities Scheme lists seven 'asses' or Roman copper alloy coins of Carausius, all from the East Midlands.

[3] This coin is drawn and described in detail in a letter from Beaupré Bell to Johnson, 9 February 1734 (see *Correspondence*, letter 209). It was by then the property of Sir Richard Ellys. By a 'bijugate' coin, Johnson meant one showing two heads; P. J. Casey describes such a coin as showing 'conjoined busts of emperor and Sol' (*Carausius*, 95).

[4] 'Adversaria' is a collection of notes or a commonplace book. This MS work by Johnson contained his information about the coins of the two Roman emperors Carausius and Allectus; he was urged to publish his work but never got it into printable form. See Adam Daubney, 'Maurice Johnson: An Eighteenth-Century Numismatist', *British Numismatic Journal* 82 (2012), 146–63.

[5] This was the well-known Revd William Dodd (1729–77: see *ODNB*); see Appendix 3. He had no connection with Emmanuel College, Cambridge, having attended Clare College from 1746 to 1749. His book *The Hymns of Callimachus*, a Greek writer (*c.*310–240 BC) was published in 1755.

[6] Henry Fielding, *The History of the Adventures of Joseph Andrews and of his Friend Mr Abraham Adams* (1742). Parson Adams is one of the novel's heroes. It was noted at the time that his character was derived from that of the Revd William Young of Gillingham, Dorset: see M. C. Batteston, *Henry Fielding: A Life* (1993) and F. Ribble, 'Fielding and William Young', *Studies in Philology* 98(4) (Autumn 2001). Later Young became a freelance author, working on classical MSS such as those brought back from his travels by Dr Ayscough.

[7] Dodd had visited Johnson on Tuesday 18 September 1750 to see a drawing of Callimachus by Beaupré Bell, given by Bell to Johnson's brother John, and an edition of Callimachus's poems by the Greek grammarian Lascharis who had worked in Constantinople in the early sixteenth century. The best early Greek edition, perhaps by Lascharis, of these poems was published in Florence by the Aldine Press in 1513. Bell had also been working on these poems and had made the drawing of a bust of the poet, which Dodd then used for the title page of his 1755 edition. Bell's papers are held today by Trinity College, Cambridge; Johnson had hoped to organise their publication but a study of them reveals that they are not ready for publication.

[8] William Fulman and Thomas Gale (eds), *Rerum Anglicarum Scriptores Veteres* (1684) contained John Fell's edition of Ingulphus's *Croylandensis Historia*. A pinax is a tablet or plate bearing a painting or engraving.

[9] Henry Savile (ed.), *Descriptio compilata per dom. Ingulphum Abbatem Monasterii Croiland, Natione Anglicum, quondam, Monachum Fontanissensem* (1596). By 'Nader', Johnson perhaps means 'nadir', the bottom point on a celestial sphere.

[10] 'From shelves to shelves see greedy Vulcan roll,
And lick up all this physic of the soul'   Alexander Pope, *The Dunciad* III, 73–4

[11] 'Of which you were a great part'; the minute book of the Egyptian Society, of which Stukeley was not the author, is in the British Library. The other Latin phrase, a quotation from Horace's *Epistles* implying that happiness can be gained anywhere if the spirit is not lacking, was already quoted by Johnson in his letter to Stukeley on 13 July 1739 (see **Letter 33**, n.3, above).

12 The SGS had originally met as an informal journal-reading group of Spalding gentlemen in 1710.
13 The son of Stukeley's brother Adlard, apothecary of Grantham, was also called William.
14 Henry Eustace Johnson.
15 Anthony Birks, SGS member 1753, surveyor, accountant and Master of Gosberton School, just north of Spalding. Birks was the author of *Arithmetical Collections and Improvements Being a Complete System of Practical Arithmetic* (1766), 2nd edn 1774.
16 The earthquake of August 1750 was approximately 4.7 on the Richter scale. It is recorded in SGS, MB5, fol.63r (entry for 23 August 1750). Spalding was divided into areas known as 'vintings', literally the twentieth part of a parish.
17 The Boston organist was Mr Allen. The SGS had held annual anniversary concerts from 1733 to 1746 and the programme was recorded in the minute book. On 2 August 1750 a letter was read to the SGS meeting from Dr Heighington (see Appendix 3), who had often directed the concerts: 'a Lr to the Ps from Dr Heighington a Member Orgainist at Leicester offering to assist our Gents of the Concert for celebrating our Anniversary this month as usual, but the Soc. excus'd that' (MB5, fol.61r). The concerts had officially ended in 1747 'as the performers were reduced to very few' (MB4, fol.116r).
18 i.e. non-local.

70. Maurice Johnson to William Stukeley, Spalding, 13 October 1750
Bodleian, MS Eng. misc. c.113, fols 367r–368v

Spalding 13 Octr 1750

Dear Dr

Since I last did my Self the pleasure of writeing You, which was on the 22nd of last Month and therein gave you some Account of an Earthquake very sencibly felt here for many Miles chiefly in a Direction from South to North on the 23^d of August Last. Wee've again been terrifyd on Sunday the last day of last Month Septr with another Earthquake^1 as Sencibly felt here as the former & in the like direction, a Tenant of mine in Moulton the Tuesday after told me he was sitting in his house and reading to his Family & was So violently Shook in his Chair he thought he should have [*sic*] thrown out of It and his Wife was herself so shaken as to be much affrighted thereby. on relating this to our Company at our last Meeting, with a Letter from my son Henry Eustace from Gosberton (which lyes NW, as Moulton Chapell gate where the other man John Griffin lives lyes SE from Us) several of the Gentlemen present declared they felt and Observed the Shake and Tremor, about the time mentiond in that Letter, which as It mentions Other remarkable appearances I take the Liberty to transcribe^2 – 'Wee had a very sensible shock of an Earthquake on Sunday about half an hour after 12, which was so great as to crack a strong house, the People thought the House would fall, I was reading at that time, heard a Noise like Thunder at a distance, I thought it was a Coach going by Got up to look through the Window, and before I was well up, I was in the Chair again, which Surprizd Me: the House shook with a sort of Tremor very odly – A Farmer of credit in Holbeach reports he saw about 3 o'clock [p.2] on Monday Morning a very strange Light N.W. forming a Triangle 2 of the Angles or Points of a red Colour, the third like those in the Rainbow. And the Night after being Tuesday about 8 o'Clock Mr Birks^3 and I observd a most beautyful Phænomenon in the Air, which moved as it were near Us, tending towards the same quarter (i.e.) N.W.'

As these Notices may prove acceptable to You Dear Sir and Such of Our friends as You may think them worthy of being communicated to, and I can assure you You needn't doubt of their Veracity I send them you, who have so considerd, and to me illustrated these wonders of the Allmighty Power, whos Mercies Wee hence ought too to esteem as infinite.

Wee were greatly entertaind with an elegant Poem on the Air by Mr Vivian of Oxford thence sent my Son by Couz. Geo. Johnson[4] of Brazen Nose who is himself too a good Latin Poet, and has favourd us (when at Durham School) with Several of his Performances, at mine and his Uncle Dr Green's requests. Who shewd us that Evening the Orbis Piscis aculatus, sive Histrix Marinus[5] he lately received a Present from Jamaica. which he says Piso mentions as taken also in the Seas on the Coast of Brasil. It seems not to have any Gills, but one Continued Tooth & that alike in both Jaws as our Dr Lister observs in Ray's Syllogi. Neither has It any Scales, but an hard Skin at equal distances from head to tail armed with triangular Prickly Points, very like the End of the leaves of the common Aloe.

[p.3] The Dr shewd us a Pretty effect of an Experiment he had made of taking of both Sides of an elegant Butterflies Wings on Paper gummd according to Mr Edwards's directions published lately in the Gentleman's Magazine[6] an Expeditious Method of taking and perhaps of Securing and preserving them, thô he little needs it, for no body I know draws more accurately nor limnes more like the life. an Advantage he gives Us in our Minute Book when the Object wee desire to have perpetuated is very Curious and uncommon.

In the Inscription sayd to be taken out of Herculan[eum] on a Pedestal to an Equestrian Statue of M. Nonius Balbus stiled PR. PROCOS. can It be otherwise read than Prætor or Prætorius Proconsul – were not the Offices Compatible – or might it not signify he was sometime a Prætor, then Procos. or Governour of Campania?[7] Is Father Gori's account of the valuable Treasures in the King of Sicilies Palaces of Portici & at Naples furnished from that Subterranean City yet published and come to your hands, how does he read it? I think I've seen Similar Instances in the Titles of Great Roman Govern[ors] in their Provincial Inscriptions to their Honour in Greevius Gruter and Reinesius.[8] but wee want the 2 former to Consul on such Occasions.

Our Drought and consequently want of fresh water continues still, but having scourd out my Canal and deepend It at foot I came to a White quick Sand which has afforded me & many of my Neighbours excellent soft, sweet, clear & well tasted Water both for washing & Brewing and all sorts of Household Uses, a great Blessing.

[p.4] You see Sir I Can't part with you so long as my paper lasts, thô I've now little more to detein You than to tell you They've lately had a Grand Concert at Boston to the Orgainist Mr Allens benefit of 40 Guineas whereat Many Gent[lemen] some of our Concert were performers.[9] Wee hope You, your Lady & Daughters are well all whom our Compliments, who are so, Attend. Last Week his Grace the Duke of Bedford with the Earles of Sandwich & Gower[10] & several Gentlemen were at Croyland and viewed the sumptuous Remaines of that Abbey. & having surveyd some works doing by the Corpor[ation] of that Levell towards repairing the old South Eau & Shire dreyn had a Meeting as I'm informd at Wisbeach thereon.

I am Dear Dr your most affectionate & obedient Servant M. Johnson

To the Rever^d Dr Stukeley
Rector of St Georges

Queen Square
By Ormondstreet
London

1   The earthquake of 30 September is recorded as having been approximately 4.1 on the Richter scale (British Geological Survey).
2   The full text of Henry Eustace Johnson's letter, addressed to his mother, with further details annotated by Maurice Johnson, is transcribed in *Correspondence*, 188–9.
3   See **Letter 69**, n.16, above.
4   Mr William Vivian, Fellow of Corpus Christi College, Oxford, is recorded as voting in Oxford in the General Election of 31 January 1750. For George Johnson, see Appendix 3.
5   This fish was described in seventeenth- and eighteenth-century literature as a large fish with a long nose; it is perhaps of the sturgeon family. For an account of the sturgeon, see John Ray, *Synopsis Methodica Avium et Piscium* (1713), 112.
6   *Gentleman's Magazine* (September 1750), 400.
7   This is read today as 'prætor and proconsul'; M. Nonius Balbus was prætor and proconsul of Crete and Cyrene and restored buildings in early first-century AD Pompeii. The expanded Latin text is 'prætori proconsuli': see A. E. Gordon, *Illustrated Introduction to Latin Epigraphy* (1983).
8   Antonio Francesco Gori (1691–1757), a founder member of the Florence 'Societa Columbaria', the predecessor of the Accademia Toscana, published *Notizie del memorabile scoprimento dell'antica città Ercolano ... Aggiunto la Statua ... di M. Nonio Balbo* (1748); the book mentioned by Johnson does not seem to have been published. Johannes Grevius (1632–1703), professor at the University of Utrecht, published *Thesaurus Antiquitatum Romanorum* (12 vols, 1694–99). Jan Gruter (1560–1627), a Dutch antiquarian, published *Inscriptiones antiquæ totius orbis Romanæ* (2 vols, 1603). Thomas Reinesius (1587–1667), a German scholar, extended Gruter's work with *Syntagma inscriptionum antiquarum cum primis Romæ veteris, quarum omissa est recensio in vasto Jani Gruteri opera* (1682).
9   See **Letter 69** above.
10 John Russell, fourth Duke of Bedford (1710–61), Whig politician and Fenland landowner; John Montagu, Earl of Sandwich (see **Letter 66**, n.11, and **Letter 67**, n.10, above); John Leveson-Gower, Earl Gower (1694–1754), Tory politician. The Bedford Level Corporation was responsible for extensive Fenland drainage in north Cambridgeshire.

71. William Stukeley to Maurice Johnson, London, 13 April 1751
SGS/Stukeley/27

[Annotated by Johnson:] Letter from the Rev^d Dr Stukeley recommending to SGS Dr Hill's Literary Gazett,¹ to be taken in.

My dear friend,
   On Munday afternoons, we generally rendezvous at my neighbor Dr Hills, where Dr Parsons² & some more of the literati meet. last munday I had the pleasure to hear of your health, in a letter from you, which he read. but I was not reconcil'd to your notion of leaving off going abroad.³ I hope we shall see you in town, once more, at least.

[*Sketch by Johnson of a pointing hand, to emphasise this section of the letter.*]

   Dr Hill is a man of fine parts. he now writes the daily paper, calld the literary gazette, where is some amusing subject, every day presented to the public. I help him out now & then, with a discourse. particularly I gave those of the nature & purpose of mankind: & shall continue it. inspector no.26.⁴

I advise you to order your man Norris[5] to send them down regularly to you. they would be a great & constant entertainment to the Society. for it will be continued with spirit.

I gave to Norris, long ago, my second edition on earthquakes, with a second part added, on your Lincolnshire earthquakes; which I suppose, you have received.

the death of the Prince of Wales[6] has chagrin'd the virtuoso part of us very much; [p.2] who had conceiv'd great hopes of the revival of arts under his administration. his highness had a good taste for painting & many other matters of curiosity.

the antiquarys are in high spirits, in hope of obtaining a charter.[7] I never go to their meetings. tis absurd to run from Royal Society to a new kind of entertainment: whereby both are jumbled out of our mind.

I enjoy as much retirement here, as in the country: frequent no Courts, levys, nor coffee houses. but having now got a library, by a purchase I made of an adjoyning room, am busy in fitting it up. & at the same time I got a stable, & shall have a horse, which will, I hope enable me, to make you a transient visit this summer.

a very good piece is lately come out by Peters:[8] a critical dissertation on Job: proving it to be an antient author: & solidly overthrowing my friend Warburtons notions, about the Jews not having a proper notion of a future state.

about 30 noblemen & people of rank have dyed in little more than the last year. the Prince, the Duke of Montague, Richmond, Lord Carpenter, [p.3] Lord Pembroke, Dartmouth, Torrington, Coventry, Rockingham, Ganesborough, Weymouth, Mansel, Orford, Stafford, Crawford, Tylney, Donerail, Colerain, Lonsdale, Cobham, Leigh, Bristol, Harborough, Rolle. to these may well be added Sir Sam. Pennant lord mayor, baron Clark, judg Abney &c.[9]

most of these were contemners of sacred things. few, very few deserving praise, or a longer date.

it seems to me, that the great ones have brought up this absolute neglect of religion: which must needs begin in our robberys, maiming, murdering, forgery, perjury &c. & must end in ruin.

Dr Hill has been plaguing our Royal Society.[10] I am not unmindful of you, thô I have lost my amanuensis: & will take care that you shall have another volume, of minutes.

very little of learning goes forward. the booksellers have put a perpetual damp upon it, by their roguery to us poor authors. & nothing now goes down but magazines without end, or meaning.

I have pleasure in congratulating your Society, in having you President, the father and nourisher of it.[11] with my service to all your body, I am
                Your faithful humble servant
                    Wm Stukeley
Lond. ap. 13 1751

---

[1] John Hill edited and was the main author of the daily journal *The Inspector* from 1751 to 1753, which appeared in the *London Advertiser and Literary Gazette*. Johnson would appreciate this news of a new journal for the SGS to read and discuss, as it helped to solve the problem of finding suitable material for its weekly meetings; it had begun by reading the *Tatler* and *Spectator* and subscribed to Dr Samuel Johnson's *The Rambler*.

[2] For Dr Parsons, see **Letter 65**, n.3, above.

3   Stukeley is concerned that Johnson has given up travelling from Spalding on grounds of ill health and age, particularly as Stukeley is the same age. On moving to London, Stukeley thought he had the prospect of meeting Johnson who would come to London for the legal term, but Walter Johnson was now taking his father's place.
4   Stukeley contributed to Hill's *Inspector* from time to time. It began publication in March 1751 and the *Inspector* no. 26 discussed a ramble around Primrose Hill, concentrating on observations of plants, animals, bees and birds.
5   Johnson's bookbinder; see **Letter 60**, n.4, above.
6   Frederick, Prince of Wales (1707–51) died on 20 March 1751; he was heir to the throne, leaving a son who became George III in 1760.
7   The Society of Antiquaries received its Royal Charter on 2 November 1751. They met on Thursdays, as did the Royal Society; at this time Stukeley preferred the Royal Society.
8   Charles Peter (1690–1774: see *ODNB*) wrote *A Critical Dissertation on the Book of Job* (1750). It contained critical comments on William Warburton's account of the Jewish views on a future state in his *Divine Legation of Moses* (1738–41).
9   See G. E. Cokayne, *Complete Peerage*, new edn revised and much enlarged by V. Gibbs and others (13 vols in 14, London, 1910–98). The Earl of Gainsborough was Baptist Noel, fourth Earl (1708–51). The Duke of Montagu was Stukeley's patron; for Lord Sandwich, see **Letters 66** and **67** above.
10 John Hill's complex relationship with the RS is discussed in detail in George Rousseau's rather negative study *The Notorious Sir John Hill* (2012).
11 Maurice Johnson was the moving spirit behind the foundation of the SGS; he was its Secretary from 1712 to 1748 and President from 1748 to his death in 1755; Dr John Green took over as Secretary in 1748.

72. Maurice Johnson to William Stukeley, Spalding, 15 April 1751
Bodleian, MS Eng. misc. c.113, fols 369r–370v

Spalding 15 April 1751

My good Friend

The Prospect you give me in your obligeing Letter this morning's very pleasing but I must insist on your being my Guest for what time you can spare me, and contriving that may be as long as you can. I congratulate you on your having accomodated your Self with a room for spending your best part of life in, as a Library is to any man of Learning, and send my Compliments to your Monday Companions.[1] Wee go on as well [*sic*] this place & times will permitt: have admitted several new Members lately Some Veterans in Re Literaria as Archdeacon Sharpe, surveyor General Ch. Frederick & Dr Tathwell, and Six or Seven Young Gentlemen in Mortalitatis Suppletionem[2] for that I may leave them whenever Providence pleases that shall be, fully Stocked. I've putt them in a Method, which if they pursue they may ever continue of bethinking of all their Acquaintance old and young, and making Annual Indraughts of such as have not been admitted, to supply their Losses, which they must in the Course of nature yearly sustein. And without applying for a Charter have found out a Method by Meanes of Two Subsisting Charters under their Great Seales of Queen Elizabeth and King Charles II of perpetuating, and Establishing this Institution, by Regulations of the Governours of our Free and Royal Grammar School here, and preserving the propertie & Use of Our publick Library and all thereto belonging from future Embezilment Or Dissipation: which pleases Me much.[3] Your Minutes whilest they lasted, being read at our Meetings as you kindly recommend, afforded our Company Much Improveing Entertainment: Wee've since then been obliged by a Member, with an Endeavour by way of Essay not attempted amongst all his Dissert[ations] by Spanh[eim] de Usu Nummi vet.[4] to prove the Truth of Christianity or prædictions about, & the Actual Coming of Christ our Saviour from profane Authors both Historical, & Poetical, Inscriptions Gemms & Coines, the same being so divided into several Sections, and so Communicated and read by one Section at one time of our Meeting:[5] I gave him a drawing done by my Daughter[6] from a Cast taken by B. Bell of a Gemm, very large, On the Destruction of Hierusalem & triumph Over Judæa, with an Illustration thereof – Shewing that the Jew standing by the Palm tree, Under which Judæa sits deploring, represents Simon Ben Giola the Jewish General, who was led in that Triumph, bound as there represented, Manibus post Terga revinctis, and after that Triumph was hanged in the Forum, as Josephus acquaints Us, who was an Eyewitness, or at lest there in Rome.[7] Spanheim gives a Medal or Coine – IVDAEA: CAPTA: of Titus,[8] with All the same Designe – to exemplify the Palma dactilifera under his Dissertation on Trees & Vegetables; but says nothing about the man so bound: who had he not been deserving of It, had not met with such a severe Sentence from so humane a Conqueror. Wee're aboundantly obliged to You Dear Dr for intending us more of your excellent observations, and I hope you're not unmindfull of the favour I requested of you of those of the Egyptian Society. I thank you Good Sir for intending me the Second Edition of your Philosophy of Earthquakes,[9] with a 2 pt added on those here, but I have not yet received such from my Bookbinder, thô I have other parcells, since the time you probably left it with him, so I suspect he may have mislayd, & overlookd It being not a bulky thing, the former publishd in 8° by Corbet 1750, with a sermon, I have, & am obliged to you for it. I shall propose to our Gentlemen the Ordering the Literary Gazett[10] being sent down for our meetings. But our best way will be for the Editor with an Order for our Knights of the Shire for franking them (as Gosling did by the Tatlers, Spectators, Lovers & Laymonks) to send them. [p.3] Wee have the Honour of Both those Senators being Members, & Mr Vyner enrich'd Our Library with Rays Synopsis 3 Volls folio, a noble & usefull benefaction.[11] You'd do us a fav^r if as You see either of those Gentlemen you'd [sic] one Cover to Me, so franked & his Order or Leave for their being so. Or that Such Editor might wait on him with Covers to be franked to Me for that purpose. Mr Heron was our constant Benefactor that way, when wee took in those papers beforementioned. Be pleasd Sir to order that this Literary Gazett may come henceforth duely so to me – & pray let all preceding be deliverd to Mr Christopher Norris[12] my Bookbinder in Chapter House Alley by St Pauls with orders to Send them me down, with your 2nd on Earthquakes, & what else he may have by him ready, by the first Carryer, that Wee may have the thing Compleat for on Your Recommendation, & as there Are works of Yours in it,[13] whether the Soc. chuse to take them in Or no, I will answer payment for them, & Mr Norris Shall duly defray the Price of the Papers, And with my service to Dr Hill, if any thing amongst our Papers may be of Service to Such, Or Any his undertakings, I will endeavour to render them So. As he & you, & Dr Parsons, whom you mention of your Mondays meeting are Members, You'd add to Obligations by induceing the rest to become So, you see how Sollicitous I am to encrease the Numbers, & consequently, I think, the Creditt of our Cell.

I [sic] long been very ill, occasioned by a Fever which settled upon my face and gums, & afflicted with violent pains in my Teeth confind me to the House and for tenn days to my Chamber, but thô much better, could not finish this Letter on Monday when I began it. Wee're told his Royal Highness the late Prince of Wales[14] was promoteing an Academy of Painting & Sculpture in London, whereto he had subscribed very liberaly, & which, 'tis feared, may not now be carryed on, at lest with that Vigour his Encouragement would have probably given It.

[p.4] I'm reading the 3rd Vol. of Dr Mackenzies Lives of Scots Authors.[15] He says the Rebels when Mary their Q[ueen] surrenderd herself to them led her in triumph through Edenburgh, & lodgd her at the Provosts, under a Guard, & Set up a Banner displayd Over against the Window having the Murder of her Husband King Henry depicted, & her son on his knees, with Judge & defend my Cause, O Lord: proceeding out of his Mouth as in our friend Vertues Historical Prints of those transactions. This Book was printed by Wilson at Edinburgh in 1722 & the 3 volls in Folio Given us by our Lord Patron the Duke of Buccleuch who (I'm sorry to see by the News Papers) is or has been dangerously sick of late, the passage above is in his Account of that Queen's Life and writings, but not noted by Mr Vertue in his printed Account given of those pictures,[16] But confirms Them. My Gardens delight me after so long a Confinement from them, &, by the Sweet Effect of this growing Weather are full of Bloom both of fruit & flowers, where I hope to take a pleasant Walk with you e'er long. But you must not come to fetch fire from

    your most affectionate friend M. Johnson

To the Reverend Dr Stukeley
at his house in Queen Square Ormond street
   London.

1 See **Letter 71** for an explanation of these comments.
2 See Appendix 3 for entries on these new members of the SGS. The Latin phrase means 'to fill the places of those who die'. Johnson aims to keep the Society going by recruiting young members.
3 This is a reference to the provisions eventually made in Johnson's will, originally drawn up by him on 16 December 1752. The Master of Spalding Grammar School will 'by an Instrument under his Hand and seal in Writing duly attested covenant Premise grant and agree to and with the said Governours and their Successors that he will conscientiously constantly and honestly take charge and care of the Museum Books Papers Suppellex literaria of and belonging to the Spalding Gentlemen's Society' (PRO, PROB 11/815/439 (Will of Maurice Johnson, 1755), fo.299v).
4 Ezechiel Spanheim (1629–1710), *Dissertationum de Praestantia et Usu Numismatum Antiquorum* (1664). 'He is still revered today as one of the fathers of modern numismatology. In addition to his important publications he is said to have founded the first numismatic society in London in 1710.' (See S. Pott, M. Mulsow and L. Danneberg (eds), *The Berlin Refuge 1680–1780: Learning and Science in European Context* (2003), 49.)
5 During February, March and April 1751 sections of 'The Truth of the Christian Religion', a MS dissertation by the Revd Benjamin Ray, were read to the SGS by the Secretary (MB5, fols 72r–77v).
6 Anne Alethea Johnson (b.1731), Johnson's youngest daughter, a talented artist several of whose drawings are in the minute books; she married Richard Wallin and went to Jamaica with him.
7 Simon bar Giora, a radical Jewish military leader, was defeated in AD 70 at the destruction of Jerusalem by the Romans and executed in Rome. The Latin phrase means 'with his hands bound behind his back'. Titus Flavius Josephus (AD 31–100) wrote an account of this in *The Jewish War*.
8 The emperors Vespasian and Titus had a range of coins struck to record their defeat of the Jews in AD 70, with the inscription 'Judea Captured'.
9 This is Stukeley's book *The Philosophy of Earthquakes, Natural and Religious, Or, An Inquiry into their Cause and their Purpose*, 2nd edn (1750).

¹⁰ See **Letter 71**.
¹¹ The two 'knights of the Shire' or MPs for Lincolnshire in 1751 were Thomas Whichcote (1770–76) and Robert Vyner (1685–1777), both SGS members; MPs had the privilege of 'franking' letters so that they would travel free. Vyner is recorded in the SGS's eighteenth-century library catalogue as presenting John Ray's *Historia Plantarum* to the Society in 1733. Henry Heron, SGS member in 1722, had been MP for Lincolnshire from 1722 to 1727.
¹² See **Letter 60**, n.4, above.
¹³ One of Stukeley's most significant contributions to John Hill's *Inspector* was an article in which he exposed the practice of adulterating bread-flour with alum.
¹⁴ Frederick, Prince of Wales, who had died on 20 March 1751, was a significant collector of paintings; George Vertue was his art adviser in his plans 'to support an academy for British painters' (see *ODNB*).
¹⁵ George Mackenzie MD, *The Lives and Characters of the most eminent Writers of the Scots Nation* (3 vols, 1708–22). It gives an account of the death of Henry Stewart, Lord Darnley, husband of Mary Queen of Scots and thus referred to by Johnson as 'King Henry' though he was simply her consort. It was presented to the SGS by their patron the Duke of Buccleuch (see Appendix 3) whose illness did prove serious; he died later in 1751.
¹⁶ George Vertue, *The Heads of the Kings of England proper for Rapin's history* (1736).

73. Maurice Johnson to William Stukeley, Spalding, 11 May 1751
Bodleian, MS Eng. misc. c.113, fols 371r–372v

Spalding 11º May 1751
Dear Dr
Yours by last post gave us double pleasure, accordingly having tother Night communicated Dr Hills generous Intentions in favour of our Institution¹ to our Company at their Meeting I by this post Send Sieur Norris my old & trusty Agent with Instructions & a Letter therein to the Dr, which He will wait on him & deliver (for I as yet know not his address) for all the Papers past that Wee may read them regularly a Principio,² as Wee did the Tatlers, Spectators, Lay Monks, & Lovers in their times, and the Dr's Orders for the delivery to him of the future to be by him sent down to me for same purpose as occasions serve. thanks to you Sir for Your good offices and ready advise to me of this Boon, for Your account of your having obteind so great a blessing as a convenient Library, & for still intending me the pleasure of your Company: but not for not engaging some Brother to officiate for You a While, that you needn't be so much in hast to return. I must submit to What your convenience will allow me, be thankfull, as I ought for the blessing of seing, as I hope, an old friend in good health, and endeavour to have in readyness something in my House and Gardens for your reception & Entertainment, & in my Stable for your New Nagg.³ The Coll^{ll}.⁴ talks to me in his Letters now & then of his Garden in Mortimer Street, abutting upon a Rideing house, as I think yours does on your Vestry, your quondam Bibliothec. Never was seen a fuller sweeter Bloom of all fruits, but Wee doubt few stand for fruit, and the Mornings are so frosty, the winds so severely cold that my Gardiner fears I shall not have more Winter fruit than last yeare, which was indeed but little: this spring I have suffered sadly in my Wall trees themselves, that my Walls look bare, which had several hopeful Peach & Nectarine Trees young & vigorous on them.
[p.2] Wee have had a Company of Strolling Players here this Month, Herbert M[aste]r,⁵ who're likely for ought I find to remain a Month at lest longer, enter-

taining the Town. They have No Harlequin, Singers, nor Dancers: So are more tolerable than meer Monkeys. Since my Lord G–'s death his first fiddle Blathwayt sometime Essex & Nivelons deputy is Sett up as a Dancing Master at Stamford[6] and Charles T. – [7]one of his Chaplains, & Violoncello's came to officiate as Coadjutor to his old superannuated Dad at Pinchbeck, which Living will be his on his Decease, he got one lately of my Lord in Rutlandshire of 80l. p.ann. which he getts officiated in by a Curate.

Mr Berridge has almost finished a fine Room for entertainment of Company to be furnished with a Suit of old Flemish Tapistry lately Bequeathed to him (with a good Estate in Terrâ firmâ) wove by Martin de Vos of Antwerp, the figures in full Size, the History of Moses the Jews Legisferor[8] from his Invention in the Rush Ark by the Daughter of the Egyptian King. These were made a Century since, but Captain Pilliod when there about 15 Yeares agone, see some such workes in hand by a descendant of that Artist. They were offerd me to purchase by this Gents Father, about 12 yeares since, but I could not well spare the Price the Lady expected for them, or should have thought them well worth purchaseing, for theyd have suited & furnished Two of my Bed Chambers very well; and much cheaper and genteeler than any wainscott. the Plagia on the Selvage is, as I remember, thus marked:

[Sketch by Johnson of a maker's mark.]

The Minute Account of It; Vol 2 of the Acts and Observations SGS fo:34b, 10th September 1730:
'The Secretary shewd the Company a Plagia Sett on the Selvage of a curious Sett of Tapistry Hangings representing the History of Moses in possession of the Revd Mr Beridge.'[9]

I'm pleasd with the Extract of the Monthly Reviewer for April 1751 of Mr Peters's Critical Dissertation on the Book of Job, a book I greatly admired, and (as to the Legislative part thereof) had the pleasure to be assistant to my Learned Friend the old Rector of Epworth,[10] therein in his Essays published in folio some yeares agone. [p.3] Were not the Places and People I prate to you thus about, known to you 'twould be triflieng to trouble you, Sir, with these notices, but as they are, there's some amusement in them, & Wee may be allowd such Chitt Chat inter Nos. I hoped e'er this to've received the favour of answers to Letters I sometime since wrote both to Dr Hill and Dr Parsons, but suppose they've been so engaged, they could not spare me so much time. I must when I've the pleasure Sir of seing you here Communicate to you my method for Perpetuating, and rendring my Institution of Our Gentlemens Society here very noble, and useful beyond what I myself could ever have Imagined or hoped, but not so proper to committ to Paper yet. For I depend on an Event may [sic] probably soon come to pass, which I could not have expected & which yet may not happen. Remind me but of telling It you when wee shall be together in my Garden & wee'll discourse It over, as inter Sylvas Academi, under those fine Elmes which I'm beholden to your bounty for. They afford me many a Shady morning walk, support me fragrant Woodbinds & bring you my Friend, and many Pleasant houres I've spent with you to my Mind, and from the Terrace they stand on I've a delightful View of my Canal, which I this last dry summer scowred out to the Very Springs & is full of good Water. to which my Neighbours, as well as my Self were beholden for many brewing of good Beer, Washings, & other Household Uses. I've moreover by laying a flight of Stone Stepps to the Very Bottom of It which I bought from the demolition of Duckhall,[11] renderd It safe & Useful for Batheing, & ready for the Gardiners constant Services in Watering the Trees and Plants, without breaking and defaceing the slope of the Terrace which I made exact & beautyfull. By our great Drought and want of Water & loss of my Fish I was so discouraged one While as allmost to've determined to plant the Sides with Aquaticks & left It wild, but my Sons prevailed on me to Sett a Gang of workmen well experienced on & to be at the Charge of Scowring out the Canal & repairing the Slopes, which I do not repent of, and hope will give you pleasure & have your approbation.

Dr Green who's just returnd from a Visit to our Relation the Rector of Great Coates near Grymesby[12] see there the antient Statue of St Gryme or Hero Gryme the founder of the Grandeur of that Antient Burgh, now not distinguishable whether he was a Clerk or Layman.[13] At Brocklesby Mr Pellams he see some good paintings especialy of a Fruiterer & fruit &c by Sneyders. at Mr Jenkynsons Seat called Wickham many fine Plantantions [sic], and Two noble Peices of Water, Each of several Acres. but says thô He went by Horncastle, & see Scrivelsby,[14] and returned by Louth, the Woulds afford not much worth a Travailers notice.

I am My Dear Friend with all our humble Services to Yourself Lady & Daughters Your most obliged Servant & Sincere Friend
M Johnson

To the Reverend Dr Stukeley
At his house in Queens Square
    by Ormond Street
        London

[1] SGS, MB5, fol.78v (entry for 9 May 1751) records the SGS agreeing to take John Hill's *Literary Gazette*. Hill had agreed to send all previous copies also to the SGS. Johnson is pleased that this mirrors the Society's initial activity of reading and discussing the latest London journals in 1710.
[2] 'From the beginning': the SGS still possesses these *Literary Gazettes*.
[3] Stukeley had recently bought a new horse.
[4] Johnson's eldest son, Col. Maurice Johnson.
[5] Mr Herbert's company of 'Strolling Players', a travelling theatre company; see S. Rosenfeld, *Strolling Players and Drama in the Provinces 1660–1765* (Cambridge, 1939).
[6] This is Lord Harry Grey, third Earl of Stamford (1685–1739). Blathwayt was a member of a Stamford family who appears here to have become a dancing-master there; he had worked with two well-known London dancers: François Nivelon, a famous French dancer, celebrated for serious and comic performances, who wrote *The Rudiments of Good Behaviour* (1737); and John Essex who translated Rameau's *Le Maître à Danser* (1728).
[7] Charles Townsend (*c*.1715–79): ordained deacon 1737 and priest 1750, Vicar of Pinchbeck (1752–79) and also Rector of Pickwell (Leics) 1750–79. His father, Thomas Townsend, was Vicar of Pinchbeck from 1726 until his death in 1751.
[8] 'Law-giver'. The tapestry of Moses perhaps comes from an engraving by Marten de Vos (1532–1603), painter in Antwerp, printed in Gerard de Jode, *Thesaurus Sacrarum* (1585).
[9] The Revd Basil Berridge (1684–1737), Vicar of Sutterton (1722–37) and Rector of Algarkirk (1716–37). His son Dr Charles Berridge (d.1782) became Rector of Algarkirk in 1737.
[10] This is Charles Peters (1690–1774), *A Critical Dissertation on the Book of Job* (1751). Johnson had assisted SGS member Revd Samuel Wesley (1662–1735) with advice when Wesley (the father

of John and Charles Wesley) was writing his *Dissertationes in Librum Jobi* (edited by John Wesley and published posthumously in 1735).

11 See **Letter 15**, n.27, and **Letter 56**, n.10, above.

12 The Rector was Revd Arthur Bransby (SGS member).

13 The legend of the foundation of Grimsby attributes it to a Danish fisherman, Grim, who helps the hero Havelok, as told in the late thirteenth-century East Midland poem *The Lay of Havelok the Dane*. There may be some confusion with the Norse god Odin who was also known to the Vikings as Grimr.

14 John Green's journey: the Brocklesby Estate in north Lincolnshire has been owned by the Pelham family since 1565; Charles Anderson-Pelham, grandson of this Mr Pelham, became the first Baron Yarborough in 1794 while MP for Lincolnshire. The painting was probably by Frans Snyders (1579–1657), an Antwerp painter known for fruit and flower pictures; Sir Robert Walpole had four paintings by Snyders in his outstanding collection at Houghton Hall. The Jenkynson family owned property in East Wickham, south-east of Grimsby. Scrivelsby Hall suffered a severe fire in 1761; it was the property of the Dymoke family, hereditary champions to the King.

74. Maurice Johnson to William Stukeley, Spalding, 3 January 1752
Bodleian, MS Eng. misc. c.113, fols 373r–374v

Spalding 3 January 1751/2

Dear Friend,

At our Last nights meeting I had the first opportunity of laying before our Company Your useful, entertaining, & kind Communication to Us of your 2^d Vol. of MS Memoirs of Observations made at the Royal and Ægyptian Societies Lond[on][1] for which those Gentlemen and I are obliged to you very much, and return you many Thanks: I had sooner acknowledged the receipt of your last Letter and the favour of the Print of ORIVNA AUG, but deferrd, daily expecting your Volume,[2] which Dr Tathwell sent me, I believe, as soon as he had a safe opportunity after his returne to Stamford, whilest at Hitchin being a Member he obliged Us with several Critical & curious Remarkes on the times of composing and occasions of several Odes of Horace and pointed out many beauties in them for which illustrations Wee were much obliged to him & since he came to [*gap in text caused by removal of seal*] for an History of the Dangerous Case and Cure of a Patient in a most Violent Feavour, which [*gap in text*] therefrom sometime before he left Hertfordshire, attended with his Observations on [*gap in text*] Barke, saline mixtures and Acids, which seemed to me to be very Juditious, with corroborating References to Dr Mede's, Huxham's, Professor Monro's & the Edenburgh Physicians'[3] Sentiments, given as Reasons for his Prescriptions and Method of the Cure. His reflexions shew him to be a good well-thinking and well read Man, and as he ever expressed an Esteem for our Institution, will I trust continue a good Correspondent, which are the most Beneficial Members, to It. when next you see Dr Hill I pray present our Services and Thanks to him for his 2^d Parcell of Literary Gazettes,[4] They as the former have been, will be very agreeable to our Company & afford Us, as Your Memoires do, many delightful Readings & Topics of Conversation. Wee began the 1st lecture of your 2^d Volume on Thursday and are gotten to the 64th Inspector. For haveing first perused those Papers, I marke those I take to be proper for our purpose with our plagia SGS at top – and over the Dissertation I write briefly what It treats on, which is generaly (as Wee have the Papers) as much as need be minuted. I remember in May last (when you gave me hopes of seing You here, & which I will hope I may this summer), You advisd us of Dr Hills kind Intention towards our Soc in bestowing as he has done those Papers on Us; which Wee could not but be the more desirous of from the Character You Sir had before then given us of Them, & from our Knowledge of your Editor. A Method I've proposed to our Members, & taken my self, of Exhibiting a Drawing, sketch or Print, with some Account of the Person has been Acceptable, & the minutes of 'em may be of some Use.

[p.2] 16 May at our Meeting Mr Grundy[5] a Member gave a full Account of the Great Improvements made by Charles Jennyns Esq another Member in his Gardens & Seat at Gopsal in Leicester shire, and the Elegant & proper Manner in which that Worthy & Ingenious Gentleman has fitted up his Hall, Chapell, Library and Musick room of which Science he is a Master, & has a grand Collection both of Instruments & Compositions and his Library well stored with all manner of other Books, Mathematical & all other Philosophical Instruments.

The President[6] gave the Company the Method of disposition of the Barberini Library from a MS. Read from Mr Geo Johnson[7] then of Brazen nose now of Magdalen College in Oxford His Greek Anacreontic Elegy on the Death of his Royal Highness the Prince of Wales.

23d May the President shewd the Company an Indenture of Leas of Lands at Struggs Hill in Sutterton, 15 [*gap in text caused by removal of a seal*] with a beautyfuly red colourd wax, of the Letter H between 2 branches, & [*gap in text*] & gave them some account of the Welby Family, one whereof a Lawyer made & attested It.[8] From the Revd Mr Smyth[9] of Woodston An Account of the Statues & Pictures at Longthorpe the Seat of Sir Francis St John's Bartt near Peterborough, with the Revd Mr Gibson's remarks. Notice of a Lusus in a red Tulip growing in Mr Rustatt's Garden at Holbeach.[10] Having 5 large & fair flowers growing from One Stalk, seen & observd by several Members present who mentioned It.

30th. From Dr Hill a Member were brought in his kind present to this Society of the 66 first No of his Literary Gazetts, which have since been occasionaly read. Mr Sands Architect, a Member, gave to the Museum of our Society a Concave Geodes – Hill of Fossils 54.[11] also a Specimen of an Oval Cornice made of factitious matter, that bears a polish with a very beautiful Specimen, highly polishd, of white & red Siena marble. The Treasurer shewd the Company Brass coines of Tiberius, Nero & Domitian, found at Hitchin.

6th June from Mr Wm Burrwell Schoolmaster & Clerk of Tirrington in Norfolk (lately a Labourer at Cowbitt) an Algebraical Solution & answer to the 6th Question in the Ladies Diary 1651[12] [*sic*] as to the content of a Cistern in Liquid measure neatly written and figured. this Genius made a Pack of Chards all himself like playing cards when at Cowbitt, & since presented the Revd the Dean of Rochester a Member with a Pourtrait of Mr Lock of his painting.

[p.3] 13th June read a Poem against Gameing sent by Coll. Johnson a Member.[13]

20th From Mr Geo. Johnson of Brazn Nose College Oxon that Mr Jn. Swinton[14] of C[hrist] C[hurch] hopes to restore the knowledge of Phoenician or Punic & Hetruscan languages. a large milk white Spider taken on a flower of Hemlock was given to the Museum.

27th a Flower & Leaf of the Pavia, or Scarlett flowering Chesnutt were produced, & reposited in an Hortus Siccus in the Societys Museum. from Mr Benjamin Cook Registrar of this Soc.[15] a Drawing of a Saxon thin round Gold Plate with an Image, designed perhaps for the Blessed Virgin Mary, & these Characters round her C++cm11M1+Tvr – It is of the Size of a Shilling, &

plain on the other Side, but seems to've had a Loop on the Edge to hand it by, as amulett; [*gap caused by removal of a seal*] sent Mr Giffard[16] a Sketch and Account of It, the workmanships very rude. this was plowd up at Chesterton in Huntingtonshire. Wee had from him an Account of many Curious Woodworks in Parquetage & inlaying done by Mr Taylor of Kates Cabbin[17], near where it was found: & a discourse by a Member on Opera Musiva, tesserata, Vermiculata & Assarota of the Antients.

4th July from Mr Dale Ingram Chirurgeon, a Member, his examination of a Porpus or Sea Hogg.[18]

11th Letter from Rev^d Mr Smith with account of Sir John Cottons MSS. Rolls from Exchequer Records and many curious particulars therefrom extracted by that Industrious member.[19] Another Letter from Mr Dacosta a Member and a List & arrangement of Fossils in his Cabinett and in Sir Hans Sloanes, with some account further of his Collections, Library, & museum.

18th. The President brought in Dr Stukeley Discourse & philosophy of Earthquakes[20] his kind present to this Society and the Public Library thereof. & the Secretary from Mr Dacosta many Specimens of curious, most of them forreigne Fossils, being a Continuation of his obligeing enrichment of this Society's museum.

25th Brought in some Prints the Usual present to this from the Society of Antiquaries London & a short treatise for reduceing the Duty on Starch by John Brooke a native of Spalding & Drakes view of Boston taken from Hussey Tower being his present to the Society.[21]

[p.4] You see, Sir, what Wee had those 3 Months, except Pourtrait Prints, & printed Papers & Inspectors generaly, & now and then a Rambler,[22] or other like, which have been sent us by Mr Rob. New a member of our and of the Society of Antiquaries London Clerk of the Papers in the Court of King's Bench, who has a large Collection & many MSS of History and Heraldry, He was my Son Walters Master as an Entring Clerk, who is also a Member of that and succeeded his Uncle as Treasurer of our Soc., & Clerk of our Court of Sewers. I hope he'll shortly marry and Settle in his Dear Mothers house next mine which was heretofore your Relations the Hobsons where Wee hold our Societys Meetings.[23]

And am with all our Families Good Wishes & Compliments of the Season to You & yours

    Dear Friend your affectionat humble Servant
      M Johnson

To
 the Reverend
Dr Stukeley at his House
 in Queens Square
  Ormondstreet
   London

---

[1] For Stukeley's memoirs of the RS and the Egyptian Society, sent to the SGS, see **Letters 61**, n.9, **66**, n.11 and **67** above.

[2] *Paleographia Britannica* III (1752), containing 'Oriuna wife of Carausius, Emperor of Britain'. For 'Oriuna', see **Letter 61**, n.12, above.

[3] For Dr Cornwall Tathwell and Dr Richard Mead, see their entries in Appendix 3. Dr John Huxham

(1691–1768: see *ODNB*), FRS 1739, trained at Reims and practised in Devon; his writing on fevers brought him a considerable European reputation. James Munro (1680–1752) was a successful London physician; Sir Robert Walpole was one of his patients.

4   See Appendix 3 for John Hill; his arrangement to send the SGS his *Literary Gazette* is discussed in **Letters 71** and **73** above. Johnson was always keen to find material for SGS meetings.

5   The remainder of this letter is a summary of the SGS minutes for the past few months, in return for Stukeley's summaries of the RS meetings. John Grundy junior gave the report: see Appendix 3. This is minuted in detail in SGS, MB5, fols 78v–80r (entry for 16 May 1751), an important description of this significant but now-vanished house. Charles Jennens (1702–73) is best known for creating the libretto for Handel's *Messiah* and was known as 'Solyman the Magnificent' for his 'profuse hospitality' at Gopsal (Moore, *The Gentlemen's Society at Spalding* (1851), 38). The well-known hymn tune 'Gopsal' was named after his house.

6   Maurice Johnson had become President on the death of the Revd Stephen Lyon in 1748. There is a full account by Johnson (SGS, MB5, fol.78) of how the Barberini Library in Rome catalogued its books, taken from Hieronymus Tetius's edition of *Aedes Barberinæ*; see *Journal of the History of Collections* 20(2) (2008), 308–9. In 1902 this library went to the Vatican.

7   See Appendix 3.

8   For an account of the Lincolnshire Welby family and a lease of land in Sutterton, Lincolnshire, see SGS, MB5, fol.80v.

9   See Appendix 3. For an account of Thorpe Hall, Peterborough, see MB5, fol.80v. Johnson had already described it to Stukeley some years before in **Letter 10** above.

10   William Rustatt, who lived in Stukeley's home town of Holbeach.

11   See Sands' entry in Appendix 3. The Treasurer at the time was Walter Johnson, Maurice Johnson's son; see his entry in Appendix 3.

12   This must be 1751 as the problem is set in the *Ladies Diary* for 1751 (p.40). In the *Ladies Diary* (1752) the answer is given (pp. 37–8) where nine names of those giving the correct answer, all men, 'and others' are listed. William Burwell of Terrington St Clement, Norfolk, was not among those listed. It is interesting that a publication aimed at women at this time included mathematical problems. The Dean of Rochester was the Revd Dr John Newcome (1653–1765), Master of St John's College, Cambridge, and Lady Margaret Professor of Divinity.

13   Johnson's son Colonel Maurice Johnson (see Appendix 3) sent 'A New Poem much commended & cited by several of our best modern writers: New-Market, a satire on excessive hazards at Horser-aces' (MB5, fol.82r).

14   John Swinton (1703–77: see *ODNB*), FRS 1729; of Wadham and Christ Church, Oxford, worked on Parthian, Samnite and Phoenician inscriptions.

15   See Appendix 3.

16   Andrew Gifford (1700–84: see *ODNB*), FSA 1748: Baptist minister and chaplain to Sir Richard Ellys, well-known as a numismatist and assistant librarian at the British Museum 1757.

17   Kate's Cabin is a point on the A1 road west of Peterborough, between Chesterton and Alwalton, today marked by a café.

18   See Appendix 3. Ingram's letter giving a detailed account of his examination of a porpoise is in the SGS archive (see *Correspondence*, letter 553).

19   Sir John Cotton, third Baronet (1621–1702). His grandfather Sir Robert Cotton created a remarkable collection of mediæval MSS and books. Sir John organised the sale of this to the state by Act of Parliament in 1701 and this Cottonian Library became the basis for the library at the British Museum, today the British Library. For Da Costa (Mendes da Costa) and Sloane, see Appendix 3.

20   Stukeley's book on earthquakes; see **Letter 65**, n.6, above.

21   John Brooks, *A Short Treatise for Reducing the Duty on Starch* (1751). Brooks was born in Spalding in 1694. For Nathan Drake, see Appendix 3.

22   The SGS had been purchasing Dr Samuel Johnson's twice-weekly journal *The Rambler* which was published from 1750 to 1752.

23   Walter Johnson (see Appendix 3) married Mary Fairfax and moved into Gayton House, the property of his mother, next door to Johnson's home at Ayscoughfee Hall. At the time, the SGS was meeting there. The Society later moved to rooms on the other side of the river near the High Bridge, belonging to Michael Cox, the SGS's Curator.

75. William Stukeley to Maurice Johnson, London, 24 April 1752
SGS/T3

[Attached is an engraving of a coin of the Emperor Carausius: 'R.Brunet deline. et fecit'.[1]]

[Note by Johnson:] To M. Johnson who answered the same the post or 2 after recd.

My dear Friend   24 Apr. 1752

Master Allen[2] your old schoolfellow, with whom I am acquainted, inquired after you. this day we celebrated the Antiquarian festivity. by tiezing, they have induced me to continue my self a member: & because I would not do any thing to discorage an Institution, whereof You & I were the parents & the nurses. but I have no great liking to their getting a charter: a mean imitation of the Royal Society! & will be prejudicial to learning in general, by dividing the Stream.[3]

I presented to them in 24 pages 4to. my memoirs toward the history of the antiquarian Society;[4] addressd to Lord Macclesfield. what I had formerly collected, when I was Secretary. the history of its commencement in queen Eliz. time; the names of the members; places & times of meeting; heads of inquiry: project [p.2] of a Petition to the queen for Incorporation; for a place of Meeting; of a Library &c. then the dissolution of the Society in K. James I time; as thinking it dangerous to government.

then I recite <u>our</u> Meeting, & erecting the present Society: & that the original paper purporting thereof, wrote in my hand, & subscribed by the founders, is in your hands. & I desire you to send me a copy of it, for them.

lastly I give an obituary of the Antiquarys; as far as come to my hands. I tell them what assistance I can give 'em, shall not be wanting; but that I never can be present at their Meetings: because on a wrong day, & too late at night for me. in truth, I draw my self off more & more, from public company, levys & attendance on great men. I reduce my self chiefly to my own parish; & enjoy a [p.3] great deal of Solitude: which is extremely agreable to a mind not ill stockd with matter to think on.

but the Society, at last, desired me to ask of you, the original paper its self, to be laid up in their Archives.[5] They are going to hire Essex house in Essex Street.[6]

I am now in the press, to show ORIVNA to be the wife of Carausius. I shall send you the treatise.[7] what I most value in the thing is the State of Christianity, about that time, in our island. I am fully satisfy'd, that S. Paul preached the gospel, in the Southern parts of Brittain, about Chichester.

your coz. Dr Lynn & I din'd together – lately at Dr Hill's. Dr Hill made interest to get him the astronomy professorship at Gresham, but without success.[8]

I am now purposed to call & see you this summer; for one evening. I am here [p.4] ty'd to a constant Sunday duty; & can't be out, longer than necessary.

our Secretary Mortimer dy'd of a jaundice, which he neglected, till it became a dropsy. our President Folks has had a paralytic stroke: but was an infidel even in philosophy. for we have good reson to believe, that electrifying is highly useful in the case. he is in a very poor condition.

Geo. Vertue looks as old as Poul's. Brown Willys is much decay'd, & now has the gout. Sa. Gale looks thin. You & I are almost the last of our founders.[9]

I am very well, but not fat. for I am obliged to omit drinking good liquors, to stave off the gout: which I do successfully enough. but cannot induce one single soul man or woman, to come to the same method.

I am affectionately yours
Wm Stukeley

24 apr. 1752 Lond.

1   Brunet's engraving is in Stukeley's *Paleographia Britannica* III.
2   'Master Allen' is unknown; he was a fellow-pupil and friend of Johnson's, either at Spalding Grammar School or at Eton.
3   The Society of Antiquaries received its Royal Charter in 1751 and was celebrating this in 1752. Stukeley became its Secretary and Johnson was appointed Librarian at the end of 1717, when it was re-founded after the original Elizabethan society had lapsed.
4   Society of Antiquaries: 'Memoirs towards an History of the Antiquarian Society, Addressed (fol. ii) to George 2nd Earl of Macclesfield FSA, 23 April 1752'.
5   Marginal note by Johnson: 'the Revd. Mr North hath my papers'. There is no record at the Society of Antiquaries of Johnson's 'original paper'.
6   For Essex House and the Society of Antiquaries, see Joan Evans, *A History of the Society of Antiquaries* (1956), 110.
7   This is Stukeley's *Paleographia Britannica* III in which he claims that the inscription on the coin he illustrates shows a female figure to be 'Oriuna', wife of the Emperor Carausius. This mistake was caused by a chip in the coin obscuring the full inscription, probably 'Fortuna'; Stukeley had not been able to see the actual coin and was working from a drawing of it. Johnson was more dubious about this identification. For fuller discussion, see **Letters 61**, n.12, **68**, n.5, and **69** above.
8   The new Gresham's Professsor of Astronomy, appointed on 21 April 1752, was William Cockayne (1717–98), Vicar of Doveridge (Derbys) and chaplain to the Lord Mayor of London in 1750. The post did not require expertise in astronomy. For Dr Walter Lynn and John Hill, see Appendix 3.
9   Cromwell Mortimer, Martin Folkes, George Vertue, Browne Willis and Samuel Gale were all members of the SGS; see Appendix 3. Vertue, Willis and Gale had all been founder-members of the Society of Antiquaries in 1717, together with Johnson and Stukeley.

76. Maurice Johnson to William Stukeley, Spalding, 1 May 1752
Bodleian, MS Eng. misc. c.113, fols 375r–376v

Spalding Mayday 1752

Dear Dr,

I much [*sic*] obliged to you for Your last favour of the 24th Ult. And to Master Allen and everyone so kind as to have me in remembrance who not quite out of the World here, am out of the Way of the most part of It who frequent your Metropolis, and thô subject to Paines in my head frequently returning, which my son Green[1] takes to to [*sic*] be rheumatick & treating as such has done me much good: Yet my friends here tell me I look well, which is more than It seems can be sayd of most of our old Stagers, & I and my Family and all fellow Members here shall have much pleasure when you favour Me as you purpose with your Company this Summer in seing you well.

So long since as 1738 when Dr Cr[omwell] Mortimer was about to Publish an Account of All our literary Societies out of Universities[2] and for that purpose (as he pretended) prevailed On me to take that Trouble: I extracted from my Papers and transmitted him the best I could and those pretty fully too of Our Institution here, and also of the Restoration and reestablishment of the Antiquarian Society in London, thô frequently Urged by me and my Friends to make the Use He promisd, which might have turnd to our Service, he disingeniously declined It. If there be any Paper Or other thing my possession [*sic*] may be of service to you you shall be wellcome to a Copie or Copies thereof: But I believe what you mean[3] was nothing a schæme or plan: signed by nobody, but written and half torn thrô, by you: which I preserved at the time from being destroyd by you: and made some Memorandums myself upon It, not by any meanes proper to be reposited in the Archives of the Antiquarian Society: In the Minute Books whereof all proper was written by you Sir as Secretary. What those Gentlemen read write or Do of late I can't tell, this I know that They ask but take not advice given them fully and friendlyly by some of the oldest Acquaintance, Who wish them Well: & could have prevented their going into Such Expences[4] as will prove too Heavy for their more Usefull Members, and not fix them upon the Establishment they aim at. As I Concieve they might have obteined. At [p.2] our first Meeting for this yeare 2[d] Janurary 1752 Wee began to read the MS Memoires of Observations made by you Sir at the R.S. & Elsewhere you favour us with & have at due times continued them since to our great Improvement & pleasure:

9[th] of Jan. Wee had by Mr Calamy Ives a Member[5] a very romantic MS. account communicated from some pretended Travailer of the rem[ain]s & statues discoverd at a Villa near Tusculum, sometime belonging to the great M.T. Cicero, but thô very romantic and Surprizing I believe all a mere figment and Incredible.

16[th] of Jan. A letter from Mr Da Costa[6] a member with an ample Account of his Intended work about Fossils with a MS Poem after Le Fontaine's fables or Tales, entitled The Sceptic and the Painter – pretyly told.

23[d] of Jan. Mr Major Thompson[7] brought in some specimens of Sea Urchins in their natural State & Shells blanchd on the shore of our Coast, Echinus communis Marinus, and Echinus Spatagus & Brissus.

30th of Jan. I shewd the Company a Petrifaction of a Nautilus levis seu Græcorum like one publishd in the Phil. Trans. in 1748 and part of a Nautilites in a Flinty Substance of the rugose kind, or those called Fluviatiles. Mr Cox our Operator shewd Us an Impress of fine antique of Dr Meads of Æsculapius.

6 February. I shewd the Company a Fungus Scindalina which grew out of Oake in the Bellfry of Hitchin in Hertfordshire, given me by the Vicar there, a Member,[8] and an Asteria stellis minoribus, a beautyfull milk white Specimen, & a draught of the Brazen Image of Judge Ludington by Mr Stennett.

13th. The Pourtrayt & Character of Master William Lambard of Kent with some account of his many learned Labours.[9] he was an Eminent Antiquary, good Justice, & very honest Lawyer in Q[ueen] Eliz[abeth's] time.

27. The Treasurer sent us a good account of the Peny yard Pence and the X Commandments thus comprized in 6 Hexameters and Pentametres.

Decalogus

[p.3]   Me solum venerare Deum, nec sculpe Quod oras
              Impia nec Vox sit: Luce quiesce Sacrâ;
    Majores reverenter habe: nec sanguine Dextram
              Infice, Nec sancti pollue Jura Thori:
    Pura manus Furti: sit Falsi nescia Lingua:
              Nullius optetur Verna, Marita, Pecus.[10]

Dr Green, Secretary, communicated a Letter with many curious remarks on fossils by Mr da Costa.

5 March. Some Account of a Coine of Hiero, King of Sicily[11] from the Treas-

urer read and of several elegant drawings presented to the Antiq. Soc. by Mr Edwards, and of a Grand Gold Medaglion of his late Majesty King George 1st.

12 Mar. I shewd the Company a Silver Stater or Tetradrachma of the Leontines – now Lintini in the Vale of Noto in Sicily, a City sometime the rival of Syracusa,[12] whereof I gave them some Account, a Lyons head between 4 Peascods. Dr Green communicated the residue of a Long Letter from Mr Da Costa.

19th. The President communicated a Letter conteining much of the Present State of the R.S. from their Reverend ~~President~~ Mr Birch[13] to him, especialy the future Phil. Trans.

26th. A Solution of a Question, (viz.) 3 Numbers in Musical Proportions their Summe 39 and the summe of their Squares 549. The [*sic*] find those Numbers answered. 9, 12 & 18, solved Algebraicaly by Mr William Burwell sometime a Labouringman at Cowbitt, now School Master of Tyrington,[14] communicated by Revd. Mr Ray. I shewd the Company a Brass Key of this Size and Shape dug up lately in our Abby Yard.

[*Sketch of antique key just over 3½ inches long.*]

and a pourtrait of Justus Lipsius[15] engraved by L. Vosterman under which: 'Justus Lipsius Iscanus sui sæculi Lumen Ætat. An. XXXVI' in an high crowned hat & staring Eyes.

[p.4] My Couz. Geo. Johnson of Maudlin in Oxford sent his Uncle Dr Green a beautyfull Latin Ode on the return of Spring read to our Company the 9th [*April*]. He is a Demy of that College.

16th. I shewd them the Ichnography and Upright of an house neatly drawn in Indian Ink by Mr Hawks of Norwich:[16] and on the last of the last Month from the Chairman of the Medical Soc. of Navy Surgeons, their plan of that noble Institution, sent Us by Mr Austin a member, with the devise for their Annual Golden Prize Medall to Encourage Correspondency, the Spiritt of all Institutions, & a full Explanation of both Sides of the said Intended Medall.[17]

So I've given you Sir, the heads of all our minutes from our last, saving your own kind Communications and our friend Dr Hill's which are of very great use and Improvement. Our Compliments to him when you see him; Wee much wish for his Volume of animals.[18] and with the Services of all my Family to your good Lady & all yours I heartyly wish You Your health and a good Journey being
    Dear Dr Your Affectionate Friend & Servant
        M. Johnson

To the Reverend
Dr Stukeley in Queens Square
  Ormondstreet
    London.

---

1 Dr John Green, Johnson's son-in-law and now Secretary of the SGS.
2 Cromwell Mortimer, Secretary of the RS, a member of the SA and SGS and a corresponding member of the Royal Academy of Sciences in Paris and of the SGS, planned to affix to the RS's *Philosophical Transactions* 'the history of the learned societies of Great Britain and Ireland' but unfortunately nothing came of this plan, see Appendix 3.
3 Johnson refers to Stukeley's request (see **Letter 75**) to send him an account of the foundation of the AS, which Stukeley believed Johnson to have written in detail.

⁴ Johnson, like Stukeley, had argued against the AS spending a large capital sum on the acquisition of a Royal Charter in 1751.
⁵ See SGS, MB5, fol.97r (entry for 9 January 1752). This letter, like others of Johnson's letters in the 1750s, features a summary of the minutes of recent SGS meetings, in return for Stukeley's memoirs of RS meetings. For the members named in this account, see Appendix 3.
⁶ Emanuel Mendes da Costa's book *A Natural History of Fossils* was published in 1757. John Green MD and Maurice Johnson are listed among the subscribers. The poem referred to, 'The Sceptick and the Painter', was by William Jackson, a SGS member, of the Custom House, Boston (see MB5, fol.97r).
⁷ Mr Major Thompson (his name, not a military rank) became a regular SGS member in 1755.
⁸ Revd Mark Hildesley, see Appendix 3.
⁹ William Lambarde (1536–1601: see *ODNB*); his concern was 'to emphasise the rule of law as the foundation of society'. Johnson showed his portrait and discussed his legal role (MB5, fol.97v).
¹⁰ This Latin versification of the Ten Commandments was made by Dr Arthur Johnston (1579–1641) of Aberdeen.
¹¹ Hiero II, the final and very successful independent King of Sicily from 265 to 215 BC. He rebuilt Syracuse with the help of Archimedes.
¹² The ancient Greek city of Leontinoi, today Lentini, close to Noto in Sicily, was mostly destroyed by an earthquake in 1693.
¹³ This letter, sent by the Revd Thomas Birch to Johnson and dated 17 March 1752, is largely transcribed in *Correspondence*, 197. Birch promises to send the RS's *Philosophical Transactions* to the SGS.
¹⁴ *The Ladies' Diary*, followed by the *Gentleman's and Lady's Palladium*, contained large numbers of complex mathematical questions such as this, besides a variety of puzzles and essays. See J. Albree and S. Brown, 'A Valuable Monument of Mathematical Genius', *Historia Mathematica* 36(1) (February 2001). For Mr Burwell of Terrington St Clement (Norfolk), see also **Letter 74**, n.12, above.
¹⁵ Justus Lipsius (1547–1606); an etching of this portrait of him by Lucas Vorsterman, engraved by Robert Gaywood, is in the British Museum collections, number 1i, 1, 30.
¹⁶ Thomas Hawkes (see Appendix 3) was a tin-plate worker of Magdalen Street, Norwich: see SGS, MB5, fol.96r (entry for 19 December 1751). He made an orrery for the SGS, the remains of which still exist in a rather battered state in the SGS's museum.
¹⁷ This is a valuable reference to a little-known society of Naval Surgeons which flourished in the 1740s and 1750s. There is a reference to this letter in *Correspondence*, 197–8; the details of the Prize Medal and of the society's plan to publish an account of surgical cases are on the back of the letter.
¹⁸ Presumably Johnson is referring to John Hill, *A History of Animals* (1752).

77. Maurice Johnson to William Stukeley, Spalding, 9 March 1753
Bodleian, MS Eng. misc. c.113, fols 377r–378v

Ayscough Feehall in Spalding
9 Mar. 1753

My Dear Friend,

'Twas with much Gratitude Wee remembred your great Beneficence Last Night, at our Soc's Meeting when our Secretary gave us the Last reading of your MSS Memoires of the 2ᵈ Volume of your judicious and entertaining observations made at the meetings of the Royal & Egyptian Soc.¹ &c. of which most Acceptable Favour Wee can't but wish, & I, their unworthy, but Indefatigable & Zealous Founder, & President, Earnestly request a Continuance; and to induce you, Sir, to indulge Us, give me leave to acquaint you of our Institution flourishing in the Accession of Three new Regular, that is, Resident Members, as all such by our Rules must be, lately at their own Instances Elected, Mr Buckworth, Dr Samuel Dinham, & Mr Jnᵒ Richards Junʳ all Etonians, and half a Score honourary,² of the Neighbouring Clergy, my Couzen Wingfield of Tickencoat, now of Hertford

Coll. Oxford; my Godson, Mr Bogdani Jun[r] of Kings Coll. Cambridge; both good Scholars & Correspondents, Mr James Verney a Painter who has travailed much, & resided here a While; Mr Pole, a Prussian, Jeweller, Engraver, & Seal Cutter, who has Done Several Good Works here, & seen many foreigne Countries; & other Ingenious Gentlemen which Indraught I've for some years passd found about the beginnings of the New Yeares, to be necessary to keep up a Good Number not only to supply Mortality, but to engage & Cultivate Correspondence, the life & spiritt, you know, of such Institutions which depend only on pleasure of Improvement in Knowledge from all Arts & Sciences. The late [p.2] Mr Bazil Berridge[3] was a Benefactor to Us in Our Musæum and Library; he has left his Brother Dr Berridge a Fine Estate, and an House Much Improved and well furnished; and very large Legacies to his Brother Johns 3 Sons and Daughter. He was on Wednesday last Interrd with his Ancestors at Algarkirk –

On the death of Mr -- late Lecturer of Boston that Corporation Invited young Mr Lenton of Freiston to Accept of, & gave him that Lecture;[4] & Harry Smyth being since dead, he has taken his house, he marryd the younger Miss Boulton. Wee hear Sir You've disposed of a Daughter in Marriage to Your Mind, and heartyly congratulate you thereon, my Youngest[5] I did so to Mr Wallin, a Jamaica Gentleman lately with whom she is gone thither, I've lately heard from my Youngest son Henry Eustace in the Service of our E. I. Company at Fort St. George, he had the Small Pox on Board in the Voyage but is perfectly well recovered.

Wee have of late had little in the way of physic, or natural history communicated at our Meetings here; the Account of the remarkable Whirle wind which carryd a Waterspout out of Dieping Fen across Cowbit & beyond my Chapel at Moulton throwing down or destroying every object that gave any resistance in the way, I sent yee to the Royal Soc. from our Minutes as communicated to Us from the Rev[d] Mr Benjamin Ray,[6] who was an Eye Witness thereof. Our Treasurer[7] brought us from the Cellar of his Wifes house at Fleet, a Lichen or such like Fungus from an Oaken beam, smooth, in various protuberances on the surface or upper part, & dark brown colourd but underneath wavy & of a Mixd Grey Colour & silvery white.

[p.3] Wee've frequently had productions of this Nature exhibited, but none more curious than One given Me by the Rev[d] Mr Hildesley Vicar of Hitchin a Member, or much the same size with this (but piped, not gilld) of a Light brown Colour the breadth of the Palm of my hand, circular & Convex, & extreemly in Appearance like what is calld Brainstone, but very light, as that Corallin is heavy, taken off from the wooden frame in Which a Bell hung in his Steeple there.[8] This has been a wet yeare, & Wee had a greater Number of small Carp, taken in Our Wash, southward above this Town, than I ever knew which has given Me opportunity of stocking my Canal with them at a Reasonable rate, which I have done with Tench too which Fish wee have more plenty, Generaly, than the Other.

Our Secretary from Capt. Proud[9] who uses the Streights trade brought us the Nutlike fruit a Trigoli, or aquatick seed vessel Eat [sic] at Venice, & produced a Vegetable growing in or near the afflux of a River that discharges it Self into the Gulf, or the Lagunes, but what he met with in No other place. This Gentleman has made frequent Voyage to all the tradeing Towns there & to some in the Archipelago – is a Curious & Observing Man & become a Neighbour, & Wee hope will become a good Member and favour Us with what he thinks worth while

out of his Journals which I'm told are accurate; He has a pretty Collection of Shells, Seeds, fruits and some good Drawings & Prints he brought from Venice, & Naples, where when he lately was He went down into Herculaneum, of which he gives a good Account, of which You may have the pleasure to hear more from, Dear Doctor,
Your most affectionat Friend & Servant
M. Johnson

To the Revd Dr Stukeley
Rector of St George's in
    Queen Square
      Ormond Street
        London

1   See **Letters 69**, **72** and **73** above for the reading of Stukeley's memoirs of the RS and the Egyptian Society sent to the SGS.
2   For these new members of the SGS, see their entries in Appendix 3, except for James Verney, painter, about whom no further information appears to be available. The minute book lists the following proposed members: Anthony Birks, William Maurice Bogdani, William Burwell, Adam Colclough, Peter Daval, John Harrison, Joseph Pole, Rev. W. R. Reynolds, Rev. John Tatham, James Verney, John Wingfield; all were accepted for membership (MB5, fol.113r, for 25 January 1753).
3   Basil Berridge of Pinchbeck Place (d.1753), patron of the living of Algarkirk, not a member of the SGS. For details of an ancient painting of Christ that he owned, see MB4, fol.77v.
4   Dr John Linton (1722–82) held livings at Freiston, Mavis Enderby, Boston and Skirbeck and Leverton. Johnson left the blank space because he was not sure of the name of the previous Lecturer, which is not recorded.
5   Stukeley's eldest surviving daughter Frances had married Richard Fleming on 7 December 1752. Anne Alethea Johnson married Richard Wallin, a merchant of Jamaica, in 1750; they were known to the family as Nancy and Dicky. Wallin became a member of the SGS in 1751. Anne Alethea's brother Henry Eustace (see Appendix 3) worked for the East India Company in Madras. Johnson is pleased that his youngest children are now settled in life; his notes on scraps of paper in the SGS archive indicate his concerns about financial provision for them.
6   Benjamin Ray's account of the whirlwind and waterspout on 5 May 1752 is recorded in detail in MB5, fol.100. It was sent to George Shelvocke for passing on to 'Mr Birch Secr. RS'. On 16 April 1753 Johnson recorded (MB5, fol.117) Stukeley's opinion that 'the wonderful Phaenomenon of o[u]r Water Spout (of which wee sent Mr Rays Acct. to RSL) without doubt was Electrical'. For the letter to the RS, see *Phil.Trans.* 47 (1751), 477–8.
7   Walter Johnson; see Appendix 3.
8   Revd Mark Hildesley (1698–1772: see *ODNB*), Vicar of Hitchin and later Bishop of Sodor and Man, see Appendix 3.
9   The *Gentleman's Magazine* for August 1747 mentions a naval officer, Captain Proud, of the ship *Roman Emperor*. Many members of the Proud family were mariners. Captain John Proud died in 1773; see his will (PRO, PROB 11/986/76). He did not become a member of the SGS. The 'Straits trade' is the Mediterranean trade.

78. William Stukeley to Maurice Johnson, London, 9 April 1753
Spalding, SGS/T3

9 apr.1753
Dear Sir,
   I stay'd till this time, before I answer you obliging letter. for now I congratulate you & the publick, in that yesterday the Parliament accepted of Sir Hans

Sloan's Museum. further, they give £10,000 for the Oxford MSS, being 60,000 volumes, & as many charters &c. to these the Cotton library is to be join'd; & a grand repository for the whole is to be prepar'd for their reception. some think of Montagu house: others of the banqueting house: a gallery round the inside, & two superb pavillions at the ends.[1]

They raise £700,000 by lottery, the government to take the overplus money.

I am oblig'd to you for mentioning the marriage of my daughter. her husband Mr Fleming is of the Chancery office, a very pretty gent. of good fortune, & business. [p.2] She will not be able to visit you again. but my daughter Ann is to come with me, this summer; & that without fail. Mr Flemings estate is in Herefordshire.[2]

we had your paper at R.S. about that wonderful phænomenon of a water spout[3] which without doubt is electrical. I have another volume half written thro', destin'd for your Society. but I have at present lost my amanuensis.[4]

our Antiquarys, to whom I never go, have after a huge struggle got out of a tavern; & fix'd their tabernacle in a great upper room over the Master of the Rolls's gate-way.[5] they have great bickerings, & ballotings among 'em.

Monsr. de Boze[6] sent me the 6 copper plates of Genebrier's Carausius. I have ingrav'd one more, & intend 5 more, containing 10 coyns in each plate. [p.3] & then I may have thoughts of publishing a short account, which I have drawn up, of that emperor.[7] I know you have collected a vast deal of materials that way, but as there is but little to be depended on, & that chiefly the medals, I intend to be very concise. Genebrier has given us enough of conjecture.[8] indeed theres very little encouragement now, for printing anything but romance. routs, concerts, ridotto's, &c. &c. have wholly engrossd all curiosity, & all money. the world is strangely alterd from what you & I first knew it: & infinitely for the worse. the men have been so weak as to throw the reins out of thir hands: & now one may imagin how diversion, & wickedness governs.

we have got a very good president at the R.S. Lord Macclesfield,[9] & he is a man of religion (as I think) & thats a great [p.4] rarity among our philosophers. they are generally great enemys to Moses, the prophets, & apostles. our late president Folkes a deplorable spectacle.

your neighbour Dr Berridg[10] was at the R.S. I saw him, but had no time for converse. I always hurry home thence. & for that reason never go to the Antiquarys. for one entertainment in a day, is enough for me. the rest fill their heads with cruditys, & indigestions.

my friend Kennedy the divine[11] has publishd an extraordinary piece on the Mosaic chronology. tis difficult to be understood but there seems somewhat right: he has maul'd my friend Jackson[12] about his L.XX chronology, which I always held erroneous.

if you have any coyns of Carausius unpublish'd, you must send 'em up to me. you may depend on thir being return'd: or any particular remarks in his history.

Yours &c.
Wm Stukeley

Lond. 9 mar 1753 [*sic*]

---

[1] This is a very useful account of the parliamentary establishment of the British Museum in Montague House as a result of Sir Hans Sloane's bequest.

[2] For the marriage of Stukeley's elder daughter Frances, see **Letter 77** above. The Fleming family

were instrumental in ensuring the survival of Stukeley's personal papers. His second surviving daughter Ann, or Anna Stukeley, married Richard Fairchild in 1758.

3   See **Letter 77** above.

4   Both Stukeley and Johnson are beginning to find problems with writing extensive letters and memoirs; both employed amanuenses, or secretaries. This is often evident in the change of handwriting and of spelling, as in Stukeley's memoirs of the RS and Johnson's final letter in this collection. The writing of both Johnson and Stukeley increased in size over the years, presumably to avoid eye-strain.

5   The AS moved in 1753 from the Mitre Tavern into rooms in Chancery Lane, London, which had belonged to the seventeenth-century Master of the Rolls. This, together with the acquisition of a Royal Charter, signalled the rise in status and aspirations of the society.

6   M. de Boze was keeper of Louis XV's collection of coins and medals. He organised the engraving of the famous coin of Carausius which Richard Mead had given to the French king, and which Stukeley misread as 'Oriuna' (see Stukeley's *Paleographia Britannica* III, 24 and **Letters 74**, n.2, and **75**, n.7, above). For Claude Genebrier, see **Letter 68**, n.7, above.

7   Eventually Stukeley published *The Medallic History of Marcus Aurelius Valerius Carausius, Emperor in Britain*, vol. I (1757), vol.II (1759), drawing partly on Johnson's MS material.

8   There is a note by Johnson at this point: 'Dr Kennedy showed me this Book, and truly I think it a romance.'

9   George Parker, second Earl of Macclesfield (1699–1764: see *ODNB*); he became President of the RS 1752–1764. A significant astronomer, he was the principal proponent of the 1752 change in the calendar from the Julian to the Gregorian system.

10   See **Letter 77** above.

11   This is presumably Revd John Kennedy (1698–1782), an Anglican clergyman in Derbyshire who published *A New Method of Stating and Explaining the Scriptural Chronology upon Mosaic Astronomical Principles, Mediums and Data* (1751). He is not to be confused with Dr Patrick Kennedy the numismatist with whom Johnson and Stukeley had had dealings over coins of Carausius.

12   The Revd John Jackson (1686–1763: see *ODNB*). His major work was *Chronological Antiquities* (1753). His *ODNB* entry states, 'he was strongly criticised by a fellow clergyman John Kennedy who argued in *An Examination of the Reverend Mr Jackson's Chronological Antiquities* (1753) that they ought, more properly, to have been astronomical in form'.

79. Maurice Johnson to William Stukeley, Spalding, 18 August 1753
Bodleian, MS Eng. misc. c.113, fols 379r–380v

Ayscoughfeehall by Spalding
18 August 1753

Dear Friend

this morning the Post (after 3 years appointment) brought me Yours of the 16th[1] full of curious matter indeed, but after many Expectations and Long tarrying I fear a disappointment having promisd my Self the pleasure of Seing You here and Enjoying Your Company Personaly, who're one of the few Cotemporaries left me: after many kind Invitations by repeated Letters from my Kinsman Geo. Lynn, I found an opportunity this Summer of being carryd to his Seat;[2] & See with pleasure the many great Improvements he has made there; I have also been able to make Some, which render this place more Comfortable, as You still give me some small hopes for Imagining you may this Yeare see, surely some Vacation you allow your Self and for what better purpose than to Visit your old Friends, See your own native Country and your Own Estate. Your Discours of It must be agreable to me, who have much of the Amor patriæ,[3] & have never faild, to make what Collections I could, to perpetuate Its History: and vindicate It's Honor. the County in general in my history of Lincoln mint[4] & this Town &

the neighbourhood in 2 large Voll: in Folio much of my own hand writing thô Chiefly indeed on subjects in my Profession as best coinciding with my Younger Studies, & opportunities; which may prove a good Foundation for some of my Familie to treat more fully of those Matters. I have asserted from Its Names Spalding, Salamboe, Aphrodisia, and the fragment of the Bas-Relief, dug up from under the Foundation of her Temple here[5] (whereof long afterwards our Conventual Church rededicated to BVM) was built. Our most antient Mercat, being by prescription held on Fryday, her Day of the Week, these I lately shewd my Friend Mr Hunter (when here last Month) & he agreed in Sentiments the Roman name was SALINÆ GŸRVIORUM. Sed de hoc tantum[6] only observe the Sea came up to our very Doors, & this was a Port to the Phœnicians of Tyre and Sidon, & continued to be stiled so PORTUS on Its Customers large Silver Seal, the Impression whereof I lately sent our friend Sir Jno Evelyn by my son the Coll^{ll} on Occasion of my recomending to his favour your Kinsman Mr Hinson our surveyor of the Lenda & Coast.[7]

[p.2] You know Sir there were several Salinæ, this might be a proper distinction for ours: and Mr de la Prime[8] of this Country in the Philos. Trans. relates Salt works & Cisterns here at Spalding, of very Antient work – but in his original Letter, though I searchd for with Dr Jurin (when S.R.S. Secretary) Wee could never find; but such were and that learned & communicative Gentleman did See and gave Account of 'em, which I was led to by Dr Battely[9] in his Antiq. Rutupinæ fol.38. S31 where they are cited thus Acta Philosoph. No. 279. p.1158, wherein I hoped that perhaps something more full might be found. I suspect they might be by the Bankside on the antient Efflux of Lenda or our River Welland in the Castlefield and that could not be far from the Castle itself doubtless a most antient site for such purpose.[10] But when our Castle the Traces whereof still incontestably & Visibly remain in the small but deep Fossa was built [*sic*] which was of British work, and Wee know the residence of Saxon Mercian Princes Or when & by whom & on what Occasion dismantled & afterwards demolished I've frequently Enquired & hitherto in all Authors sought in Vain. It was standing at the Conquest & sometime after for there the Lady Lucia[11] Countess of Lincoln Leicester & Coventry Lady of All Holland & Heiress of Mercia, lived & died & was interrd by the High Altar of our Conventual Church of St Mary & St Nicholas near her Husband Ivo or Jehan de Talbois Count d'Anjou of whom & his Pedigree, I can thence obtein no Account tho' by my Friend Mr Secretary Shelvock, I sometime sent proper Quæres to Angiers i.e. To the Abby St Nicholas, whereto he sometime made It subject as a Cell, for a proper resolution, and where they have an Academy or University;[12] that Great Lady carried the Dignity & Title of our County to the several Noblemen she marryd, But I want to know how her husband Ivo de Talbois stood related to the House of Anjou? and when and by whom, on her Decease, which did not happen till AD 1141, our Castle, which was her Mansion, at her death was demolished?

[p.3] Our Spalding Gentlemens Society much beholden to you Dear Sir I may safely assure you, & with much pleasure, flourishes, and gratefully acknowledges your favours and will esteem your promised continuance of your philosophick Memoires as a more that usual and valuable present, because it will more than usualy contribute to their food & subsistance in Re literariâ because the Members are here to be not only Entertaind but Improved thereby.

On the 10th Instant our Theatre was opend in Crackpole,[13] with a Suitable

Prologue written & spoken by Mr Geo. Alex^r Stevens, a player on the Dublin Stage, here occasionaly, with his Wife, the Daughter of Dionis Herbert Master of our Company who go home to Lincoln: being but Local compliments not so well worth transcribing by your Correspondent – less good at writing than in former days, which makes me chuse to lend you my Decennium[14] thô bound up with Several Juvenile studies Which you'll amuze yourself with as You please and Extract what you like from It being free to do So if any thing may assist your noble undertakings, with It.

You'll recieve Catalogue & Casts of all my Carausius & Allectus's for like Use, that are or can be of any Service to you, by our Peterborough, Spalding & Boston Carrier, (if I can) the very next Opportunity of his setting out hence or Some Safe hand. The little sayd to be relyd on, in this Period of Decennium, you'll find very faithfully related, & some things of those few you may not have Noted, or It may be they have escaped your Notice. Thrô Dr Smithsons Hands I sent Dr Genebrier[15] a parcell of Carausius & Allectus, & desird a few Common in France in return, but never received any, nor any kind of Acknowledgement. In this Society's Collection[16] Wee have [*illegible*] deface Paxs Carausii. In Dr Greens Collection he hath a Brass Coine of good conservation of Carausius in Busto Armd with an Helmet on & spear in his right hand & shield on his left Arm VIRTUS CARAUSII, on reverse PAX AUG, between S & C, he has I with the 3G for Augustorum – another with CONCORDIA AUGGG. IMP. C. ALLECTUS P. F. AUG. his Busto with a radiate Crown and Long beard, on reverse a figure holding a Flowr in the Right hand SPES PUBLICA in Exurg. G.[17] Another very sharp, on reverse a Figure standing a bridle in the Right, & walking staff in his righ left hand, between S. and A. in Exurg. M.L. for Moneta Lindicolini percussa as I concieve the Legend round the Emperors Head is LAETITIA AUG. I walkd down on Purpose to see what Dr Green had that were well preserved. He presents his Service to you.

Sir Francis Whichcott[18] I hear has allmost rebuilt his Hall at Aswarby. Mr Buckworth[19] the Merchants House here building by his Wifes Father is got up to the Chamber windows. Mrs Johnson & all my Family are much yours, Your Ladys & Daughters and none of them more so than, Dear Sir,

   Your very much obliged and faithfull old Friend M. Johnson

[p.4] P.S. I heard lately our old Friend Mr Geo. Vertue[20] was struck with the Palsie, But hope its Either a Mistake, or that stroke was not So Severe as to deprive him of his understanding, or to put him past recovery of his abilities to complete his Account of old Symonds and his Excellent Works for which I furnishd him with an Oval Cast of General Lambert, & another, I take to be of Coll^ll Rossiter[21] our Countryman, under whom when a very young man my Grandfather sometime was Commissary. You see Sir, by my filling every Side this Sheet how desireous I am to Converse with you, thô I've little New to Say to you – my Kinswoman our late Ministers Daughter, & widow of Mr Brandsby[22] late Rector of Great Coats near Great Grymesby is marryd again to Mr Murray vicar of Folkingham near us, and Chaplain to our Merchant Factory at Hamburgh, whither he has Exported her. She having left some of her Pictures in my Possession particularly a large one of her Father & Mother with her Self and Sisters all in one peice by Gemelli,[23] which I believe you've seen. Her sisters were drawn by Idea long after their Deaths by their Father, and inserted. 'Twas this Ladys affaires & she her

Self carryd me to Southwyke, where I exerted my Self all I could which made me seem so full of Spiritt, so I should be to see You Sir, But frequent returns of Pains in the Head render Me but Dull.

To the Reverend Dr Stukeley
Rector of St Georges in Queens Square
    by Ormond Street
        London

1 There is no letter from Stukeley dated 16 August 1753 in the SGS archives; it has presumably been lost.
2 The Lynn family lived at Southwick (Northants): see Johnson's final sentence in this letter. Members of the family were keen supporters of local learned societies such as the SGS and Stukeley's Brazen Nose Society at Stamford.
3 'Love of one's native land', here narrowly interpreted as 'love of one's own home town or district'.
4 Johnson's dissertation on the Lincoln Mint is in the archives of the SGS, together with many other MSS relating to Johnson's historical, numismatic and legal studies. Whilst his findings about the Mint were later proved incorrect, the extent of his learning was considerable.
5 This fragment of a bas-relief was associated by Johnson with Venus rising from the waves, an apt symbol for a Fenland town which was then much closer to the sea and was involved in draining the surrounding countryside. It led to the engraving by George Vertue for the SGS bookplate (see illustrations in *Correspondence*), in which Venus is held aloft by two Tritons. The connection with the Blessed Virgin Mary, to whom, with St Nicholas, the parish church of Spalding is dedicated, demonstrates historical study through analogy, a common technique in the eighteenth century. Johnson believed that Spalding was a Roman foundation.
6 'But enough of that'. Ptolemy, in the second century AD, mentions 'Salinae' in his *Geography*, book II, chapter 2, which deals with 'Albion, the Island of Britannia'. He places it in the territory of the Catuvellauni, further inland and to the south of the location of Spalding. 'Gyrviorum' was taken to relate to the 'Girvii', a tribe based in the Fens and associated with Ely, mentioned by Bede, *Ecclesiastical History*, book IV, chapter xix.
7 Johnson's Lincolnshire patriotism makes him look for the oldest possible origins for Spalding. It was widely accepted, up to the twentieth century, that merchants from Tyre and Sidon travelled by sea to Britain, particularly for the Cornish tin trade. Current views tend to favour the trade between Britain and the Mediterranean at that period passing over the Channel and then by river transport to the Mediterranean. For Hinson and Evelyn, see Appendix 3.
8 Abraham de la Pryme FRS (1671–1704: see *ODNB*), famous for his Diary (see Charles Jackson (ed.), *The Diary of Abraham de la Pryme, the Yorkshire Antiquary*, Surtees Society 54 (1870). There are six letters from him published in the *Phil.Trans.* but the one referred to here by Johnson does not exist among them. The only published letter of his about Roman finds describes items found north of Lincoln. For Jurin, see Appendix 3.
9 John Battely (1646–1708: see *ODNB*). His work was published as *Opera Postuma viz. Antiquitates Rutupiæ et Antiquitates S. Edmundi Burgi ad annum 1272 perductæ* (1745). Rutupiæ was the Roman fort of Richborough in Kent, close to salt-producing areas. His work was quoted in *Acta Philosophorum*, a journal published between 1715 and 1726, edited by Christoph Heumann in Halle, Saxony. It has recently been reprinted.
10 Johnson was concerned to establish Spalding as the site of Ptolemy's 'Salinæ'; he was aware of salt-workings in Lincolnshire and was speculating on possible salt-making sites in Spalding. In this paragraph he presents his historical understanding of Spalding Castle and the connection with Ivo Tailbois and Countess Lucy. For this, see Neal Sumner, 'The Countess Lucy's priory? The early history of Spalding Priory and its estates', *Reading Medieval Studies* 13 (1987), and Nancy Snowdon, *Ivo Taillbois* (2010).
11 For Countess Lucy, see Katherine Keats-Rohan, 'Antecessor Noster: the parentage of Countess Lucy made plain', *Prosopon Newsletter* 2 (1995).
12 Spalding Priory was an alien priory of the Abbey of St Nicholas at Angers, France. The Académie Royale des Belles Lettres d'Angers was established by the Paris Parlement on 7 September 1685. In

1747 both Voltaire and the scientist Réaumur were made members. In 1760 it took the title Académie des Sciences, Belles Lettres et Arts d'Angers. Like all French academies, it was suppressed at the Revolution but was revived on several occasions, the latest being post-World War II in 1947, and it still flourishes today.

[13] Now Broad Street in Spalding; the theatre no longer exists there. Herbert's touring theatre company, based in Lincoln, had visited Spalding on previous occasions. George Alexander Stevens (1710–84: see *ODNB*) had acted in Lincoln where he married Mr Herbert's daughter Elizabeth. Stevens was famous for his comic speeches and prologues, eventually touring the country with a satirical monologue imitating a range of people, a precursor of today's 'one-man shows'.

[14] Johnson's extensive MS notes on emperors Carausius and Allectus and their coinage still exist in the SGS archives. They were lent by Johnson to Stukeley, who used them extensively in preparing his volume on Carausius. This is fully explained in an article by Adam Daubney, 'Maurice Johnson: an eighteenth-century numismatist', *The British Numismatic Journal* 82 (2012).

[15] Johnson apparently sent coins of Carausius and Allectus to Claude Genebrier in France (see **Letter 68** above) via Dr Smithson, who it has not proved possible to identify.

[16] The SGS still has a wide-ranging collection of coins, well catalogued by the Curator of Coins.

[17] For information about the coins of Carausius and Allectus, see P. J. Casey, *Carausius*.

[18] Sir Francis Whichcote (1692–1775), Whig MP for Cambridgeshire 1718–22. Aswarby Hall was demolished in 1951.

[19] This must be Theophilus Buckworth, whose brother Revd Everard Buckworth (see Appendix 3) became SGS Secretary in 1756. The family eventually became Lords of the Manor of Spalding-cum-Croyland. Their father Everard Buckworth had built the Manor House in Crackpole Lane (now Broad Street) in 1727. Theophilus's house in High Street, completed in 1764, is Cley Hall: see Neil Wright, *Spalding: An Industrial History* (1973). Theophilus married Elizabeth Cley of Bourne who brought him a fortune of £1,000 (*Gentleman's Magazine* (April 1751), 188).

[20] George Vertue (see Appendix 3) lived until 1756. In 1753 he published his account of Thomas Simon (1618–65: see *ODNB*), the medallist and seal-engraver who worked for both Cromwell and Charles II.

[21] General John Lambert (1619–84) and Colonel Edward Rossiter (1618–69) were significant parliamentary officers during the Civil War. Johnson's grandfather Walter Johnson (1620–92) was a JP, an attorney and Captain of the Trained Bands.

[22] For Bransby, an SGS member, see Appendix 3. Grace Bransby, née Lyon, had moved to Hamburg with her second husband, Revd William Murray (1705–79). The English church at Hamburg, founded in 1611, has registers going back to 1617, in the Staatsarchiv at Hamburg and is today an active multi-cultural Anglican church. For further details of the church, see SGS, MB5, fol.124r (entry for 13 September 1753).

[23] An artist of this name cannot be traced.

80. Maurice Johnson to William Stukeley, Spalding, 3 December 1753
Bodleian, MS Eng. misc. c.113, fols 381r–382v

Ayscoughfeehall in Spalding 3^d Decr 1753

Dear Dr

You know our County Meeting, for Races, is in the first week in Septr yearely, upon Lincoln Heath: that of this Town & Neighbourhood (which are chiefly the Villages adjoying in South Holland) for like purpose, in our adjoyning Common, calld the Greens or Horse race Peice, is the Week before.[1] Our old fair's 14th Sept^r, or Holy Rood, 6 Dec^r, St Nich[olas], our modern Tutelar, added to B.V.M. by Yvo Talbois our Anjouin Lord – Our modern Marketts by Charter on Tuesdays; Our antient, by Prescription, on Frydays, dies Veneris.[2] Before any Embankation, when the Phœnician came here for Salt, wooll, Leather, Saffron or other our then Staple Commodites, this was a Port, and has thence so continued – Salambena, Aphrodisione, Salinæ Gÿrviorum, Spaldelinges, all of the same

Signification, when converted, ad spumam maris, Venus was changd to B.V.M.³
– her Temple (out of the foundations of which Wee have a Bass Relief of Venus
dug up, & preservd in the Museum of SGS)⁴ was rededicated (as usual) to B.V.M.
& when the Saxon Cell was renderd a Convent it was consecrated to her, & by
the first Norman Lord subjected to his Abby of St Nicholas at Angiers,⁵ & he
made Joint Tutelar – Neptune as said to make, & delight in Horses, & usually
Represented drawn by Sea-Horses, might invent Horse Races, his Children by
the most antient Greeks reported the first eminent Horsemen. [p.2] As God of
the Sea Carausius Commander on these Coasts was devoted to him & calld
Neptunius; avowed his Tutelage on Coines, as Diocletion Joves & Maximian
Hercules'; about Holy rood Stagg Huntings, & Races were Antiently thought
to End and general Hunting was celebrated on that occasion. the Contention by
Races on Horseback coemeing first from the Great Use of that Creature to Man
in Hunting, & takeing Beasts of Food of which the Stagg (the best, & swiftest)
requiring more than the Speed of Man to come up with, & take or Overcome – so
that Æsop makes this to be the Very Original Cause of Horsemanship, to which
Fable, Horace aptly alludes.⁶ This Islett lay Antiently on the Broad bay, which
(before the Roman Embankations)⁷ extended very far & Expanded very Wide,
where It joyned with or became an Arm of the Sea. No signes I ever heard from
our most Juditious Considerers of the late Fangled French Fantacy of this coast
ever having joyned to France as a Continent:⁸ Camden, Llhuyd, Samms, Britan,
Chichely⁹ who had viewd & surveyd Both Coasts shores & Bay never thought
so. this Bay & the Coast It in great measure Surrounds was antiently deemed one
of our Kings Camera Regis in Mare.¹⁰ [p.3] Whatever Country man Carausius
might be by Birth, & whatever Menapius Civis may signify,¹¹ I am apt to believe
he fixed the seat of Empire & his Mint was principaly Used at Lincoln, from the
vast number of his Coines & Medals bearing the Notes of that City coinage on
the reverse of them, as in my History of that Mint,¹² I long since proved to the
Antiq[uarian] Soc. and our S.G.S. and the Imense Number of the Best of those
Coines & Medals there frequently found & through all this & the Neighbouring
Counties where I presume in the Ports of this Bay or that of Waynfleet his Navy
frequently Stationd; at the Efflux of Rivers, then best, as most Natural to the
East. the Romans I believe in so distant a Province, not giveing themselves much
Trouble or Charge to make Harbours or Moles for the security of their Shipping
an Opus vere Regium as was the Siccandæ Paludes or Embanking and Dreying
[sic] the fertile Country, overflowd for want of Restraining the River Banks &
keeping their waters within their Channels to keep Open their Outfalls to Sea,
which Silting up gradualy created Salt Marshes & left the land next the Town
Morasses, Morey or Mirey, & what Wee call the Fenns lying between the High or
Hilly Country & the Sea, Saltneau or Salt Marishes – Marisci – this is the case of
ours & all sea Coasts. when Broad there are, as in ours were, many Isletts in them
which when dreyned become one Country & passable by Banks, throughout.

[p.4] Dyke Gereeves, not so properly Fossarum, as Aggerum Curatores seu
Præpositi:¹³ the Scalp. statio Carinarum ad ostium Fluminis Lendæ.¹⁴ Our shipp's
Station at the Welland Mouth. Caput fluminis Lendæ, juxta les Deeps in our Bay,
now by the Cutting our Channell streight to Fossdyke & the Embanking our Salt
Marshes, thence so named, carryd down several Leagues lower to Sea which
formerly foamed up against this very place Naturaly an Islett & higher than the

adjacent Lands.[15] As still the Levells when taken, the Antient build up thereon & the Names of the Place all speake.

Tantum raptim[16] from Dear Dr your very affectionate Friend

M Johnson

P.S. Last Thursday at our Meeting of Spalding Gentlemens Society the Members were pleasd to Elect my Kinsman Mr Geo. Johnson of Brazen Nose Oxf[or]d Mr Jo Milles of Jesus Coll. Cambr[idge] & my Son Henry Eustace Members thereof.[17]

To the Rever^d
Dr Stukeley at his House
in Queensquare
   By Ormond Street
      London
         Present

[1] The Race Ground still exists as a site and place-name in south-west Spalding. The annual horse races for the area took place there during the eighteenth century. Mr Richards (see Appendix 3) erected stables along London Road and stands for spectators beside the race-course. The last race was run in 1788. See P. Faulkner, H. Healey and T. Lane, *Wide Horizons* (2010).

[2] During the eighteenth century there were five annual fairs in Spalding: 27 April (stock, hemp, flax), 29 June (stock, hemp, flax and horses), 25 August (horses), 25 September (horned cattle and other stock, hemp, flax and other merchandise) and 6 December (general). See B. Clark, *Spalding, the Evolution of a Fenland Town* (1978).

[3] Johnson worked out from analogy with a range of classical and early mediaeval place-names, some of them mythical rather than attached to Spalding in historical reality, that the origin of Spalding lay in salt-making. He then connected the myth of Venus arising from the sea with the Christianisation of pagan beliefs so that references to her were turned into references to the Blessed Virgin Mary; this analogical method of historical reasoning was the norm in the early eighteenth century.

[4] The discovery of a bas-relief carving from Roman times was taken by Johnson as conclusive evidence for the analogy referred to in n.3 above. It was found near Spalding parish church, dedicated to St Mary and St Nicholas, so Johnson assumes that there was a Roman temple to Venus, re-dedicated to Mary when the church was built, thus linking Roman to Christian Spalding.

[5] Johnson assumes the existence of a Saxon monastic cell of Crowland in Spalding, before the Norman Conquest, and refers to the founding of Spalding Priory by the Norman Ivo Tailbois as a re-foundation. Tailbois founded the Priory as a cell of the Abbey of St Nicholas at Angers, France.

[6] Johnson continues the analogy, relating the sea god Neptune with his sea-horses to the significant horse-races in Spalding and making a further connection to the Emperor Carausius and his naval victories; ships are a frequent feature on coins of Carausius (see P. J. Casey, *Carausius*, plate 3.3). Horace refers to Æsop in his *Satires*, e.g. II, 6.

[7] The Roman Bank was assumed to be an embankment raised by the Romans to protect 'the low lands of Lincolnshire from the inroads of the Ocean' (Thomas Allen, *The History of the County of Lincoln* (1830), 8), hence its name.

[8] The 'late Fangled French Fantacy' was, in fact, correct, as France was only separated from England after the dramatic rises in sea level following the melting of the ice-sheets after the Devensian glaciation: see D. Knight, B. Vyner and C. Allen (eds.), *East Midland Heritage* (2012), 45. This is, of course, a recent geological discovery.

[9] William Camden (1551–1623), Humphrey Llwyd (1527–68), Aylett Samms (1636–79); the other two cannot be identified.

[10] Literally 'The Royal treasury in the sea'. Camera Regis was the Royal treasury, so this means the ancient royal right of profit from the sea-shore.

[11] Johnson is now questioning his and Stukeley's certainty that the Emperor Carausius was a Briton. Casey points out that 'Aurelius Victor states that Carausius was a "civis Menapiæ" [a citizen of Menapia] this being the coast of Gallia Belgica' (P. J. Casey, *Carausius*, 47).

[12] Johnson argued in a dissertation at the SGS (see MB5, fol.132r–v) that Lincoln was the seat of an imperial Roman mint; the mint at Lincoln dates from late Saxon times.
[13] 'The caretakers or supervisors of ramparts'.
[14] 'The anchorage for ships at the mouth of the River Lenda [Welland]'.
[15] Johnson assumes that Spalding was a sea-port in Roman times, before the build-up of marshland necessitated the cutting of a channel for ships.
[16] Literally 'So much quickly', i.e. 'all I have time to write'.
[17] For these three new members, see Appendix 3.

81. Maurice Johnson to William Stukeley, Spalding, 19 January 1754
Bodleian, MS Eng. misc. c.113, fols 383r–384v

Ayscough Fee Hall Spalding 19th Jany 1754

Dear Dr

From my Son the Coll,[1] so soon as I could, (after I had received your Curious Memoirs of the Royall Society the Vol III & IV) I at our last Meeting of the Mbers [*sic*] of Spalding Gent. Society carryed those your Valuable & highly Acceptable Presents[2] into that good Company, for which & all your other many Benefits bestowed on us, I beg you to Accept mine and those Gentns Grateful acknowledgements by the Hands of my Amanuensis.[3] For a Newyears Gift we had a Celestial Armilary Sphære of Tin painted with the Globe of the World in the Center of the Circles pretty Large made & presented to our Museum by the Engenious Mr Hawks of Norwich[4] brought in & given us by our Operator Mr Michael Cox, And at our last Thursdays Meeting In a Letter from Couzin G. Johnson[5] of Magd. Coll. Oxford a member of our Society Several curious & some Ancient Latin Epitaphs, This young Gent. who is very hopefull with Couzn John Wingfield of Hartford Coll. Oxford, my Son Henry Eustace at Madrass (who has sent us an Entertaining Journal of his Voyage to Asia, Attended with Drawings in Indian Ink of the Johannia and Comorha Islands) Couzn Jos. Mills of Jesus Coll. Cambr., Mr Buckworth , Dr Dinham, Mr John Richards Junr of this Town, Mr William Dodd late of Clare Hall, Mr John Harrison Gardiner & Bottanist in Cambridge (who has presented our Physick Garden with a noble plant of the true Turkey Rhububb), Mr John Landen Mathematition at Walton, Mr James Muscott Schoolmaster of Boston, Mr Anthony Oldfield of Cheveley, The Revd Mr Richard Reynolds of Peterborough, Dr Thos. Sharp Archdeacon of Northumberland, Revd Richard Southgate of St Johns Coll. Cambr., Dr Cornwall Tathwell of Stamford, Mr James Verney Painter, Richard Wallin Esqr of Jamaica & Mr James Weeks Limner & Mr Joseph Pole a Prussian of Berlin Jewler & Sculptor have all lately been Elected a noble Suply of Youth for Continuing my Good Institution here.

[p.2] Wee've read with much pleasure Mr Avison[6] of Newcastles Essay on Harmony and arguments to rectifying Church Musick, with a Critick another Orgainist thereupon – and have Enterd on the Analysis of Beauty[7] – to rectify our Tast in Musick, Sculture & Painting. I hope Dear Friend you'll favour me with your Company, so long promisd & so much longd for, & find our little Cell improvd, that Institution being the Greatest Good I could propose to my Native place which no friend I have has Contribute more the [*sic*] Advancement & honour of than your Self. You see how well I've Supplyd It for a Successsion. Dr

Green youll find has greatly augmented his Pinacotheke[8] particularly an Usurer & Jeweller by Q. Metsys, a Large noble painting and for the age well preserved & others, and I have added some good Items to my Pictures. I wish you could make out my last Scrawl, rather worse written than Even this – my Head being more than affected – I am gott into a Milk Dyet (under Dr Greens good direction) which I thank Providence agrees well with Me and by the aid of frequent Bleeding and proper Evacuation my Life becomes much more Comfortable. But I abstain from so incessant Application to reading and writing as I have to my great Detriment formerly Used, and find that absolutely necessary turning my Mind to Gardening and Improvement of my Environs & have a Grandaughter of 5 yeares of Age whom I am making a florist[9] of in order to her becoming a Bird and flower painter in Water Colours.

[p.3] I am now (as Advisd) obliged to make use of anothers hand pretty much and my Friends will excuse that I dictate and Subscribeing my Love and Services to them & having so Good a Substitute to Carry on the main of our Societys Correspondance which I held with my Own hand as fully as I could by Sir Iz. Newtons & Dr Jurin my dear Friend and esteemed Tutors Advice[10] for upwards of 30 yeares: And never lost, or mislayd a Versall[11] of Paper which papers I should esteem Inestimable, and I hope my s[?successor: *gap in paper caused by removal of a seal*] will as I have Indexed them all for ready Use to this time – and they have proved of Service to many Editors of Learned Works and Members of our Spalding Gent. Society. I am glad my Sons House[12] and his Pictures pleasd You, I do what I can to give them a Rational Manly method of Enjoying Life & being Usefull to their King and Country & friends to my Family & friends. And of Consequence Valued by Them, & a share in the Esteem I trust Every of my Sons will have for their Fathers Sake who from Infancy has Enjoyd and highly valued your Friendship. Im pleasd you've found any things in my MSS of my Younger Yeares[13] Worthy your Notice: the best things in It and what Use you please to make of them are of right at your Service. Only don't publish any part of Dr Kennedys Letter or my answer to him[14] – Hogarth has not the same Opinion of that Gentleman you and I have. You'd oblige me Much in taking notice of our Spalding Gentlemens Society in Inscribing your intended work in hand about Carausius to Them as Edward Walpool of Dunston Esq did his Translation of de Partu Virginis B.M. revisd by Mr Pope.[15]

[p.4] the More and Best part of my Decennium Carausii & Allecti being Yours Sir. Mr Roger Gales, Beau: Bells, & other Members of It who Gave me the Transcript from Metzo Barba in Occo, Banduri, Pagi, Nichol. Hayme[16] &c which render It truly valuable – I request no mention of me in the Case but have a laudable Zeale for the Honour of the Institution and a Love for the Memory of those Worthy Members and their Judgement. Our late Worthy Member the Revd Mr Stephen Lyon,[17] had an Antique Cornelion of Neptune in a Chariot drawn by Sea Horses with the express Countenance of Carausius as seemd to me on Comparing It with his Coines of best Impression now his Daughters Mrs Murrays[18] & at Hamburgh which justufys, with Cottons Coin his being Neptunius.

     Yours Dear Friend most affectionatly
      M Johnson

To the Revd Dr Stukeley
Rect[r] of St Georges Queen's square

By Ormondstreet
London

1   Colonel Maurice Johnson.
2   Stukeley's latest volumes of memoirs of the RS meetings.
3   This letter begins in the handwriting of someone other than Maurice Johnson, probably his clerk; Johnson's health was deteriorating, as the letter indicates, and he was obliged to use assistance in writing his letters.
4   This is almost certainly the armillary sphere still held by the SGS, presented by Thomas Hawkes (see Appendix 3).
5   For George Johnson and most of the SGS members listed here, see their entries in Appendix 3.
6   Charles Avison (1709–70: see *ODNB*), composer and writer on the aesthetics of music. His work reflects the taste of the English public of his times; it is interesting that he preferred Geminiani to Handel.
7   The recently published book by the artist William Hogarth (1697–1764), *The Analysis of Beauty* (1753). The SGS is keeping up with the latest publications on music and art.
8   Dr Green's picture gallery or collection of paintings. Quentin Matsys (1466–1521) of Antwerp is best known today for his painting of the money-lender and his wife, dated 1514, now in the Louvre.
9   The eighteenth-century meaning was 'an expert on flowers and plants'. Johnson refers in his will to his only grand-daughter, Anna Maria Elizabeth Charlotte Archer, child of his late deceased daughter Mary Johnson (1723–41). It may be this child he is referring to, though there is a problem about her age.
10 Dr James Jurin (see Appendix 3). The reference to Jurin as Johnson's 'tutor' is difficult to substantiate. Johnson may have attended Jurin's public lectures in London as a young man. An alternative speculation is that Jurin may have spent a little time as private tutor to the Johnson brothers in his young days; Jurin was at Trinity College, Cambridge, from 1702 to 1708 when the Master of Trinity was Richard Bentley, who had been Master of Spalding Grammar School. Jurin was only four years older than Maurice Johnson.
11 'Versal' is defined as an ornamental letter beginning a section in a book or document; here it is used to mean 'a scrap or small item of paper'.
12 Col. Maurice Johnson's house in London; evidently Stukeley has visited him recently. Johnson's son has inherited his father's interest in paintings.
13 See **Letter 79**, n.14, above. Johnson's MS study of the coinage of Carausius had been bound by him in a MS volume including his early papers such as his Latin journal of a tour to Bath in 1710 which is still at the SGS.
14 For the correspondence between Dr Patrick Kennedy and Johnson about coinage of Carausius, see *Correspondence*, 92–3. In his *Analysis of Beauty* (1753) Hogarth acknowledges gratitude to Kennedy for drawing his attention to Michelangelo's view of the 'Line of Beauty' which forms an important part of Hogarth's discussion; he describes him as 'Dr Kennedy a learned antiquarian and connoisseur'. See Charles Davis (ed.), *William Hogarth: The Analysis of Beauty* (2010).
15 Edward Walpole (1702/3–40) of Dunston (Lincs); see Appendix 3. For the reference to Pope, see Walpole's letter to Johnson (dated 19 June 1736), transcribed in *Correspondence*, 104–5. Stukeley did not dedicate his book on Carausius, published in 1757, to the SGS as Johnson hoped.
16 Roger Gale and Beaupré Bell (see Appendix 3) had also contributed material and examples of coins for Johnson's very detailed study of Carausius's coinage, on which Stukeley drew for his own published work. Johnson details his other sources: Adolfo Occo (see **Letter 18**, n.16, above; both Johnson and Stukeley had copies of his work); Anselmo Banduri (*c*.1675–1743), *Numismata Imperatorum Romanorum* (1718); Antoine Pagi (1624–99), *Dissertatio hypatica, seu de consulibus Caesaris*, of which Stukeley owned a copy; Nicola Francesco Haym (1678–1729), an Italian musician who settled in England and also wrote *Tesoro Britannico, overa il Museo Nummario* (2 vols, 1719); Stukeley had a copy.
17 The Revd Stephen Lyon (see Appendix 3). For his daughter, see **Letter 79**, n.22, above.
18 Mrs Murray: see **Letter 79**, p.188.

82. Maurice Johnson to William Stukeley, Spalding, 18 November 1754
Bodleian, MS Eng. misc. c.113, fols 385r–386v

Spalding 18th Novb[r] 1754

My dear Friend,[1]

I Thank you much for your Last favour and am glad my Collections concerning Carausius and Allectus have been of use to you – I have also been this Summer at Cambridge in my way to newmarket for Change of Air and Health which I thank God is some what Better thereby shall hope to receive you here in may as you kindly proposed[2] with any of your Family or other friend of yours with you. our Society here return your kind Compliments with the most Grateful acknowledgements and at our next meeting wee Enter upon your fourth Ingenious Memoirs of R.S. etc. Mr Hawks of Norwich[3] obligingly sent us a Tin painted Armillary Sphære of his makeing as a new years Gift for our museum our Secretary Dr Green gave us a beautiful Bird shot by his son Picus Albonigroque Variegatus.[4]

14th February[5] Read an Associator written by the Operator Mr Cox of the analogy between anamals and vegitibles[6] and another on the same subject 28th March when the Librarian shewed the Company a Striking movement in a Case added to his Watch occasionally which repeats the hours and Quarters made by Mr John Ingram a watchmaker in this town who made our metal thermometer.

25th of april Mr Calamy Ives a member brought a Specimen of the Alium marinum and a Curious Nidus with the Eggs of Some Incect therein.

23 May Mr Grundy a member presented the Museum with Large Specimins of the Asbestos Rameantus Stone Secondly an Incrostation of Sand and Shells andhereing [sic] to the upper straton of rock adjoyning to the River Dee near Land Fracture in Flintshire. 3dly the Rattlesnake 4thly an Hummingbird 5thly a very large Large [sic] Barnicle Cut off from a back of a Whale [?resembling] Wyncles by the Surgeon of the Ship Royal Bounty [p.2] On the Coast of Greenland in the year one thousand seven hundred and fifty. Seromphius of Shells plate 32 No.2 Fol.7.[7]

6th June the Librarian compleated the reading of Mr Howgarths a Nalicus of Beauty. 13th June president shewed the Company two dishes of Aubany Ware by Vasair one Imbost of Venos between Seris and Bacquis[8] a nother plane but wholl Couloured of Venus Rising from the Sea with Neptune and the Tritons attending 1515. The Secretary shewed the Company neatly preserved in Glass Cases from the Coast of Malabar Sent him by Mr Henry Eustace Johnson some Curious East Indian Butterfly's black and Scarlet large and of the kind we call Swallow Talles. 20 June Mr Grundy presented Specimons of Various Byvalves[9] out of Chalk with some of Currals and Micetite with Chrystols of five Angles from Westchester.

4th July The president Brought in a Brance [sic] of the Acatia in flower bearing white flowers like the pea and Sweet as the orange flower In Blow in his Garden. The Secretary Shewed the Company a Small Copper piece of the Empirer [sic] Gallienus Reversies Adoption of his son young Valerian as Cesar. 11th July Mr Operator Cox brought In from Mr Ingram Surgean a Member the Mason fly of Berbadeus See Dr Huses History of Berbadus.[10]

1st Aug[t] the Treasurer gave an account to the Company of a Water spout by him that day seen at Spalding somewhat resembling an Elifants Trunk. 22 Augt a Saler brought into the Museum part of a fin of a Whale which grows within its mouth.

Sept.r 19th Mr Grundy presented the Museum with Some specimens of Ores and a Nut of the Citra morabolan and Showed the Company several Elegant Skins of marl from Wyburg Sables or Pelle Zibelanæ Also of some Delicate Irmon skins from Siberian in Russia.[11]

26 Sept.r the president Shewed the Company a drawing about three Inches long of a Coper plate Studed with Silver Stars and flames of an old man with A long Beard in a long Gown bearing a fool on his back with a fools Cap and bells on it [p.3] Found among the Ruins of Waverly Abbay in Surry.[12] The seal of Thomas Orby hunter Esquire a Member who in flanders was told it was the Badg of an order called Mere De Follie whereof the Prince of Conti and some other noblemen of France where, but bycoming disolute it was suppressed for Ill behaviour. Note Waverly was a great Susturtian abbay patronised by the Byshops of Wynchester.

Also Showed the Company a ponderous Grinder Tooth Dugg up very Deep out of Deeping Fenn and turned Brown Weight three ounces three fourths of a grain Ribbed with deep Channels and Crooked[13] given him by Mr blades [*gap in text*] Day Surveyor of Sewers for Spalding parish. Dr Tathwell a member [*gap in text*] lately called at Cates Cabbin Told us part of the Inscription of the Taylors or tessura there found at the beginning an End seemed to him to be great Characters of Words to the like affect with VTERE FELIX which are stil plainly remaining thereon as Mr Benjamin Cook late our Register Drew and sent them me and that the Brass Frame, of Alabarum was dug up near that monument at Alwalton.[14]

3 Oct. plan and views of St Petersburg taken and Ingraved there 1753 where produced at this Society Also the flower of the Caltha Americana[15] with a floscular production in the Center very large.

31st Oct. The Secretary gave an Acas Marinas or Gardfish taken in the Welland whose Boans when Boyled were Green.[16]

14th Nov.br Showed a Conger powte or young Cong. Eel there taken fresh Four feet 8 inches long weight fifteen pound.

Mr Jackson of Boston a member sent the Impression in Wax of an antient Vicontial seal of Lincoln Castle Gate.[17]

My Humble Service to your Good Lady Family and all friends and be assured I am tho very tiresome with my phylosophical Correspondence my Dearest friend
              Yo.rs M Johnson[18]

To
    The Rev.d D.r Stukeley
Rector of St Georges in QueensSquare
Ormond Street
        London

---

[1] This letter is in the handwriting of an assistant, probably Johnson's clerk. The clerk has some problems in following Johnson's dictation on technical points and understanding the terms used; he therefore makes spelling mistakes inconsistent with Johnson's usual style. It is Johnson's final surviving letter to Stukeley.

[2] This visit was not to happen, as Johnson died early the following year and was buried at Spalding on 11 February 1755.

[3] See **Letters 76**, n.15, and **81**, n.4, above. It is still in the SGS museum, see Appendix 3.

[4] The greater spotted woodpecker; see John Hill, *The History of Animals* (1752), 396.

[5] Johnson is dictating summaries of minutes from the weekly meetings of the SGS which he thinks

will be of particular interest to Stukeley, perhaps with the hope that some of them will be communicated to the RS. They give an idea of the wide range of topics covered at meetings. In some cases Johnson repeats information he had communicated in earlier letters, an indication of his deteriorating health.

6   The assistant's spelling begins to show interesting variations. The 'Associators' were MS dissertations written by SGS members on erudite subjects and matters of general interest, on the lines of those published in the London journals, and read to Society meetings in addition to extracts from Dr Samuel Johnson's *Rambler*. Michael Cox wrote several on medical subjects; in addition to the two mentioned here, he is recorded as delivering 'Associators' on clothes, education, literary controversy and the positive value of association (i.e. sociability, a prime theme of Johnson's thought). They were read between 22 February 1753 and 29 January 1756, with Cox delivering the final one, 'a genteel compliment' to the late President, Maurice Johnson. Cox himself was buried on 20 April 1758. Many of the 'Associators' survive at the SGS.

7   The writer has evidently misinterpreted Johnson's dictation of 'See Rumphius of Shells', his usual way of referring a reader to a specific book. Georgius Everhardus Rumphius (Rumpf) (1627–1702), a German botanist employed by the Dutch East India company, produced *D'Amboinsche Rariteitkamer* (1705) which contained information on East Indian shells and *Herbarium Amboinense* (1741), a catalogue of Indonesian plants; this is a rare book and it is suggested that the plates were prepared by Maria Sibylla Merian.

8   Col. Maurice Johnson had sent his father a set of eight dishes of Italian Albani ware, valued then as a collector's item. Johnson showed two of them to the SGS meetings on 6 and 13 June 1754 (MB6, fol.9v). There are some interesting spellings here, as the writer attempts to cope with the dictation of Hogarth's *Analysis of Beauty* and the classical deities Ceres and Bacchus.

9   John Grundy junior, the drainage engineer, showed the SGS fossil bivalves or molluscs that he had from Chester (MB6, fol.10r), see Appendix 3.

10   The Revd Griffith Hughes (c.1707–58), FRS 1748, wrote *The Natural History of Barbados* (1750). The SGS are keeping up with the latest publications.

11   Citron myrabolan, a citrus fruit from India, the size of a plum. The minutes record that John Grundy junior showed the SGS some 'elegant' ermine skins, [pine]marten skins and 'sables, pelles Zibellinae he had presented him from Russia' (SGS, MB6, fol.12r, entry for 19 September 1754). The writer is again having difficulties with the terms dictated by Johnson.

12   In 1626 Henri de Bourbon, Prince de Condé, established a society in Dijon for wild entertainment, named after a local saying relating to 'La mère de folle'. It was banned and abolished by an edict from Lyons in 1630. The drawing mentioned here is copied into MB6, fol.12r (entry for 26 September 1754). Waverley was the first Cistercian abbey to be established in England, in 1128.

13   MB6 (fol.12v) has several drawings of animal teeth; the suggestion at the SGS was that they were those of oxen and horses; they may be prehistoric remains.

14   Kate's Cabin: see **Letter 74**, n.17, above. It was formerly the Dryden's Head Inn, during the rebuilding of which in 1754 several Roman dwelling-places and burials were recorded. Amongst the Roman remains found on this site, this letter records 'a brass frame of Alabarum'. This is his clerk's rendering of 'a labarum', a Roman military standard; it is correctly written on the relevant page of MB6 (fol.12v). The Latin phrase means 'Use Happily'.

15   Philip Miller (1691–1771) in his *Gardener's Dictionary* (1732) records the Caltha Americana as 'a marigold with an upright branching stalk oblong hairy leaves growing opposite and flowers proceeding from the sides of the stalk'.

16   The garfish, named after the Anglo-Saxon word for a spear, 'gar', is also known as the needlefish. Linnaeus named it Belone belone. It does indeed have green bones.

17   The seal of the sheriff of Lincolnshire bore a device consisting of a castle with two side towers, domed and topped by a flag, having a round-headed portal with portcullis down. See W. de G. Birch, *Catalogue of Seals in the Department of Manuscripts in the British Museum* (6 vols, London, 1887–1900) II, 105. For William Jackson of Boston, see Appendix 3.

18   The signature is in Maurice Johnson's own hand.

ADDITIONAL LETTERS

Seven letters are placed here, for a range of reasons. Two letters from Johnson, which are not present among Stukeley's papers and collection of letters held in the Bodleian Library, were transcribed and published in John Nichols, *Bibliotheca Topographica Britannica* (1781). They are included here as **Letters 83** (dated 14 October 1719) and **86** (dated 21 June 1750) since they help to fill out the correspondence and exchange of ideas between Johnson and Stukeley. **Letter 83** was also transcribed and published in *Surtees* I (1873). **Letter 85** (dated 17 March 1744) from Johnson to Stukeley, was transcribed and published in *Surtees* II (1876). Since these three letters have been reproduced from published editions, we have not seen the originals and cannot vouch for their reproducing exactly the spelling and punctuation of the original letters.

Letter 84 is a letter from Stukeley, in Grantham, to Johnson in 1728 which is not in the Spalding collection but in the Wingfield papers in the archives of the Northamptonshire Record Office; it is transcribed here by their kind permission. It has been placed here because it is not part of the collection of letters in the Spalding archive.

Of the three remaining letters, two (**Letters 87** and **88**) were written to Stukeley in 1755 and 1756, after Johnson's death, by the Revd John Johnson, third son of Maurice Johnson. They are in Stukeley's letter-book at the Bodleian Library. The final one (**Letter 89**) is a letter from Stukeley in 1756 to Dr John Green, Secretary of the SGS, which is kept with Stukeley's letters to Maurice Johnson in the Spalding archives. These final three letters are relevant as they are the final stages of this correspondence relating to the many years of friendship between Stukeley and Johnson and to their shared interest in the Spalding Gentlemen's Society.

83. Maurice Johnson to William Stukeley, Spalding, 14 October 1719[1]

Spalding, October 14 1719

Dear Doctor,

It is so long since I enjoyed your good company, and you are so much in my thoughts, that I presume you will excuse an old friend's enquiring this way of your state of health, and progress in the practice of your profession; for, believe me, Sir, you have friends no where more earnestly wishing you felicity and success than in your own country, to which you must give me leave to say, you are an ornament: and amongst your countrymen let me beg you will be assured no one can be rejoiced more in your prosperity than I do. But your gains are our loss, that your assistance when we want health, and your good company for its preservation, are too remote; this epidemic distemper[2] has rambled and raged so throughout our parts of England from Borough Bridge to your metropolis. 'Tis true indeed from all we can hear, that the malady has not been attended with such fatal consequences in our Fenny Tracts as in what we vulgarly call the High Countries.³ Perhaps, Doctor, your Epidaurean Serpent,⁴ sprung from the slimy mud of such a level, protects us as a good genius; however, the like of this illness has not ever been known here, and as it is from an infected air, the curious enquirers of your humble cell at Spalding would hold themselves much obliged by an historical account from you of any such universal contagious fever in England before this time, which we doubt not but the history of physic and distempers may have furnished you with, for other physicians tell us not of one instance of a general yet not fatal fever in so large a tract of country. With God's blessing, and the care and learning of your good friend and mine Dr Nutton,⁵ whose judgment I believe very sound, and who particularly desires me to remember him to you, I see my only son sprightly and active again, who was the most severely handled of all our numerous family, out of which, being 21 in number, all, save my spouse and brother, who are very much yours. He was, Sir, seized with it as other people, but the fever grew so fierce by degrees, and lasted so long, as to throw him into the most violent convulsions I ever did see, which when the Doctor had carried off, the poor rogue seemed lifeless, and without the least motion, having, as his fond relations perhaps alone thought, not so much as the power to breathe left. It has twice handled me severely, one fit of a fever for two days and a night without remission, and a second for 34 hours; but I thank God, I am well again; and it did interfere with my business, which I find will increase upon a young man if he perseveres, and I trust we may both live to do more than bear the charges of liberal educations. I should be glad to hear you had taken to you a female to your mind, for the continuance of your family, and question not but your successors will have reason to esteem you as much as any of your progenitors, though some of them (as I have remarked according to your commands) good and great men, of considerable interest and abilities in their country. I shall ever be most ready to serve you in any thing, and the instance I give you in this particular, by the little extracts from divers authors, only serves to evince by my diligence, my perpetually bearing you in mind when any thing occurs, that is, what you desire to preserve. These, as I believe them properly and peculiarly to relate to you, will I hope be acceptable to yourself; and I wish I could any way contribute to the entertainment of my good friends at the Mitre, whose healths we drink every Wednesday night duly.⁶ It is not the affectation of being otherwise fully employed, which prevents my endeavouring it; but the little abilities I have for communicating any thing not before observed by and well known to most of you, and the few opportunities I have of seeing here any thing but what is in print and within every man's purchase, deter my attempting it, lest I should only prove my ignorance, by making a common object, and what so well-read men meet with every day, a matter of wonder; but as a friend who will look with the favourablest eyes on my performance, I dare venture to tell you thoughts which I dare not speak out in company even the most candid. All our friends here are pretty well; your godfather and Joshua,⁷ who is yet unmarried, present their services to you. I don't need to tell you I wish I had been at home when you was in the country, that I might have had the satisfaction of endeavouring to amuse you agreeably a while, which I almost despair of doing by any thing I can communicate from hence concerning the learned world. However, what I am told I will tell you, and though it be no more than what you knew before, yet I shall only then do as they who greet us with its being a very sickly time, cold weather &c. –

The University of Cambridge is upon erecting a theatre,[8] and have for that purpose lately turned several tenants out of houses which they some time since purchased, to build it upon the ground where they stand, and resolve, as I am told, to chuse the same vice-chancellor again, and he to accept it, and to cite Dr Bentley as master of Trinity, to shew reasons why he will not consent that an instrument they call the Programma should not be fixed upon the public schools, and other such places. Our friend Sparke of Peterborough[9] has lately put into good order and a new method the earl of Cardigan's library at Dean in Northamptonshire, in a noble large room which that lord has assigned for that purpose, and fitted up accordingly. Mr Young,[10] now LL.D. who wrote the poem on the Last Day and Busiris, is taken into the Earl of Exeter's family as tutor to his Lordship's eldest son Lord Burleigh, and is going to travel with him. Your townswoman and my pretty neighbour Sally Hibbins[11] has written a very diverting comedy since she has been in Shropshire. I must not forget to let you know how our little Society goes on, which is very well. We meet constantly, but are likely to lose one of our members, Mr Atkinson,[12] who through a complication of distempers is brought so low that I fear we shall lose him very soon. Your own parish Holbeach affords one remarkable article in the parochial charge, where the last year the churchwardens paid 4l. 6s. for the destruction of the urchins or hedgehogs, at but one single penny a piece, and the present officers have paid above 30l. on the same account already: the vast stocks of cattle in this noble parish and some coney burroughs, have drawn those creatues from all parts hither, as one would think.[13] You know that ingenious old gentleman your townsman Mr Rands[14] is dead there, the remaining part of whose collection of prints devolve upon me by purchase, and I wish he had not so far indulged the ignorant as to have let them cull out some of them. I desire you will send me word, good Mr Secretary,[15] how the impression of the Registrum Honoris de Richmond goes on, and to set down Edward Horseman of Lincoln's Inn, Esquire for a subscriber for one copy, and let Mr Treasurer know I am much his humble servant, and will answer the subscription for that gentleman to him when next I have the pleasure to see you all. I have not yet been able to gain any thing worthy the press relating to that book, which I yet hope to do, and will endeavour; the whole and large Soke of Kirkton, in our fens, being parcel of that Honour, and now the possession of the Earl of Exeter, Lord thereof, and my father Steward of the Courts of that Soke.[16] I have not yet procured what I wrote for, a MS of that Earl's, relating, as I hope to find, to that district or jurisdiction; but more of this hereafter. I beg of you, when next you see Mr Norroy, our learned President,[17] to present my humble service to him, and desire him to tell you the meaning of these words not unfrequent in Domesday, title Lincolnshire, *Tailla*, & *Berew*, which last is by Ingulphus rendered Manerium, but desire him to tell you what sort of manor he takes it to be, and, if I shall not be too troublesome to him, I would beg of him to tell me whose coate of arms is, Az. on a chief Argent, 3 (I don't know what they are except Buckles) Az. and this bearing enquire about also; Jacob's staff Or between a chevron Or. charged with 5 Mullets Az. and for the Crest to this coast, an horse's head erased Gules, bridled Az. or rather a blue ribband tied round his neck.[18] My humble service also to Mr Hare and to Mr Homes,[19] and tell him I beg of him to let me have copies of the inquisition, and also of the claim at the coronation of king Richard the Second, made out for me against I come to town, where I long to be for the sake of conversing with you, Sir, and the good company at the Mitre. I hope Mr Hill[20] goes on with his Hereford; but he either has not finished the poem he read part of to us, or forgot his promise of sending me a copy of it. Pray how does Mr Baxter's Grammar go on?[21] If you have any where met with any thing relating to my ancestors in your turning over your old books or papers, I beg you in return to send it me with an answer to my queries, &c. in your own good time; and am, wishing you very much joy of all your honours and long health, dear Sir, your sincere ready friend, and humble servant,

Maurice Johnson, jun.

P.S. I had almost forgotten another coat of arms which I beg you to ask of Mr Le Neve or Mr Hare, as of the others, whose name it belongs to. Gules, 3 sinister wings, Or, between a fesse Argent, in the middle of which is a Lion Or, in a round spot Gules; two Wings above the fesse and one below it. I believe I should say a fesse charged with such a thing, but he will pardon my want of proper terms, and teach me better from your answer.[22]

---

[1] This letter was transcribed and published in John Nichols, *Bibliotheca Topographica Britannica II, Reliquiæ Galeanæ* (1781), 90–5, and also in *Surtees* I, 163–9. It was presumably among the papers of the Gale brothers which Nichols drew on for his publication; it is not among Stukeley's papers in the Bodleian Library. As this version is taken from Nichols and not from the original, it is possible that the editor has modified some of Johnson's spellings.

[2] Possibly smallpox; there was a serious epidemic of smallpox in London in 1719. Johnson states that the outbreak of illness stretches from the north of Yorkshire to London.

[3] The High Country is the higher area to the west of the Fens, notably the Cliff Edge in north Kesteven and the Kesteven Uplands.

[4] The symbol of Asclepius, the Greek god of medicine, was the serpent-entwined rod, the serpent of Epidaurus; today that symbol is the crest of the Royal Pharmaceutical Society of Great Britain.

[5] Dr John Nutton (1657–*c.*1736), MD Cambridge (1685), physician in Spalding (see *Surtees* I, 13, 35, 42).

[6] The SGS met on Wednesdays for a time during its early years, before moving to the Thursdays which are still its meeting evenings. At meetings they remembered the Society of Antiquaries, meeting at the Mitre Tavern in Fleet Street from 1717 onwards.

[7] William Ambler and his son Joshua; see Appendix 3.

[8] The university did not build a theatre in Cambridge at this time, but a local magistrate, Joseph Kettle, constructed one on private ground. The Vice-Chancellor of Cambridge from 1717 to 1720 was Thomas Gooch (1674–1754), Master of Gonville and Caius College, Bishop of Norwich 1738–47 and of Ely 1748–54. Dr Bentley (see Appendix 3 and *ODNB*) was well known to Spalding as he had been the Master of the grammar school in 1682. As a Whig he quarrelled with the Tory Gooch over college and university administration.

[9] Revd Joseph Sparke (see Appendix 3) catalogued the library at Deene Park, Northamptonshire, for George Brudenell, third Earl of Cardigan.

[10] Revd Edward Young (1683–1765: see *ODNB*), a poet best known for *Night Thoughts*. His *Poem on the Last Day* was published in 1713 and his play *Busiris* was performed in London in March 1719. Young became tutor to John Cecil (1700–22), Lord Burghley and later Earl of Exeter from 1721–22. Nichols and Surtees both have long footnotes on this.

[11] Though there were a number of successful women playwrights at this period, Sally or Sarah Hibbins cannot be traced.

[12] William Atkinson, Treasurer of the SGS, died in 1719 and Revd Timothy Neve took over the office; see Appendix 3.

[13] A vindication of the poor hedgehog was published in *Gentleman's Magazine* 49 (1780), 395.

14   Perhaps a member of the same family as Henry Rands (d.1551: see *ODNB*), Bishop of Lincoln, who came from Holbeach.
15   Stukeley was Secretary of the Society of Antiquaries (1717–25) and one of the Gale brothers, Samuel, was Treasurer. Roger Gale published his *Registrum Honoris de Richmond* in 1722 under the Society's direction. Edward Horsman also subscribed to the *General Abridgment of Common Law* (1713); his will, dated 6 November 1721, was proved 6 March 1732 by his brother Dr Samuel Horsman.
16   Johnson's father, as Steward of the Soke of Kirton for the Earl of Exeter, would be aware that the Soke was a parcel of the Honour of Richmond, which owned much of Boston and Kirton.
17   The antiquary Peter le Neve (1661–1729: see *ODNB*), President of the Society of Antiquaries at its revival in 1717. He was Richmond Herald (1707–21) and Norroy King of Arms (1704–24), both significant heraldic offices. His antiquarian knowledge led Johnson to enquire about two Domesday Book terms, 'tailla', a customary payment widespread in Lincolnshire, and 'berew', an abbreviation for 'berewica (berewick)', an outlying settlement.
18   Nichols and *Surtees* identify the first of these as the Thorowgood family and the second as the family of Evington of Hastead and Spalding.
19   John Hare (d.1720), Richmond Herald (1704–07), FSA (1717), of Snetterton (Norfolk), involved in research which led eventually to Gale's publication of the *Registrum* in 1722 (see n.15 above) and probably George Holmes (1661–1749: see *ODNB*), founder-member of the SA, close associate of Peter le Neve and Keeper of the Records at the Tower of London.
20   James Hill (1697–1727: see *ODNB*), FSA (1718), FRS (1719), historian of Hereford; his papers are all now in Hereford City Library and Hereford Record Office.
21   William Baxter (1650–1723: see *ODNB*), author of *Glossarium antiquitatum Britannicarum* (1719). In 1733 William Stukeley and Edward Lhuyd published a second edition.
22   The arms described in the postscript are identified by *Surtees* as belonging to Porter of Cornwall. According to *Surtees*, 'other coats drawn in this letter and explained by Le Neve were those of Richard Fitz John, Adam Fitz John and Johnson of Boston'.

84. William Stukeley to Maurice Johnson, Grantham, n.d. but soon after 13 April 1728
Wingfield Papers, Northamptonshire Record Office[1]

Dear Friend,

I received yours[2] with a deal of satisfaction. tis true enough that it was an uneasyness to me not to heard [*sic*] from you sooner, & seemingly to have wholly lost a friendship of long standing, when I imagin'd it would revive with fresh vigor, upon my removing so much nearer you into the same province.[3] tho' I had rode twice thro' your town yet never alighted, & once I know you was out upon the circuit, & that ought not to have been construed a neglect, for I judg, it was a point of right on my side to insist upon the first visit, or notice. but no more of such matter. I heartily congratulate you upon the success of your Society whereof you ought to be accounted the father. I have not attempted any thing of that nature here conceiving it would be a matter of great difficulty. But I have thoughts about it, which at present I defer a little longer, being taken up with establishing my character & interest.

we have lately had Dr Wallis[4] here to settle, from Cambridg, imagining there was money to be got. but I am sure he will be mistaken, for if there was only one physician, as now there are three beside practising apothecarys, one could not get much above £100 per ann. which was one reason why I fell upon practise, as knowing it would not wholly engross my time. & I think I have by my own interest & my wives numerous relations, such a prospect as will preclude any others invasion. I am grown in love with business near home, &

have disclaim'd all long journeys. for I have, I thank Providence, every thing at home so very agreabl to my own humor & gusto, that I am never so happy as when at home. my old house I have brushd up a little to make it commodious, & to my liking handsom enough. my study is finishd, looking over my gardens & a very delightful prospect of our river, heath & pastures. it has an east southern window. my garden which I have now finishd with great expedition is spacious enough, & I avoyded in it every things which I imagin'd of a little taste. I am far ~~enough~~ from coming into the modern whimsy of banishing all greens & flowers, & reducing it to grass & forest trees: that may well enough become a hunting seat, lodg in a park &c but is dissonant from the nature & design of a mansion house. nevertheless I have not crouded 'em so thick & in such diminutive knots & fancys, as that a hoopt petticoat or rather ones own feet in common progression can't handsomely walk between. I think gardens are chiefly designd for walking, & therefore should consist mostly of walks, for tho' mine be 230 foot by 130, yet I have only 4 parterres, each 40 foot square. between these only is a gravel walk in form of a cross. & this part of the garden is elevated a step or two above the common level, declining [p.2] to the South east & may be calld a terrace garden.

[*Sketch plan of the garden at the side of the text of p.2, see Illustration 8.*]

beyond this is a bason or amphitheatre 100 foot diameter 5 foot deep: planted with tall fruittrees of various sorts as apples, pears, plumbs, walnuts, mulberrys, services, medlars, cherrys. this makes an agreabl shade & is the *sylva academi*[5] for philosophers to walk in. tis underfoot grass only. quite round all this is a broad grass walk, & the wall is high enough only to exclude thieves but not to hinder the prospect of the country. for I have raisd the whole accordingly. the little diagram I have sketchd out[6] will make you understand the nature of it. I have a great deal of gardenroom more to the east & north planted much with fruittrees &c but I have done nothing at them yet. & the river runs at the bottom. the corners by the amphitheater have alcoves & seats. to the south of the house is my hermitage vineyard, so calld because the walls are all planted with vines, & in the wall I have built a grotto or cell sufficiently romantic. the plain of the garden is full of the most odoriferous herbs. herein is a stone terrestrial globe set conform to the true globe. & my roman altar from northumberland in a ragged niche overgrown with ivy &c. in a wall I have placed this inscription cut in large letters [*sketch of plaque*] in a battering wall (as technically calld) which I built to support my terrace to the east I have placd the following. it faces the river.

[*Sketch of second plaque.*[7]]

by those things you may guess I have throughly fixt my *lares*,[8] my fortune, my ambition. & truly no one was ever more satisfyd with their change or their station than my self. not having the least inclination ever to see London again. but treat it with the utmost contempt, or as the angel says in Milton
    and with retorted scorn his back he turnd
    on those proud towers to swift destruction doom'd.[9]
in the time I spent there, I took a full draught of what London could afford, & rightly resolvd to retire in time, to the serene pleasures flowing from the contem-

plation of pure & uncorrupted nature. with what delight doe I ride ore the [p.3] tops of our hills enjoying the sweetest air, & surveying the noblest prospect that can be imagind, within half a mile of my house,[10] far more magnificent than that from Hampsted Southward. hence we can see beyond Boston, Lincoln & within a mile or two of Derby, the forest of Sherwood, the Trent &c. we have the noble hermenstreet & very perfect within a mile of us.[11] the curious camp at Honington; on one side the roman city at Ancaster, on the other that of Paunton which I glory in establishing for the *Causennis* of *Antoninus*.[12] & which Mr Gale thanks me for in a letter he sent me lately. that ingenious old friend of mine has wrote to me twice lately. he sent me word of the death of our old acquaintance James Hill[13] a lad of excellent learning. His imperfect history of Herefordshire is put into Mr Gales hands. I have an original picture of him by his namesake Hill, which he sent me. I have likewise an original of Camden. Mr Gale sends me word he purposes to visit me in the latter end of August.

We lately discoverd a curious mosaic roman pavement upon a hill by Denton,[14] I sent a draught & description of it to the royal society which pleasd 'em. I was at Lincoln last week where Mr Pownel[15] expressd a concern you should take it ill, that he did not give you the famous coyn of Carausius. I discoverd again the old roman wall on the south side the castle. so that the Norman conqueror made his deep ditches in the ground of the old roman city. at Newark last Monday I saw the ingenious Mr Warburton[16] he is gone to Cambridg to take his degree. next week I goe to Nottingham to visit among others our old friend Mr Hardy who *proh deum atque hominum fidem*[17] has chang'd his religion. as if there was any thing so very essential in the forms & modes of the *cultus divinus*, which I think consists in honesty & sincerity. in action & practise & beneficence, more than belief & speculation. we have several men of excellent learning near us, & I enjoy 'em with more pleasure than we usd to doe in London where they are so common, that tis rudeness to talk of any thing that way. but my study is an endless sourse of learned amusement. & now & then I touch a little upon the huge mass of papers I have formerly wrote, & may possibly once more trouble the public with something, especially upon the Celtic antiquitys – where I have discoverd some very curious & remarkabl [*sic*] matters.

I hear the french author of Carausius is broke.[18] I hope you will not delay publishing your curious collections of the life of that brave briton or hibernian at least. I expect to see you in a months time at Spalding & hope I may have the pleasure too of seeing you at Grantham.

My Spouse sends her service to your Lady & hopes they shall be acquainted: my service waits on the Gentlemen of your Society. I am always
      My Dear Friend
           Your most affectionate
               humble Servant
                  W[m] Stukeley

To Maurice Johnson jun[r] Esq[r]
   at Spalding.
Turn at Stilton

---

[1] The Wingfields of Tickencote were related to Johnson's family and John Wingfield, called by Johnson 'Couzen Wingfield', became a member of the SGS in 1753. The letter was perhaps lent to a

member of this family and remained with the family papers, thus becoming separated from the SGS's collection of Stukeley's letters.

2   Johnson's letter of 16 April 1728 (**Letter 23** above).

3   Johnson and Stukeley had been friends since childhood, when their fathers, both local lawyers, were fellow-officers in the same unit of the local militia. Stukeley had moved to Grantham in early 1726.

4   Perhaps Thomas Wallis (c.1698–1753) MB, MD Cambridge (1725).

5   'An academic wood' or 'the wood of the Academy', a reference to Plato's original Academy which contained a grove of olive trees.

6   On the second page of the letter Stukeley has drawn a detailed plan of his garden, together with two sketches of plaques he has placed in the garden. At the top, left side and bottom of the diagram, Johnson has added notes at a later stage, probably when reviewing the letter. They are as follows: at the East end of the plan: 'here abouts beyond an Osier bank lyes the River in View'; just beyond the North edge of the plan: 'on this Side Lyeth a Large Orchard which the Dr hath since bought & layd to his Garden'; at the foot of the plan: ' I had the pleasure of Seing [sic] this retirement & my Friend at It in 1729. MJ'. The plan is reproduced as Illustration 8.

7   The inscriptions on the two plaques read: 'BEATÆ TRANQUILLITATI P. W. STUKELEY 1726' ('To blessed tranquillity by W. Stukeley') and FLUMINA AMEM SILVASQUE INGLORIUS. CHYNDONAX 1726. This is a quotation from Virgil, *Georgics* II, 'let me be lacking in fame and love rivers and trees'. 'Chyndonax' is the name Stukeley adopted in the Society of Roman Knights and was allegedly that of an ancient Druid; the Druids were known for their love of woods.

8   'Lares' were the Roman gods who protected the household.

9   The last lines of Book V of John Milton's *Paradise Lost*.

10 Grantham is surrounded by hills on three sides; the most likely site from which he gained this view is Hall's Hill, across the Witham, about half a mile east of Stukeley's house; Gonerby Hill, and Barrowby Hill, also good viewpoints, are further away.

11 Stukeley was pleased to have Roman remains so near his house. Ermine Street, or the High Dyke, is actually two miles from the site of his house in Grantham. Honington Camp, a British fortification, is several miles north of Grantham and about 1½ miles west of Ermine Street, on which he correctly places Ancaster. The two villages of Great and Little Ponton are to the south of Grantham, in the upper Witham valley about a mile west of Ermine Street.

12 Stukeley sited the Roman settlement of Causennæ at Ponton in his endeavours to locate the forts specified in the *Antonine Itinerary*. A later view placed it at Ancaster. The latest view is that it was located even closer to Grantham, at Saltersford: see J. B. Whitwell, *Roman Lincolnshire* (1970), 65. Roger Gale's father, Dean Gale of York, had studied and edited the *Antonine Itinerary*; see **Letter 28**, n.9, and n.10 above for further discussion.

13 See **Letter 83**, n.20, above.

14 Whitwell, *Roman Lincolnshire* (see n.12) states that 'the villa at Denton was first known in 1727 … close to the intersection of the Salt Way and Ermine Street' (81–2). Stukeley's account, which puts the villa close to 'the great Roman Road called Hermen street' and to the Witham 'at Salter's Ford', was published in *Phil.Trans.* 35 (1727). The discovery was as a result of 'plowing in the open fields of Denton'.

15 William Pownall (d.1735), military officer and keen local antiquarian in Lincoln.

16 William Warburton (1698–1779: see *ODNB*), not yet ordained but later Bishop of Gloucester and theological writer, was a close friend of Stukeley while Warburton was Rector of Brant Broughton (Lincs) from 1728 to 1746. He was granted an MA degree at Cambridge during the King's visit in 1727.

17 A Latin phrase quoted in Terence's play *Hecyra*, meaning 'in the name of god(s) and men' / 'I call god(s) and men to witness'. Hardy (see Appendix 3) had just changed from being a Presbyterian minister in Nottingham to become an Anglican priest, Vicar of Kinoulton (Notts) and later Vicar of Melton Mowbray.

18 Claude Genebrier: see **Letter 68**, n.7, above. Stukeley is convinced at this point that the Emperor Carausius was of British or even Irish birth.

85. Maurice Johnson to William Stukeley, Spalding, 17 March 1744[1]

Spalding, Saturday 17 March, 1743–4

As you were pleased, good Sir, to express so great friendship towards me and my family, to declare so much approbation of my institution,[2] and the conduct of it, which I've at times submitted to your consideration, and seem to be pleased with what I'm able to communicate to you in a literary way, I'm emboldened more frequently to converse this with you, and return you mine and our Societie's [sic] hearty thanks, the more due in how much I'm sencible the poor notices I can send you, Sir, can add nothing to your vast store of knowledge, and that your kind acceptance flows from your universal bene[volence to] mankind, your ardour for encouraging any tendency to promote arts and sciences, and your promptitude to patronize those, who like me, earnestly covet to be in your esteem, as you yourself must highly be in that of all who have the honour of knowing and conversing with you. We had lately, at our meeting here, the Secretary or the Gentlemen's Society at Peterborough[3] (who was long schoolmaster here, and treasurer of ours, and thence their founder.) That gentleman acquainted us he had prevailed on the Lord Bishop[4] to bestow on them the use of the old Saxon gate-chamber in the minster yard, leading to his pallace, for their meeting; but has not yet been able to prevail on that prelate to countenance them with his company. They have made an ordinance, that in case their society drop, and their meetings are but very thin, that all their books and supellex shall be then lodged in the library of the dean and chapter. Dr Thomas, their dean,[5] and now our diocesan, is their president. Wee had done the like for bestowing ours in the vestiary of our parish church, and in our Free grammar school, on such contingency, which, with God's blessing, I shall (if he spare my life), endeavour may not happen (though realms and all communities have their periods) of ages to come. Our meetings are continued constant to every Thursday's evening, and as well frequented as I find it possible to make the place bear (or the number of people here, or hereabouts, who can be induced to attend a thing of that nature), where neither politicks, in which every man thinks himself wise, can have part: nor any sort of gaming goes forward, which allures most young men as their beloved evening's recreation. But under God, I depend chiefly on the strength of my own children and my near relations, whom I have taken care to train up to a likeing of it from their infancy, and I trust will keep it up when I shall leave them.

Wee had, last Thursday, a letter from Mr W. Boyer,[6] [sic] the printer, a member, who wrote that his friend Mr Wm. Clerke[7] a prebendary of Chichester (likewise a [very] learned and worthy member), [sic] had acquainted him there has [lately] been found in that city, a Roman coin, representing Nero and Drusus, sons of Germanicus, on horseback, and on the rev. C. CAESAR. DIVI. AUG. PRON. AUG. PM. TR. P III. PP. In the middle S.C. (which I find in Dr Occo. Caligula[8] A.V.C. 791 A.D. 46, p.69) which (says he), though the very same which Palm on Sueton-Mediobarbus, &c, have given us before; yet brings one advantage to the place where it was found, as it is a confirmation of the antiquity of the Chichester inscription, which you know, Sir, is a little contested in Horsley,[9] and proves the early intercourse of the Romans with the Regni, contrary to the opinion which Bishop Stillingfleet[10] concieved for want of such remains. That ingenious gentleman Mr Bowyer, in a post-script to his letter, informs us he is printing Mr Folkes's[11] tables of our silver coins from the conquest, about 5 sheets, I presume at the expense of the Soc. of Antiq., and believe it will be the most accurate account extant.

On the 1st inst., Mr Hinson,[12] a member, brought a broad thin copper medal, having the arms of Zeeland in an oval shield, with a coronet over it, 1589. NON. NOBIS. DOMINE. NON. NOBIS. *rev.* several shipps as in a sea fight, SED. NOMINI. TVO. DA. GLORIAM. The workmanship is good, and the piece well preserved, and probably then made on occasion of the assistance that province gave us the year before when …

[*The text in Surtees stops at this point; the editor notes 'The remainder of this letter is torn off and lost.'*]

1 This letter is not in the collection of letters to Stukeley in the Bodleian Library. It is published in *Surtees* II, 285–7. As this is a transcribed version, the editor may have altered some of Johnson's spelling and punctuation. It is given here to complete the sequence of the available correspondence.
2 The Spalding Gentlemen's Society.
3 Revd Timothy Neve; see Appendix 3.
4 The Rt Revd Robert Clavering, Bishop of Peterborough (1729–47), an oriental scholar. He did not join the Peterborough Gentlemen's Society.
5 Revd John Thomas (1691–1766: see *ODNB*), Dean of Peterborough (1740–44) and Bishop of Lincoln (1744–61).
6 William Bowyer; see Appendix 3.
7 Revd William Clarke (1695–1771: see *ODNB*), Prebendary of Chichester; his main book was *The Connexion of the Roman, Saxon and English Coins deduced from observations on the Saxon weights and money* (1767).
8 Adolf Occo (1524–1606), physician and numismatist, was best known for *Imperatorum Romanorum Numismata* (1579).
9 John Horsley (1686–1732: see *ODNB*), author of *Britannia Romana* (1732).
10 The Rt Revd Edward Stillingfleet (1635–99: see *ODNB*), well-known in the eighteenth century for his book *Origines Britannicae* (1685).
11 Martin Folkes; see Appendix 3.
12 Captain Joseph Hinson, SGS member 1742; see Appendix 3.

86. Maurice Johnson to William Stukeley, Spalding, 21 June 1750[1]

Spalding, June 21, 1750

Dear Sir,

Give me leave to shew you how good a taste some folks had here so early as in king Henry the Third's time, about 1230, in the priorate of Simon Haughton,[2] surnamed the Munificent, and first perpetual prior of this our priory of Spalding, which liberal lord I believe caused their conventual seal to be made, whereof I here send you a sketch from an impression of both the sides, [*sketch, fig.1 on p.100 of Nichols, of the two sides of a monastic seal, reproduced as part of a plate associated with letters from other writers*] as perfect as it remains to a lease granted by a successor of his lordship's, Richard Ellsyn Palmer,[3] our last prior, 2d of January, 29 H. VIII, 1538, to Rauff White, then of this place, yeoman, in my possession, which, considering the age, is not bad work: the N in Spalding correct thus, [*gives examples of the lettering*]

On the foreside the B.V. Mary,[4] who here, as in many other places, was introduced to be tutelar of this place instead of Venus, whose name it originally bore, as some sea-coast towns in Greece did Αφροδισεα,[5] in the most amiable attitude of a mother as giving suck to the infant Jesus. I presume the entire reading on this side might be *S. Prioris & Capituli Beatæ Mariæ Virginis*, and thus continued on the other side or counter seal, *Et Sancti Nicholai, Spalding*,[6] where St Nicholas, the bishop to whom the abbey of Aungere[7] was dedicated, (and who had it when this cell was taken from that of St Guthlake at Croyland, and subjected thereto by Ivo Tailbois,[8] earl of Anjou, nephew of William I.) is represented *in pontificalibus* and posture of benediction, being joined with the B.V. as co-tutelar Saint, a practice formerly not unfrequent in the Romish church, abounding much in saints and holidays. This deed concludes thus, 'In witness, &c, the said *Prior and Convent put to their common seal in their Chapterhouse at Spalding*, to one part, and the said Lessee his seal to the other part. It is marked on the turning up thro' which the label that the seal is appended to is drawn in the middle, THOMAS CECIL of … and ANTHONY LYME. Those were, I suppose, the then officers of the King's Court of Augmentation of his Revenues from the dissolved houses of superstition arising,[9] who were to inspect and register all demises made by the religious, that his majesty might know what lands were let upon lease, where they lay, to whom demised, for what term of years, under what reserved rents payable when, and other covenants before this, and another conventual lease, the seal whereof is appendant but less perfect. I had with our old friend Saunderson[10] some years since searched the Augmentation-office, Westminster, to procure sight of and draw out this seal, but found there only a very small part of but one left: it is, therefore, I assure you, the more valuable, and seems extraordinary that in so short a space as 212 years, of the many hundred acts that must have passed under this public seal, as leases, grants of offices, and corrodies, and augmentations of them, presentations to benefices, manumissions of villans, licences to niefs to marry, dispensations of various kinds, petitions to kings and parliaments, appeals to popes, instruments of associating into the fraternitie to lay-lords, ladies, and other liberal and pious benefactors, no more than this should have occurred to my diligent and inquisitive search of 300 years transactions. Im many acts the lord prior's own seal was sufficient; of such I have never so much as met with one of any of our lord prior's, or any impression of one. Such as I have you see and are welcome to.[11]

The errors of my amanuensis I have corrected. As to the forms of the letters, which are those of the first Norman times, Romano-Saxon, a sort of mixed characters of the Roman and Saxon, as in Domesday capitals and other MSS. we meet with them thus; the P, B, and T. here are Roman, the rest Saxon: as in a Latin copy of St Paul's Epistle I have, written as in Edward the Confessor's time on vellum, with the plea of Pinnendun between the earl of Kent and the archbishop of Canterbury and the bishop of Rochester, with the confirmation of the sentence of the bishop of Coutance and the whole county-court of Kent by William I. and Henry I therein written, whereof see Eadmerus, and Camden, Spelman, and Selden's Commentary[12] This is a very eminent and most valuable record, and formerly belonged to Christ Church, Canterbury.

You have much obliged me, my good friend, with your History of the Institution of the Egyptian Society, London,[13] for which accept mine with the Society's thanks. What pity it is it should have been discontinued, from whence we might have hoped such rare erudition as your exposition of the Sistrum, which I approve as just, but could never have conceived the true meaning and use of.

Whilst vagrant gypsies pester all countries in plenty, I am sorry the capital of the kingdom should not be able to keep up a meeting of such noble and learned travellers, which might have been of benefit to those who have not means or opportunities, as the antient Greek philosopher, of going to and fetching knowledge thence; a more rational cause of taking such a voyage than any pilgrimage, or even a crusado. When you see here what good use we make of your excellent Memoirs of another learned Society, I hope and trust, Sir, you will indulge us farther with the remains relating to that, and those of this Egyptian too. I have an Orus, or Egyptian god of plenty, without head or feet, but with the ananas and abundant other fruits in his lap, a dog between his legs, and a Banana or Musa leaf spread behind him, being of *terra cotta* he served an honest tar as a tobacco-stopper from Alexandria hither.[14] I have also in an hæmatites an intaglio of Cakodæmon Typhon, wherewith I impress the wax that joins this paper, a double-tail'd Python; these may be justly thought *Genii boni & mali* to mankind; the terrible, and the agreeable. The horrid face and flagellum of this monster threaten destruction, and he seems compounded of many mischiefs.[15]

We had at our last meeting the result of the Rev. Mr Robert Smith of Woodston's visiting lately more than 60 churches in and about Lincoln, many corrections and critical historic-heraldical remarks relating to the lists, arms, seats, and families of those highest peace-officers the high sheriffs of this county: he promises me a visit, and purposes to inspect those of Kesteven and our Hollands. I believe and trust, for the credit of our county, that his list of ours will be as ample, compleat, useful, and entertaining as any, and far exceed the best of the Fasti Consulares.[16] A beautiful plant of a *Lichnoides flore rubente* in full blow, with another of the *Citisus verus Virgilio flore luteo*,[17] I made my gardener (as frequently I have done) carry thither in their pots to shew the company. I wish, by the bye, you would *put my lord*[18] (as you call him) *on being beneficent to our Society.* You or I should long ere this have desired [him] to become a member of so good an institution, and shewn our good will, and befriend this thing so far as to ask him to let you or me propose his becoming a member.

I am sorry, Sir, you are like to take so long a journey *solus*, but must insist on your accepting the best accommodation I can make you here, and that my house may be your home for what time you can spare me, but must allot me more of it than you talk of; be sure be here on a Thursday, to favour our Society with your company; we should meet at four, and may stay till ten; but our *readings* and *shew* begin at midway about eight o'clock or somewhat sooner.

I have indexed all our minutes,[19] and am upon our Dissertations, Essays, and other valuable papers; having also indexed all the MSS. of my own composing or collecting, chiefly of law and history, very full as to this place, much about Boston, Stamford, Hitchin, Croyland, Peterborough, and some other towns and places where my business has lain, as counsel, recorder, or steward of the Soke or Manor; who am, I thank God, much better, and, with all my family's compliments to you and yours, dear Sir, your affectionate friend and obedient servant

Maurice Johnson

---

1   This letter was transcribed and published in John Nichols, *Bibliotheca Topographica Britannica II, Reliquiæ Galeanæ* (1781), 100–5. It was presumably among the papers of the Gale brothers which Nichols drew on for his publication. As this version is taken from Nichols and not from the original, it is possible that the editor has modified some of Johnson's spellings.

2   Also known as Simon of Hautberg, Prior of Spalding for over twenty years (1230–53).
3   Richard Elsyn or Palmer, last Prior of Spalding during the 1530s.
4   William Page (ed.), *Victoria County History of Lincolnshire* II (1906), 118–24, describes the common seal of Spalding Priory: the obverse representing the Virgin with crown, seated on a carved throne, the child on the left knee. In base, under a pointed arch, slightly trefoiled with gables of church-like structure at the sides, the Prior half-length to the left in prayer.
5   Aphrodisea, after the goddess Aphrodite, known in Latin as Venus. See Johnson's views on this in **Letter 80** above.
6   'The Seal of the Prior and Chapter of the Blessed Virgin Mary … and Saint Nicholas, Spalding'.
7   Angers, France.
8   Ivo Tailbois or Taillebois established Spalding Priory as a cell of the Abbey of St Nicholas, Angers, in the 1070s. It is still debated whether Croyland Abbey had a cell at Spalding prior to the Norman Conquest; Croyland did possess a berewick of land in Spalding before the Conquest.
9   The Royal Court of Augmentations of Henry VIII was established in 1536 to organise the process of receiving income from the dissolved monasteries. It became a part of the Crown exchequer in 1554. Spalding Priory was a rich monastic house at the time of its surrender to the Crown in 1539/40. The Priory had an annual income of between £500 and £1,000 which was passed on to Charles Brandon, Duke of Suffolk. Maurice Johnson wrote an extensive account of the Priory (SGS, MB1, fols 1–11); it is printed in John Nichols, *Bibliotheca Topographica Britannica* III (1790), 1–17.
10 Robert Saunderson (1663–1741), FSA (1717), Clerk of the Rolls and Usher of the Court of Chancery; a significant archivist.
11 The seal was illustrated as fig.1, opposite p.100 of Nichols, *Bibliotheca Topographica Britannica* III, *Reliquiæ Galeanæ*.
12 The chroniclers listed here were Eadmer (*c.*1060–1126), who wrote the account of the life of St Anselm; William Camden (1551–1623), author of *Britannia* (1586); Sir Henry Spelman (1563/4–1641), whose papers were published by Edmund Gibson in 1698; and John Selden (1584–1654), who published a critical edition of Eadmer's work.
13 See **Letters 66**, n.11, and **67** above.
14 Tobacco stoppers were used to tamp down lit tobacco in the bowl of a tobacco pipe.
15 The wax stamp or seal was illustrated opposite p.100 of Nichols (see n.11 above), as fig. 2. In Egyptian legends a cacodemon was an evil spirit; Typhon was their king.
16 The Fasti Consulares were the official Roman chronological lists of the consuls, carved in marble.
17 Lichnoides: a plant from Siberia, possibly a variety of leadwort, though its pre-Linnean classification makes exact identification difficult; Cytisus: the broom; see **Letter 66**, n.4, above.
18 Samson Gideon, Lord of the Manor of Spalding: see Appendix 3. He did become a member of the SGS in 1751.
19 Johnson's MS index to the minutes of the SGS still exists in the SGS archives and has proved very useful for editing these letters.

87. Revd John Johnson[1] to William Stukeley, Spalding, 15 February 1755
Bodleian, MS Eng. misc. c.113, fols 291r–292v

Spalding
Feb. 15. 55.

Dear Sir,

As I have been for some Years a Witness to the Friendship which subsisted between my dear Father & You, & which he has oft told me was cultivated long before I could be supposed to remark it: I think it but a due Respect to his Memory, & to the Literary Correspondence You have indulged us with, to acquaint You with his Decease.

Our House has been for many Months the House of Mourning: in August last we lost our Sister Green,[2] who had long laboured under a Complication of ~~Distempers~~ Infirmities, which reduced her to, all but a Shadow; & carried her off under the Appearance of a Dropsy. – My dear Mother was on the 1st of Decr taken away from her faithfull Attendance on my Father, (whom we then thought on his Death-Bed) by the Stroke of an Apoplexy[3] & poor Man he has not long survived her; for he was taken from us in the Attack of a Third Fit of an Epilepsy, last Saturday Morn[4] –

[p.2] His Afflictions were much alleviated to him by the tenderest Care & Assiduity of my Sisters. – I hope, dear Sir, that your Friendship for my Father will long subsist to his Family. – We much wish You lived here to preside over our Society, in the Room of my dear Father: hope Colll Johnson will make his House here his Residence, & succeed to my Father in that place;[5] & that we shall be still favoured with Your ingenious & learned Communications: which have been a great Pleasure & very high Amusement to all here, & particularly to,
  Good Dr,
    Your very obliged, humble Servant,
        John Johnson

Bro' Walter & Sisters[6] beg to joyn their best Regards with mine to Yourself, Lady, & Family.

To
 The Revd Dr Stukely
  Rector of St George's
    Queen's Square
      London

[1] Third son of Maurice Johnson; see Appendix 3.
[2] Jane Green (née Johnson, 1711–54), the eldest child of Maurice and Elizabeth Johnson, married Dr John Green in 1736 and was buried on 17 August 1754.
[3] Elizabeth Johnson, Maurice's wife, died on 1 December 1754 and was buried on 4 December.
[4] This was 8 February 1755.
[5] Colonel Maurice Johnson, eldest son of Maurice Johnson, inherited Ayscoughfee Hall and eventually returned to live there for the final years of his life. He married his second wife Mary in London in December 1755.
[6] Walter Johnson was John's only surviving brother living in Spalding. His surviving sisters in Spalding in 1755 were Elizabeth Butter (died 1784) and Henrietta Johnson.

88. Revd John Johnson to William Stukeley, Spalding, 30 March 1756
Bodleian, MS Eng. misc. c.113, fols 291r–292v

                Spalding
              March 30 1756
Good Dr,
 I had the Pleasure on Thursday Night last to present Your 5th Manuscript Vol. of the Transactions of the Royal Society, with Your own Observations thereon, & Your Dissertations on the late Earthquakes to our Society here;[1] who were highly entertained with the first Reading, profess themselves greatly obliged, &, for the kind Continuance of Your Favours to us, desire their best Thanks may be made acceptable.
 On the Friday after I dined with You, I was introduced to a private Subscrip-

tion Concert of antient Musick,[2] at the Crown & Anchor; where was present amongst other Company Dr Birch,[3] Secretary of the Royal Society, whom I made myself known to, as well remembering that a Correspondence subsisted between the D^r and my late dear Father.

The Dr kindly asked after the State of our Society; was so good to bestow upon us his History [p.2] of the Royal Society; & to promise a Continuance of the printed Transactions to us, if he found any Order of that Appointment; which I told him, I believed was made when Dr Jurin was Secretary:[4] but of this I will more fully acquaint myself from the Minutes of our Society, when I shall be a little more at Leisure; for I am at present busied about the Title we set up to Moulton Living,[5] having waited upon Mr Wilbraham before I left the Town, & having received good Encouragement from his Opinion, that our claim will bear supporting.

I am with proper Compliments to the Ladies of your Family, Good D^r
    Your much obliged, humble Servant
        John Johnson

I am desired to ask the Favour of your Vote & Interest, as a Governor on the Behalf of Mr Joseph Roberts, that he may succeed his late Father Mr Roberts as Apothecary to Christ's Hospital.

It may I hope be some Recommendation that the present Candidate was educated in the Hospital; & during his Father's Illness has wholly done the Business of it for the last 12 Months.

[1] Stukeley has continued to produce and send to the SGS his MS memoirs of RS meetings which were read and discussed. He has also sent a copy of *The Philosophy of Earthquakes, Natural and Religious*, second edition, which was published in 1756; he had sent a copy of the first edition to the SGS in 1750 (see **Letter 65**, n.6, above.)
[2] 'Antient Music' at this period meant music from at least twenty years earlier, as distinct from the latest compositions, not music from several centuries previously, as today. In 1776 the Earl of Sandwich established the 'Concert of Ancient Music', a society which lasted until 1848. The Crown and Anchor tavern was in the Strand, London. Private rooms in taverns were a popular venue for musical concerts.
[3] The Revd Thomas Birch, Secretary of the RS (1752–65); SGS 1743. He wrote *The History of the Royal Society of London for Improving Natural Knowledge* (1756).
[4] This was indeed the case. In 1725 Jurin wrote to Maurice Johnson sending the RS's *Phil.Trans.*; the letter is transcribed in *Correspondence*, 64.
[5] John Johnson became curate of Moulton (Lincs) in 1755 and Vicar in 1757, having been curate at Spalding from 1746. We cannot find Stukeley as a governor of Christ's Hospital.

89. William Stukeley to Dr John Green, London, 2 October 1756
SGS/Stukeley/ 28

                                              Queensquare 2 oct. 1756
Dear Dr

I received yours, am glad that curious gold coin of Edw[ard] III is fallen into so good hands. I think you should send it up to be ingraven, with those going forward in Town.[1] I buy all those prints, think them well done, & valuable: at least they are fit for a public library.

Our Antiquarian Society are about publishing an account of Mr Folkes's plates,[2] which wil [*sic*] give you a good knoledg of our English money.

We shall have a noble sale, I suppose of poor Mr Vertues[3] plates, prints, drawings &c. this winter.

I am glad you are likely to have a good road, thrô Littleworth to Stamford.[4] [p.2] It must needs prove a vast advantage to Spalding.

I hope you or Mr Johnson[5] received the MS volume, which your father Johnson lent me, about Carausius; as also the coins of Carausius; most of which I have ingrav'd: I sent them by my coz. Stukeley of Holbech.[6]

my medallic history of that emperor is almost printed.[7] I have ingraved XXXI plates of his different coins. 10 in each plate. the work alredy, which I call the I book is swelled to a sufficient bigness. I shal not publish the plates till book II. I describe all the coins in this: & show a way intirely new, to arrange the coins in order of time: & point out the days when generally [p.3] they were struck. as deitys generally fill up the reverses, all or most of thir coins were as acts of religion stampt, for testimonys of the piety of the emperors & people, in rightly celebrating the offices of religion, pertaining to the days.

for instance. the coins of Lætitia Aug. & Lætitia Auggg. hilaritas Aug. hilaritas Auggg.[8]

can we entertain so poor a notion, as that an emp[eror] or three emp[eror]s agreed together, to take a chearful cup on such a day: & to perpetuate that noble event by a medal?

the truth is, lætitia was struck on 11 feb. annually. the celebration of the ludi genealici when indeed they were excessively merry: but in a religious [p.4] way: as were the feasts of the Jews. when they rejoiced before Jehovah. vizt. a feast upon the sacrifice.

Hilaritas Auggg. regards the high festivity of 25 march called Hilaria sacred to Mater deum. whence we see, the heathen had some prophetic notices of the great event of that day, which Christianity celebrates.[9]

the coins therefore were stampt on that day, by annual rotation, in honor to the deity. & all money was really of a sacred character.

indeed I have diverted medallic learning purely into a religious channel.[10] not solicitous whether my brother vertuoso's approve it or not. with my respects to your Society,

I am your faithful servant
        Wm Stukeley.

---

[1] It is interesting that Stukeley is still in contact with the SGS after Johnson's death. Walter Johnson was still writing to him in 1764; see *Correspondence*, Appendix 4 for his letter. Stukeley, as a well-known numismatist and still a member of the Society of Antiquaries, would be a very suitable person for John Green to contact about his coin collection.

[2] Martin Folkes (see Appendix 3).

[3] George Vertue (see Appendix 3 and *ODNB*) died in July 1756, having been unwell for some time: see Stukeley's comment about his appearance in **Letter 75** above. He was buried in Westminster Abbey. The Society of Antiquaries acquired his plates and republished them. His extensive papers and notes became a valuable resource for British art history and have been published by the Walpole Society.

[4] For earlier comments about Littleworth, south of Spalding, see **Letter 44**, n.7, above.

[5] Walter Johnson (see Appendix 3), Treasurer of the SGS. Stukeley is returning Maurice Johnson's MS study of the coins of Carausius, which still survives at the SGS and was used by Adam

Daubney for his article 'Maurice Johnson: an eighteenth-century numismatist', *The British Numismatic Journal* 82 (2012).

6   Adlard Stukeley.

7   Stukeley self-published his *The Medallic History of Marcus Aurelius Valerius Carausius, Emperor in Brittain*, vol. I in 1757 and vol. II in 1759; it includes engravings of some of Johnson's coins, lent for this purpose.

8   Lætitia Augusta, the Joy of the Emperor, and Hilaritas Augusta, the Happiness of the Emperor, inscribed on second- and third-century Roman coins, especially in the time of Gallienus. Stukeley's explanations of these inscriptions are interesting; the preferred explanation today is: 'in advertising happiness as a benefit of empire, the Roman state employed two other types of the imperial coinage, *hilaritas* and *lætitia*, that reinforced the message of *felicitas* [good fortune]. Both *hilaritas* and *lætitia* referred mainly to the personal happiness, joy or merriment of individuals and the two terms are often used together ... both terms had festive overtones and could be related to public celebrations sponsored by the Emperor.' See Carlos Norena, *Imperial Ideas in the Roman West* (2011), 172.

9   The Christian church celebrates 25 March, Lady Day, as the date of the Annunciation to the Blessed Virgin Mary that she was to be the mother of Jesus.

10 Stukeley's claim that 'all money was really of a sacred character' has validity as the Roman Emperors were seen as God-like figures. Lætitia was a Roman divinity and the Hilaria was an ancient Roman religious festival, celebrated on 25 March.

APPENDIX 1
TWO DISSERTATIONS ON LINCOLNSHIRE TOPICS BY WILLIAM STUKELEY

Both of these are in the SGS's collection of Stukeley's papers.

(a) On the Alleged Burial of Danish Vikings at Threekingham, 14 March 1729
SGS/Stukeley/13

This dissertation was prepared by Stukeley to be read by him at the first meeting of the Ancaster Society, organised jointly by him and Maurice Johnson in 1729 (see **Letters 24**, **25** *and* **26** *and SGS, MB2, fol.4r, entry for 20 March 1729). The Society met immediately following the Lincoln Assizes, and was intended to meet twice yearly. Only this one meeting took place; by late 1729 Stukeley had been ordained as a priest and had obtained his living of All Saints' Church, Stamford. As* **Letters 27** *and* **28** *indicate, Stukeley was unable to attend the meeting because of a call on his services as a physician. The dissertation was therefore sent to Johnson to be read by him at the meeting. It is of interest in showing their hopes for the Ancaster Society and Stukeley's approach to historical studies, based on the sources available and accepted as reliable at the time. It retains Stukeley's corrections, inserted as he wrote, so that we are enabled to see his work in progress. Stukeley's footnotes and additional material are indicated by the symbols he used.*

    The historical account Stukeley gives is based on that in the Historia Croylandensis, *the chronicle of Croyland Abbey ascribed to Ingulf, or Ingulphus; Stukeley owned a copy, printed in Sir Henry Savile's* Rerum Anglicarum Scriptores post Bedam *(1596). This chronicle was generally accepted as an authentic account of happenings in Anglo-Saxon and early mediæval Lincolnshire until the nineteenth century, when it was proved to have been created in the early fifteenth century to give credence to the territorial claims of Croyland Abbey against those of Spalding, Peterborough and the men of Holland. Modern historians can find no evidence to support the existence of the battle and the burial of the kings as recounted by 'Ingulf'; there is no mention of it in the Anglo-Saxon Chronicle. The legend has in all probability grown up from the place-name 'Threekingham'. However, Stukeley shows a very good grasp of place-name development and of the relation of settlements to their landscape.*

Gentlemen,   14 March 1728–9.

I cannot but congratulate my self on meeting you here: & whether I reflect on the persons present, or the place appointed for this congress, tis matter of great pleasure to me. to see so ~~great and~~ splendid an appeareance from this neighborhood, of persons of excellent learning in all kinds, must needs be a satisfaction of a high nature, to all that have a relish for the entertainments of the mind. & more ~~especially we are more~~ particularly are we obliged to the gentlemen of the Spalding Society, for favoring us with their company at this distance. if we consider the place of our meeting, we are within the walls of an old roman city, upon the most considerabl of their roads in the island of Britan, viz. the hermenstreet. Many are the roman Emp^{rs} & innumerabl legions have marchd past the door, in their journeys northwards to guard the scotish frontiers: & we may truly be said to be on classic ground. tho' the antient roman name of the place be lost to us, yet it may receive a new splendour equivalent ~~to that loss~~ from these conferences of ours; which, 'tis hop'd, may be celebrated twice in the year, without interruption, & that we may begin a custom which shall be continued by our posterity. it must be confessd that the advantages of meeting men of learning cannot be so frequent here in the country as at London, but that should animate us to meet as oft as we can, & should give a better relish to these opportunitys of conversation, with people that think in our own way. & seeing the country life has some ~~advantages~~ pleasures agreeabl to regular minds which tis impossible to obtain in a populous Metropolis; we may in a great measure supply the want of ~~them~~ others, by keeping up this & the like meetings. some gentlemen here present may furnish us with a noble example, much to their honor, of what may be done by constancy & perseverance: ~~by founding~~ in a society of <u>literati</u> in a neighbouring town, which has subsisted with great reputation for near 20 years: the founder & father whereof [1] we have the pleasure to see assisting at this solemnity. I on my part, to show my willingness to contribute all I can, toward this laudabl design, have presum'd tho' with the greatest submission, to endeavor to divert you in the subsequent discourse, ~~hoping for~~ trusting in the candor natural to men of learning, ~~for~~ to excuse the boldness or ~~for~~ the defects thereof.

In riding abroad in the country ~~whether on business or diversion~~, tis no incosiderabl part of the pleasure, to know or to inquire into the antient state & history of a town or place in ones eye. by this means, the mind is agreably amusd, whilst the body receivs the benefit of the air & exercise. I judg, tis filling up every vacancy of our life innocently & usefully. tis reading old history out of ones study, & reaping the advantages of it most, when we seem to have least to doe. the following dissertation is the result of such a self conversation, in sight of a village belonging to Grantham calld London thorp vulgarly, but rightly & antiently Laundon thorp.[2] whence I had an opportunity, as I imagin, of setting to rights, in some particulars a very memorabl & antient transaction that happen'd in our neighborhood & in that village; & of restoring to its proper place, the honor of being the sepulture of three Danish kings, as calld, slain in battle by our fathers, valiantly fighting in defence of their country. I mean the famous battle fought between the ravaging Danes & our Saxon ancestors upon our heath, which was in the year 870. of which <u>Ingulfus</u>[3] abbot of Croyland in the time of Wm Conq^r ~~gives us~~ writes a long & very particular account. in the first place I shall give you the detail of the history, ~~what belongs~~ as far as relates to this action, as ~~related~~ told by <u>Ingulfus</u> & then my observations upon it.

all the summer of that year, the Danes were plundering the province of Lindsey, or the country between the Humber the Trent & the Witham. towards Winter their swarms retiring southward with the sun, they pass the Witham, most probably because most commodiously at Lincoln, & so march along the heath, that they may ravage the villages on both sides. there were 8 of their kings, & 5 earls, who commanded this host, & it seems to have been their method (& very wisely, when in an enemys country,) to divide their forces by turns, three kings guarded the camp & the plunder, whilst five kings & as many earls went abroad the country to plunder, burn & take booty, which was brought from time to time to the camp. tis reasonabl to suppose their camps were remov'd from one eminent place to another, & in all probability they chose, what we call, the cliff,[4] or the western edg of our heath, much as the hermenstreet road goes, because tis the highest part of the heath all along; & commands a prospect both ways; toward the low country westward upon the Trent, & toward the towns on the edg of the fens eastw^d. hence by fire or smoak they might make signals from the camp, upon any distress, & all partys best relieve one another.

In the mean time our ancestors of Holland & Kesteven appeared not to be idle, nor tamely to submit, like the inhabitants of Lindsey coast, to these barbarous depredations. Algar surnamed the younger Earl of Holland as I suppose ~~who seems to be a relation of Ethelred Muchel as he was surnamed which signifys the great, who liv'd about Ganesborough & was Earl of Mercia aat that time, this Algar~~ [stet] bestird himself to relieve his injurd country. he summond ~~together~~ his two knights or seneschals Wibert who denominated the town of Wiberton near Boston where he liv'd, & Leofric, whence the name of Leverton his seat. these drew together all the youth of Holland, both north Holland (where they liv'd) & south, for those of Gedney & Sutton are particularly mentiond. with them joind Toly the Girvian or Marshman, ^{x} [*Stukeley's footnote:* ^{x}who probably liv'd in south holland] a famous soldier, who after his conversion to christianity livd as a lay bro^r in Croyland monastery. it seems as if the family of Tooly now subsisting ~~at Boston~~ were his descendants. this Toly commanded a body of 200 men that belongd to Croyland abby. they likewise raisd about 300 more stout men from the towns of Langtoft, Baston & Deeping. they were joined by Morcar lord of Brun or Bourn, I suppose a relation of Earl Algars, Morchar [*sic*] was a very powerful man & consequently brought a considerabl body of men into the field of his family & dependants. Osgot at that time sheriff of Lincolnshire, a brave old soldier brought his troop of 500 men, of Kesteven side. moreover Harding of Ryal commanded the forces that came from Stamford side. these in the whole amounted to about 8000 men. they muster'd together upon Lincoln heath as we may well suppose, & that with so much secrecy & expedition, that they fought the Danish forces which ~~that~~ guarded the camp & gave them a great overthrow, before the rest could come to their relief. they drove them into their very camp with the sloughter of 3 of their kings & a great number of common soldiers. this happend on St Maurice's day which is the 22. Sept. 870.

the night following the rest of the Danish kings & earls return to the camp sufficiently exasperated at the slaughter of their men. they bury the 3 kings that were slain, early in the morning at a place then calld Laundon (as our historian relates,) but afterwards from this buryal Trekingham,[5] & then prepare to fight the christians again. I have no need to ~~relate~~ tell any more of the story, only observe Ingulfus his words following <u>per totam planitiem</u>, I suppose most plainly import that the battles were fought upon Lincoln heath: which made me first suspect that Trekingham or Frekingham as we commonly call it, which is 3 mile off the heath, could not be the place ~~where the battle was fought~~ of action, notwithstanding the specious pretext of the towns name^x [*Stukeley's footnote:* ^{x} but that in all likelyhood & justice it ought to be referd to our Londonthorp, which undoubtedly is the Laundon of Ingulfus.] & when I came to examin into the thing within my own mind, I had several reasons ~~that~~ suggested to me to believe that the historian tho' undoubtedly ~~true~~ faithful as tho the fact of the battle, yet had mixd history & old fable together in some measure, & so among his other etymologys added that of Trekingham from fanciful tradition, ~~thinking to corroborate the truth of his~~ [*Stukeley's note:* stet] narration thereby. & consequent to this history, the parish ever since fond of it, show three gravestones in the churchyard where they pretend the 3 danish kings were buryed, the place from that time losing its name of Laundon. now tho' I have nothing to object ag.t Leofric being denominator of Leverton,[6] & Wibert of Wiberton, I may add that our Earl Algar livd at Algarkirk so calld from him, as commonly affirm'd there, & if Ingulfus had added that his Ofgot the sheriff of Lincolnshire livd at Osgodby so calld from him, should I have dissented, but as to Trekingham[x] [*Stukeley's footnote:* x being the place of battle, & so named from the 3 kings buryd there] I crave leave to differ from him, for the following reasons.

1. first we may note, tis very rare, that a town changes an old name for a new one, on any account whatever, without a revolution & change of people, nor can I easily be induc'd to think, that Laundon which according to my etymology signifies in ~~the~~ Saxon, the hilly farm or the farm on a hill, any whit suitabl to the parish of Frekingham, tho' most eminently so of our London thorp. & the termination of ham in Frekingham is enough to stagger ones faith, in supposing it derivd from the burial of the kings, because it has no propriety in the case[+] [*Stukeley's footnote:* +unless in the Egyptian sense who calld their graves their houses, but in our case, at the end of a towns name] ham signifies a home, a dwelling, a town or village for the living & by no means a burial place; & tis notorious enough that ingham is a common termination of towns hereabouts, & relates no more to kings in Trekingham, than in Helpringham, Sempringham, Fokingham, Lessingham, Metheringham. &c. particular parts of a country generally abound in a particular manner of appellation of towns ~~names~~ . thus upon Lindsey coast the towns generally end in by w.ch signifys an abiding place, home or house, as Spilsby, Eresby, Hagnaby, Kirkby, & innumerabl more. near the place we are speaking of, ham is common, as besides thos mention'd, Edenham, Bitham, Grantham, Witham, Clipsham, Iernham &c. in other parts the towns end in ing, as Spalding, Quadring, Deeping, Horbling &c. in other places they end in ton, thorp & the like, & those words are often compounded as our inghams, for instance Donington, Levington, Billingborough &c. now if to Threking had been added a termination implying a burial place, a tomb, <u>tumulus,</u> cairn or the like, there might have been at least a specious claim to this report in question; since it is otherwise I esteem it intirely fanciful, & that Laundon is our Londonthorp ~~not Trekingham~~ which is 7 or 8 mile distant from Trekingham, quite across the heath, but upon the heath, & much more likely to be the place of the Danish camp, & where the battles were struck & where the 3 kings were buryd.[7] For

2. from consideration of the story & from what we mentiond before, of the method the Danes observ'd, in dividing their forces into several parts, & keeping a camp as a place of defence to resort to in case of need, & because they were but just come into Kesteven & had not tryd the strength of the country; it is much more likely they should pitch their camp at London thorp, which is a very great eminence whence you may see to a prodigious extent, ~~& that~~ which is rich

ground, & well waterd with springs, than at Trekingham, which is incommodious upon many accounts, tis 3 mile off the heath, tis low in scituation, & has no view around it by reason of woods, they could not see any danger at a distance from hence, they could make no signals of distress to the foraging partys, dispersd abroad the country, who yet we find were within ken of the camp, & were advertisd of the battle, as we may reasonably judg by their returning together so punctually the night after, the battle add to this, Ingulfus his description of the country, the per totam planitiem, the eminence which the christians retird to when hard pressd, & the like quadrates extremely well with Londonthorp which stands upon the heath but not at all with Trekingham. I my self have observd that in all the cliff row, there is not a more commodious advantageous place for an encampment, for good land, water & prospect. in a summers even, when the air favors, the eye may reach a very great way into Derbyshire quite across Nottinghamshire, so into Leicestershire, Rutland, yorkshire, to Boston, the fens & seacoasts. I suppose at this time it might be only a farm: in process of time when other dwellings were added to it, it got the additional name of Thorp, which sig imports a village.

3. let us consider the affair of the 3 gravestones laid in Trekingham churchyard, & which among the vulgar is a most invincible argument in favor of the cause. It is most plainly no more than a bungling artifice to countenance the story, for the honor of the town as they imagine. in the first place, granting the 3 danish kings, as calld (I suppose them dukes or of the highest quality) granting, I say, they were killd & buryed here: tis ridiculous to suppose the Danes who were pagans would bury them in a christian churchyard, or that the christians would afterward remove them thither. they must needs look upon the ground as defild that coverd them, without casting into the scale the horror & detestation the people, at that time of day, must have of 'em for their barbaritys & depredations. further tis manifest from inspection, that the gravestones are purely christian, pickd up from est other graves in the church or churchyard, & laid there together, not many years agoe. perhaps, by some fantastic zealot of the parish, to keep up the credit of the relation. & should we even suppose that the inhabitants might possibly erect these 3 stones, upon the real graves of these kings, & ignorantly shape them like christian; yet it happens very unfortunately in the case, & which much invalidates the supposition, that among the rest they have displac'd the monument of a lord of the mannor. for on one of the stones is cut HIC INTUMULATUR IOHANNES QUONDAM DNS DE TRIKINGHAM as I read it some years agoe. nor would one readily suppose that a lord of the mannor should chuse to be buryd in the danish kings graves, or that he was so poor as not to afford a gravestone of his own. further still its not to be disputed but that the danish manner of burial at that day, was to lay the deceasd under a tumulus of earth or under a heap of stones, as we find in all old writers of the danish history, innumerable monuments of that sort remain still in that country, erected before & after christianity introduced there. which was the antient british way too, in times of heathenism, as we may see them all over the british isles, calld barrows or cairns or the like. & one of these very captains viz. Hubba 9 years after, being slain at the battle of Kinwith upon the Severn, was interrd under a great heap of stones, calld corruptly Hubblestone[8] to this day, as Asser menevensis Mr Camden[9] and others relate. & tho' in all probability our 3 kings were buryd immediately in the earth, nor can we reasonably expect, that the

Danes in a nights time & after the hurry of a dubious battle, could find leisure to erect those three tumuli over them; yet we must own they had much less time to erect 3 hewn gravestones.

4. as we showd before, how vain it is to derive the name of Trekingham from the three kings: so it is easy to hint to you a more natural etymology of it. the word ings signifys medows or low grounds: & all the towns that have ing in their names, are observ'd to be scituate near or upon such grounds. thus Folkingham signifys the habitation or town by the common medows, Helperingham I supposed in my Itinerary, to be Hale parva ingham or the dwelling near little Hale medows. Lessingham signifys the uncultivated medows Metheringham the Math or hay medows, & so of the rest.[10] now by our town of Trekingham a long medow or ings runs parallel to the road from Grantham to Brigend, for a mile together, which I suppose gave name to the town, meaning in Saxon the dry ings or medows, Drig [*Stukeley uses the Anglo-Saxon form of these letters*] aridus, dry, & so it is in effect; for in winter time when the common road is bad, travellers generally strike out into this medow for better riding. & I suppose the true & antient reading of the Towns name to be Trickingham, or the dwelling upon the dry ings or medows. so it is wrote in Hugo Candidus pa.43 & other old writers, & upon the very tombstone I just mentioned before, which is antient. however, the whole with great submission is defer'd, to the exact judgment of this learned Auditory.

1   Maurice Johnson.
2   Today's form is 'Londonthorpe'. The Domesday Book version was 'Lundetorp'; Kenneth Cameron derives it from Old Norse 'lundr', and Old Danish 'thorp': 'the secondary settlement of the grove ... the modern spelling London- is not common till the 16th century' (*A Dictionary of Lincolnshire Place-Names* (1998), 81).
3   Stukeley possessed Sir Henry Savile's *Rerum Anglicarum Scriptores post Bedam* (1596) which contained chronicles by William of Malmesbury, Henry of Huntingdon, Roger Hoveden and 'Ingulphi Abbatis Croylandensis historiarum lib[er] 1'.
4   Still called the Cliff Edge, this feature goes north from Grantham to Lincoln.
5   The modern place-name Threekingham was 'Trichingeham' in Domesday Book. Both Cameron (*Dictionary of Lincolnshire Place-Names*) and Eilert Ekwall, *The Concise Oxford Dictionary of English Place Names* (1960), state that the first element, 'trich' is of doubtful etymology but is of either British or Germanic origin. Historical research into the name has not been able to support the local legend that it derived from the burial of 'three kings'.
6   Stukeley takes many of these derivations from the account in 'Ingulf'; some are wide of the mark but others correct, though the persons who gave their names to the settlements cannot be as precisely identified as the chronicler claimed and may be older or more recent than the date given for this incident. Modern place-name research gives the meaning of the names as: Leverton, 'the farmstead where rushes, reeds ... grow'; Wyberton is indeed 'the village of Wibert', an old English or Germanic name; Algarkirk is 'the church of Algar or Ælfgar'; Osgodby is derived from 'Osgot's farmstead'.
7   Stukeley shows considerable understanding of place-name structure; in addition, he places the villages into their landscape in a manner approved by modern landscape historians.
8   Kenwith Castle is an earthwork in the parish of Northam in Torridge near Barnstaple (Devon). 'Hubblestone' is today Hubbastone, close to Appledore (Devon). Stukeley's explanation is derived from the legendary battle of Kinworth and the alleged death of the Viking leader Hubba there.
9   Asser Menevensis (d.909: see *ODNB*), bishop of Sherborne and author of the Life of King Alfred; William Camden (1551–1623: see *ODNB*), author of the widely used *Britannia* (1586).
10 For the accepted modern derivations of these place-names, see Kenneth Cameron, *Dictionary of Lincolnshire Place-Names*. Stukeley's comments throw an interesting light on riding conditions on the Grantham to Boston road in the early eighteenth century.

(b) On the Statues of the West Front of Croyland Abbey, 30 December 1746
SGS/Stukeley/9α

*This is part of Stukeley's investigation of the remains of Croyland Abbey near Spalding (see also **Letters 45, 46, 47, 49**), an interest which he shared with Johnson. It is written as a dissertation to be read to the SGS; it was read to the Society in January 1747. Stukeley himself admits that these are 'my conjectures' and his identifications of the statues on the West Front of the Abbey ruins with actual historical personages are purely speculative, though based on the knowledge of the time about this period of English history; some, like the image of St Guthlac, appear more accurate than others.*

To the learned Maurice Johnson esq[r] secretary to the Gentlemens Literary Society, Spalding.

In obedience to the injunctions of your Society, I have sent my conjectures of the images in the front of Croyland abby. The parochial dutys of the christmas season, have hindred me, from doing it sooner, or larger. but your sagacity & knowledg in these matters, will easily confirm & inlarge upon my opinions, or correct them.

I have sent you drawings of those images I am to speak of, being 12 in number; 6 on one side of the great west window, 6 on the other side. above the window, are 10 images of apostles, which are easily enough known from their symbols: & are only the imaginations of the sculptor, discharg'd in stone-work. but the others probably, have a real resemblance of the persons design'd: & are works extremely valuable.

1. the first is the royal founder, king Ethelbald, who built the monastery AD 716. he has a sceptre in his right hand, the mound with a cross atop, in his left. he likewise built the bridg, one of the oldest, as well as the most remarkable works of this sort, in the kingdom. the kings statue sitting, with the like mound, in his left hand, is still to be seen by the side of the bridg.[1]

2. is the first abbot Kenulf. he holds a knife in his hand, on account of the custom of giving a knife, to every guest entertain'd by the monastery, on the great festival day of S. Bartholomew; to whom with S. Guthlac, it is dedicated. a vast number of those knives were found 3 or 4 years ago, on scouring the river, by the abby: which we may well imagin, were thrown in there, on abolishing the custom.
   we observe, abbot Kenulf has no miter on: that dignity being not confer'd on the first abbots.

3. is a curious statue of S. Guthlak: the first english anchorite. he holds his famous whip or discipline, in his hand, with which he drove away the demons, that infested those deserted regions, when he went to live there. one of these demons is represented lying under his feet.[2]
   S. Guthlak's cell was that piece of brickwork, in the southwest angle of the church, on the outside. it was originally made of stud & mortar (as is the manner

of the country) or perhaps only of turf, cover'd with sedg. but as that decay'd, the convent repair'd it of brick.

such was the hermitage of the great S. Chad, founder of Litchfield cathedral, at the northwest corner of S. Chads church near Litchfield; of which I have taken drawings. such was the scituation of our neighbor S. Tibba's cell, at Ryhal. the east end of it still remains, on the north-west side of the church, without. these churches, when built, were purposely set close to these cells. others I know of, of like nature.

4. is the image of king Witlaf, AD 825. this monarch was a great benefactor to the abby. abbot Siward hid him 4 months, in S. Edelreda's cell, on the south side the choir, over against the high altar: when persecuted by Egbert king of the west saxons.
Correct, *in quadam parte cellæ reclusæ* in the list line of pa. 7 *Ingulfi historia. dele parte,* write *cella reclusæ*.[3]

he visited Croyland, every year, during his life; buryed his son Wymund here, in the choir, on the right hand of Edelreda's tomb, which was on the north of S. Guthlaks shrine. he buryed his queen Celfreda, on the other side of Edelfreda's [*sic*] tomb. she dyed AD 836.

5. is the great lord abbot Turketyl. who was a noble saxon; & lord chancellor to many of the saxon kings. & the first lord chancellor, we read of. this great & good man, smote with the charms of religion, resign'd his great dignitys & estates, into the kings hands, & became abbot here, AD 948. he reserved only 6 mannors, which he gave to the abby. whereof Cotenham by Cambridg was the occasion of founding, at least of refounding that University.

some years agoe, our great friend Roger Gale being possessor of that mannor, I visited him there, & took pleasure in viewing the scite & remains, of the old mannor house, & ground about it.

Worthorp, near Stamford, was another mannor, which Lord Turchetyl [*sic*] gave to Croyland abby. that was the occasion of founding the university here.[4]

in august 1744 Mr Samuel Gale & I visited Croyland abby together. the summer after, I gave him at London, a magnificent drawing of the intire front of the abby. but in the winter between, the ornamental work of the niche over the head of this figure, fell down, & carry'd off along with it, lord Turchetyl's head, & the head of his crozier join'd to it. it broke off by the neck, & fell luckily upon the crozier. whereby breaking its fall, the face was preserv'd.

after a good deal of pains in hunting for it, I rescu'd this head from being broke into grit, for the women to scour their floors withal. I carry'd it home, & set it up, in an old fashion'd niche, made purposely in my garden.[5]

from this head I learn't, that all these statues are of Bernake stone; of which the whole abby is built. an ingenious carver, on sight of it, was charm'd at the elegance, & at the good understanding of the carver; in adapting his lights & shades, so as to produce the proper effect, in such an elevation. Mr Gale observ'd too, that all the statues were cut with a very good taste.

I need not repeat any thing of the life of the excellent lord Turchetyl, which Ingulfus gives us copiously. but he was absolutely the refounder of the abby; after the horrid Danish devastation & massacre in AD 870. therefore deservedly merits a statue, directly under the first founder king Ethelbald: & the only mitred abbot, before the Conquest.

6. as soon as Mr Gale cast his eyes on the next figure, he calld out with great joy, the Conqueror! exceedingly pleasd with seeing so perfect an image of that monarch. he is represented in compleat armor, holding his sword upright, in his right hand.

he gave to the abby a new charter, at the sollicitation of abbot Ingulfus; who was made abbot here, by the king.

7. I take to be Maud, queen to William the conqueror, the great patron of Ingulfus; & who assisted him very much, in his applications to the conqueror, for obtaining new muniments to his abby.

8. is the statue of Lanfrank archbishop of Canterbury, another great friend of Ingulfus's. he calls him *omnium artium liberalium doctor, & in temporalibus experientissimus: vitaque ac religione sanctissimus.*[6] he holds the archiepiscopal crozier in his right hand, an open book in his left, denoting his great learning.

when I had suggested to Mr Sam. Gale who this statue was design'd for, he approv'd of my opinion, & of the propriety of the statue. & says he, I will inform you, in my turn, & tell you what book that is, which he holds in his hand. nay, says he, I can tell you further, I have that very book, now in my possession: perhaps the individual book, you see there carv'd: at least, one copyed from it, in that time, vizt. the Concordance, which Lanfrank wrote. in the summer after, at London, he show'd me the book. tis the oldest concordance of the Scriptures, which we have.

9. abbot Ingulf, to whom we are indebted for his accurate history of the abby. he wrote likewise the life of S. Guthlak. but it was lost in the general havoc of the librarys, of the religious houses, at the time of the dissolution. he dy'd AD 1109.

10. king Henry I *pulcherrimus adolescens,*[7] says Peter of Blois; a learned prince. he gave a new charter to the abby: & was extremely favorable to the church in general: as that author mentions, pa.126. his queen Matilda was a great patroness of Croyland abby. pa. 129.

11. the next figure is in compleat armor, leaning his hands on a battle ax. a dog between his feet. I apprehend, it represents the great Northumbrian Earl Waltheof, who marryed Judith the conquerors niece. he has a very just right to this station, who gave to the abby, Bernake: & the very quarry of which the abby is built, & this statue made. he was a great warrior, & a very stout man. when the conqueror besieg'd york he stood in a breach of the wall, & slew half a score Normans, with his battle ax.

he was likewise earl of huntingdon, & lived sometime at Ryhal near us; sometime at Conington, by Saltrey. He was seduced by the conquerors enemy, to enter into a conspiracy, & was beheaded. at last buryed in Croyland abby, & even thought to be a Saint.

it was usual in these times, for warriors to carry a dog along with them, in battle.

12. is abbot Joffrid, so constituted AD 1109 by king Henry I. a relation of the great Alan de Croun, of Frieston by Boston. this abbot, says Peter of Blois, was, *omnium predecessorum suorum abbatum Croylandiæ literatissimus, qui literas omnes a cunabulis cum lacte matris ebiberat.*[8] a man too of infinite diligence. he rebuilt the church & abby; & was the happy instrument of founding the universitys of Cambridge & of Stamford. as may be read at large, in Peter of Blois.

Wm Stukeley
Stamford 30 dec. 1746

The captions to the two pages of drawings read:

The upper part of the imagery, on each side of the great west window of Croyland abby, inscribd to the gentlemen of the Literary Society, Spalding, by W. Stukeley.

The lower part of the imagery on each side the great west window of Croyland abby, inscribd to the gentlemen of the Literary Society, Spalding, together with the explication of them, by W. Stukeley. 1746.

[1] The seated figure, holding an orb, at the Triangular Bridge in Crowland has come from the ruins of the Abbey; it may have occupied a position above the West window. It has been variously identified as King Ethelbald, the supporter of St Guthlac, or as a figure of Christ in Majesty, an identification preferred by Pevsner. Local tradition gave it the name of 'Oliver Cromwell with a penny bun', presumably referring to the siege of Crowland by the Parliamentary forces during the Civil War. The bridge in its current form dates from the later fourteenth century, though there are records of an earlier bridge, including a very early wooden bridge.

[2] Stukeley's enlarged drawing of the statue of St Guthlac is reproduced as Illustration 16.

[3] Stukeley, like the other historians of his time, relied for his history of Croyland Abbey on the chronicles attributed to Ingulf but actually written later in the Middle Ages. Here he suggests a correction to the version he and Johnson own, suggesting that they correct the phrase 'in some part of the cell of a recluse' by deleting 'part' so that it reads 'in the cell of a recluse'. Stukeley also used Dugdale's *Monasticon Anglicanum.*

[4] When resident in Stamford, Stukeley developed the view that the University of Cambridge was founded in Saxon times, originally with funds from Croyland Abbey's manor of Cottenham (Cambs). It was widely held, until the nineteenth century, that both Oxford and Cambridge had Anglo-Saxon foundations. As a Cambridge graduate, Stukeley was keen to give his university as early a foundation as possible. He also conjectured that funding and support from Croyland, known to be an Anglo-Saxon abbey, was responsible for founding a university at Stamford prior to the attempt made by Oxford scholars in the 1330s. For a full account, see N. J. Sheehan, *Stamford University: the Stuttering Dream* (2012). For Abbot Thurcytel (d. 975), see his entry in *ODNB*.

[5] See Letters 45 and 55 above.

[6] 'A teacher of all the liberal arts and with great experience in worldly matters; most holy in his life and faith.'

[7] 'Very handsome as a young man.'

[8] 'The most literate of all his predecessors as abbots of Croyland, who had drunk in all learning in his cradle with his mother's milk.'

APPENDIX 2
CHRONOLOGY OF THE LETTERS

	from Stukeley		*from Johnson*
1714			
		1.	**6 April**, Spalding [draft 6 April, at SGS]
	2. **19 May**, Boston		
		3.	**8 November**, Spalding [draft 7 November, at SGS]
1715			
		4.	**6 February**, Spalding, from M. Johnson senior
	5. **23 July**, Boston		
		6.	**28 July**, Spalding
		7.	No date [1715 London]
1716			
	8. **6 June**, Boston		
		9.	**6 October**, draft at SGS
		10.	**6 October**, Spalding
1717			
	11. **13 June**, London		
1718			
		12.	**10 March**, Woburn
	13. **10 April**, London		
	14. **19 June**, London		
1719			
		83.	**14 October**, Spalding [printed in Nichols]
		15.	**23 November**, Spalding
	16. **29 November**, London		
1720			
	17. **7 October**, London		
1721			
		18.	**14 October**, Spalding
		19.	**3 April**, Spalding
1722			
		20.	**3 August**, Spalding

	from Stukeley	*from Johnson*
[1723]		
1724		
	21. **12 November**, London	
1725		
		22. **8 March**, Lincoln
1726		
	[journal extract, **15 July**]	
[1727]		
1728		
	84. Soon after **13 April**, Grantham [in Northamptonshire Record Office]	
		23. **16 April**, Spalding
1729		
		24. **31 January**, Spalding
	25. **15 February**, Grantham	
		26. **15 February**, Spalding
	27. **13 March**, Grantham [14 March 1728/9 dissertation]	
		28. **24 March**, Spalding
1730		
		29. **2 October**, Spalding
	30. **9 October**, Stamford	
1731		
		31. **20 April**, Spalding
	[**5 July** – to Revd G. Hinson]	
1732		
	[**26 September** – diagram of Roman road]	
1733		
		32. **8 January**, Spalding
[1734–38]		
1739		
		33. **13 July**, Spalding
[1740]		
1741		
		34. **21 August**, Spalding
[1742]		

CHRONOLOGY OF THE LETTERS 229

	from Stukeley		*from Johnson*
1743			
	35. **27 November**, Stamford		
1744			
	36. **5 January**, Stamford		
		37.	**9 January**, Spalding
		38.	Undated fragment [**9 January 1744**], Spalding
	39. **18 February**, Stamford	85.	**17 March**, Spalding [printed in *Surtees* II]
		40.	**14 July**, Spalding
[1745]			
1746			
	41. **8 March**, Stamford		
		42.	**15 March**, Spalding
	43. **14 May**, Stamford		
	44. **17 December**, Stamford		
		45.	**20 December**, Spalding
1747			
		46.	**10 January**, Spalding
	47. **20 January**, Stamford		
	48. **28 January**, Stamford		
		49.	**6 February**, Spalding
		50.	**20 June**, Spalding
	51. **21 September**, Stamford		
		52.	**24 October**, Spalding
		53.	**6 November**, Spalding
1748			
	54. **25 May**, Stamford		
		55.	**27 May**, Spalding
1749			
		56.	**10 April**, Spalding
		57.	**19 April**, Spalding
		58.	**16 December**, Spalding
	59. **20 December**, London		
1750			
		60.	**8 January**, Spalding
	61. **16 January**, London		
		62.	**3 March**, Spalding
	63. **9 March**, London		
		64.	**12 March**, Spalding

	from Stukeley	*from Johnson*
	65. **15 May**, London	
		66. **13 June**, Spalding
	67. **16 June**, London	
		86. **21 June**, Spalding [printed in Nichols]
	68. **13 September**, London	
		69. **22 September**, Spalding
		70. **13 October**, Spalding
1751		
	71. **13 April**, London	
		72. **15 April**, Spalding
		73. **11 May**, Spalding
1752		
		74. **3 January**, Spalding
	75. **24 April**, London	
		76. **1 May**, Spalding
1753		
		77. **9 March**, Spalding
	78. **9 April**, London	
		79. **18 August**, Spalding
		80. **3 December**, Spalding
1754		
		81. **19 January**, Spalding
		82. **18 November**, Spalding
1755		
		87. **15 February**, Spalding, Revd John Johnson to Stukeley
1756		
		88. **30 March**, Spalding, Revd John Johnson to Stukeley
	89. **2 October**, London, to Dr John Green	

APPENDIX 3
MEMBERS OF SPALDING GENTLEMEN'S SOCIETY REFERRED TO IN THE LETTERS

Many of these were correspondents whose letters are preserved in the archives of the SGS; see Diana Honeybone and Michael Honeybone, *The Correspondence of the Spalding Gentlemen's Society 1710–1761*, LRS 99 (2010). *ODNB* signifies that this person has an entry in the *Oxford Dictionary of National Biography*, which will give fuller information. William Stukeley and Maurice Johnson II are omitted as they are discussed in the Introduction.

Ambler, Joshua (1694–1734): SGS founder-member in 1712, brother of Johnson's wife Elizabeth (née Ambler). His father William Ambler owned Gayton House which passed to Elizabeth (and consequently to Johnson) on Joshua's death. His will is dated 15 December 1734. He was buried at Spalding on 3 January 1735.

Atkinson, David (*c.*1692–1770): Of Fanthorpe Hall, Louth; educated Eton and Cambridge, Lincoln's Inn 1711, Gray's Inn 1717, barrister 1717, SGS 1733; he may be related to William Atkinson.

Atkinson, William: a Spalding attorney, SGS 1714, who was Treasurer from 1716 till his death; he was buried at Spalding on 28 October 1719. His will is in LAO, LCC Wills 1719/i/3.

Bayley, Harry (d.1730): SGS 1725, appointed Operator 1729; Surgeon in Spalding.

Bell, Beaupré (1704–41): *ODNB*. Of Beaupré Hall, Outwell (Norfolk); educated Westminster School and Trinity College, Cambridge, to which he left his papers; SGS 1726, 'beneficient member'; FSA 1725, PGS member 1731; second cousin to Maurice Johnson through his mother Margaret Oldfield; numismatist and antiquary, particularly interested in churches and Roman coins on which he was an expert.

Bellinger, Dr Francis (1690–1721): *ODNB*. Physician in Stamford and an original member of the SGS in 1712. He wrote about smallpox and nutrition of newborn babies.

Bentley, Dr Richard (1662–1742): *ODNB*. He was Master of Spalding Grammar School in 1681–2 before moving to Cambridge where he was Master of Trinity College. In 1720 he proposed a new edition of the Greek New Testament but never completed it despite obtaining many subscriptions. SGS 1731; a portrait of him hangs in the Society.

Bertie, Peregrine (*c.*1688–1743): Of Low Leyton, Essex, SGS 1722, lawyer, antiquary and art collector. His son Peregrine (1723–86) was MP for Westbury.

Bogdani, William (1699/1700–1771): Tower of London, 'one of the Clerks to the Ordnance'; Lord of the Manor of Hitchin (Herts); his wife Penelope (previously Bowell) was said to be a relation of Maurice Johnson; SGS 1724, 'beneficient member' and visited the SGS in 1735; FSA 1726, FRS 1730; interested in mathematics and music; son of the London-based Hungarian Protestant artist Jacob Bogdani (1658–1724); referred to in Jacob Bogdani's *ODNB* entry.

Bogdani, William Maurice (*c*.1733–90): Son of William Bogdani, godson of Maurice Johnson, of King's College, Cambridge. Visited the SGS on 5 October 1752; SGS 1753.

Bold, Peter (d.1720): Apothecary in Spalding; SGS 1719; he was buried at Spalding, 3 December 1720 (for his will, see LAO, LCC Wills 1721/i/51).

Bowyer, William (1699–1777): *ODNB*. Of London; educated Hadley (Surrey) and St John's College, Cambridge 1716–21; FSA 1736, Stationers' Company 1738; SGS member 1743; printer and editor; society printer to the SA 1736 and to the RS 1761; Printer of Votes for the House of Commons 1729–77; printer to the Society for the Encouragement of Learning; his best-known apprentice, John Nichols, called him 'the most learned Printer of the eighteenth century'.

Bransby, Revd Arthur (d.1752): BA Oxford, Curate of Spalding in 1730 and Rector of Great Coates (Lincs), 1733–52. SGS 1730. In 1735 he married Grace, daughter of the Revd Stephen Lyon (see below) the President of the SGS.

Brittain, Revd John (*c*.1675–1723): Born Sleaford, educated Oakham School and Christ's College, Cambridge (entered 1692); ordained deacon 1699 and priest 1700; Master of the Free School, Holbeach, and Curate of Gedney Fen; SGS 1714, 'beneficient member'.

Brooke, Revd Dr Zachariah (1716–88): *ODNB*. Educated Stamford School and St John's College, Cambridge; Fellow 1739–1765, Lady Margaret Professor of Divinity, Cambridge 1765, Royal Chaplain; published *Defensio Miraculorum* (1748); SGS 1746.

Buckworth, Everard senior (1693–1751): Educated Eton, Trinity College, Cambridge and Lincoln's Inn. SGS 1721. His will, dated 11 May 1751, listed extensive estates in South Lincolnshire.

Buckworth, Revd Everard (1729–92): Lawyer and cleric; he was the elder son of Everard Buckworth of Spalding (SGS 1721) who had attended Eton just before Maurice Johnson. Educated Trinity Hall, Cambridge 1747 and Lincoln's Inn (entered 1747); Rector of Washingborough (Lincs), Prebendary of Lincoln 1773 and of Canterbury 1775; SGS 1753, SGS Secretary in 1756.

Buckworth, Theophilus (d.1801): Second son of Everard Buckworth senior. SGS 1755.

Butter, Robert (fl.1730s–40s): Spalding merchant and coastal surveyor, married Maurice Johnson's daughter Elizabeth, nicknamed by the Johnson family 'Madcap Bet'; SGS 1730; interested in music (helped to organise SGS Anniversary concerts and played the bassoon there) and numismatics.

Clerk, Sir John of Penicuik (1676–1755): *ODNB*. 2nd Baronet; of Penicuik near Edinburgh; educated Penicuik Parish School, Glasgow University, Leiden University (law); Commissioner for the Treaty of Union between England and Scotland, 1707, Baron of the Court of Exchequer 1708; Vice-President of the Edinburgh Philosophical Society; FSA 1725, FRS 1729; SGS 1740, introduced by Roger Gale; coalmine owner, antiquary, advocate, musician.

Coleby, Dr Dixon (1680–1756): Born Kirton (Lincs); educated Merton College, Oxford 1696, BA 1700, MA 1703, BD and DD 1710; MD, Physician at Stamford; SGS 1733, but not listed as a member of Stukeley's Stamford Brazen Nose

Society in 1737; keen gardener and plant grower, interested in new varieties of imported plants.

Collins, Richard (d.1732): An East Midland artist, working from Peterborough, SGS 1727; official painter to the SGS, discussed his own paintings and those of other European artists at the Society on several occasions. His death is recorded in the SGS Minutes. He trained under Michael Dahl (1659–1743) 'most Eminent Master in that Art & practice chiefly in Portraiture' (SGS, MB1, fol.116v). He drew several East Midland buildings which were made into engravings, chiefly the West Front of Peterborough Cathedral, the Abbey and Triangular Bridge at Crowland and features of Northampton. His painting 'A Family of Three at Tea' in the Victoria and Albert Museum is well known and his portrait of William Stukeley is in the Society of Antiquaries.

Cook, Benjamin (fl.1740s): Of Spalding; 'Register' (legal clerk) and personal assistant to Maurice Johnson; assistant to the Secretaries of the SGS; SGS 1746.

Cox, Michael (d.1758): Surgeon-apothecary in Spalding, SGS 1729, Operator of the SGS who organised the Society's move from Gayton House to his Rooms by the High Bridge, where it remained for many years. He wrote fifteen dissertations, the 'Associators', for SGS meetings between February 1753 and January 1756. His will is in LAO (LCC Wills 1758/44).

Degg, Dr Simon (1694–1729): From Derby, physician and antiquary, FRS 1723, FSA 1724, SGS 1724, published in the RS's *Phil.Trans.* (October 1727), 'An Human Skeleton of an extraordinary size found in Repton'. Died 8 November 1729; buried at Graveley (Herts). Grandson of Sir Simon Degge (1612–1704: see *ODNB*), who married Alice Oldfield of Spalding.

Dinham, Dr John MD (1695–1754): Educated Eton, St John's College, Cambridge, Leiden 1715. SGS 1722; he lived in London Road, Spalding. His portrait and that of his wife are in the SGS's rooms. His will is in LAO (LCC Wills 1754/53).

Dinham, Revd John (c.1725–82): Son of Dr John Dinham; educated Emmanuel College, Cambridge; Perpetual Curate of Spalding 1758; SGS 1749; became President of the SGS in 1759. His will is in LAO (LCC Wills 1782/62).

Dinham, Dr Samuel (1724–61): Son of Dr John Dinham and brother of Revd John Dinham. Educated St John's College, Cambridge, MD; physician in Spalding; SGS 1752.

Dodd, Revd Dr William (1729–77): *ODNB*. Born Bourne (Lincs), educated Clare College, Cambridge, ordained priest 1753, LLD 1766, one of the King's chaplains; theological author, charity promoter and fashionable preacher, popularly known as the 'macaroni parson'; visited the SGS 1750; SGS 1751; published a translation of the poems of Callimachus 1755; condemned to death for forging a signature on a credit bill for £4,200 and was not pardoned despite the efforts of several thousand petitioners including Dr Samuel Johnson.

Drake, Francis (c.1696–1771): *ODNB*. Of York, apprenticed to a York surgeon and became City Surgeon of York; FSA 1735, PGS member 1735, FRS 1736; SGS 1747; antiquary and author, publishing the history of York, *Eboracum* (1736).

Drake, Nathan (1726–78): *ODNB*. Born and educated at Lincoln, distant relative of Francis Drake (above); FSA 1743; SGS 1751; Fellow of the Society of Artists 1771; painter, specialising in landscapes.

Edwards, George (1694–1773): *ODNB*. SGS 1743, FSA 1752, ornithologist and artist; won the Copley Medal of the RS in 1750 for his ornithological work.

Ellys, Sir Richard (1682–1742): *ODNB*. 3rd Baronet; of Nocton (Lincs) and Bolton Street, London, possibly also Place House, Ealing. A noted classical and biblical scholar; SGS 1730, 'beneficient member'; MP for Grantham, and later for Boston; book collector with extensive libraries at both of his houses (his Nocton library now at Blickling Hall in Norfolk); Calvinist, patron of the nonconformist chapel in Princes Street, London and biblical scholar, wrote *Fortuita Sacra* (1727), a study of disputed New Testament texts; patron of authors, notably John Horsley, William Stukeley, Edward Walpole and Thomas Boston.

Evelyn, Sir John (1681/2–1763): Born Dartford (Kent); Balliol College, Oxford 1699; MP for Helston (Cornwall) 1708–10; 1st Baronet 1713; grandson and eventual heir of the diarist Sir John Evelyn of Wotton (Surrey); FRS 1723, FSA 1725, SA Vice-President 1735–6; SGS 1733; Tory Postmaster General, Commissioner of Customs; letter writer, diarist, antiquarian and bibliophile, very extensive subscriber to books.

Folkes, Martin (1690–1754): *ODNB*. Educated privately and at Clare College Cambridge (entered 1706); inherited his father's extensive estate; FRS 1713, Vice-President 1723, President 1741; FSA 1720, President 1750, obtained a Royal Charter for the FSA; member of the Egyptian Society 1741; SGS 1743, 'beneficient member'; Freemason, Deputy Grand Master 1725; foreign Fellow of the Académie Royale des Sciences; LLD Oxford and Cambridge 1746; antiquarian, numismatist and mathematician, published on coins.

Frederick, Sir Charles (1709–85): *ODNB*. London, Berkeley Square; educated Westminster School and New College, Oxford (entered 1725); Middle Temple (entered 1728); FSA 1731, Director 1736 and 1740; FRS 1733; SGS 1751; MP for Shoreham 1741–54 and for Queenborough 1754–84; Surveyor General of the Ordnance, active member of the Honourable Board of Ordnance for thirty-six years from 1746 under the patronage of the Duke of Montague, Master General of the Ordnance; responsible for the 1749 Royal Fireworks and for small arms during the Seven Years' War; an eminent antiquarian.

Gale, Roger (1672–1744): *ODNB*. Of Scruton (Yorks), son of Thomas Gale (1635–1702), Dean of York; educated St Paul's School, London and Trinity College, Cambridge (entered 1691), Fellow 1697; FRS 1717, Treasurer; FSA 1717, Vice-President; SGS 1728; MP for Northallerton (Yorks) 1705–13; civil servant, commissioner for stamp duties 1714, commissioner for excise 1715–35; retired to his Scruton estate on losing his post under Walpole's reorganisation of Civil Service posts; antiquary and numismatist.

Gale, Samuel (1682–1754): *ODNB*. Brother of Roger Gale. Educated St Paul's School. Customs House official and antiquarian who also helped to re-found the SA in 1717, SA Treasurer 1717–40. SGS 1733; he sent at least one dissertation to the SGS; correspondence of the Gale brothers was published in John Nichols (ed.), *Bibliotheca Britannica Topographica, Reliquiæ Galeanæ* (1782). Roger and Samuel Gale were brothers-in-law of William Stukeley by his marriage to his second wife, their sister Elizabeth.

Gay, John (1685–1732): *ODNB*. Born in Barnstaple (Devon); poet and dramatist; created the extremely successful *The Beggar's Opera* in 1728. He came to London as a draper's apprentice and became secretary to the Duchess of

Buccleuch; as a result became a personal friend and correspondent of Maurice Johnson and through him of Stukeley. SGS 1728.

Gideon, Samson (1699–1762): *ODNB*. Financier, best known for his financial acumen which he used to support the Government, especially in the 1740s. He purchased the manor of Spalding, though he resided in London; SGS 1751.

Goche, Revd Barnaby (*c*.1677–1730): Born Bedfordshire, educated at Biggleswade and Peterhouse, Cambridge (entered 1693); ordained deacon 1698; Rector of Crowland and Chaplain of Cowbit; SGS member 1723.

Gonville, William (1697–1748): Of Alford (Lincs); SGS 1727; drainage lawyer, Clerk to the Court of Sewers of Lincoln and a relation by marriage of the Johnsons via Maurice Johnson's father's third wife, whose first husband had been a Mr Gonville. His will is in LAO (LCC Wills 1748/67).

Gordon, Alexander (*c*.1692–1754): *ODNB*. Born probably Aberdeen, educated Aberdeen University; his patron was Sir John Clerk; FSA 1725, Secretary 1735–41; member of the Society of Roman Knights, 1720s; Secretary of the Egyptian Club 1732/3, set up to publish engravings of Egyptian mummies (not to be confused with Stukeley's Egyptian Society of the 1740s); Secretary of the Society for the Encouragement of Learning 1736; SGS 1737; antiquarian, interested in Roman antiquities in Scotland and Egyptian antiquities, attempted to decipher Egyptian hieroglyphs; famous as a singer and musician, nicknamed 'Singing Sandy', who performed in Italy and Britain; Secretary to the Governor of Carolina, America, from 1741, also nicknamed Sawny Gordon.

Green, Dr John (1708–56): Born at Spalding, son of John Green of Dunsby Hall and Mary Johnson; his grandmother was a Lynn; educated at Spalding Grammar School (under Revd Timothy Neve), St John's College, Cambridge (admitted 1725, aged seventeen), Leiden University 1731 where he studied under Boerhaave; MD, physician; SGS 1729, 'beneficient member', Second Secretary 1729, dealing with correspondence relating to natural philosophy, medicine and mathematics, Secretary 1748; PGS member 1734; FSA 1739; married 1736 Jane, eldest daughter of Maurice Johnson; a capable artist, also interested in natural history.

Grisoni, Giuseppe (1699–1769): *ODNB*. Artist of Italian descent, born in Belgium. He travelled to Italy where he met the collector John Talman and came to England with him. He worked as a painter from 1715 to 1728 when he returned to Italy. He became an honorary member of the SGS in October 1741 while in Florence; was described as 'an eminent painter and Antiquary' (MB4, fol.127v). Both Talman and Grisoni submitted design sketches for a museum for the SGS when it was proposed in 1725 to create a new building (see John Harris, 'Designs for the museum and library of the Spalding Gentlemen's Society', *The Georgian Group Journal* 19 (2011), 39–49).

Grundy, John (senior) (1696–1748): Born Congerstone (Leics): 'of Market Bosworth in Leicestershire a Land Surveyor and Mathematician who made an Actual Survey of this Lordship [Spalding] & many others in this Neighbourhood & presented the Soc: with a Plan of this Town for an Ornament to their Museum' (1732); lived at Congerstone and Spalding, taught mathematics at Market Bosworth Grammar School and Spalding Grammar School; surveyor of Charles Jennens' estate at Gopsall Park; SGS 1731, 'beneficient member', came to Spalding to survey the Duke of Buccleuch's estates; worked for the Deeping Fen Adventurers creating drains and experimenting with pumping engines;

published pamphlets on drainage and wrote a MS 'Art of Drainage'. Mentioned in his son's entry in *ODNB* (see below).

Grundy, John (junior) (1719–83): *ODNB*. Son of John Grundy senior (see above), born Congerstone; family moved to Spalding in 1738, lived there and was buried in St Mary and St Nicholas church, Spalding; SGS 1739, 'beneficient member'; consultant drainage engineer working in Lincolnshire, Norfolk and Yorkshire; Agent for the Deeping Fen Adventurers 1748–64; founder-member of the Society of Civil Engineers 1771.

Hardy, Revd John (1679/80–1740): *ODNB*. FSA 1718, SGS 1724; nonconformist minister and schoolmaster in Nottingham and student of antiquities; conformed to the Church of England in 1727, becoming first, Vicar of Kinoulton (Notts) and then Vicar of Melton Mowbray (Leics). He presented Caxton's edition of John Gower's *Confessio Amantis* to the SGS library.

Harrison, John (fl.1750): Cambridge University's gardener and botanist; SGS 1753.

Hawkes, Thomas (d.1784): Of Magdalen Street, Norwich; visited the SGS in 1753; may be the Thomas Hawkes who became a member in 1782, or else a relative; tinplate worker in Norwich and maker of mathematical instruments; astronomer, mathematician, land surveyor and mechanic; made an orrery or celestial sphere for the SGS in 1750, still in the SGS's museum (described in MB5, fol.64v, 20 September 1750); observed transit of Venus in Norwich in 1761, published details in the *Norwich Mercury* 13 June 1761 and sent them also to the SGS. His will is in LAO (LCC Wills 1784/34).

Heighington, Dr Musgrave (1680–1764): *ODNB* and *Grove's Dictionary of Music*. Born at Durham, 'sometime of Queen's College, Oxford'; musician and composer; organist at Hull 1717–20; performing in Dublin in the 1720s; City Organist and organist of St Nicholas' church, Great Yarmouth, 1730s; SGS 1736, 'beneficient member', organised the SGS's Anniversary Concerts 1737–47, writing music for them, including settings of poems by SGS members and of odes of Horace and Anacreon, and performing there with his family; organist at St Martin's church, Leicester, 1748, visited SGS from there in 1751; *c*.1756 organist at Dundee where he founded a musical society. Very little of his music survives; several MSS in Christ Church, Oxford library.

Hepburn, Dr John (*c*.1685–1766): Originally from Spalding; surgeon in the army, later surgeon in Stamford; SGS 1723; wrote to the SGS in 1742 about a case in 1734 when he extracted a stone from the urethra of a child. The reference to him as a 'Brother' in **Letter 34** is probably a Masonic reference; Stukeley was a Freemason and there is evidence to suggest that Johnson was also.

Hildesley, Revd Mark (1699–1772): *ODNB*. Vicar of Hitchin (Herts) 1732–55; Prebendary of Lincoln 1754–73; Bishop of Sodor and Man 1755–72; organised the translation of the Bible and Book of Common Prayer into Manx; SGS 1741.

Hill, Sir John (1714–75): *ODNB*. Son of Dr Theophilus Hill of Peterborough, a PGS member; SGS 1740, PGS 1747; MD St Andrews 1751; apothecary in London 1730; writer and natural philosopher specialising in botany and fossil collection; published *A History of Fossils* (1748), edited a journal, *The Inspector* 1751–3; produced a 26-volume publication *The Vegetable System* between 1759 and 1775; maintained a correspondence with Linnaeus, awarded the Swedish Order of Vasa 1774; called by Dr Samuel Johnson 'a very curious observer'. See his biography: George Rousseau, *The Notorious Sir John Hill* (2012).

Hinson, Capt. Joseph (d. *c*.1782): Military surveyor, working on surveys of the Welland and the South Lincolnshire coast; SGS 1742.

Holmes, George (1662–1749): *ODNB*. FSA 1717, SGS 1728, FRS 1741, Archivist and Keeper of the Royal and Government records at the Tower of London.

Hunter, Major-General Robert (1666–1734): *ODNB*. Born Edinburgh, educated as an attorney; FRS 1709; SGS 1726; was ADC to the Duke of Marlborough in the early years of the War of the Spanish Succession, fought at Blenheim and Ramillies; prisoner of the French in Paris 1707–09; became an effective Governor of New York and New Jersey 1710–19; Controller of Customs under Walpole 1720–7; Governor of Jamaica 1727–34; Lord of the Manor of Crowland, Lincolnshire, through his wife Elizabeth Orby; Maurice Johnson was his steward and was thanked by Hunter for improvements.

Ingram, Dale (1710–93): *ODNB*. Born at Spalding; worked as a surgeon in London. 'Mr Dale Ingram chyrurgeon at Aleppo or in Turkey elsewhere' was listed as an SGS in 1733 but crossed out and 'Neg X' written after his name (MB1, fol.108A); surgeon at Barbados 1743–50; surgeon at Tower Hill, London 1750; eventually SGS 1751; published *Practical Cases and Observations in Surgery* (1751) and *Essay on the Plague* (1755); surgeon at Christ's Hospital, London 1759–91.

Ives, Calamy (b. *c*.1719): Born probably in London; apothecary's apprentice perhaps in Spalding; almost certainly an apothecary at Wisbech; SGS 1745; sent to the SGS an account of a journey to Ireland in 1747; visited the SGS 1748; described as being 'of Wragg Marsh' near Spalding, so perhaps had property there; leased property in St Martin's in the Fields, London, in 1745.

Jackson, William (fl.1740s): Schoolmaster: 'usher of the Petit School, Spalding' in the early 1740s; Customs official in Boston 1740s; SGS 1746, sent a present of a stuffed snake for the museum; one of the SGS's poets, producing a translation of poems by Horace; his poem 'All Hail the Day', an extract from his 'Ode on St Cecilia's Day', was set to music by Musgrave Heighington and performed at the 1743 SGS Anniversary Concert.

Johnson, Revd George (*c*.1733–86): Born at Spalding, son of Revd Walter Johnson, who was later Rector of Redmarshall (Co. Durham); cousin of Maurice Johnson; educated Spalding Grammar School, Durham School and Brasenose College Oxford (entered 1750), Demyship (scholarship) to Magdalen College, Oxford 1751, fellow of Magdalen 1757–65; SGS 1753; wrote informative letters to SGS from Oxford; ordained priest 1757; Vicar of Norton (Co. Durham); Prebendary of Lincoln 1781, Rector of Lofthouse (Yorks), Rector of Frinton (Essex). From Oxford, when a student, he wrote regularly to the SGS between 1750 and 1751: see *Correspondence*, letters 529, 539, 545, 549, 551 and 554.

Johnson, Henry (1687–1760): *ODNB*. Relative of Maurice Johnson; AS member 1720, SGS 1724 and regular correspondent, a merchant and eventually President of the Royal Asiento in Panama; travelled in Central America, produced translations from Spanish and contributed letters about his travels in Spain and Central America to the SGS. He then retired to an estate in Berkhamsted (Herts), where Maurice Johnson was his estate steward.

Johnson, Henry Eustace (1733–?): Born Spalding, youngest surviving son of Maurice Johnson and his wife Elizabeth (née Ambler); educated Spalding and probably at a school in Gosberton (Lincs); SGS 1753; factor of the East India Company, EIC assistant secretary in Madras, India; wrote letters to the SGS from his travels, which have not survived; died at St Helena on a voyage back to England.

Johnson, John (brother) (1690–1744): Born Spalding, younger son of Maurice Johnson senior by his first marriage to Jane Johnson and younger brother of Maurice Johnson; educated Spalding Grammar School and the Inner Temple; barrister specialising in drainage law and interested in mathematics; a founder-member of the SGS, member 1712, Treasurer 1729–42; FSA 1718. On his death, it was recorded: 'the death of John Johnson of the Inner Temple Esquire Clerk of the Court of Sewers for Elloe Holland & Steward of the Soke of Kirton and manners of Spalding, Bichar Beaumont, Croyland Holbeach Whapload and of the Mannor of Hitchin in Hertfordshire. Late the Prudent & Worthy Treasurer of this Societie & Great & liberal Benefactor both to that & the Concert here' (MB3, fol.190A).

Johnson, Revd John (son) (1722–58): Born Spalding, third surviving son of Maurice Johnson and his wife Elizabeth (née Ambler); educated Spalding Grammar School and St John's College, Cambridge, 1740; ordained deacon 1744, priest 1746; curate of Ramsey (Hunts), then incumbent of St Mary and St Nicholas' church, Spalding and Vicar of Moulton; SGS member 1742, Second Secretary 1748, President 1755 following the death of his father Maurice Johnson; unmarried.

Johnson, Maurice (senior) (1661–1747): Barrister-at-law, of Spalding, married Jane Johnson (d.1703) in 1683 and gained Ayscoughfee Hall, Spalding, through his wife's right of inheritance in 1685; two sons, Maurice (the founder of the SGS) and his younger brother John (see above). Founder-member of the SGS, 1712. Two further wives, Elizabeth Oldfield (d.1724) and Ann Falkner (d.1742) but no other children.

Johnson, Maurice (son) (1714–93): Born Spalding, eldest surviving son of Maurice Johnson and his wife Elizabeth (née Ambler); educated Spalding Grammar School and Foubert's [military] Academy, London; SGS member 1733; contributed regular full letters from his army travels and London residence; officer in the First Regiment of Foot (the Guards), serving as Captain and later Colonel, travelled in Europe during the campaigns of the War of the Austrian Succession, fought at the Battle of Dettingen 1743, served on staff of the Duke of Cumberland, took part in the campaign against the Jacobites in 1745–6, perhaps present at Culloden; married Elizabeth daughter of Sir Edward Bellamy in 1749 and later married Mary Baker in 1755; gained an estate at Stanway (Essex) from his first wife; later returned to Ayscoughfee Hall after his father's death but took little part in the activities of the SGS in the second half of the eighteenth century.

Johnson, Walter (1720–71): second surviving son of Maurice Johnson and his wife Elizabeth (née Ambler); educated Spalding Grammar School and the Inner Temple; barrister in Spalding, lived at Gayton (Holyrood) House when he married Mary Fairfax; SGS 1741; SGS Treasurer from 1742; active member in the 1760s. FSA 1749.

Johnson, Revd Walter, LLB (1686–1760): Second cousin of Maurice Johnson and grandson of Walter Johnson senior by his first marriage. Ordained deacon 1723, priest 1725; curate of Tansor (Northants) 1723, Vicar of Leek (Staffs) 1735–7. Later he became Rector of Redmarshall (Co. Durham) 1737–60. His son George became an SGS member in 1753 and correspondent while a student at Oxford.

Jurin, Dr James (1684–1750): *ODNB*. Physician and natural philosopher, born London, educated Royal Mathematical School at Christ's Hospital, London and Trinity College, Cambridge; Fellow 1706; attended Leiden University; Headmaster of Newcastle Grammar School 1709; MD Cambridge 1716; FRS 1717, Secretary of the RS 1721 and prominent Newtonian supporter; SGS 1723, a 'worthy & beneficient member' (MB1, fol.69); Maurice Johnson attended his lectures on mathematics and philosophy, perhaps in London, and William Stukeley claimed that 'Mr Johnson' had sent for Jurin to tutor his son before Jurin moved to London; Jurin helped Johnson in gaining Sir Isaac Newton as SGS member; FRCP 1719, President of Royal College of Physicians 1750; physician at Guy's Hospital, worked on inoculation against smallpox; published a series of pamphlets in the 1720s, *The Success of Inoculating the Small Pox.* In 1724 he married Mary Douglas, a wealthy widow; they had five daughters and a son.
Lake, Richard (d. early 1720s): Of Wisbech Castle (Cambs), built in the mid-seventeenth century by Oliver Cromwell's secretary and leased by the Bishop of Ely to the Lake family; it was replaced by the Crescent *c.*1814. A founder member of the Wisbech Gentlemen's Society, published the catalogue of its library in 1718. SGS 1721.
Landen, John (1719–90): Of Peakirk near Peterborough; mathematician and land surveyor, developed a theory of rotatory motion; SGS 1749; FRS 1766.
Lawrence, Edward (1674–1739): *ODNB*. A Stamford land surveyor, SGS 1731, member of Stukeley's Brazen Nose Society.
Lockier, Very Revd Francis (1669–1740): *ODNB*. For some years Chaplain to the English Church at Hamburg. Dean of Peterborough 1725–40; SGS 1726; PGS 1730s. He donated his excellent library to Peterborough Cathedral.
Lynn, George (junior) (1707–58): Of Southwick (Northants). Son of SGS member George Lynn (1676–1742), a relative of Maurice Johnson. Educated St John's College, Cambridge, and the Inner Temple; SGS 1723. Married Anne Bellamy, daughter of Sir Edward Bellamy of London and sister to Elizabeth who married Col. Maurice Johnson (son of SGS founder Maurice Johnson).
Lynn, Dr Walter (?1678–1762): *ODNB*. Born Southwick, son of George Lynn the elder of Southwick and Mary Johnson of Spalding; uncle of George Lynn junior (above) and second cousin to Maurice Johnson; educated Spalding Grammar School and Peterhouse, Cambridge (entered 1695); MB Cambridge 1704; medical writer and inventor; published *Essay toward a more easie and safe method of Cure in the Small Pox* (1714); early member of the SGS 1714; wrote *Nyktopsia* 1726, a satirical account of his invention of a candle-snuffer; published a pamphlet on steam-powered pumping engines, *The Case of Walter Lynn MB* (1726); travelled widely, including a visit to Carolina, America; published *The Anatomist Dissected* (1740), opposing experimental surgery; died in Grantham.
Lyon, Revd Stephen (*c.*1674–1748): Of French Huguenot origins, born Rouen. Educated Oriel College, Oxford, and Emmanuel College, Cambridge; vicar of Merewoth (Kent) 1702–1748 and perpetual curate of Spalding 1710–1748. Founder-member of SGS 1712, President of the SGS 1715–48.
Manningham, **Sir Richard** (1685–1759): *ODNB*. He became FRS in 1719 and Licentiate of the RCP in 1719 at the same time as Stukeley. He became a specialist in obstetrics and the best man-midwife of his time, establishing lying-in beds for his patients in the house next to his own. SGS 1724.
Mead, Dr Richard (1673–1754): *ODNB*. A famous and popular London physi-

cian and book-collector; Stukeley undertook hospital experience under him in London. FRS 1703, member of the Council of the RS for fifty years; SGS 1746.

Mendes da Costa, Emanuel (1717–91): *ODNB*. Born in London of a Portuguese Jewish family; natural historian and merchant in fossils and shells; member of the Aurelian Society 1740; employed by the Army contractors in Europe in the 1740s; SGS 1746, corresponded about fossils and the organisation of the SGS's collections in their museum; FRS 1747; FSA 1752; Clerk to the RS 1763, expelled 1768 for financial irregularities; published *Natural History of Fossils* (1757) and *British Conchology* (1778).

Middleton Massey, Dr Richard (1681–1743): Born Cheshire, educated Brasenose College, Oxford (entered 1697), non-juror so did not take his degree; 'he practised many years at Wisbeach & with Mr Rd. Lake put the Library there into very good Order & published some account & a catalogue of It'. MD Aberdeen 1720; practised as a physician in Wisbech, where he organised a learned society, then moved to London and finally practised in Cheshire, died at Rostherne (Cheshire); FRS 1712; FSA 1718, Secretary of the A.S.; SGS 1721; subscribed extensively to books.

Milles, Revd Joseph (1733–1805): Educated Jesus College, Cambridge; Curate of Spalding and of Cowbit; Rector of Dembleby, Lincs 1780–1805 and Vicar of Weston 1787–1805; SGS 1753.

Mitchell, René (d.1729): Surgeon in Spalding; SGS 1723. His will is in LAO (LCC Wills 1729/ii/258).

Montague, Very Revd John (1655–1729): Master of Trinity College Cambridge to 1700; Dean of Durham 1700–29. SGS 1723.

Mortimer, Dr Cromwell (1693–1752): *ODNB*. Born Essex to a Dissenting family; MD Leiden 1724, a friend of Professor Boerhaave; LRCP 1725; MD Cambridge 1728; FRCP 1729; physician, secretary and antiquary, practising as a physician in London and as assistant to Sir Hans Sloane 1729–40; FRS 1728, RS Secretary 1730–52; FSA 1734; PGS 1735; SGS 1737; very active corresponding member of Paris Royal Academy of Sciences; supported by the SGS in his application to be Secretary of the Society for the Encouragement of Learning 1737.

Muscat, Revd James (1708/9–58): Educated Merton College, Oxford (entered 1725 aged sixteen), then transferred to Corpus Christi College, BA 1729; schoolmaster at Boston Grammar School 1745–59; SGS 1746; Rector of Little Staughton (Beds) 1735–58.

Neve, Revd Timothy (1694–1757): *ODNB*. Born near Ludlow (Shropshire); educated Ludlow School and St John's College, Cambridge (entered 1711); ordained priest 1718; Headmaster, Spalding Grammar School 1716–29; SGS 1718, Treasurer 1718–29; Minor Canon of Peterborough Cathedral 1729–45; Rector of Alwalton 1729–57; Archdeacon of Huntingdon 1747; Prebendary of Lincoln Cathedral 1744–1757; founded the PGS on the model of the SGS 1730; Secretary and Treasurer of the PGS, author of articles on astronomy, published in the RS's *Philosophical Transactions* and the *Gentleman's Magazine*.

Neve, Revd Timothy (junior) (1724–98): *ODNB*. Born at Spalding, son of Revd Timothy Neve senior; educated Corpus Christi College, Oxford (entered 1737), Fellow 1747; SGS 1746; PGS member 1747; ordained deacon 1747 and priest 1748; chaplain to the British community in Hamburg 1751; Rector of Middleton Stoney (Oxon) and Geddington (Northants); Bampton Lecturer at

Oxford, lectures published as *Eight Sermons* (1781); Lady Margaret Professor of Divinity, Oxford, 1783; Prebendary of Worcester Cathedral 1783.

Newton, Sir Isaac (1642–1727): *ODNB*. Became an honorary member of the SGS in 1724 at Johnson's request, though he excused himself from taking an active part in the Society's activities on the grounds of his age and health. Johnson wrote in the SGS Minutes a full account of his interview with Sir Isaac, which is quoted in *Correspondence*, 26–7. Johnson frequently quoted Sir Isaac's advice to build up the correspondence of the Society as a means of ensuring its survival and prosperity. The SGS was particularly proud to have him as a member because of his international fame and his Lincolnshire origins.

Norcliffe, Richard (fl.1730s–40s): Described by Johnson as a 'merchant, Kingston upon Hull'; merchant exporting timber from Scandinavia to England, based in Friderickshald (modern Halden) in south-west Norway, near the Swedish border; SGS 1734; wrote letters describing Norwegian flora and fauna and sent geological and botanical specimens for the SGS museum; translated the history of Greenland by Norwegian missionary Revd Hans Egede; introduced Revd Andreas Bing, formerly one of Hans Egede's missionaries to Greenland, to the SGS.

Oldfield, Anthony (born *c.*1710): Descendant of Sir Anthony Oldfield of Spalding, probably son of John and Mary Oldfield and related to Maurice Johnson; assistant to the agent at Petworth House (Sussex), then assistant agent of the Duchess of Somerset; wrote from her house, Cheveley Park, south-east of Newmarket, a house later taken over by the Dukes of Rutland; SGS 1746, corresponded about a family inheritance as well as his antiquarian interests.

Parsons, Dr James (1705–70): *ODNB*. Born Ireland, educated Dublin and Reims, medical degree 1736; London-based physician, obstetrician and anatomist, opposed Joanna Stevens' treatment of internal stones by soap lees (see her entry in *ODNB*); keen antiquarian, friend of the artist William Hogarth; FRS 1741, foreign secretary of the RS 1751–62, had thirty-one papers published in the RS's *Philosophical Transactions*; SGS 1746; FSA 1748.

Pegge, Revd Samuel (1704–96): *ODNB*. Born Chesterfield (Derbys), educated Chesterfield and St John's College, Cambridge; ordained priest 1730, Vicar of Godmersham (Kent) 1731, Vicar of Heath near Whittington (Derbys) from 1751 to his death; Prebendary of Lichfield 1757–96; SGS 1730, introduced by his university friend Revd Benjamin Ray; PGS member 1731; FSA 1751; keen and successful antiquarian, book-collector, numismatist and author, had fifty articles published in *Archæologia*; his letters in the SGS collection demonstrate his incisive mind.

Pole, Joseph: Described as a 'Prussian, Jeweller, Engraver & Seal Cutter', visited Spalding in 1752 and in a letter from Peterborough sent a sample of rhinoceros skin for the SGS museum and a description of the animal from which it came. SGS 1753.

Powell, Revd Morgan (*c.*1725–74): Born Llanddeusant (Carmarthen), educated St Catharine's College, Cambridge 1742, BA 1746; University friend of Revd John Johnson (*q.v.*); ordained deacon 1746, priest 1746; SGS 1747; curate at Kirton (Lincs); Vicar of Walsingham and West Barsham 1756; Rector of Berwick St Leonard (Wilts) 1767.

Ravenscroft, George (*c.*1719–52): Of Wykeham Grange, near Spalding, descendant of the famous glass-maker George Ravenscroft (1632–83). Educated at Douai together with the natural philosopher Turberville Needham, which implies that he was a Roman Catholic. SGS 1742.

Ray, Revd Benjamin (1704–60): *ODNB*. A relative of Johnson's, born Spalding, educated Spalding Grammar School (under Revd Timothy Neve) and St John's College, Cambridge (entered 1721); ordained priest 1729; Master of Sleaford Grammar School 1723–36; Curate of Spalding 1727; perpetual curate of Cowbit and Surfleet 1729–60; SGS 1723, 'beneficient member', antiquary and numismatist, contributed several dissertations to the SGS, including one on the benefits of learned societies; PGS member 1731.

Reynolds, Rt Revd Richard (1674–1744): *ODNB*. Dean of Peterborough 1718; Bishop of Lincoln 1723–44; SGS 1727.

Reynolds, Revd Richard (1724–73): Educated St John's College, Cambridge; Vicar of Leighton Buzzard 1759–73; SGS 1753. No relation of the Rt Revd Richard Reynolds (*q.v.*).

Richards, John (1699/1700–1767): Son of John Richards gent. of Spalding; admitted St John's College, Cambridge 1716/7; SGS 1720, a significant local Spalding member of the Society, probably a merchant. His son John Richards junior also became a member in 1752.

Romley, Revd John (*c.*1711–54): Born Burton (Lincs); his father William Romley had been curate of Epworth; educated Magdalen College, Oxford, 1735, and Lincoln College, Oxford; charity school master at Wroot near Epworth and curate of Epworth to 1751; SGS 1746, corresponded with the SGS about flax-dressing machinery (see *Correspondence*, 168).

Rowning, Revd John (1701–71): *ODNB*. Fellow of Magdalene College, Cambridge; Rector of Anderby (Lincs) 1735–71; author of *A Compendious System of Natural Philosophy* (1735), Master of Spalding Grammar School and Librarian of the SGS 1755–71.

Rutherforth, Revd Dr Thomas (1712–71): *ODNB*. Born Papworth St Agnes (Cambs), educated Huntingdon and St John's College, Cambridge, BA 1730, MA 1733, BD 1740, DD 1745; fellow 1733–52; ordained priest 1737; SGS 1742, FRS 1743; Chaplain to Frederick, Prince of Wales and to his widow after his death; Rector of Barley (Herts) and Brinkley (Cambs) 1751; Archdeacon of Essex 1752; Regius Professor of Divinity at Cambridge 1756–71; Rector of Somersham (Hunts) 1756; Rector of Shenfield (Essex) 1767; keenly interested in natural science, which he taught at Cambridge, and in moral philosophy; published *Ordo Institutionum Physicarum* (1743), converted his course of lectures into a popular textbook, *A system of natural philosophy, being a course of lectures in mechanics, optics, hydrostatics and astronomy* (1748) and published *Institutes of Natural Law* (1745 and 1746).

Sands, William (d.1751): SGS 1745, architect living and working in Spalding. See Colvin, *A Biographical Dictionary of British Architects 1600–1840* (1995).

Scott, Francis, second Duke of Buccleuch (1694–1751): Son of James Scott, Earl of Dalkeith and grandson of James, Duke of Monmouth and Frances Scott, Duchess of Buccleuch in her own right, who owned lands in Spalding for which the Johnsons were stewards; while he was Earl of Dalkeith he was educated at Eton College, at the same time as Maurice Johnson; SGS 1722, Patron 1732, 'beneficient member'; presented the SGS with valuable books and maps; a significant Freemason, Grand Master 1723–4; FRS 1724; Knight of the Thistle

1725; succeeded as Duke of Buccleuch 1732; Lord Paramount of the Manor of Spalding.

Sharp, Revd Dr Thomas (1693–1758): *ODNB*. Son of Rt Revd John Sharp, Archbishop of York, whose biography he wrote; educated Trinity College, Cambridge, graduated 1716, became a Fellow and later DD; Chaplain to Archbishop Dawes and Prebendary of Southwell 1716; Prebendary of York 1719; Rector of Rothbury (Northumberland) 1720; Archdeacon of Northumberland 1722; Prebendary of Durham 1732; antiquarian and book-collector; SGS 1751; published numerous sermons and pamphlets which were collected and published posthumously in six volumes in 1763.

Sloane, Sir Hans (1660–1753): *ODNB*. Successful physician, FRS 1685, Secretary of the RS 1695, President 1727–41; member of the SGS 1733. He is best known for his well-catalogued and very varied collections which formed the basis of the British Museum. He bought a dead elephant for Stukeley and his fellow-physicians to dissect in October 1720.

Smyth, Revd Robert (*c*.1700–61): Educated Westminster School and St John's College, Cambridge (entered 1717); ordained deacon 1722; chaplain to Catherine, widow of Sir John Leveson Gower; Rector of Woodston near Peterborough 1728–61; SGS 1726; early member of the PGS 1730 and its Secretary at one stage; historian who worked on listing all the Sheriffs of England; his MS account, with introduction by Maurice Johnson, is now lost; made voluminous notes on heraldry and monuments; assisted with Carter's history of the town and university of Cambridge (1753), see p.210 for an account of his work.

Southgate, Revd Richard (1729–95): *ODNB*. Educated St John's College, Cambridge; curate of Haddon (Hunts) 1742, Rector of Woolley (Hunts) 1754–61; curate of St Giles in the Fields, London, 1765–95; Rector of Little Steeping 1782–95; numismatist and Assistant Librarian at the British Museum with the care of coin collections; SGS 1753; FSA 1793.

Sparke, Revd Joseph (1682–1740); *ODNB*. Educated Peterborough and St John's College, Cambridge (entered 1699 aged sixteen), BA 1704; ordained deacon 1705, priest 1710; curate at Eye, Peterborough, 1710; Librarian, Chapter Clerk and Master of Works, Peterborough Cathedral 1714; not a member of the PGS although his *ODNB* entry claims this; FSA 1720; SGS 1722; published *Historiæ Anglicanæ Scriptores Varii* (1723), a transcription of mediæval chronicles of Peterborough; owned premises in Spalding which he rented to the SGS as a meeting-place from *c*.1727–44.

Stennett, William (fl.1740–50): A merchant, painter and surveyor from Boston where he built the bridge over the Witham; SGS 1746.

Stevens, George (junior) (fl.1720–30): Attorney in Spalding; SGS 1721.

Stevens, George (senior) (fl.1700–30): Attorney in Spalding; SGS 1723.

Tathwell, Dr Cornwall (*c*.1723–73): Of Louth, educated St John's College, Oxford (entered 1741 aged seventeen), BA 1745, MA 1749, MB 1751, MD 1755; Fellow of St John's; physician in Stamford; SGS 1751.

Verney, James (fl.1740s–50s): Painter, SGS 1753. The SGS thought highly of him but it is difficult to find any further information about him or his paintings.

Vertue, George (1684–1756); *ODNB*. Outstanding engraver, trained with Michael Vandergucht and Sir Godfrey Kneller. Made notes on travels with Lord Harley (Earl of Oxford) and Lord Coleraine (both SGS). Member of the SGS in 1729 and engraved the Society book plate in 1746. Vertue's notebooks survive and were used first by Horace Walpole and now by all art historians to understand the art of the 18th century and earlier.

Wallin, Richard (d.1761): Merchant, son of John Wallin of Spanish Town, Jamaica. Educated Bury St Edmunds Grammar School (entered 1740), SGS 1751, married in 1751 Johnson's youngest daughter Anne Alethea and returned with her to Jamaica where she died in 1758 leaving a daughter Anne Alethea Wallin (born 1758); married in 1760 Catherine Shippen of Philadelphia, died in Philadelphia 1761. Anne Alethea Wallin, Richard's heiress and a descendant of Maurice Johnson, was sent to England and married the Revd Charles Stewart of Long Melford in 1774.

Walpole, Edward (1702/3–40): Of Dunston (Lincs); a Roman Catholic landowner and poet; translated in 1736 *De Partu Virginis* by the Italian writer Jacopo Sannazaro into English verse and dedicated it to the SGS; also wrote *The Sixth Satire of the First Book of Horace, Imitated* (1738), which he dedicated to Sir Richard Ellys; SGS member 1733.

Ward, John (1678/9–1758): *ODNB*. Born London; a Dissenter; clerk in the Navy Office, schoolmaster 1710 in London; Professor of Rhetoric at Gresham College, London 1720; FRS 1723, RS Vice-President 1752; FSA 1736, AS Director 1747, AS Vice-President 1753; Trustee of the British Museum 1753, LLD Edinburgh 1751; antiquarian, numismatist and author, published *Lives of the Professors of Gresham College* (1740). SGS 1746.

Waring, Revd John (1675–1716): Educated St John's College, Cambridge. Chaplain of Wykeham Chapel near Spalding and Master of Spalding Grammar School 1695–1716, taught Maurice and John Johnson there; Maurice Johnson's Latin MS 'Iter Bathonense' describing an antiquarian journey to Bath is dedicated to him. SGS 1714. On his death the SGS bought his books for their library.

Weeks, James (fl.1740s–50s): Educated St Paul's School, London; 'limner and painter', artist and musician playing the harpsichord and violin; taught drawing and painting to some of Johnson's children; SGS 1748, 'beneficient member', made a drawing of Lady Jane Grey (MB5, fol.17A), which still exists at SGS, and a crayon sketch of Walter Johnson (MB5, fol.19A) now lost; worked at Welbeck Abbey for Lady Oxford.

Whiting, Revd Samuel (d.1757): Born Boston; educated Clare College, Cambridge, BA 1727, MA 1730; ordained deacon 1731–2, priest 1733; Usher at Spalding Grammar School 1729, then Master 1741–57; incumbent of Wykeham Chapel near Spalding 1743, Vicar of Weston (Lincs) 1748–57; SGS 1729.

Willis, Browne (1682–1760): *ODNB*. Born Blandford (Dorset); educated Westminster School and Christ Church, Oxford (entered 1700); Inner Temple; MA 1720, DCL 1749; Tory MP for Buckingham 1705–1708; founder-member of the SA in 1717; PGS member 1746; SGS 1747; lived at Whaddon Hall (Bucks); ecclesiastical antiquary and numismatist; published *Notitia Parliamentaria* (3 vols, 1715 onwards), *A Survey of Cathedrals* (1727 and 1730) and *The History ... of Buckingham* (1755).

Wingfield, Revd John (1733–73): Of the family which owned Tickencote Hall near Stamford, being Lords of the Manor from the seventeenth century; graduate of Hertford College, Oxford; SGS 1753.

APPENDIX 4
CONTEMPORARY TRIBUTES TO JOHNSON AND STUKELEY

These two accounts are included to supplement the material in the Introduction with biographical and professional details and to give views of these two remarkable men as seen by their contemporaries. As Johnson died first, in 1755, we have tributes to him by Stukeley, though of course we do not have his tribute to Stukeley, which would undoubtedly have expressed the admiration for his friend that is frequently shown in his letters. For Stukeley, it was decided to use the rather longer account published by John Nichols within a few years of his death.

Tributes to Maurice Johnson

(i) William Stukeley's MS account of Johnson, from his book of portraits in the Bodleian Library (MS Eng. misc. e.136), written after Johnson's death in 1755. See Illustration 3 for this text, written opposite a sketch of Johnson by Gerard Vandergucht.

my countryman & old acquaintance. unwearyed in his endevors to establish the Literary Society at Spalding, which he erected in[1] & supported with credit, to the time of his death. so great a lover of learned liesure, & Antiquitys, that he chose it, before the lucrative pursuits of pleading at the Bar; in which he was well versd: being a good Orator, & skilful in the business of Law. a great lover of a garden, which he had in fine perfection: an admirable collection of flowers, & plants: & of all kind of Antiquitys, fossils, medals &c.

[1] Stukeley leaves a gap for the insertion of the date of the founding of the SGS.

(ii) William Stukeley's MS account of Johnson, from his diary for 1754–5 in the Bodleian Library (MS Eng. misc. e.135, fols 48r–50r).

On Saturday 8 feb 1755 dy'd Maurice Johnson Esqr of Spalding Lincolnshire, Councellor at Law; a fluent Orator, & of eminence in that profession. but to an extravagant acquisition of riches, which he ever had in his power, he prefer'd the serene sweets of a country life, learned leisure, study & contemplation. he is one of the last of the Founders of the Antiquarian Society, London, begun in the year 1717, the only survivors being Brown Willis esq^r & Dr Stukeley.

what is singular in Mr Johnson's praise is that he was the Founder of the Literary Society in Spalding, which memorable Transaction happen'd on 3 nov^r 1712. This Society, thro' his unwearyed endeavors, interest, & applications in every kind; by his infinite labours in writing, collecting methodizing, indexes, & the like, has now subsisted in great reputation, for these 40 years, & excited such a spirit of learning & curiosity, in that level part of Lincolnshire, called

South Holland, as probably will never be extinguished. by this means, they have got an excellent Library, & all conveniences for their weekly Meeting, have establishd a most extensive correspondence, even to both Indies, are very exact in answering all communications, have made vast collections of MSS, letters, written historys, coins, medals, antiquitys of every denomination, fossils, all kind of natural & artificial Curiositys, drawings, surveys, prints & the like. they keep exact minutes of every thing that appears before them, have members in every branch of knoledg, try useful experiments & improvements, tending to the common benefit or entertainment of Mankind.[1]

Mr Johnson was a great lover of gardening & planting, had an admirable collection of flowers, flouring shrubs, fruit trees, exotics, [and] an excellent cabinet of medals, in which he had great knoledge & judgment.

Many years agoe, particularly, he made large collections of memoirs of the history of Carausius, which he sent to me last summer, & is still in my custody, as a generous assistance in my work on that head, together with all his coins of that emperor & the coins especially, which he always took to be Carausius's son, 1 of which I here give a sketch. [*Sketch of Roman coin*] The face is like that of the young Tetricus but singular in this, that the legend begins with CÆSAR, the name SILVANUS or whatever else, obliterated, which is the more to be regretted. Mr Beaupré Bell, a young gentleman of most excellent learning & knoledg in medals now dead, to the great loss of this science, was confident that the coin belongs to Carausius's son.

in general, the Antiquitys of the great mitred priory of Spalding, & of this part of Lincolnshire, are forever oblig'd to Mr Johnson's care & diligence, being rescued & preserv'd from oblivion, thereby.

thus much I thought proper to commemorate concerning the just *elogium* of my friend and countryman.

[1] A printed version, from the beginning to this point, and with a few minor differences from this text, was published in the *Whitehall Evening Post*, Saturday 22 February 1755.

(iii) From *Literary Anecdotes of the Eighteenth Century*, edited by John Nichols, vol.6 (1782), 22–6.

Mr Johnson acquired general esteem from the frankness and benevolence of his character, which displayed itself not less in social life than in the communication of his literary researches. Strangers who applied to him for information, though without any introduction, except what arose from a genuine thirst for knowledge congenial with his own, failed not to experience the hospitality of his board. Whilst their spirit of curiosity was feasted by the liberal conversation of the man of letters, their social powers were at the same time gratified by the hospitable frankness of the benevolent Englishman. A trifling anecdote, of the truth of which I have been well assured, may serve to illustrate the justice of this remark. Pl.XX of Simon's seals, &c, engraved by Vertue, consists of medals of Generals Lambert and Rossiter, James Ash and Charles Seton, second Earl of Dunfermline. These were in the possession of Mr Johnson. A gentleman from London, unknown to the possessor, took a journey to Spalding on purpose to be gratified with the inspection of one of these medals; which he ever after mentioned with pleasure, and considered himself most amply repaid for the trouble of his journey by his introduction to so polite and universal a scholar, and by the very kind reception he met with during his residence at Spalding. It appears also, from the Minutes of the Society, that Mr Johnson gave the original medal of General Lambert, by old Symons, having behind the head J. LAMBERT, and engraved by Vertue, to a gentleman of his name and family, 1712.

The following elogium on him by Dr Stukeley is transcribed from the original, in the Minutes of the Society of Antiquaries: [here follows a shortened account of passage (ii) above]

Maurice Johnson, esq. was in the latter part of his life attacked with a vertiginous disorder in his head, which frequently interrupted his studies, and at last put a period to his life, on the 6th day of February, 1755 … [1]

Mr Johnson married early in life the daughter of Joshua Ambler, esq. of Spalding. She was the grand-daughter of Sir Anthony Oldfield, and lineally descended from Sir Thomas Gresham, the founder of Gresham College and of the Royal Exchange, London. By this lady he had 26 children, of whom 16 sat down together to his table. Of his sons, the eldest, Maurice, was a lieutenant in the Duke of Cumberland's regiment of foot guards, and served under his Royal Highness, in 1746–7, in Flanders; from whence he, being a good draughtsman,[2] sent to his father, and to the Society, whereof he was a member, several drawings of coins, &c, some drawings of Roman antiquities at Nimeguen, three statues, in length about twenty inches, of Jupiter sitting between Æsculapius and Minerva, five sepulchral inscriptions for soldiers of *Leg. X. Germ.*, two votive altars to Jupiter, one to Minerva by a *IIvir. Colon. Morinorum; sacerdos Romæ & Aug.*, one in honour of Trajan; also an antient painting of Mars, in Batoburg castle, five miles from Grave, taken out of his temple there. He was afterwards a colonel in the same regiment of foot-guards, and now resides at Spalding, and has two sons and three daughters.

Walter, the second son of the founder of this Society, was called to the degree of barrister-at-law, and admitted F.A.S. 1749, and treasurer of the Society at Spalding, where he practised in full business; and died 1779; leaving only one son Fairfax, who in 1782 was living at Spalding, to whom we are obliged for this account of his family. The third, Martin, was in the Navy, and died young. The fourth, John, was educated at St John's College, Cambridge, ordained deacon and curate of Ramsey, in the county of Huntingdon, 1745 (of which church he then sent an account to the Society) afterwards vicar of Moulton, which is in the gift of the family, minister of Spalding, and F.A.S. 1748, and president of this Society 1757, about which time he died. His fifth and youngest son, Henry-Eustace, was a factor in the service of the East-India Company, and F.A.S. 1750,[3] and died at the island of St. Helena.

He had also six daughters, who lived to maturity, five of whom were married. Jane, the eldest, married Dr Green, who practised physic with great eminence at Spalding. The second[4] married Mr Butter, a merchant, who retired to Spalding, and died there. Catharine married Mr Lodge, vicar of Moulton. Henrietta died single. Mary married Mr Maclellan, rector of Stratton, in the county of Durham, and school-master of Spalding; and Anne-Alethea[5] married Mr Wallen, of Jamaica, and left a daughter, married to Mr Stuart, of Long Melford, in the county of Suffolk.

[1] There follows an account of Johnson's ancestry and connections; in fact he died on 8 February 1755.

2   The original text has the footnote 'Mr Johnson taught all his children to draw at the same time that he taught them to write. Reliquiæ Galeanæ, p.407'.
3   Henry Eustace Johnson became a member of the SGS in 1753 but was not a member of the Antiquarian Society.
4   This was Elizabeth Johnson, known in the family as 'Madcap Bet'.
5   The original text has a footnote 'Many neat specimens of this lady's drawings appear in the Minutes [of the Spalding Gentlemen's Society]'.

Account of William Stukeley

From William Bowyer, *Literary Anecdotes of the Eighteenth Century*, edited by John Nichols, vol.5 (1812), 499–510 and note to 705. We have retained the spelling of the original.

Dr William Stukeley, descended from an ancient family in Lincolnshire, was born in Holbech in that county, November 7, 1687. After having had the first part of his education at the free-school of that place, under the care of Mr Edward Kelsal, he was admited into Bene't College in Cambridge, Nov. 7 1703,[1] under the tuition of Mr Thomas Fawcett,[2] and chosen a scholar there in April following. Whilst an under-graduate, he often indulged a strong propensity for to drawing and designing; but made physick his principal study, and with that view took frequent perambulations through the neighbouring country, with the famous Dr Hales,[3] Dr John Gray of Canterbury, and others, in search of plants; and made great additions to Mr Rays 'Catalogus Plantarum circa Cantabrigiam'; which, with a map of the county he was solicited to print; but his father's death and various domestic avocations, prevented it. He studied anatomy under Mr Rolfe the surgeon; attended the chemical lectures of Signor Vigani[4] and taking the degree of M.B. in 1709, made himself acquainted with the practical part of medicine under the great Dr Mead[5] at St Thomas's Hospital. He first began to practise in Boston in his native county, where he strongly recommended the chalybeate waters of Stanfield near Folkingham. In 1717 he removed to London, where, on the recommendation of his friend Dr Mead, he was soon after elected a fellow of the Royal Society,[6] and was one of the first who revived that of the Antiquaries, in 1717–8, to which last he was secretary during his residence in town.[7] He took the degree of M.D. at Cambridge, in 1719, and was admitted a fellow of the College of Physicians in the year following, about which time he published an account of 'Arthur's O'on' in Scotland, and of 'Graham's dyke', with plates, 4to. In the year 1722 he was appointed to read the Gulstonian Lecture, in which he gave a description and history of the Spleen: and printed it in folio, 1723, together with some anatomical observations on the dissection of an elephant and many plates coloured in imitation of nature. Conceiving there was some remains of the Eleusinian mysteries in Free-masonry, he gratified his curiosity, and was constituted master of a lodge,[8] 1723 to which he presented an account of a Roman amphitheatre at Dorchester, 4to.

After having been one of the censors of the College of Physicians, of the council of the Royal Society, and of the committee to examine into the condition of the astronomical instruments of the Royal Observatory at Greenwich, he left London in 1726, and retired to Grantham in Lincolnshire; where he soon came into great request. The Dukes of Ancaster and Rutland, the families of Tyrconnel, Cust, &c. &c. and most of the principal families in the country, were glad to take his advice. During his residence here, he declined an invitation from the Earl of Hertford to settle as a physician at Marlborough, and another to succeed Dr Hunton at Newark. In 1728 he married Frances daughter of Robert Williamson, of Allington, near Grantham, gent., a lady of good family and fortune. He was greatly afflicted with the gout, which used generally to confine him during the winter months, on account of which, for the recovery of his health, it was customary with him to take several journeys in the spring; in which he indulged his love of antiquities, by tracing out the footsteps of Cæsar's expedition in this island, his camps, stations, &c. The fruit of his more distant travels was his 'Itinerarium Curiosum; or, an Account of the Antiquities and Curiosities in Travels through Great Britain, Centuria I.' adorned with one hundred copper-plates, and published in folio, London, 1724. This was reprinted after his death, 1776, with two additional plates; as was also published the second volume (consisting of his description of The Brill, or Cæsar's camp at Pancras, Iter Boreale 1725, and his edition of Richard of Cirencester, with his own and Mr Bertram's notes) illustrated with 103 copper-plates, engraved in the Doctor's life-time.

Overpowered with the fatigue of his profession and repeated attacks of the gout, he turned his thoughts to the Church; and, being encouraged in that pursuit by Archbishop Wake, was ordained at Croydon, June 20, 1729; and in October following was presented by Lord Chancellor King to the living of All Saints, in Stamford. At the time of his entering on his parochial cure (1730), Doctor Rogers of that place had just invented his Oleum Arthriticum; which Dr Stukeley seeing other use with admirable success, he was induced to do the like, and with equal advantage: for it not only saved his joints, but, with the addition of a proper regimen, and leaving off the use of fermented liquors, he recovered his health and limbs to a surprising degree, and ever after enjoyed a firm and active state of body, beyond any example in the like circumstances, to a good old age. This occasioned him to publish an account of the success of the external application of these oils in innumerable instances, in a letter to Sir Hans Sloane, 1733; and the year after he published also 'A Treatise on the Cause and Cure of the Gout, from a new Rationale'; which, with an abstract thereof, has passed through several editions. He collected some remarkable particulars at Stamford in relation to his predecessor Bp. Cumberland; and in 1736 printed an explanation, with an engraving, of a curious silver plate of Roman workmanship in basso relievo, found under ground at Risley Park in Derbyshire; wherein he traces its journey thither, from the church at Bourges, to which it had been given by Exsuperius, called St. Swithin, bishop of Thoulouse, about the year 205. He published also the same year his 'Palæographia Sacra; No. I, or Discourses on the Monuments of Antiquity that relate to Sacred History' in 4to, which he dedicated to Sir Richard Ellys, bart. 'from whom he had received many favours'. In this work (which was to have been continued in succeeding numbers) he undertakes to shew, how Heathen Mythology is derived from Sacred History; and that the Bacchus of the Poets is no other than the Jehovah in the Scripture, the conductor of the Israelites through the wilderness. In his country retirement he disposed his collection of Greek and Roman coins according to the order of the Scripture History; and cut out a machine in wood (on the plan of an Orrery) which shews the motion of the heavenly bodies, the course of the tide, &c. In 1737 he lost his wife; and in 1738 married Elizabeth the only daughter of Dr Gale, dean of York, and sister to his intimate friends Roger and Samuel Gale, esquires; and from this time he often spent his winters in London. In 1740 he published an account of Stonehenge, dedicated to the Duke of Ancaster, who had made him one of his chaplains, and given him the living of Somerby, near Grantham the year before. In 1741 he preached a Thirtieth of January Sermon before the House of Commons; and in that year became one of the founders of the Egyptian society. In 1743 he published an account of Lady Roisia's sepulchral cell lately discovered at Royston, in a tract, intituled, 'Palæographia Britannica, No. I' to which an answer was published by Mr Parkin in 1744. The Doctor replied in 'Palæographia Britannica, No. II' 1746, giving an account therein of the origin of the universities of Cambridge and Stamford, both from Croyland Abbey; of the Roman city Granta, on the North side of the river, of the beginning of Cardike near Waterbeach, &c. To this Mr Parkin again replied in 1748; but it does not appear that the Doctor took any further notice of him. In 1747 the benevolent Duke of Montagu (with whom he had become acquainted at the Egyptian Society) prevailed on him to vacate his preferments in the country, by giving him the rectory of St George, Queen Square; from whence he frequently retired to Kentish Town, where the following inscription was placed over his door:

> 'Me dulcis saturet quies
> Obscuro positus loco
> Leni perfruar otio
> Chyndonax Druida
> O may this rural solitude receive,
> And contemplation all its pleasures give
> The Druid priest!'

He had the misfortune to lose his patron in 1749; on whose death he published some verses, with others on his entertainment at Boughton, and a 'Philosophic Hymn on Christmas-Day'. Two papers by the Doctor, upon the Earthquakes in 1750, read at the Royal Society, and a Sermon preached at his own parish church on that alarming occasion, were published in 8vo, 1750, under the title of 'The Philosophy of Earthquakes, Natural and Religious'; of which a second part was printed with a second edition of his sermon on 'the Healing of Diseases as a Character of the Messiah, preached before the College of Physicians Sept. 20, 1750.' In 1751 (in 'Palæographia Britannica, No. III') he gave an account of Oriuna the wife of Carausius; in Phil. Trans. vol. XLVIII art.33, an account of the eclipse predicted by Thales; and in the Gentleman's Magazine, 1754, p.407, is the substance of a paper read at the Royal Society in 1752, to prove that the coral-tree is a real sea-vegetable. On Wednesday the 27th of February, 1765, Dr Stukeley was seized with a stroke of the palsy, which was brought on by attending a full vestry, at which he was accompanied by Serjeant Eyre, on a contested election for a lecturer. The room being hot, on their return through Dr Stukeley's garden, they both caught their deaths; for the Serjeant never was abroad again, and the Doctor's illness came on that night. Soon after this accident his faculties failed him; but he continued quiet and composed until Sunday following, the 3d of March 1765, when he departed, in his seventy-eighth year, which he attained by remarkable temperance and regularity. By his own particular directions, his corpse was conveyed in a private manner to East-Ham in Essex, and was buried in the church-yard, just beyond the east end of the church, the turf being laid smoothly over it, without any monument. This spot he particularly fixed on, in a visit he paid some time before to the vicar of that parish, when walking with him, one day in the church-yard. Thus ended a valuable life, daily spent in throwing light on the dark remains of antiquity. His great learning and profound skill in those researches enabled him to publish many elaborate and curious works, and to leave many ready for the press. In his medical capacity, his 'Dissertation on the Spleen' was well received. His 'Itinerarium Curiosum', the first fruits of his juvenile excursions, presaged what might be expected from his riper age, when he had acquired more experience. The curious in these studies were not disappointed; for, with a sagacity peculiar to his great genius, with unwearied pains and industry, and some years spent in actual surveys, he investigated and published an account of those stupendous works of the remotest antiquity, Stonehenge and Abury, in 1743, and hath given the most probable and rational account of their origin and use, ascertaining also their dimensions with the greatest accuracy. So great was his proficiency in Druidical history, that his familiar friends used to call him 'The Arch-Druid of this age'. His works abound with particulars that shew his knowledge of this celebrated British priesthood, and in his Itinerary he announced a 'History of the ancient Celts, particularly the first inhabitants of Great Britain', for the most part finished, to have consisted of four volumes folio, with above 300 copper-plates, many of which were engraved. A great part of this work was incorporated into his *Stonehenge* and *Abury*.

In his *History of Carausius* in two vols. 4to, 1757, 1759, he has shewn much learning and ingenuity in settling the principal events of that emperor's government in Britain. To his interest and application we are indebted for recovering from obscurity Richard of Cirencester's Itinerary of Roman Britain.

His discourses or sermons, under the title of '*Palæographia Sacra*, 1763,' on 'the vegetable creation' &c. bespeak him a botanist, philosopher, and divine, replete with ancient learning, and excellent observations; but a little too much transported by a lively fancy and invention.

He closed the last scenes of his life with completing a long and laborious work on antient British coins, in particular of Cunobelin, and felicitated himself on having from them discovered many remarkable, curious, and new anecdotes, relating to the reign of that and other British kings. The 23 plates of this work were published after his decease; but the MS (left ready for publishing) remains in the hands of his daughter Mrs Fleming, relict of Richard Fleming, esq; an eminent solicitor and one of the six clerks in Chancery, who was the Doctor's executor. By his first wife Dr Stukeley had three daughters; of whom one died young; the other two still survive him; the one Mrs Fleming already mentioned; the other, wife to the Rev. Thomas Fairchild, rector of Pitsey in Essex. By his second wife Dr Stukeley had no child. To the great names already mentioned among his friends and patrons, may be added those of Mr Folkes, Dr Berkeley Bishop of Cloyne (with whom he corresponded on the subject of Tar-water), Dr Pocock Bishop of Meath, and many others of the first rank in literature, at home; and among the eminent foreigners with whom he corresponded were Dr Heigerthal, Mr Keysler, and the learned Father Montfaucon, who inserted some of his designs (sent him by archbishop Wake) in his '*Antiquity Explained.*' A good account of Dr Stukeley was, with his own permission, printed in 1755, by Mr Masters, in the second part of his '*History of Corpus Christi College*'; and very soon after his death a short but just character of his life was given in the Gentleman's Magazine for 1765, by his friend Peter Collinson. Of both these, the compiler of the present memoir has availed himself; and has been favoured with several additional particulars from Dr Ducarel and Mr Gough.

After Dr Stukeley's death, a large medallion of him was cast and repaired by Gabb; on one side his head adorned with oak leaves, inscribed 'REV. GVL. STUKELEY, M.D. S.R & A. S. Exergue æt. 54. Reverse, a view of Stonehenge, OB. MAR.4 1765 ÆT. 84; (but this is a mistake; for the Doctor was but 78.) There is a portrait of him by Kneller from which a mezzotinto was scraped by J. Smith in 1721, before he took orders, with his arms, viz. Argent, a Spread Eagle double-headed Sable. Mrs Fleming has another portrait of him in his robes, by Wills, and Mrs. Parsons (relict of Dr James Parsons) has a fine miniature, which is esteemed a good likeness.

[1] This is an error for 20 November. Bene't College was the popular name for Corpus Christi College, Cambridge.
[2] Thomas Fawcett (c.1680–1717).
[3] Dr Stephen Hales (1677–1761: see *ODNB*). Mr Ray was the botanist John Ray (1627–1705: see *ODNB*).
[4] Rolfe was Professor of Anatomy at Cambridge in 1707; John Francis Vigani (?1650–1712: see *ODNB*) was Professor of Chemistry, Queens' College, Cambridge.
[5] Dr Richard Mead (1673–1754); see Appendix 3.
[6] In 1718.
[7] He was Secretary of the Society of Antiquaries of London from 1717 to 1726.
[8] The lodge met at the Fountain Tavern, 1722.

INDEX OF PEOPLE AND PLACES

In this Index, Maurice Johnson is referred to as 'Maurice Johnson II' to distinguish him from other members of his family of the same name, such as his father and his eldest son. The abbreviation *n* following a page number indicates that a reference is to be found in the notes on that page.

Alford, Lincs: 51 *n.*2, 143, 235
Algar, Earl: 219, 220
Algarkirk, Lincs: 120–1, 220
Allen, Mr, organist of Boston: 165
Allen, Mr, Maurice Johnson II's schoolfellow: 178, 179
Ambler family:
    Elizabeth: see Johnson, Elizabeth
    Joshua: 32–4, 76, 200, 231
    Mary: 112, 113, 126
    William: xviii, xxi, 34 *n.*12
Ancaster, Lincs.: xvii, xxiv, xlii, 59, 60, 62, 63, 205, 217
Ancaster, Duke of: *see* Bertie, Peregrine
Angers, France: 187
Arthur's O'on, Fife: xlvii, xlix, lv, lvi, 44, 45, 248
Aswarby, Lincs: 57, 188
Atkinson, David; 33, 231
    William: 5, 7, 31, 96, 201, 231
Avebury, Wilts: 86, 125
Ayscough, Dr : 159
Azlacke, William: 1, 3 *n.*1

Bacon, Francis: 22, 23 *n.*17
Balam, William: 33
Banks, Joseph: 57
Barbados: 196
Bardney, Lincs.: 138
Baston, Lincs: 219
Bayley, Harry: 96, 231
Bede, the Venerable: 64
Bedford, Dukes of: *see* Russell family
Bedford Level: xxv, 125
Bell, Beaupré: xxvii, xxxi, xlv, 72, 92, 131, 134 *n.*3, 169, 194, 231, 246
Bellamy, Sir Edward: 125, 238, 239,
Bellamy, Elizabeth: *see* Johnson, Elizabeth (2)
Bellinger, Dr Francis: 56, 96, 231
Bentley, Revd Dr Richard: 39, 201, 231
Berridge, Revd Basil: 172, 183, 185
Bertie, Charles: 95
Bertie, Peregrine, lawyer: 28, 57, 231

Bertie, Peregrine, third Duke of Ancaster: 56, 89, 250
Birch, Revd Dr Thomas: 181, 213
Bishops of Lincoln: *see* Lincoln, Bishops of
Blankney, Lincs: 3, 5
Bobart, Jacob junior: lxiii, 11, 12, 14, 133
Bogdani, William: xxv, xxvi, xxxii, 72, 111, 117, 119, 231
Bogdani, William Maurice: 183, 232
Bold, Peter: 96, 232
Boleyn, Anne: 73
Borlase, Revd. William: 146, 148
Boston, Lincs: xi, xxiv, xxv, xxxiii, xxxvi, xlii, lxiv, 4 *n.*19, 16, 30, 32, 54, 85, 88, 92, 97, 98, 141, 146, 148, 153, 155, 162, 166, 176, 183, 205, 210, 219, 221, 234, 240, 243, 244, 248, Illustration 7
Boston, Massachusetts: 139, 141, 146
Boudicca (Boadicea): 18, 19 *n.*4, 21, 22
Boughton House, Northants: 125, 156, 250
Bourne, Lincs: 161, 219
Bowyer, William: 128, 132, 207, 232, 248
Bradley, Dr James: 91
Bransby, Revd Arthur: 188, 232
Bridge End, Lincs.: 49, 222
Britons, ancient: xli, 2, 3, 6, 8, 44, 205
Brittain, Revd John: 129
Brocklesby, Lincs: 173
Brooke, Revd Zachariah: 143, 232
Brutus son of Æneas: 6
Buccleuch, Duke of: *see* Scott, Francis
Buckworth, Revd Everard: 190 *n.*19, 193, 232
Buckworth, Theophilus: 188, 232
Burwell, William: 175, 181,
Butter, Robert (son-in-law of Maurice Johnson II): xxxi, 80 *n.*4, 117, 232, 247

Cæsar, Julius: lxii, 1, 6, 18, 21, 69, 144, 249
Cambridge, University of: xix, xxxii, xxxvi, l, lxiii, 20, 31, 54, 103 193, 196, 201, 226, 250
    colleges of:
        Corpus Christi College (Bene't College): xxxii, xxxviii, xlvi, 248

INDEX OF PEOPLE AND PLACES

King's College: 183
St John's College: 126, 143, 247
Trinity College: 70 *n*.3, 92, 231
origins of: 103, 224, 226
theatre of: 201
Camden, William: 127
Carausius, Emperor: xix, xxvii, xxxix, xli, xlvii, 49, 50, 51, 141, 148, 159, 161, 178, 185, 188, 191, 194, 196, 205, 214
Cartagena, Spain: 48
Catesby, Mark: 85
Caxton, William: 13, 14, 236
Cecil, Hon.and Revd Charles: 61
Cecil, David: 72, 95
Cecil, John, Earl of Exeter: 95
Chetwynd, Mary (Lady Blundell): 37
Chichester, Sussex: 178, 207
Chichley, John: 29, 36
Cirencester, Richard of: *see* 'Richard of Westminster'
Claudius, Emperor: 68, 69, 71, 72
Claudius Gothicus, Emperor: 50
Clerk, Sir John: xxxii, xxxiii, 78, 232, 235
Clipsham, Lincs: 89
Coke, Sir Edward: 14
Coleby, Dr Dixon: 54, 93, 95, 114, 232
Coleraine, Lord: *see* Hare, Henry
Collins, Richard: 233
Cook, Benjamin (SGS registrar): 147, 175, 197, 233
Cornwall: 146, 157 *n*.9
Cotterstock, Northants: 116
Cotton, Revd John: 141, 146, 147
Cowbit, Lincs: xxxii, 33, 48, 88, 89, 104, 175, 181, 183, 235, 240, 242
Cox, Michael (SGS Operator): 79, 96, 180, 193, 196, 233
Cressy Hall, Lincs: 13, 126
Crowland, Lincs: xvii, xviii, xxi, 56, 108, 110, 148, 210, 233, 235, 237
Bridge: 223
Croyland Abbey: xx, 51, 54, 88, 89, 103, 105, 107–9, 110, 111, 122, 134, 135, 161, 165, 209, 217, 218, 219, 223–6, 250
Crowle, Yorks: 116
Curl, Edmund: 28

Dalkeith, Earl of: *see* Scott, Francis
Danes (Vikings): 104 *n*.5, 134–5, 139, 217–22; 224
De la Pryme, Abraham: 187
Deeping Fen Adventurers: 235
Deeping, Lincs: xxv, xxvi, 68, 89, 133, 148, 183, 197, 219, 220
Degg, Dr Simon: 51, 57, 233
Denton, Lincs: 62, 205
Dinham, Dr John: 54, 233
Dinham, Dr Samuel: 182, 193, 233

Dodd, Revd William: 161, 193, 233
Doncaster, Yorks: 92–3, 115 *n*.15
Donington, Lincs: 88
Drake, Francis (surgeon and antiquary): 82, 135–6, 233
Drake, Nathan: 176, 233
Drayton, Lincs.: 47
Dunstable, Beds: xxvii, 26–7

Edenham, Lincs: 120
Edmundthorpe, Rutland: 102
Edward III: 213
Edward VI: 2
Edwards, George: 165, 233
Egede, Revd Hans: 83, 241
Elloe Stone, Lincs: 117
Elloe, Wapentake of, Lincs: 47, 133, 238
Ellys, Sir Richard: 32, 51, 63, 138, 161, 233, 249
Erasmus, Desiderius: 44
Ermine Street, Lincs ('Hermenstreet'): 218
Ethelbald, King: 223, 225
Ethelred, King: 138–9

Falkner, Richard (Maurice Johnson II's stepbrother): xxvi, xxxii
Falkner, Thomas: 3, 17
Fleet, Lincs: xxxvi, 33, 89, 183
Flower, Robert: 79
Folkes, Martin (President of the Royal Society): 114, 118, 136, 141, 156, 178, 185, 208, 214, 234, 251
Fountaine, Sir Andrew: 90
Fox, Bishop Richard: 63
Frederick, Sir Charles: 168, 234
Frederick, Prince of Wales: 167, 170, 242

Gale, Elizabeth: see Stukeley, Elizabeth
Gale, Roger: xix, xliii, xlix, lxiii, 28, 30, 36, 37, 39, 40, 47, 53, 57, 61, 80, 82, 86, 108, 128, 141, 194, 205, 232, 234, 249
Gale, Samuel: xix, xxxvii, 178, 224–5, 234, 249
Gale, Revd Dr Thomas, Dean of York: 64, 128, 249
Gale, Revd William: 87, 92
Gay, John: xxii, xxx, 25, 57, 234
Gedney, Lincs: 89, 219
Genebrier, Dr Claude: 49, 159, 185, 188,
Gideon, Samson: 136, 150, 155, 159, 210, 234
Gifford, Revd Andrew: 146, 176
Gildas: 64
Glastonbury, Somerset: 125
Glen, River: 63, 89, 125
Goche, Revd Barnaby: 235
Gopsall, Leics: 175, 235
Gordon, Alexander: xlix, 153, 157, 235
Gosberton, Lincs: 88, 162, 164, 237
Gower, Earl (John Leveson-Gower): 165

Grantham, Lincs.: xi, xvii, xviii, xix, xxxii, xxxiii, xxxvi–xxxviii, xlii, xlix, l, lv, 57, 59, 62, 63–5, 162, 199, 203–6, 218, 220, 222, 239, 248
 Bishops of: 65
 Earthquake at: 159
 St Wulfram's Church: 65
 view from hills around: 205
Great Coates, Lincs: 173, 232
Great Yarmouth, Norfolk: xxix, 79, 236
Greeks, ancient: 8, 83, 191
Green, Edward, surgeon: 30, 53
Green, Jane (née Johnson) wife of Dr John Green: 211, 247
Green, Dr John: xiii, xxxi, 57, 78, 79, 92, 96, 103, 117, 119, 132, 133, 144, 153, 165, 173, 179, 181, 188, 194, 196, 199, 235, 247
Greenland: 83, 196, 241
Grimsby, Lincs: 173
Grimsthorpe, Lincs: 89, 119
Grisoni, Giuseppe: 118, 235
Grundy, John junior: xxvi, 85, 125, 175, 196, 197, 235–6
 senior: xxv, xxvi, 85, 125, 235

Hardy, Revd John: 45, 47, 61, 161, 205, 236
Hare, Henry, Lord Coleraine: 57, 134
Harley, Edward, second Earl of Oxford: 45 *n*.3, 56, 61, 111, 185
 Robert, first Earl of Oxford: 25, 36,
Harrison, John (gardener): 193, 236
Hauksbee, Francis: 135
Hawkes, Thomas: 161, 181, 193, 196, 236
Hearne, Thomas: lxi, 28, 37, 59 *n*.9
Heckington, Lincs.: 138
Heighington, Musgrave: xxix, 79, 164 *n*.17, 236
Helpringham, Lincs: 89, 222
Hengist: 108
Henry I: 209, 225, 226
Henry II: 2, 103
Henry IV: 2, 64
Henry VII: 2, 118
Henry VIII: 2, 29,
Hepburn, John: 57, 72, 82, 95, 236
Herbert, Thomas, eighth Earl of Pembroke: xviii, xliii, 36, 44, 141, 167
Herculaneum: 85, 165, 184
Herod Agrippa: 143
Heron, Henry: 25, 28, 33, 34, 49, 57, 169
Heron, Mrs, wife of Henry Heron: 13, 25, 31, 36, 37
Hertford, Lady: *see* Seymour, Lady Frances
 Lord: *see* Seymour, Edward
Hildesley, Revd Mark; 183, 236
Hill, James, antiquary: 37, 202, 205
Hill, 'Sir' John: xlviii, 100, 106, 111, 122, 150, 153, 166, 167, 169, 171, 172, 174–5, 178, 181, 236

Hill, Dr Theophilus: 16, 106, 111, 150, 236
Hinson, Capt. Joseph: 54, 187, 208, 236
Hitchin, Herts: 174, 175, 183, 210
Holbeach, Lincs: xvii, xviii, xxxii, 48, 82, 89, 121, 151, 164, 175, 201, 214, 232, 238, 248
Holmes, George: 57, 136. 203 *n*.19, 236
Horace: 153, 174
Hovingham, Yorks, Roman pavement at: 114
Howgrave, Francis: 101, 106
Humber, River: 218
Hunter, Major-General Robert: 57, 237
Hunter, Thomas Orby: 125, 187, 197
Hussey, Sir Edward: 6
Hussey Tower, Lincs: 176
Hutchinson, Revd Samuel: 3
Hutchinson, Dr Samuel: 114

Ingram, Dale: 176, 196, 237
Ingram, John: 196
Ingulphus: 161, 217, 218, 220, 221, 225
Ives, Calamy: 180, 196, 237

Jackson, William: xxx, 197, 237
Jennens, Charles: 175
Jerusalem: 70 *n*.6, 169
Joffrid, Abbot of Croyland: 226
Johnson, Arabella (née Clinton) of New England: 139
Johnson family of Spalding: 32, 72–3, 88, 95, 120
 Johnson, Anne Alethea (daughter of Maurice Johnson II): 169, 183, 243, 247
 Johnson, Elizabeth (née Ambler) wife of Maurice Johnson II: xix, xxi, 3 *n*.2, 23, 53, 72, 78, 148, 212, 247
 Johnson, Elizabeth (née Bellamy) wife of Maurice Johnson III: 133, 148, 238
 Johnson, Elizabeth (daughter of Maurice Johnson II): xxxii, 94–5, 100, 247
 Johnson, George (son of Revd Walter Johnson): xxxii, 126, 165, 175, 181, 192, 193, 237
 Johnson, Henry (cousin of Maurice Johnson II): xxv, xxxi, 139, 143, 237
 Johnson, Henry Eustace: 78, 80 *n*.12. 162, 164, 183, 192, 193, 196, 237, 247
 Johnson, John (brother of Maurice Johnson II): xxi, 27, 47, 81 *n*.18, 96, 237–8
 Johnson, John (son of Maurice Johnson II) xiii, xxxi, 97, 104, 144, 199, 211–13, 238, 247
 Johnson, Martin (uncle of Maurice Johnson II): 147
 Johnson, Mary (daughter of Maurice Johnson II): 112
 Johnson, Maurice I (father of Maurice Johnson II): xvii–xviii, xx, 9–10, 78, 96, 117, 119, 238

Johnson, Maurice II (antiquary, SGS founder): xi, xii, xx–xxxii, 238, 245–7
  antiquarian interests: xiv, xxvi–xxvii, xlii, 32, 43–5, 53, 111; *see also* 'Spalding Gentlemen's Society: Activities of' in Index of Topics
  attempts to found learned societies: xxiv, xxvi, 97–8, 245
  books belonging to: xxx, 37, 70 *n*.3, 82, 132, 144, 148
  death of: 211–12
  dissertations by: 73, 79, 80
  education of: xxi
  family portraits of: 72, 132, 148
  founder of the SGS: xxii–xxv, 245
  friendship with Stukeley; xvi–xviii, 7, 13, 25, 52, 75, 95, 103,
  gardens of: xiii, xviii, xxvii, xxxi, 39, 53, 56, 78, 87–8, 124, 132, 148, 154, 170, 171, 172, 194, 245–6
  historical interests: 1–3, 18
  history of Spalding by: 186–7
  ill health of: xvii, lxii, 137–8, 144, 147, 155, 169–70, 179, 194, 196, 200, 247
  interest in drawing: 72
  journey to Bath: xix, 23 *n*.2, 244
  legal practice of: xix, xxi, xxv, 26, 33–4, 43, 47, 73, 245
  love of home and family: xix, xxxi–xxxii, 53, 78
  musical interests: 41, 123
  numismatic collection: xxvii, 18–9, 21–2, 40, 41
  President of the SGS: 167
  theories on the origin of Spalding: 187, 190–2
  view from his tower: xiv, 88–9
  views on marriage; 52–3, 200
  writings by: xix, 188, 194, 196, 246
  written style: lxi–lxiii
Johnson, Capt. then Col. Maurice III (son of Maurice Johnson II): xxxi, 1, 78, 104, 112, 124, 125, 133, 136, 144, 161, 171, 175, 193, 194, 200, 212, 238, 247
Johnson, Walter (grandfather of Maurice Johnson II): xx, 72, 95, 188, 238
Johnson, Walter (son of Maurice Johnson II): 78, 96, 104, 152, 154, 175, 176, 177 *n*.23, 183, 212, 244, 238, 247
Johnson, Revd Walter (cousin of Maurice Johnson II): 72, 92, 147, 238
Johnson, Isaac of New England: 139
Johnson, Lieut-Gen.John: 139
Johnson, Col. Richard: 143
Johnson, Archdeacon Robert: 95
Johnson, William, Stukeley's brother-in-law: 139, 143, 146
Jurin, Dr James: 50, 57, 150, 187, 194, 213, 238–9

Kelsall, Revd Edward: 3, 7, 13, 248
Kennedy, Revd John: 185
Kennedy, Dr Patrick: 142 *n*.12, 159, 194
Kennet, River: 59
Kennett, Bishop White: 128
Kenulf, Abbot of Croyland: 223
Kesteven, Lincs: 219–22
Kirkhall, Elisha; 92, 131
Kirton, Lincs: xxi, xxv, 88, 129, 141, 232, 238, 241
Kemp, John: 18
Kneller, Sir Godfrey: 35, 36–7, 252

Lake, Richard: xvi, 55 *n*.19, 98, 239
Landen, John: xxvi, 193, 239
Lanfranc, Archbishop: 225
Langtoft, Lincs: 219
Lawrence, Edward: xxv, 239
Leland, John: 127
Le Neve, Peter: 32, 96, 201, 203 *n*.17
Lennox, Charles, second Duke of Richmond: xliii, 111, 146, 150, 156, 159, 167
Leofric: 219–20
Leverton, Lincs: 219–20
Lhuyd (Llwyd), Edward: 14, 191, 203 *n*.21
Lincoln: 5, 6, 7, 26, 48, 57, 60, 63, 66 *n*.6; 78, 85, 93, 97–8, 102, 153, 154, 155, 190, 205, 210, 218–19
  attempt to found society at: xvi, xxiv, l, 97–8
  Bishop of: lv, 53, 65, 97, 104, 105 *n*.10, 242
  Castle: 197, 205
  Cathedral: 51
  Cliff: 219–22
  Heath: 219–22
  Mint: 186, 191
  race meeting at; 190
  theatrical company from: 188
Lincolnshire: 217–22
  villages: 220–2
  Wolds: 173
Littleworth, Lincs: 101–2, 121, 214
Locke, John: li, 1, 3
Lockier, Very Revd Francis: 53, 55 *n*.14, 239
Lodington, Revd Thomas: 33
London:
  Foundling Hospital: 151
  map of: 123, Illustration 11
  Queen Square: xi, xx, 141, 150, 250
  Westminster Bridge: 151, 159
Londonthorpe, Lincs: 218–20
Longthorpe, near Peterborough: 20–1, 175
Lucy, Countess: 187
Lynn family of Southwick, Northants: xxxi, 57, 189 *n*.2
  George junior: 125, 133, 186, 239
  George senior: xxvi, 57, 61, 234, 239
  Dr Walter: 88, 178, 239

INDEX OF PEOPLE AND PLACES 257

Lyon, Revd Stephen: 79, 96, 146 *n*.1, 188, 194, 239

Macclesfield, Lord: *see* Parker, George
Manningham, Sir Richard: 39, 40, 45, 48, 239
Marlborough, Wilts: 58, 249
Martin, Thomas: 40
Massingberd, Sir William: 32
Mary Queen of Scots: 170
Matilda (Maud), Queen to William the Conqueror: 225
Matilda, Queen to Henry I: 225
Mead, Dr Richard: xxxiii, xli, 28, 36, 39, 141, 159, 174, 180, 239, 248
Melrose Abbey, Scotland: 82
Mendes da Costa, Emanuel: 105, 146, 150, 162, 176, 180, 239
Metheringham, Lincs: 222
Middleton Massey, Dr Richard: xvi, 57, 98, 240
Milles, Revd Joseph: 57, 192, 240
Milton, John: 1, 6, 204
Mitchell, René: 96
Mitre Tavern, London (meeting-place of the AS): 30, 31, 36, 42, 43, 114, 200
Montagu John, second Duke of Montagu: xviii, xliii, 125, 135, 155, 156, 167
Montagu, John, fourth Earl of Sandwich: 156, 165
Montaigne, Michel de: 32
Mortimer, Dr Cromwell: 85, 138, 178, 179, 240
Moulton, Lincs: xx, 48, 88, 89, 117, 164, 183, 213, 238, 247
Moulton Chapel, Lincs: 89, 183
Muscutt (Muscat), Revd James: 153, 162, 193, 240

Needham, Turberville: 105, 106, 241
Neve, Timothy junior: 112, 240
Neve, Revd Timothy senior: xxiv, 20, 96, 113 *n*.12, 207, 235, 240
New, Robert: 176
Newark, Notts: 205
Newmarket, Cambs: 196, 241
Newton, Sir Isaac: xv, xviii, xxvi, xxviii, xxxiii, xxxvi, xliii, l–lv, lviii, lx, 36, 53, 56, 76, 79, 97, 144, 194, 240–1
Noel, William: 102, 121, 122
Norcliffe, Richard: 83, 241
Norden, Capt.: 156
Norris, Christopher: 138, 144, 167, 169, 171

Oakham, Rutland: 132, 133, 144, 232
Oldfield, Anthony: 193, 241
Oldfield, Sir Anthony: 88, 120, 241
Osgodby, Lincs: 220
Ovid: lxii, 44, 45 *n*.19, 61
Oxford: xxvi, xxvii, xxxii, 11, 12, 18, 96, 226 *n*.4
    Botanic Garden: xxvii, 11
    colleges of:
        Christ Church: xxix, 107 *n*.9, 175
        Corpus Christi College: 112
        Hertford College: 182, 193
        Magdalen College: 175, 181, 193
Oxford, Earls of: *see* Harley

Pacey, Richard: 7, 33–4
Paris, Matthew: 64
Parker, George, second Earl of Macclesfield: 35 *n*.30, 150, 178, 185
Parkin, Revd Charles: 101, 102 *n*.4, 104 *n*.1, 122, 250
Parsons, Dr James: 111, 150, 166, 169, 172, 241, 252
Paston, near Peterborough: 89
Peck, Revd Francis: 61, 73
Pegge, Revd Samuel: xxxii, 143, 241
Pembroke, Earl of: *see* Herbert, Thomas
Perry, Dr Charles: 153, 155, 156, 158
Perry, Capt. John: xxv, 73
Perry, Dr Marten: xxxi
Petavius, Dionysius: 1
Peterborough: xxiv, 54, 89, 153, 175, 188, 210, 217, 233
    Cathedral: xxi, 89, 233, 240, 243
Phoenicians: 187, 190
Pilliod, Capt. Francis: 172
Pimlow, Ambrose: 3, 159
Pinchbeck, Lincs: 89, 154 *n*.6
Pluche, Abbé Nicolas: 82
Pococke, Revd Dr Richard: 106, 156, 251
Pole, Joseph: 183, 193, 241
Ponton, Lincs: 205
Powell, Revd Morgan: 129, 241
Pownall, Capt. William: 51, 57, 60, 97
Ptolemy: 64, 189 *n*.6

Quadring, Lincs: 88, 220

Radcliffe, Dr John: 37, 159
Ravenscroft, George: 113, 241
Ray, Revd Benjamin: xxxii, 68, 78, 92, 104, 143, 183, 241–2
Redmarshall, Co. Durham: 92, 126, 237, 238
Reynolds, Revd George: 51
Reynolds, Rt Revd Richard, Bishop of Lincoln: 53, 57, 242
Reynolds, Revd Richard: 193, 242
'Richard of Westminster': xx, xlvii, 127–9, 132, 135, 159, 249
Richards, John: 20, 57, 182, 193, 242
Richardson, Jonathan: 141, 148, 151, 152
Richmond, Duke of: *see* Lennox, Charles
Ripon, Yorks: 117
Rippingale, Lincs: 89
Robinson, Mrs (singer): 36
'Roisia, Lady': xx, 101, 103, 122, 250
Royston, Cambs: 101, 103, 122, 250

Romans: xli, lvi, 1–2, 8, 17, 21, 49, 83, 116, 129, 132, 191, 207
Roman deities:
  Bacchus: xlviii, lvii, 90, 121, 138, 249
  Ceres: 69, 90, 138, 198 *n*.8
  Cybele: 138
  Flora: 121
  Hecate 82
  Neptune: 191, 194, 196
  Terminus: 44–5
  Venus: 90, 189 *n*.5, 191, 196, 208
Russell family, Dukes of Bedford: 56, 125, 165
Rutherforth, Revd Dr Thomas: 118, 242
Ryhall, Rutland: 224, 225

St Bartholomew: 105, 108, 223
St Gilbert of Sempringham: 75
St Guthlac: 105, 107–9, 110, 111, 121, 223–6,
  Illustrations 16–17
St John, Sir Francis: 20, 175
St Paul: 178, 209
Sands, William (architect): 125, 126, 175, 242
Sandwich, Lord: *see* Montagu
Scaliger, J.C.: 1, 68
Scott, Francis, Earl of Dalkeith then second
  Duke of Buccleuch: xviii, xix, xxi–xxii,
  xxv, 75, 78, 79, 123, 170, 234, 242
Searle, Revd Radcliffe: 33
Seymour, Frances, Countess of Hertford: 58, 59
Seymour, Edward, Earl of Hertford: xliii,
  50 *n*.6, 249
Shap, Westmorland: 86
Sharpe, Ven.Thomas: 168, 193, 242
'Sitomagus' (Roman fort): 40
Sleaford, Lincs.: 57, 60, 241
Sloane, Sir Hans: 111, 138, 153, 176, 240, 243
Smyth, Revd. Robert: 144, 153, 175, 210, 243
Spalding, Lincs: xxiv, xxx, 88–9, 187, 190
  Ayscoughfee Hall: xx, xxi, xviii, xix, xxvii,
    xxviii, xxxi, 39, 120, 238, Illustration 4
    painted glass in: 124, 132
    view from tower of: xiv, 88–9
  castle: 187
  Duck Hall: 33, 126, 173
  Gayton (Holyrood) House: xviii, xix, xxi,
    77 *n*.11, 113 *n*.17, 120, 126, 177 *n*.23,
    231, 233, 238
  Grammar School: xxi, xxix, xxx, 32, 40,
    53–4, 73, 88, 96, 111, 120, 168, 207,
    231, 235, 238, 241, 244, Illustration 6
  High Bridge: 73, 127 *n*.13, 233
  history of : 186–7
  map of: xxv, 127 *n*.4, 235, Illustration 12
  Parish Church: xxi, 88, 120, 187, 207
  Parochial Library: xxii, xxiii, xxx, 96, 111,
    207
  Priory ('the Abbey'): 152, 189 *n*.12, 191,
    208–9, 246
  races: 41, 190

  schoolmaster's house: 48
  theatre: 187–8
  Town Hall: 31, 39, 89, 120, 125
  Westlode (stream): 125
  White Hart inn: xxiii, 33
Spanheim, Ezekiel: 169
Sparke, Revd Joseph: 32, 201, 243
Stagg, William: 79
Stamford, Lincs: xiii, xviii, xxiv, xxv, xxxv,
  72, 75, 89, 95, 98, 101, 108, 151, 210, 214,
  219, 224, 231, 232, 239, 249
  Brown's Hospital: 95
  castle: 108
  dancing-master at: 172
  earthquake at: 159
  university at: 101, 103, 224, 226, 250
Steele, Sir Richard: xv, xxii, 10, 34 *n*.17, 98
Stonehenge: xxxiii, xxxvii, xlvi–xlvii, l, lv, lvi–
  lvii, 17, 36, 250, 251, 252
Stovin, George: 116
Stukeley, Adlard: 42, 115 *n*.7, 214
Stukeley, Elizabeth (née Gale) second wife of
  William Stukeley: xix, 78, 123, 249
Stukeley, Frances (née Williamson) first wife of
  William Stukeley: 52–3, 72, 249
Stukeley, John, father of William Stukeley:
  xvii, xviii, 10 *n*.1
Stukeley, William: 248–52
  antiquarian interests of: xxxvii–xli
  astronomical interests: xlviii, 16–17, 86
  attendance at RS: liii, 121
  birth of: 36
  contributions to the *Literary Gazette*: 166
  dissertations by: 62, 68, 72, 105, 115, 123,
    135–6, 150, 217–26
  duties as clergyman: 94, 100, 223
  education of: 248
  foundation of societies by: xlii–xliv, 54, 94
  friendship with Johnson: 24
  gardens of: xxxiii, xxxvi–xxxvii
    at Grantham: 56, 204, Illustration 8
    at Stamford: xxxiii, xxxvii, 84, 87, 121
  health of: xxxv, xxxiv–xxxv, lxii, 92,
    249–50
  interest in Druids: 6, 86, 206 *n*.7
  interest in Stonehenge: 17, 36
  life in Stamford: xxxvii, xlii–xliii
  love of antiquity: 5–6, 10–11, 12 *n*.2, 49
  map of Holland, Lincs: xxv, 47
  marriages: first: xix, 52–3
    second: xix, 249
  marriage of daughter: 183, 185
  medical practice: xxxiii–xxxvi, 62, 203–4
  membership of AS: xlii–xliii, 121 , 180
  memoirs of RS by:138, 141, 144, 147, 162,
    168, 174, 180, 182, 185, 187, 193, 212
  move to Grantham: 203–5
  move to London in 1717: 24
    proposed in 1733: 75

in 1747: xx, 121, 141
  move to Stamford: 70 *n*.1
   house on Barn Hill: 87 *n*.6, 121
  proposed visit to Spalding: 137, 144, 168, 171, 174–5, 178, 179, 185, 196, 210
  publications by: xlvi–l
   Abury: 86
   Dissertation on the Spleen: xxxiii, 251
   Itinerarium Curiosum: xlvi, 49, 249, 251
   Medallic History of Carausius: xli, 185, 215 *n*.7, 250, 251
   Palæographia Britannica: 101, 102 *n*.1, 103
   Palæographia Sacra: xlviii, 249
   Philosophy of Earthquakes: xlviii, 167, 176
  Royston controversy; 101, 103
  Secretary of the AS: 180
  theological interests: lv–lix, 71, 86, 100, 167, 205, 214
  views on music: 36
Surfleet, Lincs: 88, 242
Sutterton, Lincs: 88, 175
Sutton (Holland, Lincs): 89, 219

Talman, John: 29 *n*.10, 36, 118, 235
Tanner, Dr Thomas: 43, 92
Tathwell, Dr Cornwall: 168, 174, 193, 197, 243
Tattershall, Lincs: 139
Terminus: *see under* Roman deities
Terrington, Norfolk: 175, 181
Thetford, Norfolk: 40, 42
Thomlinson, Dr: 13
Thorpe Hall, Peterborough: 20–1, 175, 177 *n*.9
Thorney, Cambs: 54, 89, 127 *n*.8
Threekingham, Lincs: 62, 217–22
Tickhill, S. Yorks: 92–3
Tilliol family: 93
Torkington, William: 156
Trafford, Sigismund: 28, 57
Trent, River: 218
Turketyl, Abbot of Croyland: 103, 123–4, 224
Tuxford, Notts: 92

Urry, John: 106, 107

Verney, James: 183, 193, 243
Vernon, Revd. Edward: 57, 61

Vertue, George: 29, 30, 54, 114, 142 *n*.14, 170, 178, 188, 214, 243, 246, 247
Virgil: lxii, 16, 108, 153, 158 *n*.13, 206 *n*.7, 210

Wainfleet, Lincs: 81 *n*.21, 191
Wales, Prince of: *see* Frederick, Prince of Wales
Wallin, Richard (husband of Anne Alethea Johnson): 183, 193, 244
Walpole, Edward: 194, 234, 244
Waltheof, Earl: 225
Wansford, Cambs: 22
Warburton, Revd William: 57, 61, 86. 150, 167, 205
Ward, John: 114, 244
Waring, Revd John: xxi, 23 *n*.2, 96, 244
Warkhouse, Thomas: 27
Wastneys, Sir Hardolf: 143
Weeks, James: 193, 244
Welby family: 62, 175
Welland, River: 63, 73, 88–9, 125, 129, 187, 191, 197
 deepening of: 73
Weston, Lincs: 89
Whaplode, Lincs: 89
Whichcote, Sir Francis: 57, 188
Whichcote, Thomas: 116
Whiting, Revd Samuel: 148, 149 *n*.15, 244
Whittlesea, Cambs: 89
Widdrington, Hon.Ralph: 3
William I: 2, 209, 225
Willis, Browne: 28, 64, 146, 150, 152, 178, 244, 245
Wing, Tycho: 125
Wingfield family: 205 *n*.1, 244
Wisbech, Cambs.: xvi, 19, 33, 99 *n*.21, 237, 239, 240
Witham, Lincs: 220
Witham, River: 63, 85, 157 *n*.3, 206 *n*.10, 218, 243
Witlaf, King: 224
Woodward, Dr John: 11
Wren, Sir Christopher: 16–17, 38 *n*.21
Wykeham, Lincs: xxix, 88, 241, 244

York: xxvii, 30, 76, 82, 92, 132, 134–6, 138, 233

INDEX OF SUBJECTS

Abacus: 79–80
Accidents: 36, 148, 162, 250
Alphabets, ancient: 6, 44, 76
'Ancients and Moderns': 10
Anglo-Saxon Chronicle: 64, 69, 128
Antiquities:
   Egyptian: xliii, 82, 153, 235
   Celtic: 205
   Greek: 159
   Horn of Ulf: 30
   Inscriptions and epitaphs: xxvii, 26, 159, 165, 169, 193, 247
   Keys: 16–17, 27–9, 181
   Lamina ferrea (iron plates): 3, 5, 8
   Mithraic carvings: 134–6, 138
   Preserved body in peat bog: 116, 118
   Rings: 6, 8, 29, 152
   Roman: *see* 'Roman'
   Saxon gold plate: 175–6
   Shrines: 109, 134–5, 138–9, 153, 224
   Standing stones: xl, 22, 86
   Stone tools: 135
   Tumuli: 221
Antonine Itinerary: l, 66 *n*.8, 67 *n*.10
Armillary sphere: 193, 196
Astronomy:
   Aurora: liii, 162
   Comet: 85–7, 91
   Conjunction of Jupiter and Venus: 17
   Moon: liv, 17, 36
   Satellites of Jupiter: 17
   Saturn: 17
   Transit of Venus: 236
   Zodiac, signs of: 83, 162

Bat: 84–5, 86
Beetle: 153
Bible, books of:
   Epistle to the Hebrews: 86
   Genesis: 87 *n*.7, 156
   Job: 156, 167, 172
   Leviticus: 69
   St Luke: 68–9
Birds: 86, 156, 196
   owl, Stukeley's pet: 56, 58 *n*.3
Bosworth, Battle of: 2
British Museum: xiii, 112 *n*.3, 140 *n*.10, 177 *n*.19, 243
Butterflies: 165, 196

Cat, Johnson's pet: xiv, 32, 56, 58 *n*.6
Cattle disease: xiii, 112, 117, 133
Churches:
   Doncaster Parish Church, Yorks: 92
   Dunstable Priory Church, Beds: 25–7
   St Clement Dane's, London: 37
   Tuxford Parish Church, Notts: 92
Coins: xviii, xxvii, xli, 21, 131, 169,
   Anglo-Saxon: 132, 144
   British: 18, 148, 251
   English: 115 *n*.13, 213
   Greek: 180–1
   Roman: 20, 41, 50–1, 69, 141, 152, 175, 196, 207, 214, 231
      Coins of Carausius: xlii, 159, 161, 185, 188, 191, 205, 214, 246, 250, Illustration 21
      'Oriuna' coin: xvii, xx, xli, xlvii, 141, 142 *n*.12, 159, 161, 174, 250
Correspondence, value of: 72, 76, 144, 174, 183
Cottonian Library: 114, 185

Dissection, medical: 24, 54
   of elephant: xxxiii, 39, 40, 243, 248
Domesday Book: 32, 37 *n*.2, 65, 201
Dragon: lxiii, 11–12, 14, 133, Illustration 13
Drainage and draining: xxi, xxv–xxvi, 73, 85, 125–6, 165, 191, 235–6
Drought: 165, 173
Druids and Druidism: xx, xxxvii, lvii–lix, 1, 6, 85–6, 88, 146, 206 *n*.7, 250, 251

Earthquakes: xlviii, liii–liv, 146, 149–50, 159, 162, 169, 212, 250
Eel: 197
Egyptian beliefs and practices: lvii, 8, 69, 86, 156, 220
   costume: 156, 157
   gods: 210
   hieroglyphs: xl, xliii, 76
   learning: xlvii, 82, 83
   rattle (sistrum): 156, 209
Egyptian Society: *see under* Societies, London-based
Elephant, dissection of: *see under* Dissection
Etruscan:
   customs: lvii
   language: 175

script: 76
vases: 90

Fevers: 117, 155 *n*.12, 169, 200
Finance:
    French Louisiana speculation: 37
    South Sea Bubble: 38 *n*.23, 39, 40
Fossils and minerals: xxiii, xxxiii, 56, 83, 105, 106, 111, 121, 175, 176, 196, 197, 239–40, 245–6
Freemasonry: xxii, xxxviii, xlii, xlvi, 75, 79, 125, 234, 242, 248
Fungi: 180, 183

Gardens:
    Johnson's: *see under* Johnson, Maurice II in Index of People and Places
    Stukeley's: *see under* Stukeley, William in Index of People and Places
Genealogy: xxxviii, 49, 72–3, 141, Illustration 19
General Resurrection: 86
Geography: xiv, xlix, liv, 1–2, 6, 128
Glass, painted: 132, 136

History, study of: xxv, xxvi–xxvii, xli, lxii, 1–2, 3, 96, 111, 129, 132, 162, 210, 218
Horse racing: 97, 136, 152, 190, 191

Immortality of the Soul: 10
Inscriptions: *see* Antiquities: Inscriptions and epitaphs

Jacobite rebellions: 14, 15, 102 *n*.6

Languages:
    Etruscan: 175
    Phœnician: 175
Latin verse: 180
Legal:
    Assizes: xxi, 19, 33, 48, 57, 60, 97, 217
    documents: 175, 209
    inquisitions *post mortem*: 143
    Midland Circuit: xix, xxiii, 18, 43
    Terms: xiii, xvii, xxii,
Libraries: 171, 175, 177 *n*.19
    Johnson's: *see under* Johnson, Maurice II in Index of People and Places
    of the SGS: *see under* Spalding Gentlemen's Society

Maps: xxv–xxvi, l, 1, 21, 83
    by 'Richard of Cirencester': xlvii, 129
    of Lincolnshire: xxv, l, 28, 47, 85, 88, Illustration 12
    of London: 123, Illustration 11
Marine life:
    barnacle: 196
    fish: 69, 165, 183, 197

    nautilus: 180
    porpoise: 176
    sea-urchin: 180
    shells: xxvii, 83, 105, 153, 196
    whale: 196
Marshes: 191
Mathematics: xxvi, xxxviii, li, lv, 175, 181, 235
Mithraic rites: 135–6
Mosquito nets ('knatt nets'): 153
Moth: 41
Music: xxix, xliii, li, 31, 41, 75, 79, 82, 96, 123, 125, 175, 193, 213
    concert at Boston: 162, 165
    Handel's *Messiah*: 151
    organs and organists: 79, 162–4, 165, 193, 236

Numismatics: *see* Coins

Orrery: 161

Painting, art and profession of: 44, 133, 193, 194, 233, 244
Paintings, collections of: 20, 148, 170, 173, 188, 194
Peace of Aix-la-Chapelle: 125
Periodicals:
    Censor, The: 10, 11, 14, 25
    Gentleman's Magazine: lii, 133, 165, 240, 250, 251
    Inspector, The: 176
    Lay Monk, The: 98, 169, 171
    Literary Gazette: 166, 169, 173 *n*.1, 174–5
    Lover, The: 98, 169, 171
    Rambler, The: 167 *n*.1, 176, 198 *n*.6
    Spectator, The: 98, 169, 171
    Tatler, The: 98, 169, 171
Plants:
    Acacia: 196
    Broom: 153
    Chestnut, flowering: 175
    Rhubarb: 193
    Tulip: 175
Plays: xiii, 31–2, 36, 41, 171–2, 187–8
Politics: 14, 24–5, 30
    Elections: 32–3, 114, 115 *n*.2
Pottery:
    Albano ware: 90, 196
    Dresden china: 90

Rattlesnake: 83
Ridottos: 146, 185
Roman:
    altar: 124, 204, 247
    baths: 114
    buildings: 44
    camps: 51, 249
    coins: *see* 'Coins'
    drainage works: 132

inscriptions: 165, 169, 197, 247
jewels: 144, 169, 194
mosaics: xxvii, 205
roads: xxv, xxvii, l, 49, 74, 114, 206 *n*.14, 218
silver plate: 249
urns: 50, 121
villas: xxvii, 49, 116, 180

Sacrifice of animals: 71
Societies, local:
    Ancaster Society: xv, xvii, xxiv, xlii, 57, 59, 60, 62, 63, 218–9
    Attempts to found societies: xv–xvi, 97–8
    Belvoir Society: xlii, 54, 55 *n*.17
    Boston Society: xlii, 97, 153–4
    Brazen Nose Society, Stamford: xiv, xvii, xxiv, xlii-xliii, xlvi, 85–6, 92, 94, 189 *n*.2
        attempts to revive: xxiv, 94, 95–7, 114
        original society: 54, 95 *n*.5, 100
    Deepings Club: xlii, 68, 71, 100, 133, 134 *n*.13
    Doncaster Society: 114
    Peterborough Gentlemen's Society (PGS): xiv, xv, xxiii, xxiv, 97, 98, 207, 240
    Spalding Gentlemen's Society (SGS): xv, xxii–xxxi, 218, 223
        activities of: 40, 41, 43, 53–4, 75–6, 79–80, 96–7, 105, 111, 114, 117, 126, 143, 161, 165, 168–9, 174–6, 180–1, 191, 193, 196–7, 200, 207, 210, 212, 245
        'Alphabet of Arts and Sciences': lxi, 81 *n*.13, 82
        concerts at: xxix, 75, 79, 82, 162–3
        connections with the AS: 37, 43, 49, 79
        connections with the RS: 79, 213
        correspondence of: xxiii, 98, 143
        female members, possibility of: 75
        foundation of: 3, 54, 75
        future of: 75
        library of: xxviii, xxxi, 53, 79, 96, 111, 123, 153, 169, 246
        meeting places of: 53–4, 89 *n*.3, 112, 176, 177 *n*.23
        minutes of: xvii, xix, xxiii, xlv, lxii, 98, 138, 165, 172, 183, 210, 213

museum of: xxviii, 53, 73, 76, 96
officers of: 79, 96
physic garden of: xxvii–xxxviii
recruitment to: xxv, 3 *n*.1, 51, 53–4, 56–7, 168, 182–3, 193, 246
rules of: 95–6
success of: xxviii–xxix, 8, 56, 61, 75, 79, 187, 193
Wisbech Gentlemen's Society: xvi, xxiv, 54, 98
Societies, London-based:
    Antiquarian Society (Society of Antiquaries): xiii, xv, xvi, xxviii, xxxiv, xlii, xliii, xlvi, xlviii, 25–6, 27, 28, 29–30, 31, 37, 43, 49, 61, 114, 167, 178, 179–80, 185, 191, 201, 214
        charter of: 167, 178
        history of: 178
        minutes of: 180
        re-foundation of: 76, 178, 245
        sending their publications to the SGS: 79
    Egyptian Society: xliii, 153, 155–7, 162, 169, 174, 182, 209–10
    Medical Society of Navy Surgeons: 181
    Royal College of Physicians: xxxii, xxxiii, xlii, 36, 150, 159, 239, 248
    Royal Society: xiii, xiv–xv, xxii, xxiii, xxv, xxviii, xxxiii, xlii, xliii, xlvi, xlvii, lii, liii, lv, 36, 61 *n*.4, 79, 84 *n*.13, 85, 106, 111, 133, 135, 150, 156, 162, 167, 174, 178, 179–81, 182, 185, 191, 205, 212–13, 248, 250
        Philosophical Transactions of: 81 *n*.13, 85, 138, 213
    Society of Roman Knights: xiv, xxvii, xliii, xlvi, 77 *n*.6, 206 *n*.7, 235
Statues: 20–1, 105, 123, 175, 223–6, 247

Tapestry: 90, 101, 172
Telescope: xxviii, 16–17
Thermometer: xxviii, 196
Tin mining: 155–6
Trigoli fruit: 183

Waterspout: 183, 185, 196
Waxworks, medical: 24